THE NEW KEY TO ECUADOR AND THE GALÁPAGOS

"If you buy only one guidebook for Ecuador, make it *The New Key to Ecuador and the Galápagos.*"
—*Washington Times*

"A first-rate guidebook, the authors really have visited every nook and cranny of this diverse region. Highly recommended."
—*San Diego Union-Tribune*

"A thorough guide with special attention [given] to conservation issues."
—*Vancouver Sun*

THE NEW KEY TO ECUADOR AND THE GALÁPAGOS

Third Edition

DAVID L. PEARSON
DAVID W. MIDDLETON

DOUG McCARTHY
GLENN KIM
Illustrators

DAVID W. MIDDLETON
Photographer

Ulysses 🐝 Press

Published by: Ulysses Press
                3286 Adeline Street, Suite 1
                Berkeley, CA 94703

ISSN 1096-8962
ISBN 1-56975-199-4

Printed in Canada by Transcontinental Printing

10 9 8 7 6 5 4 3

Executive Editor: Leslie Henriques
Managing Editor: Claire Chun
Copy Editor: Steven Schwartz
Editorial Associates: Lily Chou, Lynette Ubois, Leslie Van Dyke, Aaron Newey
Typesetter: David Wells
Cartography: Stellar Cartography; Otavalo, Loja, Salinas, Esmeraldas, Tena
   and Puerto Ayora maps by Pease Press
Cover Photography:
   Front: Markham Johnson/Robert Holmes Photography (Lago Cuicocha,
   Northern Highlands)
   Circle: Robert Holmes (Blue-footed booby in the Galápagos)
   Back: Michael Warren (Huao man working on canoe paddle in the Oriente)
Cover Design: Leslie Henriques
Indexer: Sayre Van Young

Distributed in the United States by Publishers Group West, in Canada by Rain-
coast Books, and in Great Britain and Europe by World Leisure Marketing

Table of Contents

Maps

Foreword

Ecuador is a small country, but, as Ecuadorians say, "what makes an *empanada* so delicious is its filling, not its size." Now you might wonder what's inside. With close to 1600 species of birds, Ecuador exceeds all of North America combined, as well as every other country in South America except Perú and Colombia (and we may surpass them with more exploration). With 4500 species of orchids, Ecuador claims one-third of the total number found in all of South America. More than 200 species of trees can be found on a single site the size of four football fields—and in one single kapok tree, over 100 species of insects new to science have been recorded. Thousands of species of butterflies flash their brilliant colors everywhere. If we were to make a map based on numbers of plant and animal species and diversity of habitats, Ecuador would be one of the largest countries in South America—and probably in the entire world. But these are just a few of the ingredients.

Ecuador's human history predates the Incan Empire by thousands of years. Some of our earliest inhabitants produced the first ceramics in the Western Hemisphere, and we were melting platinum at 3272°F for exquisite filigree jewelry long before the time of Christ. Even today, diverse ethnic traditions are part of our everyday life. We are a living testimony of what archaeologists dig up—in the food we eat, the music we play, the markets we shop, and the language we speak.

Uniting the Northern and Southern Hemispheres, the habitats you will enjoy range from sea-level stretches of sandy Pacific beaches to one of the tallest and most dramatic snow-capped volcanoes in the world, Volcán Chimborazo. The isolated Galápagos Islands will delight you with their animals, but our verdant Amazonian forests, which contain more than 30 percent of all known medicines, and the crystal-clear alpine regions we call páramo will impress you beyond belief. Sixty million years of naturally chaotic events bear the promise of life and continuity that have evolved into this country containing three of the world's 12 recognized "hot spots" for biodiversity!

Please excuse me if I sound like I am bragging, but it is only my immense pride in Ecuador speaking and my hope that I can share some of this spectacularly diverse beauty with you. Of course, having so much to offer means we also have a lot to guard and protect. For the past decade, the Ecuadorian Ecotourism Association (EEA) has been playing a major role in uniting conservation and travel with private and government agencies both here in Ecuador and abroad. The EEA conducts workshops involving naturalist guides, hoteliers, lodge owners, airlines, indigenous communities, scientists, educators, tour operators, conservationists, travel agents and artisans to communicate and coordinate the sensible, long-term use and protection of Ecuador's natural wonders through ecotourism.

Much of the success of the first edition of David Pearson and David Middleton's "user friendly" book, *The New Key to Ecuador and the Galápagos*, came from their awareness of the need to involve all these players in a joint effort to guard our natural resources by empowering the tourists themselves. The second edition helped unearth even more of what we believe to be one of the best-kept travel secrets in the world.

And now, this third edition comes at the threshold of the millennium—a time to reflect on how far we have traveled as a humane species and how we *should* travel in the future. I believe that we love what we know and protect what we love. That is also what travel is all about—the shortest distance between your hometown and Ecuador is learning and understanding. This book will get you started in the right direction because it deals not only with facts but also with attitudes.

We are honored by your visit to Ecuador—where smiles are an everyday way of communicating, and where you can advance your film and horizons simultaneously in this unique land of discovery. And remember, you are playing a leading role in Ecuadorian conservation efforts.

Happy exploring!

Oswaldo Muñoz
Consultant for Ecotourism Development/
Ecuadorian Ecotourism Association

Acknowledgments

Neither one of us would have dreamed of taking on this project without the other. Our team effort, however, included many other players as well. In Ecuador, Dolores Diez, Oswaldo Muñoz, Antonio Perrone and Raul Garcia combined decades of ecotourism experience in Ecuador to provide us with advice that saved us months of valuable time. In Guayaquil, Jaime Buestán and Ronald Navarrete helped us over and over. In Quito, Oswaldo Muñoz and Mercedes Rivadeneira sought out new locations and made contacts when the fax and telephone didn't get through. In the Galápagos, Juan Carlos Naranja filled in many gaps for us. For more than 20 years, members of the Instituo Lingüístico de Verano unselfishly supported tiger beetle and bird research at Limoncocha and at the same time enthusiastically shared their knowledge of the cultures and biology of the Oriente.

In the U.S., our editor, Joanna Pearlman, helped make the writing process fun again and taught us a lot at the same time. Anne Becher graciously shared her green rating from *The New Key to Costa Rica* and helped us apply it in what we hope is a fair and consistent way to *The New Key to Ecuador and the Galápagos*. The Department of Biology at Arizona State University supported the writing of this book in many ways, and colleagues there gave advice on technical aspects of ecology, evolution, conservation, anthropology and biology. Most important of all, however, was the loving support at every step from Nancy Pearson and Claire Beck.

The New Key to Ecuador
Green Rating

Although we cover many aspects important to a tourist visiting Ecuador, including accommodations and logistics, one of the main reasons we wrote this guidebook was to introduce you to Ecuador's unique geography, culture and native species—and at the same time encourage you to help preserve the country's natural wonders. Among the hundreds of destinations in Ecuador, a growing number use ecotourism as their primary reason for doing business. When you choose which of these natural sites to visit, there are a few rules of thumb to follow. There are places where you can actually be comfortable and still see pristine forest, and some that are easy to get to where you will also see wildlife. In general, though, the more comfortable the lodging, the less wildlife, and the more accessible the location, the less pristine the habitat. If you want to see pristine environments, you are going to have to endure some hardship—either by long hours of travel or some discomfort. We think you'll find, however, that these tradeoffs are a small price to pay once you are immersed in an untouched forest or riding down an unspoiled river.

We will help you as you plan your trip by describing what we saw and experienced when we visited these remote places. However, beyond the clean sheets, delicious food and memorable canoe trips, one other factor should be considered when choosing which lodges to visit. Tourist destinations with nature listed as a significant part of their mission may or may not be sensitive to the goals of conservation. The claims of being "green" may refer only to the color of their profits and not to the rational use of natural resources under their aegis. As an ecotourist, you can have a direct impact on the future of natural areas in Ecuador by making sure "green" means rational and sustainable use of natural resources.

CONSERVATION ETHIC

Because of conflicting political and economic pressures, the environmental branch of the Ecuadorian government (Ministerio de Medio Ambiente) and its national park service (INEFAN) often get bogged down in bureaucratic processes. The saving grace of the system is that formal and informal partnerships are often formed with nongovernment organizations (NGOs), tour operators and national universities to develop long-term national conservation goals. So despite the daunting intransigence typical of government agencies around the world, the Ecuadorian system of conservation policy has evolved into an interactive system that depends on input from many sources.

As in other countries throughout the world, Ecuadorian economists and government officials are searching for a dependable source of foreign revenue on which they can make long-term plans for development. The three top earners of foreign exchange (petroleum, bananas and shrimp) either have limited reserves or their world market fluctuates drastically and unpredictably. As the fourth-most important foreign exchange earner, tourism has caught the attention of these economists, and they have forced even hardhearted politicians to take notice. Nearly 500,000 foreign tourists now visit Ecuador annually. Of these, more than 17 percent are interested in seeing parts of natural Ecuador. Large numbers of tourists paying hard cash to see birds, scenery and anthropological sites are finally having an impact on national environmental goals. You as an ecotourist can help by making your interests and priorities known. Your dollars already speak for themselves, but that is largely a passive influence. There are many simple ways for you to become more actively involved. Consider supporting Ecuadorian conservation efforts during your visit to the country by asking relevant questions. Let Ecuadorians know that you as a tourist want to see positive changes. In the following pages we suggest some pertinent questions that you can use to make your feelings clear. You might also try making contacts with local conservation groups (see Chapter Two) and, following your visit, continue to support them with letters and contributions. Cooperate with the **Ecuadorian Ecotourism Association** (EEA) (Avenida Coruña 1349 and Orellana, Quito; 2-552-839, fax: 2-565-261). This association regularly solicits letters to be written to government officials concerning specific issues affecting the Ecuadorian environment. Letters can also be written directly to the director of INEFAN at the Ministerio de Medio Ambiente in Quito to provide this hardworking but often frustrated office with information and ammunition to influence political decisions at the highest levels of government.

Finally, to help you make positive environmental choices, we evaluated each of the lodges that advertises itself as primarily an ecotourist site, and rated them on their environmental ethic. To determine this green rating, we relied solely on our own observations and interviews of employees, tourists and operators about the environmental impact of each lodge. For subsequent editions, we hope to rely on you as concerned ecotourists to help determine this rating. You have the power to change this ethic for the better. A letter to our publisher and to the lodge operator can bring about positive changes very quickly. By asking the right questions and demanding environmentally sound practices, you can help strengthen Ecuador's conservation effort. Here we target the lodge owners and operators directly, but many if not all of these questions could also be directed at the national and international tour companies operating within Ecuador.

Checklist of questions (ranked by importance, 1 = highest, 10 = lowest):

1) Are visitors educated about environmental problems and, if so, how? Are there formal talks, slide programs, printed information, guided tours, meetings with local conservation groups?

2) Are the local people treated sensitively or are they only objects of curiosity? How respectful to and familiar with the local culture is the owner/manager?

3) Do the local people profit directly from the presence of the ecotourists? Are the local people only hired as waiters and boat operators or do they also function as guides?

4) Is there evidence of a long-term program, one that is set up to operate over several to many years? Is the lodge sponsoring scientific research? Do construction techniques include fast-growing native materials that can be replaced in a sustainable long-term way with minimal impact on the local habitat? What evidence is there that the tour operator is thinking about the future and not just using the site for a quick return regardless of long-term effects on the environment? Are alternative energy sources being used?

5) How are garbage and sewage disposed of? Are digester toilets available? Is there an adequate septic system? Are there regular programs to test the water near the lodge for contaminants? Is there a recycling program? Is the garbage just burned and buried?

6) Are there formal programs to prevent and monitor habitat degradation and effects on wildlife by the presence of the tourists? Are wild animals kept as pets on the grounds?

7) Is the lodge involved in environmental outreach programs to local people? Are any of the profits donated to Ecuadorian environmental groups?

8) Are tourists informed of local and national environmental problems and how they can write or contact local politicians, newspapers and international development agencies to address these problems?

9) Are ways provided by which concerned tourists can be informed of progress and follow up on environmental problems after they leave Ecuador?

10) Is there a conservation message in the advance material or other claims of environmental awareness? After you have visited the area, would you consider these claims to be realistic and honest?

CONSERVATION ETHIC INDEX

☻☻☻   Meets 80 percent or more of the weighted criteria above. (Highly sensitive to conservation efforts.)

☻☻   Meets 70 to 79 percent of the weighted criteria above. (Doing a good job, but needs improvement on some important issues.)

☻   Meets 60 to 69 percent of the weighted criteria above. (Trying, but falling short in several areas.)

Lodges whose goal is practicing sustainable ecotourism and a green rating for each (three icons is the best rating) are listed below.

* These lodges are highly involved in local conservation and environmental education efforts as well as ecotourism. At these lodges, you should neither expect nor demand the same level of attention as at the lodges whose sole goal is ecotourism. These environmentally active sites are likely to have paying guests work as volunteers on local conservation problems.

NORTHERN HIGHLANDS
Hosteria El Carmelo de Mindo *(pages 153–54)* ☻☻
Mindo Garden *(pages 154, 156)* ☻☻
Friends of Mindo–Nambillo Forest Riverside Shelter *(page 156)* ☻☻
Bellavista Reserve Lodge *(pages 158–59)* ☻☻
*Maquipucuna Biological Reserve Lodge *(pages 160–61)* ☻☻☻

CENTRAL AND SOUTHERN COAST
Hosteria Alandaluz *(pages 300–301)* ☻☻☻

NORTHERN COAST
Steve's Lodge *(page 333)* ☻
Playa de Oro *(pages 334–36)* ☻☻☻
San Miguel *(pages 334–36)* ☻☻
*Bilsa Biological Reserve and Station *(pages 344–45)* ☻☻☻

Introduction

Other tropical destinations for tourists can claim what they will—none of them can stand up to the variety offered by Ecuador. There is no place else in the world with more species of plants and animals than the tropical rainforests. There is no tropical rainforest in the world with more species of plants and animals than the slopes and associated lowlands along the eastern base of the Andes Mountains from Venezuela to Bolivia. This geographic *arc of biodiversity* contains a richness of life that is difficult to imagine without experiencing it personally. Of all the countries within this most diverse biological realm, however, only Ecuador provides both peaceful internal politics and extensive tourist facilities. As if this claim to accessible biodiversity were not enough, Ecuador also supplies the enchantment of the Galápagos, where the animals still behave as though man is not the enemy.

The diversity of plants and animals found in Ecuador is caused largely by the variety of habitats, scenery and climates. On a two-hour drive from Quito, you quickly move from the high-elevation grasslands and towering snow-covered volcanoes of the paramo to cold-adapted *Polylepis* forests, alder woodlands, moss-covered cloud forest and, eventually, to lowland rainforest and desertlike deciduous dry forest filled with cactus. Drive a little farther, and you will be in coastal mangrove swamps and beautiful sandy beaches that go on for kilometers. Quito claims to have eternal spring, but if it's winter you want, the slopes of Mt. Pichincha just above Quito can accumulate snow in an afternoon. If it's summer you desire—wet summer for part of the year and dry summer for the rest—the coast from Guayaquil to Esmeraldas can accommodate you all year-round.

In 1998, almost half a million tourists visited Ecuador, more than half from Europe and the rest from other Latin American countries and North

America. A large proportion of these tourists were what are known as "eco-tourists." Ecotourists are tourists whose travel is both recreational and educational and focused primarily on nature and natural areas. Each year, ecotourism increases in Ecuador. In response to this demand, the facilities for tourists who want to experience the adventure of places barely, if at all, touched by humans have become available in more than reasonable numbers and levels of comfort. But if, in addition, your goal is just kicking back and being pampered, Ecuador has many alternatives to choose from. Discovering an Indian market where few other gringos are around is not difficult. However, if you prefer to blend native experiences with the company of other travelers, those places are available as well. Looking for picturesque scenes of snow-covered volcanoes with ox-drawn plows in the foreground? Ecuador has it. After a day of exploring, do you want a luxurious hotel with HBO and live entertainment? Ecuador has it, too.

As the authors of this book, we want to share Ecuador with you in a way that no other guidebooks can match. One of the authors (DLP) first visited Ecuador in 1971, and he has worked there almost every year since, conducting scientific studies of animals, plants, and forest conservation. He has published over 60 scientific articles on the ecology of tropical organisms from tiger beetles, orchid bees and single-celled *Paramecium*, to coral, birds and robberflies. His contacts in the academic and government community have made him welcome in Ecuador for almost three decades. The other author (DWM) is a widely published nature photographer and has led ecotours around the world, both independently and for Joseph Van Os Tours, for over 15 years. Eighteen of these tours have been to the Galápagos and mainland Ecuador, and his contacts with the national and international tourism industry in Ecuador is extensive. Together, we combine a depth of basic knowledge and common-sense experience that few other travel book authors can claim. With this *The New Key to Ecuador and the Galápagos*, we will open the door for you to experience the natural diversity of Ecuador as well as the generous and proud people who live there.

This book can be used by tourists with major or even only minor interests in the natural and cultural wonders of Ecuador. Some of you are planning your own personal itinerary and will use the book to maintain your independence. Others may prefer to go on a more organized tour, but the various brochures and itineraries provided by the tour companies will give you only a vague idea of what is waiting for you. This book will empower you to choose the level of comfort, adventure and interest that suits you.

Since the second edition of this book, much for the ecotourist has changed in Ecuador. There are two more national parks and reserves; several recently-constructed roads to explore exciting habitats; and a whole slew of new ecotourist lodges that are now ready to accept ecotourist visitors. We have done our best to update this third edition with additions of interest to ecotourists. We have also had to make deletions as some lodges have closed down and others we no longer consider appropriate ecotourist destinations. This variety is part of why we continue to enjoy exploring Ecuador.

David L. Pearson
David W. Middleton
September 1999

ONE

Ecuador: A Brief History

Ecuador has a surprisingly long and varied history for such a small country, but its culture has often been forgotten in the midst of much more prominent cultures in neighboring Colombia and Perú. Archaeological evidence dating from before 12,000 B.P. (Years Before Present) shows that the southern coast, the Loja area and El Inga near Quito were home to the earliest cultures living in Ecuador, with evidence of several sites continually inhabited for 8000 years. The coast had the best-developed early cultures. Evidently, the favorable ocean currents and prevailing winds off the southern coast encouraged settlement of the area. Based on the number of archaeological sites and the extent of ancient agricultural fields, well over a million people lived along the Ecuadorian coast at this time. Anthropologists distinguish four periods of development for pre-Colombian cultures in the southern coast of Ecuador: The Pre-ceramic Period includes all cultures before about 5200 B.P. Most of the archaeological remains for this group have been found on the Santa Elena Peninsula, west of Guayaquil. These people were hunters of small game and gatherers of inshore marine animals and wild plants. They also developed primitive, corn-based agriculture, buried their dead in cemeteries, lived in beehive-shaped huts, worked wood with polished stone tools and had some navigational skills.

The Formative Period, between 5200 B.P. and 2500 B.P., is divided into the early Valdivian and the later Machalilla and Chorrera cultures. Valdivian pottery shards from the southern coast of Ecuador were made of ceramic and are some of the earliest known from anywhere in the New World (5200 B.P.). Similarities between Valdivian and Asian pottery of the same time period led anthropologists in the 1970s to hypothesize a trade contact between the Valdivians and the Jomon culture of Japan. Evidence for advanced navigational skills reinforced this hypothesis of trade between South America and Japan. However, this hypothesis of transpacific contact lately has been reconsidered. Archaeologists now realize that many primitive cultures produce similarly designed pottery due to their similarly designed universal pottery tools. Also, a proto-Valdivian culture was found inland, suggesting a connection to highland cultures and not Asia.

The Valdivian culture is divided into seven phases lasting until 4000 B.P. (The most investigated Valdivian site is known as Real Alto on the south side of the Santa Elena Peninsula.) During this phase, the Valdivians changed from being primarily hunter-gatherers to being farmers. The early Valdivians lived in permanent wood-and-straw huts in villages that were arranged in a horseshoe pattern around a shell-paved central plaza. This plaza was used for ceremonial purposes and later for the communal storage of corn and grains. Some later Valdivians moved away from the central village to farm small plots on nearby river floodplains. The Valdivians are the first of Ecuador's cultures in which urban and rural lifestyles were separated and in which a social stratification developed between high religious/ceremonial leaders and all others.

Coincident with the late Valdivian culture of the coast is the Cerro Narrío culture of the southern highlands of Loja, Cañar and Azuay provinces. The Cerro Narrío culture is an amalgam of several different cultures. There is strong archaeological evidence showing that trade connections among the highlands of Perú, the Oriente of Ecuador, Perú and Brazil, and the coast of Ecuador were well established by 4000 B.P. During the subsequent Machalilla and Chorrera cultures (4000 B.P. to 2500 B.P.), more complex and technologically sophisticated pottery and tools than those of the Valdivians were produced. Also at this time, the first powerful chiefdoms arose to protect the economically and socially important trade routes.

The Regional Development and Integration Period, 2500 B.P. to 500 B.P., includes the time up to the Spanish Conquest. This period includes considerable differentiation of cultures—in art, politics and technology—all of which permitted expansion of populations. For the first time, there is evidence that people had learned how to manipulate their environment by digging wells, constructing canals and building raised fields to farm. Cities of 30,000 people developed along the coast—where goods were being imported on 30-ton balsa rafts that could easily have sailed long distances. Archaeologists know that chieftains began to control distant lands, forming kingdoms, and that they were trading with the Mayan culture of Mexico during this period. It was also during this time that gold, platinum and copper metallurgy was developed.

At the end of the Integration Period there were three great kingdoms in the highlands of Ecuador: the Cañari, centered around the present-day city of Cuenca; the Quitu, occupying the area surrounding the present-day city of

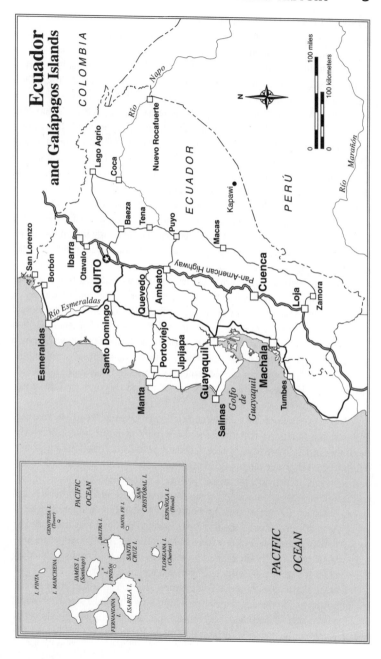

Ecuador
and Galápagos Islands

Quito; and the Caras, who lived to the north of the Quitu. These three king-doms stood in the way of northern expansion by the then very powerful Incas. The Incan culture started in the 11th century in the Lake Titicaca area of Bolivia. During the 12th century, the Incas migrated west to what is now Perú and established as the center of their domain the Andean city of Cuzco. Dur-ing the 14th and 15th centuries, this originally small band of people developed into a large, territory-hungry society complete with armies, generals, forts and well-established supply routes. The Incas aggressively expanded and even-tually incorporated many of the cultures and lands of what is now northern Chile, Perú, Bolivia and Ecuador. Led by the royal Inca Tupac-Yupanqui, the Incas invaded Cañari territory in 1460. Five years later, the Cañaris fell, and the royal city of Tomebamba, near present-day Cuenca, was built over the ruins of the Cañari capital. Incan expansion continued north from Tomebamba and, in 1492, the Quitu kingdom was conquered. Still not satisfied, Huanya-Capac, the son of Tupac-Yupanqui, lay siege to the Cara kingdom in the region of present-day Otavalo. Seventeen years later the Caras succumbed and Incan expansion to the north was complete.

The Incas were in Ecuador for less than 100 years, but their influence was profound. Tomebamba became the center of Incan power and ceremony. It was designed to be the royal city of the northern Incan Empire and was said to rival Cuzco in its opulence and grandeur. Connecting Tomebamba with Quito to the north and Cuzco to the south was the Imperial Highway, known as Capac-nan, a distance of over 2400 kilometers. Another road ran along the coast from the present-day city of Santiago, Chile, to Guayaquil, a distance of more than 4800 kilometers. A network of side roads connected these two primary highways.

Many people think that the term "highway" or even "road" is an exag-geration and that these paths were nothing more than dirt tracks. However, the Imperial Highway was 26 feet wide and paved with interlocking stones. A ditch of fresh water ran alongside the road, and trees were planted at reg-ular intervals to provide shade and shelter for travelers. The road crossed high mountain passes, traversed steep forested ridges and wide deserts and spanned at least 100 large rivers by impressive suspension bridges. The long-est of these bridges crossed the Río Apurimac in Perú, and was measured by Spanish missionaries as 148 feet long and 118 feet above the river at its low-est point. Tragically, the Incan road system was left to ruin or dismantled by the Spanish for stones to build their own monuments to power.

Huanya-Capac was born in Tomebamba, the son of a Cañari princess. He, in turn, married the daughter of the Quitu king and had a son, Atahualpa. On Huanya-Capac's deathbed, his favorite son, Atahualpa, was granted con-trol of Tomebamba and the northern half of the Incan Empire while his half-brother, Huascar, the rightful heir of Huanya-Capac, was granted control of Cuzco and the southern half of the Incan Empire. Apparently, if you are the direct descendant of the Sun God, as Incan rulers were considered to be, sharing was not a concept with which you were familiar. The once mighty and unified empire was now divided, and war soon broke out between the two brothers for ultimate control. In 1532, after five years of civil war, Huascar was captured and Atahualpa became the sole Incan ruler. Only nine months later, however, the entire Incan Empire lay in ruins.

This was accomplished primarily by Francisco Pizarro, an arrogant, brutal, ruthless and greedy Spaniard fully infected with "gold fever." Encouraged by Cortez's conquered riches from the Aztecs in 1521, Pizarro set off in a ship from Panamá in 1527 for the fabled riches of Perú. Landing in the coastal city of Tumbes, Pizarro received a friendly greeting and was given a tour of the city. Over the next several weeks Pizarro sailed his ship into other coastal towns and in each he was treated as a friend. But in this lamb's clothing lay the vicious heart of a conqueror, for this trip was merely for reconnaissance, and Pizarro would return.

In 1531, Pizarro did return to the South American coast with the intention of conquering the entire Incan Empire and in turn becoming fabulously rich. Pizarro was nothing if not wildly optimistic, for his army consisted of only 180 men and 27 horses, and ahead was a huge unknown empire protected by 250,000 troops. Pizarro landed north of the present city of Guayaquil and headed south down the coast, looting, burning and murdering everything in his path on the way. This time, though, the word of his acts spread before him, and Pizarro found little of the wealth he so desperately sought.

Pizarro marched through Ecuador into what is now northern Perú. Here, weak and discouraged, he realized that he would never be able to march the remaining 2000 kilometers to Cuzco to confront the Incan army and its ruler, Atahualpa. But luck was on Pizarro's side, for he learned that Atahualpa was not in Cuzco but instead less than 500 kilometers away in the city of Cajamarca. Four months later, Pizarro and Atahualpa stood face to face, Pizarro now with only 168 men and Atahualpa surrounded by a garrison of 7000 men and an army of 80,000 men camped nearby. In what has to be the greatest meeting of arrogance and unpreparedness (by Atahualpa) and confidence and ruthlessness (by Pizarro), Pizarro captured Atahualpa and killed 6000 Incans —supposedly without sustaining a single serious injury to any of his men. Seven months later, on July 26, 1533, after promises of safety to Atahualpa and several rooms filled with gold as ransom for Atahualpa's release, Pizarro ordered Atahualpa's death.

With the Incan Empire in disarray, Pizarro marched south to plunder Cuzco while his lieutenant, Sebastian de Benalcázar, marched north to conquer what is now Ecuador. Benalcázar was not alone in his desire to conquer the northern Incan Empire. News of the Incan riches had spread, and in early 1534, Pedro de Alvarado landed in Manta and in equally ruthless style marched toward Quito. Alvarado, who was eventually bought off by Pizarro, returned to Spain leaving Quito to Benalcázar. On December 6, 1534, Benalcázar arrived in Quito to find it in ruins—razed by one of Atahualpa's loyal generals to prevent its riches from falling into Spanish hands. Pizarro later marched through Perú and settled in Lima, where he was hacked to death by rival conquistadors in 1541. Still, Ecuador was largely in Spanish control by 1549.

Life for the indigenous people of the Andes was not good under either the Incas or the Spanish. After all the gold and silver ornamentation was taken, the Spaniards continued their never-ending quest for gold by mining the raw ore. To make laborers in the mines work longer and harder, the Spaniards plied them with coca leaves. The chemicals in coca leaves reduced hunger and thirst, and made possible work sessions that would have otherwise totally exhausted laborers. Most of the mines were in Perú and Colombia, and thus little coca was introduced by the Spanish to what is now Ecuador. This coincidence best explains why there is relatively little cocaine traffic in Ecuador today. It has been conservatively estimated that over nine million Indians died in the mines of Colombia and Perú. Equally devastating were the ravishes of European diseases, especially smallpox, that killed the indigenous people by the thousands. Beyond these deadly concerns, daily life for the conquered was filled with misery and suffering. The Spaniards considered anyone who was not a Christian to be subhuman, without a soul and heading for eternal damnation. "Why not brutalize and murder such people since they are already condemned?"

In the 17th and 18th centuries, Spain had a choking grasp on its vast territory in South America. Governors and viceroys, native and loyal to Spain, in conjunction with the church, controlled all aspects of life in Ecuador. There was no opportunity or freedom unless granted by the king's representative. An officer in the Royal Navy wrote in 1818 that "no South American could own a ship, nor could a cargo be consigned to him; no foreigner was allowed to reside in South America unless born in Spain, and non-Spanish capital could not be put to use in the colonies. Orders were given that no foreign ship should touch at a South American port; even ships in distress were not received with common hospitality, but were seized as prizes and the crews imprisoned." It is not hard to understand why in this environment, cries of "Independence" were soon to be heard.

The seeds of the eventual wars of South American independence were planted in armed conflicts across the continent. In 1692 and 1730, Peruvians staged an armed protest against the suffocating Spanish rule that was followed by an uprising in Venezuela in 1749. In 1780, 60,000 Quechua-speaking Indians took control of the central Andes for six months before they were defeated and then massacred by the Spanish. On August 10, 1809, Ecuador received its first taste of independence when Juan Pío Montúfar captured Quito and took its governor prisoner. This uprising lasted 24 days before Spanish troops from Colombia and Perú retook the city and killed all of the revolutionary leaders. Their heads were put on public display as a warning against future uprisings.

The final wars of independence that released South America from Spanish rule were like crashing waves that swept across the Andes. These wars were led in the south by José San Martín, the liberator of Perú and Argentina, and in the north by Simón Bolívar, the liberator of New Grenada—Venezuela, Colombia and Ecuador. Bolívar was born in Caracas in 1781. Ian Cameron describes him as "a small man, no more than five feet six inches, with a narrow tubercular chest and delicate hands and feet; yet he was capable of driving his whipcord body to amazing feats of endurance. He had dark eyes, curly hair, the nose of a patrician and the lips of a Negro. It was said by his contemporaries that women found him irresistible." Bolívar first tried to liberate Venezuela in 1815 but was defeated and cast into exile. He returned within a year, rejoined the battle for independence and liberated Colombia and Venezuela in 1819. From Caracas, Bolívar then marched south and helped Guayaquil gain its freedom on October 9, 1820. Two years later, Bolivar's most respected field commander, Antonio José de Sucre, defeated royalist troops on May 24, 1822, in the battle of Pichincha and liberated Quito.

In July of 1822, San Martín and Bolívar met in Guayaquil (a meeting commemorated by a famous statue on Guayaquil's waterfront) to plan the future of what Bolívar called "Gran Colombia"—the unification of Venezuela, Colombia and Ecuador. Gran Colombia lasted seven years, 1823–1830, until Ecuador was officially established in 1830 by General Juan José Flores.

The 19th and 20th centuries have seen much growth and turmoil in Ecuador. In the mid-1800s there was a 15-year period with 11 different governments and three new constitutions. Since then, military rule through coups has been more common than civilian elections, but the spirit of democracy has held on tenaciously. Ecuador was the first country in Latin America with a true democratic government, and today it remains one of the most stable countries in South America. The only external source of instability is from Perú on Ecuador's southern border. During World War II, with international interest obviously focused elsewhere, Perú invaded Ecuador and virtually uncontested acquired almost half of Ecuador's territory in the Amazon and the Province of Tumbes on the coast. A treaty was signed in Rio de Janeiro in 1942 that legitimized Perú's conquest by war. Chile, Argentina, Brazil and the United States also signed as guarantors of the protocol, but because of preoccupations with a global conflict, they pressured Ecuador into an unfavorable treaty. Later, after more careful consideration of the ramifications to this treaty, Ecuador rescinded its signing and claimed the original boundaries of Ecuador south to the Río Marañon and all of Tumbes on the coast. In reality, Perú undeniably controlled all of this land and appeared unlikely to ever give it up. The boundary officially defined in the Treaty of Rio de Janeiro was the actual separation of the two countries no matter what Ecuador's official maps indicated. However, the authors of the Treaty of Rio de Janeiro did not have access to satellites and electronic navigational aids in 1942, and the most rugged parts of this international boundary in the Andes, especially in the vicinity of the Cordillera del Cóndor, were left as *tierra incognita* with no way to concretely establish the location of the boundary. Both Perú and Ecuador placed numerous army camps along this ill-defined border, and periodic outbreaks of bloody skirmishes resulted. The most recent of these battles took place in 1981 and in early 1995. Recently, there has been some talk of making this area an international park and both sides backing off militarily, but testosterone levels, national pride and purported mineral reserves in the area will make a rational solution difficult.

The most serious recent event to challenge the democratic system in Ecuador came with the election of Abdalá Bucarám in the presidential elections of August 1996. Because of his erratic behavior, blatant nepotism (even by Latin American standards) and his bad singing (he recorded a CD of his favorite songs), newspapers and people on the street quickly dubbed him *"El Loco."* His six months in office led to a crisis brought about by embarrassment internationally but even more seriously by his systematic rape of the Ecuadorian treasury for his personal gain. In February of 1997, the legislature conducted a constitutional coup by voting Bucarám out of office and exiling him from further political actions in Ecuador. The legislature skipped over ambiguous parts of the constitution to appoint their own legislative leader, Fabián Alarcón, as acting president until the next scheduled elections in 1998. In the meantime, the elected vice president, Rosalía Arteaga, cited constitutional succession and claimed to be the new president. Of course *El Loco* was not silent in all this, and he, too, still claimed to be president. On one day Ecuador had at least three people all claiming to be the legitimate president of Ecuador. Finally Bucarám figured out he was no longer welcome, and he and his extended family fled to Panamá to live in the lap of luxury stolen from the people of Ecuador. Arteaga agreed to be reappointed vice president, and Alarcón continued as interim president. In all of this, the military never stepped in overtly, and Ecuador met yet another challenge to its democratic government.

A popularly-elected president, Jamil Mahuad, was chosen in July 1998, but with only a tiny 2% majority. He had served as a progressive and honest mayor of Quito, and the country had high hopes for his abilities to lead Ecuador into increasing prosperity and away from their overwhelming problems. The best laid plans of mice and men, however, are often waylaid in Ecuador by natural and unnatural events. The severest El Niño storms of the century battered the coast for five months in early 1998. Entire cities like Santa Rosa, Bahia de Caráquez and Manta were cut off for weeks by flooding and damage that destroyed roads all up and down the coast. Then in August a severe earthquake destroyed large parts of Bahia, and in September the volcano Pichincha, on whose sides Quito is built, began to show signs of impending eruption. Oil market prices went skidding in 1998–1999. Then the main oil duct from the Oriente to the coast, built in 1971 to last 25 years, began to rupture and explode with distressing regularity—killing hundreds and polluting large areas along its route. In March of 1999, draconian economic reforms caused the sucre to fall 25% in value in a single day, and general strikes of protest became more regular.

In the midst of all these problems, however, Mahuad did live up to one of his election promises in that finally a formal peace accord was signed with Perú in October 1998. With this treaty the ambiguities of the border and the deadly conflicts are hopefully now over forever. Much of the national budget to support the armed forces can be diverted to other priorities, and international investment is much more likely without the constant specter of war hanging over the country. Ecuador seems always to be staggering from one state of emergency to another, but somehow it survives. Expectations for the political leaders are often unrealistic, but life continues, the psyche of Ecuador is mysteriously preserved, and yet another problem is overcome or circumvented.

Today, Ecuador's main problems all stem from overpopulation and rapid urbanization. A hacienda-centered economy less than 20 years ago, more than 25 percent of Ecuador's population has now moved from rural areas to cities. The cities are ill-prepared to accept this human inundation. Full-time work is a luxury barely half the population enjoys. Housing, electricity, sewage treatment and potable water are still beyond the reach of most of Ecuador's population. Yet, paradoxically, with all of Ecuador's natural resources and economic potential in oil, gold, agricultural exports and fisheries, only a small minority of Ecuadorians live the good life. By some estimates, nearly 70 percent of the population lives below poverty lines defined by the United Nations. These problems, together with South America's densest population, make preserving the environment, protecting national parks and developing ecotourism seem like idealistic luxuries to most Ecuadorians. Overcoming poverty and preserving the environment obviously need not be a conflict, but more and more it is being perceived as such. Only a delicate balancing act among political, economic and environmental concerns has a chance of succeeding in Ecuador. Ecotourism is one aspect of this balancing act, and it has great potential for positive influence because it can directly and immediately speak to all these concerns.

TWO

The Ecological Picture

ECOTOURISM

Ecuador has a long history of ecotourism. Tourists from Europe started coming to its Galápagos Islands more than 150 years ago. They may have called themselves sailors, scientists or adventurers, but in many ways they walked like, talked like, and looked like ecotourists. With the establishment of the Galápagos Islands National Park and the involvement of tour companies providing easy access to this shrine to biology and natural history, full-blown ecotourism has become a way of life in Ecuador. Another change came in the 1970s, when the discovery of oil in the Amazonian lowlands of Ecuador led to the creation of many new roads, towns and airstrips in the "jungle." An increasing number of tourists attracted to Ecuador by the Galápagos decided to add on a short mainland excursion to see the now-accessible Amazon. More and more lodges were built to meet this increasing demand. By the late 1980s, the ecotourists visiting the mainland were becoming as important to the national economy as those touring the Galápagos. In a way, despite the obvious historical and biological interest in the Galápagos, adding on a few days to tour the Ecuadorian "jungle" was a bit like the "tail wagging the dog." In terms of diversity and species richness, natural wonders are thousands of times greater on the mainland. Darwin was able to perceive nature's evolutionary laboratory on the Galápagos largely because it was on such a simple scale. These same evolutionary processes have taken place on the mainland, but again they are multiplied thousands of times and as a result can often be mind-boggling. On the other hand, the diversity and complexity of the mainland habitats can also be considered thousands of times more interesting than the Galápagos just because so much more is available to challenge the senses and open the mind. Now, with the Galápagos reaching saturation levels of tourists and the mainland sites offering the access and variety of comfortable lodges to attract far greater numbers of tourists interested in seeing natural and cultural wonders not available on the Galápagos, we are finally seeing the "dog wag the tail."

Things have come a long way in the last 20 years, but the threat to mainland reserves continues. In 1977, when one of the authors of this book (DLP) led the first floral and faunal survey of the Río Yasuní in far eastern Ecuador, we went up rivers that no white man had been up for 80 years. We had to carry around a tape recorder with a recording in the language of the local and often aggressive people, the Huaorani. In case we encountered some of them, we knew we would have only a short time to use the recording to explain that we were harmless and not there to exploit them. Together with Ecuadorian colleagues, we were able to establish borders for the largest national park in Ecuador, a park that would protect one of the highest diversities of plant and animal species in the world. Within 12 years, however, the borders of Yasuní National Park were changed three times to accommodate other priorities. At some point the park could become so reduced and fragmented that it will neither adequately protect habitats and species nor attract tourist interest and dollars. Ecotourism dollars could be the power that finally establishes the park borders and the protection needed to have a real Yasuní National Park and not just a park on paper.

Oil interests have had a major impact on Ecuador's land use policies. Since the 1950s, a number of oil companies have been given leases throughout the Amazonia of Ecuador, including Shell, Texaco and Conoco. Although the oil reserves are not as extensive as those of Venezuela and Saudi Arabia, oil dominates virtually all national planning. With more than 50 percent of the national economy coming from oil, Ecuador's politicians will give away rights and ignore laws to accommodate the wishes of the oil extractors. The dominant international oil company now is a consortium called YPF, based in Argentina. Primarily because of public relations pressure in the U.S., this com-

Red-eyed Tree Frogs

pany is making environmental policy that is far ahead of what the Ecuadorian government requires. YPF appears ready to say that, yes, we have the technology to control the enormous oil leaks of the past, and we are ready to spend what it takes to introduce this technology to eastern Ecuador. Yes, we will build our roads and control our gas burn off to help preserve the integrity of the natural habitats we are exploiting. Yes, most importantly of all, we are ready to actively control the access of newly opened oil fields so colonists cannot invade and establish themselves in supposedly protected areas. Wherever the oil companies have opened up the forest in the past, it has been the illegal colonists entering on the access roads who have done the long-term damage. The colonists apply uncontrolled forest cutting and poor agricultural practices to a habitat for which they have received no training or education to be able to manage on a long-term basis. The result is that once-verdant habitat filled with food and useful products is reduced to a barren moonscape. No trees, no soil nutrients, lots of erosion and local climate changes all combine into catastrophe—both in terms of nature and in human suffering.

Ecotourists can best influence the oil companies by leaning on them and keeping their corporate feet to the fire of public relations. Now if a way can be found to pressure the banana companies and African oil palm companies (who cut down thousands of square kilometers of Amazonian and coastal forest for economic returns that are at best cyclic) to reduce their appetite for native forest, Ecuador's natural treasures will have a chance. If the shrimp companies, who indiscriminately destroy thousands of acres of coastal mangroves to produce an export crop sometimes so laden with chemicals that foreign markets will not accept it, can be similarly reasoned with, other natural areas of Ecuador also may still have a chance. Even if you have never thought of yourself as an activist, your visit to Ecuador to see and enjoy natural sites automatically makes you a participant. How much more you want to do beyond this passive participation is up to you.

ECOSYSTEMS

GEOGRAPHY

Ecuador is a small country (270,678 square kilometers, or about the size of Colorado or Italy), but what it lacks in size it more than makes up for in geographic variety. There are four main geographical regions in Ecuador: The Coastal region, the Andean highlands region (the Sierra), the Amazonian region (called *El Oriente* in reference to the eastern part of Ecuador), and the Galápagos Islands region. With a population of more than ten million, Ecuador has the greatest density of inhabitants (35 per square kilometer) of any country in South America, but the population is not evenly distributed.

Guayaquil, the largest city in Ecuador and the largest port on the Pacific coast of South America, has a population of over 1.8 million. Quito, the capital city high in the Andes, has over 1.4 million. Forty-six percent of the population lives in the Andean highlands region and 49 percent lives in the coastal region. Only 5 percent lives in the Oriente.

The coastline is made up of white-sand beaches broken in a few areas by headlands and dramatic cliffs rising directly from the high-tide line. In other areas, the beaches are interrupted by large estuaries at the mouths of rivers emptying into the ocean. Here fresh water and seawater mix to produce mangrove forests and fertile areas for fish, birds and many marine invertebrates to breed. The rivers associated with these streams flow from the mountains and are relatively narrow in the north and south, but in the central coastal plain, meandering rivers have formed extensive flat valleys that become immense swamps in the rainy season. Inland, the coastal plain rises abruptly into the heights of the west slope of the Andes mountains.

The Andean highlands region runs north to south the entire length of the country. It is made up of a western and eastern ridge of mountains separated by a narrow plateau (*altiplano*) 6600–9900 feet (2000–3000 meters) in altitude and 10–20 kilometers at its widest point. The two ridges are about 9900–13,200 feet (3000–4000 meters) high, punctuated by gigantic, snow-covered volcanoes extending to breathtaking heights at intervals along either ridge. The names of the volcanoes are as exotic as their appearance on a clear day or in a brief break in the cloud cover—from north to south they include: Cayambe (19,107 feet/5790 meters), Pichincha (15,820 feet/4794 meters), Antisana (19,001 feet/5758 meters), Cotopaxi (19,460 feet/5897 meters), Iliniza (17,368 feet/5263 meters), Chimborazo (20,823 feet/6310 meters), Altar (17,553 feet/5319 meters) and Sangay (17,259 feet/5230 meters), as well as many other "lesser" mountains. The Pacific slope is much steeper than the eastern slope into the Amazonian region, but no matter which way you are descending, it is obvious you are going down fast.

Nearly 50 percent of Ecuador's territory is in the Amazonian region (more if you follow the official Ecuadorian maps that extend the boundary with Perú 400 kilometers to the southeast to the Río Marañón). The Amazonian area of Ecuador is called *El Oriente*, or "the East." Four principal rivers drain this immense area: the Río Putumayo, Río Napo, Rio Curaray and Río Pastaza. They flow southeast to meet the Amazon or one of its main tributaries in Perú or Brazil. From the eastern base of the Andes (990 feet/300 meters elevation), the terrain toward the east is flat and uninterrupted by mountains as far as the horizon.

The Galápagos Island region (officially the Archipiélago de Colón) is a group of 13 major islands, 6 lesser islands and 42 named islets in the Pacific

Ocean 970 kilometers from the mainland coast. These islands either origi- nated as submarine volcanoes that eventually built up sufficient lava and ash to emerge from the ocean, or are the result of blocks of seafloor raised or tilted up by movements in the molten inner layers of the earth's crust. These volcanic islands (as well as many of the Andean volcanoes) are among the most active in the world.

CLIMATE

A deep ocean trench runs just offshore along the west coast of South Amer- ica. Winds and ocean currents bring cold but nutrient-rich water from the bottom of this trench to the surface. This upwelling of the Pacific Ocean is known as the Peruvian Upwelling or Humboldt Current. It reaches its north- ern limit in the southern part of coastal Ecuador. There it bends west toward the Galápagos. However, at irregular intervals of several years, movements of the warm equatorial current from the north can force the cold water up- welling south of Ecuador for 6–18 months at a time. The warming effect from this equatorial current is termed El Niño, "the Child" (because it is generally noticed about Christmas, the time of the Christ child). The presence or absence of the cold surface water off the coast has a dramatic effect on weather pat- terns and in turn affects the flora and fauna. Cold ocean air passing over rel- atively warm land produces an effect like a sponge sucking up the air's mois- ture and drying the atmosphere. On the other hand, warm ocean air passing over relatively cool land produces rainfall like a wet sponge being squeezed —the greater the differential between the ocean and land temperature, the greater the drying or moisture-producing effect.

The equatorial region receives the most direct rays of the sun of any area in the world. Here, the sun's rays strike at near right angles to the earth's sur- face and thus deliver the greatest energy. Much of this incredible level of energy is released to heat up the earth's surface and the air over it. Any mois- ture in the air rises as it heats until it gets so high it begins to cool and turn into rainfall. The combination of so much energy and so much moisture in the air explains why all of the worlds tropical rainforests are concentrated around the equator.

Lying on the equator, all four of Ecuador's geographic regions are obvi- ously affected by this combination of energy and moisture, but each region is also affected by local peculiarities. These interwoven conditions produce dramatic differences in weather patterns over a small area, and Ecuador has many different rainy seasons and habitats as a result.

In the high elevations of the Andean region, much of the moisture has been stripped from the air by the time it reaches the high ridges. The high- land interior plateau and slopes of the mountainous ridges facing the plateau tend to be very cool because of the high altitude and desertlike in dryness (dry shadow) because of the little rain left over to reach them.

In the Amazonian part of Ecuador in the east, little moisture is available from the winds passing from the Pacific over the Andes and down into the Amazon Basin. Instead, even though the Atlantic and Caribbean sources of moisture-laden air are much farther away than the Pacific, storm fronts from the north and east carry 30 to 40 percent of the precipitation to these forests. However, the majority of Amazonian precipitation is self-produced. Trees circulate water and nutrients from the ground through their roots and up to the highest branches and leaves via a process called evapotranspiration. This process involves evaporation of large volumes of water from the leaves. This water vapor, multiplied thousands of times by the density of trees and other plants around, rises over the forest canopy. If there is sufficient heat energy, the moisture-laden air will rise high enough to begin to cool, condense and turn into rain that falls back on the forest. Depending on the movements of local prevailing winds and the shape of the land, this locally recruited rain will be heavier in some areas than others, especially at the base of the eastern slope of the Andes. Largely because of this self-produced rainfall, the rainfall seasonality is not as extreme in the Amazon as on the coast, and instead of a dry season and a rainy season, you can expect a rainy season and a rainier season.

In years of El Niño, the warm equatorial waters intrude much farther south than normal and can extend into the Galápagos area. This change brings water and land temperatures closer together, and rain can increase dramatically, especially in the Galápagos and the southern coast of the mainland.

FLORA

Ecuador has one of the richest flora of the world. An estimate of 20,000 species of plants is likely low. Of these, more than 4500 or 23 percent are endemic (they occur nowhere else in the world) to Ecuador. More than 4500 species of orchids alone can be found here. Several distinct regions, based on the types of plants present, have been identified in Ecuador. Each region consists of large numbers of unique plant species that characterize and distinguish it from other regions.

Because of heavy rainfall, the forests of the extreme northern coast of Ecuador have evolved many plant species uniquely adapted to this type of habitat. The predominance of these specialized plants form a distinct vegetational region called the *Chocó*. To try and describe this forest you quickly discover that there are more shades of green, turquoise, teal, aquamarine and chartreuse than any five languages could handle. On one of the rare sunny days in this habitat, the spectrum of green colors goes into orbit. Although many of the species found here are shared with Central America and Colombia, a large proportion (up to 20 percent at some sites) are endemic. This area has the greatest diversity of plant species in the country. On one small study plot south of Santo Domingo de los Colorados, more than 1250 species from 136 families of plants have been found.

The coastal plain south of the *Chocó* to the Peruvian border is dry tropical forest. Here, little or no rain falls six months of the year, and the vegetation is adapted to a dry climate and short rainy season. Trees lose their leaves, roots go deep, cactus is common and most of the tall trees are along the rivers (called gallery or riparian forest). Where fresh or brackish water is predictable, like at the ocean's edge in estuaries, mangroves are common and form another floral region distinct from the tropical dry forest.

On both slopes of the Andes, small changes in altitude can produce some major changes in rainfall, cloudiness, and temperature. Many plant species adapted to a specific combination of rain, sunshine and temperature thus can only occur in a narrow range of altitude. Numerous distinct floral regions run in belts north and south. Some of the plant and animal species in these belts occur over a 3000-kilometer area from Venezuela to Argentina, but that area is restricted to a narrow, 660-foot band, above or below which they cannot exist. The vegetation in these attitudinal bands includes lower Andean forests such as the *Chocó*. A little higher, rainfall is supplemented by dense fog that forms regularly as the water vapor rising from the lowlands cools and condenses. The gatherings of trees here are called cloud forests and are typically festooned with thick layers of moss, orchids and pineapple relatives (bromeliads). In areas disturbed by landslides, large patches of alders grow. Higher on the slopes, the moisture levels drop off and the temperature falls considerably. Low bushes form impenetrable fortresses for birds and mammals. In protected gullies (*quebradas*) temperate forests grow, the most intriguing of which is a tree in the rose family called *Polylepis*. Its shaggy red bark is a signal of the presence of an entire community of plants and animals that are almost only associated with this tree species. Above the *Polylepis* forests, shrubs and trees quickly disappear to form a wet, grassy area known as paramo. Here the cold windy conditions influence the evolution of plants that hug the ground and look for all the world like an Alaskan tundra scene. The paramo eventually gives way to glacial scree of bare gravel and rocks just before the permanent snow line at about 5500 meters (18,000 feet).

In the Amazonian region, the forest is made up of numerous patches of forest types, many types often occurring within a small area. Tall, cathedral-like tree species grow on higher ground that is rarely if ever flooded by rising rivers. This forest type is called *tierra firme*. A series of forest types occurs between *tierra firme* and the forest found closest to the river. Each successive forest type is adapted more and more to the increasing chance of flooding. The fruits of plants in these seasonally flooded forests and the seeds inside them are more likely to be eaten by fish than by birds or monkeys. Near the river's edge is a forest type adapted to growing quickly in clearings created by the water's scouring action. These fast-growing plants include the hollow cecropia, five-meter grasses (*caña brava*) and willows. They also predominate on islands in the larger rivers.

Other types of forest vegetation are associated with the meandering river systems that are more common in eastern parts of Ecuador. Closer to the mountains the steep inclines and gravity force water to flow in relatively straight lines—cutting through most impediments by force of volume and speed. However, as this water reaches the Amazon Basin, the flow slows down. The total altitudinal drop from Coca on the Río Napo in Ecuador to Belem, Brazil, where the Amazon finally empties out into the Atlantic Ocean, is 990 feet/300 meters over a distance of 2200 kilometers. This gradual descent allows the rivers to wander (meander) in snakelike movements. As a meander forms, the momentum of the water continuously cuts out the banks on the outside of the curve. Eventually, the meander becomes U-shaped. Then, as the water continues to undercut the banks, the two tails of the "U" come closer and closer until, in a surge, the river cuts through the top of the "U." The meander is completely cut off from the river except at highest flood levels. In Ecuador, these cut-off meanders form lakes called *cochas*. A *cocha* no longer has a constant current to scour out accumulated trunks, sand and floating vegetation. The *cocha* slowly fills in, and a series of forest types replace each other in an often predictable sequence. Floating lily pads and grasses die and accumulate to give more terrestrial plant species a toehold. Cecropia gives way to semiterrestrial species such as Mauritius and chonta palms, which in turn give way to flood-forest species, which eventually give way to *tierra firme* species if the substrate rises high enough to escape flooding.

In the Galápagos Islands, the vegetation varies from island to island, but on the main islands it is characterized by deep green mangroves on the water's edge, a low arid zone with xerophytic (dry tolerant) shrubs and yellowish tree cacti from the coast to about 594 feet elevation. An intermediate altitudinal zone (to 1815 feet) is dominated by waxy-leafed Scalesia forests. The next higher and more humid zone has many low shrubs (*Cacaotillo*) of the genus *Miconia* with brilliant pink and lavender flowers at the beginning of the rainy season. In the most elevated and humid areas there are ferns, grasslands and distinctive trees adapted to low sunlight and foggy conditions.

Plants are uniquely adapted for one very important process: converting some of the light energy from the sun into chemical energy. This process is called photosynthesis, and it can only be done by plants. Without it, animals would have no food. The rate at which this conversion process takes place is called production. Tropical rainforests make up only 7 percent of the land surface of the world, yet they convert more light energy into plant products such as leaves, roots, trunks and fruits than any other terrestrial ecosystem.

To survive, plants must protect green leaf surfaces, the site of photosynthesis, from being removed or destroyed by animals eating them (herbivores). Sometimes this protection comes in the form of spines or thick, leathery leaves. More often, however, the plants use chemical protection. These chemicals are stored in the leaves, and when a hungry caterpillar tries to take a bite out of the leaf, it gets a mouthful of a chemical that may just taste bad or may be deadly. Even common plants we know in North America and Europe have these chemical protectants—nicotine, caffeine, digitalis, aspirin. By coincidence, some of these chemicals also have physiological effects on human beings. Ecuador is famous for having one of the best-known plant chemicals—quinine. It comes from the bark of the cinchona tree and was the first effective medicine found against malaria.

Almost every plant in Ecuador has a different chemical to fight off herbivores. With more than 20,000 species of plants in Ecuador alone, the chances that some of these plant chemicals have potential medicinal value is high. Fewer than 2 percent of the plants have been screened for their medicinal value, yet already many medicines have been found. The potential for medicines yet undiscovered is fantastic. So popular and lucrative has this search become, it has been given a name—chemical prospecting. Unlike temperate zone plant species that often have extensive geographical ranges, many tropical species grow in very restricted areas. That means in Ecuador forest destruction over relatively small areas can easily wipe out entire plant species. Along with the extinction of the plants goes the secret of the medicines that might have cured ovarian cancer, multiple sclerosis and many other plagues on humans.

Because plants cannot get up and move, they are faced with some problems animals don't have. To make babies, plants can't just get together and have sex. They have to rely on a third party—a *ménage à trois* if you will. In North America and Europe many plants use the wind to transfer pollen from one flower to the next. In the tropics, almost all plants use animals—such as bees, butterflies, bats and hummingbirds—to transfer the pollen that fertilizes new seeds. These animals are usually attracted to the flower by a sweet nectar, a scent or color. As the animal enters the flower for this reward, it gets pollen brushed on its head, legs or body. When it comes to the next flower for more dessert, the pollen falls off on the female part of the flower and fertilization takes place. Many pollinators and flowers have become dependent on each other. One species of hummingbird will only go to one species or genus of flower. The advantage of this codependency for the animal is that usually it has some special adaptation like a curved bill or extra-long tongue that other animals lack. This makes it impossible for the other animals—with straight bills or short tongues—to get to the flower's nectar and compete for food. The advantage to the flower in having only one pollinator species is that the pollen from the first flower is always going to go next to another flower of the same species. This efficiency means the flower doesn't have to make as much pollen as would a flower whose pollinator may go to five or six other flower species before finally coming to another flower of the same species. The disadvantage of this codependency is that if either flower or pollinator becomes extinct, it will drag the other one down with it. There's usually no time to evolve adaptations to change to another pollinator or flower species. In the tropics, conservation of even insignificant insects can mean the conservation of large trees that could not regenerate without that insect pollinator.

Another problem many plants have to face because they aren't mobile is how to get their seeds away from the mother plant. The worst place for a seed to try and grow is in the shade of its mother. The adult tree competes for food and water in the soil and for sunlight for photosynthesis. Also, in the tropics, specialized beetles seek out seeds in which to lay their eggs. These young beetle larvae hatch out of the egg and completely eat the seed, destroying its ability to germinate. These seed predators can most easily find seeds that are concentrated below the mother tree. Any seed that can get away from the mother has a much better chance of surviving to grow up to be an adult tree. In North America and Europe, seed dispersion is often done by the wind. In the tropics, wind is used by some plants, but even more common is the use of animals to transport seeds away from the mother tree. Seeds that are wrapped in a sweet pulp (fruits) attract these animals. Birds, monkeys, rodents and bats eat these fruits, often whole, and the next day or so when they defecate, the undigested seeds are passed and deposited on the soil, usually far from the mother tree. This dependency on animals affects the timing, size, hardness, flavor and number of seeds. It even affects the distribution of individuals of each plant species within the forest.

FAUNA

There are more than 320 species of mammals known from Ecuador, and 25 of them are endemic. Seventeen of these mammal species are monkeys, and a large number are bats and small rodents. Three species of tapirs (the largest mammal in South America and related to the rhinoceros) occur, one each in the coastal region, the Amazonian region and the Andean region. The mountain or hairy tapir (*danta*) is the least known and is found in cloud forests where few people have ever seen anything but tracks. This mountain habitat is also home to another enigmatic species, the Spectacled Bear (the only species of bear found in South America). It occurs in small numbers throughout the Andes from Venezuela to northern Argentina. Other large mammals include the Amazonian manatee and two species of river dolphin, all of which live in eastern Ecuador, but only in the lower reaches of the large rivers and associated *cochas*. The pink dolphin is by far the easiest of these aquatic mammals to see as it often surfaces near boats or canoes.

Jaguars, mountain lions, ocelots, margay cats and jaguarundi (otter cat) are found in many regions of Ecuador, but as is typical throughout their range from Mexico to Argentina, these large predators are sparsely distributed and very elusive. Chances of seeing one are so remote that you should be thrilled just to find a paw print. Even their favorite prey, which includes several species of deer and two species of wild pigs, are difficult to see. Three species of anteaters and an extremely rare forest dog are also present, but so rare they are almost impossible to spot.

BIRDS   Although plant and mammal species are numerous in Ecuador, it isn't until you start comparing bird species that it really becomes obvious that species diversity is unbelievably high in this small country. In all of North America north of Mexico, there are only about 700 regularly occurring bird species. In Costa Rica there are 830 species of birds, but in Ecuador there are more than 1550 species of birds! South America is the birdiest continent, with 3200 species of the world's 9000 species, and little Ecuador, the size of Colorado, has half the species found in all of South America. For instance, 115 species of hummingbirds are found in Ecuador. Their common

White-tipped Sicklebill

names reflect both the breadth of their adaptations as well as the frustrations of scientists trying to maintain some semblance of order in naming this abundance of species—the Giant Hummingbird, the Long-billed Starthroat, the Band-tailed Barbthroat, the White-whiskered Hermit, the Spangled Coquette, the Glowing Puffleg, the Mountain Avocetbill, the Sword-billed Hummingbird, the Amethyst-throated Sunangel and the White-tipped Sicklebill, to name only a few.

In Ecuador, at single sites the size of a small farm in Iowa, more than 400 species of birds have been recorded. At any one of these sites, it is possible to find more than 30 species of hawks, 20 species of parrots, 50 species of blackish-gray (and nearly impossible to distinguish) antbirds and 60 species of tanagers. However, in mature forest, where most of these species occur, you can walk for a half-hour and not see a single bird. Then, all of a sudden, a flock will move through the canopy or the undergrowth and be around or over you for two or three minutes—50 or 60 individuals of 20 species all moving together. Then, as fast as they appeared, they are gone. More often than not, you heard rather than saw these birds, and the few you could get your binoculars on were a leaf-obscured vision of an eyebrow or a bit of the breast. Evidently, predation on these birds by hawks, snakes and other sharp-toothed animals is so intense, it pays the forest birds to stick together. With so many eyes watching out, it is harder for the predators to get close. The tradeoff is that, in a short visit, you will not get much of a chance to see these birds. In secondary forest and cutover areas there are fewer species of birds, but they are easier to see, even in their flocks.

REPTILES AND SNAKES   Other groups of animals also show high levels of species diversity in Ecuador. Among the 350 species of reptiles are crocodiles in the coastal mangroves and several species of closely related caiman in the Amazonian region. Because the eyes of these crocodilians reflect bright orange or red in the beam of a flashlight at night, they are easy to spot from a quiet canoe—but, unfortunately, they are also easy to shoot if that is the goal. Poisonous snakes such as the fer-de-lance and bushmaster are present in many regions, but they are not common. Most snakes you see will be nonpoisonous. The large (17 feet) anaconda lives throughout the Amazonian region in rivers and *cochas*, but is difficult to spot. If you are lucky, you might see one sunning itself on the beach by a river.

FROGS   Some 375 species of frogs and toads make their home in Ecuador. The most interesting are the poison-arrow frogs (*Dendrobates*). These species usually are spectacularly colored—red, black or day-glow orange and green. They exude a poison from their skin that Indians used to tip their arrows. These and most other frogs are only active at night and after considerable rainfall. If you want to see them, go out on forest paths at night with a flashlight. Listen for the male to give its call from leaves of undergrowth bushes or from within a bromeliad. Most of these frogs will not be in the water itself but in moist parts of the forest undergrowth or even the canopy.

FISH   The fish of Ecuador are not well known, but there are more than 450 marine species and perhaps 800 freshwater species found in the country. Many of the bright tropical fish kept in aquariums back home come from the black-water rivers of this area, and these fish have become an important source of foreign exchange. Of all the fish in the Amazonian region, the piranha is probably the most infamous. In the tourist's imagination, the horror of being attacked en masse and eaten down to the bone in a matter of seconds is a frightening certainty for those foolish enough to enter the water. Actually, the piranha found in Ecuador are most dangerous when a freshly caught one is flopping around in the bottom of a canoe next to lots of exposed bare feet. We have gone swimming in *cochas* and rivers with these fish without any problems. Paradoxically, most of the species related to piranhas make their living by eating fruit. Only a few fish have teeth and behavior adapted for attacking and eating aquatic animals. One of the most notorious fish in the Amazon is a tiny catfish. Normally, it is parasitic on the gill tissue of large fish. It locates the large fish by detecting water currents passing through the gills and swims upstream into the gills. There it erects its sharp dorsal spine, so it cannot be dislodged as it feasts on the host's blood. Reportedly this tiny fish can mistake a stream of human urine underwater as a cue to swim upstream. It then swims up the urethra of the unfortunate and unsuspecting skinny-dipper and erects its spine—to be removed only surgically.

INSECTS   All of these "oh my" stories and mind-numbing numbers of species for animals and plants pale when the topic switches to insects. Instead of hundreds or even thousands, insects can be spoken of only in terms of millions. Perhaps 80 percent of all species—plant and animal—in Ecuador are insects. As a frame of reference, a scientist sampling insects from the canopy of forests in Ecuador has found more than two pounds of insects in one tree crown. These two pounds of insects consisted of at least 2000 species, of which fewer than 100 had been named previously by scientists. All the rest were unknown. Among their many duties in Ecuador, insects pollinate, disperse seeds, break down the wood fibers of dead logs, eat leaves, control other insect populations, spread diseases and serve as food for many large animals. The large plants and animals we normally associate with tropical environments have relatively little impact on the habitat in comparison to the tiny insects we usually consider insignificant pests. For the tourist, however, the common image is of a mosquito-filled jungle where every movement in the open is uncomfortable. Except for a few areas such as coastal mangrove forests and exceptionally wet weeks in the Amazon, tourists will be amazed at how unobtrusive stinging and biting insects will be. Most days in the forests of Ecuador will have far fewer mosquitoes than a summer day in Minnesota.

Butterflies appear throughout Ecuador in numbers and colors unimaginable. The first time you see the electric blue wings of the giant morpho butterfly, you will never forget it. Monstrous but harmless scarab beetles with a wing span of 8 inches fly at night. Also active at night are large click beetles, flying slowly through the understory with their two glowing headlights and a red taillight. At 6 p.m. every night in the tropical parts of the country, hundreds of cicadas simultaneously begin their earpiercing trills. Ironically, they use their eardrums to make the noise. Perhaps the most dangerous animal you are likely to encounter during your stay is the large (1 inch) black ant called *conga*. They do not walk in large swarms but are instead solitary. Their sting is extremely painful and can even cause hallucinations. The hundreds of other species of ants, however, are relatively harmless. Even the notorious army ants that raid in enormous swarms through the understory are not dangerous. They are after other insects, not human beings. The leaf cutter or umbrella ants clear broad paths along which they parade in long lines carrying bright green leaf sections. They march from the tree whose leaves they have cut with their sharp jaws to their large underground nests. Here they culture tasty fungi on the leaves to feed themselves and their young—and at the same time add nutrients to the soil.

Both by day and by night insects of every color, shape and size perform their life-providing function critical for habitats throughout the country. Look around and watch carefully. You will see more important ecological interactions among these six-legged creatures than for all the Jaguars, monkeys and macaws combined.

ENVIRONMENTAL EXPEDITIONS

You'll find a large number of companies available for environmental-oriented touring of Ecuador. Some of these companies are narrowly focused, such as the bird tour companies. Others specialize in photography, butterflies or orchids. Many are general and cater to a wide range of needs and interests. The North American and European companies often subcontract to local Ecuadorian companies, and you end up paying commission several times over. There are hundreds of Ecuadorian companies that claim to be able to plan your trip for you, and some are excellent. However, by Ecuadorian law, only those companies having tourism licenses issued by the government through its Ministry of Tourism, the government agency in charge of tourism, plus permits from the Ecuadorian National Park Service (INEFAN) for specific nature reserves like Cotopaxi, Cuyabeno or Yasuní, are permitted to operate and lead these tours.

This law is not just there to hassle tourists and make their lives more difficult. It is a way of protecting tourists who could not otherwise know if the company they are dealing with is reputable and dependable. Many of the unauthorized companies are far less expensive, but if you book a domestic flight to Coca with them and it is canceled or a road is closed and you are forced to return to Quito, there may be no alternative transportation available or you may have no hotel room in Quito while you wait for the next flight. If your time is limited, and delays only frustrate you, stick to the reputable and legal Ecuadorian tour companies. They always have plans for contingencies and will find the most convenient alternatives when the unexpected happens.

Even if you have time and want to be independent (unless you are the type of independent tourist who actually likes to brag about how bad the trip was, how many times you got lost, how awful the roads were, and so on), we strongly recommend that you plan your trip through these legal ecotourist companies in Ecuador. The country is quickly improving its tourist facilities, but roads wash out, bridges give way and mudslides can block major highways for days, delaying you and interrupting your enjoyment unless someone knows how to avoid or get around the problem.

Another irritating but common problem for independent travelers is the absence of road signs and directions throughout the country. Even Quito and Guayaquil, which have more highway signs than anywhere else in Ecuador, can be extremely frustrating if not downright impossible to navigate. Hiring a car with a local driver will save you countless situations where you have no idea where the road to Mindo went, or why the car all of a sudden won't start, or whether you should go off hiking into the forest and leave the car alone. These tour companies can also supply guides that are very familiar with Ecuadorian wildlife and flora. Not only will you get to know an Ecuadorian well, he or she will make it possible for you to know Ecuador much better than on your own.

For more details on ecotours in Ecuador and updates on related conservation issues, contact: Oswaldo Muñoz, past President, **Ecuadorian Ecotourism Association** (the private national organization dealing with ecotourism), Avenidas Coruña 1349 and Orellana, Quito; 2-527-577, fax: 2-565-261. Mr. Muñoz is actively using his position and contact with local and foreign environmental/tourism organizations to bring about a positive change in the attitude of government and industry toward Ecuador's environment. He speaks fluent New York City English and will be more than happy to let you know how you can help support conservation efforts in Ecuador.

National tourism operators who participate actively in the Ecuadorian Ecotourism Association are:

CUENCA

Ecotrek, Calles Larga 7-108 and Luís Cordero, Cuenca; 7-834-677, fax: 7-835-387; e-mail: ecotrek@az.pro.ec.

Expediciones Apullacta, Calles Gran Colombia 11-02 and General Torres, Cuenca; 7-837-815, fax: 7-837-681; e-mail: apu@az.pro.ec.

GUAYAQUIL

Canodros, Calle Urdaneta 1418 and Avenida del Ejército, Prolab Building; 4-280-164, 4-280-173, 4-280-143; in Quito 2-222-203; fax: 4-287-651; e-mail: eco-tourism1@canodros.com.ec.

Etica, Calle Isla Santa Cruz 103 and Avenida de las Américas, Guayaquil; 4-284-666, 282-348, 393-042, fax: 4-280-933; e-mail: cmoncayo@etica.com.ec.

LAGO AGRIO

Caiman Safaris, Avenida Quito 414 y Fco. de Orellana, Lago Agrio; 9-824-302, 6-830-115, fax: 830-177.

LOJA

Biotours Ecuador, Calles Colón 1496 and Sucre, phone/fax: 7-578-398; e-mail: Biotours@uio.satnet.net.

QUITO

Adventour, Calama 339 y Reina Victoria, Quito; 2-223-720, fax: 2-223-720; e-mail: adventou@uio.satnet.net.

Amerindia, Avenida Shyris N39-237 Edificio Autocom, 3rd floor, Quito; 2-439-736, fax: 2-439-735; e-mail: ecuador@amerindia.net.

Andes & Equinox, Foch 747 and Amazonas, Quito; 9-495-428, fax: 9-492-060; e-mail: eco-trek@uio.satnet.net.

Angermeyer's Expeditions, Calle Foch 726 and Avenida Amazonas, Quito; 2-569-960, 2-546-013, fax: 2-553-097; e-mail: angeme1@angemeyer.com.ec.

Centro Cofán, Los Crisantemos 186, Barrio Los Laureles, Quito; 2-437-844, fax: 2-437-844; e-mail: tranturi@uio.satnet.net.

Cruceros and Expediciones Dayuma, Avenida 10 de Agosto 3815 and Mariana de Jesús, Villacís Pazos Office Building, 4th floor, Office 301, Quito; 2-564-924, 664-490, fax: 2-564-924; e-mail: dayuma@hoy.net.

Ecuadorian Tours, Avenida Amazonas 329 and Calle Jorge Washington, 2-560-488, 2-560-494, fax: 2-501-067; e-mail: ecuadorian@accessinter.net.ec.

Empresa Metropolitana De ASEO-EMASEO, Calles Briceño 605 and Guayaquil, 2-519-622, 2-515-278, fax: 2-583-413; e-mail: emaseo1@ecuanex.net.ec.

Explorandes, Wilson 537 and Diego de Almagro, Quito; 2-556-937, 222-699, 556-936, fax: 2-556-938; e-mail: explora@uio.satnet.net.

Klein Tours, Avenida de Los Shyris 1000 and Calle Holanda, 2-430-345, fax: 2-442-389; e-mail: kleintou@uio.satnet.net.

Latitude Cero, Calles Austria 128 and Checoeslavaquia, Quito; 2-464-938, fax: 2-464-939; e-mail: mlopez@accessinter.net.

Metropolitan Touring, Avenidas República del Salvador 970 and Naciones Unidas; 2-465-868, fax: 2-464-702; e-mail: lmr@metropolitan.com.ec.

Native Life Travels, Foch E4-167 and Avenida Amazonas, 2-505-158, 2-550-836, fax: 2-229-077; e-mail: natlife1@natlife.com.ec.

Neblina Forest Birding Tours, Madroños 1152 and Avenida El Inca conjunto Santa Barbara, Casa 46, 2-407-822, fax: 9-703-939, or 800-538-2149 in the U.S.; e-mail: mrivaden@pi.pro.ec.

Neotropic Turis, Calle Robles 513 and Reina Victoria; 2-521-212, fax: 2-224-271; e-mail: neotropic@uio.satnet.net.

Nuevo Mundo Travel and Tours, Avenidas Coruña 1449 and Orellana, 2-552-617, 2-553-818, fax: 2-565-261; e-mail: nmundo@uio.telconet.net.

Pamir Travel, Juan León Mera 721 and Veintimilla, Quito; 2-220-892, 542-605, fax: 2-547-576; e-mail: htorres@pi.pro.ec.

Quasar Naútica, Avenida de Los Shyris 2447 and Calle Gaspar de Villarroel; 2-446-996, 2-446-997, fax: 2-436-625; e-mail: qnautic1@ecnet.ec.

Transturi, Calles José Pinzón 701 and Victor Hugo (Jipijapa); 2-245-055, fax: 2-466-295; e-mail: tranturi@uio.satnet.net.

Tropic Ecological Adventures, Avenida República 307 and Calle Diego de Almagro, Office 1-A; 2-225-907, fax: 2-560-756; e-mail: tropic@uio.satnet.net.

Viajes Orion, Avenidas Atahualpa 955 and República; 2-462-004, fax: 2-432-891; e-mail: vorion@uio.satnet.net.

U.S. AND EUROPEAN-BASED NATURE TOUR COMPANIES   The companies listed below are among the most conservation-minded international tour companies working in Ecuador. They differ greatly in their costs and how flexible they are in meeting your needs. Some will emphasize general natural history, some will include cultural exposure as well as natural history, others are very narrowly focused, such as the intense birding tours. If you like to sleep in until 7 a.m. and identify a few birds coming to feeders, do not sign up with one of these intense birding tours. Not only will you be disappointed, but your bird-twitching companions will quickly come to dislike you as well. Choose the tour group to fit your passion and intensity. In general, they conduct small (10–20 people) tours, but some will plan individualized tours for you. Some will have their own guide accompanying you from North America or Europe. This guide will serve as naturalist, problem solver, and facilitator. Those companies that have much lower prices for the same tour are likely keeping their costs down by relying solely on local guides, who may change from site to site. In this case, the tour company is probably working through one of the Ecuadorian companies listed above and adding on an additional commission. If you work directly through the Ecuadorian company, you would likely get the same tour for 15 to 20 percent less. Ask questions of these tour companies, so you get what you want out of them. How many people are on each tour? Do they supply their own guide? Do they organize individualized tours? Do they have access to group international air fares to give you greatly reduced prices on even the best airlines? And please let us know if any of these companies conduct their tours with insensitivity to conservation ethics.

Birdquest
Two Jays, Kemple End, Birdy Brow
Stonyhurst, Lancashire BB7 9Q
England
1254-826317, fax: 1254-826780
Small-group intense birding tours on the mainland and the Galápagos.

Borderland Tours
2550 West Calle Padilla
Tucson, AZ 85745
520-882-7650, 800-525-7753
Small-group natural history and cultural tours of the mainland with emphasis on birds.

Cheesemans' Ecology Safaris
20800 Kittredge Road
Saratoga, CA 95070
408-867-1371, 800-527-5330,
fax: 408-741-0358

e-mail: cheeseman@aol.com
Small-group natural history tours of the mainland.

Eagle-eye Tours
P.O. Box 94672
Richmond, BC V6Y 4A4
Canada
604-231-9661, 800-373-5678,
fax: 604-231-9482
e-mail: birdtours@eagle-eye.com
Small-group intense birding tours of the mainland.

Field Guides
P.O. Box 160723
Austin, TX 78716-0723
512-327-4953, fax: 512-327-9231
e-mail: fgileader@aol.com
Small-group intense birding tours of the mainland and the Galápagos.

Focus on Nature Tours
P.O. Box 9021
Wilmington, DE 19809
302-529-1876, fax: 302-529-1085
e-mail: font@wittnet.com
*Small-group intense birding tours of
the mainland and the Galápagos.*

Footloose Forays
P.O. Box 175
Sebastopol, CA 95472
phone/fax: 707-829-1844
e-mail: mjnature@aol.com
*Small-group broad natural history
tours of the Galápagos and mainland
Amazonian jungle.*

Forum International
91 Gregory Lane #21
Pleasant Hill, CA 94523
510-671-2900, fax: 510-946-1500
e-mail: forum@ix.netcom.com
*Small-group and individually tailored
tours for education, trekking,
white-water rafting and nature
observing.*

Galápagos Travel
P.O. Box 1220
San Juan Bautista, CA 95045-1220
408-623-2920, 800-969-9014,
fax: 408-623-2923
e-mail: 74072,1127@compuserve.com
*A specialized travel company that
only works in the Galápagos Islands
and operates natural history tours
and photography workshops there
throughout the year.*

GEO Expeditions
P.O. Box 3656
Sonora, CA 95370
209-523-0152, 800-351-5041
e-mail: geoexped@mlode.com
*Small-group natural history tours of
Galápagos as well as some mainland
tours.*

Gerlach Nature Photography
P.O. Box 258
Mack's Inn, ID 83433
phone/fax: 208-558-7053
*Small-group nature photography tours
of the Galápagos.*

Holbrook Travel
3540 NW 13th Street
Gainesville, FL 32609
800-451-7111, fax: 904-371-3710
e-mail: travel@holbrook.usa.com
*Small-group or individual natural
history and photography tours of the
mainland and the Galápagos. Also
plans group tours for the elderly
together with Elderhostel.*

Inca Floats, Inc.
1311 63rd Street
Emeryville, CA 94608
510-420-1550, fax: 510-420-0947
e-mail: incafloats@aol.com
*Small-group natural history tours of
the Galápagos and some tours of the
mainland.*

International Expeditions
One Environs Park
Helena, AL 35080
205-428-1700, 800-633-4734,
fax: 205-428-1714
e-mail: intlexp@aol.com
*Galápagos tours as well as mainland
tours to the highlands and the Oriente
jungle.*

Journeys
4011 Jackson Road
Ann Arbor, MI 48103
313-665-2945, 800-255-8735,
fax: 313-665-2945
e-mail: info@journeys-intl.com
*Nature and culture travel for individu-
als and small groups.*

Mountain Travel-Sobek
6420 Fairmont Avenue
El Cerrito, CA 94530-3606
510-527-8100, 800-227-2384,
fax: 510-525-7710
e-mail: info@mtsobek.com
*Trekking in highlands and Oriente
together with white-water rafting.*

Oceanic Society Expeditions
Fort Mason Center
Building E
San Francisco, CA 94123-1394
415-441-1106, 800-326-7491,
fax: 415-474-3395
*Small-group natural history tours of
the Galápagos.*

Overseas Adventure Travel
625 Mt. Auburn Street
Cambridge, MA 02138
617-876-0533, 800-221-0814
e-mail: boberlander@bitnet.net
*Small-group tours or individual treks,
nature and wildlife viewing mainly on
the Galápagos Islands, but there are
some trips to the highlands of the
mainland.*

Questers Tours and Travel
381 Park Avenue South
New York, NY 10016-8806
212-251-0444, 800-488-8668,
fax: 212-251-0890
e-mail: quest-one@msn.com
*Group natural history and cultural
tours of the Galápagos and highland
areas of the mainland.*

Victor Emanuel Nature Tours
P.O. Box 33008
Austin, TX 78764
800-328-8368
e-mail: ventbird@aol.com
Small-group and individual intense

*birding tours on the mainland and the
Galápagos.*

Voyagers International
P.O. Box 915
Ithaca, NY 14851
800-633-0299
e-mail: voyint@aol.com
*Group and individual travel to the
Galápagos, highland markets and
Amazonian jungle.*

Wildland Adventures
3516 N.E. 155th
Seattle, WA 98155
800-345-4453
e-mail: wildadve@aol.com
*Small groups on Galápagos, Andean
and Amazonian treks.*

Wings
1643 North Alvernon Way
Suite 105
Tucson, AZ 85712
520-320-9868, fax: 520-320-9373
e-mail: wings@rtd.com
*Small-group intense birding tours on
mainland.*

Woodstar Tours, Inc.
908 South Massachusetts Avenue
DeLand, FL 32724-7022
904-736-0327
*Small-group birding and natural
history tours on mainland.*

Zegrahm and Eco Expeditions
1414 Dexter Avenue North, Suite 327
Seattle, WA 98109
206-285-4000, 800-628-8747,
fax: 206-285-5037
e-mail: zoe@zeco.com
*Small-group natural history tours of
the Galápagos with limited mainland
extension.*

HOW TO HELP

FOLLOW A CODE OF ENVIRONMENTAL ETHICS

A **code of ethics for sustainable tourism** was devised several years ago by the Costa Rican Department of Responsible Tourism of the Institute for Central American Studies (Apartado 1524-2050, San Pedro de Montes de Oca, San José, Costa Rica; e-mail: mesoamer@sol.racsa.co.cr). We feel that this set of guidelines is appropriate for ecotourism in Ecuador as well, and with permission of the Costa Rican DRT, we repeat it here.

1. **Wildlife and natural habitats must not be needlessly disturbed.** Visitors should stay on the trails, remain within designated areas, and not collect anything except litter. Visitors should keep their distance from wildlife so it is not compelled to take flight. Animal courtship, nesting or feeding of young must not be interrupted. Bird nests should be observed from a safe distance through binoculars. Marine mammals should be observed only with the assistance of a trained guide. Photographers also should keep their distance: foliage should not be removed from around nests, and animals should not be molested for the sake of a picture. Monkeys and other wild animals should never be fed, because this alters their diet and behavior.

2. **Waste should be disposed of properly.** Tour operators should set a good example for visitors by making sure that all garbage is confined to the proper receptacles. Boats and buses must have trash cans or bags. Special care should be taken with plastic that is not biodegradable. No littering of any kind should be tolerated. When possible, tourists and tour groups should use returnable or reusable containers.

3. **Tourism should be a positive influence on local communities.** Tourism and tour operators should make every reasonable effort to allow communities near natural areas to benefit from tourism. By hiring local guides, patronizing locally owned restaurants and lodges and buying local handicrafts, tourists can help convince residents that wild places are worth saving.

4. **Tourism should be managed and sustainable.** Tour operators should encourage managers of parks and reserves (including the Ecuadorian government) to develop and implement long-term management plans. These plans should prevent deterioration of ecosystems, prevent overcrowding, distribute visitors to underutilized areas and consider all present and future environmental impact.

5. **Tourism should be culturally sensitive.** Tour operators should give visitors an opportunity to enjoy and learn from (Ecuador's) mix of cultures. Tourism should serve as a bridge between cultures, allowing people to interact and enrich their understanding of how other people live. Tours should be designed to provide participation in and enhance appreciation of local traditions.

6. **There must be no commerce in wildlife, wildlife products or native plants.** There are strict international laws prohibiting the purchase or transport of endangered wildlife. Tourists should not buy or collect any wildlife, and should make sure that the natural products they wish to purchase are commercially grown. Wood crafts generally constitute a viable economic option for local artisans, and tourists should encourage local production from sustainable timber sources.

7. **Tourists should leave with a greater understanding and appreciation of nature, conservation and the environment.** Visits to parks and refuges should be led by experienced, well-trained and responsible naturalists and guides. Guides should be able to provide proper responsible supervision of the visitors, prevent disturbances to the area, answer questions of the visitors regarding flora and fauna, and describe the conservation issues relevant to the area.

8. **Ecotourism should strengthen the conservation effort and enhance the natural integrity of places visited.** Companies offering "ecotourism" must show even greater concern for the natural areas visited, involving tourists in conservation efforts. Tour operators should collaborate with conservation organizations and government agencies to find ways to improve Ecuador's environmental programs.

Visitors should be made aware of Ecuador's great achievements as well as the problems. The best tour operators will find ways for interested tourists to voice their support of conservation programs: by writing letters of support, contributing money, volunteering to work in a park or reserve, or other creative outlets for concerned activism.

If tour operators, tourists, government agencies, conservation and development organizations work together, ecotourism in Ecuador can continue to grow, visitors will leave the country satisfied and enriched, and local efforts to conserve our natural heritage will be stronger and more diverse.

Many private conservation groups (nongovernment organizations or NGOs) have sprung up in recent years in Ecuador. Some of them are focused on a single geographical area or habitat. A few are more national in scope, but all of them are deserving of your help. From the following list, pick out a group or two that work in a part of Ecuador you visited or that work in an area that interests you personally—such as children's environmental education or birds. Direct communication with Ecuadorians who will appreciate your interest and help can be a satisfying reward. That they can get so much done with even small gifts is more evidence that your trip to Ecuador can keep on helping save habitat for future generations even after you have returned home. For detailed information on local environmental programs, read *Directorio Verde: Organismos Ambientalistas en el Ecuador* (in Spanish) by A. Varea, A. Maldonado and C. Barrera. Published in 1993 by Comité Ecuménico de Proyectos and Central Evangélica de Ayuda al Desarrollo. Below, we list the most active of these nongovernment conservation organizations by region with their addresses and phone/fax numbers, and urge you to contact them.

COCA

Capuchina Mission
Nicolás Lopey s/n, Coca (Casilla 17-2101918, Quito)
2-241-281 (Quito)
This church-based environmental group was founded in 1945 and works in the Coca area to create economic incentives to conserve tropical forests. It is especially focused on agricultural plans that avoid plantations of single plant species (monoculture). These tend to need large capital investments and exclude local people except as indentured workers. The group also works to legally contest contamination of the environment by oil companies and limit road building into pristine forest areas inhabited by indigenous people.

CUENCA

Ecuadorian Corporation for the Conservation of Nature–Ecological Group "Tierra Viva"
Gran Colombia 520, Cuenca
7-842-621, fax: 7-842-621
This group was founded in 1986 and concentrates on controlling contamination of the environment and erosion. It provides legal assistance to local communities, as well as monitors industrial pollution in the Cuenca area.

ESMERALDAS

Ecological Foundation Plantemos Ahora
Malecón and Manuela Cañizares, Esmeraldas
6-713-000

The participants in this foundation, founded in 1992, want to transform the passive attitude of the public and local government into active participation in the development and rational use of natural resources. They sponsor research, academic training, environmental education and lobby politicians to make positive decisions about the environment.

GALÁPAGOS

Charles Darwin Foundation for the Galápagos Islands
6 de Diciembre 4757, Casilla 17-01389, Quito
2-244-803, 2-241-573, fax: 2-443-935

One of the oldest (it was founded in 1964) and most influential environmental organizations in Ecuador, the Charles Darwin Foundation has an international reputation. Its goals are to conduct scientific studies, conserve and protect all habitats in the Galápagos Islands. They also serve as the primary consultant to the Ecuadorian national government on matters of conservation in the Galápagos Islands. Their programs of environmental education and influence on political decisions reach far beyond the Galápagos to the entire country and often to the international community.

GUAYAQUIL

Andrate Ecological Foundation
Edificio Inca, García Moreno 804 and 9 de Octubre, 1° piso,
Casilla 5800, Guayaquil
4-292-860, fax: 4-290-740

This foundation was founded in 1993 and owns and manages 5000 acres of tropical dry forest within the Churute Mangrove Ecological Reserve located south of Guayaquil. The organization supports scientific research as well as management of forest restoration.

Corporation for the Protection of Natural Resources (Corporacíon Protectora de Recursos Naturales)
Jambelí 206 and México, Guayaquil
4-330-950

Founded in 1988, this group's focus is the environment in the city of Guayaquil. They are fighting problems of industrial pollution, uncontrolled urban expansion into estuarine areas, and deforestation of mangrove and local forests. They provide legal help to local communities and groups as well as sponsor environmental management plans, education and academic training.

Ecuadorian Foundation for the Conservation of Nature (Fundación Natura, Guayaquil)

Avenida C. J. Arosemana Km. 2.5, 2° piso,
Casilla 09-01-11327, Guayaquil
4-201-628, 4-205-152, 4-205-482, fax: 4-202-703

As the Guayaquil chapter of Ecuador's most well-known and powerful nongovernment conservation group, this group was founded in 1984 and has a high profile. It sponsors a broad array of environmental programs from reforestation to community projects and park planning. It coordinates many local and national government projects throughout the southwestern part of the country. Its relation with the parent chapter in Quito is somewhat autonomous, and it often has regional priorities that differ from those of the Quito chapter.

Ecuadorian Orchid Association

José Salcedo and El Oro 106, Guayaquil
4-343-346

This association is made up largely of Ecuadorian orchid fanciers. They have worked together since 1975 to protect natural habitats with endemic and rare orchid species, especially in the tropical dry forests of the coast. They were also instrumental in the establishment and maintenance of the Guayaquil Botanical Gardens.

Foundation Pedro Vicente Maldonado

Malecón 100 and Loja, Guayaquil
4-308-163, 4-307-670, fax: 4-307-370

Education is the primary goal of this group, which was founded in 1984. They seek to change attitudes of the public and private sector toward the environment, especially regarding mangrove and estuarine habitats. They maintain relations with the tourist industry, as well as with local fishing and artisan industries, through training workshops and economic programs that are pro-environmental.

Foundation Pro-Bosque

Km. 15 vía a la Costa, Casilla 09-01-04243, Guayaquil
4-871-900, fax: 4-873-528

Founded in 1992, the foundation's main goal is to protect, conserve and regenerate native forests of the Ecuadorian coast. They operate under the auspices of the National Cement Company and administer 2000 hectares of tropical dry forest in a private reserve, Cerro Blanco, only 20–30 minutes from downtown Guayaquil. They have a well-trained staff that conducts educational programs and sponsors field trips into the Cerro Blanco. Scientific inventory and biological research are also high priorities.

LAGO AGRIO

Ecuadorian Foundation of Popular Progress (FEPP)
10 de Agosto and 12 de Febrero, Lago Agrio (Nueva Loja)
6-830-232
This organization has worked since 1980 to protect Amazon habitats by introducing logical agricultural practices and use of the nation's soil. Pollution of the air and water, deforestation and soil erosion are major targets. Technical training, environmental education and legal aid are the principal means by which their goals are reached.

LOJA

Ecological Foundation Arco Iris
Olmeda 984 and Miguel Riofrío, Loja
7-572-926, fax: 7-572-926
This award-winning group is one of the most active and successful in the country. They were founded in 1990 primarily to protect the Podo-carpus National Park, and their efforts made legal history in Ecuador. Because of them and their ability to raise the consciousness of politicians, gold miners were largely evicted from the park boundaries. The group participates actively in community schools and town councils, and they provide technological alternatives to the peasant farmers of the province of Loja. With this valuable experience and relatively high profile, they have expanded their goals to control forest fragmentation throughout the Andes as well as limit destruction of mountain watersheds.

Foundation Danta
Zoilo Rodríguez 178, Loja
7-561-730, 7-573-075, fax: 7-573-075
The main objectives of Danta (founded in 1990) involve environmental education. They want to create an environmental conscience in the general population that will protect and conserve natural resources.

Foundation Vilcabamba
Pío Jaramillo and Brasil, Loja
7-561-145
The focus of this group, founded in 1993, is the Vilcabamba Valley and the rational use of it as an ecosystem. This group of grassroots activists operate out of their own homes and work with local environmental problems such as loss of surface water, deforestation, overgrazing and destructive use of the soil.

OTAVALO

Center of Ecological and Cultural
Study and Education (CIDECO)
Los Corazones 113, Otavalo
2-921-163
CIDECO was founded in 1990 and works on problems of pollution of the air, lakes and soil as well as deforestation in the province of Imbabura. They are trying to change the conscience of the local people to understand and appreciate the impact of environmental problems on their lives. They also are working to change laws that affect reforestation along the edges of lakes and rivers.

QUITO

Corporation for the Defense of Life (CORDAVI)
Juan Montalvo 200,
Casilla 17-120309, Quito
2-17-120309
This organization was founded in 1987 and is considered by many to be the best environmental law group in Ecuador. It is associated with a national network of environmental lawyers. Its goal is to advance the concept and application of law to protection of the environment in Ecuador. It litigates environmental problems and sets precedents to make the law a useful force for advancing conservation. Besides court actions, this group informs the public as to their legal rights and educates the young and old on the power of using the legal system.

Ecuadorian Corporation for the Conservation
of Nature–Ecological Group "Tierra Viva"
Calle Italia 832 and Mariana de Jesús, 2° piso,
Casilla 17-211907, Quito
2-230-746, fax: 2-569-650
This group was founded in 1986 and works on problems of deforestation in the Amazon, contamination of natural habitats by oil companies, destruction of mangroves on the coast, and control of herbicides and pesticides on crops. Much of its work is in research projects and training.

Ecuadorian Council for the Conservation and Research
of Birds (CECIA)
La Tierra 203 and Avenida de los Shyris,
Casilla 17-17-906, Quito
phone/fax: 2-464-359; e-mail: cecia@uio.satnet.net

Specializing in one of the most popular groups of wildlife, this organization's goal since 1986 has been to develop programs of research and conservation of birds and their habitats. They concentrate on controlling large-scale deforestation and illegal colonization of protected areas in Ecuador. They have a broad international reputation and have been very effective influencing enforcement of environmental laws and protecting national parks and reserves within Ecuador.

Ecuadorian Foundation for the Conservation of Nature (Fundación Natura-Quito)

Avenida América 5653,
Casilla 17-01253, Quito
2-447-341, 2-447-342, 2-447-343, 2-447-344, fax: 2-434-449

This is the largest and most widely recognized nongovernment environmental group in Ecuador. It was founded in 1978 and publishes hundreds of useful reports, has many volunteers and scientists working on numerous projects and brings in hundreds of thousands of dollars in international funds to support its work. Its high profile and extensive financial support provide this group with many advantages, but these same factors result in an often complicated bureaucracy. However, there is no doubt that its studies of protected areas, its access to the media and its ability to mobilize pro-conservation propaganda are unequaled in Ecuador.

Ecuadorian Foundation of Ecological Studies (EcoCiencia)

Tamayo 1339 and Colón, Casilla 17-12-257, Quito
2-526-802, 2-548-752

This is one of the most effective nongovernment organizations in the country. Founded in 1989, it fields some of the best-trained scientists and educators in the country to carry out its projects. It is studying the biodiversity of Ecuador, developing national plans for environmental education and implementing plans for uses of natural resources in a way that will benefit all Ecuadorians.

Foundation Antisana (FUNAN)

Mariana de Jesús and Carvajal, EMAP-Q, Casilla 17-03148, Quito
2-433-849, 2-433-850, 2-433-851, fax: 2-433-851

The goal of this group, which was founded in 1991, is to have declared the 200,000 hectares around the Volcán Antisana a protected area. In connection with this work, they are actively involving residents of the area in education and community projects that promote economic development without destruction of the habitat.

Foundation Jatún Sacha
Río Coca 1734 and Amazonas, Casilla 17-12-867, Quito
2-253-267, fax: 2-250-976
With its research station and private protected forest reserve on the upper Río Napo, this group's priorities since 1989 are the conservation and protection of the Jatún Sacha Biological Reserve as well as other critical forest habitats in coastal and highland Ecuador. It is primarily involved in basic research and academic workshops. It also works with local people in ecotourism projects, school environmental education, forest management projects and botanical training. It has been honored as only the second Children's Rain Forest in the world.

Foundation Llanganati
Eloy Alfaro 2013 and Suiza, Quito
2-435-146, 2-434-311, fax: 2-437-645
This foundation was founded in 1986 and works to protect the Cordillera de los Llanganates, and to educate the local people and promote scientific investigation of the area.

Foundation Maquipucuna
Baquerizo 238 and Tamayo, Casilla 17-12167, Quito
2-507-200, 2-507-201, fax: 2-504-571
The objectives of this group, founded in 1988, are to promote the defense and conservation of renewable natural resources, implement sustainable developmental projects and study biodiversity. Members conduct basic and applied research, provide technical training courses and conduct general environmental education.

TULCÁN

Foundation Frailejón
Junín and Pichincha, Tulcán
2-980-150
The goals of this organization (founded 1992) are focused on local environmental problems. They are trying to raise the status of the wilderness area of El Ángel to one that is officially protected by the Ecuadorian government as a National Protected Area. Reintroduction of the Andean Condor to this area is also a high priority. More generally, they are involved with identifying causes of erosion and soil conservation. They work with local people to control deforestation and unlimited colonization of the paramo habitat. Much of this information is made public through an environmental education program to local schools and clubs.

INTERNATIONAL

The following international conservation groups are active in Ecuador and often work in association with national NGOs. Donations to these organizations result in responsible and timely conservation efforts in Ecuador that local and national NGOs could not accomplish on their own:

Conservation International

1015 18th Street, N.W., Suite 1000
Washington, DC 20036
202-429-5660, fax: 202-887-0193

One of the most innovative and industrious international NGOs working in Ecuador, this organization established the Rapid Assessment Program for critical habitats. It also supports biotic surveys and management-training throughout Ecuador.

The Nature Conservancy

1815 North Lynn Street
Arlington, VA 22209
703-841-2711, fax: 703-841-1283

Usually associated with creative and original financing to acquire critical habitats in North America, this organization also has extensive education and management-training programs throughout tropical countries of the world, including Ecuador.

The Wildlife Conservation Society

NYZS, International Programs
185th Street and Southern Boulevard
Bronx, NY 10460
718-220-5155, fax: 718-364-4275

Actively involved in sustainable and rational use of Ecuador's natural resources, this organization supplies funding and expertise in coordination with Ecuadorian counterparts. It trains nationals and helps manage habitats in danger of destruction.

World Wildlife Fund-US

1250 24th Street N.W.
Washington, DC 20037-1175
202-293-4800, fax: 202-293-9211

This organization has a long and important history in Ecuadorian conservation. It was a key to helping found Fundación Natura and continues to fund this national NGO as well as a few separate projects in southern and western Ecuador.

THREE

Planning Your Trip

WHEN TO GO

In Ecuador there are two high tourist seasons: late May through late August and mid-November through January. These times correspond more to the popular vacation times in North America and Europe than they do to any particular season in Ecuador. During these high tourist periods, reservations and advance planning are needed to travel anywhere in Ecuador. If you can be flexible in your travel plans, try September to early November. The hotels have few guests, the beaches are deserted and the jungle lodges are likely to be virtually empty except for you. These are the months when you may successfully bargain for better rates. This is also the time for tourists who like trips with no concrete itinerary—what we call using the FIT (Fake It Through) method. February through April is another low foreign tourist season, but this is also spring vacation for many of Ecuador's schools. Popular mountain and beach destinations will be absolutely jam-packed with vacationing Ecuadorians. The Galápagos Islands are a popular destination any time of the year, so you will always need to plan in advance for island trips.

CLIMATE

This close to the equator, day length remains constant throughout the year at about 12 hours a day, but rainfall (and its cooling effect on temperature) varies markedly. On the coast, hot dry days and hot humid nights last from September through November. The rainy season begins in December or January and continues through April. May to August are fairly dry and cool. In the mountains, the cool dry season runs from June to December. The rest of the year has sunny, warm mornings and cloudy afternoons and evenings, often with downpours. Anywhere in the highlands a sweater is appropriate at night and

Frigate

even during some of the more cloudy days. In the Oriente, the rainy season is from November to February and the rainier season is from March to October. In the Galápagos, the hot season runs from December to June and the rainy season from January to March. April and May can end up in either season depending on the year.

HOLIDAYS

At least 19 days each year are celebrated nationwide in Ecuador. Many of these days are holidays for everyone, and travel or services can be very difficult to arrange. Other holidays are just celebrated regionally or only by some part of the population. At any rate, be prepared for some inconvenience on these days or consider avoiding some regions of Ecuador during their holidays. (On the other hand, experiencing these national and regional celebrations can be an exciting and memorable experience.) Stay away from all the beaches on the coast in February and early March. All of Quito goes on a final vacation fling before school starts up and seems to camp out on any little stretch of sand at this time. The roads are clogged with traffic, litter and garbage are everywhere, and the restaurants and hotels are completely booked.

JANUARY

Countrywide: On **New Year's Day** most shops and services close to recover from the previous night's celebration.

Countrywide: The religious holiday **Three Kings' Day**, held on January 6, also sees the closing of many shops and services.

FEBRUARY–MARCH

Countrywide: February 12 celebrates the **Anniversary of the Discovery of the Amazon River** with a few local parades and speeches.

Puyo, Tena, Macas, Zamora: Each of these towns celebrates the land on February 12 in an **Annual Agricultural and Livestock Fair**.

Galápagos: The February 12 **Province Day** festivities include local speeches and colorful parades.

Countrywide: February 27 brings flag waving, patriotic speeches and parades on **Patriotism and National Unity Day**.

Countrywide: Intense partying and revelry mark **Carnival**, the three days prior to Ash Wednesday. Many shops and services close to celebrate the major holiday of the year. (Beware of flying water balloons.)

APRIL

Countrywide: Shops and services close up and everyone heads to the beach during **Holy Week**, a religious festival that inspires various religious parades during the week-long celebration.

Riobamba: The **Agricultural, Livestock and Arts and Crafts Fair**, which falls during April 17–21, brings locals together to celebrate the land and the local arts.

MAY

Countrywide: May 1 is **Labor Day**, and most shops and services stay open. Celebrations feature parades and speeches focusing on workers.

Countrywide: The **Anniversary of the Battle of Pichincha** is celebrated most dramatically on May 24 in Quito; but every town hosts big parties and memorable parades.

JUNE

Countrywide: Religious processions through most towns take place on Thursdays mid-month, for the **Corpus Christi** holiday.

Otavalo, Guamote, Tabacundo: **Saint John the Baptist Commemoration** falls on June 24; people gather for religious processions through town.

Countrywide: The religious processions lead into great fiestas during the June 28–29 **Saint Peter and Saint Paul Festival**.

JULY

Countrywide: July 24 heralds the arrival of lots of parties and celebrations commemorating Ecuador's liberator on **Simón Bolívar's Birthday**. Celebrations last two days on the coast (see below) and one day in the highlands.

Countrywide: The celebration continues on July 25 with recognition of the **Anniversary of the Foundation of Guayaquil**. Fiestas are especially big in Guayaquil.

AUGUST

Esmeraldas: During August 3–5, many local artisans and land workers gather for the **Agricultural, Livestock and Arts and Crafts Fair**.

Countrywide: Ecuadorians celebrate **National Independence Day** on August 10, leaving few shops and services open.

Santa Rosa (El Oro): At the **International Crayfish Fair**, the local crustacean serves as an excuse for great celebrations the last week of the month.

SEPTEMBER

Otavalo: The first week of September celebrates the harvest through parades and celebrations at the **Yamor Festivities**.

Cotacachi (Imbabura): The **Jora Corn Festival** is a celebration of the harvest with parades and parties during the first week of September.

Guayas: During the second week of the month the **Milagro Agricultural Fair** is celebrated with parades and parties.

Loja: **The Virgin of Cisne Festival** starts during the third week of September with a religious procession that leads into several days of street parties.

Portoviejo (Manabí): Many unique souvenirs can be found at the **Arts and Tourist Fair** which also falls during the third week of September.

Machala (El Oro): **The International Banana Fair**, held the last of the month, is a celebration of appreciation for the fruit that brought much of El Oro's wealth to town.

Latacunga: A religious procession is followed by parties and festivities to celebrate **Our Lady of Mercy Festival** from September 23 to September 24.

OCTOBER

Durán (Guayas): During the first week of October, you'll find arts, crafts, new machinery and technology spotlighted at the **International Fair**.

Guayaquil: October 9 is **Guayaquil Independence Day**. Residents celebrate it with speeches, parades and long parties. Don't expect to move anywhere in Guayaquil today.

Countrywide: Discovery of America, or **Colombus Day**, is another excuse for speeches, parades and parties on October 12.

NOVEMBER

Countrywide: The **Day of the Dead** is observed on November 2. Everyone goes to the cemetery to lay flowers and offerings on the graves of loved ones.

Cuenca: November 3 marks **Cuenca Independence Day** with big celebrations and parades.

Latacunga: **Latacunga Independence Day**, which falls on November 11, is celebrated with parades and festivities.

Pichincha: There is a religious procession followed by celebrations for the **Virgin of the Quinche Festivities** on November 21.

DECEMBER

Countrywide: The **San Francisco de Quito Foundation Day** starts a week before the actual holiday on December 6, which opens the bullfighting season in Quito. The holiday acts as an excuse for many parties, although it is not celebrated much outside of Quito.

Countrywide: **Christmas** is fairly quiet in Ecuador. Almost all shops and services are closed.

Countrywide: Although too soon after Christmas and too soon before New Year to be a big celebration, the **Day of the Innocents,** held on December 28, is an excuse for a few more parties.

Countrywide: **New Year's Eve** is a big night in Ecuador with huge festivities ringing in the New Year at midnight.

COMING AND GOING

ENTRY REQUIREMENTS

Visitors must hold a passport valid for at least six months beyond the entry date into Ecuador. (For U.S. passport information, try the U.S. Passport Service web site: http://travel.state.gov/passport_services.html). A visa obtained from an Ecuadorian consulate is required of citizens of some countries, but the list of these countries changes constantly. Check with your local travel agent or consulate for the current requirements for your nationality. Citizens of the U.S. and Canada, most EC countries, and Latin American countries do not need a visa and have only to fill out a tourist card and present it to Ecuador immigration along with the passport. The tourist card is available from the airlines or ship company or from immigration officials at the port of entry into Ecuador. Each tourist is allowed to be in Ecuador a total of 90 days per 12-month period. Upon your arrival, the National Police official will generally ask you how long you expect to stay in Ecuador on this particular trip and write that number of days on the entry stamp in your passport and on the back of your tourist card. At the same time, the official will search through the rest of the passport to see if you have made other trips to Ecuador that same year. They are fairly strict about not letting anyone accumulate more than 90 days per 12 months, but extensions are fairly easy to obtain once you are in the country. The passport lines are relatively efficient and hassle-free at international airports, but can be somewhat more laborious at other entry points. We are generally impressed with the National Police in Ecuador and their relatively friendly attitudes serving as immigration officials.

Carry your passport with you at all times, and do not lose your copy of the tourist card. It must be returned to the immigration official when you leave the country. These documents are checked at police and army checkpoints on highways throughout the country, and your passport is often checked against your airline ticket when you take domestic flights within Ecuador.

CUSTOMS REGULATIONS

You are allowed to bring in up to 300 cigarettes or 50 cigars and a bottle of liquor tax-free. You cannot enter or leave the country with firearms, ammunition, narcotics, fresh meats and any type of plant or animal without prior approval from the Ministry of Agriculture and Livestock (MAG). At the international airports in Quito and Guayaquil the customs procedures are fast and efficient. Ecuadorian nationals arriving with monstrous suitcases full of microwave ovens and jeans are much more the target of customs agents than are gringo tourists. Usually, just showing your passport and smiling is enough to be waved through. However, crackdowns do occur at irregular intervals, and more-thorough search procedures may be applied to tourist luggage as well.

EXIT AND EXTENDED VISAS

Ecuador charges one of the highest departure taxes in Latin America, $25 or equivalent in Ecuadorian sucres. At the international airports you pay this fee after checking in and obtaining your boarding pass. Check that the tax official has placed the two "tax paid" stickers on your boarding pass. Confirm your return reservations 72 hours before leaving. Arrive at the airport two hours ahead of departure time to allow for long lines and possible overbooking.

When leaving Ecuador, police security will inspect all your checked luggage as well as hand-carried bags with x-ray machines. Airline security may also search your hand-carried bags visually just before entering the departure lounge for your flight. Before boarding some flights, all passengers are asked to stand in a line with their hand-carried bags in front of them on the ground. An officer of the National Police or military and a drug-sniffing dog will then come down the line checking each and every bag. It turns out that the U.S. Drug Enforcement Agency (DEA) pays rewards to the police for finding drugs before departure. As that dog comes down the line toward your bag, it is hard not to become apprehensive—no matter how innocent you are. On occasion, officials from the Ministry of the Environment will also inspect bags for animal skins, butterflies, stuffed crocodiles, feather crowns, orchids and other biological contraband. These articles are all illegal to export without a permit and can be confiscated. They are also illegal to import into the U.S. and most European countries, so do *not* buy any souvenirs made from wild animals or plants.

Visas can be extended at National Police offices in the major cities. If you are extending your visa but will not go over the 90-day limit within the 12-month period, there is no cost. If you are staying more than 90 days within a 12-month period, several different visa types are available—such as student or scientific study—at a cost scaled to the type of visa. Each one has its requirements, but most will include proof of return passage to your home country, minimum amount of cash and written evidence of your purpose for staying in the country. Some of the more stringent visa types, such as resident alien, will require police records from your home town and extensive medical records. Check with your local Ecuadorian consulate for details on your specific case.

U.S. CUSTOMS REGULATIONS

Even if you are an American citizen, the U.S. can be harder to enter than Ecuador. When returning home, U.S. residents may bring $400 worth of purchases duty-free (including the value of any gifts received while in Ecuador). Anything over this amount is subject to a 10 percent tax on the next $1000 worth of items. In case customs agents question the values you declare, have receipts handy.

Fruits, seeds, fresh foods, live animals or animal parts are not allowed into the U.S. Any parts of endangered species are prohibited and will be confiscated. Someone in Ecuador who wants to sell you an ocelot skin or sea turtle shell is probably going to swear on a stack of Bibles that it is legal. Don't believe it. The same is true of ancient relics and pre-Columbian art.

For more details, contact **U.S. Customs** (1301 Constitution Avenue, Washington, DC 20229; 202-566-8195; www.customs.treas.gov); the **U.S. Fish and Wildlife Service** (Department of the Interior, mailstop 430, Arlington Square, 1849 C Street NW, Washington, DC 20240; 202-208-5634); or the **U.S. Department of Agriculture**, Animal and Plant Health Inspection Service, Plant Protection and Quarantine (4700 River Road, Riverdale, MD 20737; 301-734-7799; www.aphis.usda.gov/ppq).

To avoid confiscation of prescribed drugs, label them carefully and bring along a doctor's certificate of prescription. If you get caught carrying illegal drugs, you will rue the day of your temptation as well as the day of your judgment.

Customs and immigration personnel at the U.S. border use traveler profiles as a tool to keep the lines moving. If you do not fit the "normal" profile (including clothes, behavior and other indicators), you may be the subject of more detailed questioning and search.

INOCULATIONS

No vaccinations are required for entry into Ecuador, but other countries in Asia and Africa require proof of yellow-fever inoculation to enter their borders if you have been in South America within the previous three to six months. If you are going to be in the forests of coastal or Amazonian Ecuador, a yellow-fever shot is a good idea anyway. It's good for ten years and most regional clinics in the U.S. provide it. Because the vial must be refrigerated and then all used once it is opened, most clinics have a restricted calendar of days of the month or week when the vaccination is available. Diphtheria-Tetanus (DT), polio, and measles shots are a good idea to update regularly whether you are traveling or not. More controversial is immune serum globulin (formerly called gamma globulin). It is commonly used against hepatitis A, but it provides marginal protection at best. On top of that, it is only good for four to eight weeks. An inoculation series specifically against hepatitis A is now available (Smith-Kline Beecham) that provides protection for up to one year, longer with a booster. Know that this type of hepatitis can best be avoided by being careful about the food and water you consume. If there is any chance you will be coming into contact with human blood samples or secretions or having unprotected sex in Ecuador, a series of shots is available against hepatitis B. If you plan an extended trip to Ecuador that involves time in rural areas, typhoid fever (inoculations or booster pills) and preventive rabies shots are recommended. Be sure to check with the Centers for Disease Control (CDC) in Atlanta for information about any last-minute outbreaks or health updates for travel to Ecuador (404-332-4555; www.cdc.gov/travel/travel. html). For other up-to-date information, we recommend subscribing to *The Latin American Advisor* (P.O. Box 17-17-908, Quito; fax: 2-562-566) or *Latin America Traveler* (P.O. Box 62921, Phoenix, AZ 85082-2921; e-mail: nbc@ primenet.com). Both these newsletters publish current information and advice on health, safety and travel budgets.

TRANSPORTATION

AIRLINES SERVING ECUADOR

Most tourists arrive in Ecuador by air at one of its two international airports —Mariscal Sucre in Quito and Simón Bolívar in Guayaquil. Both of these airports have money-exchange facilities, duty-free shops and tourist information centers run by the Ecuadorian Tourism Corporation (CETUR). Despite Ecuador's interest in expanding tourism and the high departure tax, neither airport has covered walkways connecting the gate with the airplane. Instead, steps mounted on trucks are driven to the doors of the plane and passengers must climb up or down. This lack of technology can be a tremendous barrier for handicapped passengers and frustrating for many others. Depending on where the plane parked, buses will transport you between the plane and the terminal or you will walk—sometimes several blocks in the rain or heat. At the Quito airport you are at almost 9900 feet/3000 meters elevation. Tourists coming from low altitudes with heavy carry-on bags should walk slowly. If you feel faint or your pulse becomes rapid, stop and rest. No matter how fast you get through the immigration line, you will have to wait 20 minutes or so anyway for your baggage to begin to arrive. Check both baggage carousels as there is seldom any indication which one is being used for your flight.

The following airlines have international flights to Ecuador:

American Airlines (Guayaquil—Edificio San Francisco 300, General Córdova and Avenida 9 de Octubre, 4-564-111, 4-561-856, 4-561-857; Quito —Avenida Río Amazonas 353, 2-561-144, 2-434-610, 2-434-653) has two daily nonstop flights between Miami and Quito and one daily flight between Miami and Guayaquil. Try to avoid the second flight from Miami to Quito. It arrives late at night, and the Quito airport is frequently fogged in after 10 p.m. This airport closes up and the lights are all turned off at midnight. If the flight cannot land at Quito, it is diverted to Guayaquil where you will spend the night in a hotel and then fly to Quito the next morning. Two additional caveats: First, if you are flying through Miami in March, the thousands of vacationing college students there will make it virtually impossible to change reservations for flights out of Miami to other parts of the U.S. Second, at any time of year, you are more likely to be well taken care of by the airlines if you use the same carrier within the U.S. as you use to fly the international leg of your journey to Ecuador. Transfer between airlines can raise the probability of lost luggage as well as delay your arrival if connecting flights are missed.

Continental Airlines (Guayaquil—Avenida 9 de Octubre between Los Ríos and Esmeraldas, Edificio Finansur, 11th floor, 4-453-600, 4-287-311; Quito—Avenidas Naciones Unidas and Río Amazonas, Edificio Banco La Previsora, 3rd floor, 2-461-485, 2-461-486, 2-461-492) has daily flights between Houston and Quito (one stop in Panamá) and daily nonstop flights between Houston and Guayaquil. They also have daily flights between Newark and Guayaquil (one stop in Panamá) and daily flights between Newark and Quito (one stop in Bogotá).

SAETA (Guayaquil—Vélez 226 and Chile, 4-203-999, 4-200-600, 4-200-614, 4-329-855; Quito—Avenida Amazonas and Santa María, 2-542-148, 4-564-969, 4-502-712, or 800-827-2382 in the U.S.) is a flag-carrying airline of Ecuador. It has six flights weekly from New York's JFK (Delta, Terminal 2), with a stop in Miami.

KLM (Guayaquil—Aguirre 411 and Chile, Unicentro 7, 4-328-028; Quito —Avenida Amazonas 3617 and Juan Pablo Sanz, Edificio Xerox, 2-455-233, 2-455-562, 2-442-804) and **Iberia** (Guayaquil—Avenida 9 de Octubre 101 and Malecón Simón Bolívar, 4-320-664, 4-322-603; Quito—Avenidas Amazonas 239 and J. Washington, 2-560-546, 2-560-456, 2-562-930) fly directly between European cities and Ecuador.

The national air carriers from Argentina (**Aerolineas Argentinas**), Brazil (**VARIG**), Colombia (**Avianca**), Costa Rica (**LACSA**), Panamá (**COPA**), Perú (**Aero Peru**), and Venezuela (**AVENSA** and **VIASA**) service Quito from their capital cities, and most also service Guayaquil. SAETA and its affiliate SAN also service many Latin American cities from Quito and Guayaquil.

CRUISE SHIPS

Only six or seven cruise ships visit Ecuador each year, and they all stop at the ship terminal docks in southern Guayaquil. Tours to the more interesting northern part of the city can be made directly with the cruise company.

INTERNATIONAL BUS COMPANIES

Entry into or from Ecuador by bus is limited almost entirely to the Pan-American Highway at Tulcán on the Colombian border and at Huaquillas on the Peruvian border. The best Ecuadorian bus company for international travel is **Panamericana International**. Their luxury buses (with attendants) have private terminals (except Guayaquil) throughout the country. Their personnel assist in crossing the border into Colombia or Perú and transferring to the bus company in that country to continue your international trip. In Quito, the terminal is a refurbished, salmon-colored mansion located at Colón and Reina Victoria (2-501-585, 2-501-584). In Guayaquil (4-297-638, 4-284-491), their buses use the *terminal terrestre*. In Cuenca (7-840-060), the private terminal is located on the corner of Avenida Huaynacapas and España.

PACKING

Experienced travelers learn quickly that the trick is to pack light. Depending on how many different altitudes and habitats you will visit on your trip, a small carry-on bag and one checked suitcase should be the maximum you need to bring. Whether you are staying two weeks or two months, the basics are about the same and should make little difference in how much you have to pack. Do not pack any valuables in the check-in luggage as virtually all airports have problems with dishonest baggage handlers rifling baggage. Also, do not pack new clothing or equipment such as cameras in their original boxes and wrapping. First of all, they will take up much more room and second, they will look more suspicious to customs agents who are not too thrilled about tourists coming to Ecuador to sell hard-to-get goods on their "vacation."

In the Galápagos, the dress is very informal and repeating outfits is the name of the game. You will wear shorts and T-shirts all day, every day. A long-sleeved shirt or pullover for cool nights or while you are motoring between islands is very handy. With a bit of laundry detergent, you can do a quick wash and hang out your wet clothes on the boat to dry in the breeze. Be sure to fasten your clothes to the line securely, or else you will make an unwanted contribution to the marine environment. The easiest thing to wear on your feet are the new rugged-style sandals, such as Tevas. They are perfect for both wet and dry landings because you will not have to hassle removing your shoes and then putting them on again. Remember to put sun block on the top of your feet as well if you are wearing sandals. If you are an avid snorkeler (if you are not, you will be), a wet-suit top or "shortie" allows you to linger a bit longer in the sometimes cool waters of the Galápagos.

In the highlands, from Otavalo and Quito to Cuenca and Loja, a hooded sweatshirt or light jacket will be useful on cloudy days and cool evenings. During the rainy season, torrential downpours frequently occur in the afternoon —often after a pleasantly sunny morning. A fold-up umbrella or light rain parka will be useful here, as well as in the jungle. Shorts are considered inappropriate by local custom anywhere in the highlands—especially on women. Shorts are tolerated on tourists on the beach and in the jungle, but few other places.

In the Oriente, calf-height rubber boots are very handy for walking the muddy trails. Most lodges will rent or lend them to you free of charge during your stay. If you have exceptionally large feet, and plan on spending extended time in muddy jungle areas, you may do well to bring your own pair along. They do take up a *lot* of room in your suitcase, however. If you don't mind getting your feet wet, tennis shoes will often work for short periods. Bring your own thick and high socks for inside the boots. They will keep you from most blisters. A pair of light rain chaps that go on each leg separately and tie to your belt can be very handy. Wear your pants legs inside the boots and the chaps outside the tops of your boots. This will not only keep your pants from getting wet and muddy, it will keep mud from falling down inside your boots. Do not bring jeans to Ecuador. They take forever to dry out once they get wet, and they are very hot. Cotton-polyester pants, shirts and socks are the best. Shorts are useful here only in your cabin. In the forest, shorts will only increase your exposure to biting insects and stinging plants. A heavy rain poncho will be useful at higher elevations or when sitting in an open canoe during rainstorms at lower elevations. In the rainforest, however, a broad-brimmed cloth hat (not a pith helmet) and a small fold-up umbrella are most effective. Alternatively, depending on your companions, a very effective method is to take off all your clothes and place them in a plastic bag until the rain stops. Then put them back on. Plastic Ziploc and garbage bags, by the way, are very good ideas. Keep your cameras, binoculars, field guide and toilet paper in separate sealed bags inside your rucksack. For hiking trips or on canoes and horseback, always pack all of your clothes and equipment inside a plastic garbage bag lining your carrying bag or backpack.

On the coast, in the Galápagos, at high altitudes and in open canoes anywhere, the sun is your main worry. The intensity of energy reaching the equator can fry skin much faster than anything you are used to. Even thin shirts are little protection in themselves. A broad-brimmed hat and lots of 30+ SPF sun block are needed to avoid a sunburn. Long-sleeve shirts can be rolled up or down as you want, but short sleeves and short pants will leave much of your tender limbs exposed. The resulting pain of a sunburn can spoil the rest of your trip. If your friends back home complain that you have returned without a deep tan, tell them you are a seasoned traveler and have other priorities.

A hooded sweatshirt or a light windbreaker can serve you in the mountains when it gets cold but can be comfortable even in the Amazon jungle on some cooler evenings. At any rate, it is always a handy pillow to lay your head on or to sit on when the canoe seat gets too hard. A pair of flip-flops, dry tennis shoes and light cotton socks will be very useful. A small rucksack is essential for carrying needed things on travel days, and keeping other items handy on day excursions. A regular flashlight and a smaller backup—together with a set of extra batteries for each—are also needed. Please do not throw your used batteries from your flashlight or camera into the water or roadside. Even small amounts of the chemicals they often contain, such as mercury, can pollute large areas. If viewing wildlife is a high priority for you, avoid outer clothing that is bright yellow, chartreuse or red. You will be seen easily by the wildlife and avoided. Instead, wear deep green or dark blue. Although Ecuadorian officials are not as paranoid as their counterparts in Colombia and Perú, avoid any clothes that have camouflage patterns resembling military-type styles. Even Vietnam "jungle boots" can elicit negative reactions from police and soldiers at checkpoints. This is especially true along the Colombian border in the Oriente and anywhere along the Peruvian border.

Most hotels in the larger cities have *bodegas* in which you can safely store your suitcase and extra clothes while you make a sojourn off to the jungle or some other side trip. Your carry-on bag and rucksack should be sufficient to tote all you need for three to four days. You can save room by wearing your rubber boots (citified with pants legs outside the boots) on the short plane trip to the Oriente and packing tennis shoes. A small pin-on compass has saved us more than once when we thought we could take a shortcut through the jungle. A referee's whistle is also handy to have if you ever have to locate your group or signal an emergency. Glasses wearers should carry an extra pair of glasses in their rucksack.

We've noticed how few tourists visiting Ecuador to see its natural wonders bother to bring along a pair of binoculars. This purchase can increase your enjoyment of Ecuador a hundred times, so consider bringing a pair along. All binoculars are sized by two numbers, such as: 6 x 20, 8 x 35, 10 x 40. The first number is the magnification power of the binoculars. The second number is the diameter of the lens and reflects its light-gathering capacity. Because higher-power binoculars let in less light, the second number needs to be larger as the power gets larger. As a rule of thumb, the diameter (second) number should be five times larger than the power (first) number. Small pocket binoculars (6 x 20) costing $75 to $150 are very handy because they are so easy to carry along. They are also easy to focus on very close objects like insects. Their disadvantage is they often do not magnify objects adequately, and they are not very good in low-light situations. For general wildlife viewing we recommend 7 x 35 or 8 x 40 binoculars. They are not too large, but they will not fit into a pocket either. Avoid nonfocusing binoculars, and make sure yours have a center focus knob. They should be in alignment—where both eyepieces focus on the same object. If you see two of everything as you look through the binoculars, you will have to cross your eyes to bring the object into focus, and this extra work can be hard on your eyes and cause headaches.

Here's a list of handy items to take along and still keep your packing down to one checked suitcase and a carry-on bag:

__ Passport
__ Photocopy of passport picture and number
__ Plane tickets
__ Cash
__ Traveler's checks
__ Pocket notebook
__ Extra pencils and pens
__ (3) long-sleeve work shirts
__ (1) short-sleeve sports shirt
__ (1) long-sleeve sports shirt
__ (3 pair) long hiking pants
__ Bermuda shorts
__ Hooded sweatshirt
__ (5 pair) undershorts
__ (3) T-shirts
__ (2) bras
__ Swimsuit
__ (7 pair) regular socks
__ (2 pair) dress socks
__ (2 pair) long, thick socks
__ Broad-brimmed cloth hat
__ Light rain jacket
__ Rain chaps
__ Walking shoes

__ Sneakers
__ Rubber boots (optional)
__ Daypack or rucksack
__ Flip-flops
__ Fold-up umbrella
__ (2) flashlights (one larger and one pen light)
__ Extra batteries for flashlights and camera
__ Pocketknife
__ Notebooks and pens
__ Small travel alarm clock
__ Extra prescription glasses
__ Eyeglasses strap
__ Sunglasses
__ Small mending-sewing kit
__ Field guide(s)
__ (5) large Ziploc plastic bags
__ (3) heavy duty garbage bags
__ Binoculars
__ Camera
__ Extra film
__ (2) plastic water bottles (half-liter)
__ Earplugs

__ Toiletries in kit
__ Sufficient prescription
medicines and copies of
prescriptions
__ Tampons or pads

__ Small first-aid kit
__ Sunscreen (SPF 25 to 30)
__ Flowers of Sulphur powder
(against chiggers)

If you will be using a wide variety of classes of accommodations that include rustic or primitive sites, the following additional items are recommended:

__ Sturdy drinking cup
__ Water filter
__ Cotton bed sheet
__ String and clothespins
__ Powdered clothes soap
__ Towel
__ Packages of dried fruit

__ Emergency cans of
sandwich meat
__ Nonmelting granola bars
and similar snacks
__ Small compass
__ Referee's whistle

ELECTRICITY

The electricity used in Ecuador is 110 watts AC and 60 cycles. The sockets are two-pronged, North American–style, but rarely have the third hole for a grounding prong. High-resistance appliances like hair dryers should not be used at places operating only with on-site generators. You could blow the power for the entire complex.

An increasing demand for electricity combined with a lack of new generating facilities has led to blackout periods for 4 to 8 hours per day throughout the country from September to December. The bigger hotels have emergency generators to provide lights and power during the blackouts, but in smaller hotels be prepared to use candles and forgo the elevator.

TRAVELING EXPENSES

All prices listed in the book are in U.S. dollars unless indicated otherwise. We have listed lodging and restaurant prices to give you a standard of comparison, but know that prices are always subject to change without notice. Most travel in Ecuador is cheap by North American or European standards. The top luxury-class hotels in Quito and Guayaquil are way overrated and offer little more than an inflated bill over lesser luxury class accommodations or first class. Many very good hotels are considerably cheaper and a much better deal than similar hotels in the U.S. Hotels in the provinces are almost always inexpensive, and if you look around, they can be quite clean even if humble. If you are willing to share bathroom facilities, the price comes down even more. Watch out, however, for the cheapest places in outlying towns. Filthy and unhealthy accommodations can ruin the rest of your trip for you.

Buses go almost everywhere and are very cheap. But even the domestic airlines have flights that cost only $25 to $80 one-way. Rental cars with insurance can run $65 to $135/day. Some companies offer completely unlimited kilometrage (mileage), so shop around when renting. Other places offer 1000 free kilometers per week and then $0.25/kilometer after that. Sometimes it is cheaper to rent a taxi and driver for a day than to rent your own car. Water-taxis on some river systems are cheap and a fine introduction to Ecuadorian culture. Depending on your comfort level, expect to spend anywhere from $10 to over $200/day for all expenses.

ACCOMMODATIONS IN ECUADOR

Ecuador has no shortage of places to stay, especially in the popular resort towns and large cities. The simplest is a *residencial*, which is an extra room in someone's house reserved for guests. A *posada* is a small home that has been converted for guests and is similar to a bed and breakfast. A *hostal* is bigger than a *posada*, up to 12 guests, and often has shared accommodations and baths. A combination of a *residencial* and a *posada* is called *casa* (e.g., Casa de Linda or Casa de Verónica). These types of accommodations can be found most easily in areas where tourists are common, such as in Baños and Salinas, and are quite inexpensive ($2–$10). *Aparthotels* tend to have larger rooms or to emphasize suites.

In the highlands of Ecuador, the large, historic farms are called *haciendas*. These typically date to the 16th or 17th century and were granted to prominent Ecuadorians by the King of Spain. The amount of land allotted to some haciendas was staggering—36,000 acres to one near Volcán Cotapaxi—and often encompassed all that could be seen from the hacienda. Land reform broke up these huge parcels but some of the colonial haciendas remain and several have been converted into tourist accommodations.

The top hotels in Ecuador will usually have a pool, a 24-hour coffee shop and a generally high level of luxury. Prices and cleanliness are not always related though. We have visited many of these establishments in Ecuador, and our comments on service, rooms, cleanliness and price should serve to make your choice relatively easy.

In the large cities of Guayaquil, Quito and Cuenca, and in a few smaller cities like Machala, there are many well-known hotels from which to choose. They are generally operated by international hotel corporations, so each hotel, no matter where you are, is basically the same as one in the U.S. or Europe. These hotels are extremely well run with highly professional and very friendly staff. They offer all the amenities a traveler could want—international cable TV, minibar, exercise rooms, faxes, complimentary toiletries, laundry service, direct dial phones and more. Of course you pay a rate two or three times more than in other classes of hotels to feel like you haven't even left home. These hotels tend to insulate you from much of the culture and flavor of Ecuador, except for what you can find in the lobby gift shop.

If you want to stay at a hotel that's more Ecuadorian, there are usually several very nice ones in cities and large towns where tourists are likely to go. These hotels often are remodeled colonial homes or refurbished haciendas, so they are rich in the culture and history of the area. They are usually in the $20–$40 range. Refer to the specific geographical chapters of the book for our favorites. There are also many budget or economy accommodations throughout Ecuador where rooms can be had for $2–$10. Some of these are fine for a single night and offer clean rooms with some privacy. Ask for a private bath with hot water and a double bed (*cama matrimonial*), and be sure to see the room before you pay for it.

You should be aware that not every hotel accepts credit cards and even those that do don't accept *all* credit cards. Be sure to ask before you register.

In the Oriente, it is sometimes impossible to find a nice place to stay even in the main towns. If you are wandering about and traveling without an itinerary, you will find yourself occasionally sleeping without basic comforts such as clean beds, clean bathrooms, private rooms and quiet nights. To some, this is part of the adventure of travel. To others, it is a night from hell. These primitive accommodations can be avoided if you plan your trip carefully and call ahead for reservations. If you are going to a "jungle lodge," plan on spending the night of the day you travel at the lodge. All the lodges included in this book have far nicer rooms than those in the nearest towns.

Wherever you stay, basic hotel safety is always appropriate. The nicer hotels in bigger towns and cities have their own security, but be cautious nonetheless. Be sure your room does not have a roof just below your window or a balcony that is easily accessible from the ground. Make sure all your doors lock securely, and take valuables such as your cameras and extra money to the desk for safekeeping while you are out. When we leave the room for a short time, we leave the TV on just loud enough so that it can be heard from outside the door.

One word of caution: **never stay in a motel** unless you are there for a clandestine meeting with sexual overtones. In Ecuador, as throughout almost all of Latin America, motels are located on the outskirts of cities, have high walls surrounding the buildings and parking lots, and charge an hourly rate.

NOTES FOR WOMEN TRAVELERS

Ecuador is not very liberated when it comes to women's issues, but at the same time, women can expect a relatively hassle-free time. A woman traveling alone or several women traveling together can expect to be stared at or honked at by passing cars, but little more. Ecuadorian women have learned to absolutely ignore these attention-getting devices by Ecuadorian men. The worst thing you can do is acknowledge this behavior. Don't even look at the man to register your distaste. A woman traveling with a man will receive none of these overtures. Blonde women have more problems. Light hair is considered so exotic and different in a culture with almost universally dark hair, it will always be an attention-getter. In addition, by Ecuadorian men's conventional wisdom, only two types of Latin women bleach their hair blonde— movie stars and prostitutes. With much of their knowledge of gringas based on movies, many Ecuadorian men will see their fantasies in a woman tourist walking along a road. If you ignore them, and if your behavior belies their fantasies, they will quickly lose interest in you.

NOTES FOR TRAVELING WITH CHILDREN

In Ecuador, children are considered life's greatest blessing. If you choose to travel with your children, you will quickly become used to strangers stopping to coo over them. You will also quickly see the benefits of jumping in front of a line, having everyone making way for you, and having Ecuadorians in general falling all over themselves to help you out.

If you plan to travel to parts of Ecuador that are set up for family vacations, such as beach resorts and mountain resorts, you'll have a ball. Playgrounds, entertainment, playmates of the same age and child-friendly facilities are all in place. If, however, you want to try more isolated places like remote jungle lodges and mountain trekking, Ecuador will disappoint you.

Stores in Quito and Guayaquil will have most of the diapers, baby food, vitamins, toys and other such items in speciality stores and large department stores (but at import prices much higher than you would pay back home).

NOTES FOR SENIOR TRAVELERS

Age is respected in Ecuador, and you will find Ecuadorians eager to help you. Read the descriptions of lodges and markets carefully to estimate the physical abilities required for each. We have tried to indicate which hotels have elevators, which tours are very rigorous, and which sites have physical demands beyond the normal. **Elderhostel** (75 Federal Street, 3rd floor, Boston, MA 02110-1941; 617-426-8056; www.elderhostel.org) has teamed up with **Holbrook Travel** (800-451-7111, fax: 352-371-3710; e-mail: travel@hol brooktravel.com) to sponsor numerous trips to Ecuador and the Galápagos specifically oriented to travelers over the age of 55.

Be cautious about your health. Bring any medications you use with you, along with copies of your prescriptions. Consider carrying a medical record with you—including your current medical status, medical history, your doctor's name, address and phone number. Check with your health care provider and insurance agent to find out if you are covered while traveling in Ecuador. Ecuador has some world-class health facilities in Quito and Guayaquil.

NOTES FOR TRAVELERS WITH DISABILITIES

Ecuador is in general very poorly set up to accommodate handicapped travelers. Even some of the most luxurious hotels have elevators accessible only after ascending a staircase. Many hotels have no elevators. Except for a few streets in the center of Guayaquil and Quito, the curbs have no wheelchair crossings, and virtually no government or private buildings have wheelchair ramps. Even the arrival at the two international airports will prove a problem for many handicapped travelers, as there are no terminal bridges to the airplanes, and very high portable stairs must be maneuvered. Within buildings, frequent two-step barriers separate building sections. Handicap parking places do not exist.

NOTES FOR STUDENT TRAVELERS

There are few organized student tours to Ecuador, but the country is well-suited for young people traveling on a budget. Several of the conservation organizations, like Jatún Sacha, accept volunteers to work on their projects, and Hostelling International has just included Ecuador in their youth hostel program. Contact the Ecuadorian office for information on this chain of 20 (and growing) facilities catering to young travelers in mainland Ecuador and the Galápagos (National office: Hostelling International, Pinto 325 and Reina Victoria, Quito; 2-226-271, fax: 2-543-995).

NOTES FOR GAY TRAVELERS

As with many Central and South American cultures, Ecuador is quite intolerant of homosexuality. With that said, it is best to be discreet about your lifestyle. Even discussion of gay rights with liberal Ecuadorians is likely to elicit negative reactions. Recently, however, the first gay association in Ecuador was formed and has requested legal standing from the Ministry of Social Welfare. It is called **La Asociación de Gays Trans-género Coccinelli**. Its goals are to work for legal benefits of Ecuadorian gays and lesbians and eliminate prejudice and discrimination in the country.

NOTES FOR TRAVELING WITH PETS

If you want to bring a pet into Ecuador, you should have an International Health Certificate for Dogs and Cats (Form 77-043) signed by a U.S. veterinarian verifying the animal's health and immunization record. For further details, check with the nearest Ecuadorian consulate or embassy. You will also need these records to bring your pet back into the U.S. Sometimes a mandatory quarantine is placed on all pets entering the U.S., so check with U.S. customs before leaving the country.

SAMPLE ITINERARIES

Even though Ecuador is relatively small, the distances are deceptive as the ground transportation can be very slow. If you are planning to spend all of your time on the mainland, budget at least a week. If you are primarily interested in the Galápagos, most tours are 5–10 days. Many tourists add a mainland tour onto their Galápagos trip. Anything less than four days on the mainland extension will be so superficial as to be more frustrating than enjoyable.

Most Galápagos tours have relatively inflexible itineraries. The main differences between the tours will be the length of your stay and which islands are visited (see Chapter Sixteen). Here are some itineraries we can recommend for the mainland:

FOUR DAYS

Day 1	Fly to Quito and overnight.
Day 2	City tour in the morning and then drive to Otavalo—overnight.
Day 3	Visit Otavalo market in the morning and other craft towns or Lago Cuicocha in the afternoon; return to Quito in the evening.
Day 4	Morning departure on international airline from Quito airport.

Alternatively, buy a four-day package tour to one of the jungle lodges on the lower Río Napo or Agua Rico. These tours leave and return on set days of the week, so check with the tour company you are using. This plan will mean you have to already be in Quito the day before the tour leaves as you cannot otherwise make the morning flight to Coca or Lago Agrio–Tarapoa.

ONE WEEK

This itinerary includes the highlands, markets, and forests of the coastal plain and Amazon Basin. A lot of travel is necessary, but also you will see a lot of Ecuador.

Day 1	Fly to Quito and overnight.
Day 2	Drive to Cotopaxi and return to Quito.
Day 3	Drive to Otavalo and return to Quito.

Day 4	Drive to Tinalandia or Mindo Garden—overnight.
Day 5	Spend the day exploring the area; return to overnight in Quito.
Day 6	Drive to Papallacta and Baeza and return to Quito.
Day 7	Morning international flight.

TWO WEEKS

This itinerary takes you to most of the major ecosystems in the country as well as exposes you to Ecuadorian culture.

Day 1	Arrive on evening flight to Quito—overnight.
Day 2	Drive to Cotopaxi, return to Quito—overnight.
Day 3–6	Morning flight to lower Napo or Agua Rico jungle lodge (4-day package); return to Quito—overnight.
Day 7	Fly to Cuenca or Loja—overnight.
Day 8	Drive to El Cajas or Podocarpus National Park; return to Cuenca or Loja—overnight.
Day 9	Drive to Gualaceo or Zamora; return to Cuenca or Loja—overnight.
Day 10	Fly to Quito—overnight.
Day 11	Drive to Otavalo—overnight.
Day 12	Drive to El Ángel for hiking or sightseeing and return to Otavalo—overnight.
Day 13	Drive to Quito and afternoon city tour—overnight.
Day 14	Early morning international flight home.

Pottery

FOUR

Once You Arrive:
Getting Around in Ecuador

LANGUAGE

Spanish is the official language of Ecuador. Quichua and various indigenous languages of native people in the lowlands are also considered national languages. Few signs, even in tourist areas, are in English.

"MODISMOS"—ECUADORIAN SPANISH

From the taxi driver to your local guide, Ecuadorians are in general enthusiastic about any gringo who tries to speak Spanish. They are amazingly patient and will inevitably tell you how well you are doing—even when in your heart you know you are doing lousy. As is typical of the Latin American culture, they will not correct you unless you absolutely insist. In many parts of Ecuador, you cannot communicate without basic Spanish. Mastering key phrases and words before you arrive in Ecuador can increase your enjoyment of the trip immeasurably. If you are traveling on your own without tour guides, it is virtually mandatory. Don't rely on the old saw, "I had a year of Spanish back in high school, and I know it will all come back to me as soon as I am forced to use it." Take some time before you leave on the trip and learn as much Spanish as you can.

As is true with every country and region in Latin America, there are local uses of words that are unique to each place or country. In English, we call these words or phrases idiomatic expressions. For instance, the word for the animal "gopher" means a turtle in the southeastern U.S., a ground squirrel in the Midwest and a burrowing rodent in the rest of the U.S. Sometimes words from one region have absolutely no meaning in other regions. For instance, in Minnesota, a "bismark" is what the rest of the U.S. calls a jelly-filled donut.

Ecuador has its share of these *modismos*, but the most common and obvious one is *Siga, no más*. Literally, this should mean "Don't continue," but it actually means "Keep on going." The grunted "uh-uh," which in English means "no," means "yes" in Ecuador. In Ecuador, *cola* can mean "soda," a "line" (such as at a bank window), a "bribe" or a "tail." Throughout Latin America, however, the distinctive regional word uses are being slowly but surely homogenized, especially in the big cities. Many blame television and the *novelas*, or soap operas, from Venezuela and Mexico. When *quiteños* refer to a car's tires as *cauchos* and not *llantas*, it is obvious that this purely Venezuelan *modismo* has infected the Ecuadorian vocabulary. One *modismo* shared by Mexico, however, cannot be blamed on television, and we are hard-pressed to understand how it came about. Throughout all of Latin America, the common response to a question or statement not well heard or understood is *¿Cómo?* (in English, "What?"). Only throughout Mexico, some parts of Central America and in Ecuador, especially coastal Ecuador, is the word *¿Mande?* substituted. Literally, it is from the word *Mándame*, or "command me." How this peculiar and unique *modismo* got from Mexico to Ecuador is not clear, but it happened long before television.

MONEY MATTERS

CURRENCY

The currency unit is the sucre. Bills come in denominations of 100, 500, 1000, 5000, 10,000, 20,000 and 50,000. Some coins are available, but because of inflation, they are next to useless except for paying small children to watch your car. The larger denomination bills can be difficult to use in rural areas where change is often unavailable. Rumors abound that soon the present currency will have the last three zeroes lopped off and be renamed.

CHANGING MONEY

It is always a good idea not to exchange too much money at one time. That's because whatever inflation rate there is favors those who wait. Often the money exchange places in Miami, Houston or Los Angeles airports give a poor rate that is 5 to 10 percent lower than that at the money exchange counter in the Ecuadorian airport arrival area. The best rate, however, will almost always be in the banks and money exchange offices (*casas de cambio*) in the bigger cities. In Quito and Guayaquil, many taxi drivers and businesses will accept dollars directly. In rural areas, however, this is not the case. As a matter of fact, in some rural areas it is almost impossible to exchange foreign currency of any kind. In an emergency, gas stations often prove to be a place to change money when no other alternative is available, but don't expect the best rate. Most tourist hotels will exchange foreign cash and some will exchange traveler's checks, but again their rate is always considerably lower than that of money exchange offices or banks. Except for souvenir value, there is no economic advantage to holding on to sucres when you leave the country. The departure tax at the airport is a good way to clear your wallet of the last of your sucres.

There has been a trend for money changers not to accept foreign currency with tears or holes, even if the bills otherwise are valid. Often only the larger banks will accept these damaged bills. More recently some money changers have been accepting only the new $20, $50 and $100 bills with large presidential portraits. To avoid these problems, make sure you are carrying only undamaged and new bills to Ecuador. Of course, no such standard of excellence is maintained for the Ecuadorian sucres you receive in exchange. Many of the smaller denomination bills look like they were used to line someone's shoe for several months before finally being spent.

Counterfeit currency is a problem for both Ecuadorian sucres and U.S. dollars. Many of the money exchange offices and banks now use UV-light detectors, but experience and a trained eye are still the main way to detect the phony bills. In general, money exchangers at banks and other official exchange sites are authorized to confiscate and destroy counterfeit bills with no compensation. Having one of your dollar bills (or even worse, a $20 bill) punched full of holes before your eyes is very frustrating. Recently minted U.S. bills of higher denomination ($100, $50, $20 and $10) now have a thin, vertical polyester strip embedded in the paper one inch to the left of the president's portrait. Hold it up to the light and you can see it even has the denomination of the bill printed on the plastic strip—"USA 10," "USA 20," "USA 50" or "USA 100." Just because a bill lacks this strip, however, does not mean it is counterfeit. Authentic older bills still in circulation will not have the strip. The newly formatted US$20, $50 and $100 bills have several features beside the polyester strip (security thread) to foil counterfeiters. They have a larger, off-center portrait of the president; a duplicate image (watermark) of the president is visible on the side opposite the security thread when held up to a light but cannot be photocopied; and the numeral value of the bill in the bottom right hand corner on the president's portrait side of the bill looks green when viewed straight on but black at an angle.

Banks are open Monday through Friday from 9 a.m. to 1:30 p.m. Some branches are open in the afternoon as well. More and more banks in the bigger cities feature automatic teller machines, some of which are connected to North American credit card companies. Ask which banks will exchange foreign currency and which will exchange traveler's checks. Most banks will accept both, but others will only accept one or the other, and some will not exchange foreign funds in any form.

Street money changers, while legal, are not common in Ecuador. If you encounter them, be advised against using their services as they may try short-changing your exchange. Normally, so many reputable businesses will exchange money, there is little reason to use these street changers.

CREDIT CARDS

In the larger cities and at the tourist-oriented lodges and restaurants away from the major cities, credit cards are readily accepted. However, not all types of cards are always accepted at these businesses. For instance, Diners Club is probably the most universally accepted foreign credit card, with Visa and MasterCard next. American Express is more problematic, as many establishments specifically exclude AmEx. However, if you lose or have your credit card stolen, the major credit card companies have their own offices in Ecuador and can replace your card the same or next day.

American Express—in Guayaquil, Ecuadorian Tours, Cia Ltza, Avenida 9 de Octubre 1900, P.O. Box 3802, 4-287-111; in Quito, Ecuadorian Tours, Avenida Río Amazonas 339, P.O. Box 2605, 2-560-488.

You can also receive local currency and traveler's checks with a personal check presented with your credit card at these offices.

Diners Club International—in Quito, Edificio Diners, Avenidas de la República 710 and Eloy Alfaro, 2-221-372, 2-509-929; in Guayaquil, Urdesa, V. E. Estrada 306 and Las Lomas, 4-884-500, 4-880-500; in Machala, Rocafuerte and Guayas, 1st floor; 7-936-060, 7-936-062.

Visa—in Quito, Avenida de los Shyris 3117 and Isla Tortuga; 2-459-391, 459-000; or call collect to the U.S., 410-581-9944. Have your card number and home bank name available. Two to three days after making the call you should receive the card via courier at your hotel or residence in Ecuador.

MasterCard—in Quito, Avenida de Las Naciones Unidas 825 and Shyris; 2-462-770; or call collect to the U.S., 214-994-9843. Have your card number and home bank name available. Two to three days after making the call you should receive the card via courier at your hotel or residence in Ecuador.

TIPPING

Tipping in Ecuador, like anywhere else in the world, is based on the level of service you received. Taxi drivers, guides, boatmen, etc., are all very appreciative of any extra money you give them. If they have gone out of their way to make you happy, give them more; if they have been surly or unprofessional, give them less or nothing at all. A general rule of thumb is 50¢ per bag for baggage handlers. If they have to carry them particularly far or if your bags are bigger or heavier than normal, tip $1 per bag. If you have had a guide or driver for a day or more and they have done a good job, a tip of $5 to $10 per day is standard. If they have been exceptional, tip them more. In good restaurants the tip is almost always included on your check.

The paradox in tipping with cash is that it can lead to negative behaviors for those people who are not used to large sums of cash suddenly appearing in their hand. This is particularly true for indigenous guides in the rainforest. Unfortunately, too much cash can be overwhelming. By rewarding someone who has helped you, you may inadvertently cause problems. This doesn't happen all the time, but it has happened enough for us to be careful when tipping guides. There is no easy solution to this paradox. You could try tipping with field guides or sweatshirts from home instead of cash. It is best to ask the manager of the lodge for suggestions and, if still in doubt, get your guide's address and send him something when you return home.

BARGAINING

Part of the fun for many tourists is trying out their bargaining skills in Ecuador. It can only be used in the rural villages and Indian markets, and the practice is somewhat deceptive. You probably only bargain once or twice a year, but these people at the markets do it all day all year. Guess who is going to come out ahead? If you approach it like a game, you will enjoy it. Tricks like walking away when the price won't come down usually work well. Being the first customer of the day holds some "lucky charm" association for some vendors. They will let you get away with almost anything to increase the chance for sales for the rest of the day. In grocery stores, pharmacies, big-city department stores, and wherever price stickers are placed on sale items, do not try bargaining—it is considered rude.

LOCAL TRANSPORTATION

TAXIS

Taxis are very inexpensive by North American or European standards. In the larger cities of Quito, Guayaquil and Cuenca, taxis are legally bound to have and use meters. However, because gasoline prices are always rising and the meter commission is always six months behind in granting permission to adjust the meter rates up, quite often the taxi drivers will not use the meter. Only in Quito do they regularly use them anyway. If the meter is not to be used, be sure to establish the fare to your destination *before* you get into the taxi. Ask at the hotel desk or airline counter what the *tarifa* is to your location, so you will have at least a ballpark estimate of what you should be paying. Taxis assigned to a hotel always charge more than taxis at stands away from the hotel. Taxis can be a good alternative to renting a car if you want to go on an excursion for a day. Often the price of the taxi and driver is less than the cost of a rental car for the same time, and you don't have to drive to get there. Bargain with a taxi driver the day before, and pick a taxi that is relatively new and in good condition.

HITCHHIKING

Because bus service is widely available and relatively cheap, hitchhiking is not a tradition in Ecuador. Foreigners trying to flag down a private car with their thumb are likely to be charged for the ride. You can ask for a lift from a truck driver if you can talk to him at a rest stop or gas station, but unless it is an emergency, don't try stopping private vehicles on the road.

BUSES

Buses are the most common and inexpensive way to travel in Ecuador. They connect the smallest of towns as well as large cities. The large inter-provincial buses are the most comfortable and the most expensive ($15 between Quito and Guayaquil). Some of these large intercity lines are express and make no intermediate stops. Most, however, stop for everyone and his chickens. The most remote areas are serviced by buses converted from trucks (*rancheras*). Their seats are wooden and have adequate leg room only for contortionists and very short people. The smaller buses have little room for baggage inside the seating area, so it is piled on top of the bus. Pilfering and pickpocketing of gringos is not uncommon on buses, so watch your baggage all the time. Most larger towns and cities have a central bus station (*terminal terrestre*), and this makes life easier for the foreign traveler. You can compare prices, service and schedules side by side to pick the best bus for your trip. In many towns, however, there is no central bus station, and you have to hunt from one end of town to the other for each bus company (*cooperativa*) office and parking area. For long trips, be sure and ask if the bus has a bathroom (*servicio*) on board; otherwise, carry a tennis ball can along. The express (*directo*) buses are not only faster, but because they do not stop along the way, there is little chance for the occasional stick-ups that occur along some routes at night. Be prepared for long hours, dusty roads and very cramped seating. You can, however, experience a part of Ecuador that tourists taking airplanes or rental cars never will. International bus service is available, but you have to change buses at each border crossing (see Chapter Three).

TRAINS

Historically, railroad lines in Ecuador were built to service isolated communities that otherwise couldn't get goods to market and back. As more and more highways have been built throughout Ecuador, the train service has become less and less necessary. Not long ago, the government announced it was suspending virtually all railroad subsidies (only the lines that still served communities with no highways would keep their subsidies). That means the railroad from Guayaquil to Riobamba to Quito will likely become extinct soon. The only railroad that now meets the subsidy criterion is the Ibarra–San Lorenzo line. Now there is construction of a highway along that route as well, and railroads in Ecuador are probably going to cease to exist within a few years.

DOMESTIC AIRLINES

Two major airlines and an up-and-coming newer company serve an amazing number of Ecuador's cities and towns. The domestic fares on these airlines run between $20 and $80 one-way depending on the competition and distance. SAETA and its domestic company, SAN, fly Boeing 727s to Quito, Guayaquil and San Cristóbal (Galápagos), and between Quito and Cuenca. With direct computer linkups in its offices in Los Angeles, Miami and New York City, it is easy to make reservations from the United States or Europe.

The Ecuadorian Air Force flies several types of civilian aircraft, under the name TAME, to most of Ecuador's major towns. They have flights between Quito and Baltra (Galápagos), Coca, Cuenca, Esmeraldas, Guayaquil, Lago Agrio, Loja, Macas, Manta, Portoviejo and Tulcán. They also have flights between Guayaquil and Bahía de Caráquez, Baltra (Galápagos), Cuenca, Quito, Loja and Machala. Unfortunately, TAME has no direct linkup by computer outside Ecuador. International carriers such as American Airlines or SAETA can only make inquiries for you on TAME, and then they will pursue these reservations only if you are flying with them to Ecuador. The best way to make reservations on TAME is to work through a travel agency in Ecuador or contact them directly. To but a ticket on TAME in Ecuador is a horrendous experience. They have computers, but the offices are always filled with long waits even if you just want to reconfirm a reservation. In the airport, they make you go through three separate lines—one to make the reservation, one to buy the ticket and one to accept your ticket and baggage and receive a boarding pass. Most flights on either TAME or SAN do not have assigned seats. Space for hand luggage is very limited, especially on some of the smaller planes flown by TAME. Be sure to confirm your reservations at least 24 hours ahead of time. This is one place that will throw you off the passenger list and replace you immediately if you don't, so beware.

Pre-embarking tickets are available from both TAME and domestic SAETA flights. You can request one 48 hours ahead of your scheduled flight time. This enables you to skip the wait at the ticket counter and take your luggage right up to the front of the line to be checked. If you change your mind and want to fly on a different flight, however, you must pay a small fine.

A new and fairly small airline, Aerogal, is trying to make inroads by offering competing service between some cities. They fly small, 20-passenger prop planes and may or may not be around next year. Several charter plane companies and air-taxi services are also available, but are, of course, tremendously expensive.

BOATS

On rivers of the Oriente and the coast, boats and motorized canoes are often the only mode of transportation possible. These boats operate just like water-buses or water-taxis. Always ask the price *before* you get into the boat.

DRIVING IN ECUADOR

Exploring by rental car is the most independent and easiest way to see Ecuador. Being able to stop wherever and whenever you want is ideal for the independent traveler. The tradeoff, however, is enduring the vagaries of Ecuadorian drivers, the almost complete lack of road signs, the danger of trucks passing on blind curves, and the uncertainty of leaving your vehicle unattended anywhere while you explore side trails or spend the night in a local hotel. We cannot imagine or recommend driving around Ecuador without a good command of Spanish.

Always assume that vehicles will pass you no matter if you can see ahead or not. Drive defensively, but do not drive so overcautiously that you become a danger to yourself and everyone else on the road. Even though the driving techniques of Ecuadorians may seem totally out of control according to your gringo sensibilities, they at least know what to expect out of each other. That's why there are relatively so few accidents. If you come along driving like you were still back in Omaha, none of the other drivers around you will expect you to give way at the intersection or to stop at the traffic circle when everyone else is jockeying for an opening. You end up creating problems that may cause an accident.

The police have permanent traffic control points, but they also often set up temporary control points on the major highways. If a policeman signals you, stop and have your driver's license and car registration ready. More often than not, when they see you are a gringo driving a rental car, they will wave you on through. The military checkpoints are permanent control points with barricades, speed bumps and armed soldiers. Not only will you need to show your driver's license and car registration, but usually you will have to get out of the car and show your passport and tourist card to the National Police also at the control point. They will record your passport number and ask you where you are going. This normally takes only a few minutes, unless you are driving near the Peruvian border soon after one of the irregular flareups over the long-disputed border position between these two countries.

In 1996, seat belt use was made mandatory for the driver. Although this law is only rigorously enforced in Quito, don't give the local traffic cop an excuse to stop you. Wear your seat belt!

While driving, don't assume that stop signs, lane division stripes or speed limits really mean anything. The one sign that is usually respected is the tiny little arrow that indicates a one-way (*una vía*) street. Unfortunately, these are usually so inconspicuous or so high up on a building that unless you already know they are there, you are likely to miss them. The other drivers will let you know, however, if you are going *contra flecha* (against the arrow).

Many Ecuadorian roads have no shoulder. On the open highway, a pile of green-leafed branches means "watch out for a stalled vehicle ahead." If the vehicle has been repaired and driven off, not only will the pile of branches be left on the road but the large rocks placed behind the rear tires of the stalled vehicle will also still be there. Ecuadorians have a frustrating habit of not caring at all about the problems these rocks cause drivers who come after them. In general, drive only in the daytime to be able to see these rocks, potholes and other obstructions that would be impossible to spot at night.

Never leave your vehicle unattended. If you want to go off into the forest or explore some paramo habitat along the road, a companion or driver should stay by the car. Not all Ecuadorians are bandits, but a car filled with cameras, clothing and other valuables can be a temptation for many. At night, park your vehicle in a protected compound or garage provided by the hotel.

City driving is the most challenging place for foreigners. Cutting off other cars, racing for position and ignoring the traffic lights is considered normal driving. At night some motorists will drive without their lights to save the battery, and nobody stops for a red light. Ecuadorian drivers are getting better about using turn signals, but do not depend on them always to tell you what the driver in front of you is planning. Besides the one-way arrows, the one thing you should never ignore is a traffic policeman. Either on the corner or in the middle of the intersection, their directions always take precedence over the traffic light or stop sign. If his (or, more and more frequently, her) back or front is toward you, STOP! If his side is toward you, proceed. These policemen all rely on referee's whistles to communicate their wishes. They can chirp, warble or scream at you with these whistles. Sometimes all they have to do is strike the opening on top of the whistle against their hand to produce a sharp sound. Whatever you do, don't make a policeman dodge your vehicle—you'll hear that whistle scream like there is no tomorrow. If he gets really mad, he can confiscate your driver's license and car registration on the spot. Getting them back can mean days of red tape or a bribe (which we do *not* recommend). If you are in an accident with another car or strike a pedestrian, you are in BIG trouble no matter whose fault it was. This strange situation might be called THE PARADOX OF THE PEDESTRIAN. As a pedestrian you have absolutely no rights. You always give way to vehicles whether they are turning in front of you, stopping on the sidewalk right in your path, or wherever. However, if you are hit by a car or, God forbid, killed by a vehicle, you automatically receive the benefit of the doubt and are conveyed complete rights. The vehicle driver is considered guilty no matter the circumstances. He (or she) is expected to convey you to the nearest doctor or hospital and pay your expenses. If you are killed, the driver automatically goes to jail and only after negotiations with the victim's family for financial compensation is there a chance for release from incarceration. You would think with this type of punishment hanging over the head of all drivers they would have more regard for pedestrians, but such is not the case and thus the paradox. Of course, the other ramification of this system is that a driver hitting a pedestrian is likely to try a hit-and-run tactic to avoid punishment.

All in all, we strongly suggest that you consider *not* driving while in Ecuador. For the independent-minded traveler, we know this is a very difficult idea to consider. But the hassles and stress of getting around will not enhance your trip. Contact one of the large tour operators and hire a driver. Not only will you get to where you want to go, but you will meet and get to know an Ecuadorian and perhaps learn something about the people and land. Trying to sightsee, navigate, drive and enjoy yourself at the same time is a sure way to have a frustrating trip or an accident. Trust us, hire a driver.

CAR RENTALS

You will find that in Ecuador almost everything from food to photocopies is considerably cheaper than in North America or Europe. The one outstanding exception is a rental car. For even the smallest car, expect to pay $35 a day (including insurance but not taxes of 20 percent) plus $0.11/kilometer.

The average car rental costs, with insurance, about $65 to $135 per day. Larger cars and four-wheel-drive vehicles (*tracción doble*) cost up to $75 per day and $0.50/kilometer. (Some companies now offer international rates paid in dollars that include unlimited kilometers.) Plan out the total driving distance ahead of time so you don't have any major surprises when you pay your final bill. On top of this, of course, you must pay for gasoline, which now is as expensive if not more expensive than in the U.S. ($1.65/gallon for super). Weekly and monthly rates are a better deal, with two to ten free days and 1000 kilometers per week free. Some car agencies and travel agencies can provide a driver, but of course that costs more—$35–$50/day plus room and board. (In several cases, we have found it cheaper and much more convenient to rent a taxi and driver for several days.) You must have a credit card to rent the car, otherwise a cash deposit of $1000 to $1500 is needed. Valid foreign drivers' licenses can be used up to 90 days, and after that an International Driver's License is required. During the high tourist season, advanced reservations, especially for four-wheel-drive vehicles, are often necessary. Insurance is included, and the better (also more expensive) companies will replace your vehicle if it has mechanical problems. A driver will get your new vehicle to you as soon as possible depending on where you were stranded. Ecuador is so small that in most cases you will be no more than 4–6 hours away from Quito or Guayaquil.

Flat tires are a way of life and are not covered by insurance. Be prepared to change the tire at least once on your trip. Fortunately, tire repair shops (*vulcanizadora*) are common along highways. They usually have an old tire hanging outside a little building or shack that serves as the shop. Before you leave the rental car agency, check the spare to see that it is inflated and has reasonable tread. Don't assume that the jack (*gata* in Spanish) is in the car, so check for it, too. Before signing the rental contract, note every scratch on the outside and inside of the vehicle, and record missing equipment like radio knobs, antennae, rear windshield wiper, etc. Some companies are very strict about charging for these things upon return of the vehicle. Several times we have rented a four-wheel-drive vehicle from major international companies that did not go into four-wheel drive when we needed it. Once you leave the rental car lot, these minor inconveniences become your problem, and they can ruin your trip once you get away from the city. Rental car agencies in Ecuador include the following:

AMBATO

Localiza Rent-A-Car
Calle Montalvo y Avenida de los Copulíes: 3-828-249, 3-825-251

CUENCA

Hertz Rent-A-Car
Hotel Oro Verde, Avenida Ordóñez Lazo: 7-831-200, fax: 7-832-849

International Rent-A-Car
Airport: 7-801-892, 7-804-063

Localiza Rent-A-Car
Avenida España 1485 and Granada/Airport: 7-863-902, 7-860-174

GUAYAQUIL

Arrancar Rent-A-Car
Airport: 4-288-179, 4-283-473, 4-286-279
Avenida de las Américas: 4-283-473

Avis Rent-A-Car

Airport: 4-395-554

Federico de P. Ycaza 425 and Calle General Córdova: 4-562-815

Budget Rent-A-Car

Airport: 4-288-510

Avenida de las Américas 900 and Calle N: 4-394-314, 4-284-559

García Moreno and Hurtado (Sucursal): 4-328-571, 4-329-898,
    fax: 4-283-656

Pichincha 334: 4-523-952

Colcar Cia., Ltda.

Airport: 4-288-475, 4-281-129, 4-281-149

Delgado Rent-A-Car

Airport: 4-287-768

C. C. Plaza La Garzota: 4-232-752, 4-232-753

Edificio San Francisco 300, Calle General Córdova and Avenida 9 de
    Octubre: 4-561-669, 4-560-680, 4-564-613, fax: 4-314-596

García Moreno 917 and Avenida 9 de Octubre: 4-398-687, 4-398-704,
    4-398-337, fax: 4-323-845

Driol-Fax Rent-A-Car

Airport: 4-399-707, 4-399-703

Ecuacar Rent-A-Car

Airport: 4-285-533, 4-283-247

Adace, Calle A SI 23 Calle 7: 4-293-651, 4-293-811, fax: 4-286-247

Fiesta Rent-A-Car

Airport: 4-290-513, 4-290-372

Gran Hotel Guayaquil, Boyacá and Calle 10 de Agosto: 4-328-439

Hertz Rent-A-Car

Airport: 4-293-011, fax: 4-293-012

Escobedo 1213 and 9 de Octubre: 4-511-316, 4-511-317,
    fax: 4-511-318

International Rent-A-Car

Airport: 4-284-136

Jorsan Rent-A-Car

Airport: 4-284-876, 4-289-708

Localiza Rent-A-Car

Airport: 4-281-462, fax: 4-380-372

Avenida de las Monjas 125 and V. Emilio Estrada: 4-889-353, 4-381-113

Super Rent

Airport: 4-284-454, 4-285-354

Aguirre 406 and Chile (in front of Unicentro): 4-324-598, 4-324-599

LOJA

Hidal Rent-A-Car

Hotel Ramsés, Colón 14-31 and Bolívar: 7-571-402, fax: 7-581-832

MACHALA

Localiza Rent-A-Car

Avenida Paquisha and Kilometer 1 C. C., Unioro: 7-937-330, 7-931-504

MANTA

Hertz Rent-A-Car

Centro Comercial Manicentro, Local No. 8, Avenida Flavio Reyes
between Avenidas 24 and 23: 5-627-519, fax: 5-627-526

Manabi-Rent-A-Car

Calle 10 kittycorner from the Filanbanco near the terrestrial terminal:
5-621-434, 5-921-432

QUITO

Arrancar Rent-A-Car

Airport: 2-450-688, 2-433-357

Avis Rent-A-Car

Airport: 2-440-270

Avenidas Cristóbal Colón 1741 and 10 de Agosto: 2-550-238,
2-550-243

Budget Rent-A-Car

Airport: 2-459-052, 2-240-763

Avenidas Cristóbal Colón and Río Amazonas: 2-237-026, 2-548-237

Hotel Colón: 2-525-328, 2-548-388

Ecuacar Rent-A-Car

Airport: 2-247-298, 2-448-531

Avenidas Cristóbal Colón 1280 and Río Amazonas: 2-529-781,
2-523-673

Expo Rent-A-Car

Airport: 2-433-127

Avenida América 1116 and Bolivia, Plaza Indoamérica: 2-501-203

Hertz Rent-A-Car

Airport: 2-254-258, fax: 2-254-257

Localiza Rent-A-Car

Avenida 6 de Diciembre 1570 and Wilson/Airport: 2-505-986,
505-974, fax: 2-506-005

Premium Rent-A-Car

Avenidas Orellana 1623 and 9 de Octubre: 2-238-582, 2-552-897,
2-565-253

MAPS

By law, all maps of Ecuador must include the disputed area of northern Perú as part of Ecuador. Although most Ecuadorians now accept that Iquitos will never be part of Ecuador, it is a matter of pride when a foreigner speaks disparagingly of this strange addition to Ecuador's boundaries. In the airport and in many tourist shops, there are large colored maps of Ecuador. These are only good for tacking to your wall when you get home. One of the most useful maps we have found is a very accurate and detailed road map (2nd edition, 1996) produced by ITMB Publishing/World Wide Books and Maps, Ecuador No. 278 (345 West Broadway, Vancouver, B.C., Canada V54 1P8; 604-687-3320, fax: 604-687-5925). The other useful map is *Guia Vial del Ecuador*. It is published in the form of a booklet (4 x 8½) with 13 fold-out detailed maps of each of the regions of Ecuador. It is published in Ecuador by the Instituto Geográfico Militar and is available in most hotel souvenir shops and bookstores (*librerias*) in the larger cities.

The **Instituto Geográfica Militar** (El Dorado section of Quito, Senierguez and Paz y Mindo) sells detailed topographic maps for many sections of the country. Just pass through the gate, after leaving an identification card or driver's license with the soldiers on guard, and ask for the map store. Don't forget to reclaim your card when you leave.

GAS

As a rule of thumb, never let the tank of your vehicle get below half-full. Filling stations (*gasolineras*) are found in most towns and rarely are you more than 25 kilometers from the next one. Only in the very remote areas of Zamora Chinchipe and Pastaza are there likely to be problems. Gas is sold by the U.S. gallon and is relatively expensive. Most stations offer several types of gasoline and diesel fuel, so make sure you use the pump that delivers fuel appropriate for your vehicle. "Extra" is the same as regular-leaded ($1.35 per gallon). "Super" is the highest octane and is also leaded ($1.65 per gallon). Diesel is the cheapest fuel ($0.85 per gallon). The pumps are always operated by the employees, and self-service stations are nonexistent. Gas stations are a good place to change those large-denomination bills no one else will accept. Also, as an emergency, gas stations will sometimes change U.S. dollars, but at a very poor rate. If soon after filling your car with gas, the motor begins to run very poorly with lots of engine stops, you likely have water mixed in with the gas. If you have a vehicle with fuel injection, you will quickly stall and have little hope unless you are stalled near an auto mechanic (*taller*). If you have a vehicle with a carburetor, run the car over bumps to mix the water and gas. The water tends to separate out and fall to the bottom of the tank. Get to the nearest mechanic and have the tank drained. If you have some pure alcohol along and are far from a mechanic, pour the alcohol into the tank. It will combine with the water and burn off fairly well.

Be aware that even if a gas station advertises that it accepts credit cards like Visa or MasterCard, the phone call needed to authorize a foreign-held card is usually more than the attendants are willing to do. Be prepared to pay for fuel in cash.

ACCIDENTS

The procedures for reporting an accident are somewhat hazy, but everyone agrees that you must report to the nearest police station as soon as possible. The police will try and divide the fault between the parties according to the evidence. Usually the car in back is blamed for most accidents. If you are in a rental car, you will need this police report for the insurance claim. However, the deductible for most car insurance is $1000 to $2000, so you will be responsible for that amount out of your own pocket. If the police report indicates that your part of the fault in the accident is low or none, you can legally make the other driver pay this deductible. Most Ecuadorian drivers, however, do not have this kind of money on them, so you will have to get the other driver's address and telephone number. Count on a month before you will even have a prayer of seeing this money. Although no policeman would admit it, there is strong indirect evidence that fault is often determined partly by who can most afford to pay. As a result, a gringo involved in an accident is likely to receive more of the fault no matter what.

If the accident results in injury or you hit and injure a pedestrian with your car, a whole different set of standards is used. This kind of accident is considered so serious, you need to react appropriately and immediately. The vehicle driver is expected to take the injured person to the nearest hospital or doctor's office quickly. You are expected to pay for the medical bills and show considerable remorse and repentance. Do not act haughty or uncaring, even if the fault was entirely the pedestrian's or the other car's. If a fatality is involved, you will most likely be put in jail with no questions asked. Contact the nearest consulate or embassy as soon as possible. Depending on how quickly the police decide to proceed, you can expect to stay a week or more in jail. This would happen even to another Ecuadorian involved in a fatal accident, so don't feel that it is just a conspiracy against gringos. However, a gringo would be expected to pay a higher fine and settlement to the victim's family.

ROAD TROUBLE

If you break down away from a city or town, be sure to place branches on the road 50 yards in back and ahead of your car. Someone will stop if you signal them and take you to the nearest town and garage mechanic (*taller*). Someone should stay with the vehicle if possible until you return. If the road is very remote and little traffic goes by, trucks often have all the tools you might need for simple repairs. Bus drivers are usually so hassled with their schedule, they virtually never stop. If you have rented from one of the better companies, get to the nearest phone and have them send a replacement car. Flat tires are a way of life for anyone driving in Ecuador. Be prepared to change a tire at least once during the trip. Our record is seven flat tires in two weeks—five caused by nails, one by a screw and one by a broken bone we picked up by inadvertently driving over a dead dog in the road!

STREET ADDRESSES

In small towns and cities, the address system is based on the fact that everyone knows where everyone else lives. Even in big cities, signs are few and far between, and those that are around are tiny and placed high up on the sides of corner buildings. At best an address will have the street, a number and the closest cross street. When you get close, just start asking people where such and such is. If the address is in a large building, remember that numbering floors is different in Latin America. What we call the first floor or ground floor is *planta baja*, and the first floor is our second floor and so on. In elevators, "PB" is the ground floor, and numbering of rooms and offices begins with the 100s on the next floor up.

In 1997 the municipality of Quito introduced a new address system for the city based on a grid. Every house and business now has an address that includes letters and numbers. Unfortunately not even taxi drivers have been able to divine how the system works, and most everyone continues to rely on the old system.

BUSINESS HOURS

The siesta or lunch break is very important in Ecuador. Most businesses open between 8 a.m. and 9 a.m., close for two to three hours at mid-day, and then reopen at 2 p.m. or 3 p.m. They close for the day at 5 p.m. to 6 p.m. Many tourist-oriented businesses remain open throughout the day with no siesta period.

TIME ZONES

Mainland Ecuador is on Eastern Standard Time year-round. The Galápagos are on Central Standard Time year-round.

COMMUNICATIONS

TELEPHONES

The telephone system in Ecuador is quite good. National and international calls can be made from most phones with only the necessary country and city codes. For the most reliable and cheapest tolls, use the national phone company (EMETEL) office. There is one in virtually every village and town in the country. Depending on the sophistication of the equipment in the EMETEL office, the operator there will either dial for you, or sell you tokens (*fichas*) that can be used in phone booths lining the EMETEL office waiting room. You dial your own number and use as many tokens as you need, or as much time as your tokens permit.

Ecuador's country code for calls from abroad is 593. Ecuador in turn is divided into six area codes. Zone 2 includes Pichincha Province and Quito. Zone 3 includes the provinces of Bolívar, Cotopaxi, Chimborazo, Pastaza, and Tungurahua and the cities of Ambato, Puyo and Riobamba. Zone 4 includes the province of Guayas and the cities of Guayaquil and Salinas. Zone 5 includes the Galápagos and the provinces of Los Ríos and Manabi and the cities of Manta, Portoviejo, Quevedo and Babahoyo. Zone 6 includes the provinces of Carchi, Esmeraldas, Imbabura, Napo, Orellana and Sucumbios and the cities of Esmeraldas, Tulcán, Ibarra, Latacunga, Tena, Coca and Lago Agrio. Zone 7 includes the provinces of Azuay, Cañar, El Oro, Morona Santiago and Zamora Chinchipe, and the cities of Cuenca, Machala, Azogues, Gualaceo, Loja and Zamora.

From most hotels, national and international calls can be made through the hotel operator. In the bigger hotels, credit calling cards can be used, so you can dial yourself. To connect directly and without extra cost to an English-speaking operator in the U.S., dial 999-119 for AT&T, 999-170 for MCI and 999-171 for Sprint. For an operator in Canada, dial 999-175 (Teleglobe).

A word of warning. The big hotels hate these calling cards, and they will do anything to make sure you do not make a call abroad that they cannot charge somehow. Even though these calling-card calls cost the hotel no more than a local call, many of them make you go through their hotel operator and then charge up to $0.50/minute on your call. You will still have to pay the international toll on your next phone bill when you get home, but you will also have a horrendous charge on your hotel bill. If you don't like this rip-off, say something to the hotel administration. Fax transmission machines are very common in Ecuador. The cost for sending an international fax out of Ecuador, however, can cost more than $5/page.

MAIL

Post offices are found in even the smallest towns throughout Ecuador. If you are sending a letter that must get to its international destination, be sure to register it. The extra cost is worth it. Some tourists have souvenirs and extra baggage sent back home via mail at the end of a trip. Sometimes vendors will include this mailing service when you buy something expensive at their shop. Be sure to ask to see receipts for other people who have had their valuable souvenirs sent home via mail. If the shop owner has a letter or two thanking him for the service, all the better. If you want to receive a package in Ecuador from back home, be prepared to pay big bucks for duty. Even a box of chocolate-chip cookies can cost $15 in duty, and the Ecuadorian officials won't let you see what's in the box before you pay for it. Mail can be received from the United States at the American Express office or at your embassy. Some courier services also deliver mail and packages to and from Ecuador. The costs are high, but the delivery time is fast and reliable. We recommend DHL International as the most reliable for service to and from Ecuador (Avenida de la Republica 396, Quito; 2-565-059, 554-177).

LAUNDRY

Dry-cleaning is available at shops in Quito and Guayaquil. Laundry is either done by the better hotels (very expensive) or by yourself in the hotel bathroom sink. At the ecotourist lodges, laundry is not usually included or even available. Bring powdered soap, clothesline and clothespins if you will be in an area without laundry facilities, which in Ecuador means almost everywhere away from the big cities. In Quito, we have found two reliable and relatively inexpensive laundries in the central hotel district: **Burbujas Laundry** (6 de Diciembre 1868 and Juan Rodríguez; 2-231-511, 228-444; 9 a.m.–7 p.m. Monday–Saturday) and **Calama Laundry** (Calama 244 between Diego de Almagro and Reina Victoria; 8 a.m.–8 p.m. every day).

PUBLICATIONS

U.S. magazines, newspapers and paperback books can be found in the bookshops of the first-class and luxury hotels. A few bookstores, like Libri Mundi in Quito, have a large selection of English-language publications. The Quito and Guayaquil airports also sell English-language publications at their small bookshops.

THE METRIC SYSTEM

Whether you're buying bottled drinks, checking the thermometer or looking at road signs, you'll notice the difference: most everything is metric. Ecuador measures temperature in degrees Celsius, distances in kilometers, and most substances in liters, kilos and grams. However, a person's weight is still given in pounds (*libras*) and gasoline is sold by the U.S. gallon (*galón*).

To convert from Celsius to Fahrenheit, multiply times 9, divide by 5 and add 32. For example, 23°C—the average temperature in Ecuador during the winter—equals [(23 x 9)/5] + 32, or (207/5) + 32, or 41.4 + 32, or about 73°F. If you don't have a pocket calculator along (but you probably should), just remember that 0°C is 32°F and that each Celsius degree is roughly two Fahrenheit degrees. Here are some other useful conversion equations:

- 1 mile = 1.6 kilometers. 1 kilometer = $^3/_5$ mile
- 1 foot = 0.3 meter. 1 meter = $3^1/_3$ feet
- 1 pound *(libra)* = 0.45 kilo. 1 kilo = $2^1/_5$ pounds
- 1 gallon = 3.8 liters. 1 liter = about $^1/_4$ gallon, or about one quart

PICTURE TAKING

Almost everyone who travels to Ecuador goes with a camera. With the sophistication of today's cameras and film, good photos can be expected from any trip. Many of you will want to take pictures of the friendly people of Ecuador. *Always* ask permission before you do so. Many of the *campesinos* of the highlands believe their souls will be taken when photographed and thus do not want their picture taken. Respect their wishes as you would want to be respected. Never force your will on someone for the sake of a photo—no picture is more important than the welfare of the subject. If you are patient and perhaps willing to pay a small fee or buy some merchandise, some of these people will cooperate.

If you are serious about photography, see the section on nature photography in Chapter Five. If you want to concentrate on the wonderful faces of the Ecuadorian people, get permission, pay a few dollars and carefully set up your shot. Spontaneous photography of people is almost guaranteed to be mediocre. Take your time, find a cooperative person to model and snap away. If you are creative and friendly, your results will be what you want, and the shot will appear spontaneous.

HEALTH PRECAUTIONS

WATER

Most brochures and tourist information claim that water in the better hotels and restaurants in Ecuador is safe to drink from the tap. Maybe that is so for Ecuadorians, who have received natural immunization after drinking it their whole life. Do *not* under any circumstances be lulled into a false sense of security about water in Ecuador. Never take a chance. Bottled mineral water (*agua mineral*) or bottled noncarbonated water (*agua sin gas*) is available now even in remote towns of Ecuador. If not, beer or soda (*gaseosa* or *cola*) is. If you want to be extra cautious, make sure the waiter opens the bottle in your presence. Ordering ice in your drink defeats all the caution in the world, because normally the ice is made from tap water. Tap water is also used to wash freshly cut fruits and vegetables. Avoid tap water and don't worry about how much of a wimp you may appear to your fellow travelers, or how paranoid you look. You can have the last laugh when your macho colleagues are on their backs groaning in pain and running to the bathroom all night long.

A micropore filter has saved the day for us more than once in remote areas where boiled or bottled water was unavailable. The metal or plastic pump filters are a lot of work, but they can filter out all but the smallest viruses. Some of the new models also automatically inject iodine into the filtered water, but that means there's just one more thing on it to break. Katydyn is a quality brand and is available in most outdoor recreation stores.

FOOD

Once again, common sense should prevail. If the food is so hot you have to blow on it to cool it off, it is likely to be safe. Never eat food from street vendors' carts, and eat only fresh fruit that you have peeled yourself. Be especially cautious of seafood in coastal areas because hepatitis and cholera, if they are going to occur, are most likely to be contracted by eating tainted seafood.

ALTITUDE

Due to the high altitude of many areas in Ecuador, tourists with heart problems or high blood pressure should consult their physicians before traveling here. Quito has an elevation of 9356 feet/2835 meters, and several of the popular tourist sites like Papallacta Pass and Cotopaxi are considerably higher in elevation. Most tourists acclimate within a day or two to the altitude of Quito. Try taking it easy carrying bags or climbing stairs until you have adjusted.

MALARIA

This mosquito-borne disease is now limited in Ecuador to some coastal areas and more remote sites in the Oriente. Consult the CDC (Center for Disease

Control) in Atlanta and local tour agencies for the latest updates. Resistant strains of the malaria microbe (*Plasmodium*) have evolved in Ecuador, so check locally as well. Most of the prophylactic medicines (like Aralen, Chloroquin, Mefloquin and Primaquin) if taken long-term, can also have severe side affects. If you do not need to take them, some doctors advise avoiding unnecessary exposure.

CAUTION: Some anti-malaria medicines can react severely with other simple medicines like anti-diarrheal drugs, as well as with alcohol. Read the label on your medicine and be aware of any dangers of mixing medicines. One measure of prevention is to avoid going out at night in malaria-prone areas. The primary mosquito carrier (genus *Anopheles*) of malaria is active mainly at night. It is immediately recognizable because as it bites, it raises its abdomen and its hind pair of legs high in the air over its back and appears to stand on its head. Other species of mosquitoes keep their rear legs low and their abdomens more or less parallel to the skin surface.

CHOLERA

Strong public education and aggressive measures to clean up areas where cholera has occurred have been very effective. Cholera is present now in Ecuador only in small numbers. Tourists can avoid it by taking minor precautions in what they eat and drink. Avoid tap water, raw or undercooked seafood (including uncooked ceviche), cold seafood salads, raw vegetables and ice from unknown origins. There is an inoculation against cholera, but it is only partially effective and is good for no more than six months.

EMERGENCY HEALTH CARE

In Guayaquil the general emergency telephone number is **199**, but in both Guayaquil and Quito there are also separate emergency numbers for police (**101**) and for fire (**102**). If you do not speak Spanish, this is no time to try and learn. The chances are that no one will understand English, especially if it is an emergency situation and you are excited. Try to get an Ecuadorian from the hotel desk or tour operator to call for you. If you are on an organized tour, the best tour operators will have contingencies and resources to take care of the emergency. They will know which is the best hospital to take you to and mobilize the vehicles, boats and helicopters that might be needed to get the job done. Do not depend on the police or fire department to do this. A case in point happened recently, when a 55-year-old Dane had a heart attack while diving off the Galápagos. Luckily for him, he had chosen one of the best and biggest tour companies for his expedition. The Ecuadorian officials had absolutely no idea what to do despite the $80 fee each tourist pays to visit the Galápagos. Only because the tour company was willing to spend the money to get a decompression chamber available, charter the helicopter and get him into the best hospital in Guayaquil, did he survive. Any time you choose a tour company just because it is the cheapest, you are losing out on this important fringe benefit.

In Quito the best hospitals for emergency care are **Hospital Metropolitano** (Avenida Mariana de Jesús and Avenida Occidental; 2-431-520, 431-521) and **Hospital Voz Andes** (Villalengua 267 and Avenida 10 de Agosto; 2-241-540, 241-541). In Guayaquil there are three excellent emergency hospitals: **Clínica Guayaquil** (downtown), Padre Aguirre 401 and General Córdova (4-563-555); **Clínica Alcívar** (south), Coronel 2301 and Azuay (4-444-287); and **Clínica Kennedy** (north), Avenida San Jorge between 9th and 10th in the Kennedy District (4-286-963).

MOSQUITOES AND OTHER PESTS IN PARADISE

Mosquitoes are a problem limited mostly to the rainy season in coastal areas and in a few areas along rivers in the Oriente. Most tourists are underwhelmed with mosquitoes and have little use for anti-bug ointments. By the way, the active ingredient in most bug ointments, DEET, is so active it will eat away at plastic on binoculars and glasses. What it can do to your skin and body may not be healthy, so avoid overuse. If you have burning sensations and prolonged red skin reactions to application of the anti-bug ointments, stop using them immediately. Tourists who bring the spray forms of these ointments can be especially obnoxious spraying a cloud of the chemical around them every couple of minutes. The applicator sticks are the most economical and friendliest form in which to apply the chemical to your skin and clothes if it is absolutely necessary. Yellow fever, dengue fever and malaria are spread by mosquitoes. Avoiding night-time activity in infected localities and sleeping under mosquito netting can control some transmission.

Bot flies are an inconvenience for some long-term visitors to Ecuador's forests. The female bot fly captures a female mosquito, lays her eggs on the mosquito and then releases her. When the mosquito lands on a human to bite, the bot fly egg instantly hatches out (cued by the body heat) and crawls down the mosquito's legs to bury itself in the skin of the human arm or wherever. A few days later, the bot fly larva constructs a breathing hole in the skin and takes ten weeks or so to grow under the skin. If you have a little hole in your skin with a tiny, white straw sticking up out of it periodically, this is likely the snorkel-like spiracle of the larval fly. It can be easily and safely removed only if it is first anesthetized so it cannot hold on to the inside of its burrow with its hooks. If any problem is likely to arise from the bot fly presence in your skin, it will be from secondary infections trying unsuccessfully to remove the larva and having part of it break off in the skin. One suggested cure is to put a piece of bacon tightly over the hole. The larva then burrows up into the bacon to be able to breathe and can be thrown away with the strip of bacon. We have successfully used clear finger nail polish over the hole to suffocate the larva and then two days later pop it out like a large pimple. If you want to experience the entire development of the larva, let it stay in your skin for the ten weeks it takes to mature. Then it will emerge on its own as an adult. A major danger is returning to the U.S. and going to a doctor who has had no experience in tropical medicine. We know several people who now have large scars where an inexperienced doctor removed a core of skin and muscle around the larva to extract it.

Chiggers are microscopic-size ticks that live in pastures and open areas of forests—especially if cattle are present. When you walk through the pasture, they crawl onto your legs, walk to the nearest skin and take a meal of your body fluids. Evidently, they can best burrow their mouth parts into your skin where there is tight clothing—socks, underwear waistband, bra, etc. Because they are so tiny, you have no idea they are there until it's too late. While sucking your body fluids, they inject proteins. Your body reacts to these foreign proteins by producing histamines that become raised, red spots. These spots itch, but as you scratch them, the itching only intensifies and can go on for days. To avoid chiggers, stay out of pastures or wash vigorously with soap and water immediately after crossing the pasture. One easy method to prevent the chiggers from getting to your skin is to apply powdered sulphur (Flowers of Sulphur) liberally inside your socks, around your waist and other areas constricted by tight clothing. The chiggers apparently do not cross these areas or bite in them. Peremethrin 0.5% appears to be very effective against chiggers, ticks, fleas and mosquitoes. It MUST NOT be sprayed on your skin, however. It is instead sprayed on your long-sleeved shirts, long pants and hat before you put them on. This product remains imbedded in the cloth and keeps its potency for up to five launderings. The most common brand names are Coluston's Duranon Tick Repellent and Sawyer's Peremethrin Tick Repellent. If you already have the red spots, a friend recently discovered that Preparation H (1% Hydrocortisone), an over-the-counter hemorrhoid treatment, stops the itching immediately and the spots go down. For some people, the cream has to be reapplied several times a day to have an effect, so be careful about using the cream too often or over too much of your body, and check with your doctor to make sure this and any other medications are safe for you to take personally. Chiggers tend to be highly seasonal, so ask local guides if there is any trouble with *garapatas* in the grass. Most local people have become immune to the bites, so make sure the guides are making a judgment based on other tourists who have visited the area recently.

Africanized bees were first introduced into the Western Hemisphere in Brazil because they make greater quantities of honey than the European variety. They quickly escaped their Brazilian hives and began moving north, reaching Ecuador some 20 years ago. When they first arrived, especially on the coast, there were noteworthy events of mass attacks. Dogs were killed and humans aggressively and repeatedly stung—some even died. However, an entomology colleague in Guayaquil told us that now these reported attacks have become very rare. Other experts have seen the same pattern in Brazil and Mexico. After an initial bout of aggressive attacks following the first wave of invading swarms, the frequency of attacks falls off after about five years. Some experts theorize that the aggressive genes become diluted by inter-breeding with more-docile European honey bees already present. Others theorize that papers and television just don't spend so much time reporting these incidents after a few years. At any rate, these bees appear to be a minor problem, and one that you are unlikely to face during your visit. The advice given to those unlucky enough to encounter the bees is to run through brush and vegetation as fast as you can and as far as you can. Do not hit at the bees or flail your arms. Freshly killed bees can give off a powerful aroma that incites the rest of the hive to protect the area. If you are allergic to bee stings of any kind, you should travel with an injection kit of epinephrine (adrena-line) or some other substance to fight the anaphylactic shock associated with severe allergic reactions to these stings. The kits are available by prescription so check with your doctor. Those with severe allergic reactions to bee stings are often just as susceptible to hornet and ant stings.

Ocelot

DRUGS

The history of drugs in Ecuador is very different from its neighboring countries, Colombia and Perú. Cocaine is not used in the highlands by indigenous people to make their long day endurable as it is in other Andean countries. There is no major market for marijuana. It is not consumed or grown commonly, and no tradition justifies it. Perhaps the best-known psychedelic drugs in Ecuador are used by the lowland indigenous people of the Oriente. Sap from trees and vines are drunk, inhaled or eaten to have visions. But this tradition has not made its way into the mainstream life of Ecuadorians.

Drugs can be found in Ecuador, but they are generally not considered appropriate. In this type of social environment, you can expect little support for a tourist caught using drugs. The laws and their enforcement are often inconsistent, but that is all the more dangerous for a foreigner. Ecuadorian jails are not fun places, and the Ecuadorian judicial system can be slow. If you are arrested on drug charges in Ecuador, you will be tried as a criminal. Your United States passport will have no bearing. Stay away from drugs in Ecuador.

SAFETY AND THEFT

In general, Ecuador is a safe place to travel, especially in comparison to its more notorious neighboring countries. As Ecuador becomes more economically sophisticated, however, it is also in danger of losing its reputation as an island of tranquility in the midst of chaos and danger. Quito has rising numbers of armed robberies and assaults. Parts of Guayaquil and Esmeraldas are considered dangerous even by Ecuadorians. The northern parts of the province of Sucumbíos on the Colombian border have even experienced kidnappings and assaults from Colombian rebels crossing the border. Car break-ins are a common type of crime that tourists must deal with. As a tourist, your main exposure to crime will likely be in crowded areas such as busy streets and on buses where pickpockets often work. Do not carry open bags, like purses, over your shoulder. You will never know when you are being pickpocketed, and the straps are too easy to cut, leaving your bag in the hands of a vanishing thief. Daypacks with outside pockets can also be easily sliced open by a razor, so never put anything valuable in the outside pockets. Men should try putting a large rubberband around their wallets, and keeping it in the front pocket of pants. Anyone else trying to sneak it out will have a very difficult time because of the friction caused by the rubberband. If you are in a crowd, put your hand in your pocket over your wallet. Another alternative is to use a belt or waist pouch for your valuables. If you carry binoculars or a camera, cover it up with a windbreaker so it isn't so obvious. If the windbreaker has a drawstring bottom, tie it off so someone cannot reach under the windbreaker.

Women should carry their purses under their arm and not hanging free from a shoulder. Rucksacks and fannypacks should be worn on the chest or stomach. A current favorite of petty thieves in Quito is to cut purses, rucksacks or even pockets with a razor blade so skillfully that the owner doesn't even realize that the contents have already been pilfered until back at the hotel room. First-class and luxury hotels supply lock boxes for your valuables. They are only a minor inconvenience to use and well worth the peace of mind, to say nothing of the protection.

A scam at airport security points has spread worldwide. You are more likely to have this problem in the U.S. than in Ecuador, but watch out whenever you walk through an x-ray security check. A passenger with obviously valuable hand-carried luggage, like a laptop computer, is spotted by one of a team of thieves. He (or she) steps in front of you right after you have placed your baggage on the x-ray conveyer belt and just before you go through the security portal. With a metal object in a pocket, this person then sets off the alarm. During the ensuing confusion of trying to find whatever set off the alarm and passing back and forth through the alarm portal several times, your luggage is casually picked up by a confederate waiting on the inside of the secured area. Often it is passed off immediately to another member of the gang, who then walks back out into the ticket area of the airport and quickly disappears with your property. To avoid this scam, never place your luggage on the x-ray conveyer belt until you are sure that you will be the next person to pass through the portal. Also, remove all coins, notebooks, keys and other metal objects and place them in the basket provided. If you set off the alarm and have to fumble around passing back and forth through the portal, you may lose your luggage the same way.

If you are robbed, many U.S. insurance policies will cover at least some of your losses when you return to the U.S. and report the loss, but generally you must have evidence of a police report filed in Ecuador. This means filling out a report (*denuncia*) in the closest police office. Speaking only English will be of little help in most parts of Ecuador outside the major cities, so try to get a Spanish speaker to come with you to the police station. Check with your insurance agent before leaving the U.S. as to what losses are covered by your policy and what evidence is needed to receive payment from the insurance company. With all these precautions, remember that most problems like this are not unique to Ecuador. They could just as well apply to most metropolitan areas in the U.S. and much of Europe. You will only spoil your trip to Ecuador by taking such ultra-defensive precautions that you are never able to get out and enjoy the wonderfully honest majority of Ecuadorians.

LITIGATION

Thankfully, most tourists to Ecuador will have no need to deal with one major cultural difference between Latin America and North America—personal injury accidents and legal responsibility. However, knowing how best to avoid this potential culture shock can be vital to your safety, as well as to the enjoyment of your trip.

In the United States and to a lesser degree in Europe, we have come to depend on the power of litigation to protect us from accidents and injury. We assume that the canoes will not tip over with all of our luggage, the walkways and cabin floors will not break through, and the canopy tower will be secure. If anything happens, surely the proprietors know they will be sued to within an inch of their economic existence. In Ecuador, this safety net is largely nonexistent. Here the philosophy of *"es la vida"* rules, and fate is often blamed for things broken or mislaid. In other words, you are responsible for your own well-being. Most of the isolated "jungle" lodges require you to sign a waiver before the trip, but only two of these lodges in the entire country regularly hire an Ecuadorian doctor to accompany the tourists and/or have a reasonably well-supplied clinic. All the rest have vague to nonexistent plans for emergency medical situations. Several lodges depend on the fact that medical doctors are often visiting as tourists. Be aware of this situation by taking sensible precautions. Watch where you walk. Always wear your lifejacket on the water. Keep well back from anyone wielding a machete. In general, however, try to maintain a balanced attitude that avoids being either naive or paranoid, both of which can make your trip as painful as a broken leg.

EMBASSIES AND CONSULATES

Canada

Quito—Consulate: Avenida 6 de Diciembre 2816 and James Orton; 2-543-214, fax: 2-503-108. Hours: Monday to Friday, 9:30 a.m. to 12:30 p.m.

Guayaquil—Consulate: Calles General Córdova 810 and Victor Manuel Rendón, 21st floor, office 4; 4-563-580, 4-566-747, fax: 4-314-562. Hours: Monday to Friday, 9:30 a.m. to 1:30 p.m.

Colombia

Quito—Embassy: Avenidas Cristóbal Colón 133 and Río Amazonas, 7th floor; 2-508-106, fax: 2-566-676. Hours: Monday to Friday, 8:30 a.m. to 1 p.m. and 2:30 to 4 p.m.

Consulate: Avenidas Atahualpa 955 and de la República, third floor; 2-458-012, fax: 2-460-054. Hours: Monday to Friday, 8:30 a.m. to 12:30 p.m. and 2:30 to 4 p.m.

Guayaquil—Consulate: Calles General Córdova 812 and Victor Manuel Rendón, 2nd floor, office 11; 4-563-308, fax: 4-563-854. Hours: Monday to Friday, 9 a.m. to 12:30 p.m. and 2:30 to 4:30 p.m.

Cuenca—Consulate: Luís Cordero 955 and Pasaje Hortencia Mata, 2nd floor; 7-830-185. Hours: Monday to Friday, 9 a.m. to 1 p.m. and 3 to 4 p.m.

Great Britain

Quito—Embassy: Gederico González Suárez 111; 2-560-670, 2-560-671, fax: 2-560-730. Hours: Monday to Friday, 8:30 a.m. to 12:30 p.m. and 2 to 5 p.m.

Guayaquil—Consulate: Calle General Córdova 623 and Padre Solano; 4-560-400, 4-563-850, fax: 4-562-641. Hours: Monday to Friday, 9 a.m. to noon and 2:30 to 5 p.m.

Japan

Quito—Embassy: Juan Léon Mera 130 and Avenida Patria, Edificio de La Corporación Financiera Nacional, 7th floor; 2-561-899, fax: 2-503-670. Hours: Monday to Friday, 9:30 a.m. to noon and 2:30 to 5 p.m.

Guayaquil—Consulate: Avenidas 9 de Octubre and Quito, Edificio Inuauto, 5th floor; 4-283-482, fax: 4-285-716. Hours: Monday to Friday, 9 a.m. to 5 p.m.

Mexico

Quito—Embassy: Avenidas 6 de Diciembre 4843 and Naciones Unidas; 2-457-820, fax: 2-448-245. Hours: Monday to Friday, 9 a.m. to 1 p.m.

Guayaquil—Consulate: Tulcán 1600 and Calle Colón; 4-372-928, fax: 4-250-251. Hours: Monday to Friday, 9 a.m. to 1 p.m.

Perú

Quito—Embassy: Avenidas Río Amazonas 1429 and Cristóbal Colón, Edificio España; 2-520-134, fax: 2-562-349. Hours: Monday to Friday, 8:30 a.m. to 1:30 p.m.

Consulate: Avenidas Río Amazonas 1429 and Cristóbal Colón, Edificio España, 5th floor; 2-527-678. Hours: Monday to Friday, 8:30 a.m. to 1:30 p.m. and 3 to 5 p.m.

Guayaquil—Consulate: Avenida 9 de Octubre 411 and Calle Chile, 6th floor; 4-322-738, fax: 4-325-679. Hours: Monday to Friday, 8:30 a.m. to 1:30 p.m.

Machala—Consulate: Bolívar and Calle Colón, Edificio Coronel; 7-930-680, fax: 7-930-680. Hours: Monday to Friday, 9:30 a.m. to 12:30 p.m.

Loja—Consulate: Sucre 1056 and Miguel Riofrío, 3rd floor; 7-571-668. Hours: Monday to Friday, 8:30 a.m. to 1:30 p.m.

Macará—Consulate: Bolívar 127 and 10 de Agosto, Barrio Juan Montalvo; 7-694-030. Hours: Monday to Friday, 8:30 a.m. to 1:00 p.m.

United States

Quito—Embassy: Corner of Avenidas 12 de Octubre and Patria; 2-562-890, fax: 2-502-052. Hours: Monday to Friday, 8 a.m. to 12:30 p.m. and 1:30 to 5 p.m. (after hours: 2-561-749).

Guayaquil—Consulate: Avenida 9 de Octubre and García Moreno; 4-323-570, fax: 4-325-286. Hours: Monday to Friday, 8 a.m. to noon and 1:30 to 5 p.m. (after hours: 4-321-152). The consulate in Guayaquil is in charge of U.S. interests in the Galápagos.

NATIVE FOOD AND DRINK

Just as it offers geographical and biological diversity, Ecuador is blessed with a fine diversity of local foods. We will include the distinctively regional food types within the discussion of each of those areas. Throughout Ecuador, however, some types of food can be considered typically Ecuadorian (called *criolla*). They may be prepared a little differently in each part of the country, but they will be recognizable. In general, Ecuadorian food is not prepared spicy, but *ají* (hot sauce) is available in virtually every restaurant and family home. It's the orange soupy stuff in the small dish or bottle in the middle of the table. Its *picante* (from the word *picar*, "to bite or sting") intensity varies from place to place, so test it first before dumping it all over your food. The mid-day meal is generally the big meal of the day, but on weekends and special occasions, the evening meal can be very big, too.

The most typical and common appetizer in Ecuador is **ceviche**, even though the Peruvians claim to have originated this delicacy. It is cooked or uncooked shrimp, shellfish or fish marinated in lemon juice, onions and other spices. It is often served with popcorn for some unfathomable reason, but tastes super. Unfortunately, because of diseases such as cholera and hepatitis, eating raw or undercooked seafood of any type anywhere is not recommended.

sopas ("soups" not "soaps")—commonly the first course for meals

caldo de mondongo—beef tripe soup cooked like a stew

caldo de patas—beef shank soup simmered for hours

caldillo de huevo—a beef broth with spices and hard-boiled egg slices.

locro de cuero—a pork and vegetable cream soup

chupe de pescado—a fish and vegetable soup most typical of the coast but now served in the highlands as well

Main meals of typical Ecuadorian cuisine include:

seco de pollo—a fried chicken served with rice and often garnished with avocados *seco de chivo*—a goat stew also served with rice

guatita criolla—another type of stew; it is made with tripe and peanut sauce

lomo salteado—a thin beef steak that is covered with tomato sauce and onions

carne asada con menestra y patacones—a grilled steak usually served with rice and cooking bananas

camarones al ajillo—shrimp fried in a garlic sauce and is no longer a meal restricted to the coast

Desserts are not a big thing in Ecuador. For breakfast, *pan dulce*, a sweet roll, is common. For other meals, *flan* is the most common dessert eaten by Ecuadorians. It is a sweet custard covered by a burned sugar sauce. Tree tomato (*tomate de árbol*) is a delightful local fruit often served as a blended drink or as a dessert. In tourist areas, ice cream, pie and cake are relatively common. For a cheap snack, the Ecuadorian national candy bar is the *Manicho*. It is made of milk chocolate and peanuts.

ECUADORIAN CUSTOMS AND TRADITIONS

You will find that, in general, Ecuadorians are kind, thoughtful and friendly. Just as in any country, however, there are bad-tempered people and bad days for even the kindest people. Three areas, however, are bound to bring out the worst in the mildest Ecuadorians. *Never* ask someone to turn down the music on the radio. Even if it means you cannot sleep at 2 a.m., it is considered completely rude to suggest that the volume is too loud—the same applies with a party next door. Wear earplugs or move your room, just do not pull a gringo power play and force your own wishes off on those enjoying themselves. Second, *never* ask someone not to smoke. Even in areas such as the airport waiting rooms where officially smoking is not allowed, do not approach the smoker yourself and step on his vice. Ask an airline or airport official to do it for you, but then make sure you are out of sight and cannot be blamed. In a restaurant or airplane, forget any thought of raising an objection. You may start a riot instead. And, *never* speak disparagingly of bullfighting, especially in the highlands in late November and early December when the bullfighting season has everyone's testosterone levels at super-high levels.

If you end up driving in Ecuador, you will quickly learn that the polite and courteous Ecuadorians as pedestrians become monsters behind the wheel. Cutting each other off, running red lights and hogging two lanes are all part of the accepted behavior of driving in Ecuador. No one gives the finger, waves a fist or shoots a gun at violators of the gringo road ethic. Get used to it and don't hold a grudge—otherwise hire a driver and forget driving altogether in Ecuador.

Ecuadorians are also very fond of using car horns to communicate their moods. A taxi driver waiting impatiently for traffic will make his rising impatience clear with his horn. On rural roads, cars, trucks and buses will always toot to let you know they are coming. Sometimes a car that has just been cut off more precariously than acceptable will honk in a way that is obviously a curse. Young attractive women can expect to hear cars honking frequently, the equivalent of a wolf whistle.

One of the most pleasant customs is the *abrazos*, a hug sometimes accompanied by a kiss. There are only a few rules. Generally, whether a man or a woman, you only shake hands the first time you meet. If you are a man meeting a woman, let her initiate the handshake. The second or third time you meet her, as you are shaking hands, lean over and touch her right cheek with yours. On a subsequent meeting, she may actually kiss your cheek. The same procedure usually is followed when saying good-bye. For many male gringos, this is interpreted as a come-on, but it should never be considered so. Latin Americans in general are much more affectionate than North Americans, and Latinos are able to recognize that no sexual overtones are mandated by this physicality. Men tend only to shake hands with each other, both when meeting and when saying good-bye. *Abrazos* between men is reserved for meeting a friend who has just arrived from an extended absence or saying good-bye to a friend who is leaving for some time. The hug between men starts with a handshake. Then the right hand and arm are slipped around to the back of the other and a few masculine slaps are administered. The more audible these back slaps, the longer these two men have known each other. After slapping each other a couple of times, you shake hands one more time.

Know that in Ecuador and throughout Latin America, people stand closer together when talking than in North America. Arms, shoulders and hands are often touched. Don't back away as this would be an insult. To motion for someone to come to you, wiggling your forefinger with palm up as we do in North America will accomplish little except for producing confused looks. Instead, turn your palm down and waggle all your fingers together toward your body.

There are many other subtle customs and traditions you can learn by keeping your eyes open and trying to be aware. For instance, watch when an Ecuadorian is describing how tall someone is. They never show the height with their hand raised flat but instead turn the hand with the palm facing inward, and the lower (little finger) side of the hand at the proper height. A flat hand, as we would do, is reserved only for showing the height of an animal and is considered rather rude if applied to a person.

INDIAN MARKETS

The indigenous people of Ecuador represent 30 percent, some say more, of the total population of the country. They live in small villages throughout the country, from the cold highlands to the humid lowlands, raising crops and tending animals to sustain their simple way of life. The indigenous people cling tightly to traditional ways and yet embrace parts of today's society and thus they straddle Ecuador's historic and modern worlds. To us, this paradox is much of the fascination we find in getting to know the indigenous cultures of Ecuador.

The best way to begin to experience the indigenous cultures of Ecuador is to visit one, or several, of the Indian markets. In these markets you will step into their world. If you allow yourself to slow down and absorb what is around you, there is much to learn and appreciate. To us, the food section of each market is the most interesting. There are all kinds of fruits and vegetables on display, although you probably will not recognize most of what you see. There are also all kinds of bags and boxes full of grains, types of corn and fresh-ground flours, bundles of herbs for cooking and medicinal use, live chickens in burlap bags or in someone's hand hanging by their feet, guinea pigs (*cuy*) in crates and various cuts of unrecognizable farm animals hanging in shadowed alleys. There is a bustle of sound as much as there is a jostle of people. Andean music blares from stereos over Quichua and Spanish voices. Barkers cry their wares, oil fries, a flour mill grinds, bare feet shuffle, cars honk, scales shake, bags crinkle open, camera shutters click, rattles rattle, chickens chatter, knives slice, grains pour and mallets whack as the market clatters on. Exotic smells waft from every motion. Cilantro and chile, coffee and cocoa, sweet perfumes from sliced fruits, industrial aromas from packaged goods, faintly rancid whiffs from hanging meats and cooking rice and pork. There are some places where it smells better the faster you walk away.

Not every market is the same, though. There are city and country markets, as well as traditional markets and those for tourists. Some markets are inside buildings with goods displayed in booths, while others sprawl across village squares with goods piled on cobblestones. Some markets are chaotic and seemingly randomly arranged; others have organized sections and even permanent booths for vendors. In general, tourist markets sell mostly handicrafts such as weavings, leather goods, jewelry, clothing, etc. Otavalo is the most famous tourist market (see Chapter Seven). Traditional markets have mostly food and housewares for sale to and by locals. The most traditional markets will have a line of sewing machines for the weekly mending and/or barber's chairs for the monthly haircut.

The best time to go to a market is as early as you can get there. All markets start at dawn and are fully active an hour or so later. This is the time when the locals arrive to buy and sell their goods. Animals to be sold are always brought to the market at the crack of dawn. If you arrive at ten a.m., the animal market will be empty. By noon, most of the indigenous are already home and there are more tourists in the markets than locals. Most markets begin to close up by mid-afternoon. Many tourists think bargaining for a better price is expected by the vendors. While it is often true that prices are inflated for tourists, the difference in price when converted is usually inconsequential. Do not barter just for the sport of bartering. If you like something and you think it is too expensive, negotiate for a fair price, but if something is one dollar do not haggle until it is ninety cents. As a word of warning, be aware of pick-pockets and thieves in crowded tourist markets and also watch out for water balloons overhead (tourists are a favorite target, so be honored) as part of the Carnival celebration at markets in February or March.

Below is a list of the nation's major markets and when they occur. There are many villages and towns that have smaller or informal markets as well, so do not limit yourself to visiting just those listed below. The famous market at Otavalo is open every day, but those on Wednesday and Saturday are the biggest.

Monday

Ambato—in a building downtown; mostly traditional, some tourist

Tuesday

Latacunga—on downtown streets; mostly traditional

Wednesday

Pujuli—south of Quito; in village square; traditional

Otavalo—on downtown streets; mostly tourist, some traditional

Thursday

Saquisili—south of Quito; on village streets; huge, mostly traditional

Cuenca—at Plaza Rotary downtown; mostly tourist

Riobamba—on streets downtown; many indigenous, mostly traditional

Guamote—south of Riobamba; in village square, mostly traditional

Friday

Salaron—south of Guamote; in village square, high in mountains, very traditional

Ingapirca—in village square; traditional and tourist

Saturday

Otavalo—see above; the biggest market day

Latacunga—see above

Riobamba—see above

Tambo—south of Ingapirca; in village square; traditional

Azogues—in town square; traditional and tourist

Zumbahua—one hour west of Hosteria La Cienaga; in village square; high in mountains and very traditional

Sunday

Pujuli—see above

Peguche—north of Quito; in village square; traditional

Sangolqui—south of Quito; in village; traditional

Machachi—near Cotapaxi; in village; traditional

Salcedo—south of Ambato; in village; traditional, some tourist

Cañar—north of Cuenca; in village; traditional, some tourist

Cajabamba—south of Riobamba; in village; traditional

Saraguro—north of Loja; in village; traditional

SOUVENIRS

The provinces of Cañar and Azuay in the southern highlands are thick with cottage industry crafts. Cuenca, the capital city of Azuay Province, is the commercial hub for most of these handcrafted products. If you do not have time to go out into the countryside and actually see the craftspeople at work you will find a sample of their work, in the stores of Cuenca. The typical items for sale are textiles, weaving, baskets, ceramic tiles, jewelry, metalwork and Panamá hats. The best places to buy souvenirs in Cuenca are in the shops along Calle Gran Colombia.

PANAMÁ HATS   Of all the handicrafts of Ecuador, the Panamá hat is the most renowned. Panamá hats are finely woven from plant fibers and are made no place else in the world, not even in Panamá. The name comes from the fame they earned when they were provided to the workers on the Panamá Canal. Ever since then these truly Ecuadorian hats have been called Panamá hats. The hats achieved their greatest fame in the late 19th and early 20th centuries when U.S. presidents, European royalty, high society and flashy gangsters sported "Panamás." Today, they are less fashionable internationally, but still very popular in Latin America. In Ecuador you will see Panamá hats on everyone from *campesinos* (farmers) to corporate executives and not just a few gringos.

There are 30,000 people employed in the entire Panamá hat industry in Ecuador. The weavers are almost entirely indigenous women and children—they do most of the work. The middlemen and sellers are almost always men of the city—they get most of the credit and profit. The weavers get about 5000 sucres (about $2.50) per hat, more if it is a higher quality weave. A finished hat retails for 10 to 100 times that amount. In the heyday of the Panamá hat, this inequality led to terrible exploitation of the weavers. Today, most sellers recognize the interdependence and treat the weavers with more respect.

The reedlike plant *(Carludovica palmata)* from which the hats are woven grows from Panamá to Bolivia but is only commercially harvested in the coastal hills west and north of Guayaquil. It grows for three years before it is cut, bundled and sent to local markets where weavers buy what they can afford. The straw, as it is called, is then boiled, dried, split, boiled again and dried again before it is ready to be woven. It takes about a day and a half to weave one good-quality hat. The best quality hats, the *superfinos*, can take several weeks to weave and are only woven in the small town of Montecristi south of Manta on the central coast of Ecuador. Finished, the *superfino* hats will cost several hundred dollars but they can hold water without a leak, so fine is their weave, and be folded up into your pocket without a crease, so pliable is the straw.

The process of finishing the weaver's work is done in factories in Cuenca. The most famous Panamá hat company in Cuenca is Homero Ortega & Sons Ltd. on Avenida Gil Ramirez Davalos 3-86. Groups, by prior arrangement, can get a tour of the factory and see the unfinished hats transformed into the magnificent hats of every style for which Sr. Ortega is famous. It takes ten days to finish a hat, most of which is time spent in the bleaching and dying vats. When they show you the finished hats, notice how fine the weave is and how carefully it is presented. Sr. Ortega's history (his father took him to Panamá as a boy to sell hats) and pride is evident in every hat he sells.

OTHER SOUVENIRS   Other souvenirs include ceramic pots and figures, leather goods, silver and gold jewelry, weavings, carved wooden statues and tagua nut jewelry. Tagua nuts are as hard as ivory and are used as a substitute. Best of all, these nuts come from intact lowland forests, and buying them supports sustainable use of this important habitat.

FIVE

The Outdoors

If your goal for traveling includes outdoor adventure, you'll be thrilled to hear that Ecuador has more natural sights, sounds and smells than you can begin to imagine. Eternally snow-capped mountains run the length of the Andes, sandy ocean beaches stretch along the Pacific coast, Amazonian rainforest extends in every direction to the horizon, waterfalls cascade hundreds of feet, and rivers spread more than a kilometer wide. Orchids, monkeys, butterflies and crocodiles all call Ecuador their home, as do more varieties of trees than even the scientists studying them can believe. Be prepared for sensory overload because Ecuador doesn't "do" nature halfheartedly. Once you've experienced what outdoor Ecuador has to offer, you'll never think of nature the same way again.

NATIONAL PARKS, RESERVES
AND NATURAL PROTECTED AREAS

The Ministry of Environment (Ministerio de Medio Ambiente) through its national park service, INEFAN (Instituto Ecuatoriano Forestal y de Areas Naturales y Vida Silvestre), is the government agency charged with establishing, maintaining and protecting natural areas in Ecuador. Twenty-one areas are officially classified as units of conservation. They include nine national parks, seven ecological reserves, two faunal production areas, one national recreation area, one biological reserve, one marine resource reserve and one geobotanical reserve.

There is a two-tier entrance fee to national parks and to some of the reserves and natural areas. For Ecuadorians and resident aliens, the cost is generally about $1, but for foreigners it's another story. Entrance fees have risen sharply for foreigners, and there is no reason to expect that they will stop climbing. The Galápagos National Park charges $80 per person (and the city of San Cristóbal adds another $30 tax per person); the mainland parks charge $10 to $30. Although there is no general pass you can purchase to get into different parks, the ticket you receive for the first entrance can be used to enter the same park at different entrances on subsequent days. INEFAN helps support its facilities and personnel with park fees. If you want to be reassured as to how your money is being used, just ask the local guide or workers at the park if they receive their salaries regularly and on time. If they respond positively, you have a good idea that your entrance fee is being used properly.

Numerous private reserves have been established throughout the country. Most of them are associated with a tourist lodge, and they tend to be well protected. Many of them, however, are seeking status as protected forest (*bosque protectora*) under the auspices of INEFAN. Private holdings are subject to illegal but effective invasions by unlanded peasants (*campesinos*), and this government status gives the forest somewhat more protection—a good sign in the long run as courts are used more and more to settle these disputes.

CAMPING

There is little organized camping in Ecuador. Small areas are set aside in most of the national parks and reserves, but often there is no single designated site. A few camping stores sell equipment in Quito, but the prices are four to five times more expensive than for the same item in the United States. If you intend to camp, bring all your own equipment and supplies from your home country. In more populated areas of the mountains, on the beach or near towns in the Oriente, land owners will often let you camp on their land if you ask. It is better to camp near a house in these more populated areas to discourage thieves. In alpine areas or remote Amazonian forest sites, the main problem is isolation in case of emergencies. Several tour companies listed in Chapter Two can organize your camping itinerary and provide guides. We also mention camping sites associated with various destinations throughout the book.

FISHING

Although not the prime motive for most tourists to visit Ecuador, there are amazingly many opportunities here to pursue fishing interests—from the alpine-like lakes of the paramo to the oxbow lakes of the Oriente and the open ocean of the Pacific coast.

FRESHWATER FISHING

Rainbow trout have been introduced throughout Ecuador's highlands. They are a mixed blessing at best. In some of the mountain lakes, monstrous trout have grown fat on unlimited food supplies. On a lake above Quito, using fishing line and worms as bait, three of us caught four trout in one hour. Each weighed between 11 and 18 pounds, and our barbecue fed 15 people easily. (On mountain streams, especially on the east slope of the Andes, these introduced trout rarely get above 4 pounds.) The downside of this introduction is that trout can have disastrous effects on the native stream ecology. No long-term studies have yet been made in Ecuador, but in other parts of the world, such as Mexico, where these trout have been introduced, large adults are voracious predators on native fish and smaller juveniles compete for food with native fish. Rainbow trout and largemouth bass introduced into Lake Titicaca have been directly linked to the extinction of an entire fish family formerly endemic to this large lake.

In the Oriente, most tourists like to fish for piranha, the notorious marauder of Amazonian rivers and lakes. Actually, the piranha found in Ecuador are not likely to attack and consume a human. They are more interested in smaller vertebrate and invertebrate life in the water. Fishing for piranha involves a simple line and hook. Place fresh meat on the hook and lower the bait into the water about a yard or two. Then, without stopping, bring the bait up quickly toward the surface. If you leave the bait in the water without moving it, the piranhas will strip the hook quickly and efficiently. By the way, these fish are very bony and hard to eat.

If you get a chance to fish for the large catfish called *bagre*, you will have a real experience. Found primarily on the bottom of large rivers, these fish can weigh up to 200 pounds or more. Their meat is delicious and well worth the patience needed to catch them. The line used to fish for them is usually a rope, and the hook needed is big enough to catch a shark. A big hunk of meat is stuck on the hook, and the long rope is then placed way out in the middle of the river. It's best if the rope is tied to a tree on shore. If you are lucky, after a few hours of waiting, the rope will go taut and then you can have the fun of pulling in the monster while you sweat and the no-see-um flies bite.

DEEP-SEA FISHING

Virtually all the deep-sea fishing in Ecuador originates from the towns of Salinas and Manta. Marlin and sailfish are the primary species sought here. See Chapter Twelve for details.

SCUBA DIVING AND SNORKELING

Most people who come to Ecuador to scuba dive or snorkel go to the Galápagos. The Galápagos are renowned for their rich marine environment and colorful and diverse animals. If you are a serious diver, be sure to sign up for a diving trip aboard a boat set up for diving. If you are a snorkeler, almost

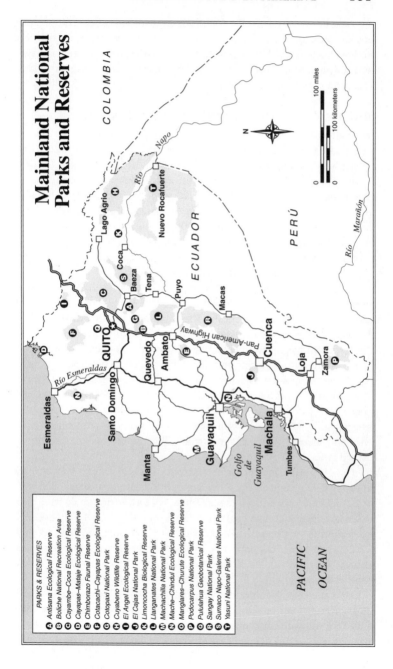

Mainland National Parks and Reserves

PARKS & RESERVES
- Ⓐ Antisana Ecological Reserve
- Ⓑ Boliche National Recreation Area
- Ⓒ Cayambe–Coca Ecological Reserve
- Ⓓ Cayapas–Mataje Ecological Reserve
- Ⓔ Chimborazo Faunal Reserve
- Ⓕ Cotacachi–Cayapas Ecological Reserve
- Ⓖ Cotopaxi National Park
- Ⓗ Cuyabeno Wildlife Reserve
- Ⓘ El Angel Ecological Reserve
- Ⓙ El Cajas National Park
- Ⓚ Limoncocha Biological Reserve
- Ⓛ Llanganates National Park
- Ⓜ Machalilla National Park
- Ⓝ Mache–Chindul Ecological Reserve
- Ⓞ Manglares–Churute Ecological Reserve
- Ⓟ Podocarpus National Park
- Ⓠ Pululahua Geobotanical Reserve
- Ⓡ Sangay National Park
- Ⓢ Sumaco Napo-Galeras National Park
- Ⓣ Yasuní National Park

COLOMBIA

ECUADOR

PERÚ

PACIFIC OCEAN

Esmeraldas

Santo Domingo

Manta

Quevedo

QUITO

Ambato

Guayaquil

Machala

Tumbes

Cuenca

Loja

Zamora

Lago Agrio

Nuevo Rocafuerte

Coca

Baeza

Tena

Puyo

Macas

Golfo de Guayaquil

Pan-American Highway

Río Esmeraldas

Río Napo

Río Marañón

N

100 miles

100 kilometers

any boat or itinerary will take you to some great spots to see fish, penguins and sea lions. Most boats have snorkeling gear onboard, but bring your own mask to assure a good fit. If you wear glasses and get discouraged underwater because everything is out of focus, buy a mask with prescription glass to bring along, so your sight will be clear.

BIRDWATCHING AND WILDLIFE VIEWING

Whether birdwatching and wildlife viewing are the primary goal for your trip to Ecuador or only a small part, a few tips can improve your chances considerably. We strongly recommend studying field guides (*A Field Guide to Woody Plants of Northwest South America*) by Gentry, 1996; *Butterflies of South America* by D'Abrera, 1984; *Guide to the Birds of Colombia* by Hilty, Brown and Tudor, 1986; *Ecuador and its Galápagos: The Ecotravellers' Wildlife Guide* by Pearson and Beletsky, 2000; *A Guide to Bird-watching in Ecuador and the Galápagos Islands* by Best, Heijnen and Williams, 1996; *Neotropical Rain Forest Mammals: A Field Guide* by Emmons, 1990) so you are more familiar with the local flora and fauna.

Knowing what to expect and where to find it is often half the secret of seeing and identifying animals and plants in the wild. Many of the lodges and parks have species checklists. These and regional checklists (*Birds of Ecuador* by West, 1989; *Aves del Ecuador* by Ortiz, 1991) help narrow down identifications by process of elimination. Your ears will often be more important than your eyes in finding and identifying wildlife in many parts of Ecuador. Cassette tapes are available (*Sounds of La Selva, Ecuador* by Moore, 1993; *Birds of Eastern Ecuador* by English and Parker, 1992; *Voices of Galápagos Birds* by Hardy, 1991), and learning even just the common sounds by listening to them before your visit to Ecuador can help you overcome the overwhelming number of strange noises you will hear while visiting Ecuadorian natural areas.

Once you arrive in Ecuador, several tricks will help increase your chances of seeing wildlife or their signs. Remember that the larger mammals and birds of Ecuador are very difficult to see. This is *not* East Africa, so do not expect to see large mammals like Jaguar or tapir on your trip. Instead, you should be excited just to see the tracks or other evidence a large cat has passed your way.

Going into the field alone or in small groups is one way to increase your chances for seeing wildlife. Even a single noisy companion can scare off some types of shy wildlife. But in the forest there are always thousands of species of plants and animals immediately around you. Most of them are insects and other invertebrates, but birds, frogs and small mammals can also be right underfoot without your knowing if you don't take the time to look. Sitting or standing still for 20–30 minutes near a creek or along a path with many animal tracks can often reward the patient observer with incredible looks at wild-life. Dawn is the time of greatest activity for many animals, and walking along paths or drifting in a canoe along a lake edge at this time of day can be very exciting.

During the day, birds travel mainly in flocks of many species together. Listen for canopy flocks as well as undergrowth flocks, and try to determine in which direction they are moving. Sometimes you can keep up with the flock for a half-hour just by walking along with them. Monkey troops can be found by listening for their birdlike chirps and noises or movement of branches and foliage as they jump from tree to tree. Macaws, parrots and toucans will often be completely hidden and noiseless while eating fruits in the canopy. How-ever, the falling of fruits to the ground is a giveaway that they are above you. The fallen fruit under these trees also attracts more earthbound species such as agoutis and tinamous. During the dry season, fallen dry leaves make every movement of ground-dwelling lizards, birds and mammals obvious—of course, your movements are obvious to them, too. During the rainy season, camou-flaged insects and frogs are all around you, but you have to learn to spot them. Often this learning process is different for each habitat, but if you work at it, you can quickly develop a knack for spotting what seemed impossible to glimpse before.

Night in most habitats is a completely different world. A strong flashlight will pick up the eye reflection of various animals. Bright red-orange eye re-flections on the surface of a lake can mean caiman, while yellow on the forest floor or in the vegetation along the river's edge can be any of several species of whippoorwill-type birds. Red may mean the nocturnal Boat-billed Heron, and various other shades of red to orange are nocturnal mammals likes cats and opossums. The white reflections that look like drops of water in the grass or bushes along the water are usually the multiple eyes of wolf spiders. Sounds are also a big part of any sojourn at night. Most frogs, katydids, night mon-keys, and some birds only call at night. Among the most spectacular is the low, steplike descending whistle of the Common Potoo. The local name of this large bird, a cross between an owl and a whippoorwill, is *alma perdida* ("lost soul") or *madre de luna* ("mother of the moon") because of the forlorn song usually called on moonlit nights.

PHOTOGRAPHY

Whether you are a beginning photographer or a seasoned shooter there are a few things to keep in mind when photographing natural Ecuador. Remember, photography is the process of capturing light on film. With film being so uni-formly good, the secret of great photography is shooting in great light. The best light is the warm rays of early morning and late afternoon. This light does not last very long on the equator—just an hour or two after sunrise and before sunset. Try to avoid shooting at mid-day because the strong equatorial sun creates too many dark shadows. This lack of contrast will be rendered as detailess black on film. This is especially a big problem in the rainforest. Wait for a cloud to come over to take your shot of the forest. If you have to photograph in full sun, try to find subjects in open shadows where the contrast is less.

If you are expecting to get great photographs of jungle animals, you will do much better at your local zoo than in the Ecuadorian rainforest. The animals in the rainforest are hard enough just to see, let alone photograph, and the light is often so dim even scenic photography is difficult. If you are intent on getting pictures of rainforest birds and monkeys, you will have to use a complicated projected flash contraption. And expect to spend weeks wandering trails and floating streams to even get a chance to fire off a few frames.

Be sure to bring an extra camera body just in case. And bring lots of extra film and batteries with you, as both are hard to find and very expensive in Ecuador. Given a choice, we always pass our film around the airport x-ray machines but unless your film is old, very fast or is zapped many times you probably will not have any problems. (See Chapter Sixteen for photography hints in the Galápagos.)

OTHER OUTDOOR SPORTS AND ACTIVITIES

For tourists who want to participate in other types of sports while in Ecuador, there is a wide range of opportunities—from the standard outdoor activities you would expect back home to the tooth-jarring and unusual.

WHITEWATER RAFTING AND KAYAKING

These two sports have just begun to be included in the repertoire of Ecuadorian travel adventures. The companies running these facilities are primarily North American–based tour companies and should be contacted before you arrive in Ecuador. Several tour companies such as the Hotel Quito, Row Expeditions and Ecotours, all located in Quito, are among the few places in Ecuador that can set up opportunities for rafting and kayaking within Ecuador, but they will need at least a two- or three-week lead time to make arrangements.

In the last two years, the popularity of whitewater rafting and kayaking has zoomed. Unfortunately many local companies have formed to take advantage of this popularity without adequate measures for safety or training of their personnel. When you choose a company to guide you on these dangerous rivers, don't choose them just on the basis of low price. Check their reputations carefully. Go with reliable companies that may cost you more but are going to get you back safely.

MOUNTAINEERING AND HIKING

Ecuador offers many mountain peaks and sheer slopes for those who want to push the envelope of excitement. Although hiking has not been as popular in Ecuador as mountain climbing, growing interest in this activity has led to the establishment of more maps and directions to the trails that do exist. Refer to books such as *Climbing and Hiking in Ecuador* by Rachowiecki, Thurber and Wagenhauser (fourth edition, 1997) for details you will need to prepare for hiking trips in the mountains as well as in a few lowland areas.

BICYCLING

This sport is just beginning to become popular among tourists visiting Ecuador. Mountain bicycles are most commonly available for rent from hotels and shops at the beach resorts of Salinas, Bahía de Caráquez, and Esmeraldas–Atacames. In the mountains, Baños is the best place. Recently a tour operator who specializes in arranging bike tours (one to five days) has begun business in Ecuador. They supply modern bikes, helmets and gloves as well as accommodations, food and jeep rides uphill. Contact Flying Dutchman Mountain Bike Tours (Foch 714 and Juan León Mera, Quito; 2-542-806, fax: 2-567-008; e-mail: dutchman@ecuadorexplorer.com). For other details of bike routes and biking in Ecuador, see *Latin America by Bike* by Sienko (1993).

SECTION I

The Highlands

The highlands of Ecuador are a narrow mountainous strip of land running north–south, squeezed between the lowland rainforest to the east and the coastal plain to the west. The highlands are characterized by fertile valleys and lush forested ridges overseen by looming mountains often topped by snowy summits. A dazzling array of orchids, hummingbirds and stunning vistas can easily be found in the region's parks and reserves. In a single day of sightseeing, it is possible to drive from the humid, subtropical forests of the coastal mountains through dense forests and shaggy paramo draped in clouds to the ice-cold barren slope of a snow-capped volcano. On the way, if your timing is right, you are likely to see an Indian market where the indigenous customs and goods for sale are as diverse and fascinating as the animals in the forest nearby. To those who live here, the highlands represent not only the physical backbone that connects the entire country but also the intellectual and creative backbone—from which radiates the inspiration for all of Ecuador's arts and sciences. This opinion is not necessarily shared by those who do not live in the highlands—especially the people of Guayaquil, who consider their business acumen to be Ecuador's foundation.

In any case, Ecuador's highlands have been inhabited for several thousand years. At first, small tribes of Indians occupied the fertile lowlands and migrated up and down the river valleys as they conquered or coalesced with neighboring tribes. By the mid-15th century, large cities (that were later to become Quito and Cuenca) were already well established. These cities were enlarged and incorporated within the vast Incan Empire and the indigenous people, like the forest and the wild game, fled to hidden highland corners or became servants to the Incan Sun God. The conquering Spaniards arrived shortly after the Incas, and the Indians, now twice conquered, were further pushed aside as they became servants to the Catholic Church.

When the Spaniards first traveled through the lands of the Quitus and Cañari, they were amazed to see crosses on top of the homes of the Indians. It is said that many Spaniards fell on their knees at the sight of these crosses for they believed that Christ had walked here before them. In fact, the crosses represented the four elements the Indians considered essential to life: air, earth, fire and water. During a breeze, these crosses would spin—symbolizing *pachacuti* or the recycling, in 500-year cycles, of all life on Earth. *Pachacuti* also symbolized the wisdom of *Pachacama* and *Pachamama*, the great father and mother Earth Gods. Today, it is not uncommon to see highland Indians walking barefoot so that their soles and therefore their souls may always be in touch with *Pachacama* and *Pachamama*. It is in small villages, off the beaten track, where you will find the purest indigenous cultures, where modern Christianity and capitalism are mixed with healthy doses of bartering and animism or *Hatun Pachacamac*—the Indian term for all that is great and holy.

It was not until three hundred years after the Spanish Conquest that the choking, repressive grip of Spanish rule was finally broken. Freedom for the people of Ecuador was hard-earned but not evenly distributed, for the Indians and the land upon which they depend still struggle for respect and autonomy. Many Indians believe that the coming of the Spaniards in 1493 marked the beginning of a 500-year cycle of darkness. Highlanders believe this cycle is now over and a new *pachacuti*, one of promise and prosperity, is beginning. Geographically, the highlands are well known as the "Avenue of the Volcanoes," a phrase coined in 1802 by the German explorer, geographer, botanist and anthropologist Baron Friedrich Heinrich Alexander von Humboldt. Humboldt made important contributions in many areas of science, but he is best known in Ecuador as a mountaineer and a daring volcanologist. What better place to satisfy both a passion for mountain climbing and a curiosity about volcanoes than in a country where active volcanoes are arrayed conveniently along the main road between two large cities (Cuenca and Quito).

Humboldt arrived in Ecuador in 1801 after exploring the Orinoco River in Venezuela. While in Ecuador, Humboldt studied the volcanoes near Quito. During this period, these volcanoes were very active and earthquakes and eruptions were commonplace. A few years earlier, a very strong earthquake had leveled Quito, killing 40,000 people. Humboldt did more than study the volcanoes from afar. He was the first person to actually climb and investigate the active craters on top of these volcanoes. He describes one such trip as follows:

Twice on 26th and 28th May (1802) I climbed to the crater of Pichincha, the volcano overlooking Quito. I managed to take my instruments with me, and was able to carry out observations and collect samples of air for analysis. The first ascent I made with a single Indian companion. On the rim of the crater were three rocky pinnacles, free of snow because it is melted by the steam rising out of the fumerole. I climbed one of these pinnacles, and found close to the top a shelf of rock, projecting like a balcony over the abyss. Here I set up my instruments. The rock . . . was shaken by constant earth tremor— we counted 18 in less than half an hour. If we lay down we could get a perfect view of the crater. It would be difficult to imagine anything more sinister. Its depth appears limitless. . . . I'm afraid we are going to have to tell the people of Quito the bad news that their volcano is active—possibly its fires have been rekindled by the catastrophe of 1797.

Humboldt was the first person to speculate that the origin of volcanoes resulted from a structural weakness in the Earth. Today, we know Humboldt's "weakness" is actually the boundary between two of the dozen or so tectonic plates that comprise the Earth's geologic crust. These plates are of two kinds: oceanic and continental. Oceanic plates are thick and hearty and are formed from deep cracks in the ocean floor where fresh magma upwells from the Earth's mantle. This upwelling causes adjoining plates to separate and pushes distant plates in a very slow geologic bump and grind. The Mid-Atlantic Ridge, a well-known example of an oceanic plate, is where new oceanic crust is forming, pushing North and South America apart from Europe and Africa. The continents are lighter and thinner hunks of crust that ride like floating islands on top of oceanic plates.

Ecuador is the result of two plates: the Nazca Plate in the Pacific Ocean and the South American Plate. These two plates collide at a rate of more than 10 centimeters (4 inches) per year, a high-speed crash geologically speaking. As you might expect, the movements of these plates are not smooth and placid. In general, tectonic plates can collide and wrinkle, slide by and shake or sink and melt. The Andes of Ecuador are formed from the subduction (passing underneath) or sinking of the oceanic Nazca Plate as it is pushed beneath the continental South American Plate. As the Nazca Plate descends, it melts, sending rising plumes of magma toward the surface of the Earth. When this magma reaches the surface, a volcano forms. Cotopaxi and Sangay are examples of active Ecuadorian volcanoes; each has a rising plume of magma below. Pichincha and Chimborazo are inactive or extinct volcanoes that no longer have magma plumes beneath them.

We cannot be sure what thoughts were going through the curious mind of Humboldt as he gazed into Pichincha's crater for his "perfect view." We do know that for today's traveler in the highlands of Ecuador, less rigorous effort is needed to get a "perfect view." With just a bit of time and planning, you can see the same volcanic peaks that Humboldt gazed upon from Quito, travel along the Avenue of the Volcanoes in his footsteps (even spending the night at the same haciendas he did), visit Indians markets that are not much changed since Humboldt's time and get to know the gentle folk of the highlands that Humboldt found so friendly and appealing. Just remember to keep your distance from the rim of a trembling crater.

SIX

Quito Area

The city of Quito is the capital of Ecuador. But it is much more than just the seat of government. Quito, in many ways, best represents the tossed salad of adjectives that describes all of Ecuador. Quito is a mixture of the colonial and the contemporary, the poor and the prosperous, the chaotic and the quiet, the highlands and the lowlands, the Indian and the international, the city and the countryside. On any day spent wandering the city it is quite possible to stand in front of a colonial church and look across a tree-shaded park at a glass sky-scraper where a hummingbird is hovering over an orchid growing on a tele-phone line while a businessman on a cellular phone and a beggar pass you by on a cobblestone street. It is this sometimes magnificent and sometimes mad-dening combination that makes Quito such a fascinating city to visit.

Quito lies on a narrow plateau between a high mountain ridge and a deep valley. The plateau is just 22 kilometers south of the equator but it is 9405 feet (2850 meters) high, so the climate is, as is popularly said everywhere in the highlands, "eternal Spring." The days are usually pleasantly warm, the nights cool, and it is more likely to sprinkle in the afternoon than not. Rising abruptly above the city to the west is Volcán Pichincha, a mountain that at 15,820 feet (4794 meters) may get a coating of snow on its summit at any time of the year. Dropping suddenly to the east is the deep valley of the Río Machángara, where fruits are grown in subtropical warmth. Farther to the east, just a 45-minute drive from downtown Quito, is the crest of the Andes. To the south, the Pan-American Highway becomes the famous "Avenue of the Volcanoes" as it stretches down to the small city of Riobamba. And to the north, the greener, milder ridges and scattered lakes are Ecuador's most vis-ited and densely inhabited region.

In Quito today you see a conglomerate of many influences. The city was founded on December 6, 1534, by the Spanish conquistador Sebastián de Ben-

110

alcázar. While it seems like this should be the beginning, it really marked just the most recent change in control of the region. The Quito area has been inhabited since pre-Columbian times. The peaceful Quitus people lived here and hunted on the slopes of Pichincha for at least 1000 years before the Spanish arrived. The Quitus were integrated into the Caras Indians when the Caras immigrated up the Río Esmeraldas into Quitus territory. The Caras were ruled by the Shyri clan and together the Caras and the Quitus became known as the Shyri Indians. The Caras brought to the highlands a sophisticated understanding of astronomy and were the first to recognize the equator as the track of the sun. In the 14th century, the Shyris intermarried with the Puruhás Indians, who lived on their southern boundary. Thus was formed a large heterogeneous Indian culture, known as the kingdom of Quitu, whose capital was located where Quito now stands. Today, evidence of the Shyri and Incan cultures in Quito is difficult to find.

The 14th and 15th centuries were also the height of the Incan Empire. This empire, known as Tahuantinsuyo, stretched from what is now northern Ecuador to what is now northern Chile, a distance of 3300 kilometers. The last great Incan ruler, Huanya-Capac, who was born in Ecuador, continued the expansion of Tahuantinsuyo and invaded northward into the kingdom of the Quitus in 1492. Shortly after, Huanya-Capac marched still farther north into the land of the Caras Indians. For 16 years, the Caras bravely held off the more powerful Incas but eventually they, too, were conquered and thus the entire Quitu Kingdom fell to the Incas. Huanya-Capac built a magnificent capital city over the ruins of the Shyris capital where Quito now stands. Huanya-Capac married a Shyri princess and had a son, Atahualpa, who ruled the northern half of the Incan Empire. Atahualpa's older half-brother, Huascar, ruled the southern half of the empire from Cuzco in what is now Perú.

The relationship between the two half-brothers was unfriendly and a bloody rivalry developed. It ended only after a devastating five-year war in which Huascar was captured and imprisoned by Atahualpa. As a result of this war, the once mighty Incan Empire was in disarray and perilously weakened. It was at this opportune time, in 1532, that Francisco Pizarro and a band of fewer than 200 conquistadors struck the blow that soon would end the period of Incan domination. Through a combination of arrogance and ignorance, Atahualpa was lured into a trap, captured and eventually killed by the unscrupulous and ruthless Pizarro. Only 40 years after his capital city had been established, Atahualpa's rule was over. The northern Incan capital was left undefended and in chaos. When he realized all was lost, Atahualpa's loyal general, Rumiñahui, completely destroyed the city before the Spaniards could plunder it. As a result, when Benalcázar founded Quito in 1534, it was on top of the ashes of several civilizations, including the rubble of a once-great Incan city. A few of the Incan chiseled stone blocks can still be seen in Quito's oldest churches and convents, but otherwise all else has been lost or buried.

Quito today is divided into the old or colonial city and the modern city. Colonial Quito is still reminiscent of how it was more than 450 years ago, even though it is but a small island surrounded on all sides by a fast-growing modern city. In colonial Quito are narrow cobblestone streets lined with whitewashed walls over which the steeples and cupolas of historic churches and a cathedral rise. The integrity of colonial Quito was assured in 1978 when the United Nations declared the city a World Cultural Heritage Site.

The Spanish designed Quito in a typical European grid pattern. The grid was centered around a central plaza around which were the government buildings, cathedral and Bishop's residence. The city was divided into 200 lots—or one lot for each conquistador. Typical Spanish haciendas were built on the lots, each with a central courtyard ringed by covered balconies. A garden and small orchard were behind the hacienda. Stables and pastures occupied the remaining land. The indigenous people lived in the surrounding hills, close enough to be of service when demanded.

GETTING AROUND QUITO

The city of Quito is 30 kilometers long in a north–south direction. Colonial Quito is in the southern part of the city, modern Quito is near the middle and the airport is in the northern part. It is not practical to try to see the entire city in a single day because many of the sites of interest are so spread out. Spend one morning wandering around colonial Quito and then another afternoon uptown, on Avenida Río Amazonas. For a bird's-eye view of the city, visit the **La Virgen de Quito** statue on Panecillo hill that overlooks old Quito or go to **La Cima de la Liberatad**, a museum on the slope of Volcán Pichincha west of the old part of town. It is best to take a taxi to both sites. The walk up Panecillo hill can be dangerous because it is a notorious site for robbers and muggers even in daylight and especially at night.

If you are in a hurry and want to see as much of Quito as you can in a short time, or if you just want a cheap means of transportation around town, the **Trole Bus** system is fast and easy to use. These double-length buses are powered by overhead electric lines and use a central set of lanes reserved only for their use. The line runs 22 kilometers, from just south of the airport at its northern terminal to the extreme southern part of the city past the *terminal terrestre*. Buses run every five to ten minutes throughout the day from 5 a.m. to 8 p.m. and every half-hour from 8 p.m. to midnight. Every half-kilometer there's a covered stop with a waiting room, ticket booth (1500 sucres per ride as far as you want to go), and attendant to answer questions. The introduction of these Trole Buses was initially met with much opposition by the bus driv-

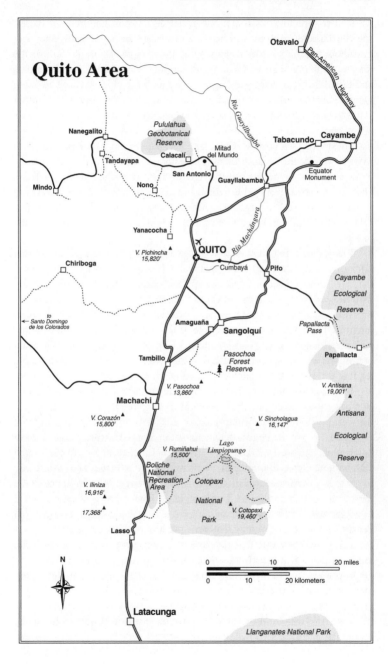

Quito Area

Otavalo

Pan-American Highway

Río Guayllabamba

Nanegalito

Pululahua
Geobotanical
Reserve

Tandayapa

Calacalí

Mitad
del Mundo

San Antonio

Tabacundo   Cayambe

Equator
Monument

Mindo

Nono

Guayllabamba

Yanacocha

Río Machángara

V. Pichincha
15,820'

QUITO

Chiriboga

Cumbayá   Pifo

Cayambe

Ecological

Reserve

to
← Santo Domingo
de los Colorados

Amaguaña

Sangolquí

Papallacta
Pass

Papallacta

Tambillo

Pasochoa
Forest
Reserve

V. Pasochoa
13,860'

Machachi

V. Antisana
19,001'

Antisana

V. Corazón
15,800'

V. Sincholagua
16,147'

Ecological

Reserve

Lago
Limpiopungo

V. Rumiñahui
15,500'

Boliche
National
Recreation
Area

Cotopaxi

V. Iliniza
16,916'

17,368'

National

Park

V. Cotopaxi
19,460'

Lasso

N

0   10   20 miles

0   10   20 kilometers

Latacunga

Llanganates National Park

ers formerly plying this route, but in one fell swoop hundreds of diesel-spewing buses were eliminated from the streets, and air pollution together with grid-locked traffic were noticeably reduced overnight. The route follows the length of the major street 10 de Agosto in its northern and central portions and then follows a more winding route through the older sections of south Quito. There are plans to extend the line north past the airport and farther south to have 33 kilometers of service eventually. We have only two caveats if you choose to ride the Trole Bus. From 6 a.m. to 8 p.m. these trolleys are usually jammed with people. Carrying a backpack or large suitcase will prove to be very difficult. Because the troles are not on tracks, it is up to the driver's experience to stop the bus just the right distance from the loading platform. Quite often new drivers get it wrong, and the metal bridge that is lowered to connect the trole exit door to the platform doesn't connect. Watch out for this problem to avoid stumbling or, even worse, falling between the trole and the platform.

Today, the central plaza is called Plaza de la Independencia (Independence Square), and it is the heart of colonial Quito. It is surrounded by the cathedral, the Presidential Palace, the Archbishop's Palace and the jarringly modern city hall. Beyond the plaza, many of Quito's original churches and historic buildings remain, although some have been extensively modified, especially their interiors. The churches always seem to be in some state of restoration but that isn't surprising when you consider that they are, after all, more than 400 years old. If you can block out the crush of traffic and the blare of taxi horns (a big if), it is still possible to imagine colonial Quito as it was four centuries ago.

There are also many opportunities for day trips in the area around Quito. You can choose to go into the mountains and explore the paramo, drop over the western slope and see subtropical forests, drive to the snow line high on Cotopaxi, or visit the largest Indian market in South America. Some of these destinations are well marked and easy to find, but most are off the beaten path without signs, so finding the route may be a challenge. The easiest way to get to any of these destinations is to hire a driver/guide through one of the large tour operators in Quito. They will know how to get to where you want to go and will also know some of the local history and culture. It is more expensive to hire a driver/guide, but we think it is well worth the cost.

You should be aware that pedestrians are fair game for vehicles in Quito but big trouble if a vehicle hits one. This means that anytime you walk in Quito you are very likely to have close calls but you will probably live to tell about it. Crossing streets is the worst. Remember, to an Ecuadorian driver, a yellow light means accelerate and a red light only applies to the driver in back. You can try to wait for the light to cross but most seasoned walkers just make a dash for it. Timid solo pedestrians do not get very far in Quito—we recommend crossing in a pack of other pedestrians. After a few tries, crossing the street will become second nature.

A WALKING TOUR OF COLONIAL QUITO

Most of colonial Quito can easily be seen in half a day of leisurely walking. There are many tourists in the area and many tour operators that can provide you with a guide. Beware of pickpockets and purse snatchers, especially in crowded areas. If you plan to take photographs, bring someone along who can watch you while you are distracted taking a picture. The most complete booklet on colonial Quito is *Colonial Quito*, published by the Libri Mundi bookstore. The entire walk described below is about 22 blocks.

Start at the **Plaza de San Francisco** on Benalcázar between Bolívar and Sucre. The plaza is an open cobblestone square, one block in size, ringed by red-tiled roofs and whitewashed buildings with ornate eaves and brightly colored balconies. The plaza becomes a hub of activity by midmorning with Indians selling religious souvenirs—crosses, crucifixion pictures, beads and candles—and *quiteños* hawking everything from shoeshines to sunglasses. You will see businessmen, young lovers, gringo tourists, barking dogs, street vendors, uniformed school children, devote indigenous highlanders, ragged beggars, pigeons, sitting old men and working old women.

The northwest side of the plaza is overwhelmed by the **Monastery of San Francisco** and its connecting buildings. Two gleaming white spires rise above a massive dark stone facade supported by four pairs of limestone columns. Local tour guides describe the architectural style as Herrera's sober baroque; we just think it is very impressive. The walls of this immense complex rose from the rubble of Huanya-Capac's royal house, which also stood at this spot. In 1535, the Franciscan friar Joedco Ricke began construction of the complex, which includes three churches, a convent, seven courtyards, a school and several orchards. The children of Atahualpa were taught reading, writing and mathematics in this school. Friar Ricke was also the first person to introduce wheat to Ecuador, grown in a garden within these walls. Above the convent door, to the right of the main entrance to the church, is the date when its construction was finished: October 4, 1605.

Inside, the church is astonishingly ornate, with every surface of every wall, ceiling, arch, dome and column covered in lavish gold leaf. In the morning, light pours into the central nave illuminating the gilded walls in an almighty golden glow. Only the wide plank floor, which creaks as worshipers walk over it, is plain and simply functional. The magnificence of this church is difficult to put into words.

There always seems to be a service going on, but you are welcome to walk around quietly and look at the artwork. This is one church where spontaneous exclamations are natural, but please be respectful of the worshipers, and do not disturb their prayers with loud conversation and camera flashes. For a closer look at more religious paintings and sculptures, go outside to the right of the main entrance to the **Franciscan Museum** (Tuesday–Friday, 9 a.m.– noon and 3–5 p.m.; admission). If you have come to Quito in part to visit the old churches, be sure to hire a guide from one of the big tour operators in town. Every nook and chapel has a fascinating history to be told. But even if you think old churches will not interest you, force yourself to visit at least the Monastery of San Francisco—it is a jaw-dropping experience.

Turning to the right (northeast) as you face the church, walk across the plaza and down the steps to Avenida de Cuenca. Even though street markets were outlawed in Quito in the early 1980s, there is always a **street market** here. Most of the goods on sale are bits and pieces of modern life: belts, socks, cassettes, watches, pants, batteries, wallets and lots of shoes. The market is nothing less than an outdoor department store stretched along three blocks. One block away, on the corner of Cuenca and Chile, is a small textile market with some *otavaleños* selling sweaters and woven goods.

Across from the textile market is the **La Merced Church**. Completed in 1742, La Merced is one of the newest churches in colonial Quito. It was built by Mercedarian priests and is dedicated to Our Lady of Mercy who, in 1575, is said to have saved Quito from the eruption of Volcán Pichincha. In honor of Our Lady of Mercy there is an almost life-size statue of the Virgin in the middle of the gilded altar. The entrance to La Merced is along Calle Chile, just up from the corner of Calle Cuenca. The gate is often hidden among the booths of the street vendors and sometimes can be hard to find. The ornate walls of the sanctuary, many with paintings of erupting volcanoes, are decorated by intricately sculpted and painted stucco. Looking up, the magnificent vaulted ceiling is adorned with arabesques of white stucco on rose background. Be sure to notice the paintings on the ceiling of the central cupola and the old pipe organ high on the wall above the entrance.

The market along Calle Cuenca spills around La Merced on its west and north sides. Behind the church is the **central market**, a maze of narrow alleys between tightly packed booths. Again, there are mostly modern goods for sale here but it is still a fascinating place to stroll around. Be careful of your wallet and valuables on the crowded streets.

Next to La Merced on the corner of Cuenca and Mejia is the **Museo de Arte Colonial** (9 a.m.–5 p.m., Tuesday–Friday, and 10 a.m.–4 p.m., Saturday –Sunday; admission). The building was the former home of Spanish nobility and is a beautiful example of period architecture. The museum has a fine collection of 16th-, 17th- and 18th-century paintings, sculpture and furniture. Featured are the religious works of Miguel de Santiago, Bernardo de Legarda and Caspicara.

From the colonial art museum turn downhill along Mejia and follow the wide brick sidewalk two blocks to the corner of García Moreno. Turn right (southwest) on García Moreno and you will be in front of the **Church and Monastery of La Concepción**. Monasteries were built, as one book says, "by widows of conquerors and poor damsels" for prayer and contemplation. The nuns who later lived within did much of the tedious labor on the elaborate decorations that adorn many of the fabulous church altars. La Concepción was once considered to be the most beautiful church in Quito, but a fire in 1878 destroyed much of its magnificence.

One block farther, on the corner of Chile and García Moreno, is the Presidential Palace on your right, the central plaza in front of you and the cathedral on the far side of the plaza. **Plaza de la Independencia** is a block in size. A monument to Ecuador's independence is in the center of the square and stone walks radiate to each side and corner. Between the wide walks are beautiful pocket gardens shaded by tall palm trees. The plaza is exceptionally clean and well maintained, with attractive street lamps and many benches. This is a wonderful spot for a picnic lunch or just to sit and watch the passers-by. In the morning, there is a view of the independence monument, the cathedral and the statue of the Virgin of Quito on the hill beyond from the northeast corner of the park that makes a stunning photograph.

The southwestern edge of the plaza is dominated by the massive stone walls of the **Cathedral**. Circular steps lead to a small arched cupola over huge wooden doors. While this offers a nice view of the Presidential Palace, the actual entrance to the cathedral is from García Moreno. There have been three generations of cathedrals built on this site. The first was started on the day Quito was founded and was built out of adobe and wood. The second, a more typical cathedral, was created out of stone and finished in 1667. This building was extensively remodeled after a serious earthquake in 1755, but some of the work was not finished until 1930.

The interior of the cathedral is much more austere than are the other colonial churches in Quito. The walls, arches and ceiling are of plain stone, and only the altar and the side chapels show any of the opulence normally characteristic of this style of architecture. Behind the altar is a very large and well-known painting, the *Rising of the Virgin*, by Manuel Samaniego. Behind the main altar is the spot where President Gabriel García Moreno died in 1875 after he was shot near the Presidential Palace and carried to the cathedral. A small plaque marks the spot. Also here is the grave of Ecuadorian hero Antonio José de Sucre, who defeated Spanish troops in the decisive battle for independence.

On the northwest side of the Independence plaza is the **Presidential Palace** (Palacio Presidencial), marked by a long arched walkway above the street.

Standing at attention at the entrance are two guards with automatic weapons. The guards are dressed in 19th-century uniforms of long-tailed royal blue coats, white pants, polished black boots with silver spurs, gold embroidered front, red cuffs and collar, white gloves and a tall blue hat with a gold emblem in front. Another good photo opportunity is in front of the guards, through the arches toward the cathedral. You are allowed to walk in and see the main courtyard and the mural of Francisco Orellana's discovery of the Amazon River but you cannot go any farther. Do not let the quaintness of the guards fool you. There has been much action here in the 20th century, including a period of 50 years when there were 39 governments, most born of force. (The last coup was more than 20 years ago so you do not have much to worry about now.) Before you leave, take a photo from the palace steps nearest the cathedral of the colorful buildings lining García Moreno.

Continue walking southwest down García Moreno past the entrance to the cathedral. The building adjoining the cathedral is **El Sagrario Church**. It was built to be the main chapel of the cathedral, but now it is a separate church. Manuela Cañizares, an early Ecuadorian patriot, held the first freedom meetings in 1809 in a room off this church to organize the "first shot of Independence" for Ecuador. Inside, the sanctuary is smaller than other churches but equally attractive. The walls and the ceiling are cleverly painted to simulate marble. Windows, high in the ceiling, cast a soft light upon the golden altar.

Across the street from El Sagrario is the **Museo de Arte y Historia** (9 a.m.–4 p.m., Tuesday–Friday, and 10 a.m.–4 p.m., Saturday–Sunday; admission), also known as Museo Municipal Alberto Mena Caamaño, but often just referred to as the Municipal Museum. The entrance is located on the opposite side of the building, on Benalcázar. In the basement of this building, the organizers of the 1809 independence movement were imprisoned and eventually executed. Wax dioramas are on display in the basement showing the grisly deaths of these patriots. Upstairs is a fine collection of 16th- and 17th-century religious art.

Just before the next corner is the most impressive church in Ecuador and perhaps in all of Latin America, **La Compañia**. The church was built by Jesuits who arrived in 1586, the last and richest of the religious orders to come to Ecuador. Construction of the church began in 1605 and was completed 163 years later in 1768. You will understand why it took so long to build when you see the interior. If you thought the Monastery of San Francisco was magnificent, you will be absolutely dumbfounded when you see La Compañia.

The first hint that the Jesuits did not spare any expense or effort on this church is the exterior facade, detailed unlike any other in Quito. There are columns, pedestals, portals and pilasters set among garlands of carved stars,

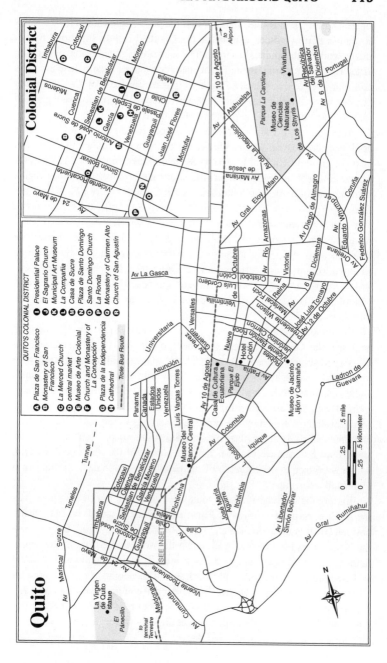

leaves and filigrees. Inside, walking into the nave of the church is like walking into a narrow golden canyon. A high vaulted ceiling supported by tall arches leads to the chancel in front. The intricately gilded walls and ceiling of La Compañia are so magnificent that superlatives become useless. It is said that it took seven tons of gold to gild the surfaces of La Compañia. Locally, it is referred to as "Quito's Sistine Chapel." There are also eight side chapels, each deserving a superlative of its own.

At the corner of García Moreno and Sucre turn left (southeast) down the brick pedestrian street where vehicles are restricted. If you are tired or short on time, turning right (northwest) on Sucre will take you, in one block, back to the Plaza de San Francisco where this walking tour began. One block ahead, at the corner of Sucre and Venezuela, is the **Casa de Sucre** (9 a.m.–4 p.m., Tuesday–Friday, and 10 a.m.–2 p.m., Saturday–Sunday)—the former home of Mariscal Antonio José de Sucre. Sucre was the general who defeated Spanish troops on the slopes of Pichincha on May 24, 1822. In his honor, the denominations of Ecuadorian currency are named after him. The museum here has a collection of art, furniture and clothing from the period of Independence, but we enjoy just walking around the beautifully preserved historic building. The hours vary, but the museum is generally open mid-morning and mid-afternoon.

Continue walking down Sucre one block to Guayaquil. On this corner is an Artesanias Otavalo Folklore store next to a Royal Burger restaurant. On the opposite corner is the El Texano Cafeteria. Guayaquil is a busy street with lots of little pocket stores and eateries. Turn right (southwest) on Guayaquil and go one block to Bolívar. Ahead of you now is the large but not very interesting **Plaza de Santo Domingo**. In the middle of the plaza is a statue of Mariscal Antonio José de Sucre pointing toward his victory on Volcán Pichincha. On the far side of the plaza rises the **Santo Domingo Church** and monastery. The church is well known for its sculpture of the Virgen del Rosario, which was given to the church by King Charles V of Spain. The sculpture is in a small side chapel.

Exiting the church, turn left (southwest) and walk out of the plaza, past the **Arch of Santo Domingo of Rocafuerte**. Walk downhill on Maldonado past the Hotel InterAmericano and Hotel Residencia Guayaquil. Do not cross the bridge ahead but instead walk down the steps to the right to the nearly hidden street underneath, known as **La Ronda**. Turn right on this narrow street and walk up the gentle hill to the northwest. This neighborhood is called La Ronda for the evening serenades that were once common here. Today, it is a picturesque street with pretty iron balconies and blue doors reminiscent of days gone by. Do not walk in this area at night, however; it can be a dangerous place because of muggers and thieves.

The next street is Guayaquil. You can turn right here and walk uphill to return to the Plaza de Santo Domingo at the corner of Viciente Rocafuerte or you can continue straight on what is now Avenida 24 de Mayo one or two more blocks before turning right on García Moreno to Viciente Rocafuerte. If you are back in the Plaza de Santo Domingo, walk up Viciente Rocafuerte (away from the church) two blocks to the corner of García Moreno. You will know you are at the right place because there is a large arch, the **Queen's Arch**, at this corner. The peach-colored arch was built in the mid-1700s and once marked the southern entry of Quito. The arch connects to the **Monastery of Carmen Alto**. On this site, Mariana de Jesús, Quito's Saint, lived between 1618 and 1645. In the small patio in front of this monastery is a revolving window where abandoned children are passed through to be taken care of by the nuns. From the arch continue one block on Rocafuerte to Sebastián de Benalcázar. A right turn here brings you back to the Plaza de San Francisco where this walking tour began.

There are many other churches and historical buildings in colonial Quito worth a visit. In particular is the **Church of San Agustín** on the corner of Guayaquil and Chile, two blocks southeast of Plaza de la Independencía behind the modern city hall. It is historically noteworthy because this is where, on August 10, 1809, the declaration of Ecuador's independence was signed. Unfortunately, a year later the bodies of these patriots were buried here. Next door is the **Museo de San Agustín** (10 a.m.–4 p.m., Tuesday–Friday, and 10 a.m.–2 p.m. Saturday) where many fine paintings of the Quito School are on display.

CUMBAYÁ

Nestled in a hanging valley fifteen kilometers east of Quito on the main highway toward Pifo and Papallacata is the trendy suburb of **Cumbayá**. This area of elegant homes, upscale shops and modern stores is a phenomenon built almost completely in the last ten years. Typical and symbolic of the entrepreneurial spirit of the highly educated and upwardly mobile residents here is the presence of the Universidad San Francisco de Quito. Founded by a small group of North American–educated Ecuadorians in 1990, this university has moved from its rundown rented facilities and financially shaky beginnings to a contemporary campus with new buildings going up every year. Intellectually it has become arguably the most advanced and sophisticated university in Ecuador—some would say in all of northern South America.

There are yet few facilities for lodging in the area, but the one place we can recommend to stay in Cumbayá is the **Hosteria la Villa de San Francisco** (formerly **Hosteria Brandenburgo**) (Cumbayá above San Patricio and San Juan; private bath, hot water, cable TV; $30–$35; 2-890-107, fax: 2-890-

304). Built 20 years ago in the timber and brick architectural style of Bavarian Germany (*Fachwerkbau*), it sits on a 12 acre (5 hectare) forested site at 7600 feet (2300 meters) elevation and overlooking the Tumbaco Valley. It has 21 comfortable and clean rooms in the lodge and in separate cabins. There are heated pools, tennis courts and isolated places to sit and watch the clouds and the birds go by. Only 20 minutes from the international airport and 30 minutes from central Quito, it is a remarkable escape from noisy traffic and crowded streets. Great for a day or two of recuperation from hectic schedules, it is also an efficient base from which you can make day trips to Papallacta and Pasachoa or even launch a longer trip to Baeza and the northern Oriente. Recently purchased by the Universidad de San Francisco, the facilities now serve as a training site for their School of Gastronomy and Hotelier. The food in the restaurant is prepared and served at extremely high standards, but the prices are reasonable ($5–$12).

GETTING THERE: By Car or Taxi: The only drawback to this hosteria is that there is no public transportation, and without a car you are rather isolated. At the first traffic circle in Cumbayá on the main road to Pifo east from Quito, turn right onto a cobblestone road that goes uphill. Take the right fork at the first "Y" in the road and then turn left onto the paved road at the "T." There are small signs indicating the hosteria all along this road, and it is about three kilometers from the traffic circle in Cumabayá.

MUSEUMS

In addition to the several museums described above in colonial Quito, there are others scattered throughout the city that are worth seeing. On the east side of Parque El Ejido is the modern **Casa de Cultura Ecuatoriana** (Avenidas Patria and 12 de Octubre; 9 a.m.–12:30 p.m. and 3 p.m.–6:30 p.m., Tuesday–Friday, 9:30 a.m.–4 p.m. on Saturday). There are actually three museums here: one of modern and 19th-century paintings, an ethnographic museum and another featuring primitive musical instruments from around the world. Near the Casa de Cultura Ecuatoriana is the Catholic University's library, which has an archaeology and art museum on its third floor. This is the **Museo de Jacinto Jijón y Caamaño** (Avenida 12 de Octubre; 8 a.m.–noon and 2 p.m.–6 p.m., Monday–Friday; admission). The archaeology display is from the collection of Jacinto Jijón, an Ecuadorian archaeologist. The colonial-era paintings are from the Quito School, which is characterized by pictures using much gold leaf and an Indian influence. All three museums have English-speaking guides available with prior notice.

The **Observatorio Astronomico de Quito** (2-570-765) is a working astronomy observatory affiliated with the National Polytechnic University (open to the public 9–noon on Saturday, or by appointment). It is located in the Parque de La Alameda (10 de Agosto and Colombia) near the border of old and new Quito. Besides housing seismographic equipment for monitoring earthquakes, it has a large Merz telescope mounted in the principle dome of the observatory. This German-built telescope was installed in 1887, and still operates on a system of pulleys and weights instead of electricity to track stars and other heavenly bodies. Aficionados delight in seeing an efficient system operating as it did in the previous century, a sight impossible anywhere else in the world.

One of the finest displays of both modern and colonial art is at the **Museo Guayasamín** (Bosmediano 543; 9 a.m.–12:30 p.m. and 3 p.m.–6:30 p.m., Tuesday–Friday). Oswaldo Guayasamín is a world-famous Ecuadorian Indian artist. The museum, located in Guayasamín's beautiful home, features his collection of contemporary and colonial paintings and colonial sculptures. Another one of our favorite museum/galleries featuring Ecuadorian artists is the **Museo de la Fundación Ecuatoriana de Desarrollo** (Venezuela 1357 and Oriente). It is in a renovated colonial home with a central patio in old town Quito and features a wide range of exquisite painting and sculpture styles. Call for hours and information on the current showings (2-210-464, 2-215-401).

There are two museums that feature natural history. The most complete is the **Museo de Ciencias Naturales** (Parque La Carolina; 9 a.m.–4:30 p.m., Monday–Friday, 9 a.m.–1 p.m. on Saturday; admission). This natural history museum is a good place to visit before you start your adventures if you are unfamiliar with the plants and animals of the highlands and tropics. A more specialized museum is the **Vivarium** (Reina Victoria two blocks north of Avenida Colón; 9 a.m.–4 p.m., Tuesday–Friday, 9 a.m.–4 p.m. on Saturday; admission). This is a museum featuring Ecuadorian frogs and amphibians and where you will find a Boa Constrictor, a fer-de-lance snake, iguanas and tortoises.

LODGING

A wide variety of lodgings is available in Quito. Most of the nicest hotels are in the Mariscal Sucre area, centered around Avenida Amazonas, of the new part of the city. There are many hotels in the colonial part of Quito, but the neighborhoods are not as nice or safe and most of the hotels appear to be a bit run-down.

DELUXE HOTELS

All of these luxury hotels have 60-plus rooms and most are fully equipped for conventions. In Quito, much more than in Guayaquil, guests in these hotels are mainly tourists. The hotels all have a 24-hour coffee shop and one or more elegant and expensive restaurants. They have numerous bars, pools, sauna, exercise room, casino, room service and laundry service. Rooms all have private baths, hot water, air conditioning, bathtubs, hair dryers, phones, cable color TV and mini-bars. Some have nonsmoking rooms on some floors. Rates for double rooms range from $75–$300. Tax adds another 20 percent. All credit cards are accepted.

Hotel Alameda Real (Vicente Ramón Roca 653 and Avenida Río Amazonas; $70–$110; 2-562-345, fax: 2-565-759). It always distresses us when one of our favorite hotels slips so precipitously in service that we can no longer recommend it. The Hotel Alameda has become a Hilton "wannabe," but it is too small and lacks the amenities to compete at this level. At the same time it has abandoned its image of comfort and individualized service. Only if you are spending a fast overnight in Quito can you expect little aggravation and discomfort over the poor service.

Hilton Colón Quito (corner of Avenidas Río Amazonas and Patria; $70–$150; 2-560-666, fax: 2-563-903), the biggest hotel in Quito, is ideally located near Parque El Ejido, where there is always something happening, and at the beginning of Avenida Amazonas, the best tourist shopping district in the city. The Hilton has more of everything than you need: pool, sauna, disco, 24-hour coffee shop, two bars, two restaurants and a casino. If that is not enough, there are also several stores on the lobby level, including a branch of Libri Mundi, the best bookstore in Quito, and Olga Fisch, perhaps the nicest art handicraft store in Quito. All the rooms are very comfortable and well appointed. There is not much Ecuadorian about this marble and chrome hotel and its large size means you should expect to be treated like a number, but it is still one of the best places to stay in Quito.

Hotel Oro Verde (corner of Avenida 12 de Octubre and Luís Cordero; $220–$300; 2-566-497, fax: 2-569-189) features a luxurious hotel within walking distance of Amazonas. The Hotel Oro Verde, like the Hotel Alameda Real and the Hotel Colón, is a huge, polished-marble and shiny chrome building with very little to indicate it is in Ecuador. That is not to say that the Oro Verde is anything but spectacularly luxurious. The hotel also offers more than you could possibly want: a bar, a café, an informal barbecue restaurant, an Italian restaurant, a Japanese restaurant, an elegant international restaurant and an exercise club with a pool, sauna and steam room and squash and racquetball courts. If you are looking for unparalleled comfort, the Hotel Oro Verde is just for you.

Radisson Royal Quito Hotel (corner of Avenida 12 de Octubre and Cordero in the World Trade Center building; $185–$285; 2-548-355, fax: 2-543-200, or 800-333-3333 in the U.S.; e-mail: quito@uio.radisson.com.ec) is the newest and in our opinion the nicest deluxe hotel in Quito. There are 112 luxurious rooms, including 14 royal suites. Each has a sophisticated security system with in-room safes and internet connections (laptops are available upon request). Even though this hotel is geared for business travelers, regular tourists are as welcome here. In fact, despite its high-class appearance, we feel this hotel is the warmest and most people-oriented of all the deluxe hotels.

MODERATE HOTELS

Double-occupancy room rates for these hotels range from $40–$80. All credit cards are accepted. Amenities in the rooms include private baths, hot water, air conditioning, phone and color TV. They each have a small restaurant and a bar, but few other extras.

Hotel Sebastian (corner of Avenida Diego de Almagro and Luís Cordero; $60–$100; 2-527-577, 2-222-400, fax: 2-565-261) is our favorite place to stay in Quito. The rooms are as comfortable and well decorated as the other deluxe hotels but you are not paying for their added pretentiousness, so the cost for a room is considerably less. Also, the Sebastian is a bit smaller than the other deluxe hotels so you will receive more personal service. The Sebastian is also the only hotel in Quito that purifies all of its water so the tap water in every room is safe to drink. There is a very good restaurant, a café, a bar, a sauna and a large conference area. The Sebastian is easy walking distance to shopping on Amazonas and is located just a few blocks from many good restaurants on Calle Calama. The Sebastian is associated with Nuevo Mundo Tours, so your complete trip to Ecuador can be coordinated with a single phone call.

Hotel Reina Isabel (Avenida Amazonas 842 and Veintimilla; $50–$100; 2-544-454, fax: 2-221-337) is a new hotel on busy Avenida Amazonas in the heart of Quito's tourist section. There are 30 attractive rooms and a restaurant and bar downstairs. This hotel combines very modern facilities with very friendly service.

Isla Isabela Hostal (Isla Isabela 321 and Isla Floreana near the Plaza de Toros; $25–$50; 2-240-222, fax: 2-257-616; personalized tour and driver arrangements possible) is perhaps the most homey and personable place to stay in Quito. Located in a quiet neighborhood near the airport with shopping and good restaurants close by, the service and atmosphere of this hostal are wonderfully warm and friendly. We were extremely impressed with the staff and the facilities here.

Hostal La Villa (P.O. Box 17-079-653, Toledo 1455 and Coruña; $75–$150; 2-222-755, fax: 2-226-082) is an elegant little inn nestled into a quiet neighborhood on the east side of Quito. If you want to feel more like a friend and not just another customer, this is a good place to stay.

Hotel Quito (Gederico González Suárez 2500; $60–$80; 2-230-300, fax: 2-567-284) was once the flagship luxury hotel in Quito. The hotel is situated on the eastern edge of the plateau on which Quito is built and thus has a magnificent view of the Machángara river valley and the Andes to the east. There is a restaurant, cafeteria, bar, conference room and casino. The hotel has 230 rooms, some of which are newly renovated, but most are a bit run-down. This hotel appears to be a tad worn out because it has been for sale for years and the owners have been reluctant to put money into it.

Hotel Chalet Suisse (corner of Reina Victoria and José Calama; $50–$80; 2-562-700, fax: 2-563-966) can be found in the middle of Quito's restaurant and shopping district. The hotel is only a block from Calle Juan Leon Mera and its many art galleries and it is on the same street, Calama, as several very good restaurants. The hotel itself has a very good Swiss restaurant that serves delicious steaks, as well as an informal cafeteria, a bar, a steam room, a sauna and a casino. The 63 rooms are comfortable and pleasantly decorated and the staff is very friendly and helpful.

Hostal Los Alpes (José Luís Tamayo 233; $40–$60; 2-561-110) is a small hotel in a big house in a quiet neighborhood in central Quito. The hotel has 24 wonderfully homey and comfortable rooms. There is an excellent restaurant, a little breakfast cafeteria and a nice bar for relaxing at night.

Hotel Tambo Real (corner of Avenidas 12 de Octubre and Patria; $45–$60; 2-563-822, fax: 2-554-964), a small highrise hotel opposite the U.S. Embassy, has 90 rooms that are spacious and clean; some have refrigerators. The Tambo Real has a restaurant and breakfast cafeteria, as well as a casino for late-night revelry.

Hotel Cesar (corner of Avenidas 6 de Diciembre and de la República; $45–$80; 2-239-778, fax: 2-232-073) is a smaller hotel a short walk from Avenida Colón, the middle of bustling Quito, and shopping on Amazonas. The 42 rooms are modern and very attractive. You'll find a bar, cafeteria and restaurant, in addition to a laundry service and a small flower shop on the premises.

Hostal Charles Darwin (La Colina 304; $40–$60; 2-529-384) offers a wonderful bed and breakfast in a two-story home in a quiet neighborhood. The hostal is run by a sister and two brothers who are extraordinarily friendly and helpful to bewildered gringos. There are six very attractive rooms and a pretty inner courtyard. This is a good place to go if you would like to get to know some delightful Ecuadorians personally.

Hotel Plaza International (Leonidas Plaza 150; $28–$50; 2-522-985, fax: 2-505-075), a beautiful colonial building located between the U.S. Embassy and the French Embassy, is just one block from the museums of the Casa de la Cultura and the Parque El Ejido. The rooms are large and attractive, many with great views over the park. The hotel has a nice restaurant and a bar but there are others so close we recommend exploring a bit to find a better place to eat. The staff is very friendly and speaks English, French and Portuguese as well as Spanish. If you do not want the polished, high-priced ambiance of the Hotel Colón but do want its central location, this is a good compromise.

Hotel Republica (corner of Avenida República and Azuay; $42–$60; 2-436-553, fax: 2-437-667) is another of Quito's small highrise hotels. There are 44 rooms in this modern hotel plus a restaurant, bar and small cafeteria. There is also a travel agency associated with the hotel to help you plan day trips in the area.

Hotel Ambassador (Avenida 9 de Octubre 1052; $44–$65; 2-561-777, fax: 2-503-712) offers big highrise hotel service in a small highrise hotel. The Ambassador has 60 rooms that have been newly remodeled, a good restaurant, a cafeteria, a pleasant bar and a pastry shop. Avenida 9 de Octubre is one block to the east of Amazonas so this is a good base from which to explore the area's galleries and shops.

Although the name suggests only a restaurant, the **Café Cultura** (Robles 513 and Reina Victoria; $58–$74; 2-224-271, fax: 2-504-078; e-mail: info@cafecultura.com) is mainly a hotel. Its 24 bedrooms are built into a huge colonial-style house that used to be the French Cultural Center. If you want a hotel with atmosphere, this one has it and more—some might even say it flirts on the margin of being funky. No two of its rooms are alike, and its downstairs library with a huge fireplace is a pleasant place to pass the evening reading or making new friends—there are no TVs in the hotel. The café is open daily from 7 a.m. to 7 p.m. and serves delectable vegetarian and non-vegetarian meals. A tour desk in the lobby (Cultural Reservation Center) can recommend and help you arrange trips to picturesque sites throughout the country.

INEXPENSIVE HOTELS

These lodgings run $15–$40 for a double-occupancy room. All have private baths and hot water. The rooms are a bit smaller than the more expensive hotels and may show a bit of wear around the edges.

Hotel Rincon Escandinavo (Leonidas Plaza 11-10 and Baquierizo Moreno; $20–$35; 2-540-794, fax: 2-222-168) is located just downhill from the Hotel Oro Verde in a nice neighborhood with a good view of the city. The rooms are simple but clean and pleasant. There is a restaurant and bar downstairs and a separate room for small groups.

Hotel Embassy (Calle Presidente Wilson 441; $19–$25; 2-522-133) features a modern hotel in a great location. It is just a few blocks from the restaurants on Calama and the galleries and stores on Juan Leon Mera. The hotel has 70 simple but clean rooms, including 15 suites. The Embassy is a restaurant and cafeteria but we recommend walking to one of the better places to eat nearby.

Hotel Floresta (Isabel La Católica 1015; $30–$40; 2-225-376, fax: 2-500-422) is a small hotel located in a residential neighborhood. The hotel has 20 rooms that are small but sufficiently comfortable. There is a restaurant, a bar and even a small swimming pool.

Hostal Los Andes (Muros 146; $15–$25; 2-550-839) can be found in a very nice residential area near the British Embassy. We have not had the chance to stay here but it has been recommended to us several times. The owners speak English and are very friendly.

Hotel Inca Imperial (Bogota 219; $15–$25; 2-524-800) is located a few blocks west of the Parque El Ejido. There is an okay restaurant and a bar. The owners are helpful, very friendly and speak English.

Hostal Santa Barbara (Avenida 12 de Octubre 2263; $20–$35; 2-564-382, fax: 2-225-121) offers a very pleasant small hostal in a beautiful Spanish-style building. The hostal has a good restaurant, a breakfast room and a small bar. Covered parking is provided.

Although primarily known for its restaurant and good food, the **Magic Bean** (Foch 681 and Juan León Mera; $10–$26; 2-566-181; e-mail: magic@ecuadorexplorer.com) also has five upstairs rooms (two with private bath).

RESTAURANTS

There are many good places to eat in Quito and a few great places. You can find everything from elegant dining experiences in fine restaurants to a quick bite to eat at a sidewalk café. All kinds of international cuisine are offered in Quito's restaurants, but do not overlook the wonderful Ecuadorian food. In many restaurants, it is possible to have a meal with a German beer, an Ecuadorian appetizer, an Argentinean steak, a French pastry and a Chilean wine!

ECUADORIAN The three most popular restaurants serving typical Ecuadorian food are the **Rincón La Rhonda** (Belo Horizonte 400; noon–11 p.m.; $12–$20; 2-540-459), **La Querencia** (Eloy Alfaro 2530; noon–11 p.m.; $10–$16; 2-461-665) and **La Choza** (Avenida 12 de Octubre 1955; noon–3:30 p.m., 7 p.m.–10 p.m.; $12–$18; 2-230-839). Each is quite elegant and located in traditionally decorated buildings. These restaurants can be crowded with early-eating gringo tour groups, so plan to eat a bit later, like native Ecuadorians, or call ahead for reservations. These restaurants have roving minstrels to serenade your table and very attentive waiters. Be sure to try something on the menu you have never heard of before—chances are you will be very pleasantly surprised. **Bambú Bar** (Almagro 2213 and Francisco; lunch only; $3–$7; 2-543-107) is an upscale restaurant that is a favorite lunch spot for business people. Everything we have tried has been delicious. **Hooters** (Avenida 12 de Octubre; 12:30 p.m.–11 p.m.; $9–$16; 2-234-994), across from the Hotel Quito, is a very nice Ecuadorian restaurant with good food that has nothing, other than its name, in common with the infamous restaurant chain based in Florida known for its scantily clad waitresses.

STEAK RESTAURANTS   We have three favorite steak restaurants in Quito. **La Casa de Mi Abuela** (Juan Leon Mera 1649; 4 p.m.–11 p.m.; $8–$12; 2-565-667), **Martín Fierro** (Inglaterra 1309; 3 p.m.–11 p.m.; $8–$12; 2-243-806) and the **Shorton Grill Steak House** (José Calama 216; 1 p.m.–11 p.m.; $8–$12; 2-523-645) offer Argentinean cuts of beef for thick and juicy steaks that are delicious. These restaurants are used to serving huge, cardiac-alert portions so if you want less, be sure to ask for a smaller cut. They also serve grilled chicken and pork. The owners of the **Adam's Rib** (José Calama 442; noon–11 p.m.; $8–$12; 2-563-196) claim to have the "best barbeque south of the equator," and we must agree.

SEAFOOD   If you are a seafood lover, Ecuador is the place for you. We think the three best seafood restaurants in Quito are **Restaurante Mare Nostrum** (José Luís Tamayo 172; 4 p.m.–11 p.m.; $7–$15; 2-563-639), **Las Redes** (Avenida Río Amazonas 845; 4 p.m.–11 p.m.; $8–$15; 2-525-691) and **Barlovento** (corner of Avenidas 12 de Octubre and Orellana; noon–11 p.m.; $7–$15; 2-231-683). They all offer delicious fish, crab, clams and calamari, but their specialties are lobster and shrimp. The shrimp come in different sizes. *Langostinos*, or little lobsters, are the largest, *gambas* are the more usual size. You can have them with lemon, in garlic sauce or just about however you want them. The restaurants will even de-shell them so you can concentrate on savoring the wonderful flavor. We have also heard good things about the less formal **El Auzuelo** (on the corner of Juan Leon Mera and Luís Cordero; 11 a.m.–11 p.m.; $7–$10; 2-547-799) and **Puerto Camaron** (Centro Comercial Olimpico; 11 a.m.–11 p.m.; $6–$10; 2-457-230).

VEGETARIAN   There are several good vegetarian restaurants in Quito that are usually crowded for lunch but less so for dinner. We like the **Magic Bean** (Mariscal Foch 681; 8 a.m.–3 p.m.; $4–$10; 2-566-181), especially for their huge breakfasts. The Magic Bean is also a coffeehouse with a small bakery full of delicious desserts (and they have five guest rooms upstairs). It's a great spot where you can relax on their pleasant patio after wandering around Amazonas. **Vitalcentro** (Lizardo García 630; 11:30 a.m.–2:30 p.m.; $4–$9; 2-520-580) and **Girasol** (Oriente 581; 11 a.m.–2:30 p.m.; $4–$10; 2-217-175) are health food stores that also serve lunches.

INTERNATIONAL   There are an extraordinary number of restaurants offering international cuisine in Quito. You can choose from several very good German, North American, Arabic, Brazilian, Russian, British, Colombian,

Korean, Cuban, Chinese, Spanish, French, Polynesian, Italian, Japanese, Mediterranean, Mexican and Swiss restaurants, not to mention vegetarian. Have fun!

POLYNESIAN   **Kontiki** (Eduardo Whymper 1094; noon–11 p.m.; $10–$16; 2-565-602) is a very attractive Polynesian restaurant with delicious food. Try the Hawaiian-style shrimp or the grilled chicken.

ITALIAN   **Il Piccolo** (Lincoln 149; 12:30 p.m.–11 p.m.; $10–$16; 2-543-552), **Trattoria del Veneziano** (Vicente Ramón Roca 562; 12:30 p.m.–11 p.m.; $10–$18; 2-523-085), **Vecchia Roma** (Vicente Ramón Roca 618; 1 p.m.–11 p.m.; 2-230-876) and **La Gritta** (Santa María 246; 1 p.m.–10 p.m.; $9–$16; 2-567-628) are elegant Italian restaurants with great food. In general, Quito's Italian restaurants are very good but a bit more expensive than the other international restaurants.

MEXICAN   **La Guarida del Coyote** (two locations: Geronimo Carrion 619 and Japón 542; 2 p.m.–11 p.m.; $8–$16; 2-503-292), **La Posada** (Gederico González Suárez 135; 11 a.m.–11 p.m.; $7–$14; 2-523-649) and **La Fonda del Cuervo** (Avenida América 5993; noon–11 p.m.; $8–$14; 2-243-287) serve very tasty Mexican food in informal settings. Listen for the difference between Mexican and Ecuadorian Spanish.

CUBAN   An exciting restaurant, **La Bodeguita de Cuba** (Reina Victoria 1721 and La Pinta; noon–4 p.m. and 7 p.m.–midnight Wednesday–Friday, and noon–midnight Saturday and Sunday; $4–$12; 2-542-476) has delicious Cuban food (try the *ropa vieja*), friendly ambiance and a charming Cuban proprietress.

FRENCH   French restaurants in Quito are also unusually common and generally very good. The three best, **Rincon de Borgoña** (Avenida Eloy Alfaro 2712; noon–11 p.m.; $10–$20; 2-446-627), the **Normandie** (Leonidas Plaza 1048; 12:30 p.m.–10:30 p.m.; $12–$22; 2-233-116) and **Chez Maurice** (Gonnessiat 239; 1 p.m.–10 p.m.; $12–$20; 2-233-566) are among Quito's most elegant places to eat and are priced accordingly. Save one of these for a special night or a celebration.

CHINESE   Just a block in back of the Oro Verde Hotel, the **Happy Panda Restaurante** (Cordero 341 and Isabel la Católica; noon–3 p.m and 6–11 p.m; 2-547-322; $5–$15) features Hunan cuisine. It is new and one of the best *chifas* in the central hotel area of Quito.

OTHER EUROPEAN   Restaurants featuring the cuisine of Europe, other than French, are not as common in Quito. **Pim's** (two locations: José Calama 413, 2-553-080, and Mariano Aguilera 326, 2-562-042; 2 p.m.–midnight; $8–$16), styled after an English pub, is an informal British restaurant and bar that serves light meals and snacks. The **Raclette restaurant** (corner of Eloy Alfaro and Avenida República; 11 a.m.–11 p.m.; $6–$12; 2-553-974) serves Swiss cuisine prepared tableside on your own grill. The **Excalibur** restaurant (José Calama 380; 1:30 p.m.–11 p.m.; $10–$21; 2-552-502) is considered by many to be the best restaurant in Quito. It is beautifully decorated and serves magnificent food with very good but very expensive wines. The European cuisine combined with the friendly Ecuadorian service makes for a delightful dining experience.

The **Avalon Restaurante Jardin** (Avenida Orellana 155 and 12 de Octubre; 1:30 p.m.–midnight; $10–$25; 2-229-993), offering international cuisine, is one of the most elegant restaurants in Quito. The food and service are excellent, and it is on a quiet side street just a block from the Hotel Quito.

FAST FOOD   **King Chicken** (Cuenca 710, 2-516-893, and Santo Domingo Plaza, 2-516-655, plus five more locations; 11 a.m.–11 p.m.) is a knock-off of KFC, but with more types of food.

Gus (Santo Domingo Plaza, 2-263-008, and Teatro Plaza, 2-567-146, and three other locations; 10 a.m.–11 p.m.) is an Ecuadorian fried-chicken chain that is inexpensive and quite good.

Tropiburger (Avenidas Shyris and Naciones Unidas, 2-435-471 and Avenidas Alfaro and Mariana de Jesús; 10 a.m.–11 p.m.; 2-568-097) is a typical fast-food hamburger joint, but the food is not bad.

PIZZA   Eating pizza in Quito is a fun experience because there is an interesting South American flavor to it that you cannot find at home. Try **Pizza Pazza** (Avenida América 4059; 11 a.m.–11 p.m.; 2-241-628), **Pizza Métrica** (Avenida Amazonas 854; 11 a.m.–midnight; 2-224-274, also home delivery), **Roy's Pizzeria** (corner of Avenidas Amazonas and Orellana; 11 a.m.–midnight; 2-460-028, plus home delivery) and **El Hornero** (Veintimilla 1149; 11 a.m.–midnight; 2-542-518, and three other locations plus home delivery).

SHOPPING

Want to buy a tablecloth? Sunglasses? Have your shoes shined? **Avenida Río Amazonas** (*quiteños* just say Amazonas) is the place for you. We are not referring to the stores, of which there are many, along Amazonas. All this commerce happens on the sidewalks of this bustling street where vendors hawking their wares pound the pavement. We have seen young men selling fists full of sunglasses; women with baskets of supposed Incan artifacts; and lace tablecloths draped between two men, like a banner at a ballgame, parading along the street crowing prices. And if you pause long enough, you will find your foot on a stand in front of a young kid with shoe polish in his hands and change in his pocket.

Avenida Amazonas is the heart of the shopping and tourist district in Quito. The two go hand in hand. Where there are tourists there will be stores and where there are stores there will be tourists. There are stores selling compact discs, weavings from Otavalo, leather goods, T-shirts, wood carvings, ceramics, cellular phones and jewelry, to name but a few. There are more stores than you can shake a tourist guidebook at. You will see gringos staggering under bags of even more T-shirts, weavings for sale in alleys, tiny highland Indians with babies clutched to their shoulder, magazine stands and lottery ticket hawkers.

Note: Avenida Amazonas is also the center of the bargain tour operators. There are dozens of these operators in tiny offices offering "fabulous" trips to an "ecological reserve" that is "paradise" and "virgin"—all at extremely low prices. Remember, if it seems too good or too cheap to be true, it probably is.

A stroll along Amazonas can start anywhere, but we will begin at the Hilton Colón, at the corner of Avenida Amazonas and Avenida Patria. Across from the Hilton is the Parque El Ejido, which is always full of strollers, impromptu art exhibits, soccer games, joggers and picnickers during the day. It is a nice place to sit and watch a slice of Quito wander by and enjoy a bit of a snack. Avenida Amazonas starts at this park and runs more or less north toward the airport. Most of the best stores are on Amazonas and Juan Leon Mera between Avenida Patria by the Hilton and Calle Presidente Wilson, about a seven-block distance. Juan Leon Mera is one block east of Amazonas and is parallel to it. The block-size Hilton anchors this area—on its west side is Avenida Amazonas and on its east side is Juan Leon Mera.

There are two good bookstores in this seven-block area. The biggest and the best in all of Ecuador is **Libri Mundi** (Juan Leon Mera 851; 2-234-791). The store is between Veintimilla and Calle Presidente Wilson on the west side of Juan Leon Mera. Most of its books are in Spanish but there is also a large section of English-language books, including Quito's best selection of natural history books and guides and a surprisingly good selection of paperbacks. Libri Mundi also has branch stores in the Hilton Colón (2-550-455) and the Hotel Oro Verde (2-567-128). The other good bookstore is **Libro-Express** (Avenida Río Amazonas 826; 2-550-527), near the corner of Amazonas and Veintimilla. It has the best newsstand of English language magazines as well as day-old *USA Today* newspapers. They also have a good selection of Ecuadorian guide books and maps. (They do not accept credit cards.) Another good bookstore that specializes in used books is **Confederate Books** (2-527-890), a few blocks away on the corner of Juan Leon Mera and Calama 410.

There are so many stores with the word "artesanias" in their name it would take several pages to list them all. But they all are very similar. They have narrow aisles crowded with every kind of cheap souvenir imaginable. Many of these stores sell pinned rainforest butterflies mounted behind glass. We recommend that you do not buy them. The butterflies have been "stolen" from the rainforest and they are illegal to bring into the U.S. and most other countries.

There are several fine art galleries in this area that sell beautiful woven rugs, handmade sweaters, paintings and jewelry. Our favorites are: **Galeria Latina** (Juan Leon Mera 833; 2-540-380), **La Bodega** (Juan Leon Mera 614; 2-232-844), **Artesanias Comunitaras-MCCH** (corner of Juan Leon Mera and Robles), **Centro Artesanal** (Juan Leon Mera 804; 2-548-235), **CDX Gallery** (Juan Leon Mera 804; 2-238-802), **Galeria de Arte** (Avenida Río Amazonas 609; 2-542-670) and the **Art-forum** (Juan Leon Mera 870; 2-544-185). All these galleries are open every day, except Sunday, until 7 or 8 p.m. and they all gladly accept credit cards.

On the corner of Juan Leon Mera and Vicente Ramón Roca is a very small cobblestone **corner square** where there are always piles of *otavaleño* weavings, sweaters and cotton clothes. The prices are not much different here than in Otavalo, so if you see something you like, buy it.

When you get hungry from wandering around, there are three sidewalk **cafés** on Avenida Amazonas between Robles and Roca. You cannot miss them—there are always waiters out front hawking menus and the day's specials. An alternative to these cafés is the **El Español Deli** next to the Libri Mundi bookstore on Juan Leon Mera. If you do not like any of these, there are at least three dozen informal eateries on Amazonas where you can get a snack or a cold drink.

For travelers desperate for a quick fix of home, take a taxi to the **Quicentro Shopping Center** (corner of Avenidas Naciones Unidas and 6 de Diciembre; 9:30 a.m.–8 p.m., Monday–Saturday, and 10 a.m.–6 p.m. on Sunday) or the newer **Mall El Jardín** (2500 Amazonas; 9:30 a.m.–9 p.m. daily). These are like typical North American upscale malls, with a large food court and over 200 fashionable stores including Nautica, Bally, Flags and Ralph Lauren. Most of the people you see here are well-dressed, upper-crust Ecuadorians (no lottery ticket sellers or beggars allowed in this sanitized bit of Ecuador). Close your eyes here for a moment and when you open them you will think you have been transported back to Dallas or Atlanta or Minneapolis.

NIGHTLIFE

Because of the constantly changing addresses and nature of the discos and bars in Quito, we feel it best not to recommend any particular establishment. Although drugs and other criminal behavior are usually well-controlled inside these establishments, on the sidewalk outside some of them drug sales and prostitution may be common. It has been our experience that those that are safe one year are not the next, and those that are at one place one time have moved to another place the next time we visit. This is not meant to discourage you from exploring the fun nightlife of Quito. We suggest that you ask at your hotel for their recommendation as to the best spot currently to enjoy Quito's nightlife.

GETTING THERE: Quito is the transportation hub city in Ecuador so all roads, tracks and flights either start in Quito or eventually get there.

By Air: Quito is the primary point of arrival and departure in Ecuador so there are plenty of international and domestic flights to chose from. Beware though that flights that arrive at night are sometimes rerouted to Guayaquil because fog or curfew often closes the Quito airport.

By Bus: There are many buses that travel the streets of Quito. Many are old and crowded and go by a system that is beyond the comprehension of a normal gringo. If you are the type of person who likes to experience a place from the point of view of the common folk, get on a bus and stay on it until—hopefully— it returns to where you got on. If you are fluent in Spanish, you will be able to negotiate the system if you ask enough questions. If you plan on figuring out the system on the go, we'll be writing folksongs about you for, like poor old Charlie on the MTA, you may never return. If you do not understand Spanish, stay off the buses.

Every community within 200 kilometers of Quito has at least one and probably half a dozen bus companies that provide transportation to Quito. Alternatively, you can just stand beside the road and stick out your hand when you see a bus with *"a Quito"* on the front approaching. Almost all buses leaving or arriving Quito do so at the *terminal terrestre* in the extreme southern part of the city. The best way to get to the terminal is by taxi, but if you do not have much luggage, the Trole Bus south has a convenient stop just 200 meters west of the terminal's main entrance. The Trole Bus stop here is called the Terminal Terrestre Stop. The terminal itself is on three floors with arrival on the top floor and departures on the bottom floor. The ticket booths on the bottom floor are arranged by destination with southern destinations in Ecuador at one end and northern destinations at the other (with many exceptions). Four gates lead to the buses after you have purchased your ticket. Ask the ticket agent which gate you should exit and at which stall your bus is located. Unlike the relatively well-organized terminal in Guayaquil, the Quito terminal is old and run-down, with many of its stores and restaurants out of business. The Quito terminal is also not a place you want to loiter around as thievery is common. Keep a close eye on your wallet and luggage at all times.

By Car: In Ecuador all roads lead to Quito or so it seems. Quito straddles the Pan-American Highway and lies at the junction of Route 28, the main road to the Oriente. Because of Quito's considerable sprawl, the difficulty is not so much getting to Quito as getting out.

By Taxi: Quito is a city of cars. There must be at least half a zillion vehicles on the streets at any one time and of these, a third will be little yellow taxis. Finding an empty one is not difficult, but finding one that knows how to go to a spot off the tourist route is sometimes a problem. Always ask if the driver knows where your destination is, and always confirm the price before you start driving away. If the taxi driver does not seem sure how to get to where you are going, go to a well-known spot close by and then walk to your destination. The taxis associated with the large tourist hotels are very good and reliable—we have even asked them for their recommendation for nearby restaurants. Hotel taxis, however, will always be more expensive than taxis hailed on the street.

DAY TRIPS SOUTH OF QUITO

The Pan-American Highway divides into two routes through Quito. The western route stays high in the Quito valley before descending to the town of Tambillo. The eastern route drops quickly away from the Quito valley to the east through the town of Sangolquí to meet the western branch of the highway at the town of Tambillo. Most drivers take the eastern route to go to the Pasochoa Forest Reserve and the western route to go to Cotopaxi National Park and points south.

The **Pasochoa Forest Reserve** protects one of the few remaining patches of native mountain forest in the highlands near Quito. It is not a large reserve, about 1000 acres, but it is important because it not only protects a rare forest environment but it is very close to the urban sprawl of Quito. To many *quiteños*, the trails of the Pasochoa Forest Reserve are their only contact with relatively undisturbed nature and the native forest that once covered the area. This is especially important for schoolchildren who come to the Pasochoa Forest Reserve to experience and learn about the natural world. The reserve is administered by Fundación Natura (Avenida América 5653 and Vozandes, Quito; 2-447-341/342/343).

Located on the slopes of the extinct Cerro Pasochoa (13,860 feet/4200 meters), Pasochoa Forest Reserve is a strip of land within the narrow watershed of Pasochoa Creek. The lowest part of the reserve (8910 feet/2700 meters), near the entrance station, is pastures and hedgerows. Climbing upstream from the entrance station is a secondary forest dominated by dense stands of chusquea bamboo. Above this bamboo forest, on the high valley slopes, is an undisturbed native forest of big trees and epiphytes, including many orchids and bromeliads. Ringing this forest on the high ridges of the valley is a band of paramo that extends to the top of Cerro Pasochoa.

At the entrance station there are restrooms and maps available of the trails. Remember to pay the $7 fee to walk the trails. Behind the entrance station is the Education Center, which contains natural history exhibits, more restrooms and a small store selling T-shirts and handicrafts. The trails start behind and to the right of the Education Center. Behind and to the left of the Education Center is a camping area ($10 per night) and a picnic area. These two areas can be crowded on weekends, so make advance reservations at the Fundación Natura office in Quito.

There is much to see in every habitat of Pasochoa. The reserve is well known for birdwatching, and over 120 species have been recorded. Even if you are not an avid birdwatcher, Pasochoa is still a great place to visit to get away from the noise of Quito. There is an extensive trail system for all levels of exertion that leads through the reserve. The trails start behind the Education Center. The trails are laid out like colored links in a chain. Each successive link or loop is progressively longer and requires more effort. It is a long day hike to get to the rim of the caldera and back to the entrance station, but the views from the high ridges are spectacular. Be aware of approaching weather if you decide to go to the rim.

The Pasochoa Forest Reserve can be busy on weekends but it is usually empty on weekdays. If you arrive early, you will most likely have the entire reserve to yourself. July through September are the hottest, driest months, while April is the wettest month. Most flowers bloom in May, which is also when the various hummingbirds are easiest to see. If you have a day to kill in Quito, this is a great place to spend it. Not only will you see interesting plants and animals and get some exercise but you will be contributing to the conservation and environmental education efforts of Fundacíon Natura.

GETTING THERE: By Bus: There are daily buses that go to the village of Amaguaña from Quito. Ask to be let off at El Elejdo. From there you will have to either walk, which will take about an hour and a half. If you are lucky, you can hitch a ride on the infrequent traffic.

By Car: The Pasochoa Forest Reserve is about a 45-minute drive (40 kilometers) south of Quito. There are two ways to get to the reserve. Both are equally confusing because of the lack of signs marking the route. The easiest way is to head south on the Pan-American Highway to the little town of Tambillo, 32 kilometers from Quito. Turn left (east) there toward the village of Amaguaña. Five kilometers along this road turn right (south) before Amaguaña on the road to the reserve. When you get lost, ask for directions. The locals know where the reserve is and are used to bewildered visitors. Alternatively, the shortest route starts from the eastern branch of the Pan-American Highway south of Quito. Before the town of Tambillo, on a near hill to the left (east) of the road is a little, two-spired, white- and blue-trimmed church known locally as El Elejdo. Turn left to the church and then bear right past the church on a narrow cobblestone road. This road passes through an old hacienda before turning right and ending at the reserve. It is 11 kilometers from Tambillo and 6 kilometers from the El Elejdo church to the reserve.

By Taxi: Many taxi drivers in Quito know how to get to Pasochoa, but some do not. Be sure your driver knows the way before you agree to hire him. For a half-day trip it will cost between $20 and $50. A taxi is the best way to get to the reserve, if you want to arrive early to birdwatch. Arrange the trip the night before so you can leave promptly at 5 a.m. to get to Pasochoa at dawn.

Cotopaxi National Park is the jewel of Ecuador's mainland parks. Located about 60 kilometers south of Quito just east of the Pan-American Highway, this 85,000-acre park is roughly square in shape and centered around the magnificent Cotopaxi volcano. Rising in a steeply symmetrical glacier-capped cone to 19,460 feet (5897 meters), Cotopaxi is Ecuador's second-highest mountain and its highest active volcano (many books write that it is the highest active volcano in the world, but Volcán Tupungato on the border of Argentina and Chile is higher). Cotopaxi dominates the surrounding highlands, and on a clear day it is easily visible from Quito. Every snowcapped mountain in Ecuador is sacred to Ecuador's indigenous people, but Cotopaxi, because of its seemingly symmetrical perfection, is the most sacred. Shamans make an annual pilgrimage to Cotopaxi to restore their power, and all Ecuadorians refer to Cotopaxi with reverence and pride.

The paradox of Cotopaxi is that while it is Ecuador's most beautiful mountain, it is also its most destructive. Eruptions of Cotopaxi have killed more people and done more damage than any other volcano in Ecuador. The first historic eruption occurred in 1534. It next erupted in 1742, destroying the town of Latacunga at its base. Cotopaxi erupted again in 1743, 1744, 1766 and 1768, when Latacunga was again destroyed. The volcano was active for several years in the mid-1850s and then erupted four times in 1877, which once again destroyed the intrepid town of Latacunga. The last significant period of volcanic activity at Cotopaxi occurred in 1903 and 1904, with minor activity in 1942. The mountain was first climbed in 1872 by a German and a Colombian and then by the first Ecuadorians a few months later. The famous South American mountaineer Edward Whymper spent the night on the summit in 1880. His route has now become the standard route to the top.

Both roads to the entrance station lead through extensive stands of introduced pines in the small **El Boliche National Recreation Area** (2500 acres). The pines represent an ill-conceived attempt by international foresters to reforest the highlands of Ecuador with exotic, non-native tree species. You might be tempted to look for wildlife in these pine forests, but you will have more success if you move on to the national park. Not many native animals thrive in non-native environments. There are picnic and camping sites in Boliche as well as herds of introduced White-tailed Deer and tame llamas. From the entrance station ($4 fee), the road quickly climbs out of the pines to the paramo that skirts the mountain. Six kilometers from the entrance station is the park's **visitors center** on the right. There are restrooms here, displays on the park's cultural and natural history, maps of the park and usually someone to answer questions.

From the visitors center, the road climbs gradually between recent lava flows to an ashy plain and Lago Limpiopungo. The lake is small, shallow and surrounded by swampy vegetation. There is a rough trail that goes around the lake that starts on the right side.

Look for the orange and black *Atelopus* frog along the margin of the lake. Twenty years ago this frog was abundant throughout the paramo, even right in Quito. Now it is found in only a few isolated areas. Scientists are not sure why its population is declining so rapidly. One theory is that increasing UV light coming through the atmosphere has had a deadly effect on this and the many other frog populations that have crashed throughout the world. Apparently, frog skin has no protection from UV light, unlike the scales of lizards and snakes, the feathers of birds and the hair of mammals.

At 12,540 feet (3800 meters) elevation, any activity is breathtaking, so be sure to take your time and plan to do less than expected. The vegetation on the plain is low and sparse, and the area can be quite dusty on windy days. If you are interested in exploring the paramo, stop either before you get to the plain or continue driving to the far side of the mountain, which is a bit lower in elevation and wetter, and thus has more lush paramo vegetation. Most of the animal life you will see in the paramo will be birds and most of them are skulkers. Wrenlike cincloides run from tuft to tuft hiding in the grass as do pipits, canasteros and snipes. Exotic sounding tit-spinetails, tit-tyrants, shrike-tyrants and ground tyrants can also be found within the park. The birds you are most likely to see are either teal, coot or pintail ducks on one of the few lakes; Puna Hawks or Carunculated Caracaras soaring overhead; or one of several kinds of hummingbirds feeding on the flowering plants of the paramo.

To see these birds you have to pull your gaze away from the gleaming summit of Cotopaxi looming to the south. It is such a massive mountain, at such close range, that the human mind cannot easily make sense of it. You might think that it can't be that big or it can't be so close, but it is. From Lago Limpiopungo, the summit is 6600 feet (2000 meters) higher and about 8 kilometers away as the condor flies. If you want to get a closer look at the mountain, weather permitting, turn right on the obvious side road just past the lake. This 8.5-kilometer road snakes up the slope of Cotopaxi to a parking lot below the Climber's Refuge. Some passenger cars cannot make this trip because of the high altitude. The parking lot is above the zone of vegetation, so the only signs of life you are likely to see are a few lichens and many dusty footprints. It is not uncommon for the parking lot to be within the cone of snow that usually adorns the top of Cotopaxi, so bring warm clothing if you want to wander. The **Climber's Refuge** is up the ashy slope from the parking lot, about a 45-minute walk, although it appears as if it should be only five minutes away. At the refuge there are 30 bunk beds, kitchen facilities, running water, outside toilets, a fireplace and lockers for climber's gear. If you want to spend the night ($4 fee), bring a sleeping bag and your own food.

The ascent of Cotopaxi from the refuge is not technically difficult, but it does require specialized gear—ice axes, crampons, climbing rope—and sophisticated knowledge of glacier travel. Because of the quickly deteriorating condition of snow under the equatorial sun, most climbers start the summit attempt between midnight and 2 a.m. It takes between six and eight hours to reach the summit (sulfury fumeroles greet you) and three to four hours to return to the refuge. If you want to climb but do not have the necessary experience, you can hire a guide in Ambato or in Quito. Inquire at one of the big tour operators for recommendations. Make sure your guide is licensed and is a member of the Associación de Guias de Montaña. For more information on climbing Cotopaxi, refer to the book *Climbing and Hiking in Ecuador* by Rachowiecki, Thurber and Wagenhauser.

There are few established trails within the park, but the possibilities for walking and hiking are just about limitless due to the open terrain and generally thin vegetation. Just park your car at a safe spot and go for a walk. Most of the terrain near the road is generally flat, so other than the altitude, you will not have to work too hard. From Lago Limiopungo, it is possible to climb Volcán Rumiñahui to the north or to just follow the informal trail part of the way. You can also circumnavigate Cotopaxi on foot in about a week, picking off a few other summits on the way. Refer to the above-mentioned book for more details on these hikes. Afternoon clouds are the rule, so plan to visit Cotopaxi as early in the morning as you can. Many visitors spend the night at the nearby **Hosteria La Ciénega** or go there for lunch after seeing the park (see Chapter Eight for more information). Many tour operators in Quito offer one- to two-day trips to Cotopaxi National Park. This is a great, hasslefree way to see the mountain. The two-day trips often offer a stay at La Ciénega and a visit to an Indian market along the way.

GETTING THERE: By Bus: Many buses travel the Pan-American Highway between Quito and Latacunga. The cheapest but most strenuous way is to ask to be let off at the park's entrance road. From there you will either have to walk or hitchhike into the park. If your intent is to get to the Climber's Refuge, this would be a long hike but an effective way to acclimatize yourself for the climb ahead. Alternatively, you can hire a truck from Latacunga or Lasso (a town just south of the entrance road) to take you directly to the Climber's Refuge for about $20. Make sure you tell the driver that you want to go to the refuge. Some vehicles cannot make the high-altitude climb necessary to get to the refuge.

By Car: There are two entrances to the national park. Both roads start from the Pan-American Highway and meet at the park entrance station to become the one road through the park. The northernmost entrance is about 16 kilometers south of Machachi or about 26 kilometers north of Latacunga. The turn is marked by a roadside sign indicating Area Nacional de Recreación Boliche and a sign for CLIRSEN, a satellite tracking station formerly operated by NASA. Follow this road past the tracking station to the entrance station, about 8 kilometers from the Pan-American Highway. The southernmost entrance is the official entrance to the park, although both routes are heavily used. This entrance is about 22 kilometers south of Machachi (53 kilometers south of Quito) and about 20 kilometers north of Latacunga. The turn is marked by a large sign for the park and is difficult to miss. The entrance station is 12 kilometers from the Pan-American Highway via this route. After the entrance station, the road continues through the northern half of the park. The park road eventually drops into the valley of the Río Pita on the park's eastern side before exiting into the remote east Andean highlands. This is not a loop road, so you will have to retrace your steps to leave the park.

DAY TRIPS EAST OF QUITO

East of Quito over the Andes is the great basin of the upper Amazon and all of its wonders waiting to be seen. In their efficiency and haste to get there, many tourists fly directly to the heart of the rainforest for the then short trip to their lodge. This is certainly the easiest way to get to the rainforest, but an important and interesting ecosystem, the paramo, is bypassed on the way. Not to worry—a beautiful extent of paramo is just a 45-minute drive from Quito.

The first thing you will notice as you leave Quito is that the city seems to go on forever. You will also observe that the mountain that rises above Quito, Mt. Pichincha, is to the west of the city toward the coast and not to the east toward the Andes as you might think. Once you have reoriented your internal map, you will notice that Quito sits on a high plateau. This is especially noticeable when you drive east because as soon as you leave the city you drop quickly into the valley of the Río Machángara, leaving the highrises of Quito high behind you. The Río Machángara soon empties into the Río Chiche, which flows north and then west eventually joining the Río Esmeraldas. The Río Chiche, the second river met, is crossed by a long bridge over a deep gorge just minutes from downtown Quito. If you have a window seat on the right side of your vehicle going east, look over the edge of the bridge into the gorge to the south. The stone arch bridge you see below is the oldest bridge in Ecuador, built by the Incas about 450 years ago.

From the Río Chiche the road begins its climb toward Papallacta Pass. The sprawl of Quito is still evident, but now more and more bits of the *campo* or countryside are seen. Small garden plots of cabbage and corn are squeezed between fences and parked cars and horses and cows tethered in the roadside ditch become more and more common. About 30 kilometers from Quito is the little town of **Pifo**. Pifo is a farming community that is becoming a commuter community as more and more people travel to Quito to find jobs. The vegetation around Pifo is still mostly introduced pines and eucalyptus—the native forest is still just a dark smudge on the hillsides far above the town. Here and there are patches of native forest hidden in the seams and wrinkles of the land but mostly what vegetation you see belongs somewhere else.

A few kilometers beyond Pifo, the left fork of the road continues to climb and pieces of the paramo become visible among the small fields of potatoes and fava beans. Soon the crops fade away and the characteristic plants of the paramo—tussocks of grass, spiky rosettes, shrubby asters, bushy lupines—cloak the hillsides. About 20 kilometers east of Pifo, you will also notice dense patches of trees clinging to the valley sides. These are *Polylepis* trees, the highest-growing tree species in Ecuador and a member of the rose family. *Polylepis* trees are short with peeling red bark and contorted trunks and limbs. Within this unique forest are several specialized birds of interest to birdwatchers, such as Giant Conebills, Tit-like Dacnis and several species of flowerpiercers. A few patches of *Polylepis* forest come close to the road and are easy to walk into from the road. Be sure to park far enough off the road so you will not be a danger to the passing traffic.

The top of **Papallacta Pass** (13,068 feet/3960 meters) is marked by a roadside shrine, La Vírgen. There are all kinds of possibilities for walking and hiking near the pass. While there are no formal trails to be found in the area, none are really needed. Just park the car and wander. The elevation makes it difficult for you to go too far and the gentle topography makes it difficult for you to lose sight of your car, so do not worry too much about getting lost. Most wildlife can be found in the wetter, more lush parts of the paramo. Just before the top of the pass on the west side of the road is a marked protected area of paramo where we have had good luck finding birds. There are also two old roads—one traveling east, the other west—on the north side of the pass opposite the shrine that are worth exploring. Between these roads is a small bog with an informal trail around it. Generally, the west side of the pass is much better for exploring the paramo. Without too much traffic or stops, it takes about 45 minutes to get to the top of the pass from downtown Quito.

The east side of the pass is more forested. About 15 minutes from the pass is the little village of **Papallacta**. There are a few tiny stores here and well-known **hot springs** nearby if you want to get some of the dust off before you continue on. Turn at the well-marked road west of town to get to the baths.

For either a day visit or to stay overnight, the tourist complex, **Termas de Papallacta**, is a restful and comfortable place just two kilometers off the

Quito-Baeza highway (at Km 65—as you enter the town of Papallacta turn north at the sign). The 615-acre (250-hectare) complex has 22 pools with naturally heated water that ranges from 85°F to 130°F (29°C to 55°C) depending how far the pools are from the source spring. There is even a pool with water from the nearby mountain stream that averages 38°F (4°C) for those that like to push the boundaries of comfort. Many of the thermal pools are located in the day-use area (entrance fee $4) with flagstone decks, sunning areas and snack bars. For those wishing more privacy and lodging for the night, the **Jamiyacu Hotel** (in Quito, Foch 635 and Reina Victoria, Office no. 4-A; private bath, hot water; $24 per person; phone/fax: 2-548-521) is at the south end of the complex. Here the hot springs pools are reserved for guests only. Thirteen new and large rooms with private baths can accommodate up to four people each. More spartan and cheaper ($13 per person) rooms with a bunk bed and communal bathrooms and showers for men and for women are also available. Two large cabins (private bath) for up to six people each are also available ($64 per night). Two restaurants are available on the compound for meals.

Situated in a valley at almost 11,000 feet elevation (3300 meters), this tourist complex on a rare clear day has a spectacular vista of sub-paramo and temperate forests climbing steep mountain sides on three sides. Hiking trails go into these relatively undisturbed habitats, and guides are available by the day ($3). November to February are the sunniest months, but expect fog and clouds even then, especially in the afternoons. In July the temperatures at midday often fail to rise above 40°F (5°C), and the days are almost guaranteed to be rainy. For us it is always a thrill, rain or shine, to be sitting in the steaming water and watching Sword-billed Hummingbirds flitting from one giant Daytura (*huanto*) flower to the next right above the deck of the pool. If you prefer solitude and quiet, stay away from here on weekends. From Friday night to Sunday afternoon, this is a popular weekend stay for hundreds of *quiteños*. The rest of the week the complex is virtually empty.

A good spot to look for wildlife is on the west side of Papallacta at a concrete bridge over a rushing mountain stream. On the west side of this bridge is an informal trail heading upstream into the forest. The other good spot to look for wildlife is 15 kilometers east of the village of Papallacta at another bridge over a rushing mountain stream marked as the Río Chalpi Grande. There is a pullout downhill from this bridge and a trail heading back into the forest. From December through April this part of the road can be very dusty so if you are looking for birds you will have to get into the forest away from the dust.

GETTING THERE: By Bus: There are several bus companies that provide service to Baeza, about 100 kilometers east of Quito and well past Papallacta Pass.

The buses will be glad to drop you off wherever you want and pick you up if it is not full.

By Car: The main road to the Oriente, Route 28, starts in central Quito as Avenida Oriental or Vía a Tumbaco. If you cannot find this street, ask for directions to the Hotel Quito. Avenida Oriental is just north of Hotel Quito and quickly descends below the hotel into the Río Machángara valley. Papallacta Pass is 58 kilometers from Quito along this road.

DAY TRIPS WEST OF QUITO

West of Quito rises the green slope of Mt. Pichincha. There are two, now little-used roads that curve around its flanks and give birders, in particular, and naturalists, in general, easy access to a few remaining patches of west-slope forests. The road to the south is known as the Old Road to Santo Domingo and the road to the north is known as the Nono–Mindo Road. These roads make easy day trips from Quito or alternative, more scenic routes to either Santo Domingo or Mindo. Beware though that road maintenance is at best sporadic on the Nono–Mindo Road so it may be impassable at the time you want to travel it.

The **Old Road to Santo Domingo** descends the western slope of the Andes on the southern flank of Mt. Pichincha. The road starts at about (9240 feet/2800 meters) elevation and drops to about (2640 feet/800 meters elevation near Santo Domingo. It used to be the only way to Santo Domingo from Quito, but a new road farther south has now taken most of the traffic. The old road is gravel and continues to be in good condition and easily passable for normal vehicles because of the maintenance necessary on the Trans-Ecuadorian oil pipeline that runs alongside it. The road is about 90 kilometers long, but expect to take most of a day if you are planning on stopping and exploring. **Chiriboga**, the only town of any size, is located halfway along this road, but there are no places to stay or restaurants there that we can recommend.

GETTING THERE: The only way to travel this road is with your own car. There are no buses that use this road to get to Santo Domingo. Once you find the road, you will have no trouble staying on it until you get to the junction of the new road to Santo Domingo near Tinalandia. Finding the beginning of this road is the hard part. From downtown Quito, travel south on Avenida Occidental and then on Avenida Vencedores de Pichincha past Old Quito to a large CEPE gas station on the right side of the road. The right turn to the old road to Santo Domingo is half a kilometer past this gas station. When you get lost, ask for the road to San Juan (near the beginning of the road) or for the road to Chiriboga. Most taxi drivers know how to get to this road. For details on exploring the lower end of this road see the Santo Domingo section in Chapter Thirteen.

Yanacocha is our favorite hiking path in all of northern Ecuador. It is only an hour from downtown Quito, but unlike Pasachoa and Papallacta, few people visit it, even on weekends. The wide path runs on top of a buried water pipeline, and it gently winds through extensive cloud forest and sub-paramo at 11,000 feet (3350 meters) with no ridges to climb. Your views of the unpopulated west side of Pichincha and the forest-covered slopes down into Mindo are breath-taking. Even on cloudy and rainy days when you cannot see far, the vegetation along the path is full of active bird flocks and several species of mammals that make a hike here full of surprises. The trail goes for almost 10 kilometers (including passing through a 75-meter concrete tunnel about 3 kilometers from the parking area). Because the trail is so flat we can recommend it to almost anyone in moderate physical shape.

GETTING THERE: There is no public transportation to Yanacocha, and while a high-clearance vehicle is desirable, it is usually not necessary. Take the Avenida Occidental to the old road to Nono (*vía a Nono* or Avenida Machala) 0.8 kilometer north of the main cross street of Avenida Legarda. If you look down into the Quito valley, this road is just north of the international airport. Turn west and go 9.5 kilometers up this narrow and windy cobblestoned road. At the EMAPA (municipal water company) sign indicating "Campamento Pichan," turn left (south) and drive up the gravel road (take the right fork at 0.8 kilometer) 7.9 kilometers to the EMAPA compound and gate. If the gate is not open walk around it and knock on the door of the main house. We have had no problem with the manager unlocking the gate to let tourists drive the final 4 kilometers to the end of the road and a parking area. The trail begins here, and the forest and vistas get better and better the farther you go on the trail.

The **Nono–Mindo Road** is the old road to Mindo. From Quito it is about 25 kilometers along this road to Nono, another 50 kilometers to Mindo (for more on Mindo, see Chapter Seven). It descends the western slope of the Andes on the northern flank of Mt. Pichincha from 9240 feet (2800 meters) elevation near Quito to 4950 feet (1500 meters) near Mindo. It is now little traveled because a new, paved road to Mindo and Puerto Quito is quicker and far more comfortable. There are several small villages along this route, including **Nono**, but there are no restaurants or places to spend the night that we can recommend. Unlike the Old Road to Santo Domingo, this road is not at all well maintained. You should expect landslides and washouts on the road, especially during the rainy season from December to April. A four-wheel-drive vehicle is recommended for this route at all times—it is mandatory during the rainy season.

The old road is worth the extra effort, though, as it is more interesting because of the patches of temperate and subtropical forests it traverses along the way. Stop at the beginning of a patch of forest and get out of your car and walk a bit along the road. If you have a driver, tell him to go ahead a few kilometers and wait for you to walk there. Remember that birds travel in flocks so there will be times when there are no birds around and others when birds are all over the place. To find a flock, listen for the quiet call notes birds use to stay in contact with the flock.

GETTING THERE: The only practical way to travel this road is with your own vehicle. Once you are on the road, it is not hard to follow. The trick is finding the start of the road. From Quito head north on Avenida Occidental and turn left (west) on Avenida Machala (see directions for getting to Yanacocha above). If you get confused, ask for the road to Nono and you should get good directions. Finding the western entrance to the road is more difficult because the new road to Mindo has broken it in several spots making through travel impossible. Ask in the town of Nanegalito on the new highway for directions to Nono.

DAY TRIPS NORTH OF QUITO

The landscape north of Quito is low and very dry. After leaving the sprawl of the city (Quito eventually does end!), the Pan-American Highway descends into the headwaters of the Río Guayllbamba that flows northwest toward Esmeraldas. The river valley, thanks to extensive irrigation, is a green oasis in a landscape of coarse, dry hills covered by low cactus and scraggly mesquite trees. As the Pan-American Highway climbs out of the low hills to the slopes of the Andes, the land becomes greener and friendlier. This is a region renowned in Ecuador for its cut flowers. Clusters of commercial greenhouses grow flowers for both national and international markets. If you have ever bought exotic tropical flowers at your local florist, they very well may have come from these greenhouses.

There are three sites north of Quito that make good destinations for day trips. The closest site is the monument marking the path of the equator, 20 minutes north of Quito. The second site is just beyond the equator monument on the ridge to the north, the Pululahua Geobotanical Reserve. The third site is two hours north of Quito, the famous Indian Market at Otavalo, claimed to be the largest Indian market in South America. Pululahua and the equator monument can easily be combined into a pleasant morning tour. Otavalo is also best done in the morning. All three sites are well known and easily accessible from Quito by public or private transportation.

The **Mitad del Mundo** is the monument that marks the closest point the equator passes to Quito. The equator is more than just a reason for another tourist site—in many ways the equator represents the very fiber from which all Ecuadorians are made. The native pride of an Ecuadorian is in part because Ecuador is defined as the country of the equator. Rather than a division between hemispheres, the naturally conciliatory Ecuadorians view the equator instead as a line that unites both halves of the world. Located just 30 minutes north of Quito, the equator is well worth a visit.

The equator has been well known and celebrated for centuries in Ecuador. Archaeological evidence indicates both pre-Incan and Incan civilizations recognized and worshiped the path of the equator as the marker of the equinox. The equinox occurs when the sun is directly over the equator. On this day, day and night are of equal length everywhere on Earth. This happens once in the spring, on or near March 21, and once in the autumn, on or near September 22. The equinox was important ceremonially to early civilizations because in spring it marked the time for planting and in autumn it marked the time for harvest. Equinox celebrations are still held by the indigenous people of Ecuador, and a big celebration occurs at the Equator Monument every spring and fall.

The first equator monument was erected in 1936. It marked the second centenary of the famous French–Spanish Geodesic Mission to Ecuador of 1736–1744. The object of this mission was to attempt to measure the shape of the Earth by determining the arc of a north–south line one degree of latitude in length, about 112 kilometers. At the time, the major scientific debate concerned whether the Earth was perfectly spherical or bulged at the poles or the equator. Without an accurate shape of the Earth, navigational maps would be frustratingly inaccurate. The measurements from Ecuador were then compared to a similar line in Lapland and it was conclusively determined that the Earth did indeed bulge around its middle. It is now known that the equator is 19 kilometers farther from the center of the Earth than are the poles.

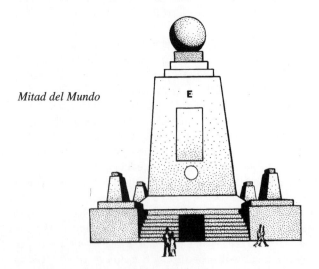

Mitad del Mundo

The only practical implications of this fact are for lovers of speed and dieters. Because of the rotation of the Earth, you are traveling at 1667 kilometers-per-hour here, faster than anywhere else on Earth and, because the pull of gravity is less on the equator (farther from the center of Earth's mass), you weigh less. Pass the cookies, fast!

In August 1979, the original monument was moved to the equator in the little town of **Calacalí**, 7 kilometers to the west of where it was. In its place a new equatorial monument was erected in 1982. This monument is much bigger and is the centerpiece for the development around the equator. The monument is 100 feet (30 meters) tall and topped by a metal globe 15 feet (4.5 meters) in diameter and weighing five tons. Underneath the globe is a balcony accessible by an interior elevator. The view from the balcony on a clear day is magnificent: to the east is Volcán Cayambe, 19,100 feet (5790 meters) high, and to the south Volcán Cotopaxi, 19,330 feet (5857 meters) high. Descent from the balcony is via a winding staircase that leads past interesting displays (all in Spanish) on the 18 different indigenous cultures of Ecuador. There are English-speaking guides available upon request.

Leading up to the monument is a wide promenade lined with large stone busts honoring the 13 men who contributed to the Geodesic Mission. Apparently, the sculptor did not have very good likenesses to work from because all the faces on the busts look the same. Due east of the monument, to the right of the promenade, is a touristy area styled after a typical Ecuadorian town with a church, plaza, bullfighting stadium, and workshops and stores selling souvenirs. Whatever you do, be sure to take the obligatory picture straddling the equator. There are more workshops selling items immediately to the north of the monument. To the north of the "town," across a dry streambed, is **INTY-NAN** (admission), an ethnographic museum with handicraft displays, archaeological exhibits and a shrunken head. Bilingual guides are present to explain the displays.

On the south side of the promenade is a cluster of four **international pavilions**—France, Spain, Germany and Ecuador—with displays and interpretive exhibits and a planetarium (admission). Next to the pavilions is an **exhibit hall** for the Fundación Quito Colonial. Inside is an amazing scaled replica of colonial Quito, hand built by Guido Falcony. The model is 26 feet by 33 feet (eight by ten meters) in size and has details such as iron railings, street lamps and curtained windows. Every 30 minutes a light show depicts a 24-hour period complete with sunrise and sunset, lighted windows and crowing roosters. There is a small entrance fee to see this incredible city model.

There are two Incan archaeological sites near Mitad del Mundo, Rumicucho and Cochasquí, but they are presently in disrepair and have no tourist facilities. There are plans to restore them, but the timetable is unclear. In the

very recent past, both ruins have been used for target practice by the Ecuadorian Air Force. A more interesting alternative is to visit the privately run
Solar Museum in the nearby town of San Antonio. The small museum was
built by and now also honors the work of Professor Luciano Andrade Marín
and is full of fascinating displays and artifacts pertaining to the equator. The
most important piece on display is a solar chronometer that shows the exact
astronomical time, day, month and season with the sun's shadow. Around the
museum, also built on the equator, are interesting plants that attract many
kinds of birds including 11 species of hummingbird. The museum is overseen
by Oswaldo Muñoz, President of Nuevo Mundo Tours, who was a close friend
of Professor Marín. Contact Nuevo Mundo Tours in Quito (2-527-577) for a
tour of this worthwhile museum.

Another place to visit near Mitad del Mundo is an **organic farm** just south
of the village of Calacalí past the little church of Rayocucho. By using 80
percent Indian methods and 20 percent modern technology, the growers are
able to maximize production and minimize effort. The goal of the farm is two-
fold: to grow pesticide-free vegetables, flower extracts and floral scents for
consumption in Quito, and to act as a demonstration farm for the local Indians.
The manager of the farm is Lawson Crichton, an earthy, expatriate Australian
who has lived and farmed in Ecuador for many years. Lawson calls Ecuador
a "privileged country. Every growing condition in the world can be matched
in Ecuador. What the world has in latitude, Ecuador has in altitude." He must
be doing something right on the farm, as he grew 3300 pounds of tomatoes
from two 25-cent packages of seed. With prior notice, guests can get a complete tour of the operation and a fresh-picked lunch. Contact Oswaldo Muñoz
at Nuevo Mundo Tours in Quito (2-527-577) for a tour of this interesting
operation.

GETTING THERE: By Bus: Buses to Mitad del Mundo leave the Avenida
America between Peréz Guerrero and Mariana de Jesús every 15 minutes and return to Quito on the same schedule. Plan to depart by midafternoon before the
clouds from the coast obscure the monument. To get to the old equator monument
in Calacalí, continue 7 kilometers past Mitad del Mundo over a low pass to the
village. The monument is in the center of the town plaza. There are two other small
monuments marking the equator in Ecuador. One is located on the Pan-American
Highway south of Cayambe (on a clear afternoon you can get the monument and
the snow-capped Volcán Cayambe in the same photo) and the other is on the coast
south of Pedernales.

By Car: Travel north out of Quito bearing left at the large highway signs for
Mitad del Mundo. The town of San Antonio is 22 kilometers north of Quito; the
monument is just west of town and cannot be missed from the road. The Incan
ruin of Rumicucho is a few kilometers north of San Antonio. Every taxi driver in

town knows where the monument is and will take you there for $20–$30. Many tour operators in Quito also have trips to the monument that usually include a bilingual guide and lunch.

The **Pululahua Geobotanical Reserve**, created in 1978, is a flat-bottomed, bowl-shaped valley 13 kilometers by 15 kilometers in size and 1980 feet (600 meters) deep. The boundary of the 8250-acre reserve traces the rim of an extinct volcanic caldera. There are two small hills in the center of the caldera rising 1320 feet (400 meters) above the valley floor. These hills are probably volcanic plugs or the corks in the volcano's throat. The valley floor is a patchwork of corn and sugarcane fields but its walls are too steep to farm and are still covered with native vegetation.

There are two ways to see the reserve. The easiest and most popular is to drive to the rim of the crater. From here, there are impressive morning views of the entire caldera. By the afternoon, the valley will be obscured by clouds from the Pacific Ocean. Notice the layers of volcanic sedimentation in the rock cut at the parking lot. There are solid layers and crumbly layers. The solid layers of rock are ancient lava flows. Closer examination of the crumbly layers will reveal lots of pieces of pumice. These pumice balls were violently tossed out of the volcano when it erupted. The holes in the pumice are from escaping bubbles of gas when the rock was still molten. Volcanologists call these rocks ejecta.

From this rimside parking lot there is a zigzagging trail that leads down to the valley floor. The trail runs mostly through native vegetation so there are great opportunities for birdwatching. The trail is also a great spot for butterflies. In fact, entomologists have recently discovered a new species of butterfly that lives only in the crater. Walking the trail takes about an hour to descend to the valley floor and about two hours to climb back up to the rim.

GETTING THERE: By Car: The Pululahua Geobotanical Reserve is located a few kilometers north of Mitad del Mundo on the road to Calacalí. A large roadside sign marks the obvious turn up to the rim of the crater. We are not sure what those large panels on the skyline are. We have been told they are cloud catchers to collect water, old billboards, military antennas or landing signals for space ships —you decide! To drive into the crater, cross the pass to the little town of Calacalí and take an unmarked right turn on the dirt road into the crater. This road can be very rough, so we suggest a high-clearance vehicle. Ask for directions in Calacalí to find the road into the crater.

The **Otavalo Market** in the town of Otavalo (for more on the town of Otavalo, see Chapter Seven) is the best-known Ecuadorian attraction to gringos, outside of the Galápagos Islands. The market has been around for at least 4000 years as the social and economic center of the northern highlands.

Before tourists descended upon the sleepy town, all kinds of goods and produce passed through Indian hands at Otavalo. Chickens, guinea pigs, cows, horses, birds, sheep, vegetables, grains, fruits from the coast and Oriente, pottery, hand tools, shawls, shoes, beads, mats, ropes and saddles were just some of the items brought to and bartered for at the market. Today, all these things are found in the market plus handicrafts for tourists—such as woven rugs, shirts, wall hangings, bags, paintings, clay figurines, carved wooden animals, musical instruments, cassettes, jewelry, Panamá hats and leather purses, vests, coats, satchels, bags and belts (we are sure we forgot more than we remembered).

The best time to go to the market is as early in the morning as possible. The earlier you go, the more local people you will see and the more you will be able to learn about their ways. The animal market, located just north of the bridge over the Pan-American Highway, is over by 8 a.m. so if you want to see the bartering you have to arrive early. If you cannot find it along the Pan-American Highway, it is probably already over. The Saturday market is the most popular for tourists. The buses from Quito arrive around 10 a.m., so if you do not want to see many gringos, get your shopping done early. The prices of goods at the market are not much different than you might find in Quito or Cuenca or any other tourist spot. You go to this market for the atmosphere, not to find bargains. Negotiating for a better price is okay to a point but do not argue over a few dollars just for the sport of it. These people are trying to make a living, not to entertain you. Beware of pickpockets on the crowded streets of the market. There is nothing like a preoccupied, camera-toting, bag-carrying gringo in sensible shoes to make a thief happy. Pockets in backpacks can be sliced open and fannypack straps cut without your having the slightest idea what is happening. Wear a light windbreaker to cover your "carry-on" or carry only what you can control with one hand. The object is to be both inconspicuous and more trouble than the other tourists.

Although every day is market day in Otavalo, Saturday is the largest market. Wednesday is the smallest, but every day the famous *otavaleño* weavings are on display and for sale. On Saturday, the market is huge. It extends for 10 to 12 blocks on three parallel streets in the middle of town. If you cannot find the market, you are in the wrong town. There are sections within the market for housewares, leather goods, textiles, food, produce and animals, but they interblend so much there is no real beginning nor end to each part. The housewares are generally to the south end of the market near the large church and plaza (the best place to meet if you get separated from your group). The famous *otavaleño* textiles are mostly in a plaza on the north end of the market. This textile plaza is the heart of the market and where you will always find vendors every day of the week. Food is on the north side of the market, on the northern edge of the textile plaza.

The food market mostly offers vegetables, fruits and grains, although you probably will not recognize most of what you see. The colors, textures and shapes of the fruits and vegetables are fantastic—leathery greens, sweet yellows, dripping pinks and screaming reds. There are also all kinds of bags and boxes of grains and bundles of fresh-cut herbs for cooking and medicinal use. At lunchtime, the sounds and smells of frying potatoes, grinding flour, butchered meat and roasting chickens can be almost overwhelming. There are times when a part of the market smells better the faster and farther you walk. If you see the food is freshly and thoroughly cooked, it is probably safe to eat.

GETTING THERE: By Bus: There are several bus companies that have regular daily service to Otavalo from Quito. The bus companies Transportes Otavalo and Transportes Los Lagos take you into town near the market. Most of the others drop you off on the Pan-American Highway, forcing you to walk about ten minutes into the market. Buses cost about $2 for the one-way trip and take between two and three hours. Many Quito tour companies offer one- or two-day trips to Otavalo for a reasonable price and a comfortable ride.

By Car: Otavalo is located on the Pan-American Highway about 100 kilometers north of Quito. The loop via Tabacundo is also paved, but offers much more spectacular scenery than the main highway. It takes about two hours to get to Otavalo by car. The Pan-American Highway wraps around Otavalo on its west side; the market is about half a kilometer to the east and then south of the highway. Parking can be a problem if you arrive late in the morning. Otherwise, you should not have much trouble finding a place to park just by cruising the streets surrounding the market. If you are staying in a nearby hotel, taxis are very reasonably priced to take you to and from the market. To find a taxi at the market, go to the south end of the market to the plaza opposite the church.

SEVEN

The Northern Highlands

The highlands north of Quito are lower in elevation, warmer and less harsh than the highlands south of Quito. Only one snow-capped volcano, Mt. Cayambe (19,107 feet/5790 meters), dominates the skyline, and it is farther away from the highway than those to the south along the famous "Avenue of the Volcanoes." The hills and ridges west of Cayambe are rounded and rolling and are dotted with lakes, leading some to call this area Ecuador's lake district. The region is famous for its weavings, leather craft, embroidery and woodworking. All these factors, combined with its proximity to Quito, make the northern highlands the most visited mainland region by tourists in Ecuador.

MINDO

Sixty-seven kilometers northwest of Quito is the small agrarian community of Mindo. Located in an isolated pocket valley surrounded by tall forested ridges, Mindo is known locally as the "Valley of Eternal Spring." Bathed by the waters of the Río Mindo, the fertile valley has a long history of producing fruits and vegetables for the markets of Quito. It was colonized in 1582, mostly by Europeans, and by the early 1700s the local farmers were transporting sugarcane, yuca, coffee, cacao, bananas and dairy products on mule and horseback to Quito. Today, Mindo is recognized as the "land of the *guayaba*" because of the many orchards in the area that grow this tropical fruit. Mindo remained relatively isolated until 1977 when the first good road to it was finished. Now a paved highway roars past just 8 kilometers away, and Quito is less than a two-hour trip by car.

To naturalists, Mindo is gaining a wide reputation as a wonderful and productive locale from which to explore the nearby tracts of untouched forest. Large, undisturbed forests are becoming increasingly rare west of the Andes.

Scientists think only 5 percent of the original forest remains on the western slope of Ecuador's Andes. Because the area around Mindo has long been difficult to get to, there is still much primary forest. In fact, Mindo is surrounded by forest on three sides. To the south and east of Mindo, the forested ridges are part of the Río Mindo watershed. To the west, the forests are drained by the Río Nambillo. These two watersheds encompass the 48,000 acres "Mindo–Nambillo Protected Forest" administered by the Friends of Nature of Mindo, a private conservation organization based in Mindo. It is a region of incredible richness, with over 400 species of birds (including the flashy Cock-of-the-Rock), hundreds of kinds of orchids, Puma, howler monkeys and countless butterflies. The life zones range from low, humid subtropical forests to higher cloud forests and up to the crowning high-elevation paramo. This forest, combined with the 35,000 acres of protected forest of the Maquipucuna Biological Reserve abutting to the north, is one of the largest expanses of native forest on the west slope of the Ecuadorian Andes.

Mindo is a sleepy little village with only a few tourist facilities geared for gringos. (Just outside the village, however, there is one nice ecotourist lodge.) The village is four by three blocks, and what activity there is can be found along the main street. Within the town center itself there are no places to stay that we can recommend, but a few places do offer rooms if you are stuck; all range in price from $3 to $10. Try the **Guadual Inn** or the **Hosteria Bijao**, both just as you enter the village. There are no formal restaurants in Mindo, but there are a few typical small street cafés where you can get a good meal. The **Salon Noroccidental** at the north side of the square has been recommended, as has the **Restaurante Omarcito** on the main street. The **Abarrotes Elenita** is the most complete store for supplies and food in Mindo, but it is very limited, so do not rely on it for your supplies.

LODGING   Outside the village of Mindo is the ✪✪ **Hosteria El Carmelo de Mindo** (in Quito, Avenido Foch 769 and Amazonas, 2nd floor; private bath, hot water; $30–$50; 2-224-713, fax: 2-295-831; e-mail: hcarmelo@ uio.satnet.net) and it is a good place to stay. The hosteria is located almost half a mile northwest of the village on 80 acres of orange and *guayaba* orchards, pastures and secondary forest. Turn left at the sign on main street on the road past the community swimming pool and then left again up the driveway at a small sign to a tall bamboo thicket at the hosteria's parking area. From the parking area, the open-air restaurant, reception area and a few rooms are to the left. To the right, across a small lawn, are six A-frame cabins for guests. The A-frames have three beds (one queen-sized downstairs and two twins in the loft). They are large enough for a family or a group of friends, and they are clean and attractive. The grounds are thickly planted with fruiting trees and shrubs, and flower gardens surround all the buildings.

It has a restaurant that serves all meals and is usually good. There are also campsites ($2 per person) available for backpackers.

The hosteria opened for guests in late 1994, but it has been the longtime residence of the López family. The owner, Señor Washington López, has always been interested in nature. Now that he manages the property, he is actively planting native trees and letting pastures go wild to make them more natural and attractive for wildlife. There are guides available (English-, German- and Spanish-speaking) to take you up into the Mindo–Nambillo Forest or to show you around the valley. A favorite hike in the forest begins early in the morning to visit a Cock-of-the-Rock lek (mating ground), followed by a walk back down the road to the hosteria for a late lunch.

If you are going to overnight in Mindo, the newly re-opened ❂❂ **Mindo Garden** lodge (private bath, hot water; $70 per person per night, meals included; in Quito: República de El Salvador 1084 and Naciones Unidos, Edificio Mansión Blanca, Office 12, 2-252-488, 2-252-489; e-mail: casablan@ uio.satnet.net or in the U.S. contact Neblina Forest 800-538-2149) is our favorite place to stay. This lodge is located 4 kilometers from the village square on the banks of the beautiful Río Mindo. Take the main street through town and turn right at the "T" in the road at the plaza near the south end of town. You will quickly come to a small stream that can be forded easily (except in March when it occasionally turns into a dangerous and deep river). Follow the rough road that turns south up the valley and continue past a "Y" taking the left fork. After another 3 kilometers you come to the parking lot and wooden arches that mark the entrance into Mindo Garden. The bridge that continues over the Río Mindo here leads to the beginning of the Mindo–Nambilla Forest Reserve.

Mindo Garden is situated on 55 acres of mostly primary forest squeezed between the top of the steep hill across the road and the verdant banks of the Río Mindo. The main building with kitchen, restaurant/common room, reception area, restrooms and game room is 55 yards off the road along a pretty garden path lined by bunches of impatiens and poinsettia. From the gardens around the main building a path leads back along the forest river bank to three thatched-roof chalets. The chalets are widely placed and surrounded by thick forest, so each is private. On the first floor is an outdoor porch, (shoes must be removed before entering any of the buildings, so make sure you don't have any embarrassing holes in your socks), entry and a very large bedroom with a king-size bed, a twin-bed and a private bath. Upstairs are two smaller but also very comfortable bedrooms, each with a queen-size bed and private bath. The large screened and glass windows invite gazing out on the forest and make you feel like you are sleeping outside. The rooms are extremely clean, well-maintained and attractive. Two of the chalets are located on the banks of the

Northern Highlands

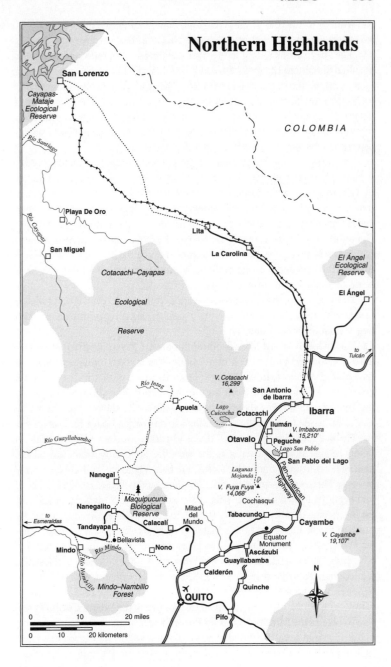

San Lorenzo

Cayapas-
Mataje
Ecological
Reserve

Río Santiago

COLOMBIA

Playa De Oro

Río Cayapas

San Miguel

Lita

La Carolina

El Ángel
Ecological
Reserve

El Ángel

Cotacachi–Cayapas

Ecological

Reserve

to
Tulcán

Río Intag

V. Cotacachi
16,299'

San Antonio
de Ibarra

Apuela

*Lago
Cuicocha*

Cotacachi

Ibarra

Ilumán

V. Imbabura
15,210'

Río Guayllabamba

Otavalo

Peguche

Lago San Pablo

San Pablo del Lago

Nanegal

*Lagunas
Mojanda*

V. Fuya Fuya
14,068'

Cochasquí

Pan-American Highway

Maquipucuna
Biological
Reserve

Mitad
del
Mundo

Nanegalito

to
Esmeraldas

Tandayapa

Calacalí

Tabacundo

Cayambe

V. Cayambe
19,107'

Bellavista

Mindo

Río Mindo

Nono

Equator
Monument

Ascázubi

Río Nambillo

Mindo–Nambillo
Forest

Guayllabamba

Calderón

Quinche

N

QUITO

Pifo

0   10   20 miles

0   10   20 kilometers

Río Mindo, so the roar of the river (loud enough to drown out the snores of a nearby companion) is constant. At the chalet farthest downstream, there is a wonderful flat rock sitting in the river—a great spot to relax and watch the peculiar Sunbittern, a cross between a small heron and a pheasant, stalking its prey on the forest floor and river edge. The other chalet is also surrounded by forest but is farther away from the river so it is quieter. The main administrative building has a covered porch that is cantilevered out over the river if you want an alternative place for reverie or watching the antics of white-headed Dipper birds walking in and out of the rushing water.

The forest around the grounds of the lodge is enchanting and full of intriguing plants and animals. For the more adventuresome, there are a number of trails that lead into the forest from the lodge. Most of them loop up toward the crest of the hills and are moderately steep in places, but nowhere as steep and demanding as the trails on the other side of the river in the Mindo–Nambillo Reserve. To enter the reserve on the other side of the river, a nominal fee of $1.50 can be paid to the administrator at the Mindo Garden office. A butterfly farm and viewing building is another attraction 1 kilometer back down the road toward Mindo. It also costs $1.50.

The service and food at this lodge are excellent, and even if you aren't a reverent bird watcher or wildlife photographer, relaxing in this natural setting is incredibly cozy and fulfilling.

The ✪✪ **Friends of Mindo–Nambillo Forest Riverside Shelter** for naturalists is located 4 kilometers from Mindo. Ask in town for directions to the now-closed Mindo Gardens Lodge. From there cross the bridge and walk downstream along a well-worn trail to the shelter. From Mindo the trail is mostly flat, and it takes about an hour to walk to the shelter. You should be able to get a ride to the trailhead near the Mindo Garden Lodge for a small fee.

The shelter is an open-sided, thatched-roofed wooden building with an outhouse just uphill. Upstairs is the sleeping area; downstairs are tables, benches and a small but fully stocked kitchen. There are no lights, showers or beds. There are sleeping pads for the floor, and you can use the kitchen if you bring your own supplies. This is a great place for birdwatchers and forest lovers who do not mind camp-style living because they are surrounded by primary forest and several trails that lead away into the forest from the shelter. With prior arrangement, you can hire a cook or a guide to make your stay a bit easier. It costs $25 per person, per day, for a guide with lodging, less just for lodging. To make reservations in Quito, contact Señora María Guerrero (Friends of Mindo–Nambillo Forest, P.O. Box 17-03-1673; 2-455-907), or in Mindo stop by the office on the main street and ask for Señora Cecilia Perez.

To hike in the **Mindo–Nambillo Forest**, a trail starts at the southeast corner of the main square in Mindo and goes past a yellow house where a minimal entrance fee is collected to walk on this private land. The first part of this trail crosses through pastures and secondary woodlots. About 1 kilometer from the square, you come to the forest. The trail eventually peters out but not until it traverses a nice part of the forest. Several other trails start near the Friends of Mindo–Nambillo Forest Shelter on the Río Mindo. If you do not have a compass or tend to become disoriented, hire a guide.

There are two advertised naturalist guides in Mindo. The best seems to be **Vinicio Perez**. Look for his sign directing you to his home as you enter town, or just ask where he might be found. A couple of blocks down the street is the sign for **Fundación Pacaso & Pacaso**, the other guiding service in Mindo. Opposite this sign is the office for the Friends of Mindo–Nambillo Forest (Amigos de Bosque Protector de Mindo–Nambillo). Stop in for the best information (in Spanish) on where to go and what to see. If you plan to go into the forest, you will have to pay a small entrance fee here ($5) and get the key to the gate at the end of the road. You can easily go into the forest without paying, but don't. This is a good organization that is actively protecting the forest, as well as conducting environmental education programs for the nearby communities; it is well worth your support. If you are impressed with the forest and want to help their efforts to protect it, stop by their office on your way out and give them a contribution.

You can drive to the ridge that separates the Río Mindo and the Río Nambillo if you have a four-wheel-drive vehicle and the road is not washed out or too wet (always a possibility). Take the road from the southwest corner of the square and continue across the stream ford. At the "Y," take the right arm and cross on the bridge over the Río Mindo. This road eventually climbs up to the high watershed ridge and enters the Mindo–Nambillo Forest. There are several trails that you will see leading from this road once you are on top of the ridge, although none of them are marked and there are not any maps of the area. The first trail on the east (left as you head uphill) leads steeply down the slope to the left and eventually to the Río Mindo near the Friends of Mindo–Nambillo Forest Shelter. A bit farther up the ridge another trail cuts off to the west or right as you head uphill. This trail leads steeply down to the Río Nambillo and then shortly to a well-known Cock-of-the-Rock lek. The lek is most active early in the morning and then late in the afternoon. You are very unlikely to find the lek and very likely to become lost on one of the many side trails here unless you have a guide with you who knows the way. At night and early in the morning, Oilbirds can be found feeding on fruits in this area. They are the only bird species known to use clicking noises to echo-locate their positions. They use this ability to navigate in total darkness as well as find their way into and out of the caves in which they nest.

Where this trail crosses the Río Nambillo, it is perhaps as close to tropical forest paradise as we have ever seen in Ecuador. The river flows in a tumbling watery chord over short cascades through a lush, verdant canyon

Mountain toucan

of tall trees draped with hanging vines and hemmed with a thick leafy border. Calls of birds filter through drooping leaves as a mist lingers amongst the limbs overhead. In the air, the sweet aroma of nectar mixes with the damp musk of the leaf mulch on the forest floor. We visited last during a sunny downpour when every raindrop in the forest glistened in the afternoon light—an experience we will not soon forget.

GETTING THERE: By Bus: There is regular bus service between Mindo and Quito by the Cooperativa San Pedro de Cayambe. A bus leaves daily from Quito for Mindo at 3:30 p.m. and leaves Mindo for Quito at 6:30 a.m. Friday through Sunday an additional bus leaves from Quito to Mindo at 6:30 a.m. and leaves Mindo for Quito at 2:30 p.m. It takes about two and a half hours to get to Mindo by bus from Quito. There is also bus service between Santo Domingo and Mindo leaving Santo Domingo at 2 p.m. and returning from Mindo at 4:30 p.m. Be sure to reconfirm these ever-changing times.

By Car: The best way to get to Mindo is from Quito on the paved highway via Mitad del Mundo, Calacalí and Nanegalito. The well-marked left (south) turn to Mindo is just past the little town of Santa Rosa. It is then 8 kilometers downhill from the main highway to Mindo on a mostly cobblestone road. Without stops, it takes roughly two hours to drive to Mindo from Quito. You can also take the old road through the village of Nono to get to Mindo. This route is much more scenic and you are more likely to see wildlife than on the new paved road, but it is a rough dirt road and prone to washouts and landslides, so the trip can unexpectedly turn into an unwelcome adventure if your timing happens to be bad. It takes about four hours to get to Mindo via Nono.

Built in 1995 and an ideal addition to any trip to the Mindo area is the ✪✪ **Bellavista Reserve Lodge** (some private baths, one shared hot-water shower; $43 to $50 per person, per night, including meals; cellular phone: 9-490-891, in Quito, phone/fax: 2-224-469; Casilla, 17-12-103; e-mail: aecie3 @ecnet.ec). The private reserve comprises 1500 acres of surrounding land that includes a mixture of primary- and secondary-forested slopes at an elevation of 5000 to 7000 feet. The plants and animals at this altitude are quite different from those down around the town of Mindo. Hundreds of species of high cloud-forest birds abound here. Five kilometers of trails lead through various habitats and make for easy access to the forest and its denizens.

The lodge consists of a tall, circular building built on a forested ridge. A bar and dining room take up the first floor. A wraparound porch lets you look out in all directions over the forest top and into the neighboring valley. Several hummingbird feeders hang over the porch and attract large hummingbirds like Buff-tailed Coronet, Collared Inca and Gorgeted Sunangel. As these spectacular birds come hovering into the feeders, it is often easy to forget the bands of tanagers and toucanets feeding in the treetops below you. On the paths around the lodge more species of orchids, bromeliads and unusual plants abound than you can imagine. Don't forget to bring along fast film (ASA of at least 400) and a strobe flash to make the plant colors obvious. This is a cloud forest, and full sunshine can be expected only in the morning and even then not very often.

On the second floor of the lodge are five large and very comfortable pie-shaped rooms for three people, each with private baths and balconies attached. On the third floor is a general sleeping area with mattresses and a single, shared bathroom. The top floor is only for the spry and athletic as it is reached by a very steep ladder. Here there are also mattresses for sleeping but no bathroom (the bathroom on the third floor below is shared). The view, however, makes up for these few deprivations. A two-story cabin for groups of up to eight was recently completed. It has private baths, balconies and large bedrooms on both floors. This cabin is a kilometer from the main compound, so most guests staying here will need their own vehicle to get to the main dining room for meals. The food is principally vegetarian, and the cook uses many vegetables from the lodge's own garden. A nearby area is available for camping, and several tents can be rented.

The owner-operators of the lodge are an English ex-pat, Richard Parsons, and his Colombian wife, Gloria. Besides being a professor of intercultural communication, Richard speaks fluent French, German and Spanish, as well as the Queen's English. Together with friends, he promotes scientific and conservation research on the reserve. Richard and Gloria are also active in promoting "Friends of Bellavista," a conservation enterprise to buy and protect more land and to promote environmental education among the local colonists. Some "Friends" have decided to buy adjacent land and participate directly in conserving this fast-dwindling habitat. For more details contact the Parsons directly.

GETTING THERE: By Bus: Take one of the buses going to the coast from Quito via the Mitad del Mundo–Puerto Quito highway and get off at the small town of Nanegalito. Contact Don Jorgé Bermudez in the grocery store "Viveres Patty." He will take you the 15 kilometers up to Bellavista for $15.

By Car: From Avenida Occidental in the northern part of Quito, take the road to Nono and continue past it to the town of Tandayapa. Here, turn left at the "T" in the middle of the village and drive 6 more kilometers to Bellavista. Alternatively, take the paved highway from Mitad del Mundo toward the coast. Just after the last bridge before the town of Nanegalito (at Km. 32 on the paved highway), take the gravel road to the left beside a former military camp. Continue up this road about 15 minutes to the village of Tandayapa. Drive straight through the village heading uphill 6 more kilometers to Bellavista, almost at the crest of the mountain. You will see the sign and arch on the right indicating Bellavista. Park inside the gate. There are alternative routes. Because rain storms and mud slides often make it difficult to get there, it is best to contact the lodge for up-to-date directions.

MAQUIPUCUNA BIOLOGICAL RESERVE

The Maquipucuna Biological Reserve is located just north of Mindo on the western slope of the Andes. Despite its proximity to Quito, the area remains mostly isolated from the rush of development due to the complex topography of the region. The reserve is a 10,000-acre jumble of very steep ridges and deep valleys within the headwaters of the Río Guayllabamba. An additional 25,000-acre protected buffer zone surrounds the reserve. This biologically rich and ecologically rare intact forest includes a variety of life zones from low-elevation (3300 feet/1000 meters) subtropical forests to high-elevation (9900 feet/3000 meters) cloud forests. Ninety-five percent of the reserve is primary forest, while the remainder is secondary forest edges and overgrown pastures.

The reserve is managed by the Fundación Maquipucuna (Baquerizo 238 and Tamayo, Casilla 17-12-167, Quito; fax: 2-507-201), an extremely professional and effective conservation organization whose president, Sr. Rodrigo Ontaneda, is an enthusiastic and tireless worker. The goals of this foundation are manyfold: to purchase and protect the area's forests, to conduct and support scientific research, to promote environmental education in the local communities, to practice sound ecotourism and to involve the local communities in ecologically sustainable economic development. This is one of the best conservation foundations in Ecuador and is worthy of your support, either by a visit to the reserve or by a contribution.

The ✪✪✪ **Maquipucuna Biological Reserve Lodge** (shared bath, hot water; $45; fax: 2-507-201, write to Baquerizo 238 and Tamayo, Casilla 17-12-167, Quito) was finished in early 1995. It is a rustic but very attractive wood and bamboo building with a thatched roof that blends nicely into its surroundings. A small generator provides electricity every evening from 6 p.m. to 10 p.m. On the ground floor is a reception area, dining room and kitchen. Upstairs is a common room with a big wood-slab bar, a central fireplace and three bedrooms, above which is a small sleeping loft. Each bedroom has a bunk bed and a twin bed, screened windows and a place to hang clothing.

Bedding is available but in limited supply, so bring a sleeping bag or some blankets. The men's and women's bathrooms are in a separate but attached building where there are hot-water showers, sinks and flush toilets. The entire building is designed with open sides that look out over the river and nearby forest. Pull up a chair to almost any view and you could enjoy quite a list of sights. Our favorite is the balcony on the top floor that overlooks a bank of trees where toucans, quetzals and even Cocks-of-the-Rock are seen feeding on fruit. Local men who work at the reserve are available for hire as guides ($10/day).

The lodge sits at the base of a hill that was once part of a farm, but which is now quickly returning to the forest. Immediately upstream from the lodge is a self-guiding nature trail. The trail starts as a boardwalk through a patch of riverside forest. It continues as a trail through overgrown pastures and secondary woodlots before returning to the lodge. It takes about an hour to walk this loop if you are wearing blinders or at least two hours if you are looking for wildlife and flowering plants. Another trail leads to an old road that climbs the short hill in back of the lodge and then heads back to the primary forest in the heart of the reserve. Along this road were once four other farms, but they were bought by the foundation. The pastures are now filling with dense stands of heliconia, shrubby thickets and trees from the forest edge as they reclaim lost territory. This disturbed forest is alive with wrens, hummingbirds and flocks of foraging birds, especially in the early morning. This place is also a good one to look for hawks perched on open limbs waiting for a meal to run or fly by.

About a 45-minute walk from the lodge is the beginning of the primary forest. Steadily climbing, the trail leads through a beautiful tall forest with hanging lianas to a lush, green cloud forest of bromeliads, orchids and mossy limbs. To get to the cloud forest from the lodge requires considerable effort and a long day. The forest along the way is very wild, and you have a chance to see many exotic birds such as Toucan-Barbet and Golden-headed Quetzal. There is a shelter for backpackers along this trail as well, and you could arrange to stay a night or two and really explore this forest. The foundation has plans for another shelter for backpackers in the forest and three canopy platforms to provide views to the treetops. If you are out on the trails during the quiet midday and there is not much animal activity, there are some Incan ruins and remnants of an Inca Trail that you can visit. Ask your guide to show you these well-hidden bits of the past.

GETTING THERE: By Bus: There is a bus that leaves Quito every day at 12:30 p.m. that goes to Nanegalito and then to Nanegal. From Nanegal, you will either have to walk or hire a local driver to take you the rest of the way. The bus takes about three hours to get to Nanegal, and it is about another two hours to walk from there to the lodge.

By Car: Even though the Maquipucuna Biological Reserve is so close to Quito, the drive there is long and rigorous. Head north out of Quito on the new road toward Mindo. At the little town of Nanegalito, turn right (north) to Nanegal. Nanegalito is a popular lunch stop for truckers, and there are several street cafés and stores if you want to buy supplies or eat a meal. There also is a regional medical clinic in Nanegalito. From Nanegal, go 12 kilometers and turn right again toward the fish hatchery. This turn has a small sign indicating Maquipucuna. The road past the fish hatchery curves right and ascends an increasingly narrow valley. As you climb this valley, the road steadily deteriorates. During the rainy season, from January to April, this road may be impassable to passenger cars. Eight kilometers from Maquipicuna and the fish hatchery, the road ends at a covered bridge over the Río Guayllabamba. Maquipucuna's new lodge is just across the bridge on the other side of the river.

The entire trip takes between three and four hours by car depending on the condition of the roads and whether or not you have to walk part of the way if your car cannot make it. Ironically, the forested slopes to the right (north) of the highway as soon as the road crosses the divide west of the town of Calacalí are part of the Maquipucuna Biological Reserve. So close to Quito, but so far because there is no way to get to those slopes. In talking with Sr. Rodrigo Ontaneda, he assured us that the rough road into the lodge was going to be improved and that there were plans to someday build an access road to a visitors center much closer to Quito on the new road to Mindo. Even if you plan to visit Maquipucuna Biological Reserve before these improvements are finished, you will not be disappointed. Set aside a day to get to the lodge so you can take your time and explore the countryside.

CALDERÓN TO CAYAMBE

The Pan-American Highway north of Quito soon drops into the fertile Guayllabamba river valley. Just outside the northern sprawl of Quito is the small town of **Calderón**. This sleepy village is known for its bread-dough figurines and is a popular stop for tourist buses headed north. The shops selling the figurines are along the main street in town and are hard to miss.

Because the Río Guayllabamba valley is at a lower altitude than Quito, many fruits and vegetables can grow here that are otherwise difficult to cultivate in the highlands. You will recognize apples, oranges, extra-large avocados and little, dark pears in the roadside stands. What you will probably not recognize is a large green fruit with dark geometric markings that looks like a cross between an artichoke and a billiard ball. This is a chirimoya, grown particularly in the area around the little village of Guayllabamba. You eat it by cutting through the hard skin to the large, black seeds and creamy white pulp inside. The seeds are not edible but the pulp has a pleasant, delicate flavor. This native Ecuadorian fruit is now widely marketed throughout the world and is becoming easier to find in your local grocery store.

Three kilometers beyond the village of Guayllabamba, the Pan-American Highway forks. Both ways lead to Cayambe about 30 kilometers ahead. The left fork leads away from civilization through a very dry, desertlike landscape of small cacti and scrubby acacia. This route is a bit longer but faster, so it is the better route to take if you are in a hurry to get north. This road crosses the equator but there is no sign indicating where. Along the way the only tourist sight is the ruins of **Cochasquí**. The ruins are north of the little village of Tabacundo—turn left toward Tocachi before you get to Tabacundo. The ruins were built by the Cara Indians before the Incas arrived and, until recently, were mostly forgotten. There are 15 low, truncated, flat-topped pyramids with long ramps leading up to them. It was long thought that they represented works in progress, probably a fortress, but recent studies have shown that the structures are precisely aligned astronomically so the ruins are now thought to be more ceremonial in nature. Interestingly, the level at which these pyramids are cut is about the same level of the ceremonial rooms inside the pyramids in Egypt. Unfortunately, there is very little on-site interpretive information for the visitor. Local guides can sometimes be found to take you around and explain the history of these fascinating and mysterious ruins. There is no entrance fee and the guides are underpaid, so if you have a good tour be sure to tip them.

The right fork goes from town to town through the heavily irrigated farming country around the town of Cayambe. Just a few kilometers down the road is the turnoff to the right (south) that leads to a wandering route back to Quito. Along the way is the little village of **Quinche**, well known for its ornate church and the Virgin of Quinche. The church's walls are lined with pictures depicting the miracles attributed to the Virgin. This is a popular spot for *quiteños* to come to get the Virgin's blessing on everything from a new car to a new child. If you continue past Quinche the road eventually leads to Pifo on the main road to the Oriente from Quito. A right turn at Pifo will take you back to Quito. Back on the Pan-American Highway heading north, just before the town of Cayambe, the highway crosses the equator. The spot is marked by a **monument** that is not nearly as impressive as the one at Mitad del Mundo, but it is also less crowded and touristy. All the required photos of people straddling the hemispheres or "walking the line" can be taken here so if you are not an equatorphile, this is a convenient place to quickly "do" the equator.

Just beyond this marker for the equator and on the east side of the highway is the entrance to the **Hosteria Guachalá** (Panamericana Norte, Kilometer 70; private bath, hot water, $30–$45; 2-363-042, fax: 2-362-426). This authentic hacienda was converted to a hotel in 1993 and combines modern amenities with traditional architecture. The buildings are constructed of rammed earth with terra cotta tile roofs. A swimming pool, bar and 24-hour restaurant are tastefully woven into a compound of buildings, gardens and fields that emote tranquility and the mystery of Incas and Spanish conquistadores who walked these very paths 400 years ago. The 21 rooms are arranged around an open patio, and their clean and tasteful furnishings will give you an idea of what it was like to visit a working hacienda in the early part of the century yet with modern facilities. The view of nearby Volcán Cayambe on a clear morning is worth the stay alone. You can also rent horses ($5 per hour) and explore much of the area.

The town of **Cayambe** is about 34 kilometers from Quito and 32 kilometers from Otavalo. There is not much for the tourist to see here but it is a good spot to pick up some local cheese and dairy products, for which the area is known. These make good snacks while you are wandering the Otavalo market later or a refreshing ice-cream stop on your return trip back to Quito. Volcán Cayambe, Ecuador's third-highest mountain, is immediately east of the town of Cayambe but it is hidden from view behind low foothills. In case anyone asks you, the south flank of Volcán Cayambe is the highest point through which the equator crosses—about 15,180 feet (4600 meters).

The Pan-American Highway north of Cayambe continues through rich agricultural land dotted with dairy farms and impressive greenhouses. These greenhouses grow magnificent flowers for flower shops and homes around the world. Access inside the greenhouses is difficult but with a bit of persistence you can probably find a grower who will let you wander around and see the operation.

GETTING THERE: By Bus: There is frequent bus service between Quito and Otavalo that stops in Cayambe. Most buses leave from Quito's *terminal terrestre* on Maldonado 3077. Alternatively, you can also wave a bus down that is going north along the Pan-American Highway and ask to be dropped off at Cayambe.

By Car: Cayambe is 70 kilometers north of Quito on the Pan-American Highway.

OTAVALO

Continuing north, the town of Otavalo is located in a valley between two extinct volcanoes. To the east is Volcán Imbabura (15,210 feet/4609 meters) and to the west is Ecuador's eleventh highest mountain, Volcán Cotacachi (16,299 feet/4939 meters). The vast Cayambe–Coca Ecological Reserve, which stretches from the Río Quijos in the Oriente south to Papallacta Pass and then east to just outside the town of Cayambe, reaches its northern limit in the high foothills due east of Otavalo. The Pan-American Highway runs through this valley north to the provincial capital city of Ibarra. The highway crests a small rise a few kilometers south of Otavalo from which the lush valley of Otavalo and the town can be seen ahead. At the head of this valley is the large Lago San Pablo, a lake that the highway passes to the west. As you descend the hill toward the lake, a road cuts off to the right (east) to the small village of San Pablo del Lago and the well-known Hosteria Cusín. On the western edge of the lake you will pass Hosteria Puertolago, another very nice place to stay or catch a meal while in the area. (For more on both of these, see lodging listings later in this section.)

The Pan-American Highway bypasses the town of Otavalo to the west before heading north toward Ibarra. On the south side are two entrances into town. The first right (north) turn, at the large gas station, is Calle Atahualpa. This street leads north as it crosses the east side of town before turning west, now Calle Quito, and intersecting the Pan-American Highway again. The second right turn off the Pan-American Highway is Calle Bolívar, which heads through the heart of Otavalo, two blocks to the west of Calle Atahualpa, before blending into the Pan-American Highway on the north end of Otavalo. One block west of Calle Bolívar is Calle Sucre. The Otavalo Indian market is centered on Calle Sucre in the middle of town.

Most people who visit Otavalo come to see the famous Indian market (for more on the market, see Chapter Six), the largest and most economically important market in South America. The market is roughly centered around poncho plaza, on the corner of Calles Sucre and Salinas, but it almost always spills more or less onto the surrounding streets. Poncho plaza is where most of the weavings and Indian cloth work can be found. Besides the market, there are plenty of stores where you can find souvenirs and handicrafts. Many people who go to the market on Saturday do not even realize there are stores in Otavalo because the vendors' booths hide them from passersby.

Most tourists who come to Otavalo do so on buses from Quito. While this is an efficient way to see the market, you will see very little of the town and none of the surrounding countryside. Also, all these buses generally arrive in Otavalo at about the same time, around 10 o'clock in the morning, so you have little chance of seeing the market without gringos everywhere. The best time to visit any Indian market is as early in the morning as you can get there. By midmorning, many of the locals have conducted their business and have left. Try to arrive by 7 a.m. if you want to see the market for what it really is—a social and economic gathering place for the region's Indians.

The *otavaleños* are attractive people of typical Andean features and stature. The young children have wide, engaging faces with dark, opal eyes and shy smiles. The elders have faces lost in a crush of wrinkles and bent bodies from years of heavy hauling. Perhaps the most noticeable are the women, who seem to be everywhere, doing all the buying, selling and hauling away. The men, when they can be found, are most often seen lost in conversation, hard at work leaning on a fender or wildly gesturing. The women dress in long dark skirts, sometimes with colorful hems, and beautiful white blouses decorated with bright embroidery. They have layers of golden beads around their necks and wrists and many do not wear shoes (so that they may be in contact with *Pachamama* or Mother Earth). They all are wrapped in long black shawls in which they cárry their purchases in the overlapping folds. We have seen every-thing from children, tires, sacks of grain, bags of potatoes and groceries to an unhappy piglet wrapped on the back, heading for home. The most charac-teristic clothing worn by the *otavaleños* are the black fedoras. You seldom see an adult without a hat on, although it is not always a fedora. Folded cloth, sweaters, bags, purses and Mack Truck baseball caps are adequate substitutes as well.

LODGING Spending the night in Otavalo makes getting to the market much easier and also allows you time to explore the surrounding country-side. There are several very nice places and one exceptional place to stay within 15 minutes of Otavalo and a few good places in the town of Otavalo itself.

The exceptional place to stay in the Otavalo area is **Hosteria La Mirage** (deluxe suites, private bath, hot water, TV, fireplace, patio; $140–$185 per suite, per night, including two meals; in Cotacachi, 6-915-237, fax: 6-915-065; call Latin America Reservation Service, 800-327-3573, fax: 941-439-2118 in the U.S. and Canada). Everything about La Mirage is exceptional—the res-taurants, the gardens, the staff, the rooms—it is one of our favorite places to stay in Ecuador. Perched on a hillside 15 minutes northwest of Otavalo, La Mirage is a contemporary hotel built to look like an old hacienda. Both work-ing farm and country inn, La Mirage is set on 15 acres of gardens, wooded hedgerows and small pastures where horses, llamas, chickens, turkeys, pea-cocks, dogs, rabbits, ducks, geese and burros can be found. La Mirage sits about 200 yards off the main road through the little town of Cotacachi. The entrance is about a block past the bus station and marketplace on the north side of town. The cobblestone drive leads through an iron gate (with gate-keeper for safety) to the main building. With prior arrangement, someone from La Mirage will pick you up at the Quito airport or at your Quito hotel for the two-hour trip to the hotel. Pass through a columned entry and you come to the front door and reception area. To the right is a small waiting area and library complete with piano and to the left is the large dining room. You will notice right away how beautifully the hotel is decorated. The furnishings at La Mirage are an eclectic blend of local and European pieces, all distinctive and interesting. You will see antique plates displayed above doorways next to old country tools in a Spanish cupboard. In the dining room, a former church confessional has been converted into a wine rack—a piece that enlivens many conversations.

To the right of the main building a wide stone walkway leads past a small chapel and, behind a garden wall, the bar. The bar is a large room decorated in fine colonial style with comfortable chairs and sofas arranged for quiet conversation, a central fireplace and oil paintings on the walls. The bar is open all day for cozy reading or relaxing storytelling after a bit of exploration. In the evening, the warmth of the decor and fire makes it hard to leave for dinner.

To the left of the main building is a gently sloping front lawn that is fringed with formal gardens. A small statue graces the center of the lawn and a water garden with hidden sculptures and quacking ducks separates the lawn

Otavalo

LODGING
Ⓐ Hotel Ali Shungu
Ⓑ Hotel El Indio
Ⓒ Hotel Otavalo
Ⓓ Hotel Yamor Continental

from the large garden beyond. There are two small patios with garden chairs and shady umbrellas near the water garden. Overhead are seven flagpoles, the tallest always for the Ecuadorian flag, the other six showing the nationalities of the guests. When we were there, the flags of Germany, the United States, France, Israel, Denmark and Colombia were waving.

Thanks to a bit of architectural wizardry and lavish landscaping, each of the 22 rooms (no two alike) seem like they are in separate, detached cottages. All the rooms are large and decorated with a country elegance. Each has two twins or a queen-sized bed, often with a canopy, a sitting area, large bathroom and a working fireplace. Upon request, the staff will come by after dark to light a welcoming fire to warm the chilly Andean night air in your room. The rooms are reached by garden paths that snake around flower-draped fountains and through vine-draped arbors. In fact, flowers are everywhere at La Mirage. There are flowers in huge, fresh-cut bouquets in the dining room, in your suite and also blooming along the paths that wander through the grounds.

A very popular attraction at La Mirage is the restaurant. Not only are the food and wine superb, but you have the delightful opportunity to look out on the broad landscape beyond to the green and earthen Andean hillsides while dining. Above the hazy foothills, the giant snow-topped peak of Volcán Cayambe rises like a thunderhead above a darkening sky. Many *quiteños* come to La Mirage just to enjoy a sumptuous meal after a day's drive in the countryside. This is especially true on weekends. Weekend lunches are very popular at La Mirage so call ahead to make sure you have a table. All of Mirage's waitresses wear the traditional long blue skirt, white apron, gold bead necklace and embroidered white blouse of the *otavaleños*.

La Mirage's combination of quality, service and value has proven extremely popular with both residents of Quito seeking a hideaway and foreign travelers who desire an extremely comfortable overnight base while visiting the famous Otavalo market. After visiting La Mirage, most visitors are so impressed by the accommodations and service that they regret not having signed on for a longer stay. Guest facilities at La Mirage also include a tennis court, a solar heated swimming pool, a gift shop with exquisite handmade products and a small conference room ideal for small groups of businessmen or ecotourists. The extensive grounds invite long strolls and serious flower sniffing. Horseback riding is available as well. For those who want a longer day of exploration, you will receive a map of the local backroads in your welcome packet. These dirt lanes provide wonderful possibilities to see the area's countryside and people at your own pace and level of interest.

Another place to stay in the Otavalo area is the **Hacienda Cusín** (San Pablo del Lago; private bath, hot water, phone, TV; $80–$150; 6-918-013, fax: 6-918-003; e-mail: hacienda@cusin.com). The hacienda is located about ten minutes south of Otavalo on the outskirts of the little village of San Pablo del Lago. Cusín is the oldest tourist hacienda in Ecuador, with parts of it dating back to 1602. But do not worry about staying in an old, run-down place —it has been extensively remodeled, most recently in 1990. This was once the largest hacienda in the area and now enjoys the reputation as being one of the best places to stay north of Quito. Unfortunately, the two times we visited we could not find anyone to talk to and were not as warmly greeted as at the other places we visited. Many tour companies use Hacienda Cusín, so do not be surprised to see buses in the parking lot. The grounds are extensively landscaped with gardens and tall shade trees. Placed about the grounds are one-, two- and three-room cabins—ask for an individual cabin if you want to have some privacy. The restaurant is also well known, serving a variety of local specialties and delicious desserts. If you want to get the feeling of staying at a 17th-century hacienda, Cusín is the place for you.

The other very nice place to stay in the Otavalo area is the **Hosteria Puertolago** (Pan-American Highway south at Km. 5.5 and Lago San Pablo; private bath, hot water, phone, TV; $40–$80; 6-920-920, fax: 6-920-900). Hosteria Puertolago is built on the shore of Lago San Pablo so birdwatching on the lake and in the nearby marsh is quite good. The main building has a reception area and a very large dining room that overlooks the lake. We did not get a chance to try the food here but judging from the number of people in the dining room, this is a very popular place to eat on the way to or from Otavalo. As one might expect being close to a lake, the kitchen is particularly known for its delicious trout dishes. The guest rooms are comfortable and very well kept with warm wood walls reminiscent of a cabin in the forest. Boats for fishing and waterskiing are available as are bicycles for guests. This hosteria is so convenient and the staff so friendly that we highly recommend it as a good place to stay while visiting Otavalo.

Another place that allows easy access to both Otavalo and the surrounding countryside is **Casa Mojanda** (Apartado Postal 160, Otavalo: private bath, hot water, fireplaces, restaurant with breakfast and dinner included in price, horseback riding and mountain biking; $25–$40; 6-731-737, fax: 6-922-969; e-mail: mojanda@srvl.telconet.net). Located 3.5 miles from Otavalo on the road to the Mojanda lakes (opposite Avenida Sucre in Otavalo), Casa Mojanda is like staying at a very pleasant country inn. There are eight comfortable adobe cottages, a Spanish and English library, beautiful gardens and live traditional Andean music almost every night. For nature lovers, this is the best place to stay in the Otavalo area because it is near the Mojanda lakes and its undisturbed paramo and a protected cloud forest called Cushmirumi. Both spots are within mountain-biking distance. Casa Mojanda can also arrange trips to local villages and longer trips into the mountains as well as classes in Andean music, cooking, organic gardening and Spanish and Quechua languages.

There are four places we can recommend within the town of Otavalo itself. All offer clean rooms, private baths with hot water and an on-site restaurant. The best of these is the newest **Hotel El Indio** (Calle Bolívar 904; phone, TV; $20–$40; 6-920-060). There are two other hotels with the same name in Otavalo owned by the same people, but this one is the best. The rooms, arranged around an interior courtyard, are clean and comfortable. There is a roof-top swimming pool with spectacular views of Otavalo and Volcán Imbabura. This hotel is located in the middle of town so it is very convenient to the market but it can sometimes be a bit noisy because of the busy streets. The small restaurant serves typical meals of the area such as potato soup and pork dishes, but their specialty is grilled chicken.

Also in the middle of town is the **Hotel Otavalo** (Roca 5-04 and Montalvo; phone, TV; $20–$40; 6-920-416). The rooms and service here are very good, as is the restaurant where breakfast is included in the price of the room. The hotel is centrally located, two blocks west of the train station, two blocks east of the main plaza and six blocks from poncho plaza. They also offer rooms with shared baths for a cheaper rate.

A close second to the Hotel El Indio is the **Hotel Ali Shungu** (Calle Quito and Miguel Egas; phone, TV; $20–$40; 6-920-750). This hotel was built in 1991 and is four blocks from pancho plaza but at the edge of town, so it is not as noisy as the hotels that are more centrally located. The hotel is operated by two people from the United States who have lived in Otavalo for many years. They also have a unique book exchange if you have finished the one you brought from home. There is a good restaurant serving both vegetarian and typical dishes and a very attractive garden with a spacious patio that overlooks it.

On the north end of town where Calle Bolívar intersects the Pan-American Highway is the sprawling **Hotel Yamor Continental** (phone, TV; $20–$40; 6-920-451). There are 40 basic rooms that are plain but clean in this former hacienda, as well as a swimming pool, tennis court, miniature golf course and a small zoo of animals from the rainforest on the grounds. The Yamor also has a restaurant, bar and breakfast room, but it would probably be better to eat in town, a 15-minute walk away. If you are traveling with a family and want to conserve your money, this would be a good place to stay.

RESTAURANTS   The best places to eat in the Otavalo area are at the hosterias outside of town. They all range in price from $5 to $10. The restaurant at **La Mirage** is the best, followed by those at **Cusín** and **Puertolago**. In town, the restaurants at the **Hotel Ali Shungu** and the **Hotel El Indio** can also be recommended. There are several informal, inexpensive restaurants

Volcán Chimborazo—Ecuador's highest mountain and the point farthest from the center of the Earth.

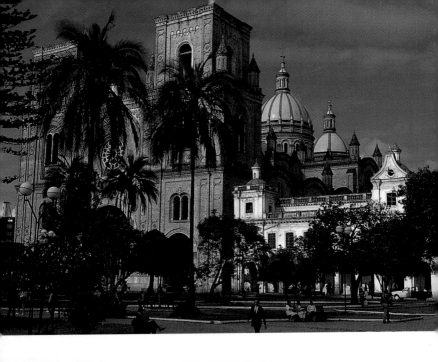

Above: Parque Calderón and the new Cathedral in the heart of Cuenca.

Left: Indigenous women bartering grains and vegetables at a highland market.

around the poncho plaza. On the southwest side is the **Shenandoah**, which has
good desserts and snacks. A few doors
away is **La Galería**, which has a bigger
selection of meals and great espresso.
On the north side of the plaza is **Ali
Micui's**, which is also a good spot for
an inexpensive meal. Just southeast of
poncho plaza is a place to get Mexican
food and breakfast called **Tabascos**.
They also have U.S. magazines to read.

GETTING THERE: By Bus: There are
several bus companies that have regular
daily service to Otavalo from Quito. The
bus companies Transportes Otavalo and
Transportes Los Lagos take you into town
near the market. Most of the others drop
you off on the Pan-American Highway,
forcing you to walk about ten minutes into
the market. Buses cost about $2 for the
one-way trip and take between two and

*Lineated
Woodpecker*

three hours. Many Quito tour companies offer one- or two-day trips to Otavalo
for a reasonable price and a comfortable ride.

By Car: Otavalo is located on the Pan-American Highway about 100 kilometers north of Quito. It takes about two hours to get there by car. The Pan-American
Highway wraps around Otavalo on its west side; the market is about half a kilometer to the east and then south of the highway. Parking can be a problem if you
arrive late in the morning. Otherwise, you should not have much trouble finding a
place to park just by cruising the streets surrounding the market. If you are staying in a nearby hotel, taxis are very reasonably priced to take you to and from the
market. To find a taxi at the market, go to the south end of the market to the plaza
opposite the church.

AROUND OTAVALO

To the east and northeast of Otavalo are several small *otavaleño* weaving
communities—Peguche, Ilumán and Agato—that make a fascinating destination for a half-day tour or a pleasant walk from Otavalo. There are no tourist
facilities in these towns but if you are lucky, friendly and speak some Spanish,
you might be able to see the weavers at work. Do not expect to go and be able
to walk uninvited into these people's homes and workshops. The best way to
see the weavers working is to hire a guide who knows some of the weavers

personally. Many of the tour agencies in Quito offer this option, as do the large tour operators in Otavalo. If this is what you are interested in, be sure to ask if it is included in your Otavalo tour before you jump on the bus.

Peguche is the closest of the three villages. It takes about an hour to walk the 4 kilometers to Peguche from Otavalo. Follow the dirt track along the railroad tracks northeast out of town to the road that leads to the village. Two kilometers south of Peguche is the **Cascada de Peguche**. This popular tourist spot is managed by Fundación Natura in Quito. A short trail leads from the parking lot through a tall forest to an impressive waterfall. There is also a mostly overgrown archaeological site here. A small entrance fee is collected at the parking lot. **Ilumán** is another 3 kilometers north of Peguche. Continue along the dirt road that parallels the railroad track to reach the village. **Agato** is due east of Peguche and northeast of Otavalo behind the low hill on the edge of town. There are several tracks that lead there from both Peguche and Otavalo —ask the locals which trail leads where.

Seventeen kilometers south of Otavalo are the **Mojanda Lakes** (Lagunas de Mojanda). These lakes, located in shallow depressions high in the paramo, are a great spot to go hiking for the day. Above the lakes is the ragged outline of the extinct Volcán Fuya Fuya (14,068 feet/4263 meters). The road ends at the biggest lake where there is a backpacker's refuge for overnight stays. Another alternative is to take a taxi to the lakes and walk back down the road to Otavalo. The road to the lakes turns hard left (south) where the Pan-American Highway turns north as it bypasses Otavalo. A taxi to the lakes costs about $5.

Cotacachi is a small village about 15 minutes north of Otavalo that is well known for its leather craftsmen. The main street is lined with well over 100 leather shops (*tiendas de cuero*) where it is possible to buy beautifully crafted leather belts, purses, bags, jackets, backpacks, briefcases, vests, skirts, hats, gloves, coats and boots. There are so many leather shops here that it is hard to find any other kind of store. The quality of the leather work does vary a bit, as do the prices, so shop around to find exactly what you want. There is an interesting little weekend food market next to the bus station on the western edge of town if you want a refreshing break from all the leather.

LODGING   There are two places to stay near Cotacachi. The best and most expensive is **Hosteria La Mirage**, located about 100 yards past the bus station west of town (see description under Otavalo lodging section earlier in this chapter). The other place to stay in Cotacachi is the **Hosteria El Meson de las Flores** (Centro Cívico; private bath, hot water; $20–$40; 6-915-009). This former hacienda is more than 200 years old and has been converted into a charming hotel. The second- and third-story rooms face an interior courtyard that is framed with flower-draped balconies. The courtyard restaurant is filled with umbrella-topped tables and serves typical pork and chicken dishes. If you are brave, ask for *cuy*, a specialty of this province (*cuy* is a large guinea pig that looks a lot like your old pet back home). Next to the courtyard restaurant is a cozy bar. Across the street is a former convent that has been restored and converted into a conference center. Whether you are with a group or not, walk here to see the lovely Colonial-style architecture and the view of the cathedral looming overhead.

GETTING THERE: By Bus: Buses leave Otavalo on the hour for the short trip to Cotacachi.

By Car: Cotacachi is about a 15-minute drive north and west of Otavalo. Take the Pan-American Highway north from Otavalo and turn right or west at the well-marked intersection, about 5 kilometers from Otavalo. This road crosses a river gorge and then leads directly into town.

Created in 1968, the **Cotacachi–Cayapas Ecological Reserve** encompasses an area of 510,000 acres. The boundary stretches from just east of Esmeraldas on the Río Cayapas on the north and to Lago Cuicocha just east of Otavalo on the south and west. With this irregular outline, the reserve protects a very broad range of habitats from lowland coastal rainforest (see Chapter Thirteen) to cloud forest to high elevation paramo. Volcán Cotacachi is the tallest mountain in the reserve at 16,299 feet (4939 meters) high.

Lago Cuicocha sits inside an old caldera on the southern flank of Volcán Cotacachi. There are two small conical islands on the far side of the lake, but they are closed to visitors. Because of the height of the surrounding rim, most of the lakeshore is inaccessible by foot. Boats can be hired to tour the lake for a closer view of the islands and the distant shore. There is a trail that circles the lake that starts from the picnic area uphill from the restaurant at the end of the entrance road. The trail takes about five hours to walk and makes an interesting day hike. For most of the way, the trail leads through lush paramo —dense, shrubby vegetation with a soft, green carpet of mosses underneath. On the far side of the lake the trail crosses several patches of *Polylepis* forest. Many of the animals of the paramo use these forest patches for cover and foods so take a break when you get to the forest and see what you can find.

For those less ambitious, walk the beginning of the lake trail from the roadside picnic area to the east. About ten minutes from the road a run-down building is located, where, on a clear day, you can see the white crest of Volcán Cayambe rising to the east. Below this part of the trail, clinging to the steep wall of the rim of the caldera, are small patches of forest where birds can be easily seen flying through the treetops. Scarlet-bellied Tanagers and Crimson-mantled Woodpeckers are two of the more colorful birds found here. In the paramo, flowerpiercers dart among the bushes and dwarf trees.

Lago Cuicocha offers the most accessible native vegetation near Otavalo. The lake is at a fairly high elevation, so the temperature will be brisk in the early morning. If you are lucky, there will be fresh snow on the summit of Volcán Cotacachi. Remember the elevation if you are planning to do some hiking. No hike at this altitude is just a walk in the park.

GETTING THERE: There are two ways to enter the reserve. *By Boat:* From the northwest, out of the town of Borbón north of Esmeraldas, you can hire a boat to take you along the Río Cayapas to the reserve. For more complete information on this part of the reserve, see Chapter Thirteen.

By Car: The easiest way to see part of the Cotacachi–Cayapas Ecological Reserve is on its eastern side, from the little town of Cotacachi, 15 minutes northeast of Otavalo. From the center of town, take Calle Antonio José de Sucre east 12 kilometers to the guard station of the reserve. There is no fee but the rangers will ask you your nationality. Beyond the guard station the gravel road crests a small hill and leads down past a picnic area to the rim above Lago Cuicocha, a distance of about a kilometer. The road ends here where a small restaurant and boat sightseeing operation are located. (Both of these businesses were closed when we visited and no hours could be found when they are open. It is most likely that they are open weekends only or by special arrangement.)

IBARRA AREA

Located about halfway between Quito and the Colombian border and 22 kilometers north of Otavalo, **Ibarra**, population 80,000, is the capital and the commercial hub of Imbabura Province. It is known as the "white city" for the quaint whitewashed buildings in the older part of town. It might also be called the "quiet city" because, despite being the provincial capital, Ibarra is really just a grown-up but sleepy little town. There is very little for the tourist to see along the cobblestone streets. Most of the attractions of interest to tourists—craft villages, Indian markets and wilderness areas—are in the surrounding area and have better, more convenient places to stay near them. Many *quiteños* come to the Imbabura area for weekend getaways in the country because the province is mostly rural and the climate is a bit warmer than Quito's.

There is very little to see in Ibarra itself. There are a couple of small parks and plazas in the city that are nice places to watch the world go by, but they are not remarkable. In the Parque La Merced, on the corner of García Moreno and Olmedo, there is a small **church** with a statue of the Virgin of La Merced on top. Two blocks to the east is the prettier Parque Pedro Moncayo. On the north side of this park is Ibarra's huge **cathedral**. On the north side of town, at the corner of Carretera Bolívar and Calle Troya, is a statue of Simón Bolívar, the great South American liberator, marking his July 1823 victory against Spain in the Battle of Ibarra. The **train station** is in the southwest corner of the city between calles Velasco and Colón.

The main tourist attraction in Ibarra has been the **San Lorenzo–Ibarra train**. This train is on the way to extinction but has for years provided the only means of land transportation to the coastal town of San Lorenzo and to the rugged mountain terrain between San Lorenzo and Ibarra. It is infamous because it is so unreliable and the track is so precarious. In fact, its very unreliability and precariousness have become its primary "charming" attraction to adventuresome tourists. We think most tourists take this train just so they can have a traveler's war story to relate to their friends back home. We have actually heard of gringos being disappointed when the trip went smoothly.

Actually, the train is really not a train in the traditional sense. It is a diesel-powered, converted old Bluebird bus mounted on railroad wheels. Up to 50 passengers can be shoehorned into the seats, with at least that many more crammed in the aisle and perched on the roof. It takes all day to complete the 200-kilometer trip if you are lucky, and includes a 5-kilometer walk in the middle where a landslide wiped out the tracks. New roads to San Lorenzo from Borbón and Ibarra will make this train even more obsolete. In fact, no one is sure how much longer the train will keep running. Evidently, the goal is to try to keep it going until the road is paved the entire way. At present, the roads are unpassable during the wet season.

In October 1995, the 120-kilometer road from Ibarra to San Lorenzo was completed, making this the best route to see a wild corner of northwestern Ecuador. Only the first 46 kilometers to just past the town of La Carolina, however, are paved. But even this paved portion can have rough detours around or over major landslides. A high-clearance vehicle, preferably with four-wheel drive, is desirable for the final 80 kilometers, but during the rainy season (February–April), it may be closed to all vehicles. An entire day descending this road will allow for many stops along the way. Then an overnight in San Lorenzo (see Chapter Thirteen) and an entire day to ascend back up the road will give you a second chance for whatever you missed on the way down. Many patches of excellent forest still stand along this road, primarily below the town of Lita. Take food and supplies with you, however, as the stores along the highway carry few groceries.

The best way to reach this road is to drive north through Ibarra. Two and a half kilometers beyond the northern boundary of Ibarra is a large customs control point (which may or may not be open). Another 18.2 kilometers beyond (north) the customs control point and at a major bend in the Pan-American Highway is a small sign for the town of Salinas. Turn left (west) here onto this smaller paved road, cross a bridge over the Río Mira and you are on the San Lorenzo Highway. The road parallels the Río Mira on its southern bank (the old train tracks can be seen across the river paralleling the north side). Initially the habitat is dry paramo and acacia scrub until just past the town of Carolina. Here cloud forest begins. After Lita, lowland rainforest predominates. This rainforest is part of the region called the Chocó and has some of the highest plant diversity in South America.

San Antonio de Ibarra (or just San Antonio as it is called locally) is on the southern outskirts of Ibarra. Well known for its wood carvers, everything from full-sized statues of people and animals down to miniatures can be found in this small village. Most of the shops are around the central plaza and you can usually find the craftsmen working on their next project in the room behind the streetside shop. The most well-known carver is Señor Luís Potosí, whose store, **Galería Luís Potosí**, sells his work all over the world.

LODGING   The best places to stay in the Ibarra area are at the hosterias outside of the city. Most of these are located off the Pan-American Highway west and south of Ibarra. The cheaper hotels, like the cheaper restaurants, are between the train station and the center of the city. Of these, the **Residencial Colón** (Narvárez 8-62 and Velasco; 6-950-052), the **Residencial Imperio** (Olmedo 8-54 and Oviedo; 6-952-929) and the **Hotel Ibarra** (Mosquera 6-158 and Sánchez; 6-955-091) have been recommended. Expect to pay between $5–$10 for a room with carpeting and a private bath, less if you do not mind sharing a bathroom and sharing your room with other creatures. Ask to see the room to be sure it is acceptable *before* you pay for it.

In Ibarra, the best place to stay is the **Hotel Ajaví** (Avenida Mariana Acosta 16-38; private bath, hot water, phone, color TV, minibar; $20–$30; 6-952-485, fax: 6-955-640). This is a modern, two-story hotel built around a very large and attractive swimming pool. The 55 rooms, including four suites, are spacious and comfortable. The hotel also has a conference room, sauna and steam room.

The **Hosteria Chorlavi** (4 kilometers south of Ibarra on the Pan-American Highway; private bath, hot water, phone, color TV; $25–$60, meals separate; 6-955-707, fax: 6-956-311) is the nicest place to stay near Ibarra. This was once the original hacienda in the area, controlling all the land from horizon to horizon. In 1830, it passed to the Tobars, an influential Ecuadorian family of businessmen and politicians, and since then seven generations of Tobars have run the hacienda. In 1972, it opened to tourists.

Hosteria Chorlavi, which translates to "nest of love," is a collection of beautiful old whitewashed buildings with worn red-tile roofs in a pretty garden setting. On the grounds are tall palms, walnuts and a large Norfolk Island Pine that welcomes visitors to the hacienda. The 46 rooms are very comfortable and arranged in blocks around the gardens. There are tennis and squash courts and a playground for children, as well. The red-brick walks lead to a swimming pool that has a bar, a glass-enclosed hot tub and two saunas next to it. Beyond the swimming pool is a cock-fighting arena that is popular with Colombians on weekends.

The restaurant here is very well known, especially the weekend lunch buffets. There is also a small Indian market, selling mostly *otavaleño* weavings, that operates on weekends on the grounds. This is a very popular place to stay, and reservations are a must if you plan to be here on a weekend. If you want a quieter time at the hosteria, avoid the weekends when buses of tourists arrive and the facilities are overrun with people.

Four kilometers south of the Hosteria Chorlavi is the newer **Hosteria Natabuela** (8 kilometers south of Ibarra on the Pan-American Highway; private bath, hot water, phone, color TV; $15–$20, 6-957-734, fax: 6-955-755). There are no grounds to speak of here, but the buildings are new and the ten rooms quite spacious and comfortable. There is a swimming pool in back and a sauna next to it. The Hosteria Natabuela is a bit isolated in the countryside, but with the restaurant and bar, everything you need is here.

Well out into the countryside northwest of Ibarra is the **Hosteria San Francisco** (Chachimbiro; private bath, hot water, phone, color TV, minibar; $50 includes meals; 6-920-387). We have not had a chance to visit this hosteria, but its food and service have received mixed reviews. There are ten rooms, a restaurant, cafeteria and bar and a swimming pool with hot springs. The hosteria is also close to the boundary of the Cotacachi–Cayapas Ecological Reserve.

RESTAURANTS   The best places to eat in the Ibarra area are at the hosterias outside of the city. They all range in price from $5 to $10. Try the **Hosteria Chorlavi**, **Hosteria La Mirage** in Cotacachi and the **Hosteria San Francisco** in nearby Chachimbiro. In Ibarra there are three good restaurants, each of about equal quality. The **Hotel Ajaví** (Avenida Mariano Acosta 16-38; all meals; 6-955-600) has a modern restaurant typical of a first-class hotel. It features *especialidades Imbabureñas*: paila ice cream and *llapingachos*, a delicious cheese and potato mixture. The **Restaurant El Dorado** (Calle Oviedo 545; noon to midnight; 6-950-699) and the **Restaurante La Estancia** (Calle García Moreno 766; noon to midnight; 6-951-930) both have excellent seafood and regional chicken and pork specialties. There are lots of other, more informal places to eat in Ibarra. Many of these are clustered around the train station and around the edge of Parque La Merced and Parque Pedro Moncayo.

GETTING THERE: By Bus: There is regular bus service to Ibarra from Quito and Otavalo.

By Car: Ibarro is located 22 kilometers north of Otavalo on the Pan-American Highway.

El Ángel Ecological Reserve was established in 1992, and not many tourists visit it yet. The 39,288-acre (15,906-hectare) reserve was created to protect Ecuador's northernmost and perhaps most ecologically diverse area of paramo. The El Ángel reserve is renowned for its magnificent specimens of Freilejones plants, which are reminiscent of a yucca on a four-foot stalk. Within the reserve are Puma, deer, Torrent Ducks and many species of hummingbirds, and it is one of the few places in northern Ecuador where Andean condors can still be found.

There is one dirt road that crosses the reserve. It goes from the village of El Ángel on the south side of the reserve to the village of Tufiño on the Colombian border, north of the reserve. Expect to take most of a day exploring this road. From Tufiño, another dirt road follows the Colombian border to the west and crosses the reserve before dropping down to the remote village of Maldonado. Both of these roads are rough and can be challenging to negotiate, so we recommend them for only the best prepared and hardiest traveler.

The best way to see this extremely rich environment is to go on the Golondrina trek, an easy multi-day hike through the reserve, offered by **Fundación Golondrina** on Calle Isabel La Católica 1559 (in Quito; 2-226-602, fax: 2-502-640), a foundation that works with communities to support alternative development and to conserve nature. It is working with local communities in the area around the El Ángel Ecological Reserve to help preserve an additional 62,500 acres of this threatened and unique paramo habitat known as the Golondrina.

One of the ways they are doing this is by offering three- to five-day guided trips through the Cerro Golondrina (Swallow Hills). These trips combine easy hiking, nature study and local community involvement. The trips start in the El Ángel Ecological Reserve, high above the tiny village of El Ángel (due south of the reserve) in the paramo, descend through incredibly rich primary cloud forest, eventually ending in subtropical rainforest in the equally tiny village of La Carolina. Each day's hike is mostly downhill and never more than six hours long, so there is plenty of time for photography, birdwatching and exploring. Tents, food and heavy luggage are transported by horses so hikers only need to carry daypacks. Some of the trail is also done on horseback. A sleeping bag, rubber boots and raingear are all that the hiker must provide. The minimum group size is six people and the daily cost is about $50 per person.

A big plus of the trip is the chance to interact with the local people. The interaction has been designed into the trip itinerary, providing both the local people and the hikers an important opportunity to get to know each other and to understand each other's way of life. This is an extremely professionally run operation that offers a vitally important opportunity to respect another culture while at the same time helping to preserve a threatened ecosystem. We think it is one of the finest community-based conservation efforts in all of Ecuador.

GETTING THERE: By Car: Access to El Ángel Ecological Reserve is easiest through the village of El Ángel. El Ángel is located west of the Pan-American Highway, 67 kilometers north of Ibarra and 48 kilometers south of Tulcán. Thirty-three kilometers north of Ibarra on the Pan-American Highway, a paved road leads through the town of Mira to El Ángel. Alternatively, a good gravel road leads 22 kilometers west from the large town of San Gabriel on the Pan-American Highway to El Ángel.

By Air: TAME has two flights between Quito and Tulcán every weekday.

EIGHT

The Central Highlands

The central highlands of Ecuador are an interesting mixture of pre-Columbian, colonial, contemporary and colossal Ecuador. It is a region peppered with historic haciendas, fascinating Indian markets, modern cities and the highest point in Ecuador, Volcán Chimborazo. The Pan-American Highway bisects the central highlands on its way from Quito to Cuenca carrying the commerce of the country north and south. The landscape is mostly high-elevation grassy meadows rising to paramo and the snowy cones of towering volcanoes. Native vegetation is mostly gone except in the most inaccessible pockets in the mountains and ridges. The region is heavily farmed but still has a rich and varied Indian culture.

Two hundred years ago, each broad valley, topped by its own snow-capped volcano, was controlled by a different Spanish family. Each family lived in a sprawling hacienda on a land grant that stretched to the near horizon. To run these huge farms, the local Indians were forced to work the fields or to weave in sweatshops, indentured for a lifetime. Land reform eventually eliminated the servitude and broke the land monopoly, but the artistry of the Indian weavers and the colonial haciendas themselves, sitting far off the road, are remnants of this bygone era.

Above the haciendas, on tiny patches of land lined with well-kept rows of potatoes and furrows of beans, you will see hard-working Indians tending their fields. Many of the Indians have been pushed off the fertile valleys to the highest, steepest land to scrape out a living on a hardscrabble farm. Although their land is poor, their culture remains rich. Three Indian markets that have changed little over the last hundred years flourish in these highlands. These weekly markets service the needs of the locals and do not cater to the whims of the gringo tourist trade and thus are absolutely fascinating to visit.

Even here amongst this bit of an earlier Ecuador are splashes of modern life. In the towns of the central highlands, glassy walls of office buildings overlook honking Mercedes and streets crowded with the business of the day. Contemporary hotels and gleaming art galleries beckon to gringos in sensible shoes and multipocketed pants. These tourists now stay in the old haciendas, but with cable TV in their rooms and colorfully costumed Indians serving them meals. While much has changed in the central highlands, much has not.

In the central highlands, the Pan-American Highway is better known as the "Avenue of the Volcanoes." Some would argue that the Avenue of the Volcanoes starts in the northern highlands with Volcán Imbabura and Volcán Cotacachi near Otavalo, but most agree that the Avenue starts as soon as you leave Quito and head south. Here, where the valleys are punctuated with dairy cows and cobbled lanes, the summits of the volcanoes loom large over the highway. On the west side, starting from Quito and going toward Cuenca is Volcán Pichincha, which rises above Quito. Heading south are Volcanoes Atacazo, Corazón, Iliniza, Yanaurcu and Carihuairazo, which sits on the shoulder of Chimborazo, the biggest of them all. On the east side of the Pan-American Highway, starting from the north are the Volcanoes Pasochoa, Antisana, Sincholagua, Rumiñahui, Cotopaxi, Quilindaña, Tungurahua, Altar and finally Sangay, just south of the city of Riobamba.

Located between Quito and Riobamba are three national parks—**Cotopaxi**, **Llanganates** and **Sangay**—and two national reserves: **Antisana Ecological Reserve** and the **Chimborazo Faunal Reserve**. Cotopaxi and Chimborazo are easily accessible and commonly visited. Sangay and Llanganates national parks are virtually inaccessible except to the most adventuresome and hardy hikers. Antisana Ecological Reserve sets aside large blocks of upper elevation forest. Most off the fresh water supplying the city of Quito also comes from this reserve. Access is principally limited to trails from the Papallacta-Baeza Highway and the Cordillera de Huacamayos on the Baeza-Tena Highway (see Chapter Fourteen). Mountaineering expeditions enter via poor roads southeast of Quito. This reserve is also a major refuge for Andean Condors.

SOUTH FROM QUITO

The drive south from Quito on the Pan-American Highway leads through green pastures dotted with cows and roadside villages filled with gas stations and truck-stop eateries. The turn to Pasochoa Forest Reserve is about 30 minutes south of Quito at the little town of Tambillo (see Chapter Six for more information on the Pasochoa Forest Reserve). About 10 kilometers past Tambillo is the larger town of Machachi. The only thing for the tourist here is the **Guitig Mineral Springs** where Guitig mineral water, the most popular mineral water in Ecuador, is bottled. The plant is open for tours 9 a.m.–4 p.m., Monday through Friday.

Beyond Machachi, the Pan-American Highway rolls into more green valleys. To the west, rising above the tiny villages and fields of corn and grain is, first, Volcán Corazón and then the twin summits of Volcán Iliniza. You may not notice Volcán Iliniza because to the east, on the opposite side of the valley, rises the eye-riveting, symmetrical cone of Cotopaxi in the middle of **Cotopaxi National Park**. There are two entrances to the park, one through Boliche National Recreation Area and the other, just south, that leads directly into the park. Both entrances are well signed. For more information on Cotopaxi National Park, see Chapter Six.

Lying in the dawn shadow of Cotopaxi is perhaps the most well-known and historic hacienda in Ecuador, **Hosteria La Ciénega** (Lasso–Cotopaxi; private bath, hot water, phone; $40–$80; 3-719-182, fax: 3-719-093, Quito office: Luís Cordero 1442, 2-541-337). Hosteria La Ciénaga is located on 30 acres of originally swampy land (*la ciénaga* translates into "the swamp"). The grounds are now covered in green lawns and formal gardens, all shaded by huge eucalyptus trees. The eucalyptus trees are over 120 years old and are said to be the first ever planted in Ecuador. The grass came from Africa and was planted here as a test to see if it was suitable for polo fields.

Several prominent families have owned this land and hacienda over the last 400 years. The original land, granted by the King of Spain, stretched from Quito to Ambato. Through the centuries, Ecuadorian presidents and foreign ambassadors have stayed at La Ciénaga as they traveled to Cuenca. Also, several renowned scientists have stayed here, including Charles Marie de la Condamine, the head of the French geodetic survey, in 1742, and Baron von Humboldt, the 19th-century geographer, while studying Volcán Cotopaxi in 1802.

The main house, built in 1580, is an impressive building and is considered a national historic landmark. The massive whitewashed walls form a typical Spanish-style square building with a lovely interior courtyard. The courtyard is a beautiful garden with cobbled walks arranged in two concentric circles around a central fountain. The hacienda's west side is a family chapel with an intricate, two-bell facade facing the fountain. The ornately carved wooden door opens to a simple room with a stone floor, side pulpit, flowered altar and painted ceiling. A confessional is tucked into a back corner.

Modern additions to the original hacienda include ten guest rooms, a large restaurant, a bar, a TV lounge, reception area and gift shop. All the rooms in the main building, including the guest rooms, are elegantly decorated with colonial and 19th-century pieces. The restaurant is particularly attractive and is a popular spot for lunch, especially on weekends. Many tours stop here after

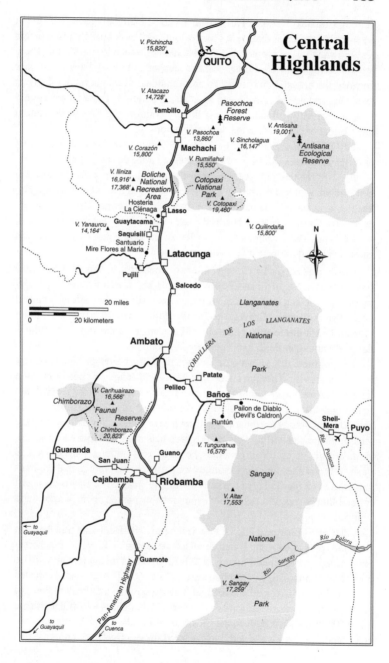

Central Highlands

V. Pichincha
15,820' ▲

✈ **QUITO**

V. Atacazo
14,728' ▲

Tambillo

Pasochoa
Forest
Reserve

V. Antisana
19,001' ▲

🌲 Antisana
Ecological
Reserve

V. Pasochoa
13,860'

V. Corazón
15,800'

Machachi

V. Sincholagua
16,147' ▲

V. Rumiñahui
15,550'

V. Iliniza
16,916' ▲
17,368' ▲

Boliche
National
Recreation
Area

Cotopaxi
National
Park

Hosteria
La Ciénaga ●

Lasso

V. Cotopaxi
19,460' ▲

V. Yanaurcu
14,164' ▲

Guaytacama

V. Quilindaña
15,800' ▲

Saquisilí □

N

Santuario
Mire Flores al Maria ●

Latacunga

Pujilí □

Salcedo □

Llanganates

| 0 | 20 miles |

LOS   *LLANGANATES*

CORDILLERA

DE

National

| 0 | 20 kilometers |

Ambato □

CORDILLERA

Patate □

Park

V. Carihuairazo
16,566'

Pelileo □

Baños

Pailon de Diablo
(Devil's Caldron) ●

Chimborazo

Faunal
Reserve

**Shell-
Mera**

● Runtún

✈ □ **Puyo**

V. Chimborazo
20,823' ▲

Río Pastaza

Guaranda

Guano □

V. Tungurahua
16,576' ▲

San Juan □

Sangay

Cajabamba

□ **Riobamba**

V. Altar
17,553' ▲

← to
Guayaquil

National

Río Palora

Río Sangay

Guamote □

Pan-American Highway

V. Sangay
17,259' ▲

Park

to
Guayaquil

to
Cuenca

visiting Cotopaxi National Park so lunch can be extremely crowded. Do not be surprised to see several buses parked out front at noon. The restaurant is less crowded in the evening but you should still make a reservation. There are wandering minstrels during weekend lunches and for all dinners to further enhance the colonial ambiance. To accommodate more guests, La Ciénega expanded and added 22 rooms in an attached building. These rooms are not quite as elegantly colonial but are still very comfortable. Ask for a room in the original building when making reservations.

GETTING THERE: *By Bus:* La Ciénega is 2 kilometers from the Pan-American Highway. Buses will let guests off at the gate if the driver knows in advance.

By Car: The turn to La Ciénega is just south of the little town of Lasso. The turn is to the west and marked by a white gate and arch marked La Ciénega. Follow this road about 2 kilometers to the formal stone gate and the tree-lined entrance drive. It takes about an hour and a half to drive from Quito to La Ciénaga.

By Train: The train from Quito to Riobamba passes the roadside gate and guests can be left off there if they tell the conductor.

Close to Hosteria La Ciénega are two wonderful Indian markets in the tiny villages of **Saquisilí** and **Pujilí**. These markets are as authentic and non-touristy as you can find in Ecuador today. Saquisilí is a few kilometers west of the Pan-American Highway, just south of the town of Guaytacama. Pujilí is about 10 kilometers west of the city of Latacunga. Market days are Wednesday and Sunday in Pujilí and Thursday in Saquisilí.

Both of these tiny villages are far enough off the beaten path that not very many tourists visit. They are important for the local indigenous people because the markets are the center of their social and economic worlds. You will not find very many, if any, handicrafts and weavings for sale to tourists here. These are food and housewares markets selling practical items for daily use by the local Indians. You will find pig parts, green bananas (used to feed cattle), all kinds of fruit, yarns, ropes, ceramics, heaps of used clothing, pails and stacks of shovels and axes for sale. Ceramics are particularly common in these markets (there is a lot of clay in the surrounding hillsides). The clay is also used for building blocks, stacks of which you probably passed on the way to these villages.

Also near Cotopaxi National Park is the exquisite **Hacienda San Agustin de Callo** (private bath, hot water, fireplace; restaurant, hiking, fishing, horseback riding and mountain biking; $100–$200, meals included; Quito office phone/fax: 2-503-656, on-site phone/fax: 3-719-160). The hacienda is located in the foothills of Cotopaxi and is small (five guest rooms), difficult to find and consequently little visited. Don't be discouraged though, as it is well worth the effort. The hacienda is built on the site of an Incan palace, and the dining room and chapel still have walls with Incan carved stones. The large rooms are furnished with antiques and are simply magnificent. This is the place to come if you want a country escape from Quito and to be pampered in comfort on the shoulder of Cotopaxi. The hacienda is located well off the Pan-American Highway on the northern edge of Cotopaxi National Park, more than an hour's drive from Quito. Detailed directions to reach the hacienda will be provided with a reservation.

LATACUNGA AREA

Ninety kilometers south of Quito is **Latacunga** (population 40,000), the capital city of Cotopaxi Province. Despite this status, there is surprisingly little to see here. To us, Latacunga is a town without an identity. There are almost no historic buildings or even any particularly attractive streets. In fact, the town has a suspiciously modern feel to it in spite of its long history of occupation stretching back to pre-Incan times. There is a very good reason for this and explains why we call Latacunga "the town that can't take a hint."

That reason looms to the northwest of Latacunga in the form of Volcán Cotopaxi. Three times in the last 200 years, Latacunga has been completely destroyed by volcanic eruptions. The first time was in 1742, but the town was quickly rebuilt. It happened again in 1768 and again the town was rebuilt. Finally, in 1877, Latacunga was razed once again by Cotopaxi and yet again rebuilt. Cotopaxi has been pretty quiet for the last century so you do not have much to worry about now (probably).

LODGING   Like the town itself, the lodging possibilities in Latacunga are pretty average. You can expect private baths, hot water and a moderately clean room but not much else. This is okay, though, because most people staying in Latacunga are just passing through and will only stay for a night. The busiest times in Latacunga are Wednesday and Saturday nights because of the Thursday market at Saquisilí and the Sunday market at Pujilí. Consequently, the limited hotel rooms tend to be full by late afternoon. If you plan to visit on these days, make reservations ahead. Alternatively, you can plan to stay at La Ciénaga, 20 kilometers north of Latacunga, or Hosteria Rumipamba de las Rosas, 13 kilometers south of Latacunga. Both are far better than anything Latacunga can offer, and La Ciénaga is also close to the markets in Pujilí and Saquisilí.

The two best places to stay in Latacunga are on the north end of town on the Pan-American Highway. The **Hotel Latacunga** (private bath, hot water, TV; $5–$20; 3-802-372) and the **Hostal Quilotoa** (private bath, hot water; $3–$15; 3-801-866, fax: 3-802-090) are modern, have friendly staff and are fine for a short stay. Ask for a room away from the highway for a quieter night's sleep. They both have small restaurants nearby for a light meal. In town we can recommend the **Hotel Cotopaxi** (Salcedo 73-21; private bath, hot water; $3–$15; 3-802-912) on the north side of the Parque Vicente León. It, too, can be noisy from the street but streetside rooms have a nice view of the park, so if you want the view you will have to hope for a quiet evening.

RESTAURANTS   There are no restaurants in Latacunga that we can recommend. There are several informal places to eat that serve simple, inexpensive meals, but nowhere you can go for a romantic or delightful dining experience. Try the restaurant in the **Hotel Costa Azul** on 5 de Junio just west of the Pan-American Highway, or in town, try **Parrilladas los Copihues** or **Restaurant La Carreta** on the west side of Parque Vicente León. There are also several small pocket cafés surrounding the park that serve chicken and roast potatoes as well as a number of bakeries for breakfast breads and rolls. If you are in the area at lunchtime, try the **Parador Tiobamba** or the **Parador de la Finca** near the basket market on the Pan-American Highway.

For those who like to do a bit of backroad wandering, head west of Latacunga to the small village of San Felipe de Latacunga and then northwest, asking for directions along the way, to the **Santuario Mire Flores al Maria**, locally known as the Tilipulo Hacienda. The sanctuary is a former monastery where, in the 16th and 17th centuries, the local indigenous people were forced to weave textiles for export to Spain. Today, the whitewashed walls of the church and hacienda are slowly being restored. There are plans to make this a hosteria and restaurant for tourists. Within the walls of the hacienda are beautiful gardens in hidden courtyards, shaded walks under arched ceilings and a small family chapel with high stained-glass windows. The hacienda overlooks a serene, green valley dotted with grazing cows and marshy reeds. The sanctuary is a hard place to find but well worth the effort, especially if you'd like to explore a historic hacienda and peek into all of its corners and nooks.

GETTING THERE: By Bus: Many bus companies offer transportation up and down the Pan-American Highway. You can go to the bus station at the main intersection to downtown Latacunga on the Pan-American Highway or you can just stick out your hand when a bus traveling in the right direction approaches.

By Car: Latacunga is about 90 kilometers south of Quito on the Pan-American Highway. Most of the city is east of the highway but it is still impossible to miss.

By Train: The main train line in Ecuador follows the Pan-American Highway but the track is always in disrepair, causing the train schedule to be at best creative writing and at worst pure fantasy. In theory, the train to Latacunga is supposed to arrive from Quito around mid-day. Check ahead if you plan to do any train travel in Ecuador.

Fourteen kilometers south of Latacunga and 100 kilometers south of Quito is the quiet town of **Salcedo**. There is not much to see in Salcedo but it is a picturesque place to wander and enjoy a small Ecuadorian highland town.

Those in the know stop in Salcedo for delicious ice cream. There are many streetside ice cream shops selling interesting fruit and combination flavors. We have been know to linger on hot afternoons around the central plaza and test flavors—for purely professional reasons, of course. The main plaza in Salcedo is also a pleasant and safe place to stroll as dusk fades to night.

A kilometer north of Salcedo on the west side of the Pan-American Highway is the delightful **Hosteria Rumipamba de las Rosas** (Pan-American Highway Km. 100; private bath, hot water, phone, TV; $40–$60; 3-726-128, fax: 3-727-103, Quito office: Avenida Orellana 1811, 2-568-884). The Hosteria is a converted historic hacienda that was built in the late 1800s. All of the 31 rooms, some with fireplaces, are large and decorated with old farm tools, tree-round tables and period antiques, giving guests a feeling of staying the night on an old working farm. There is also a very good restaurant, intimate bar in the main building, an informal café for breakfast and lunch, and outside seating for weekend brunches. Outside is a large pool surrounded by gardens, including an impressive group of cacti. If you are planning to spend the night in the Latacunga area, Hosteria Rumipamba de las Rosas is by far the best choice.

GETTING THERE: *By Bus:* Many bus companies offer transportation up and down the Pan-American Highway. Go to the bus station at the main plaza in town or just stick out your hand when a bus traveling in the right direction approaches.

By Car: Salcedo is about 100 kilometers south of Quito and 13 kilometers south of Latacunga on the Pan-American Highway.

Declared a national park in 1995, **Llanganates National Park** fills a void of unprotected highland Andean forests between Cotopaxi and Sangay national parks. Although not yet developed for tourists, several gravel roads lead to its western border from Latacunga and Ambato. A major highway is planned from Latacunga to Tena that will provide access to much of the northern portion of this park. Hopefully, the government will be able to control illegal colonization along this road, and the integrity of the park's habitats can be maintained as the road is finished.

AMBATO AREA

Traveling south of Salcedo on the Pan-American Highway, the road follows high bluffs above the Río Culuchi. There are occasional lakes in the river valley that can be interesting to scan with binoculars. Expect to see Slate-colored Coots and Andean Ducks disappearing and suddenly reappearing as they dive for food. **Lago de Yambo** is across the highway and below the Paradero Yambo and usually has large flocks of ducks. The rural landscape in this region is entirely devoted to farming. Patchwork fields of corn and wheat, worked by oxen-pulled plows, surround small homesteads where a cow, goat or horse is likely to be tethered to graze in a roadside ditch. The tall piles of green bananas you see in the paddocks are fed to the cows.

Thirty kilometers or so south of Salcedo, the Río Culuchi is joined by the Río Ambato. Together they continue to flow south and then east to become the Río Pastaza that soon flows out of the Andes and grows to be one of the major rivers of the Oriente. On the banks of the Río Ambato is the city of **Ambato** (population 150,000), the capital of Tungurahua Province and the largest and most important commercial city in the central highlands.

People have lived on the banks of the Río Ambato for several thousand years. The first inhabitants settled in this area, known then as Cashapamba. They were a combination of Hambato, Huapante, Pillaro, Quisapincha and Izamba Indian tribes that grew oca (a tuber), sweet potatoes, potatoes, corn and the grain quinoa. Cashapamba was conquered first by the Caras Indians and then by the Incas. The Incas established a *tambo*, or resting place, here on their road system between Quito and Cuenca. In 1535, Sebastián de Benal-cázar, the founder of Quito, ordered a town be created, known as Ambato, at this tambo. An earthquake destroyed the town in 1698, but a new Ambato was built soon after, a few kilometers to the south of the original town site.

Like Latacunga to the north, Ambato has felt the repeated wrath of the surrounding volcanoes. The most recent event was a very strong earthquake that devastated the city in 1949. The resilient people of Ambato have rebuilt the city, but the town, like Latacunga, suffers from the fact that much of its history is periodically destroyed. There are almost no colonial buildings and few historical artifacts and records. Consequently, there is only one small museum dedicated to Ambato's history—the **Casa de Cultura** (on the north-west side of Parque Juan Montalvo). The most interesting museum in Ambato is the **Museo de Ciencias Naturales** (corner of Sucre and Lalama near Parque Cevallos). This museum has a good collection of stuffed native animals and some historic photos of Cotopaxi erupting.

We do not mean to imply, though, that there is little for the tourist in Ambato. Ambato is an interesting city, with the largest urban market (*mercado*) in the country. In fact, there are more markets in Ambato than you can shake a tired tourist at. In the center of the city are the **Mercado Central** and the **Mercado Colombia**, markets that sell vegetables, fruits and other foods on the ground floor and serve typical Ecuadorian meals of potatoes and meats on the second floor. Other **markets** include the Primero de Mayo market, the Urbina market, the Pachano Plaza market, the Simón Bolívar Plaza market, the Ferroviaria market, the garlic and tuber market, the farm bird and live-stock market and the shoe market. Most of these smaller markets are on side streets off Calle Bolívar, three blocks northwest of the Mercado Central. There is also a small flower market next to the Mercado Central. North of the Mercado Colombia, Calle Cevallos is clogged with booths selling tourist items such as weavings, ceramics, jewelry and wooden figurines. The main market day is Monday, with smaller markets on Wednesday and Friday.

Ambato also has a rich tradition of festivals celebrating the fertility of its surrounding hills. The best-known festival is in late February: **Fiesta de Frutas y Flores**, or the Flower Festival. At this time the streets and squares are filled with flowers and fresh fruits and there are parties and parades to fill the days and nights. Associated with the Flower Festival is the International Folk Festival where musical groups from many countries come to play and perform their national folk music.

Ambato is known as the "city of the three Juans." Between 1850 and 1870, three famous and historically important people named Juan lived in Ambato. **Juan Montalvo** (1832–1889) was a writer known as the "American Cervantes" and the father of Ecuadorian philosophy who wrote about the injustices of Ecuador's dictators. **Juan Benigo Vela** (1843–1920) was a politician and a political essayist who campaigned against political corruption and who was also a champion of the underprivileged. **Juan Leon Mera** (1832–1894) was a musician and also a writer. He wrote *Cumandá*, a famous book about the life of the indigenous people in the 1800s, as well as the words to Ecuador's national anthem. He also founded the Ecuadorian conservative party. The Ambato homes of Juan Montalvo and Juan Leon Mera are now museums open to the public.

LODGING   The following four hotels range in price from $30-$80 for double occupancy. Amenities in the rooms include private bath, hot water, air conditioning, color TV and phone. Each hotel has a restaurant and a bar.

The most deluxe hotel in Ambato is the attractive **Hotel Ambato** (corner of Guayaquil and Rocafuerte; cable TV, minibar; 3-827-093, fax: 3-827-197). The hotel is located on a steep bluff above the Río Ambato in the western corner of Ambato. The rooms are extremely comfortable with posh bathrooms; many rooms have river views. There is a casino, as well as an elegant restaurant downstairs and a cafeteria that serves delicious breakfast and lunch buffets. The Hotel Ambato is an easy walk to the markets and very close to the Casa de Cultura and the Casa de Montalvo museums.

Two very nice hotels are located in the quiet, pretty residential neighborhood of Miraflores on the southwest side of Ambato. The modern **Hotel Miraflores** (Avenida Miraflores 227; 3-844-395) has 30 rooms behind a broad green lawn with picnic tables. The **Hotel Villa Hilda** (Avenida Miraflores 600; 3-822-730, fax: 3-845-571) is run by a German couple and is surrounded by gardens and attractive plantings. There is also a pool. Both hotels have clean, pleasant rooms and helpful staffs to make your stay more enjoyable. These hotels are a 20- to 30-minute walk to the Mercado Central.

Located 4 kilometers north of Ambato on the Pan-American Highway is the **Hosteria Dulce Primavera** (3-822-569, fax: 3-822-569), which has a heated pool, sauna, hot tub and playground. The entrance road to the hosteria is a bit difficult to find because the hosteria is tucked behind another building and is shielded from the highway. Turn at the large sign on the east side of the Pan-American Highway and head for the red and white brick building. The rooms are in individual cabañas scattered around the grounds so that each of the ten cabañas is very private. The large pool and nearby playground make this the best place to stay in the area for a traveling family.

The following four lodgings cost between $5–$30 for a single/double-occupancy room. All have private baths and hot water. The rooms are a bit smaller than the more expensive hotels and may show a bit of wear around the edges. These hotels are located downtown, so they may be noisy. Be sure to ask for the best rooms or else you may get stuck with a shared bath on a top floor with windows that do not open.

The hotels we can recommend in this category are the **Hotel San Ignacio** (corner of 12 de Noviembre and Maldonado; 3-824-370), one block northeast of the Colombia market; the **Gran Hotel** (corner of Lalama and Rocafuerte; 3-824-119, fax: 3-824-235), one block north of Calle Bolívar and its markets; the **Hotel Vivero** (Mera 504; 3-840-088), located in the middle of the city and close to everything; and the **Hotel Cumandá** (Eguez 837; 3-826-792), east of Calle Bolívar near the Gran Hotel.

RESTAURANTS   Restaurants in Ambato range in price from $8–$12. Perhaps the best restaurant here is in the **Hotel Ambato** (corner of Guayaquil and Rocafuerte; 3-827-197). Elegantly set tables with beautiful views over the river and an outside dining patio combined with delicious food make this our favorite place to eat in Ambato. Nearby is a very good Argentinean steak restaurant, the **Parrilladas El Gaucho** (corner of Bolívar and Quito; 3-828-969) and a very good French restaurant, **La Buena Mesa** (Quito 924; 3-822-330). These restaurants have a quiet, attractive ambiance but are on the expensive side for Ambato. The other fine Ambato restaurant is **El Gran Alamo** (Montalvo 535; 3-820-806), which is run by a Swiss couple.

For more informal dining, try the other two El Alamos: **Restaurante El Alamo** (Sucre 660; 3-821-710) and the **El Alamo Chalet** (Cevallos 612; 3-824-704). Other informal restaurants are the **Restaurant El Coyote** (Bolívar 330; 3-827-886), which is also a disco bar; the Chinese restaurant **Chifa Jao Fua** (corner of Cevallos and Mera; 3-826-987); and the **Parrilladas Los Charruas** (corner of Atahualpa and Los Shyris; 3-842-347), which serves delicious grilled steaks, chicken and trout.

GETTING THERE: By Bus: Many bus companies offer transportation up and down the Pan-American Highway. You can go to the bus station on the corner of

Maldonado and 12 de Noviembre or you can just stick out your hand when a bus traveling in the right direction on the Pan-American Highway approaches.

By Car: Ambato is about 136 kilometers south of Quito on the Pan-American Highway. Most of the city is east of the highway.

By Train: In theory, the train to Ambato is supposed to arrive from Quito in the afternoon. Check ahead if you plan to do any train travel.

CHIMBORAZO AREA

Continuing south from Ambato on the Pan-American Highway, the looming mass of Volcán Chimborazo and its sister peak to the northeast, Carihuairazo, increasingly command your attention. The highway crosses a pass on the eastern flank of Chimborazo that in good weather has spectacular views of the mountain. Many tourists have never seen a mountain this massive or this high. For several years in the 19th century, Chimborazo was considered the world's tallest mountain. As it turns out, Chimborazo (20,823 feet/6310 meters) is the highest mountain in Ecuador and is higher than any other mountain north of it in the Western Hemisphere. Also, its top is the farthest point on Earth from the center of the Earth due to the bulge around the equator. Volcán Carihuairazo is the ninth-highest mountain in Ecuador. Both mountains are extinct volcanoes, long dormant. Geologists believe that Volcán Chimborazo is, in fact, two volcanoes fused by a great dollop of ice.

El Chimborazo, as it is know locally, sits in the middle of the 146,400-acre **Chimborazo Faunal Reserve**, established in 1987. Unlike Cotopaxi, its astonishingly symmetric neighbor to the north, El Chimborazo's outline is rugged and irregular. The top of the glacier-crowned mountain is capped by five summits, four of which are over 19,800 feet (6000 meters). The highest peak, the Whymper Summit, is named for the British climber who, in 1880, became the first to ascend the mountain. El Chimborazo is an impressive mountain, reminiscent of Mount Blanc in the Alps or Mount Rainier in the Cascades of Washington State. Unfortunately, the mountaintop is often obscured by self-manufactured clouds, even on days with otherwise blue skies, so hope for good luck and clear skies to see all of this magnificent mountain.

There are two roads that enter the reserve, one from the north and one from the south. Both join and end at a climber's refuge high on the western slope of the mountain. The northern route, the Ambato–Guaranda Road or Route 50, crosses the reserve's northwest corner. The southern road starts in the village of San Juan, 10 kilometers west of Riobamba, and heads to the northwest. The southern road is the better road and the most popular way to enter the reserve. A gravel road from Route 50 intersects the southern access road about 6 kilometers from the refuge. At the end of the access road at 15,840 feet (4800 meters) elevation, is a dusty parking lot beneath the small

refuge. There are toilets at this refuge and snacks are sometimes available. The larger **Whymper Refuge** is 660 feet (200 meters) above the parking lot and the 30 minutes of steady walking is not easy at this altitude. This refuge is the one typically used by climbing parties, and there is a manager on site to supervise the building. The refuge has toilets, cold water, bunk beds for 40 people, foam mattresses, kitchen facilities, a propane stove and a fireplace. Bring your own sleeping bag and food if you plan to spend the night.

Despite El Chimborazo's stature, the reserve is not a national park, so there are no formal visitor services such as an interpretive center or marked trails. This is not to say that you cannot park and wander just about anywhere you choose. Most of the landscape is either dry or moist paramo. Dry paramo has short plants that are widely scattered on hard ground that is bare or dusty. Wet paramo is much lusher, with the ground densely packed with a wide variety of plants of many different sizes and kinds. The ground is soft as if you were walking on a mattress.

There is much more wildlife in the areas of wet paramo than in the dry paramo. Look for the unique birds of the paramo such as canasteros, the alliterative Carunculated Caracara, the Giant Hummingbird and the diminutive Chimborazo Hillstar. There are also rabbits, deer and fox to be seen. The easiest mammals to spot are the reintroduced vicuña, wild relatives of the llama. The Ecuadorian government is trying to re-establish these once-common animals to some of their former range. If you are lucky enough to get near one, they make a great subject for a photograph, especially with the mountain in the background.

You will also notice farming within the boundaries of the reserve. Remember, this is not a national park. Farming is limited, however, to traditional techniques that have been practiced for centuries on the slopes of El Chimborazo. These have to be some of the highest farms in the world and certainly amongst the hardiest farmers. To supplement their income, many of the high-elevation farmers travel to the glaciers and cut blocks of ice that are then sold to people in the communities below.

If you are interested in climbing Chimborazo, you will need to secure a guide unless you are a very experienced mountaineer. The traditional routes to the summit involve sections of very steep ice climbing where ropes, crampons and an ice ax are necessary. Tour operators in Ambato and Riobamba can arrange guides. Give yourself plenty of time to acclimatize to the high elevation. For more information about climbing and hiking in the reserve, refer to *Climbing and Hiking in Ecuador* by Rachowiecki, Thurber and Wagenhauser.

GETTING THERE: *By Bus:* The bus from Ambato to Guaranda can drop you off around El Chimborazo. Various tour operators and hotels (start at Metropolitan Tours or the Hotel Whymper) in Riobamba can arrange day trips to El Chimborazo. You can even take a taxi to the mountain from Riobamba for around $25 round-trip.

By Car: The best way to get close to the mountain is to drive up the gravel access road toward the Whymper Refuge on the volcano's west side. The well-signed trip takes about an hour from Riobamba via the village of San Juan (10 kilometers west of Riobamba on the Pan-American Highway heading south) and a bit longer from Ambato via the road (Route 50) to Guaranda. The turn on Route 50 is at the abandoned white house on the left side of the road decorated with political slogans. The house is about 56 kilometers from Ambato (there are no other houses near the turn).

RIOBAMBA AREA

From the pass on the eastern flank of El Chimborazo, the Pan-American Highway slowly descends for about 30 kilometers to the capital city of Chimborazo Province, **Riobamba** (population 70,000). Riobamba sits in a broad valley on the southern slope of El Chimborazo. To the east rise three high volcanoes: due east is the three-spired crown of Altar (17,553 feet/5319 meters), to its north is the jagged summit of Tungurahua (16,576 feet/5023 meters) and to Altar's south the ashy gray top of Sangay (17,259 feet/5230 meters). Sangay is one of Ecuador's most active volcanoes, so it is not unusual to see a steamy plume rising from its crest.

Unlike Latacunga to the north, Riobamba is a city that can take a hint. The original site of Riobamba was 21 kilometers west where the present-day town of Cajabamba is located. A devastating earthquake in 1797 leveled the town and, instead of rebuilding at that location, the survivors relocated to its present site. Also unlike Latacunga, much of Riobamba's 19th-century architecture remains, giving the city a pleasant colonial ambiance much like Cuenca. In fact, as you stroll the cobblestone streets in central Riobamba and admire the ornate balconies and colorful doors and windows along its narrow streets, it is hard not to imagine you are walking the more famous cobblestone streets of Cuenca. Riobambeños would prefer you not say anything about this little secret.

Chimborazo Province, the geographical center of the country, is a mostly rural, agricultural region with the highest percentage (about 70 percent) of indigenous people in Ecuador. Consequently, Riobamba is the Ecuadorian city where it is most likely you will see a tractor or a group of cows downtown. This is especially evident every Saturday when people from the surrounding hills pour into Riobamba for market day.

Finding a market is not difficult in Riobamba; almost every plaza in the city is filled with things to buy on market day. There are two modern market buildings—**Mercado Borja** on the corner of Guayaquil and Colón and the

Mercado la Condamine two blocks south of Chile on Montalvo—where everything from potatoes to plastic pails are sold. The best places to find local handicrafts such as shawls, hats and jewelry are the **Plaza Simón Bolívar** (corner of Argentinos and 5 de Junio) and **Parque de la Concepción** (corner of Orozco and Colón). One particularly interesting item for sale in Riobamba is tagua nut souvenirs. Tagua nuts come from a native palm that grows in intact rainforests. The nut is soft and pearly white at first but soon hardens into what looks very much like ivory. Not only does the tagua nut reduce the demand for ivory, but it provides an economic incentive to preserve intact rainforests. Several stores opposite the train station on Avenida Primera Constituyente sell tagua nut figurines, jewelry and other knickknacks.

There are other things to see in Riobamba besides the markets. The **Museo de Arte Religioso** (Religious Art Museum) in the Church of the Concepción (corner of Argentinos and Larrea; 9 a.m. to 6 p.m., with a break for siesta, Tuesday–Saturday; 3-965-212; admission) has a variety of well-presented religious paintings, statues and vestments. Be sure to see the priceless gold-, pearl- and diamond-encrusted monstrance. (A monstrance is a receptacle for the consecrated wafer used in communion.) There is also an interesting ethnographic display and modern art exhibit in the **Museo de Banco Central** downtown on Avenida Primera Constituyente.

The most famous church in Riobamba is the round **Basilica** (corner of Veloz and Alvarado) on the northeast side of the Parque La Libertad. The Basilica was built by locals between 1883 and 1915; unfortunately, it is seldom open. Riobamba's interesting **cathedral** is opposite the **Parque Maldonado** (corner of Veloz and Espejo). We think the park is more interesting than the cathedral, though, because in the park are pretty gardens, shade trees and singing birds. A great spot to watch Riobamba go by. The best place to see the sunset over Riobamba is the **Parque 21 de Abril** north of town on Argentinos. There is a platform here from which you can get a good view of Volcán Tungurahua and see a display on the history of Riobamba done in tile.

There are two villages near Riobamba worth exploring, especially if you like indigenous crafts. A few kilometers north of Riobamba is **Guano**, known for its rug weaving. These rugs are not the typical thin woven rugs that are commonly found in Ecuador. They are much thicker, knotted rugs with pre-Columbian and abstract nature designs unique to Guano. The village is so small it's easy to find the shops selling the rugs and the outdoor looms where the rugs are created. Thirty kilometers south of Riobamba on the Pan-American Highway is the village of **Guamote** featuring a mostly indigenous market on Thursdays. Most of the commerce conducted at this market is by bartering. There are piles of highland fruits and vegetables and lots of utilitarian items. Notice the llamas tied up outside the market in the llama parking lot. There is a new road between Guamote and Macas in the Oriente that we did not get a chance to explore, but it seems like a great route to take to get a cross-section of life between the cold paramo and the humid rainforest.

LODGING The best places to spend the night in the Riobamba area are outside the city. One is an elegant country hosteria, one a sprawling mini-resort, and another is a new hotel similar to a country inn. Each has large, comfortable rooms with private bath, hot water, phone and color TV, and each also has at least one restaurant.

In a class by itself in the Riobamba area, and equal to the best hosterias in the country, is the **Hosteria La Andaluza** (16 kilometers north of Rio-bamba on the Pan-American Highway; $40–$80; 3-965-575, fax: 3-904-234). The original hacienda was started in 1550 and completed in 1736. It was remodeled for guests in 1989. In the 18th and 19th centuries, the hacienda became a convenient stop on the journey between Cuenca and Quito. At this time the hacienda controlled lands that covered parts of four provinces and exceeded 375,000 acres. Consequently, there is much history associated with La Andaluza. During the 1830s, the writers of Ecuador's constitution were guests at the hacienda, as was Simón Bolívar. Ecuador's March Revolution in 1834 was also planned here.

La Andaluza is a wonderfully warm and inviting colonial hosteria filled with period antiques where guests get a sense of life a century past. The 42 large rooms are arranged, mazelike, down wooden planked corridors and stone-block steps. There are two restaurants (where the former stables were), one that is a bit cozier and more formal, and the main restaurant with its large fireplace and windows that frame El Chimborazo. Hosteria La Andaluza is the place we would stay if we were exploring the Riobamba region.

The favorite place in Riobamba for gringo tour groups is the contempo-rary **Hosteria El Troje** (6 kilometers southeast of Riobamba on the road to

Winnowing wheat

Chambo; many with fireplaces; $40–$70; 3-965-472, fax: 3-964-572). The hosteria is a sprawling complex of buildings, tennis courts, gardens and court-yards that overlook the vineyards of the Chambo river valley. The 40 newly remodeled rooms are unusually large—most have a fireplace, sitting room and an outdoor patio. The hosteria also has a pool, sauna, game room, out-door sports courts, boutique and mini-zoo. Around the grounds you will find a Galápagos Tortoise, several peacocks, a water garden full of ducks and four Scarlet Macaws. If you want a comfortable place to stay, albeit culturally sterile, Hosteria El Troje is just the place.

Alberque Abraspunga (3.5 kilometers northeast of town on the road to Guano; $30–$50; 3-940-820, fax: 3-940-819) is our favorite place close to Riobamba. The hotel is very much like a family-run country inn because of the friendly staff and the intimate rooms. There are 20 rooms that are quite spacious with high ceilings, large bathrooms and lots of room to move about. Each room is named for a mountain in Ecuador and is decorated with the photographs of the famous Ecuadorian mountaineer and Riobamba resident Marco Cruz. There is a small restaurant, and a large area in back that would be perfect for kids to blow off a little extra energy. There are also trails and horseback riding. The Alberque Abraspunga is a great place for families or for individuals. We recommend it highly.

There are also three reasonably priced hotels in downtown Riobamba that offer pleasant, clean rooms. Our favorite is the **Hostal Montecarlo** (10 de Agosto 2541; private bath, hot water, phone, TV; $20–$40; 3-962-844). Recently remodeled, the Hostal Montecarlo is the best hotel closest to the train station. The **Hotel Chimborazo Internacional** (corner of Argentinos and Nogales; private bath, hot water, phone, TV; $25–$40; 3-963-475) and the **Hotel El Galpon** (corner of Argentinos and Carlos; private bath, hot water, phone, TV; $25–$40; 3-960-983) are modern hotels west of the city center. They both have a restaurant and a bar and are a bit quieter than the Hostal Montecarlo. For the budget-minded, the **Zeus Hotel** (Daniel León Borja 4129; private bath, hot water, phone, TV; $10–$25; 3-963-100, fax: 3-968-036) and the **Hotel Whymper** (Avenida León 2310; private bath, hot water, phone, TV; $10–$25; 3-964-575) offer small but reasonably clean rooms. The Hotel Whymper is popular with mountain climbers and can arrange transportation and guides to any of the surrounding peaks.

RESTAURANTS   Restaurants in the Riobamba area are priced between $12 and $18. The best restaurant, by far, is at the **Hosteria la Andaluza** (16 kilometers north of Riobamba on the Pan-American Highway; 3-965-575). The kitchen serves delicious steak and chicken dishes, as well as fresh trout in a style best described as country elegance. Only the magnificent views of Chimborazo out the large windows can rival the flavor of the food.

In Riobamba, the best restaurant is the **Restaurante El Delirio** (Primera Constituyente and Rocafuerte; 3-965-027). El Delirio is on the fancy and expensive side compared to the other, rather plain restaurants of the city, but the food, service and ambiance are worth it. The restaurant is located in a small colonial house that was once owned by Simón Bolívar, so you get a taste of history with your dinner.

Three other restaurants in downtown Riobamba offer pleasant dining with good food for a reasonable price: **La Cabaña Montecarlo** (García Moreno 24-10; 3-962-844), around the corner from the Hotel Montecarlo, offers typical Ecuadorian fare; the **Candilejas** (corner of 10 de Agosto and Pichincha) also features Ecuadorian meals; and the **Steak House Restaurant** (corner of Dávalos and Veloz; 3-968-291) specializes in steaks and pork dishes.

BAÑOS AREA

Sixty kilometers northeast of Riobamba or 50 kilometers east of Ambato is the resort town of **Baños**. (But watch out—there are numerous towns in Ecuador named Baños. The principal one is in Tungurahua Province.) This Baños (population 18,000) is well known for its perpetually mild climate (elevation 5940 feet/1800 meters) and as a gateway to both the Oriente and the high peaks of the Andes. The town is built on a narrow bench between a high cliff on the south and the deep gorge of the Río Pastaza on the north. The cliff is part of the steep hem of the green skirt that surrounds Volcán Tungurahua, which towers over Baños. The Río Pastaza collects the waters from the rivers of the central highlands and flows through a very narrow gorge east of Baños to and beyond the Oriente gateway city of Puyo. North of the Río Pastaza is the Cordillera de Los Llanganates. These mountains are very inaccessible and have been the rumored site of the famous lost gold of the Incas, or *El Dorado*. Fortune hunters still comb the steep ridges and hidden valleys, convinced there is a fortune to be found.

Baños is where many urban highlanders come on weekends or vacations to get away from the hubbub of the city and to soak their cares away. In case you have not figured it out yet, *baños* translates to "bath" in Spanish. And sure enough, there are two popular hot springs, or thermal baths, in Baños. Many Ecuadorians believe these baths will cure many an ailment. The baths certainly will wash the dust and grime away after a day spent enjoying the area's other attractions, such as horseback riding, mountain biking, hiking, shopping, birdwatching or just relaxing.

The main bath in town is directly under the **Cascada Caballera de la Virgen** (Virgin's Hair Waterfall). The water falls in thin wisps (hence Virgin's hair) over the steep cliff on the town's southeastern edge. The waterfall is obvious from anywhere in town and is a good point to meet people or to regain your orientation. The most popular **hot springs** (open before dawn until after dark; admission) are at the base of this waterfall. There are several pools here with different water temperatures, changing rooms and attendants to watch your clothes. We do not recommend putting your head under water because the pools are cleaned only once a week and locals use the baths to bath in. The pools are nonetheless a relaxing way to start or end your day.

The other thermal baths, **El Salado Hot Springs** (open dawn to dusk; admission), are 2 kilometers west of town. Turn left just past the big bridge on Via al Salado and go to the end of the road. These hot springs are not as convenient for most tourists, so they are less crowded. It is about a 40-minute walk or a five-minute taxi ride from town. There are also buses that regularly go here.

While Baños today seems like just another tourist destination, to Ecuadorians it is more importantly the site of the **Santuario de Nuestra Señora de Agua Santa** or the Church of the Virgin of the Holy Water. The Virgin is credited with many miracles and many Ecuadorians make an annual pilgrimage to Baños to ask for the Virgin's blessing. The church is on Calle Ambato, the main street in town. Inside you will see primitive paintings depicting the miracles that have been performed by the Virgin. The captions under each painting explains the miracle that is illustrated. On the way out of the church, notice the stacks of crutches and canes that have been discarded thanks to the beneficence of the Holy Virgin.

The rest of Calle Ambato is chockablock with souvenir shops selling everything from religious figurines and Otavalo weavings to T-shirts and taffy. In fact, there seems to be an inordinately high amount of taffy being pulled in the stores lining Calle Ambato. Once the allure of stretched taffy wears out, there are lots of other things to do that are almost as fascinating. Many tour operators offer half- to full-day horseback riding trips into the surrounding hills. Some of these trips can be combined with hiking options as well. Be sure to ask a lot of questions about your trip, the guide, etc., before you give them money, so there won't be any disagreement or disappointment. Also, be sure to insist on a healthy horse with a strong and correct-size saddle.

For those who prefer riding something with real brakes, there are also lots of mountain bike rental companies in town. Most people who rent mountain bikes are told to take the scenic ride downhill to Puyo and then catch the bus back to Baños. The problem with this route is that half of the road to Puyo is narrow and gravel and you will be battling dust and large trucks for the first part of your trip. We suggest instead to go with a tour operator that offers combination jeep and bike rides. These trips usually go up into the hills around Baños where the ride back is far more relaxing and just as scenic. As with horseback-riding trips, be sure to check your equipment carefully before you start your trip and ask for a spare tire just in case.

There are many possibilities for easy to strenuous hikes based in Baños. The most popular hike starts at the trail at the north end of Calle Pastaza and crosses the San Francisco bridge to the north side of the Río Pastaza. From here there are loop trails leading into the hills or downstream to the Río Pastaza and another bridge back to Baños. You can also hike up a trail that climbs the high cliff on the south edge of town to the little village of **Runtún** and return via the Hosteria Luna Runtún (a great spot for lunch) on another trail down the cliff. The cliff trails are wide and not as scary as they look from Baños. Besides, once you are passed going uphill by a little indigenous woman carrying a heavy load, your mind will be on other things. The trails up the cliff start at the south end of Calle Maldonado and Calle Mera.

A more strenuous hike is up the slopes of Volcán Tungurahua in **Sangay National Park**. The trail starts at the park office high on the northwestern slope of the mountain. Sangay National Park covers the high, steep slopes on the south side of the Río Pastaza to the south and east of Baños (for information on southern and eastern portions of Sangay see Chapter Fifteen). The only access to the park's northern part is from the park office and this is mostly for mountaineers. There is a **climber's refuge** 3300 feet (1000 meters) in elevation above the park office that makes a good destination for a day hike. Take a taxi to the park office and remember to arrange a time to be picked up. From the high village of Runtún the boundary of the park is still a four- to five-hour hike uphill. For more information on hiking in the Baños area, refer to *Climbing and Hiking in Ecuador* by Rachowiecki, Thurber and Wagenhauser.

The **drive toward Puyo** (68 kilometers) is a good way to see some spectacular scenery that offers a cross-section from mountain to rainforest. Be warned, though, that part of the road is built on a very narrow shelf high above the Río Pastaza Gorge, so passing other cars and—especially—unheeding buses can be a bit unnerving. The rewards of the trip overcome these few inconveniences, however. Along the way you will see roadside orchids, dramatic waterfalls, cliffside farms, patches of little-disturbed forest and vistas of untouched mountainsides on the opposite side of the river.

Our favorite place to stop is the **trail to Pailon de Diablo**, or the Devil's Caldron. The trailhead is marked by a large sign that advertises Pailon de Diablo and **El Otra Lado**, a small hostal on the other side of the river. The short trail leads downhill through scrubby vegetation to a suspension bridge over the river below the falls. Before the bridge there is a small gazebo where soft drinks and conversation are available. The land the trail crosses is owned by a young man named Wilfredo who is trying to save the remaining stands of primary forest and who has developed a few trails for hikers and birdwatchers. Wilfredo is very friendly, informative and trying to improve his English, so a conversation will benefit all. Above the gazebo is a very short trail that leads to an overlook above the deep bowl into which a waterfall pours, the impressive Devil's Caldron. The best view of the main falls is from midway on the suspension bridge. The entire area around the gazebo, across the river at El Otro Lado, on the trails to the caldron and down to the river itself offers the best birdwatching near Baños. Flocks of tanagers, warblers and finches are common in the low trees and Cocks-of-the-Rock have been seen near the gazebo. Even if you are not thirsty, buy a soda from Wilfredo to help support his efforts to protect this forest.

LODGING   There are numerous places to spend the night in Baños, more seemingly than in Riobamba and Ambato combined. Many are small residencials and hostales offering a room and a private bath with hot water in a private home for just a few dollars. These places come and go as the owners alternate between wanting more privacy or more money. Try the **Residencial Lucy** (Rocafuerte next to the central park; 3-740-466), the **Residencial Timara** (corner of Maldonado and Martínez; 3-740-599) or the **Residencial Villa Santa Clara** (corner of 12 de Noviembre and Ibarra; 3-740-349). If these are full, there are several other residencials bordering the central park.

The most intriguing place to stay, the recently opened **Luna Runtún Resort** (at Km. 6 on the road to Runtún; private bath, hot water, fireplace, porch; $40–$80; 3-740-882, fax: 3-740-376) is the farthest from Baños but is worth the extra effort. The Luna Runtún Resort ("resort" is misleading— it should really be called Hosteria Luna Runtún) is a collection of 13 colonial-style buildings nestled into a shallow green fold high above Baños. The buildings are constructed on three terraces so that each of the 32 rooms has a view to the north over the valley. The rooms are very comfortable, with luxurious bathrooms and thick down comforters on each bed. Several of the rooms are built right on the edge of the cliff, providing a breathtaking view of Baños. There's also a restaurant and conference room. You could fly a frisbee from one of these porches and land it in the soccer stadium below.

The land on which the Luna Runtún Resort is built was once the family farm of the current owners. Their home has been preserved and is now a small museum on the grounds. The owners still grow crops and raise cattle in the hills surrounding the resort. The resort offers several one- to five-day excursions into Sangay National Park led by local guides. You can choose to go by horseback or on foot. For the less ambitious, you can walk down to Baños on one of the cliff trails that starts at the Luna Runtún or walk up to the typical highland village of Runtún, 40 minutes away. We very much enjoyed staying at the Luna Runtún Resort.

Similar to the Luna Runtún is the **Hacienda Manteles** (half-way between Baños and Ambato near town of Patete; private bath, hot water, restaurant, hiking, horseback riding; $30–$40; on-site; 3-870-123, Quito office, phone/fax: 2-505-230, or 800-323-3573 in the U.S.). The hacienda is located in the patchwork quilt of farm lands just below Llanganates National Park. All rooms are spacious and comfortable and the restaurant serves delicious meals. Hacienda Manteles offers a variety of outdoor activities including rides into the mountain forests and visits to isolated Andean villages. Birdfeeders around the buildings and the large flower garden make this hacienda a perfect spot for birdwatchers as well. The lodge is difficult to find unless you have been there. It is on the north side of the road between Ambato and Baños near the little village of Patate. Contact the lodge for more detailed directions.

In town, the most popular place to stay for gringos is the **Hotel Sangay** (Plazoleta Isidro Ayora 101; private bath, hot water, phone, cable TV; $30–$60; 3-740-490, fax: 3-740-917). The Hotel Sangay is just across the street from the Waterfall of the Virgin's Hair and its thermal baths on the southeast corner of town. There are 72 comfortable guest rooms in two buildings—ask for a room in the new part of the hotel. The hotel also has a good restaurant and bar with a great view of the falls and pools, as well as a tennis court, sauna, thermally heated pool, exercise room, game room and steam room. Hotel Sangay can also arrange trips into the Oriente or to the slopes of Tungurahua.

The **Villa Gertrudis** (corner of Montalvo and Ibarra; private bath, hot water, phone, cable TV; $20–$50; 3-740-441) is a lovely old home among beautiful gardens that has been converted to a guest house. The attraction of the Villa Gertrudis is its homey ambiance and the friendliness of the staff. There is also a very good restaurant and an unusually large pool on site (the owner was a former Argentinean swimming champion). This is a very cozy hotel that we highly recommend. The **Hosteria Monte Selva** (corner of Montalvo and Halflans; private bath, hot water, phone, TV; $30–$50; 3-740-566, fax: 3-854-658) is a new hotel built into the cliffside rising above Baños. There are 12 individual cabañas on a hill above a pool, restaurant and reception area. People unable to walk uphill would find the walk to the cabañas difficult, but the hillside perch of rooms gives each a nice view over Baños. The grounds are covered with beautiful gardens interlaced with cascading water. (The manager claims that there are over 300 kinds of plants on the grounds.) These gardens and the proximity to the shrubby cliffside make the Hosteria Monte Selva a great place for birdwatchers to stay.

Across the street from the Hotel Sangay is the **Hotel Palace** (Montalvo 2003; private bath, hot water, TV; $15–$40; 3-740-470). The Hotel Palace is older than the Hotel Sangay and the rooms can be a bit run-down. They do have a nice garden with tall trees nearby and a good restaurant. In the same price range as the Hotel Palace is the **Hotel Humboldt** (corner of Ambato and Halflans; private bath, hot water, TV; $15–$40; 3-740-430) near the center of town. The rooms are clean and pleasant and the staff is helpful. Our favorite place in this price range is the German-owned **Hostal Isla de Baños** (Montalvo 131; private bath, hot water; $12–$20; 3-740-609). There are 11 pleasant rooms and two kitchenettes and a spectacularly delicious breakfast bakery downstairs. The hostal is surrounded by a high fence that contains a beautiful garden where stray pet parrots can often be found. The owners can also arrange horseback and hiking trips.

RESTAURANTS   Many of the places to eat in Baños are small, informal street cafés where you can get a plate of chicken and rice or pork and potatoes for a reasonable price ($8–$12). There are also lots of bakeries selling fresh baked breads, pastries, yogurts, granolas and juices. We recommend the **Rico Pan** (corner of Ambato and Maldonado), **Mi Pan** (corner of Ambato and 16 de Diciembre) and the **Cafe Cultura** (corner of Montalvo and Santa Clara). Our favorite bakery/restaurant here is the German-run **Cafetería Isla de Baños** at the south end of Montalvo. They have the best bread in town to go with the best breakfast. The breakfast room opens to a beautiful garden where stray pet parrots often hang out. The cafeteria is part of the Hostal Isla de Baños, one of our favorite places to stay while in Baños.

There are not many outstanding restaurants in Baños. Almost all of the restaurants assume the informal atmosphere of the town, so if you are looking for elegant dining and pretentious prices you are going to be disappointed in Baños. The restaurant at the **Hosteria Luna Runtún** (on the road to Runtún, follow the signs) is as close to fine dining as you are going to find in Baños. The food is good and it is never too crowded, plus the evening view from the top of the cliff overlooking Baños and the Cordillera de Las Llanganates is sublime. If you bring a flashlight, you can even walk off your dinner descending the cliff trail back to Baños. In town, try **Le Petit** (Alfaro 246) for French cuisine, **El Marqués** (corner of Montalvo and Ibarra) and **El Higuerón** (12 de Noviembre 270) for typical Ecuadorian food, and **Villas Gertrudis** (corner of Montalvo and Ibarra) and the **Savoy** (Calle Martinez near the pool) for good steaks and seafood.

GETTING THERE: The little town of Baños is one of the most popular tourist destinations in Ecuador so there are many convenient ways to get there.

By Bus: There are direct buses from Quito to Baños, but they are less convenient than taking a bus to Ambato and then transferring to another bus to Baños. The *terminal terrestre* in Baños is in the center of town on the main plaza.

By Car: Baños is 49 kilometers southeast from Ambato and 66 kilometers northeast from Riobamba. Both routes are well marked and on good paved roads.

NINE

Cuenca Area

To many, Cuenca embodies the tourist's ideal of Ecuador: narrow cobble-stone streets, whitewashed colonial buildings with worn tile roofs and small wooden balconies, markets of flowers, baskets, woven rugs and hats, ornate churches and quiet convents, riverbanks of drying clothes, peaceful streets and cheerful faces and a sense of timelessness that can transport a visitor through centuries long faded. This is the charm of Cuenca and yet, at 350,000, it is the third-largest city in Ecuador and a thoroughly modern metropolis. There are very comfortable hotels, fine restaurants, fashionable stores and sophis-ticated offices in Cuenca. If Quito's crush of noise and people is too much and the sprawling chaos of Guayaquil is unnerving, visit Cuenca to sample the history and creativity that underpin all of Ecuador.

The original inhabitants of the Cuenca area were the Cañari Indians, who lived here between 500–1500 A.D. They had a well-developed culture based on farming and were sophisticated astronomers. They called this region *Gua-pondelig*, which translates into "land as big as heaven." In the 15th century, Incas invaded from the south. After many years of siege the Cañaris were finally conquered and absorbed into the Incan culture. The Incas incorporated the Cañari's astronomical knowledge into their own and either overbuilt or tore down and rebuilt Cañari buildings in the Incan style. The Inca renamed the area *Tomebamba* or "the Valley of the Knifes" for the weapons they car-ried. The Incas built a grand city here—Pumapungo, "the door of the Puma" —and moved their capital here from Cuzco. Much still remains of the lega-cy of the Inca in the surrounding region of Cuenca: the ceremonial buildings of Ingapirca to the north, a series of roads radiating from the old capital, now called the Inca Trail, and a network of communication posts and lookouts.

The reign of the Incas did not last long in Tomebamba. The Spanish ar-rived in the early 1530s and quickly conquered the Incas. Within 15 years,

the magnificent city of Pumapungo lay in ruins. From the rubble the Spaniards overbuilt or rebuilt the Incan buildings so that in 1557 Cuenca was re-
born once again.

CUENCA

Cuenca is located in a lush valley 7755 feet (2350 meters) in elevation and
ringed by green mountain ridges. It is known as the City of Four Rivers, or
Santa Ana de los Cuatro Ríos de Cuenca, as the Spanish named it. The northernmost river, marking the north edge of this low valley, is the Río Machangara. Through the center of Cuenca flows the Río Tomebamba, whose waters
gather in the jagged mountains visible to the west. Just north of this river
is the colonial part of the city—south are the stadium, universities and the
modern suburbs. Along the southern edge of the city flow two rivers, the Río
Yanucay closest to the city and the Río Tarqui farthest south. The rivers join
together west of the train station far in the southeastern corner of the city and
are shortly joined by the Río Tomebamba. Farther east, the Río Machangara
adds its waters to form the Río Cuenca that in turn flows into the Río Paute
and continues to trace a watery line east to the Amazon Basin.

Today in the city of Cuenca, besides the obvious Spanish influence, there
are still hints of the architecture of the Incas and just faint rumors of the works
of the Cañaris. One spot where all three building styles are visible is at the
ruins of **Todos Santos** located on the corner of Calle Larga and the Todos
Santos Bridge in the southeast corner of the city. The ruins occupy a corner
of a small city park where construction in 1970 unearthed these foundation
ruins. The ruins are easily seen from the sidewalk, or you can walk into the
park on the uphill side and explore the ruins more closely. If you look carefully at the rockwork, the three styles of construction are evident. On the
right, the long rectangular blocks with square edges are Cañari; on the left,
the smaller blocks beautifully fit together with beveled edges are Incan; and
in the middle the characteristic Spanish arch is made from both styles of rock.
This former mill of a wealthy Spaniard is now owned by the Central Bank of
Ecuador.

The Spanish were not the last to invade Cuenca. In the 1860s, 2000 Jesuits
from France peacefully entered Ecuador. Their influence in Ecuador has been
profound—religiously, intellectually and architecturally. This is especially
evident in Cuenca, where tradition and history are more a part of everyday
life than in the more modern cities of Quito and Guayaquil. There are an
unusual number of churches in Cuenca (52, or one for each Sunday of the
year) plus three universities and many museums. Many Ecuadorians consider
Cuenca to be the creative center of Ecuador. The international influence can
be seen along the city's streets. It is common to see a French-style building—

with mansard roof, domes, no eaves, ornate molding and bright paint—alongside an older colonial Spanish building that has wide eaves showing wooden beams, balconies with simple railings, a small bench outside and plain or no molding around doors and windows.

The best view of the city can be found at the indigenous village of **Turi**. Take Avenida Fray Vicente Solano south past the stadium and across the Río Yanucay and Río Tarqui to the top of the bluff immediately south of the city. A small church, the **Church of Turi**, and adjoining orphanage sit at the edge of the bluff. This white church is clearly visible from almost anywhere in the city. In front of the church is the **Mirador de Turi**, or viewpoint of Turi, with a beautiful tile panorama depicting the city below. To the west the jagged peaks of El Cajas National Recreation Area are clearly in sight when the clouds cooperate, and to the north, with a trained eye, the mountain knobs can also be seen where the communication outposts along the Inca Trail were located. Before you leave Turi, walk up the stairs to the orphanage past the gaily painted murals to a chest-high wall near the statue of Hermano Miguel,

Cuenca Area

one of the saints of Cuenca. Now you will find yourself above the trees and powerlines bordering the street. Not only is the view of Cuenca a bit better up here, but there is also a small niche with a statue of Jesus de Belén in the wall behind you. Statues of Jesus are quite common in Ecuador, but this one usually has small plastic bags filled with hair and guinea pig droppings— black magic—scattered among the lit candles at the base of the statue. The indigenous people never gave up their own beliefs when Christianity spread across Ecuador—they just added another spiritual layer.

North of the Río Tomebamba and south of Avenida Héroes de Verdeloma is **Colonial Cuenca**, a historic area of approximately 12 by 16 blocks. Outside this colonial core are the modern suburbs, factories and the airport. The Pan-American Highway, or Avenida de las Américas as it is called in Cuenca, loops around the city to the west. It is easy to tell if you are in the old city as the streets here are paved with rectangular cobblestones. Calle Gran Colombia, the main street in the city, runs east–west and bisects Colonial Cuenca. Most of the things tourists want to see are south of Calle Gran Colombia.

On the corner of Calle Simón Bolívar and Calle Benigno Malo, one block south of Calle Gran Colombia, is the main square in Colonial Cuenca, **Plaza Abdón Calderón**. The plaza is a pleasant place to relax and watch Cuenca pass by. Across from the southeastern corner of the plaza on the corner of Calle Mariscal Sucre and Calle Luís Cordero is **El Sagrario**, more informally known as the Old Cathedral. Construction of this church, started in 1557 when present Cuenca was founded, rose from a foundation of Incan stone blocks, some of which are still visible along the front of the building. The church is small and easily overlooked but it is worth a peek inside at the historic and newly renovated interior. It is open to the public but the hours are uncertain so expect to go there more than once to get a look inside. Interestingly, the church was used as one of the fixed points of measurement when French scientists determined the shape of the Earth.

Overwhelming the east side of the plaza across from the Old Cathedral is the **Catedral de la Inmaculada**, or the New Cathedral. This impressive brick building with sky-blue cupolas was started in 1885 when Cuenca had outgrown the Old Cathedral. The cavernous interior of pale alabaster and pink marble topped by three stained-glass–edged domes holds 10,000 people. The altar is a free-standing golden arch with a statue of Christ on the cross underneath. It was originally intended to be the largest cathedral in South America, but an architectural miscalculation prevented it from reaching its intended size. Still, it is the signature building of Cuenca and dominates its skyline. It is open to the public during most hours, but be sensitive to the always-present worshipers inside. The view of the cathedral for photographers is in the morning from the northeast corner of the plaza in front of the cathedral. Across the street (Calle Mariscal Sucre) from the New Cathedral is a nice restaurant for snacks and lunches, Café El Carmen. Next to the café is the **Casa de Cultura**. This small museum always has interesting displays of paintings by local artists as well as a bookstore and a small coffee shop.

Turning west and walking one block along Calle Mariscal Sucre from the Old Cathedral you will find **Plazoleta del Carmen**, a pocket plaza with a daily flower and plant market. If you are at all attracted to flowers, be sure to visit this market—especially in the morning when the air is still and the flowers and floral bouquet are freshest. There are ten or so umbrellaed flower stands crowded together on one side of the plaza and displays of house plants and pottery arrayed over the cobbles on the other side. Each flower stand is awash in fresh-cut flowers, as if each were a fort and protected by bastions of blossoms. There are roses, carnations, lilies, mums, daisies, gladioli, orchids and many more in a wide range of colors to chose from. Amid the flowers are the cheerful faces of the flower ladies dressed in white Panamá hats, colorful skirts and blouses and radiant smiles. You can buy an armload of flowers for $5 and take them back to your hotel room or give them as a present to your guide.

The flower market is tucked under the eaves of **El Carmen de la Asunción**. The church, open from 8–10 a.m. and 3–5 p.m., was built in 1682. Associated with the church is the Cloister El Carmen Alto. You can visit the entrance to the cloister by walking to the back corner of the flower market, but no one is allowed inside. There are 20 nuns inside, isolated from the modern world. They wear no shoes, have shaved heads and tend a small garden for vegetables. Three of these cloisters were established—one in Perú, one in Mexico and one here. The nuns' lives are devoted solely to prayer. They receive no medical care or outside disturbance and are never allowed to leave the building for any reason. No new nuns have joined the strict devotion of the cloister in many years. Contact to the outside world is through a revolving window near the cloister's entrance. You can watch as the local indigenous people put offerings and favors in the window for the nuns beyond.

If you have not seen enough churches, from the corner of the flower market you can turn south (left) on Calle Padre Aguirre two blocks to the **Church of San Francisco** or north (right) three blocks to the **Church of Santo Domingo**. Two other historic churches of interest are east of the main plaza. **San Blas** on the corner of Calle Simón Bolívar and Calle Manuel Vega is the second-largest church in Cuenca and towers over the whitewashed buildings around it. One block west and one block south of the main plaza is the **Church of the Conceptas** but more on this church later on our tour. Every historic church or cathedral is unique and offers interesting discoveries to those who take the time to explore them. Try to notice more than just the grandeur and magnificence of the interior, although at times that can be a jaw-dropping experience. Poke around and look for the carvings and paintings and mortar of the souls whose faith and spirit fill each church.

If you turn south (left) at the flower market along Calle Padre Aguirre, in half a block you will come to a square in front of the Church of San Francisco that always has booths of vendors scattered about. You can buy food, baskets, weaving, sweaters, shoes, blankets, rugs or just about anything you might want. This market is open every day and caters mostly to locals, although there is plenty for the tourist to see and buy. For those who will not get to the famous market of Otavalo, there are even booths with woven goods from that region. If you prefer a less traditional place to buy crafts, try the **Gallerias El Túcan** three blocks east and half a block north of the Plaza de San Francisco on Calle Presidente Borrero 7-35. They also have a store on Calle Gran Colombia 7-88.

Two blocks south of the market and the Church of San Francisco is Calle Larga and the old buildings that line the north side of the Río Tomebamba. If you turn east (left) on Calle Larga, you will be able to find a couple of narrow streets that lead down to the river. On nice days there are often women doing their wash and drying their clothes along the riverbank. It is a classic photo opportunity to capture the colorful laundry and river in the foreground and the rising colonial buildings in the background. Returning to Calle Larga, continue east to the **Museo Remigo Crespo** at the junction of Calle Larga and Calle Presidente Borrero. The museum commemorates a pioneering Italian anthropologist and missionary, "Padre Crespi," and has a fine collection of colonial and ethnographic artifacts that he collected on his wide travels. The museum is being renovated but is expected to be open soon to the public during regular business hours.

One block east of the Museo Remigo Crespo along Calle Larga at the junction of Calle Hermano Miguel is the **Museo de Artes Populares**. You have to walk down a few steps toward the river to find the entrance to the museum. This museum is operated by the Centro Interamericano de Artesanias y Artes Populares (CIDAP). It has interesting displays of local craftsmanship and art. Admission is free and it is open during the regular weekday business hours. Two other museums lie outside the historic core of the city. The **Museo de Arte Moderno**, or Modern Art Museum, is six blocks west of the main plaza on the corner of Calles Mariscal Sucre and Coronel Talbot. The museum is housed in an old convent, which contrasts the very modern art it contains. Paintings, multimedia works and sculpture are presented in revolving displays. The best museum in Cuenca is the **Museo del Banco Central**, or the Central Bank Museum. It is located near the mouth of the Río Tomebamba just east of the ruins of Todos Santos on Calle Larga. Housed in

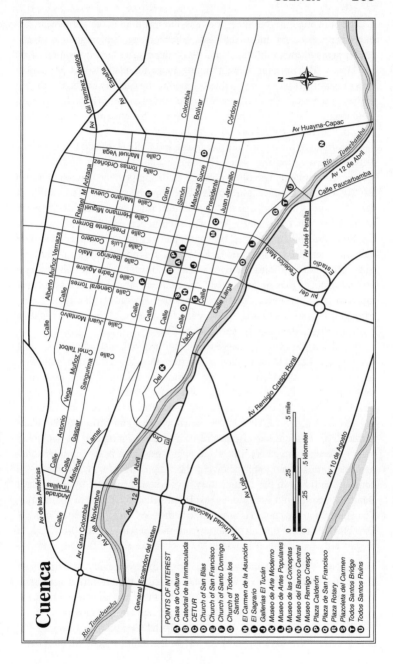

Cuenca

POINTS OF INTEREST

- Ⓐ Casa de Cultura
- Ⓑ Catedral de la Immaculada
- Ⓒ CETUR
- Ⓓ Church of San Blas
- Ⓔ Church of San Francisco
- Ⓕ Church of Santo Domingo
- Ⓖ Church of Todos los Santos
- Ⓗ El Carmen de la Asunción
- Ⓘ El Sagrario
- Ⓙ Gallerias El Tucán
- Ⓚ Museo de Arte Moderno
- Ⓛ Museo de Artes Populares
- Ⓜ Museo de las Conceptas
- Ⓝ Museo del Banco Central
- Ⓞ Museo Remigio Crespo
- Ⓟ Plaza Calderón
- Ⓠ Plaza de San Francisco
- Ⓡ Plaza Rotary
- Ⓢ Plazoleta del Carmen
- Ⓣ Todos Santos Bridge
- Ⓤ Todos Santos Ruins

a large contemporary building, the museum has impressive permanent displays of religious art, Incan and Cañari archaeology, ethnographic artifacts, photographs of historic Cuenca and revolving displays of contemporary art and issues. The museum is built among Incan foundations that are slowly being unearthed—some are visible behind the museum. Even though the interpretive signs are in Spanish, there is much to see and learn here. If you bring a dictionary with you, even better! Admission to the museum is free, and it is open during regular weekday business hours.

Returning to the corner of Calle Larga and Calle Hermano Miguel at the Museo de Artes Populares, you are presented with two choices. Still-energetic walkers can continue two blocks east on Calle Larga to the Church of Todos Santos. There is a convent associated with this church, but it is usually not open to tourists. Just beyond the church, turn south on a street that appears to cross the Río Tomebamba. You will soon notice that the bridge, known locally as the "broken bridge," only goes halfway across the river (the other half was carried away in a flood). From the bridge you will get a fine view of the old buildings lining the river and a brief respite from the cobblestones and colonial canyons of downtown Cuenca. Remember, only 400 years ago, this area from the bridge downstream was the imperial Incan city of Tomebamba. It is not hard to imagine why the Incan selected this area or, with a bit more effort, what it must have looked like.

For those walkers less energetic but still inspired, instead of continuing east on Calle Larga to the broken bridge from the Museo de Artes Populares, turn north on Calle Hermano Miguel and walk just past Calle Juan Jaramillo, about two blocks. On the right will be the tourist information office of CETUR, where you can get maps and brochures and have your questions answered. Opposite CETUR is the church, convent and **Museo de las Conceptas**. The museum has displays of many types of religious art, including nativity scenes, carved crucifixes and paintings. There is also an interesting presentation of photographs showing the simple life of convent nuns. The convent, built late in the 17th century, was restored recently by the Central Bank. Notice the old tombstones displayed inside the doors of the church. The entrance to the church is around the corner on Calle Presidente Córdova. One block east and one block north from the church will take you back to Plaza Calderón, the main square in town where we started this city tour.

LODGING   There are many lodging possibilities of every description in and around Cuenca. First we will list those places within historic Cuenca and then those outside the colonial city. All offer the usual amenities you'd expect to find, including private baths, hot water and air conditioning.

The best hotel in the city center is the **Hotel Crespo** (Calle Larga 7-93; phone, cable TV; $40–$60; fax: 7-839-473). It is built on the north bluff overlooking the Río Tomebamba and thus has beautiful views over the river and the southern part of the city. There are 41 rooms, including 15 suites, that are spacious and nicely decorated with large private baths and queen-sized beds. A few of the rooms overlook the street so would be a bit noisier, but all the rooms are comfortably elegant. There is a well-known and very good restaurant specializing in French and international cuisine that offers views of the river through large glass windows and serves all meals.

The other nice hotels in the city are usually less expensive than the Hotel Crespo but they are not quite as comfortable. Of these, the **Hotel El Dorado** (Calles Gran Colombia 7-87 and Luís Cordero; cable TV; $40–$60; fax: 7-831-663) is the best, but it is as expensive as the Hotel Crespo. The rooms are well appointed with large private baths and queen-sized beds. There is a restaurant and bar on the top floor with great evening views of the city and a cafeteria, pastry shop and sauna downstairs. The **Hotel Inca Real** (Calle General Torres 8-40; $25–$45; fax: 7-840-699) is a recently renovated two-story colonial building where you will soon feel part of old Cuenca. The rooms are located around three interior courtyards complete with hanging ferns and brick walks. The rooms are a bit small, but comfortable. There is a restaurant in the main courtyard across from the reception desk and the staff is very helpful. The hotel is extremely convenient to most of the tourist sites of Colonial Cuenca, especially the little flower market around the corner.

The modern **Hotel El Conquistador** (Calle Gran Colombia 6-65; minibar; $20–$40; fax: 7-831-291) offers 44 comfortable rooms that are nicely decorated. A breakfast buffet is included in the price of your room, as are transfers to the airport. There is a decent restaurant serving local, national and international food, as well as a bar and discotheque.

The **Hotel Presidente** (Calles Gran Colombia 6-59 and Hermano Miguel; $20–$40, fax: 7-824-704) and **Hotel Principe** (Calle Juan Jaramillo 7-86; $20–$40; fax: 7-834-369) also offer nice rooms for a reasonable price in the heart of the city. Both are modern hotels with restaurants and comfortable rooms with all the usual amenities.

There are many budget hotels in historic Cuenca offering clean rooms, friendly service and usually a small restaurant. Recommended in this category are the **Hotel Atahualpa** (Calles Mariscal Sucre 3-50 and Tomas Ordonez; $15-$30; fax: 7-842-345); **Internacional Hotel Paris** (Calles Mariscal Sucre 6-78 and Calle Borrero; $10–$30; fax: 7-831-525); **Hotel Catedral** (Calle Padre Aguirre 8-17; $10–$30; fax: 7-834-631); and the **Hotel Tomebamba** (Calles Simón Bolívar 11-19 and General Torres; $10–$30; fax: 7-835-142).

Outside the city of Cuenca are several very nice places to stay. Each has rooms and restaurants as good as any hotel in Cuenca, but with the added bonus of being quieter and having grounds and country lanes to roam when you get the urge to wander. But, if you anticipate spending all your time exploring the old churches and many museums of Cuenca, you'll find it more convenient to stay in the city.

The best place to stay in Cuenca is the **Hotel Oro Verde** (Avenida Ordóñez Lazo; $100–$125; 7-831-200, fax: 7-832-849). The Oro Verde is located 2 kilometers from the central historical district, 5 kilometers from the airport and just a couple of minutes west of the Pan-American Highway on the road west toward El Cajas National Recreation Area. It was formerly called the Hotel La Laguna and it is still referred to as that by locals, but it is formally the Oro Verde, part of the International Oro Verde luxury hotel chain. The name La Laguna comes from the fact that the hotel is built around a small lake. The lake is ringed by tall eucalyptus trees that slope down to the bank of the Río Tomebamba. Between the lake and the river are landscaped grounds with gardens and a playground for children.

All the 79 rooms have views of the lake and are large, very comfortable and have everything expected of a first-class hotel. There is a swimming pool, sauna, weight room, steam room, coffee shop, bar and a beautiful restaurant with great food that overlooks the lagoon. There are also paddle boats available for the lake and a number of animals wandering the grounds, including a family of friendly llamas. The staff is extremely friendly and helpful and can arrange trips with guides to the surrounding region, as well as to Colonial Cuenca. Because the hotel is on the west side of town, it is a great base from which to explore El Cajas—only a 20-minute drive away. If you like high-quality accommodations and a professional staff in a gardenlike setting, the Hotel Oro Verde is an excellent choice.

Southwest of Cuenca, about ten minutes by car, is the small farming community of Baños. This is *not* the famous Ecuadorian town of Baños located east of Ambato, but one of several other towns in Ecuador called Baños due to their natural hot-water mineral baths. In Baños is a delightful place to stay that is comfortable, interesting and also away from the noise and congestion of Cuenca—the **Hosteria Duran** (Km. 8 via Baños; minibar; $15–$30; fax: 7-892-488). The colonial-style hosteria is located inside a low, eroded volcanic rim on the slope below the little village of Baños. There are 17 spacious rooms, including two large suites built around the central spa/pool. The rooms are very comfortable, at half the price you would pay for similar accommodations in Cuenca. Above the reception area in the main building is a cozy bar and a restaurant. The restaurant and its French chef are well known, as is the splendid view north over the green hills and the red-tiled roofs of Cuenca. There are also tennis courts, hiking possibilities and camping sites for the tenting crowd. This is a very popular spot to come and relax for the people of Cuenca, especially on weekends, so try to time your visit during weekdays.

North of Cuenca on the Pan-American Highway is the **Hosteria El Molino** (Km. 7; $40–$60; fax: 7-890-737). The meaning of *el molino* can be inferred by the windmill that dominates the front of the hosteria. It means "the mill"—a reference to its past role in this agricultural region. Now this historic Spanish hacienda has been completely remodeled into a beautiful place to stay for those who want to be close to Cuenca but still have some peace and quiet. There are 18 rooms, including three suites and three large rooms for families. The spacious rooms are attractively decorated with antiques, fresh flowers and hanging plants. There is a very nice swimming pool with a poolside bar to relax at after a long day in town. Around the pool and grounds are extensive gardens that attract hummingbirds to the many flowers. Inside is the fine restaurant "El Quijote," which is popular with cuencaños for dinner and weekend lunch. There is also a comfortable bar with a large-screen TV and a cafeteria for informal meals and breakfast. Hosteria El Molino is a bit of country elegance on the edge of the city—a place where you can immerse yourself in the comfort and style of historic Cuenca.

RESTAURANTS   There are many opportunities to eat out in Cuenca, ranging from street vendors selling French fries with mayonnaise to elegant, intimate restaurants. Almost all of the nice restaurants in Cuenca open at 7 p.m. for hungry gringos—*cuencaños* wait to dine until at least 8 or 8:30 p.m. Also, most restaurants not in the large hotels, as well as small food stores, close on Sundays. Most of the restaurants have a full bar service, including a good selection of wines.

All the better hotels have nice restaurants where you can get a good meal. The outstanding hotel restaurants are **La Casino** in the Hotel Crespo, known for its French and international food and incredible evening views over the Río Tomebamba; **Archon de Oro** in the Hosteria Duran, with a well-known French chef, that is particularly popular for lunch; and **La Cabala Suiza** in the Hotel Oro Verde, serving international food and the best pizza in town. Our favorite restaurant in Cuenca and considered by many to be the best is the **Villa Rosa Restaurante** (Calle Gran Colombia 12-22). The restaurant is in a beautifully renovated colonial home with tables placed about the interior courtyard. Try the *pollo de mi abuela* (my grandmother's chicken). For a quick trip to heaven, order the fresh fruit fondue for dessert. In the same class as the Villa Rosa is **El Jardin Restaurante** (Calle Presidente Córdova 7-23), a cozy place with great food and friendly service. We recommend the *pollo al rey* (King's Chicken) and the langostino (a large prawn), which is served in a variety of ways.

For lovers of Italian food, there seems to be an unusually large number of pizzerias in Cuenca. Two are on the corner of Calle Gran Colombia and Calle Luís Cordero—**Los Pibes** and **La Tuna**. There is another one that has been recommended, **La Napoletana Pizzeria**, on the corner of Calle Benigno Malo and Calle Larga. All serve other Italian dishes, as well, and are popular with *cuencaños*, so they might be crowded. For authentic Mexican food, try **El Pedregal Azteca** (Calle Gran Colombia 10-29). It is not the typical Tex-Mex food found in the United States, but delicious Mexican food cooked by Mexicans in the traditional Mexican style. For light snacks, coffee and desserts, try the **Heladeria Holandesa** (Calle Benigno Malo 9-45), which has good ice cream, or the **Café Austria** (corner of Calles Simón Bolívar and Juan Montalvo) known for their European cakes and pastries. If you happen to get stuck at the airport, walk one block to the right as you exit, and kill time at the **Restaurante Rancho Chileno**. There is a covered patio to relax on and a full menu if you are hungry. They are very friendly and do not mind a pile of luggage under your table as you wait.

NIGHTLIFE   Cuenca is an unusually sleepy city for being so large. By ten o'clock at night, the sidewalks begin to empty and by eleven they are rolled up till morning. In general, the best bars are in the best hotels, especially in the Hotel Crespo and the Oro Verde. The **Hotel El Dorado** does have a discotheque open nightly, and on weekends, you can try the discos at **El Patio** (Calles 12 de Abril and Paucarbamba) and the **Hotel El Conquistador**. The two evening gathering places not connected to hotels are across from each other on the corners of Calle Luís Córdova and Calle Presidente Borrero— **La Cantina Bar** and **Picadilly Bar**. The drinks are way overpriced here, so go for the atmosphere and to relax.

SHOPPING   There are two markets in Cuenca. In the Plaza de San Francisco in front of the Church of San Francisco is the daily local market. In the **Plaza Rotary** along Avenida Gaspar Sangurima near Calle Mariano Cueva is a market on Thursdays and Sundays. This is mostly a housewares market, but it also has craft items for the tourist. Scattered about this cobblestone plaza are piles of wares that sprout blue plastic covers under the noon sun. There are heaps of baskets, stacks of brown and green glazed crockery, leaning buckets of adzes, picks and shovels, confusions of bird cages, grills and ironwork, arrays of unfinished furniture still being sanded, and coils of bright rope with strands cast to the stones. Around the edges of the plaza are food vendors and in the early morning live chickens and pigs for sale eyeing their roasting brethren.

If you walk west through the booths and cross Calle Mariano Cueva, you will find a permanent food market in the adjoining building that spills out into the alleys. The food booths are filled with all kinds of interesting fruits, vegetables and meats. To us, the attraction of these food markets—*mercados alimentos*—are the wonderful piles of tropical colors and textures and the waves of exotic scents that wash over every visitor. Take your time and allow your senses to be drenched by all the unfamiliar and bizarre sights. It is okay to buy fruits here if they have to be peeled or cut to eat. At least buy a bunch of one of the 15 (some people say 25) kinds of bananas and see what a fresh apple-banana tastes like.

GETTING THERE: *By Air:* Unless you plan an extensive tour of Ecuador, the best way to get to Cuenca is by plane. Between Quito and Cuenca TAME has a daily morning flight, except on Sunday, and a daily afternoon flight except Saturday. SAN has a daily flight, except Sunday. TAME also has two daily flights between Cuenca and Guayaquil, except on weekends when they have only a single daily flight. The SAN-SAETA flights are in all travel agents' computers, and it is easy to confirm reservations. The TAME flights, however, are typically not listed on your home travel agent's computer, or if they are, confirmed reservations are very difficult to get. It is best to contact an Ecuadorian travel agency for reservations on these flights.

By Bus: From Quito, it is a seven- to ten-hour ride that often includes dusty parts of the road being repaired and a three- to four-hour drive from Guayaquil. Both express and "milk-run" bus lines run between these two cities. Cuenca is also served by bus lines from Guayaquil, Loja and many smaller towns. All of these conveniently depart and arrive from the terrestrial terminal out by Cuenca's airport.

By Car: The Pan-American Highway is paved all the way and is a relatively fast road. Without stops, the drive between Quito and Cuenca takes five hours. The windy but paved road from Guayaquil (via Duran, La Troncal and Azogues) takes three hours. From Loja, the highway is now paved most of the way and takes only two and a half hours.

DAY TRIPS FROM CUENCA

There is much to see in the hills around Cuenca. No matter which direction you decide to go in, you will quickly enter the green rolling countryside that surrounds the city. Small hillside farms growing corn and potatoes overlook large valley ranches and scattered cattle. If you decide to explore the hidden corners of the region, you will find that paved highways quickly turn into dirt tracks or, if you are lucky, old cobblestone roads. All the native vegetation has been cut, burned or tilled under, so eucalyptus, planted as hedges and for shade, is just about the only kind of tree you'll see. The countryside is pretty nonetheless. It looks like a giant earthtone quilt of greens and browns textured by furrows and vegetable rows and held together by shaggy eucalyptus stitches.

As you travel across this earthy quilt you may find a change in weather in each valley you come to. If you find you do not like the weather where you are, go to the next valley and it will probably be different. The valleys that drain to the Oriente (open to the east) are typically warmer, more humid and less cloudy. The valleys that drain to the coastal plain (open to the west) are cooler and can be socked in with clouds pouring off the ocean, especially in the afternoon. In general, the weather in this part of Ecuador is warmer and more pleasant than in Quito, so it is unlikely that you will have day upon day of dreary weather.

Whatever the weather, there is always something interesting to see. Nature lovers can visit El Cajas National Recreation Area or take the road from Gualaceo toward Macas in the Oriente. For those with an interest in archaeology, Ingapirca—the most important ruins in the country—is just a couple of hours north of Cuenca. Interested in native culture? The Cañari Indians, who live in the region around Azogues, still cling to traditions that survived Incan domination. There are also several Indian markets (Sigsig and Gualaceo are the best) close to Cuenca. And for collectors there are a number of back roads, or craft trails, radiating from Cuenca, where you can see guitars, ceramics, weavings, Panamá hats and sweaters being made.

If you do not have a car to get around, it is well worth the money to hire a guide to show you the sites that are of interest to you. Even though all the towns in the region are easily accessible by bus or taxi, without a guide you will miss much of what there is to see. Guides know the special spots that a tourist could never find, even if the places were on a map. And more importantly, a guide will know some individual craftspeople. To witness the magic in the hands of these artists and to see where and how the pieces were created is far more satisfying than merely buying the finished product in a Cuenca shop. There are many tour operators in Cuenca that offer trips to wherever you want to go. Check with your hotel for one they recommend. An exceptional guide in Cuenca is **Eduardo Quito** (7-823-018, fax: 7-823-449). He speaks fluent English and is well-versed in the history, culture and nature of the area. Trust us, hire a guide and you will have an unforgettable experience.

EL CAJAS NATIONAL PARK

Elevated in 1997 from a National Recreation Area to a full-fledged National Park, El Cajas stretches to the west of Cuenca. In fact, it would be difficult to go west of Cuenca and not go through El Cajas. Past El Cajas, the roads continue to the coast—Guayaquil is about three and a half hours away by car.

El Cajas, or just "Cajas" as it is called locally, is the green, mountainous rim that defines the western horizon when looking from Cuenca, 12 kilometers away, on a clear day. Cajas covers 72,020 acres of mostly above-treeline tundra, or paramo, with patches of humid forest decorating the hem of its sprawling skirt. The landscape is rugged and jagged, cut up into deep valleys (from which the name *cajas*, or "boxes," originates) and coarse ridges, yet softened with several hundred sapphire lakes. There are two seasons in Cajas.

From August to January, the weather is typically clear but windy, with an average daytime temperature of 59°F and average nighttime temperature of 23°F. From February to July, the weather is cloudy and more humid, with a greater chance of rain. The average daytime temperature at this time of the year is 50°F and average nighttime temperature is 28°F. The lowest elevation in Cajas is 10,395 feet (3150 meters), while the highest point is Mt. Arquitectos —14,685 feet (4450 meters). The park's visitors center is at 12,771 feet (3870 meters), so be prepared for cool temperatures, sudden weather changes and the physical sluggishness that comes with altitude. Altitude sickness is a real possibility here; take preventive measures so you can enjoy the sights.

The main road to Cajas follows the Río Tomebamba up a narrow, steep-sided valley. Houses and small farms become less numerous as you approach the reserve, but native vegetation is found only on the highest, most imprac-tical-to-farm slopes. The entrance to Cajas is marked by a building and a swinging gate. There is apparently a small entrance fee of $10, but when we went, we were only asked for our nationality, which we gave for free. The guards did have maps and brochures (in English!) available, which is quite unusual, and were very friendly and helpful. Several kilometers before the entrance station is a hardly noticeable dirt road that leads across a rickety bridge and then up a steep valley to the south. This is the **Manzon Cloud Forest Reserve** and is the closest native forest to Cuenca. Alas, it is open by special permission only, so you must have a guide with a permit to get in. If you are a birdwatcher or a forest lover, take the effort required to see this reserve—it is very special.

The main road quickly climbs to the paramo and leaves civilization be-hind. You are now in the midst of the jagged ridges and shaggy green vales you saw from Cuenca. Eight kilometers from the entrance station on the north side of the road you will see a trout farm. In the valley below, in the cluster of buildings, on the left side, is another trout farm. This one is associated with a nice restaurant called the **Dos Chorreras**, or two waterfalls, for the two falls visible across the valley. The restaurant is a great spot for lunch after spend-ing the morning exploring Cajas. The fish the two farms grow are shipped off to restaurants in Cuenca. For those who like to catch wilder fish, many of the lakes and rivers in Cajas are stocked with Brown and Rainbow Trout, so fishing is very good and very popular with *cuencaños*.

Just past the Dos Chorreras restaurant you will see in the valley below a large white cross in front of a smaller cross and **shrine** atop a rocky knob. The shrine marks where, in 1988, a young woman from Cuenca claimed to see the Virgin Mary. The vision appeared to her over four weekends and by the last weekend thousands of believers had gathered to witness the miracle. Many who were there speak of strange atmospheric phenomena and feeling a pres-

Butterfly

ence when the Virgin Mary appeared to the young woman. It is now a popular pilgrimage for the faithful, especially for Colombians, and can be congested on weekends.

Past the shrine, higher in the same valley, are **Incan ruins**. They are visible to the north of the road across the rushing river as a crisscross of low, unassuming stone walls and mounds. Scientists think that they are the ruins of an Incan *tambo* or outpost along the Inca road to the coast. *Tambos* were located one day's walk apart along supply and communication routes radiating from the Incan capital city of Pumapungo (now Cuenca). If you look carefully at the blocks of stone you may find carved faces and designs that are very similar to those found in Perú. The Inca Trail passes through Cajas, and it is possible to follow it on foot through the reserve and down into the coastal plain. Several operators in Cuenca offer such treks for archaeology buffs and hikers. For those less hardy, you can see part of the Inca Trail (it looks like a narrow, grassy cobblestone road) from the car. A few kilometers past the information center, where the road curves around the northern edge of a small lake, the Inca Trail is visible on the opposite side of the lake as it climbs to the pass ahead. Remember, it is illegal to remove or bring home any historical artifacts you might be lucky enough to find.

Twenty kilometers of steady climbing past the entrance station is the **information center/ranger station**. There is not much to see inside the building other than restrooms. For campers there are a few beds available or you can sleep on the floor if the beds are taken and, with permission, use the small kitchen for cooking. Most people stop at the station to explore the rolling paramo. The station sits just above a rather large lake—**Lago Toreadora**—that has an interesting trail around it. It takes one to two hours to complete the circuit, depending on how curious you are and how many rest stops you need to take.

From the information station to the pass, which is the Continental Divide, there are several trails that lead off into the paramo. Because of new road construction trailheads are sometimes hard to find, but do not let that stop you from exploring. Park along the shoulder where it is safe and go wandering. If you follow a stream, it may soon lead you to a hidden lake in a wonderful valley that you will probably have to yourself. If you would rather climb, there are several inviting ridgelines to walk, especially near the divide. Even if you are not so ambitious, at least get out and walk around part of the paramo. The paramo here is like a cross between Arctic tundra and northern bog—

the plants are low and dense but the ground is soft and spongy. You will find spreading heaths, creeping berries, damp clumps of moss, bristly succulents and grassy tufts all dotted with the tiny blue, yellow and red blossoms of paramo wildflowers.

GETTING THERE: By Bus: From Parque San Sebastian in Cuenca, a bus leaves at 6 a.m. and 7:40 a.m. (except on Thursday) and travels the main road through El Cajas. You can be let off anywhere in the park if you let the driver know beforehand. The bus returns through Cajas past the visitors center at 2 p.m. and 3 p.m. This bus can be very crowded on weekends when many *cuencaños* go to Cajas to fish. For the southern route to Soldados and Angas, a bus leaves the park at the corner of Avenida Loja and Calle El Vado in Cuenca at 6 a.m. on Monday, Wednesday, Friday and Saturday. It is a grueling four-hour ride to Angas and, unless you thrive on physical discomfort and mental anguish, this is not the bus for you. An alternative way to get to Cajas is to hire a taxi for a day or to sign up with one of the many tour operators in Cuenca for a day excursion or even an overnight trek.

By Car: Two roads provide access to Cajas. The northern road is an extension of Avenida Ordoñez Lazo that runs past the Hotel Oro Verde on the western edge of Cuenca. Avenida Ordoñez Lazo is itself the western extension of Calle Gran Colombia, the main street through Colonial Cuenca. Calle Gran Columbia turns into Avenida Ordoñez Lazo at the monument of Simón Bolívar at the intersection of the Pan-American Highway. This is the main park road and is the one that is recommended for all visitors to Cajas. Major improvements to this road started late in 1994 with the intention of making it a primary highway between Cuenca and Guayaquil, so access and traffic will increase soon. From Cuenca, it is about 12 kilometers to the park entrance and 34 kilometers to the information center along this road. The southern road is barely navigable and recommended only to the most adventurous visitors. This road is an extension of the road to Baños and runs southwest through the village of Soldados and then to the tiny pueblo of Angas. From Cuenca, it is 34 kilometers to Soldados and 54 kilometers to Angas. There are no visitor facilities and no official access to the reserve along this route.

NORTH OF CUENCA

The Pan-American Highway north of Cuenca passes through green, rolling countryside. Here are raggedy eucalyptus woodlots, agave crowns, freshtilled brown hillsides colorfully dotted with shrubby lupine blues and woolly sheep whites, tethered horses, cows in pickups, roadside, hillside and even cliffside corn, orange tile roofs and white adobe walls, roadside shrines, colorful clotheslines and Coca-Cola signs. This is Cañar Province and the home of the Cañari Indians. Cañaris wear black ponchos and white felt hats with upturned rims. They are mostly farmers, but many also are weavers of Panamá hats, shawls and rugs.

Azogues, population 30,000, is 35 kilometers north of Cuenca. Despite the fact it is the capital of Cañar Province, Azogues remains a quiet town. It is known as the "town of the pigs" for all the fresh and cooked pigs hanging in roadside stores. There is not much to see here and most tourists only pass through on their way north to Ingapirca or south to Cuenca. There are two museums in town off the main plaza. The **Museo Ignacio Neira** in the Colegio Julio Maria has displays of artifacts and rocks and the **Museo del Colegio de los Padres Franciscanos** has displays of religious art and more artifacts. Both have irregular hours. There are also two interesting churches in the area and both are perched high atop hills—the **Iglesia de San Francisco** in Azogues and the **Santuario de la Virgen del Rocío** in nearby Biblián. Incas built their places of worship on top of hills to be closer to their Sun God. The Spanish, in their quest for domination, built their churches over the Inca's. The result is a healthy walk for all who want to visit these churches. You will, however, be rewarded with great views and the satisfaction of actually making the climb.

There is one nice place to stay in Azogues, the **Hotel Playa**, that we did not get a chance to visit. It is located down by the river on the west side of town. The only time it might be busy is around September 8th when Azogues fills up for the annual pilgrimage to the santuario in Biblián. There are several basic restaurants in towns serving variations of chicken or beef with rice and vegetables. The **Restaurant Gran Manila** on Calle Simón Bolívar near the main plaza and the **Pollería 87** just off the Pan-American Highway seem to be the best. If you are feeling bold you can try the *cascarita* or fried pig skin that is served in roadside stands, usually near a hanging roadside pig. It is often served with *llapingacho* (mashed potatoes stuffed with cheese). The potatoes are quite good—but we have not gotten enough courage yet to try the pig skin.

North of Azogues the Pan-American Highway crosses **Bueran Pass**, a 13,200-foot (4000-meter) high grassy slope planted in small patches of garlic, corn, fava beans and potatoes. This land is barely arable but it is the only land available to many Indians. In the 18th, 19th and early 20th centuries, land was controlled by the Catholic Church. What money the indigenous people had they gave to their local priest to hold. Inevitably, these required donations to the Church and taxes would rise and the people would eventually lose their money and their land to the Church. Interestingly, those who had the best land were the first to lose it. In 1965 the government of Ecuador passed a land reform act that dissolved the Church's land holdings, but when land was redistributed, the best land went to the wealthy and well connected. This pushed the Indian farmers onto more marginal land. The result has been the elimination of native vegetation in much of the highlands and the tilling of land unsuitable to sustained farming. This is why you see crops growing on incredibly steep hillsides and why people are trying to farm at an elevation of 13,200 feet (4000 meters).

GETTING THERE: Azogues is easily reached by both bus and taxi from Cuenca because the Pan-American Highway passes through the town. The train between Quito and Cuenca also passes through Azogues.

The best and most well-known Incan archaeological site in Ecuador is **Ingapirca**. While not as extensive or as grand as Incan sites in Perú—Incas had more than four centuries to build in Perú while they were in Ecuador for less than 100 years—Ingapirca is nonetheless a historically important and fascinating place to visit and Incan lore and culture permeate modern Ecuador. The best place to appreciate this spiritual and cultural legacy is amongst the curving walks and carved rocks of Ingapirca. Find a quiet spot and let your imagination wander through time. There are whispers of awe and reverence in the rockwork and rumors of nobility and sacrifice in the shadows. Rub your hand across a chiseled wall as the stonecutter did centuries ago and feel the pride of his craft. This is not just history lost. There is very much of the present caught in these stone walls. Not all was conquered and ruined by the Spanish.

Located on a grassy hillside offering impressive views of the valleys to the west, Ingapirca is marked by low, concentric stone walls with an elliptical-shaped stone building—an observatory/temple—at one end. Appropriately, Ingapirca is a Cañari word meaning "walls of the Incas." The ruins are 330 feet from the **entrance station** where a $4-per-person fee is collected. Ingapirca is open daily from 8 a.m. to 5 p.m. It is best to visit in the morning, as clouds often roll in and envelope Ingapirca in the afternoon. At the entrance station is **Señora Julia's**, a small restaurant that serves chicken with rice or potatoes. There are restrooms located behind the restaurant. One kilometer beyond the village of Ingapirca is a nicer restaurant called **La Pasada**. It is run by the same people who run El Jardin restaurant in Cuenca. This is where most tours stop for lunch, so service can be slow. Up on the hill across the street from the entrance station is a very nice **museum** and gift shop. Artifacts from Ingapirca are on display here and even if you do not understand Spanish, there is much to see. Most tours start at the museum, so your guide will explain the displays. Occasionally, the local Indians set up booths near the entrance station to sell handicrafts. The museum and gift shop are open whenever there are people interested in seeing them.

As you pass through the gate and enter the grounds of Ingapirca, the building ahead of you on the right is the **observatory/temple**. You will notice the flat curve of the Incan road leading from the observatory/temple toward you before it disappears to the left toward Cuenca. From above, the outline of Ingapirca forms a stylized Puma—the sacred animal of the Incas. The observatory/temple is the head of the Puma, the Incan road its spine and a square stone foundation, thought to be the remains of the **House of Virgins**, is the tail.

Before the Incas arrived at this site it was a sacred place to the local Cañari Indians. The Cañari called it *Cashaloma* or "the place where stars are pouring from the Heavens." The Cañaris were accomplished astronomers, like the Incas, and they built an observatory here to study and worship the sun and the stars. The Incas conquered the Cañaris in the early 15th century and absorbed them and their ways into the Incan culture. The Incas built Ingapirca over the Cashaloma foundations between 1450 and 1485. Very little evidence of the Cañari civilization is visible. Recently, though, a tunnel under the observatory/temple was discovered that led to a small room were many Cañari artifacts were found. As you wander the grounds, you may find a few angular stone blocks quarried by the Cañaris or some unpainted Cañari pot shards in the dirt (painted shards are Incan).

There is much controversy as to what was the function of Ingapirca. It might have been just a *tambo* or resting place along the Incan road to Quito. There were also large granaries at Ingapirca, which suggest it might have been a collection center for the region's farmers. Perhaps it was originally a Cañari fortress that the Incas used to control the valleys below. The observatory/temple argues that it was largely ceremonial. In all likelihood, Ingapirca was all of these—part ceremonial, part fortress and part *tambo*.

The best and most authentic way to see the ruins is to start off walking down the Inca Trail to the observatory/temple. This is the route visitors took 500 years ago when they came to Ingapirca. The Incan road is six men wide —the number of bearers needed to carry the high priests and nobility. The foundations on either side of the road were the homes of important and influential Incas. In the mid-1700s when the French Equatorial Expedition arrived at Ingapirca, the first scientists to do so, these walls were 10 feet (3 meters) high and some buildings still had thatch roofs. Since that time, much of the stone has been removed to serve as building material in Cañar.

The observatory/temple is still an intriguingly intricate building. The most obvious intricacy is the astounding rockwork construction of the building. Notice the beveled edges of each stone and how no more than two corners of each block ever join at one point. It is commonly written in tourist pamphlets that the stone masons never used mortar, but in fact they used a mixture of animal blood and dust to seal each joint. If you look carefully you will see a pencil-thin line of mortar between the blocks. You will also quickly notice that the shape of the doorways is not rectangular but trapezoidal. Trapezoid doors are characteristic of Incan architecture and are apparently stronger and more earthquake resistant than rectangular doorways.

The *cañaris* probably designed this building to be used as an observatory— while the Incas modified it to be a temple to worship the sun. Its construction is marvelously astronomically precise. The building is elliptical, mirroring the Earth's orbit around the sun. The long axis of this ellipsis is aligned precisely east–west. An inner north–south wall

Panamá Hat

divides the building in half and forms two interior rooms. Against this dividing wall the path of the sun was measured as it shone through four slit windows at both the east and west ends of the building. The four windows marked each solstice and equinox. The Incas covered both sides of the interior wall with gold foil so that during ceremonies golden light would highlight the High Priest, indicating the presence of their Sun God. On top of the building is a seat carved in stone with deep furrows running away from it. It is thought that this might have been an altar or the spot where human sacrifices were performed.

Because there are no interpretive signs or booklets available, this is one place where a guide is almost mandatory—not because Ingapirca is hard to find or because it is easy to get lost in but because a guide is essential to understand the significance of what you see. Hire a guide at the ruins (10,000 sucres) or in Cuenca (as part of the tour package), and allow yourself the luxury of taking a 500-year step back into the realm of the Incas.

GETTING THERE: By Bus: There are no buses that go to Ingapirca. You can take a bus north on the Pan-American Highway and get off at the turn to Ingapirca and try to catch a ride to the ruins, but traffic is light and you may be stranded for a while.

By Car: The closest town to Ingapirca is the little town of Cañar, 66 kilometers north of Cuenca on the Pan-American Highway. Two kilometers south of Cañar is a large red and white sign indicating the turn to Ingapirca. It is 15 kilometers along this sometimes rough dirt road to the ruins. This road passes through the little village of Ingapirca 1 kilometer before the ruins. An alternative route starts 1 kilometer north of Cañar at the village of El Tambo. This road is better maintained—there has been talk of paving it for years—and shorter, only 8 kilometers, to Ingapirca. The best way to get to Ingapirca is to hire a taxi or sign up for an all-day tour in Cuenca. Expect to pay $30–$50 for a tour, a bit less for a taxi from Cuenca. You could negotiate a ride from Cañar to Ingapirca but it is unlikely you would be able to find someone to take you from Ingapirca back to Cañar. You can also take the train to San Pedro, about 4 kilometers from Ingapirca, but it arrives at night, so finding a place to stay in San Pedro (there are none) is problematic. If you decide to wing it, bring at least a sleeping bag and a tarp in case you get stuck sleeping outside.

By Foot: It is possible to walk the Incan road, now called the Inca Trail, from the north to get to Ingapirca. It is an easy two- to three-day walk through a pass in the paramo that then descends through typical small highland farms to Ingapirca. Along the way are the Incan ruins of Paredones, usually the first night's campsite. The trail starts at the little village of Achupallas which is about 30 kilometers east of Alausí, Km. 290 on the Pan-American Highway. Buses go to Alausí from both Quito and Riobamba but there are no buses to Achupallas. You can hire a driver in Alausí for about $7 per person to take you to Achupallas or you can try a combination of hitching and hiking. There is usually enough traffic along the road so you will not have to wait too long. The drive to Achupallas takes about an hour and a half. The trail starts at the arch with a cross and heads south past the cemetery. It is not an obvious trail the entire way and there are many junctions and turns. For a complete description of the walk, refer to the book *Climbing and Hiking in Ecuador* by Rachowiecki, Thurber and Wagenhauser.

EAST OF CUENCA

The valleys and hills east of Cuenca are lower in elevation and therefore warmer than the surrounding region. Because of this, the main town of the region, Gualaceo, is a popular retreat for weekending *cuencaños* and *guaya-quileños*. This area is also known for its wonderful fruit—especially peaches, apples and berries. The villages surrounding Gualaceo are also becoming well known for their crafts. Some villages make nothing but guitars, others shawls, sweaters, ceramics, jewelry or Panamá hats. The dirt roads linking these cottage industries are known as the craft trails. It is worthwhile to spend a day following a craft trail and meeting the craftspeople at work. Farther to the east of Cuenca, above Gualaceo, a green shoulder of the Andes rises, marking the western edge of the Oriente. Gualaceo is also the back door to a spectacular road through the Andes and a little-visited part of the Oriente via the town of Limón (see Chapter Fifteen).

Gualaceo is a small town that looks and feels a lot like a miniature Cuenca. There are narrow cobblestone streets lined by whitewashed colonial buildings filled with friendly people in a relaxed environment. There is even a river, the Río Santa Barbara, that flows through Gualaceo much like the rivers that flow through Cuenca. Most tourists come to Gualaceo either to visit the Sunday market or to shop for the high-quality crafts of the region.

Birdwatchers who want to explore the pass to the Oriente should plan to spend at least one night in Gualaceo to eliminate the long trip from Cuenca. Gualaceo is also a good base from which to explore the craft trails of the area.

The Gualaceo **Sunday market** is the largest market in the area and the weekly center of social and economic activity. The market is held in the main plaza in town next to the cathedral on Calle 3 de Noviembre. It is mostly a food and housewares market—weavings and craft items are better found in the adjoining shops. Like any market, it is awash with the hustle and bustle of people selling, trading, bartering, comparing, rejoicing and commiserating. Jump feet-first into this market and let your senses be drenched by the exotic shapes, aromas, textures and sounds that surround you. Among the different types of fruits and vegetables you are likely to see at this market: reina cloudias, Indian cherries, naranjillas, maracuyas, zapotes, achotes, limes, chiles, grapes, papayas, pears, oranges, guavas, watermelons, mangoes, apples, peaches, pineapples, strawberries, raspberries, corn, manioc, avocados, onions, beans, tomatoes, turnips, potatoes, peppers, carrots, scallions, many kinds of grains and ten different kinds of bananas!

If you can pull yourself away from the piles of fruits and vegetables, look for an old woman sitting in front of armfuls of herbs and grasses. Herbal cures and earthy wisdom are dispensed here, for this is the Indian healer and the herbs are her pharmacy. If you watch discretely you may see parents bringing their children to her for eye problems and old folks lingering to have their aches eased. Remember, this is not a show put on for tourists—this is serious business, so be respectful. Crossing from the magical to the mundane, you are also likely to see roasted pigs on poles in the lunch part of the market. Gualaceo is famous for its roasted pork. If you are a ham fancier you will be in pork paradise here.

LODGING   There are two excellent places to stay in the Gualaceo area, and numerous inexpensive and humble residenciales. At the south edge of Gualaceo, 1 kilometer west of the main street, is the delightful **Parador Turistico Gualaceo** (private bath, hot water, cable color TV, phone, minibar; $25–$40; 7-842-443, fax: 7-830-485). The Parador is located on 1500 acres of what used to be a sugarcane plantation. The 22 attractive rooms are on three floors (no elevator) and overlook the valley or pool area. Extensive gardens and eucalyptus trees have now replaced the sugarcane. The colonial-style hacienda has two restaurants, a bar, steam room, sauna and small disco (open weekends and holidays). There is a large swimming pool, tennis courts, and several trails to wander. There are also picnicking facilities and places to camp on the grounds. This is a very popular weekend getaway for Cuencans and for market-day lunch, so plan ahead if you want to enjoy the comforts offered here. There is an artisan museum at the entrance driveway to the Parador, but it is open only on weekends and holidays.

Incomparable in facilities, service and setting, the **Hosteria Uzhupud** (private bath, hot water, cable color TV, phone; $21–$40; in Paute, 7-250-339, 7-250-329; in Cuenca, 7-807-784, 7-809-530, 7-809-529, 7-806-521, fax: 7-250-373) is nothing short of spectacular. We rate this 15-year old hotel as not only one of the most comfortable places to stay in Ecuador but also the best bargain (probably priced so low because of the road problems between Gualaceo and Cuenca). The 58 rooms look out onto magnificent gardens, trees and views of the surrounding mountains and river. Besides the restaurant, bar, pool, horseback riding and orchid house, the grounds offer a restful ambiance that makes you want to stay. Cultural events, local dances and fiestas are celebrated here to bring Ecuadorian culture to you. If requested, the restaurant will even open at 4:30 or 5 a.m. to accommodate early-morning bird trips. An associated hostel for students is also available for the backpacker set. The Hosteria Uzhupud is about half-way between the towns of Paute (7 kilometers to the south) and Gualaceo (8 kilometers to the north).

In Gualaceo proper, other places to stay are the **Residencial Gualaceo** and the **Residencial Español**. Both are cheap ($3 per person) but clean, and they are located just off the northeast corner of the city park and cathedral on Gran Colombia. The Residencial Gualaceo also has protected parking. Both have 10 to 12 rooms, all located on the second and third floors. Hot water is available in the evening. The owners are friendly and courteous, and a stay here will expose you to a side of Ecuadorian culture that is absent among the glamour and luxury of the bigger places.

RESTAURANTS   Beside the international cuisine of the restaurants at the **Parador Turistico Gualaceo** and the **Hosteria Uzhupud**, numerous small restaurants around Gualaceo's main plaza serve tasty Ecuadorian dishes. We liked the **Restaurant La Delicia** on the southeast corner of the open market square. On market day, there is plenty to eat at the market.

THE CRAFT TRAILS   Many people come to the Gualaceo region to visit the craftspeople for which the area is so famous. The countryside is dotted with villages that are renowned for one type of craft or another. One area will be home to weavers, another knitters or potters—clusters of artisans linked by a shared skill and avenue. The back roads that connect these clusters of craftspeople are known locally as craft trails. There are trails for Panamá hats, sweaters, jewelry, weavings, ceramics and guitars. Unfortunately, there are no road signs or markers that tell you where these craft trails are. Unless you like to wander and nose around, you are unlikely to find the craftspeople without a guide who knows the routes. Most guides also know some of the craftspeople as well, allowing for a more personal and interesting experience.

The best-known and most easily found cluster of craftspeople is the little town of **Chordeleg**, a few kilometers up the hill and east of Gualaceo.

Chordeleg is Ecuador's jewelry capital. There must be hundreds of *joyerias* —jewelry stores—in this little town. *Joyerias* densely line the road as you enter town and they are on every corner and side street off the main plaza. Behind rusty doors and peeling paint are displays of magnificent gold and silver rings, bracelets, necklaces, earrings, pins—every kind of jewelry you can imagine—from contemporary to traditional styles. Chordeleg is best known for its intricate filigree jewelry but only a few jewelers still spend the painstaking hours to create it. There are also potters, weavers and knitters here, but they are lonely outposts in a sea of silver and gold. There is also a small Sunday market in the main plaza.

The Chordeleg market and another market close by to Gualaceo could be combined into one day trip. In the village of **Sigsig**, 26 kilometers south of Gualaceo, is another Sunday market. It is also smaller than the Gualaceo market, but it has a wider variety of things for sale. The Sigsig market is a locals' market, and there are never very many tourists. This appeals to many because you can see a more authentic market, a market the way it used to be.

Outside the village of **Bulcay**, just north of Gualaceo, is the weavers' trail. Working on front porches overlooking the Santa Barbara River valley, women dye the thread and set the design and the men do the weaving. Using the ancient Incan Ikat technique of hand spindle and back loom, the weavers of Bulcay create shawls and throws like those their ancestors wove generations ago. You can find these same designs from Perú to Guatemala. **San Bartolomé**, south of Gualaceo, is the land of apples and guitarmakers. Glued forms and shaved sound boards line the eaves of the homes of the guitarmakers. Many of these guitars are used by the roving restaurant troubadours in Cuenca and Quito, while others are shipped to Japan and sold as Yamaha guitars. Only some of the craftspeople make the finest guitars, so ask around for the best instruments. The sweater trail is in the area around **Paute**, 23 kilometers north of Gualaceo. You will see everything from coarse pullovers to fine cardigans in bundles and in piles in the corner of the knitters' homes. Many of the knitters are girls who knit after school—their hands flashing to the metallic rhythm of clinking needles. All around Gualaceo you will find both potters and Panamá hat makers. The potters throw mostly household items—pots, bowls, dishes—but occasionally some will create decorative ceramic tiles. Many will throw 60 pots a day, their spinning cement wheel ringed by damp pots as they press and raise thin clay walls to simple practical shapes. To find Panamá hat makers, look for the drying straw in front yards and on clotheslines. Try the area around the little towns of **Lacao** and **Solano** northwest of Gualaceo. For more on the making of Panamá hats, see Chapter Four.

For nature lovers or for those who just want to explore an interesting area, try the road east out of Gualaceo toward the towns of Limón and Macas in the Oriente. The road is described in some books as **Macas Pass** but locally it is known as "la via a Limón." Sixteen kilometers from Gualaceo, the road climbs to a high paramo valley that is worth several stops to look for Giant Hummingbirds feeding on blooming agaves or Andean Condors soaring in the clouds. The pass (11,055 feet/3350 meters) is reached 24 kilometers from Gualaceo. From the top of the pass heading east, you will soon find good patches of cloud forest where great roving flocks of brightly colored tanagers and their allies can be found. The farther you continue along this road as it drops in altitude, the more hot and humid it becomes until, by Limón, the true Amazonian rainforest is reached. Limón is 77 kilometers from Gualaceo. We rate this road as the most biologically exciting and aesthetically pleasing descent into the Amazon in Ecuador.

GETTING THERE: By Bus: Gualaceo is serviced by numerous bus lines (*cooperativas*), but there is no central *terminal terrestre*. Most of the bus offices are clustered along the main street through town and four blocks east of the main plaza. There are buses every half-hour between Gualaceo and Cuenca during the day, and once every several hours at night. Several *cooperativas* also serve Limón, Méndez and Macas in the Oriente. Bus schedules, however, can be irregular because of construction and landslides in the rainy season—ask when you get to Cuenca what the current situation is.

By Car: In 1993, a huge landslide permanently closed the old main highway between Cuenca and the Gualaceo area. However, for cars and vans, the direct highway between Cuenca and Gualaceo is now open, albeit dusty and rough in places. This highway is by far the shortest and least complex route to Gualaceo, Hosteria Uzhupud, the crafts villages and the Gualaceo-Limón road to the lowlands. Drive north of Cuenca on the Pan-American Highway 15 kilometers and cross a large bridge. Less than a kilometer north of this bridge a major road, Vía El Descanso, goes off to the east (right) with a small sign indicating Gualaceo. Five kilometers down this road, a very narrow bridge, called La Josefina, over the Río Cuenca makes it impossible for large buses and trucks to pass. The paved highway then continues another 16 kilometers directly to Gualaceo. For the Hosteria Uzhupud, turn north (left) off this paved highway 10 kilometers after La Josefina bridge. Continue down onto a narrow bridge across a small river. Continue 11 kilometers on this dusty gravel road that parallels the east bank of the Río Paute and turn left at the "Y." Then within 100 meters turn right and into the entrance of the hosteria (total travel time is about 50 minutes from the Cuenca airport).

By Taxi: You can always hire a taxi to take you to the Hosteria Uzhupud, Gualaceo or the Sunday market, but most taxi drivers are not familiar with the craft trails despite what they may say. If you want to see the craftspeople at work, hire a guide who specializes in craft tours. Be sure to arrange for a time and date for the taxi to return to pick you up. Otherwise, you will have to return to Cuenca on the bus.

TEN

Southern Highlands

Other than the inaccessible parts of the extreme southeastern Oriente, this area of Ecuador is perhaps the least known and least visited by foreign tourists, and yet it is a lovely mixture of high-altitude habitats, cloud forests, and the upper limits of Amazonian forest types. Because of its lack of popularity among tourists, the southern highlands offer many chances to wander authentic towns and villages, view spectacular vistas and enjoy unspoiled habitats with few other tourists around. The people of this area are not as likely to have become jaded by tourists, and delightful encounters with local people even in the bigger towns and cities are common. At the same time, this isolation from the more heavily traveled tourist routes doesn't mean you have to suffer primitive facilities and a lack of amenities. Elegant hotels, luxury restaurants and clean camping areas are available to meet the needs of even the most particular tourist.

The city of Loja is a logical place to stay while you are exploring the region. Vilcabamba to the south of Loja is another potential base. If you want to spend some time enjoying one place without the pressures of daily destinations, Vilcabamba is a goal in itself. Podocarpus National Park is only 20 minutes away from either Loja or Vilcabamba; many visitors have found it worth the entire trip to Ecuador alone. Natural history, scenery, anthropology, art, indigenous markets and some of the cheapest prices in the entire country are all terrific reasons to make the southern highlands top the list of areas to include in your trip to Ecuador.

LOJA

Loja is one of the cleanest and friendliest cities in Ecuador. It is just like the attractive Quito of 25 years ago, before it sold its soul to modernization in the name of international banks and oil development. A city of 120,000 inhabitants, somehow Loja has been able to avoid most of the pitfalls associated with economic development and modernize without losing its soul. Perhaps its relative isolation from both Guayaquil and Quito has enabled it to develop under the philosophy of benign neglect. Whatever its secret, it works, and this part of the book will be inadequate no matter how hard we try to describe this delightful corner of southern Ecuador.

One of the few tradeoffs for this semi-isolation is Loja's unsophisticated money exchange system. Except at the top hotels, where U.S. dollars can be exchanged for Ecuadorian sucres at a rate 10 percent less favorable than in Quito or Guayaquil, no one will readily exchange currency. Even the Banco de Fomento (on the Parque Central) will only exchange traveler's checks. Also, leave your American Express Card at home, as no one in Loja accepts it. Strangely enough, nearby in little Vilcabamba, American Express is accepted in several hotels. In Loja, for now, Visa and Diners Card are the credit cards most generally accepted, and then only at the better (more expensive) hotels and restaurants.

Except for the three weeks each year (the last two weeks of August and the first week of September) when the city is one big block party celebrating the Sacred Virgin of Cisne, Loja bustles without being crowded and hustles with little crime. Its best hotels and restaurants are relatively inexpensive, and if the parks and artisans of the city were not enough additional attraction, the higher elevation portions of the spectacular Podocarpus National Park are less than half an hour from the city center.

Founded in 1548 by Alonso de Mercadillo, Loja lies at 6930 feet (2100 meters) elevation in the Cuxibamba Valley and enjoys a climate referred to by locals as "eternal spring." (Every town in the altiplano claims the same thing, so be prepared to smile and say "How wonderful.") Cool days and even cooler nights can be expected in July and August, but the average temperature is 63°F.

Every August 17th, as a demonstration of faith, thousands of devout Catholics from Ecuador, Perú, Colombia and other Latin American countries converge to carry the statue of the Virgen del Cisne (Virgin of the Swan) for three days on their shoulders the 70 kilometers from El Cisne to the cathedral in Loja's city center. The arrival of the statue also provides a Mardi Gras–like party atmosphere that finally tapers off about the middle of September.

If you have your own car or want to pay a taxi driver about $5, take a drive out on the Zamora road 5 kilometers to **Castillo Scorpio**. Here are vistas that overlook the city and offer a view of the entire valley that will provide a conversion experience at sunset. At Castillo Scorpio, intriguing ceramics are available for sale on the campus of the Universidad Técnica right next to

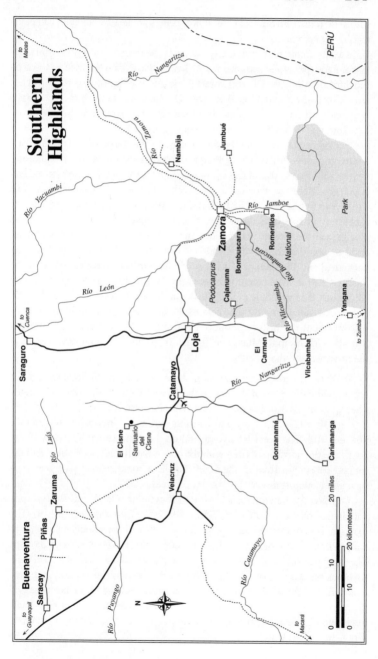

the castle (*castillo*). Several natural hot springs are nearby, and you can bathe in *el agua edionda*.

Twenty minutes from the city center is the entrance to Podocarpus National Park (pay your entrance fee of $10 at the INEFAN office in town on the third floor of the "Distrito Forestal" next to the Topoli yogurt shop at the corner of Bolívar and Miguel Riofrío. Do the Loja entrance to Podocarpus first, and you can use the same ticket the next day to enter at the low elevation entrance through Zamora and avoid paying a $20 fee).

For other places of interest in the city, try the **Banco Central** (9 a.m.– 5 p.m., Monday–Friday) on the Parque Central. It has a museum of anthropology, as well as permanent and visiting art shows, for which there's no charge. If you are interested in colonial-style architecture and art, the churches of **El Valle**, **San Sebastián** and **El Pedestal** (good view of the city), as well as the monastery of **Las Conceptas**, are all fine examples. Their hours for visitors change with the season, holy holiday and various festivals, so check with your hotel or taxi driver to find out the best time of day to visit them. The **city cathedral** and **the chapel of El Rosario de Santo Domingo**, both near the Parque Central, have recently restored nearly 100 fresco paintings by Diego Miderosas. The vestibule of the **Municipal Palace** (9 a.m.–1 p.m. and 3 p.m. –6 p.m., Monday–Friday), also near the Parque Central, has intriguing murals that represent the history, traditions and music of the area. The **Almacen Turistico Municipal** (Municipal Tourist Shop) displays representative art of the province and the country.

LODGING   Even the best hotels in Loja fall only in the moderate price range ($30–$45). One of the best is the **Grand Hotel Loja** (Manuel Augustine Aguirre and Rocafuerte; private bath, hot water, color TV; 7-575-200, 7-575-201, fax: 7-575-202). The 54 rooms are on six floors and served by a new elevator. The hotel is easy to find on the main street. The only drawbacks are the noise associated with the above-mentioned main street and the limited parking in front of the hotel. This is a popular hotel with businessmen and is almost always full except on weekends.

Our favorite hotel in Loja is **Hotel Libertador** (Colón and Bolívar; private bath, hot water, color TV; 7-560-779, 7-570-344, fax: 7-572-119). The manager is very focused on ecotourism, and through an associated tour company, Vilcatur, will help you plan day tours to all the local sites of interest. The hotel entrance is on a narrow street, and a taxi unloading guests will easily block the way for other traffic. However, an underground parking garage makes it easy for those driving their own cars. A new addition has increased the number of rooms to 65 on three floors and includes an elevator and swimming pool. The new rooms are much more spacious than the often-cramped rooms in the old wing.

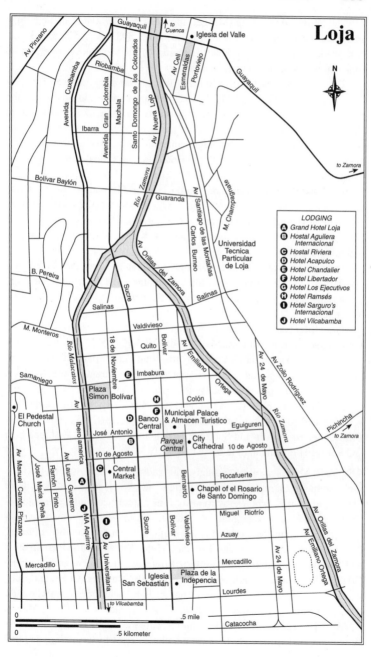

Loja

N

LODGING
- **A** Grand Hotel Loja
- **B** Hostal Aguilera Internacional
- **C** Hostal Riviera
- **D** Hotel Acapulco
- **E** Hotel Chandalier
- **F** Hotel Libertador
- **G** Hotel Los Ejecutivos
- **H** Hotel Ramsés
- **I** Hotel Sarguro's Internacional
- **J** Hotel Vilcabamba

to Cuenca
Iglesia del Valle
to Zamora
to Zamora
Pichincha
to Zamora

Guayaquil
Av Pinzano
Av Celi
Esmeraldas
Portoviejo
Guayaquil
Riobamba
Santo Domingo de los Colorados
Av Nueva Lojo
Avenida Cuxibamba
Avenida Gran Colombia
Machala
Ibarra
Río Zamora
Bolívar Baylón
Guaranda
Av Santiago de las Montañas
Carlos Burneo
M. Champagñata
Universidad Tecnica Particular de Loja
B. Pereira
Av Orillas del Zamora
Salinas
Salinas
Sucre
Salinas
M. Monteros
Río Malacatos
Valdivieso
18 de Noviembre
Quito
Bolívar
Av Ermiliano Ortega
Av 24 de Mayo
Av Zoilo Rodríguez
Río Zamora
Samaniego
Imbabura
E
Plaza Simon Bolívar
Av Ibero america
El Pedestal Church
H
Colón
Municipal Palace & Almacen Turistico
F
D
Banco Central
José Antonio
B
Eguiguren
Parque Central
City Cathedral
10 de Agosto
10 de Agosto
José María Peña
Ramón Pinto
Av Lauro Guerero
C
Central Market
Bernardo
Rocafuerte
A
Chapel of el Rosario de Santo Domingo
J
MA Aquirre
I
G
Av Universitaria
Sucre
Bolívar
Valdivieso
Miguel Riofrío
Azuay
Av Manuel Carrón Pinzano
Mercadillo
Mercadillo
Av 24 de Mayo
Av Orillas del Zamora
Av Emiliano Ortega
Iglesia San Sebastián
Plaza de la Indepencia
Lourdes
to Vilcabamba
Catacocha

0 _____ .5 mile
0 _____ .5 kilometer

The **Hotel Vilcabamba** (Manuel Augustine Aguirre and Rocafuerte; private bath, hot water, color TV; 7-573-645, 7-573-393, fax: 7-571-538) is just two blocks from the Grand Hotel Loja and on the same busy street. Its 40 rooms are on four floors with an elevator.

The **Hotel Ramsés** (Colón and Bolívar; private bath, hot water, TV; 7-579-868, 7-571-402, fax: 7-581-832) is definitely more run-down than the other three top hotels in town. Directly across the same narrow street from the Hotel Libertador, its cheaper prices mean you can pay less and still take advantage of many of the Libertador's amenities. The only reliable car rental agency in Loja is associated with the Hotel Ramsés (Hidal Rent-A-Car, see Chapter Four).

The **Hostal Aguilera Internacional** (Sucre and Emiliano Ortega; private bath, hot water, color TV; 7-563-189, 7-572-461, fax: 7-572-894) is located in the quietest neighborhood of any of the better hotels. It is smaller than the other hotels (thus the name "hostal") but offers most of the same amenities, including a sauna.

The next level of hotels are even more moderately priced ($5–$12/night). The **Hotel Los Ejecutivos** (Avenida Universitaria and Azuay; private bath, hot water, color TV; 7-560-004) is by far the best in this category, but with only ten rooms, it is often filled.

The **Hotel Sarguro's Internacional** (Avenida Universitaria 07-24 and 10 de Agosto; private bath, usually 24-hour TV; 7-960-552, 7-960-521, 7-570-552, 7-560-521) is primarily visited by traveling Ecuadorians. If you want to get away from gringos and immerse yourself in Ecuadorian culture, food and attitude, this is the place for you. With 40 rooms, it is less likely to be filled.

For budget travelers ($2–$10/night), the **Hostal Riviera** (Avenida Universitaria and 10 de Agosto), the **Hotel Acapulco** (Sucre 07-45), and the **Hotel Chandelier** (Imbabura and Sucre) are clean and respectable. A shared bath and hot water are standard at these hotels.

RESTAURANTS   Not surprisingly, the most consistent quality food is found in the restaurants associated with the best hotels in Loja. If you don't like taking chances with exotic foods or funky ambiance, and prefer international cuisine, these restaurants are inexpensive ($2–$3), solid and dependable, if not adventurous: **Grand Hotel Loja** (Iberoamerica and Rocafuerte), **Hotel Libertador** (Colón and Bolívar), **Hotel Vilcabamba** (Iberoamerica and Rocafuerte) and **Hostal Aguilera Internacional** (Sucre and Emiliano Ortega). The restaurant associated with the **Hotel Ramsés** (Colón and Bolívar) is much seedier. For restaurants not affiliated with hotels, **La Cascada** (Sucre and Lourdes), **Mezon Andaluz** (J. A. Eguiguren and 24 de Mayo), **El Arco de Legarfie** (24 de Mayo and Rocafuerte) and **La Capiata** (18 de Noviembre and Quito) are the most popular eateries featuring international cuisine. Our two favorites, however, are **La Tullpa** (18 de Noviembre and Colón), where you eat what middle-class *lojaños* would have for Sunday dinner—fried chicken and yuca or a thin steak covering a mound of rice and in turn covered by two fried eggs—and **Las Redes** (18 de Noviembre and M. Riofrio), newly reopened and specializing in seafood, chicken and beef entrées. Although not without some merit, we would put the restaurant associated with **Hotel Sarguro's Internacional** (Universitaria and 10 de Agosto) somewhere near the bottom of better places to eat.

GETTING THERE: By Air: TAME has two daily flights from and to Quito except Sunday and a single flight to and from Guayaquil on Tuesday, Thursday and Saturday. Flights are impossible to book at the last minute from early August to mid-September, and only difficult the rest of the year.

The Loja airport (La Tola) is actually located in Catamayo about a half-hour by taxi to the west. Taxis are readily available either direction, and if you agree to share the ride with other passengers, the cost one-way is less than $3 per person.

By Bus: Buses, like the airlines, carry many passengers to Loja, especially around the celebration of the Virgin of Cisne. Reservations may be needed. From and to Quito, Cooperativa de Transportes Loja, Santa and Viajeros are the three most important bus companies. The trip takes about 18 hours. Cooperativa Loja is the primary carrier for the ten-hour trip from and to Guayaquil. Cuenca is now less than four hours away via the newly refinished highway, and Cooperativa Loja, Ejecutivo San Luís and Viajeros are the main bus companies. At the city *terminal terrestre* (at the north end of town where the Guayaquil road intersects the Cuenca road), taxis are available to take you to your hotel.

By Car: If you plan to drive from Quito or Guayaquil in a rental car, plan on six to seven hours from Guayaquil on winding but well-maintained asphalt roads with relatively light traffic. If you choose the more scenic but also much dustier and bumpier route through Piñas, count on an additional two hours of driving time. From Quito, this trip is a bear to do in one day (12–14 hours), and the traffic is often very heavy. An overnight stay in Cuenca will soothe the body and revitalize the mind for the short three- to four-hour drive to Loja the next day.

Located 74 kilometers north of Loja, the town of **Saraguro** is the center of a distinct group of indigenous people called the Saraguros. They speak Quichua, but their clothing, oral traditions and other customs indicate a distinct lineage. North of Saraguro is the **Baño del Inca**, a rocky swimming area in the river said to have been used as a bathing area in Incan times. Saraguro and Loja bus companies have daily service to Saraguro. There are a few simple restaurants but no adequate lodging here, so this destination would be best done as a day trip out of Loja.

In Spanish, Santuario refers to a shrine and not a wildlife sanctuary. This Santuario is in the small but very famous town of **El Cisne** 70 kilometers northwest of Loja. An enormous Gothic temple built in the form of a mountainous escarpment houses the statue of the Virgin, which was carved from cedar wood by Don Diego de Robles at the end of the 16th century. The May 30 and August 15 are the principal festival days celebrating this statue. On August 17 each year, the statue is carried by devout pilgrims to Loja, where the celebration continues. Taxis can be rented in Loja for $20–$30 round-trip to El Cisne, depending on your bargaining skills in Spanish. Tour companies and hotels can also arrange for vans to make one-day trips.

PIÑAS AND BUENAVENTURA

Either as a day trip from Machala on the coast (see Chapter Twelve) or as an overnight stay on the way to or from Loja, natural areas near the small town of Piñas (elevation = 1000 meters) should be visited. The area's mountain forest patches are full of intriguing plants and animals. The town of Piñas, 80 kilometers southeast of Machala, is a sleepy hamlet and of marginal interest to most ecotourists. There is no lodging in Piñas that we recommend. More interesting are the back roads that pass through an area of small and large patches of natural cloud forest west of Piñas called Buenaventura. Gravel roads to these forest patches wind both south and north from the main paved highway at the landmark shrine and large Buenaventura sign at the crest 8.5 kilometers west of the "Y" in the highway in the center of Piñas (or 15.5 kilometers east of the town of Saracay if you are coming from Machala).

GETTING THERE: By Bus: Buses leave regularly from Machala for Piñas and Zaruma and less regularly from Loja. Get off at the Buenaventura Shrine and walk the gravel roads. Some of the best forest patches are within a few kilometers of the paved highway.

By Car: From Loja drive 25 kilometers past Catamayo on the main Loja-Guayaquil highway. Turn north (right) onto the broad gravel road and continue 51 kilometers toward Zaruma. Just before the city of Zaruma, cross the river and take the paved highway through Piñas and then continue 8.5 kilometers to the second crest and the large shrine and sign for Buenaventura on the north side of the road.

From Machala, drive south toward the city of Santa Rosa. Ten kilometers south of Santa Rosa take the left arm of the "Y" in the highway toward Loja. You will come to an army checkpoint where you will have to stop and register your passport number. Ten kilometers beyond this checkpoint, you again take another left at a "Y" in the highway (both arms are paved) toward Saracay and Piñas. Go 15.5 kilometers to the crest of the highway and the large Buenaventura Shrine on the left (north) side of the road. Here gravel roads go off to the south and the north.

If you are visiting Buenaventura or need a place to stop over between Guayaquil and Loja, the area's only good lodging is the **Club d'L Campo**

Romachay (formerly known as Rosales de Machay) (private bath, cold water; $20–$30; Simon Bolivar 4-56 and Mariano Cueva, Cuenca, 7-839-969, 7-836-760, fax: 7-838-694; ROSETUR, C. C. Rocafuerte Mesanine #12, Casilla 0701949, Machala, 7-946-446, fax: 7-936-445; Royal Tours, Escobedo 809 and Junín, Casilla 3420, Guayaquil, 4-307-512, fax: 4-308-134). This resort has 12 log or brick cabins with small rooms but comfortable beds. Several of the cabins are on the rushing river that flows by one side of the resort, and the rest are in the tree plantation, where Peruvian Pygmy owls can be heard calling regularly. There is a full-service restaurant and bar as well as pools, sauna, tennis court and a camping area. Avoid weekends, when screaming crowds of guests arrive from the coast to escape the heat and humidity. The only way to Romachay is by car. It is two hours from Machala, 45 minutes from Buenaventura and three hours from Loja. Follow the directions to Piñas and Buenaventura. Twelve kilometers east of Piñas and just before crossing a bridge and entering the towns of Puertovelo and Zaruma, turn north (left) onto a narrow gravel road (several signs including one announcing Club d'L Campo Romachay mark this road). Drive 8 rough but passable kilometers, all the while paralleling the west side of the river. At a small village the road comes to a bridge and crosses to the east side of the river. Turn back south along the east bank of the river and go another 2 kilometers (through a farm-yard) until you come to the gates of Romachay. Ring the bell or honk and someone will come to open the gate for you on weekdays.

VILCABAMBA

Forty-three kilometers south of Loja is the small town of **Vilcabamba**, meaning "sacred valley" in Quichua. It is located in a warm (mean temperature 68°F) and dry valley at 5775-feet (1750-meter) elevation and has a population of 2000. Twenty years ago, it was a dusty agricultural town whose only claim to fame was a large number of people claiming to be over 100 years old. Although the birth certificates of these people were never checked, and there is a strong suspicion of wanton bragging, the published reports made the town known to outsiders. The economy of the town has now become largely based on tourism, and while Latin Americans are the major tourists in Loja, North Americans and Europeans are the major tourists in Vilcabamba. Because of the large number of tourists, there are plans to build a visitors center and an additional entrance to Podocarpus National Park near Vilcabamba. At present, the most popular approach to the park from Vilcabamba is through the Quebrada Honda entrance and is a one- or two-day hike. Most tourists spend their time on day hikes into the surrounding hills (mostly cutover scrub forest and agriculture land) or along the rivers. Horseback riding is another popular pastime. Most common, however, is just hanging out and relaxing.

bromeliad

In the southeast part of the town is a recreational park, **Yamburara**, with a swimming pool, small zoo and orchid garden. **El Valle de Quinara**, 9 kilometers south of Vilcabamba, has many archaeological sites.

LODGING   Located on the north entrance to Vilcabamba, **Hosteria de Vilcabamba** (private bath, hot water; $20–$30; 7-580-271, 7-580-273, fax: 7-580-272) is the newest and most elegant in town. The hosteria has 26 spacious rooms all on the ground floor, an exercise room, sauna, pool and bar, and the grounds are covered with flowers. The manager, a retired Ecuadorian army colonel, defines efficiency.

The **Parador Turístico de Vilcabamba** (Casilla 107, Vilcabamba; private and shared baths, hot water; $7–$15; phone/fax: 7-580-272) is a pleasant surprise. Overlooking the Río Vilcabamba, it is still within a five-minute walk of the town center. Its 25 rooms are very clean. It is probably no coincidence that this lodging is just as efficiently run as the Hosteria de Vilcabamba; the manager is the wife of the colonel in charge of the hosteria.

Hostal Madre Tierra (Casilla 354, Loja; private bath, hot water; $9–$11; fax: 7-580-269) has 22 rooms made of rustic materials and designed to attract young travelers and the upscale backpacker and New Age set. The price includes a huge breakfast and the evening dinner. There's a pool and steam bath; a nightly video shown on the veranda appears to be quite popular. Look for a tiny round sign on the west side of the main road just as you enter Vilcabamba. The narrow, dusty road leads to the hostal 250 meters off the paved highway.

Mandango Hostal (private and shared baths, hot water; $3–$6) is on the west side of town near the bus terminal. It has 13 rooms and is located at the foot of Mandango, a small hill that is a popular day hike.

RESTAURANTS   The best food in Vilcabamba is found in three of the hostales and hosterias in or near the town. Most elegant and expensive (by Vilcabamba standards) is the **Hosteria de Vilcabamba** (north edge of town). **Hostal Madre de Tierra** (west of the main highway on a dusty road at north end of town) specializes in vegetarian food, but also serves chicken and some beef. Its atmosphere is definitely focused on young travelers, mainly from Europe. The **Parador Turístico de Vilcabamba** (southeast side of town overlooking the river) is pleasant, clean and inexpensive. Numerous small fast-food hamburger places and ice-cream parlors have sprung up in the city center. Many are new and may or may not pass the test of time. They are all within easy walking distance of the lodgings available in town.

GETTING THERE: By Bus: The Sur Oriente Bus Line runs buses hourly between Vilcabamba and Loja. The bus trip takes two hours. Some of these buses continue south to Yangana and Zumba if you want to see the area near the Peruvian border. Be careful whenever you get within 10 kilometers of the Peruvian border, though. After the 1995 border "war," checkpoints are frequent. Tourists with cameras and binoculars, however, are usually greeted with a smile.

By Car: From Loja, take the Vilcabamba highway 43 kilometers south. The road is paved and the only tricky place is an ambiguous jog to the left (rather than straight ahead) at the village of El Carmen, 30 kilometers south of Loja.

By Taxi: In Loja, a taxi costs about $10/person; the trip is 45 minutes to an hour depending on the driver. Getting a taxi back to Loja is likely to be more of a problem.

VALLADOLID AND ZUMBA

At Vilcabamba the pavement of the main highway from Loja gives out and continues south as a gravel road. The road is easy to drive, and there is little traffic. South of Vilcabamba the road passes through agricultural land and then begins to ascend a ridge of the Andes. Thirty kilometers (45 minutes driving) south of Vilcabamba, or 10 kilometers south of the town of Yangana, the road suddenly enters the southwestern leg of **Podocarpus National Park** (no entrance fee here) and an extensive area of undisturbed cloud forest and sub-paramo habitat. For the next 25 kilometers, there are no houses, fields or indications of man's interference other than the road itself. This area of Podocarpus National Park is the most easily accessible of all entrances, but it is still so wild that with a little luck you might see a Spectacled Bear or Mountain Tapir crossing the road in front of your car. Flocks of brightly colored birds move along at eye level all along this road.

Adventurous travelers can continue on this road south down the mountain to the tiny and isolated village of **Valladolid** and then on to the small and winding part of the road all the way to the city of **Zumba** (5000 inhabitants) on the Peruvian border (four and a half hours' drive from Loja nonstop). This is the only part of Ecuador that directly contacts the Río Marañon and its unique flora and fauna.

LODGING   The only lodging we recommend in Zumba is **Pension Rosita** (communal bathroom and shower, cold water; $2 per person) kitty-corner from the military barracks (*El Quartel*) on the town plaza. The seven rooms are all on the second floor, and they are very spartan but clean. The only telephone that connects with Loja and the rest of Ecuador is at the army barracks and is available from noon to 5 p.m. daily.

RESTAURANTS Directly across from the Pension Rosita is the best restaurant in town, **Restaurante La Choza**. A set menu is served for breakfast, lunch and dinner. The food is simple but hearty with generous portions ($1.50/meal).

GETTING THERE: By Bus: Several bus companies ply the route between Loja and Zumba each day. Local *rancheras* or pickup trucks carry passengers between Zumba and the villages of La Chonta and El Chorro closer to the Peruvian border.

By Car: The drive south from Loja to Zumba takes four to five hours depending on road conditions. Be careful of the last 35 kilometers as the road becomes very winding and narrow.

ZAMORA

The highway from Loja to Zamora is only 64 kilometers long, but it is like going back into the last century. The scenery from the road is spectacular as you descend from paramo and elfin woodland through cloud forest and finally to upper Amazonia forest at Zamora (3201 feet/970 meters). Podocarpus National Park runs along the highway's south side for much of its length.

As you drive into Zamora, you pass from clean and modern Loja into a frontier town whose facilities are not prepared for most tourists. Even though Zamora is the capital of the Province of Zamora Chinchipe, it has the aura of a small town (the population is less than 10,000) forgotten in the jungle. However, the discovery of gold at nearby Nambija and, even more seriously, the rumors of gold in the lower parts of the adjacent Podocarpus National Park have already created problems both for the town of Zamora and for the future of the park. Tourism is in many ways a much more desirable economic base upon which to plan the town's growth.

The surprisingly well-stocked store, **Comercial Zambroro**, is one of Zamora's saving graces. Numerous small restaurants are in the town center, but except for a clean bakery near the City Municipal Building, the eateries tend to be marginal to filthy. If you plan to visit the Podocarpus National Park from here, stop at the **INEFAN** offices on the south (right) side of the highway as you enter Zamora from Loja. Here you can pay your $20 fee and receive maps and directions to the entrance. There are no signs, and the entrance road from Zamora is obscure. If you were in the park previously, even if it was the Cajanuma entrance from Loja, which costs only $10, you can present that ticket to enter without further charge at either of the two park entrances from Zamora.

LODGING Finally, two good hotels exist in Zamora! The **Hostal Internacional Torres** (Francisco de Orellana and Amazonas; private bath, hot water, floor fans, color TV; $25; phone/fax: 7-605-195) has 12 carpeted rooms on the second floor for 22 guests. The owners are attentive to ecotourists, and the rooms, restaurant and lobby are very clean. Even more recently constructed is the **Gymifa Hotel** (Diego de Baca and Pío Jaramillo Alvarado; private bath, hot water; $25; 7-605-024, 606-103). It has ten clean and comfortable rooms but no restaurant. The next "best" hotel in town is the **Hotel Maguna** (Diego de Vaca near the Río Zamora on the northwest end of town; private and shared baths, cold water, fans; charges by the bed $2.50 –$5). The rooms are dingy to dirty, and the overall ambiance is one of humid deterioration.

RESTAURANTS   The nicest place to eat is at the **Hosteria Internacional Torres** (7 a.m.–9 p.m.). The food is hearty and served family-style. Another clean, inexpensive restaurant is the **Restaurant 24 Horas** (corner of Pio Jaramillo Alvarado and Amazonas; 7 a.m.–9 p.m.) where chicken, rice, local soups and stews are the normal fare.

GETTING THERE: Arrangements can be made with travel agencies or the better hotels in Loja to rent a van and driver for a day trip to Zamora. Loja bus line is the main carrier between Loja and Zamora, and buses run all day and night. The road north to Macas via Yantzaza and Gulaquiza is more than 260 kilometers of dust and mud. Only the masochistic and hardy should even consider this route.

PODOCARPUS NATIONAL PARK

Stretching across the provinces of Zamora, Chinchipe and Loja, Podocarpus National Park was established in 1982 and covers 365,700 acres. Varying in altitude from 3300–11,880 feet (1000–3600 meters), the park extends from the upper Amazonian to paramo habitats. Less rain falls in the higher altitudes; here the rainy season extends from February to March while the dry season is October and November. In the park's Amazonian part, the rainy season is March and April and the dry season is October to December. This park protects the only large expanse of undisturbed forest left in southern Ecuador. For more details on the park, its hiking trails, flora and fauna, see *Birds of Podocarpus National Park: An Annotated Checklist* by J. F. Rasmussen and Carsten Rabeck (Fundación Aage V. Jensen). It costs $20 and is available through the Corporación Ornitológica del Ecuador (CECIA) in Quito.

In the park's higher altitudes you'll also find more than a hundred lakes created by ancient glaciers. Everything from lush green cloud forest to boggy grassland paramo is typical of this area. In the higher altitudes are the park's namesake. Three species of podocarpus trees, some individuals reaching 165 feet (50 meters) in height, occur in protected groves. This is the only conifer-type tree found in northern South America. The lower altitudes have flora and fauna typical of the upper limits of the Amazonian forest. Cascading streams filled with boulders and numerous waterfalls are also plentiful here.

By some estimates, there are likely between 600 and 800 species of birds in the park, and probably 3000 to 4000 species of vascular plants make their home here. Through the combined efforts of INEFAN and the Loja-based conservation group Fundación Arco Iris, Ecuador for the first time was able to bring environmental law to the courts and force out the many gold miners who had established themselves within the park's boundaries. Although this danger is still present, especially around the lower boundaries of the park near Zamora, a precedent has been established in Ecuadorian courts that hopefully can be applied in future cases throughout the country.

CAJANUMA ENTRANCE

The administrative center for the Loja end of the park is at Cajanuma (9075 feet/2750 meters elevation). Thirteen kilometers south of Loja on the Vilca-bamba road, a dirt road on the left (east) side of the road leads to a guard station and archway. You can pay the entrance fee ($10) here, but often there is no guard until you drive up the 8 kilometers of the rest of the road to the **National Park Administrative Center**. Even better is to have paid the fee at the Loja park office. At several places along this gravel road, four-wheel drive would be nice. However, two-wheel drive and some skill are usually all that are needed. This road reaches the actual park boundary after 5 kilometers, and here the cloud forest habitat closes in on the road. Although very difficult to observe even here, this is probably the best place in all of Ecuador and perhaps all of South America to catch a glimpse of the Spectacled Bear, the only bear found south of Mexico. The rangers report seeing these large black bears with white circles around the eyes on this road several times a year. They are extremely shy and usually cross the road in early morning or late afternoon. Also, the Bearded Guan, Gray-breasted Mountain Toucan and Ocellated Tapaculo are relatively common here—all bird species that are difficult to find anywhere else in Ecuador.

At the **Cajanuma Visitors Center**, a two-story building that can house up to 20 guests is available. From the lodge are a variety of trails. Some relatively short loop trails can be done in one to two hours. The Lagunas de El Compadre Trail goes through elfin forest to paramo habitats and is 12 kilometers long. Because of the difficult climb and soggy terrain, this is an overnight hike and takes eight to nine hours one-way. Besides many unusual plants, birds and insects, this is one of the best areas in Ecuador to see the Mountain Tapir (*danta*). Camping is permitted at the Administrative Center, as well as at Lagunas de El Compadre. Be prepared for cold, wet weather and bring warm clothing and adequate tenting equipment. November and December are the best months to camp in this section of the park. You can expect to have days without rain and perhaps even see the sun. The rest of the year brings almost constant rain and cooler temperatures. Several simple but warm **cabins** have been constructed near the Administrative Center and can also be used for lodging. Make reservations through the office in Loja.

GETTING THERE: By Bus: Take any bus from Loja going to Vilcabamba. Ask to be let off at the Cajanuma entrance to the park (20 minutes south of Loja). It is then an 8-kilometer hike up the gravel road to the visitors center.

By Car: Drive 13 kilometers south of Loja on the Vilcabamba highway. Turn in left (east) at the arched park entrance and drive the 8 kilometers to the visitors center. A two-wheel-drive car can readily manage this road.

RIO SAN FRANCISCO ENTRANCE

INEFAN has recently constructed a guard station and **trailhead** at this site on the main highway to Zamora, 16 kilometers east of Loja. At this point, the paved highway forms the boundary of Podocarpus National Park, and all the lush forest on the steep south side of the highway is pristine. The elevation (6500 feet) and vegetation type (subtropical cloud forest) are similar to those of the Cajanuma entrance but much more accessible. A narrow trail leads down from the highway into the forest and continues for 5 kilometers. Beside the spectacular views of plants and animals, one of the attractions of this trail was ready access to an immense Podocarpus tree 1 kilometer from the highway—the most accessible individual in the park. In 1996, poachers cut this tree down one night and began to cart it up to their truck on the highway. They were caught, their saws, truck and the cut lumber confiscated, and they received a fine. Ironically, this confiscated lumber is being used to construct an observation tower at the point where the tree used to stand. Now to see giant individuals of this ancient conifer you must walk much farther down this path or visit the slopes of the southwestern part of the park east of Vilcabamba.

GETTING THERE: By Bus: Take one of the numerous buses going from Loja to Zamora. Ask the driver to stop at the INEFAN sign for San Francisco. The ranger station is a white building 200 meters off the road.

By Car: Take the Zamora highway from Loja and drive 16 kilometers up over the cordillera crest and then down past paramo and temperate forest habitat to the San Francisco sign. Park in the parking area and check in with the park guards. If you reach a hydroelectric plant on the south side of the highway, you have gone 5 kilometers too far.

BOMBUSCARA ENTRANCE

The Bombuscara road to Podocarpus National Park quickly becomes a narrow, grass-centered strip that continues along the river for 4 kilometers. A wide area at the end of the road is for parking. Lock your car and continue on the trail by foot another 2 kilometers. This trail passes through secondary and then primary forest. Even before you enter the park boundary proper, you are likely to see flocks made up of seven to ten different tanager species, each so eye-catching with gaudy colors, it is hard to make progress along the path. Cocks-of-the-Rock are regular here, too. The large males of this east slope race are bright red-orange with a conspicuous crest. The females and immatures are a dirty tan. In the morning and afternoon, both males and females feed in the fruiting trees and are not shy.

About a half-kilometer after passing the boundary sign for the park, this path will suddenly open up into a large clearing. The several buildings of the **Bombuscara Administrative Center** are in the center of this clearing, and here you need to register and pay your entrance fee if not already paid. Camping is allowed here, but it is best to have written permission from the INEFAN station in Zamora. A short (1-kilometer) circular path south of the buildings forks off to the right at the **orchid garden**. This small garden has been packed full of transplanted orchids from the surrounding forest. Usually one or more of 30 or so species of orchids is in blossom. Over 15 kilometers of easy hiking paths continue along the river and into the forest.

GETTING THERE: From Zamora's *terminal terrestre* take the road east (past a monument near the station) and turn right (south) at an unmarked road that parallels the west side of the Río Bombuscara. If you are driving, be sure and ask someone to point out the road to Podocarpus National Park. Do not cross the bridge over the river—this road goes to the park's Romerillos entrance 20 kilometers away.

ROMERILLOS ENTRANCE

The road from Zamora crosses the Bombuscara bridge and continues a few kilometers along the south bank of the Río Zamora. Then the road turns sharply south and follows Río Jamboe's west bank for about 18 kilometers more to the village of Romerillos. There are no stores here so don't depend on buying food or supplies. From here it is a five- to six-hour hike to the camp site at **Quebrada Avioneta**. Be prepared for a muddy slog. The wildlife viewing and the scenic vistas, however, are worth the effort. One cautionary note: rumors of gold in the park have sparked periodic invasions of Romerillos by miners. They have been controlled at the trailhead at Romerillos, but be sure and check at the INEFAN office in Zamora. Highly volatile situations can arise quickly, and backpacking gringos are not likely to be guaranteed safe passage.

GETTING THERE: There are daily buses to the small village of Romerillos, but these vehicles (*rancheras*) are open-sided trucks that have been converted to torture chambers for anyone over 5 feet tall. Alternatively, you can hire a truck in Zamora for $30 to take you to Romerillos and pick you up later.

SECTION II

The Coastal Region

One way to understand the coastal region of Ecuador is to recognize the cultural and historical differences between the coast and the sierra (highlands). Historically, the residents of the sierra were sedentary farmers dominated first by the Incas and then by the Spanish. In marked contrast, the inhabitants of the coast were hunters and fishermen who were never fully conquered by the Incas and who mounted stiff resistance to the Spanish. Labor was cheap and plentiful in the sierra, but on the coast labor was in such short supply that African slaves had to be imported by the Spanish. Stereotypes of people of the sierra and the coast are still based on these historical differences. In the sierra, people are perceived as traditional, submissive, and more community oriented. On the coast, people are seen as highly independent, aggressive, and more politically progressive.

Many of the cultural distinctions between the coast and the sierra have been exaggerated by competition for limited economic and political resources. With a less belligerent indigenous culture in the sierra, colonial rule was much easier, and the seat of Spanish government became established there. Hand in glove with the Spanish government was the Catholic Church and it, too, became dominant in the sierra. In contrast, even as late as the 1700s, the Catholic Church had few missions and converts on the coast. In the highlands, the Catholic Church had a tremendous influence on artistic and intellectual endeavors through its education programs at all levels, from primary school to university. Because of this influence, Quito became the center of the arts and higher education in the country. This legacy is reflected today in the generally higher education level of *quiteños* compared to *guayaquileños*. The coast, on the other hand, is better known for its business acumen and political activism, characters of an independent and innovative people.

Nowhere is this entrepreneurial spirit more obvious than in Guayaquil. With its front door on the giant Guayas River and the Pacific Ocean, from the beginning Guayaquil was open to the world through trade. With most of Ecuador's nonpetroleum exports leaving via Guayaquil's ports, the city became more and more dominant economically. Meanwhile, Quito, isolated in its comfortable traditions in the mountains, became less and less of an economic force but held on tenaciously to its political power. With the people of Guayaquil feeling that they were the engine driving Ecuador's economic growth, and the people of Quito perceived as using their political power to funnel large portions of the country's gross national product to the sierra, it is not surprising that regional resentments were the result. Many of these regional resentments are based on a lack of communication. To this day, even highly educated *quiteños* will talk of how dangerous the coast is and how ignorant the people living there are. Meanwhile, many of those from the coast see the *quiteños* as arrogant snobs who, through political tricks and misuse of centralized power, receive most of the profits earned by the industriousness of the *guayaquileños*. This regionalism is very slowly being eroded by decentralization of political power and by increased economic incentives. Businessmen appear to be the ones most aware that this provincialism has no place in a modern society. They know through personal experience how critical it is for Ecuador's future that the various regions work together for common goals.

The coast is much more than just the urban sprawl of Guayaquil and the sandy beaches that go on for miles and miles. The coastal region includes all the lowlands between the mountains and the ocean. Indeed, the coastal lowlands are the country's most productive agricultural land. Rice, bananas and African oil palm plantations cover thousands of acres. On the coast itself, additional thousands of acres are covered with shallow, manmade lakes for raising shrimp. Among these agricultural developments, tourism has also made an impact, albeit much more moderate in comparison. Unfortunately, much of this economic development, especially shrimp farming, has also had devastating effects on the coastal ecosystems. Thousand of acres of mangroves have been cut down so that large shallow lakes could be constructed to raise shrimp. This industry is now the largest private-sector business in the country and produces hundreds of millions of dollars worth of shrimp for export. Many of the enormous houses the size of castles along the coast are the homes of the shrimp barons, who wield inordinate power. Because the very same mangrove estuaries that have been destroyed are also the breeding grounds for much of the fish caught out at sea, a major source of protein and cash for many Ecuadorians living on the coast has crashed. Paradoxically, these native estuaries provide most of the wild shrimp larvae from which mariculture ponds are stocked.

Agricultural development inland has had an equally devastating impact. Virtually uncontrolled clearing and lumbering have changed the coastal lowlands from a lush mixture of wet, moist and dry forests to an expanse of exhausted pastureland and eroded hillsides. Silting of rivers from heavily eroded hillsides, runoff of pesticides and other chemicals used almost indiscriminately on banana and African oil palm plantations, and contamination by sewage often produce health problems and conflict with alternative economic uses such as fishing and tourism.

In the midst of all these problems, it took one of the few branches of the national government that is largely made up of people from the coast—and with interests focused on the coast—to take action. The Ecuadorian navy realized in the 1980s that management of Ecuador's coastal resources was a national priority. Besides setting aside mangrove forests (some right on the edge of Guayaquil), the navy helped initiate an International Coastal Resources Management Project together with the United States Agency for International Development (USAID) and the University of Rhode Island. This program deals with problems ranging from irrigation of drier areas, rational use of water and soil resources, pollution, education, tourism and periodic disasters that result from El Niño. If this management plan is heeded and can wield any influence, some coastal areas may not become devastated wastelands. In the meantime, remnants of natural habitat in the form of private holdings, military reservations and national parks or reserves remind us, or sometimes haunt us, with a taste of what this region was like as little as 30 or 40 years ago. For more information on management plans and details of coastal geography, read *A Profile of Ecuador's Costal Region*, by Epler and Olsen, and *Shoreline Characteristics and Management Recommendations for the Coast of Ecuador*, by Boothroyd, Ayon, Robadue, Vásconez and Noboa (both produced by the International Coastal Resources Management Project, University of Rhode Island, Narragansett, RI 02882-1197).

For visitors, Guayaquil is the biggest and most obvious jumping-off point for discovery trips on the coast, especially if you are headed south to the Machala area or west to the beaches of the Santa Elena Peninsula. More and more tourists are even using Guayaquil as a base for their trips to the rugged coastal national park of Machalilla to the north. Manta on the central coast is an alternative starting point to visit Machalilla to the south or the remote beaches to the north. Finally, Esmeraldas is the third possible starting point on the coast. It leads to some of the least-visited sites in Ecuador, with untouched mangroves and sandy beaches and potential adventures with the unique cultures and rainforests of the Río Cayapas. Wherever you journey on the coast, we think you'll find it to be a memorable experience.

ELEVEN

Guayaquil Area

As Quito is the cultural, economic and political center for the highlands, Guayaquil is the cultural, economic and political center for the coast. With nearly two million people, Guayaquil is also the largest city in Ecuador. Residents of Guayaquil are called *guayaquileños* or, more familiarly, *guayacos*. Several historical origins of the name Guayaquil have been asserted. Some historians suggest the name comes from the Huancavilca Indian language and means "Big House." Other historians claim that the city was named after the last Indian chief of the area, Guayas, and his wife, Quil, who both committed suicide rather than submit to the Spaniards.

The city was finally established at its present location in 1547 after ten years of false starts as its founders tried to evade the fierce coastal Indians. Chosen for protection from raiding pirates and Pacific storms, the final site of the city and its port was the spot where the Daule and Babahoyo rivers converge to form the short but very deep and wide Río Guayas, which readily accommodates seagoing vessels even during the driest time of year. It is only 70 kilometers from the beginning of the Río Guayas to the Gulf of Guayaquil, and the shipping channels are protected by mangrove islands, canals and straits. Guayaquil's location, however, proved to be more effective protection from Mother Nature's storms than from the marauding of Sir Francis Drake and many other pirates.

Once established, Guayaquil still faced problems getting going. The inability to jump-start the economy was caused largely by a severe labor shortage. The local Indians were either too warlike or too freedom-loving to be enslaved. The importation of African slaves was only a stopgap measure, as many of them escaped into the nearby forests and quickly adapted to an environment similar to the one they already knew in Africa. The labor shortage was finally alleviated by importing highland Indians—not as slaves but as paid laborers. The face of Guayaquil today is a mixture of these four cultures: Spanish, lowland Indian, highland Indian and African.

Incessant sackings by English, French and Dutch pirates together with numerous accidental fires destroyed Guayaquil over and over into the 1700s. Only its tremendous economic potential as a trade port kept the city from being abandoned. Even as its wealth and importance increased, the reins of Spanish rule were finally thrown off. This occurred shortly after the two great South American liberators, Bolívar and San Martín, had their first and only meeting, in Guayaquil in 1822. Ever since, nonstop growth of its population and sporadic growth of its economy have combined to turn Guayaquil into one of the largest ports on the Pacific coast of South America.

Today, Guayaquil is the economic hub of Ecuador, responsible for over 40 percent of the nation's industries and almost all of the exportation of Ecuador's agricultural products. Its philosophy and look are more Caribbean than Andean South America. Its equatorial climate means many hot and humid days during the rainy season (December to April), but even then its temperature rarely rises above 98°F. From May to November, the influence of the cold Peruvian Current can make the days cool and the nights almost cold (68–82°F).

Virtually all of the city was at one time mangrove swamp. This legacy is most obvious when you see the recent expansions of the city in its southern parts. A relatively new highway (Vía Perimetral) from south Guayaquil to Puerto Azul, connecting with the coastal highway to Salinas, passes blocks and blocks of bamboo houses built on landfill that was mangrove swamp just a few years ago. Flooding, sewage, clouds of mosquitoes, malaria and unbelievable suffering are the lot of these settlers, who have literally invaded the area. The highway goes from the established parts of Guayaquil to the new shantytowns and suddenly enters mangrove forest under the control of the Ecuadorian navy and is where all colonization stops. After seeing these invaded areas of mangrove swamps, when you return to the downtown area filled with modern skyscrapers and the older, more elite residential areas with their large mansions and quiet, tree-lined streets, it is easier to imagine how the entire city started in the same way as the poor colonists in south Guayaquil have today.

The city itself is an intriguing mixture of bustling activity, entrepreneurial mentality, and inferiority complex. It is simultaneously chaotic and enchanting. While most first-time visitors to Ecuador admire Quito immediately, their response to Guayaquil is usually not as positive. Guayaquil is like an olive—you have to learn to like it. But if you are willing to give Guayaquil a chance, it has a lot to offer.

A WALKING TOUR OF GUAYAQUIL

We have worked with a good friend of ours, Antonio Perrone, a native of Guayaquil and an active ecotourist operator, to produce this walking tour. Most visitors to Guayaquil will be staying in one of the numerous hotels near the cathedral in the downtown area. Although we start the walking tour from this area, the route is roughly a 6-kilometer circle. You can jump in anywhere on the circle and do as much or as little of it as you want. We have tried to choose streets and neighborhoods that are safe from muggers as well as heavy traffic, but depending on the time of day or the day of the week, these dangers can arise anywhere. Be cautious but don't become so overcautious that you can't enjoy yourself. The best time to take this tour is early in the morning before it gets too hot, and on a weekend when there is relatively light traffic in the area. However, on weekends many of the museums will not be open. Refer to the map and lettered sites that correspond to this walking tour. Several shortcuts are possible, and you may choose to concentrate on only the part of the tour that most suits your interest and time frame. Taxis are cheap in Guayaquil, so flag one down to take you through any part of this tour you don't want to walk.

We begin at **Seminario Parque** at Calles 10 de Agosto and Chile. The entire park is surrounded by a tall, wrought-iron fence, and the gates are closed each night at 9 p.m. The old trees of this park are well over 80 feet high and provide shade and shelter for strolling visitors as well as several species of parrots, tanagers and flycatchers. The park is also home to an unexpected animal and an unusual custom. Between 3 p.m. and 4 p.m., workers from the major hotels looking onto the park bring in discarded salads, fruits and vegetables and place them on the ground. Yard-long iguana lizards living in the trees quickly descend and consume their meal, completely ignoring the Ecuadorian kids squealing with delight or fear. Children and adults alike watch in rapt curiosity, almost as if they had stumbled upon some miniature bright green dinosaurs. This park is sometimes called Park of the Iguanas or Bolívar Park for the large statue of Bolívar on his stallion that dominates its center. Musicians and artists often have impromptu exhibitions here, and as a place just to sit on a shaded bench and watch the people around you, this park is superb. Next to the park and across from the Continental Hotel on Calle Chile is the square building that houses the city's library and a small **anthropological museum** (9 a.m.–5 p.m., Monday–Friday).

The stately city **Cathedral** faces the west side of Parque Seminario. With its neo-Gothic architecture, the cathedral has a simple elegance both inside and outside. Its appearance is in pleasing contrast to the almost garish quality of many cathedrals around the world. If you are staying at the Grand Hotel

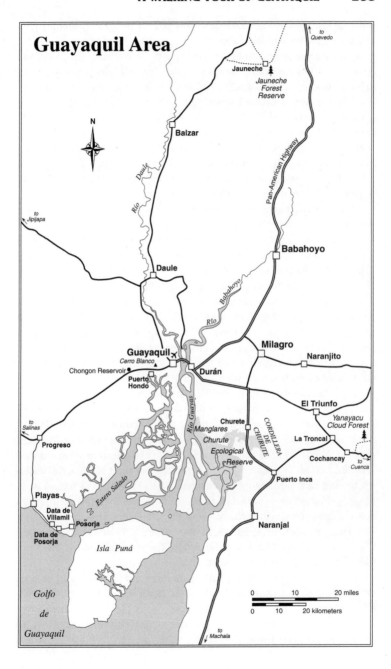

Guayaquil Area

Guayaquil, the stained-glass windows that you see over the swimming pool area are on the back of the cathedral.

Cross Parque Seminario to the side opposite the cathedral (east side) and go north (left) four blocks along Calle Chile. This will bring you to the main street in downtown Guayaquil, called Avenida 9 de Octubre. At this corner you can often find **Otavalo Indians** selling their wares, but hold off buying anything until you visit the Artisan Market later on the tour. Turn west (left) onto 9 de Octubre and walk six blocks. The second floors of the buildings along here are built out over the sidewalk and provide shade and protection from the rain. In addition to many banks, department stores and businesses, you will pass the oldest fire station in the city. Here also is evidence of "Gringolandia" in the form of Burger King, Pizza Hut and KFC.

Parque Centenario, the largest park downtown, is four blocks in size and interrupts 9 de Octubre for vehicles but not for pedestrians. The park is filled with heroic statues celebrating Guayaquil's past. The tallest statue is of Liberty, and it dominates the entire park. There are many trees and shrubs, and although the shade is not as complete as at Parque Seminario, benches are placed strategically for you to rest out of the sun.

Just west of Parque Centenario, where 9 de Octubre picks up again for vehicles going around the park, the **Casa de Cultura** building is on the north (right) side of the street. The Casa de Cultura sponsors film festivals, art expositions, and specialized classes in literature, art, language and history. There is a small archaeological museum here (8 a.m.–5 p.m., Monday–Friday); the Café Galeria next to the entrance is open the same hours.

Cross back to the south side of 9 de Octubre and continue west two more blocks to the corner of Calle José de Antepara. The large building on the southwest (left) side of the intersection is the **Banco Central** (320-576). Its giant murals of indigenous people on the outside walls are obvious. The U.S. consulate is housed in this block as well, so don't be surprised to see armored vehicles and lots of soldiers guarding the area. For most tourists, the reason for coming here is to see the best **archaeological museum** (8 a.m.–5 p.m., Monday–Friday) on the coast of Ecuador. Two recently remodeled permanent exhibits—archaeology and contemporary art—were opened in July 1995. Temporary exhibits are also featured often. Consult the arts and culture section of the newspaper for more information. The entrance is to the left, down Calle José de Antepara a few yards. There is no admission.

After visiting the museum, retrace your route back east (right) on 9 de Octubre one block to Avenida Machala. Go north (left) crossing 9 de Octubre, and walk through this area seven blocks. (Note: This is not the nicest part of the city, so if you prefer, you might want to take a taxi these seven blocks or to whatever point you next want to visit on the tour.) You now come to a street with lots of traffic—Calle Julian Coronel. Do not try crossing this busy street at its surface level. To the northwest (left and ahead) under and beyond the vehicle overpass is a white pedestrian bridge that goes over Julian Coronel. Climb these stairs and cross over the bridge and through the Gate No. 8 entrance into the **General Cemetery** (sometimes called the *Ciudad Blanca* or White City because of all the white marble used to construct its tombs and mausoleums) and turn east (right). This gigantic cemetery is like a miniature city. As you walk inside the cemetery wall that parallels Julian Coronel, you will see mausoleums that would make some New York City apartment buildings on Fifth Avenue look cheap. The less wealthy are buried in more humble surroundings higher up on the hillside called Cerro del Carmen. Other burial sites are built like housing developments, with small doors for the caskets twenty wide and ten high. Read the dates on the tombs, and you will see much of Guayaquil's history recorded. Meander past the flower vendors and on Sunday be sensitive to the many relatives visiting deceased loved ones. Continue east past Gate No. 6 three blocks to Gate No. 1 and exit back onto the sidewalk of Julian Coronel and continue east (left).

In about three blocks, the street bends northeast, and you will come to the grounds of the immense public hospital, Luís Vernaza. Turn east (right), and cross onto Loja. Go four blocks to the **Artisan Market** (Mercado Artesenal) (10 a.m.–6 p.m., Monday–Saturday), located between Calle Loja on the north and Calle Juan Montalva on the south, and between Avenida Baquerizo on the west and Calle General Cordova on the east. The market building takes up the entire block, and it is filled with 240 shops selling crafts made of leather, wood and ceramics. You'll find more jewelry, paintings, sculptures and clothing here than anywhere else on the coast. Many of the shops take credit cards, but that doesn't mean you can't bargain for prices. It is a comfortable place to browse because the shopkeepers are not pushy. They will normally let you show some interest in their wares before asking if they can help.

You may want to make the market your only goal for one day. If so, return by taxi to your hotel with your purchases. Otherwise, finishing this walking tour with your arms full will not be the most pleasant experience. If you were able to resist buying out the shops in the market, continue north (left) on General Cordova two blocks until you are again at Julian Coronel at the base of the prominent hill (Cerro del Carmen). Turn northeast (right) and follow the road as it curves around to a prominent church, **Santo Domingo**, just in back of the open-air theater called Juan Pueblo. The church is the oldest in Guayaquil (1548), but it has burned down many times and was last reconstructed in 1938. Few tourists visit this church, which is used actively by local people. Inside, the paintings over the side altars are more interesting than the rather simple main altar.

Iguana

Across the street and down a block is the entrance to a small **Fireman's Museum**. There is no entrance fee, and its hours are somewhat erratic. A few old fire engines and fire-fighting equipment from the 1800s are on display.

Just past the building housing the Fireman's Museum is the entrance to Las Peñas, the oldest part of Guayaquil. A set of stairs for pedestrians and a narrow road for vehicles leads north (left) into a small plaza with old cannons pointing out toward the Río Guayas. The single narrow road winds north through several blocks of wooden colonial buildings and eventually comes to a dead end. The old town has become less a residence area and more an artistic enclave. Several houses have been converted into galleries, and local artists are featured. A police substation (*Puesto de Auxilio Inmediato*) near the monument to Francisco de Orellana, purported founder of Guayaquil, has made the area quite safe.

Return to the entrance to Las Peñas and turn south (left) to go along Malecón Simón Bolívar, the street that runs along the west bank of the Río Guayas. Continue past the landmark Polytechnic School on your right and the large building to your left (cable TV GamaVision) to the set of small docks on your left. This is the place to watch or catch the boat to **Durán**. Every half-hour, a small launch pulls up to these covered docks and takes on passengers for the 20-minute ride across the Río Guayas to the town of Durán. The ride costs $1.50 each way and is an interesting way to see the city from a different vantage point.

Continue south nine blocks. Here the sidewalk is next to the river, with tall trees to shade much of your walk. Several **barges** are permanently moored along this stretch of the Malecón, and they serve as floating restaurants and bars. Any one makes a good place to stop for a soft drink or a beer. At Avenida Francisco de Paula Icaza, or more simply P. Icaza, in the midst of a canyon of tall business buildings, go west (right) two blocks to the **Banco del Pacífico**. On the second floor is a top-rate anthropological museum. Its interpretive signs are in both Spanish and English and are very informative. Artifacts from pre-ceramic to Valdivian cultures are emphasized. On the third floor is an elegant gallery for local artists, with the exhibits changing every two weeks. The cool, dark museum and gallery can be a pleasant and educational escape from the heat and humidity of the walking tour. Between Pichincha and 9 de Octubre, one block west of the Malecón, is the best area for money changing offices (*casa de cambio*).

Return to the river and the Malecón and turn south (right) one block to 9 de Octubre. Here is the impressive **La Rotonda**, a statue memorializing the enigmatic meeting between Argentine liberator José San Martín and Venezuelan liberator Simón Bolívar in 1822. These two great generals in the war of liberation from Spain never met before and never again. They apparently had very different visions of what a liberated South America would be. Bolívar wanted a democratic presidency and Martín wanted a king. No one recorded what was said in their meeting in Guayaquil, but at the end of the meeting Bolívar took over the rest of the war of liberation. San Martín returned to Argentina and eventually went into exile in France. The statues of these two great men shaking hands may be only an idealistic symbol of what really went on between them.

Continue south on the Malecón four more blocks. On your left is a five-story tower constructed in the style of the Moors and called the **Moorish Clock Tower** (Torre del Reloj). Across the street to your right is the **Palacio Municipal** and the **Palacio de Gobierno** (Governor's Palace). These buildings hold the political offices of the city and province.

Four more blocks south, you come to the end of the Malecón (having passed a monument to the United Nations) where Avenida Olmedo intersects it at an angle from the northwest (right). Here is **Olmedo Monument**, a statue of the first mayor of Guayaquil, José Joaquin de Olmedo. He sits in his armchair contemplating the river as it flows by him. If you are ready for some real excitement, try turning right and walking back toward your hotel in the city center along Avenida Olmedo. This section of the city is called **Mercado Sur** and is an open-air fruit and vegetable market. Farther north is **Mercado Bahía**, a black market for clothes, hardware, canned food and everything else you could think of. Be careful here, as the crowds of people make it easy for pickpockets to operate. The enthusiasm and energy of these markets, however, are fascinating to see. The markets operate almost 18 hours a day every day of the week except Sunday. After experiencing this hustle and bustle, you will never again be tempted to stereotype Latin Americans as *mañana* personalities with no work ethic.

Turn north (right) on Calle Chile and continue another five blocks to your starting point at the Parque Seminario.

LODGING

A wide variety of lodging is available in Guayaquil, with most places concentrated in and around the downtown area. Strangely, the Urdesa district with its many restaurants, nightclubs and shopping areas has virtually no lodging.

Most of the museums, theaters and tourist sites are close to the downtown hotel area. Reasonable walks or short taxi rides from your hotel will get you to most places of interest in the city center. From here, Urdesa is a 20-minute taxi ride or an hour bus ride to the north.

DELUXE HOTELS

All of these luxury hotels have 60-plus rooms; most are fully equipped for conventions. In Guayaquil, much more than in Quito, guests here are mainly business people. The deluxe hotels all have a 24-hour coffee shop and one or more elegant and expensive restaurant. They have numerous bars, pools, sauna, exercise room, casino, room service and laundry service. In the rooms, private baths, hot water, bathtubs, air conditioning, hair dryers, phones, cable color TV and minibars are all included. Some have nonsmoking rooms on some floors. Rates for double rooms are $75–$300. Tax adds an additional 20 percent.

With 90 rooms on seven floors, **Continental** (Calles Chile and 10 de Agosto; $90–$115; 4-329-270, fax: 4-325-454, or 800-333-1212 in the U.S. and Canada) probably has the best service of all the major hotels in Guayaquil. There is a parking garage, and all the rest of the amenities of a modern, international-class hotel.

Featuring an atmosphere of stated elegance and an architecture of mature taste is **Grand Hotel Guayaquil** (Boyacá and Clemente Ballén; $85–$125; 4-329-690, fax: 4-327-251), with 160 large and luxurious rooms. A pool and quiet waterfalls back up against the wall of the cathedral; guests can also enjoy the fully equipped gym, squash courts, sauna and massage. The service is personal and efficient. Our favorite of all the luxury hotels in Guayaquil, its only obvious drawback is its utter disregard for handicapped visitors. The elevators are at the top of a long and wide set of marble stairs, and there is no alternative to being carried up or down these stairs.

Finished in 1997, the **Hilton Colón Guayaquil** (Avenida Francisco de Orellana, Kennedy District; $220–$270; 4-689-000, fax: 4-689-049, or 800-445-8667 in the U.S.) is the newest and most opulent hotel in the city. With 290 rooms, several restaurants, fitness center and meeting rooms, the Hilton has all the latest amenities. It is located closer to the airport and Urdesa district than any of the other luxury hotels.

Oro Verde (Avenida 9 de Octubre and Calle García Moreno; $220–$300; 4-327-999, fax: 4-329-350) has 225 rooms, a sauna, an exercise room, pools and everything else you expect from a luxury hotel. Located on the north side of downtown, except for the Hilton, it is closer to the airport than any of the other luxury hotels. Its coffee shop serves some of the best *criollo* food we've eaten.

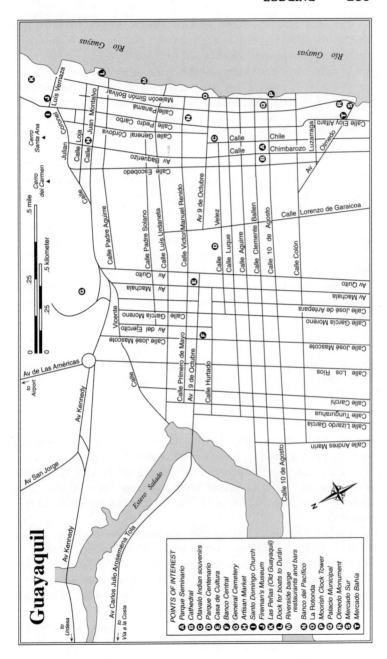

Guayaquil

Río Guayas

Río Guayas

Malecón Simón Bolívar

Calle Panamá

Calle Pedro Carbo

Calle General Córdova

Calle Víctor Manuel Renido

Calle Luis Urdaneta

Calle Padre Solano

Calle Padre Aguirre

Av 9 de Octubre

Calle Lorenzo de Garaicoa

Velez

Calle Luque

Calle Aguirre

Calle Clemente Ballen

Calle 10 de Agosto

Calle Colón

Calle Los Ríos

Calle Andrés Marín

Calle Lizardo García

Calle Carchi

Calle Tungurahua

Calle José Mascote

Calle Primero de Mayo

Av 9 de Octubre

Calle Hurtado

Calle García Moreno

Calle José de Anteparra

Calle José Mascote

Av del Ejército

Av García Moreno

Av Machala

Av Quito

Av Machala

Av Quito

Av Baquerizo

Calle Escobedo

Calle Chile

Calle Chimbarozo

Cerro del Carmen

Cerro Santa Ana

Luis Vernaza

Coronel

Calle Loja

Calle

Calle

Julian

Vicente

Juan Montalvo

Calle Eloy Alfaro

Luzarraga

Olmedo

Estero Salado

Av Carlos Julio Arosemena Tola

Av Kennedy

Av San Jorge

Av Kennedy

Av de Las Américas

to Airport

to Urdesa

to Vía a la Costa

.5 mile

.25

0

.5 kilometer

.25

0

N

POINTS OF INTEREST

- Ⓐ Parque Seminario
- Ⓑ Cathedral
- Ⓒ Olavalo Indian souvenirs
- Ⓓ Parque Centenario
- Ⓔ Casa de Cultura
- Ⓕ Banco Central
- Ⓖ General Cemetery
- Ⓗ Artisan Market
- Ⓘ Santo Domingo Church
- Ⓙ Fireman's Museum
- Ⓚ Las Peñas (Old Guayaquil)
- Ⓛ Dock for boats to Durán
- Ⓜ Riverside barge restaurants and bars
- Ⓝ Banco del Pacífico
- Ⓞ La Rotonda
- Ⓟ Moorish Clock Tower
- Ⓠ Palacio Municipal
- Ⓡ Olmedo Monument
- Ⓢ Mercado Sur
- Ⓣ Mercado Bahía

Ramada (Malecón and Orellana; $105–$195; 4-565-555, 4-312-200, fax: 4-563-036) offers 110 rooms, a sauna, an indoor pool and other amenities. Its riverside location provides views from the rooms, but it also presents a problem at night. The streets in this area of the city are not the safest after 10:00 p.m. Some rooms over the busy city streets are very noisy, and the few lights in each room make reading difficult after dark. The elevators are at the top of a staircase, and no easy access is available. There's a 24-hour parking garage.

With 138 rooms, **Unipark Hotel** (Calles Clemente Ballén 406 and Chile; $140–$180; 4-327-100, fax: 4-328-352, or 212-750-0375 in the U.S.) is divided into two towers by a small but very tasteful shopping center (Unicentro). Reception and check-in area is at the east (Parque Seminario) end on the second floor. If your room is in the west tower, you have to walk across the shopping center to the elevators for the other tower. A second-floor connection crosses between the towers, too. There is one nonsmoking floor (the seventh), and all the rooms are amazingly quiet. If your room overlooks Parque Seminario, you can watch birds and iguanas at eye level or below you. The views from the other directions are not as nice. If you want to avoid expensive hotel restaurants, the deli at the north entrance to the Unicentro is terrific for sandwiches, drinks and pastries, and is reasonably priced. The parking garage is two blocks away.

MODERATE HOTELS

Double-occupancy room rates for these hotels range from $40–$75. Amenities in the rooms include private baths, hot water, air conditioning, refrigerator, color TV unless otherwise indicated and phone. Each has a small restaurant and a bar but few other extras.

La Concorda (Avenida 9 de Octubre 1703; $50–$75; 4-522-856, 4-510-646, fax: 4-321-726) has 12 rooms all on the twelfth floor of an apartment and business building. Take the elevator to the twelfth floor, and ring the bell at the inconspicuous door down the hall. An attendant will open the door for you. The rooms are large and clean but a little run-down. The good news is the view of the city is spectacular, and you are only a block away from the U.S. consulate.

The *best* place to stay for the money in downtown Guayaquil is the **Palace** (Chile 214-216; $40–$80; 4-321-080, fax: 4-322-887). The 176 rooms are large and immaculate, and some even have king-size beds. The security locks and precautions are more sophisticated than even in most of the luxury hotels. Except for somewhat noisy rooms facing the street and the lack of a parking garage, we have difficulty making any complaints, and the Palace easily wins accolades for a comfortable stay that won't eat up your budget. Unfortunately, the hotel restaurant on the ground floor serves food that is both mediocre and expensive.

Sol de Oriente (Calles Aguirre 603 and Escobedo; $40–$50; 4-325-500, 4-325-601, fax: 4-329-352) offers 56 very nice rooms on seven of the top eight floors of a 14-story building. There is a sauna as well as an excellent exercise room. It has a large *chifa* (Chinese) restaurant on the fourteenth floor, and a 24-hour cafeteria on the ground floor. The motif is Asian throughout, but the service is somewhat slow, and the employees are not as friendly as in other hotels of this class.

Suites El Ejecutivo (Calles Escobedo 1403 and Luque; $40–$60; 4-532-295, 4-329-180, fax: 4-321-409) boasts 13 extremely large multi-room suites, including an efficiency kitchen. The rooms are a little run-down but quite clean. There is no restaurant, but 24-hour room service is available.

INEXPENSIVE HOTELS

These lodgings run $15–$40 for a double-occupancy room. All have private baths and hot water.

Metropolitana (Calles Victor M. Rendón 120 and Panamá; air conditioning; $12–$20; 4-565-251, 4-565-2500) has more quaint atmosphere than any other hotel on our list. Built with an open-air design of the early 1900s, balconies look out onto the city from each hallway, and an internal set of balconies looks down on the ground-floor foyer. The telephones in each room are the old, World War I French style, and while clean, the furniture and ambiance of each room are definitely reminiscent of another time. The reception desk is on the fourth floor, and you get there via a wrought-iron, cagelike elevator with an elevator operator. Across the Malecón from the Río Guayas, the rooms are *very* noisy with heavy street traffic below. This is also a dangerous part of town at night, so consider carefully the tradeoffs of staying here.

Plaza (Calles Chile 414 and Clemente Ballén; air conditioning in some, ceiling fans in others, phone, cable color TV, some with minibar; $35–$40; 4-327-140, 4-324-006, 4-329-7411, fax: 4-324-195) offers 48 rooms that are clean and simple, but tend to be quite noisy. There is a cafeteria.

Rizzo (Clemente Ballén 319 and Chile; air conditioning, phone, cable color TV; $30–$40; 4-325-210, fax: 4-326-209) provides 60 rooms on five floors, and a cafeteria and restaurant on the ground floor. The rooms show their age, but the location of the hotel near Parque Seminario is handy for seeing some of the more interesting parts of downtown Guayaquil.

Located in a quiet residential area across from the main campus of the Universidad de Guayaquil, **Tangara Guest House** (M. Saenz and O'Leary, Block F. No. 1 in the Bolivariana section of north Guayaquil; air conditioning, private bath, hot water; $33–$46; 4-284-445, 4-284-039, fax: 4-284-039) has lodging for 16 people in doubles and triples. It is the closest accommodation to the airport and the Urdesa district. The main attraction for this guest house is the family atmosphere of the Perrones, who run the place as an extension of their own home next door. Breakfast is served for $4, and a large kitchen is available for storing and cooking your own lunches and suppers. All cookware, plates and utensils are provided. The rooms are modern, simple and ultra-clean. There is also an in-house tourism office, and you can arrange field trips to all parts of mainland Ecuador and the Galápagos through them. The name of their guest house ("The Tanager") reflects their keen interest in the environment.

BUDGET HOTELS

Because of safety issues and sometimes unsanitary conditions, we cannot recommend most budget hotels in Guayaquil.

Centenario (Calles Vélez 728 and Santa Elena; private bath, cold water, some with air conditioning, rest with table fans, some with color TV; $5–$15; 4-524-467, 4-523-724) can count 55 rooms, but they are spartan and only moderately clean. The bathrooms are in a corner of the bedroom separated only by sliding-glass doors that do not reach to the ceiling. Some have an unpleasant odor, so look at the room before you check in. There is a small cafeteria, but no parking garage.

RESTAURANTS

ECUADORIAN   **Lo Nuestro** (Avenida Victor Emilio Estrada 903 and Higueras in the Urdesa district; 7 a.m.–midnight, open seven days a week; $2–$4; 4-386-398) is one of the best and most economical restaurants in the Urdesa district. It serves typical Ecuadorian dishes, especially *criollo*, and the large restaurant has a personal touch with excellent service.

Paradero Rustico and **La Casa del Cangrejo** (Avenida Luís Plaza Dañín near the Policentro shopping center; 7 p.m.–1 a.m., Tuesday–Sunday; $3–$6; 4-396-632) are a pair of restaurants run side-by-side by the same management. The food here is authentic Ecuadorian, including a meal of locally caught crabs boiled and served with all manner of side dishes. The food is good, but the intensity of the people filling these restaurants is incredible. Everyone comes here as much to have a good time as to eat. Both restaurants are small, with booths lining the walls, but everyone seems to be eating at a family get-together.

Juan Salvador Gaviota (Avenida Francisco de Orellana in the north Kennedy district; 8 p.m.–11 p.m. except Sunday; $4–$9; 4-298-280) is one of the most elegant and romantic restaurants in Guayaquil. It specializes in seafood that will make you want to come back soon.

El Fortin (Hotel Continental, Calles Chile and 10 de Agosto; 7 p.m.–1 a.m., open seven days a week; $6–$15; 4-329-270) is a handy place to try

Ecuadorian cuisine in the downtown area. The service is excellent, but the food is extremely overpriced.

El Patio (Oro Verde hotel, Avenida 9 de Octubre and Calle García Moreno; $7–$15; open seven days a week, 24 hours a day; 4-327-999) offers the most authentic Ecuadorian dishes we have tried at any of the big hotels. However, the prices for even simple dishes are astronomical.

STEAK RESTAURANTS   **Parrillada "La Selvita"** (Avenida Olmos and Calle Brisas in the Urdesa district; 12:30 p.m.–3:30 p.m. and 6:30 p.m.– 12:30 a.m., Tuesday–Saturday; 12:30 p.m.–3:30 p.m., Sunday–Monday; $3–$10; 4-881-000) is a large, Argentine-style restaurant in a quiet part of Urdesa. Grilled steaks and, if you insist, chicken are available.

O'Casarão (Avenida Guillermo Pareja R. at the entrance to Ciudela La Garzota; noon–midnight except Mondays; $4–$10; 4-295-763) serves more types of meat than you have ever seen in one place before. Waiters constantly roam the tables cutting great slabs of roast beef, chicken, sausage, pork and more from sword-like skewers—Brazil style.

La Parrillada del Ñato (Avenida Victor Emilio Estrada 1219 and Lureles in the Urdesa district; noon–1 a.m., open seven days a week; $8–$25; 4-387-098) is the most Argentine and red-blooded of all the steak restaurants. The food is spectacular and the portions immense, but the prices are also spectacularly immense. The restaurant has an open and airy atmosphere, and the service is excellent.

CHINESE AND JAPANESE   **Kwantung** (Avenida San Jorge 308 and 3rd Este in the Nueva Kennedy district; noon–3 p.m. and 7 p.m.–11 p.m., Tuesday–Sunday; $5–$20; 4-395-266) is a beautiful restaurant specializing in Cantonese food. This is arguably the best *chifa* in Guayaquil.

Tsuji (Avenida Victor Emilio Estrada 813 between Guayacanes and Higueras in the Urdesa district; noon–3 p.m. and 7 p.m.–11 p.m., Tuesday –Sunday; $4–$12; 4-881-183) claims to be the only Japanese restaurant in Ecuador. It is an elegant place with peaceful gardens and fountains, and the food is authentic, even if the Japanese owner speaks English with a Houston accent.

ITALIAN   **La Carbonara and Trattoría Pizzeria** (Bálsamos 206 and La Unica in Urdesa; 12:30 p.m.–3 p.m. and 7:30 p.m.–midnight, Tuesday– Sunday; $5–$12; 4-382-714) serves a wide selection of Italian foods. The atmosphere of this friendly restaurant is set by a bar that seems to extend forever and a collection of beer bottles and cans neatly lining the walls that the manager claims is the largest in Ecuador.

Ristorante Casanova (Calle 1ra 604 and Avenida Las Monjas in Urdesa; 1 p.m.–2 a.m., except Saturday 7 p.m.–2 a.m.; $5–$20; 4-882-475) is a small (nine tables) and intimate restaurant recently refurbished. The food is good, and live but quiet music at midday and after 8:30 p.m. lends atmosphere.

Trattoría de Enrico (Bálsamos 504 between Avenida Las Monjas and Ebanos in Urdesa; 12:30 p.m.–3 p.m. and 7 p.m.–midnight, Wednesday–Monday; $6–$15; 4-387-079) was voted the best restaurant in Ecuador for 1993 and 1994 by the national gourmet club. Besides the delicious menu of Italian food, the restaurant is pleasantly divided into separate but open rooms that simultaneously provide some intimacy without losing the friendly camaraderie of fellow diners. Watch out for the low entrance at the front door; after that, you can stand upright inside with no fear.

INTERNATIONAL CUISINE   **Caracol Azul** (Avenida 9 de Octubre 1918 and Calle Los Ríos, a couple of blocks west of the Oro Verde hotel; 12:30 p.m.–3:30 p.m. and 6 p.m.–midnight, Monday–Saturday; $15–$40; 4-280-461) offers, by most visitors' estimate, the best seafood restaurant in town. The menu is extensive, and the choice of wines fantastic. It is also probably the most expensive restaurant in the city.

Le Gourmet (Oro Verde hotel, Avenida 9 de Octubre and Calle García Moreno; 6:30 p.m.–1 a.m., open seven days a week; $10–$25; 4-327-999) specializes in French cuisine in an elegant setting of European paintings and atmosphere. The food—*c'est excellent*—but also *very* expensive.

Casa Baska (C. Ballén 422 on Seminario Parque; 11 a.m.–midnight except Sunday; $3–$9; 4-534-597) and its sister restaurant **Tasca Vasca** (Chile 416; 11 a.m.–4 p.m. except Sunday; $3–$5; 4-324-834) are both near the Unipark Hotel in the downtown district. They specialize in Basque food, but serve a wide array of Spanish and international cuisine. Ask for the Tartufo for dessert!

La Balandra (Calle 5 between Avenida Las Monjas and Datiles in the Urdesa district; noon–3:30 p.m. and 7 p.m.–midnight, open seven days a week; $4–$10; 4-385-807) is an exquisite place to have seafood prepared in styles ranging from Ecuadorian to Hawaiian.

Restaurant 1822 (Grand Hotel Guayaquil, Boyacá and Calle Clemente Ballén; noon–4 p.m. and 6 p.m.–midnight, open seven days a week; $5–$15; 4-329-690), while not the largest of the luxury hotel restaurants, is the one we choose to eat at over and over. The service is great, the food absolutely fantastic, and the prices, while steep, are not pretentiously overblown.

El Parque (Unipark Hotel, Calles Clemente Ballén 406 and Chile; 7 a.m.–midnight, open seven days a week, $6–$12; 4-327-100) is on the fourth floor of the Unipark Hotel and directly overlooks the Parque Seminario at treetop level. During the day you can see parrots, kingbirds and tanagers flying around at eye level. The food is good and the service excellent.

VEGETARIAN   **Supernutrion** (Chimborazo 617 and Sucre, kittycorner from the cathedral; 9 a.m.–5 p.m. Monday to Saturday; $2) is the best vegetarian restaurant in downtown Guayaquil.

SHOPPING

Guayaquil has souvenirs and handicrafts from both coastal and highland areas in a variety of stores and locations. Leather goods, wood carvings, porcelain statuettes, jewelry, weavings and embroidered shirts and blouses are among the most popular items available. The upscale chain **Modapelle** has handy stores in the major shopping centers of Albán Borja, Plaza Quil, Plaza Triángulo and Unicentro. In the Policentro shopping center, **Folklore Carmita** and **La Nuestra** are good. In the Albán Borja shopping center, **El Telar** and **Ramayana** are small but excellent handicrafts stores. In the Urdesa district, **Coosas** and **Boutique Manos** are very upscale shops for souvenirs. **Ocepa** is the government-run handicrafts store on Calle Illingsworth 111 near the Malecón along the Río Guayas. The **Mercado Artesenal** is on Calle Baquerizo Moreno near the Old Town part of Guayaquil. **Las Peñas** is the most extensive and exciting handicrafts center in town (and probably has the best prices).

NIGHTLIFE

Guayaquil's nightlife is varied and intriguing. Casinos, discotheques, nightclubs and restaurants all have a tropical atmosphere that lends a somewhat exotic air to the night. Movie theaters are a common part of the night scene, but theater, concerts and more highbrow nightlife typical of Quito are rare in Guayaquil. For information on plays (Civic Center Theater, Centro de Arte Theater, and La Garzota Theater), check the culture and arts section of the newspaper. Guayaquil has its own symphony orchestra, but its concert season (as well as that for most plays) is limited to May and June. The Plaza San Francisco in the downtown area has many street musicians and spontaneous entertainment acts most nights throughout the year. Be careful of pickpockets in the crowds.

Two areas of Guayaquil compete for most of the nightlife activities going on. Downtown around the major hotel zone near Parque Seminario and along Avenida 9 de Octubre is one, and the other area is in the northern suburb of Urdesa along Avenida Victor Emilio Estrado, Guayaquil's answer to Beverly Hill's Rodeo Drive. Downtown is somewhat rowdier and more boisterous, while Urdesa is a bit more cultured and preppy.

BARS   Most social drinking in Guayaquil is done in restaurants or discotheques. Real bars are relatively uncommon, and the few that are around shamelessly mimic North American stereotypes of bars.

In the Urdesa district is **Navajo Bar and Grill** (Avenida Victor Emilio Estrado between Ficus and Guayacanes; 6 p.m.–2 a.m., Tuesday–Saturday; 4-882-831). Navajo is transplanted from a lonely desert road in the southwestern United States with its adobe-like walls and ranch-house interior. The menu includes hamburgers, French fries and North American beer for those who need to escape the Ecuadorian culture for a night. The jukebox plays Western favorites, but they are the songs that were popular five years earlier. Ecuadorian wannabe cowboys and cowgirls are always happy to see a real live gringo, so if you are lonesome, this place is almost certain to find you friends.

Rob Roy Bar (Alborada district of north Guayaquil in the 7th Etapa, Villa 1-U2739; 9 p.m.–3 a.m. or beyond, Tuesday–Saturday) is not just a mimic, it is a perfect replica of a small, funky bar with sawdust on the floor and *loud* rock music. It's crowded and friendly, and perfect for those who miss having to shout at each other to be heard. After three beers, everyone seems fixated on signing their names somewhere on the interior of the bar. Look for our signatures on the ceiling.

DISCOTHEQUES AND NIGHTCLUBS   In Latin America, a "disco" is not the home of a music genre of the '70s; it's a place to hear lively Latin American dance music like *salsa*, *merenque*, *cumbia* and *bolero*. These distinct music types come from different regions of Latin America and then quickly hybridize with local tempos and color to produce an amazing diversity of sounds. If you are a regular, you can name the country of origin of the music being played. If you are an expert, you can identify the musician and the regions influencing the song. If you can't do either, just dance. Partner dancing in Latin America involves tremendous coordination, especially of the hips, knees and elbows, and everyone seems to be an expert. Is it genetic or do they all practice from the age of three? The hours open are usually Tuesday to Sunday, 7 p.m. to 3 a.m., or even later.

The Urdesa district is the main center of discotheques in Guayaquil. Nine of the most popular places in town are along or near the main drag through town: **Amnesia** (Avenida Victor Emilio Estrada 205 and Cedros; 4-394-969), **Arena Blanca** (Guayacanes and Calle 4), **Bola Ocho** (Circunvalación Norte and Calle Primera), **Buona Notte** (Bálsamos 504 and Avenida Las Monjas; 4-387-079), **Infinity** (Avenida Victor Emilio Estrada 505 and Ebanos; 4-383-348), **Metropolis** (Avenida Victor Emilio Estrada and Cedros) and **Tequilala** (Avenida Las Aguas and 2nd Entrada; 4-531-101).

In other parts of town, the discotheques are more spread out: **Años Veinte** (Las Lomas, Local No. 4; 4-84-293), **Los 90** (Carchi 803 and Avenida 9 de Octubre; 4-451-699) and **Santa Ana Music Hall** (Continental hotel, Calles Chile and 10 de Agosto; 4-327-029). A small concentration of discotheques is in the downtown area of Guayaquil just one block off 9 de Octubre at

Calle Zaruma and Antonio Campos. This last area is pretty rough, however, so don't go there alone, especially if you are a woman.

GETTING THERE: By Air: The airport is in the northeast part of the city. From downtown, a taxi costs about $5 to the airport. (The same taxi ride from the airport to your downtown hotel will probably cost a couple dollars more.) Let your driver know if you are taking an international *(vuelo internacional)* or domestic *(vuelo nacional)* flight as the drop-off point is different. International flights connect Guayaquil to cities throughout South America; to Houston, Newark, Miami and New York in North America; and with Amsterdam in Europe. Within Ecuador, Guayaquil has flights to the Galápagos, Cuenca, Loja, Machala, Quito and Salinas. Numerous charter companies and air taxis also fly up and down the coast from Guayaquil.

By Bus: The Guayaquil terminal terrestre is the biggest and most efficient bus station in the country. It is located just north of the airport. Besides a bus depot, there are hundreds of stores, restaurants, and banks all under the same roof of this gigantic building. Around the periphery of the ticketing area, which is a city block in size, there are 50 windows for purchasing bus tickets. They are organized by destination and bus company *(cooperativa).* That way you can compare prices and schedules to suit your budget and time frame. When you buy your bus ticket, don't forget to also get the small pass *(ficha)* that will get you through the gate into the departure stalls for the buses. The stalls are numbered, and you should have that number indicated on your bus ticket. Intercity buses within the province of Guayas leave from the first floor on the south side of the building. Interprovincial and international buses leave from the second floor. Hundreds of taxis, local buses, and vans wait outside the terminal to take you to any part of Guayaquil you want. Just ask around to find out who has a route to the section of the city you are seeking.

The price of the intercity ticket will depend on several factors. Luxury buses with video TV and stewardesses are the most expensive. *Colectivos* are small buses and are usually less expensive, *Busetas* are vans that usually are filled to overcapacity, are quite uncomfortable, and very cheap. Express service is faster than local service but is also more expensive. The 9-hour ride to Quito costs about $6; the 5-hour ride to Cuenca costs $4; the 12-hour ride to Esmeraldas costs $5; and the 12-hour ride to Loja costs $6.

By Car: For the uninitiated, driving into Guayaquil can be very confusing. From Quito and Santo Domingo via Babahoyo, follow the exit signs, and turn right to Durán at the freeway interchange just east of Durán. From Cuenca, the interchange of converging highways is an unsigned labyrinth. Ask to make sure you are on the right road to Guayaquil after the town of Delia. From Salinas to the west and Daule to the north, you are quickly dumped into the traffic and unsigned streets of north Guayaquil. Even seasoned Ecuadorian drivers from Quito pale at this frustratingly confusing route. Some friends who have crossed Guayaquil seven or eight times have taken a different route every time because they couldn't find the same route they used before. If you are driving to the coast from Cuenca or Babahoyo, after crossing the high bridges over the Río Babahoyo and Río Daule just west of Durán, follow the signs at the outskirts of Guayaquil that indicate *Perimetral.* Once you are on this bypass around the north end of the city, look for the signs to Salinas. These traffic signs are small and often placed in obscure places, so look carefully.

DAY TRIPS FROM GUAYAQUIL

Many tourists have a day's layover in Guayaquil between flights from the Galápagos Islands and Quito. Guayaquil is close to ocean beaches, mangrove swamps, tropical dry forest, high-altitude cloud forest, and remnant lowland moist forest. If you would like to use your time to see some of these very different parts of Ecuador, there are several exciting places that can be visited during a day trip from Guayaquil's city center. Some, like the Botanical Gardens and Cerro Blanco, are less than a half-hour away from downtown Guayaquil. Others, like Jauneche and Churute, will make for a long but exciting day. If you have several days, you might want to consider using Guayaquil as your base and sallying out in different directions each day to see as many as possible of the various local sights.

In 1974, a group of Ecuadorian orchid enthusiasts formed the Ecuadorian Orchid Society. One of their goals was to study the orchids of the country and document their biology, distribution and conservation needs. A second goal was to make these beautiful plants and many other Ecuadorian plants better known to their fellow countrymen. In 1989, the society obtained 12.5 acres of land on a small hill just north of Guayaquil. Here, in conjunction with the municipal government of Guayaquil, they established the **Guayaquil Botanical Gardens** (4-416-975, 4-417-004; admission). Overlooking 50 acres of secondary growth vegetation that is privately owned, this garden is a relaxing and informative escape from the hustle and bustle of nearby Guayaquil. The trees and many other native plants, including 80 percent of all the orchid species known from the coast of Ecuador, have quickly responded to the lovely irrigation systems disguised as bubbling brooks and quiet forest pools and have grown into a luxuriant and shaded forest oasis. Labels identify the plant species, and a map indicates the paths and different sections of the garden. The shaded paths attract birds and pollinating insects, and the numerous benches attract Guayaquil residents and tourists alike to take a seat and relax.

With the completion of each step in the development of the garden, it has become not only more useful for education and relaxation but also more beautiful. Recently, an auditorium seating 200 people was completed. This auditorium fits tastefully into the surrounding landscape and serves as a cultural and education center. A huge butterfly enclosure houses free-flying butterfly species native to the coast as well as the native plants that serve as food for their developing caterpillars. Additional native tree and flower species are being planted constantly, and as they grow, the garden will only become more attractive. As is true with the entire coastal area of Ecuador, mosquitoes can be a problem here during the rainy season between February and May, so bring your repellent.

The entrance fee is $4 for foreigners. If you want to walk through the gardens before the gates open at 8:30 a.m., call the day before and make arrangements. A guide can also be arranged to accompany you either from your hotel or to meet you at the garden entrance. A bookstore, plant store and small restaurant are located in the gardens.

GETTING THERE: By Bus: The garden is north of downtown Guayaquil and overlooks the residential suburb called Urbanización de Los Orchideas. Buses from downtown will require at least three transfers, and the hour and a half to two hours to get here by bus will turn this relatively short trip into an all-day affair.

By Taxi: A 20- to 30-minute taxi ride will get you here quickly and cost no more than $6. Not all cabbies will know this area, so just ask for the *"jardín botánico cerca de la Urbanización de Los Orchideas."*

As recently as 1960, mangroves covered the estuaries of coastal Ecuador. Now because of their wholesale destruction for shrimp farming, pristine mangroves are difficult to see. Most of those areas remaining are uncut primarily because of their inaccessibility. Only a few tracts, like **Manglares Churute Ecological Reserve** (in Guayaquil 4-397-730, 4-293-131, fax: 4-293-155), are accessible and largely uncut because of active efforts to conserve them. The reserve is only a 45-minute drive south of Guayaquil and the town of Duran on the coastal highway south to Machala.

The reserve was established in 1979 and officially has an area of 87,605 acres, 20,000 of which are mangroves. Unofficially, much of the area within the established boundaries is still privately owned, and active grazing, burning and farming continues. Although the mangroves and associated swamp areas were the main reason for setting aside this area, the reserve also includes considerable tropical dry forest and cloud forest in the highest elevations of the Cordillera de Churute that rise 2970 feet (900 meters) above sea level. The warm wet season is January to May, when the forest is in leaf and the mountainsides are green. The cool dry season the rest of the year is often characterized by the paradox of foggy days but brown and dried vegetation in which the green trunks of large deciduous trees stand out completely denuded of their leaf canopy. Closer to the coast, the mangroves are evergreen, but the dry season is made evident by the absence of the clouds of mosquitoes present during the rainy season.

The main highway goes right through the reserve and descends into an extensive swampy area of tall grass. Three kilometers through the swampy area on the left (east) is the headquarters building and **information center**. Here you pay your entrance fee ($6), obtain maps and view a video of the reserve. You can also arrange for guides to see the mangrove section or for various hikes up into the tropical dry forest habitat or, during the dry season, to the swampy area. Back north 4 kilometers on the main highway is the village of Churute. Off to the west is a road that goes around behind the store and soccer field. A sign indicates *Cooperativa El Mate*. This is the entrance to the mangrove portion of the reserve, but it is best done with a guide. You will need a permission slip anyway to get by the guard station, and that means you must first go to the information center.

Steep trails start from the center up into the hills, while others descend gradually down into the swampy areas. Sometimes the guards will let hikers hitchhike on the back of their motorcycles to the *El Mate* guard station, but otherwise be prepared for an 8-kilometer hike from the center to the mangrove section.

The flora and fauna of the three distinct habitats of the reserve are all very different. In the **swampy area** reside 20 to 30 Horned Screamers (locally called *Canclón*). This huge bird is related to ducks and geese, but it looks nothing like its relatives, or any other bird you may have seen for that matter. A long, thin "horn" juts out of the middle of its head, and a large, sharp spur sticks out at the bend of each of its wings. Its deep gulping calls during the breeding season carry for many kilometers. During the dry season they concentrate with herons, egrets and rails in the wettest parts of the swamps, and are fairly easy to see. This bird is normally a denizen of the swamps and marshes of the Amazon Basin. Somehow a small population found its way over the Andes, and it occurs nowhere else on the coast except here and one small area northwest of Babahoyo.

In the **tropical dry forest** many unique birds, mammals and plants abound. Two species of monkeys are found here. The less common White-fronted Capuchin is agile and moves quickly through the forest tops in troops of five to fifteen individuals seeking fruits and insects. The larger and more common Mantled Howler Monkey moves slowly, if at all, munching on leaves. You are most likely to note its presence when it calls. Somewhere between an approaching windstorm and a lion's roar, this sound will definitely get your attention. Early morning and late afternoon are the best times to hear them, and they call year-round. The path from the visitors center to *El Mirador* is the most popular and is a rigorous four hours round-trip. From the highest points on this trail you can hike to small patches of moist cloud forest that harbor isolated populations of plants and animals.

To see the **mangrove section**, it is best to arrange with the information center or one of the tour companies in Guayaquil several days in advance for a motorized canoe or boat. A park ranger must accompany the boat. The cost ranges from $60–$90 for the boat, depending on how far you wish to travel. The channels through and around the mangroves abound with dolphins, fish and birds. Wintering Osprey, Laughing Gulls and Royal Terns, as well as resident herons, egrets, ibis and Roseate Spoonbills are everywhere. At low tide the Fiddler Crabs are out by the millions running across the tidal flats. Each male waves his big "pincher" arm around like some bizarre referee at a football game, but instead of calling penalties he is trying simultaneously to attract females and intimidate his male competitors. The trees are filled with bromeliads, orchids and distinctive birds like the Mangrove Yellow Warbler.

Alternatively, a controlled-access road along the new flood control dike on the northern boundary of the reserve takes you to the backside of the tallest mangrove forest in the reserve. You can do this trip in the dry season by car or by a 5-kilometer hike from the main Guayaquil highway.

GETTING THERE: By Bus: Machala or Naranjal-bound buses leave from the Guayaquil *terminal terrestre* (windows 8, 19 or 22) throughout the day. Ask the bus driver to drop you off at the Churute information center (*Centro de información Churute*). These buses can also be flagged down on the main highway in front of the information center for your return to Guayaquil.

By Car: Take the highway from Guayaquil southeast across the high bridges that span first the Río Guayas and then the Río Babahoyo to the suburb of Duran. Drive east in the direction of the town of El Triunfo. At Km. 26, long before reaching El Triunfo, turn south and continue for about ten minutes on the road to Machala. A sign on the west side of the road will indicate the boundary of Churute Ecological Reserve.

Fundación Ecológica Andrade (Edificio Inca García Moreno 804 and Avenida 9 de Octubre, first floor, Casilla 5800, Guayaquil; 4-292-860, fax: 4-290-740), a private NGO, has purchased its own 2000 acres that now make up the northwest boundary of Churute Ecological Reserve. The foundation supports ecological and biological research both independently on its own reserve and in conjunction with Churute Ecological Reserve on the state land. They also welcome visitors. The Andrade reserve is primarily tropical dry forest, and is well protected. Trails lead through secondary and primary forest sections, and lists of animals and plants are available. The trails up into the forest are not so steep as those at the Churute Center, and monkeys are easier to find here. A stop at Andrade before or after a trip to Churute is a must.

The foundation has an office, living quarters and conference hall on the west side of the main highway just before entering the Churute reserve from the north (about 2 kilometers north of the village of Churute and 5 kilometers north of the Churute Information Center).

GETTING THERE: By Bus: Machala- or Naranjal-bound buses leave from the Guayaquil bus station (windows 8, 19 or 22) throughout the day. Ask the bus driver to drop you off at the Fundación Andrade just before the village of Churute. These buses can also be flagged down on the main highway in front of the information center for your return to Guayaquil.

By Car: Take the highway from Guayaquil southeast across the high bridges that span first the Río Guayas and then the Río Babahoyo to the suburb of Durán. Drive east in the direction of El Triunfo. At Km. 26, long before reaching El Triunfo, turn to the south and continue for about ten minutes on the road to Machala. A cluster of new, low buildings on your right (west) make up the administrative and scientific center for the foundation. A sign at the driveway indicates the foundation.

Only 20 to 30 minutes northwest of downtown Guayaquil, **Bosque Protector Cerro Blanco** (admission) is a private reserve protecting 8725 acres of tropical dry forest. More than 80 percent of this land is owned by the Cemento Nacional, and the reserve is administered by the Fundación Pro-Bosque (Km. 15 vía a la Costa, Apartado postal 09-01-04243, Guayaquil; 4-871-900, fax: 4-872-236). It is absolutely incredible that this forest and much more beyond it that is not under private or government protection exists so close to Ecuador's largest metropolis. Both its protection and its continued threat are wrapped up in the extensive white limestone deposits throughout the ridge system that makes up the Chongon Hills. This limestone is used to produce most of the cement used in construction up and down the coast. To protect the mines from illegal entry, tight security measures were set up years ago. This security also kept out hunters and tree cutters. As part of a very effective public relations program, the Cemento Nacional company extended this protection to areas of their land that are not mined. It also generously supported the founding of the Fundación Pro-Bosque in 1992 to promote ecotourism, scientific studies and conservation education in conjunction with the forest. The foundation also maintains a nursery here for growing native plants for restoration projects throughout coastal Ecuador.

Although most of the forest is secondary, some impressively large and old patches of primary forest still exist. The huge Ceiba trees grow on the dry hillsides and dwarf all the other vegetation around them. In the dry season (June to December), most of these dry hillside plants lose their leaves, and the green bottle-shaped trunks of the Ceiba stand out. In the shaded streambeds (*quebradas*), water is maintained in pools even through the driest part of the year, and a completely different array of plants grow here, most of them evergreen.

Because of its protection as well as its connection to extensive forest north of the Chongon Hills, the animal life here is very diverse. More than

200 species of birds have been recorded, and they include a phenomenal 21 species of hawks and falcons. This is apparently one of the last two areas in which the Great Green Macaw still occurs in Ecuador, with seven to ten individuals present. (The other area is in extreme northwest Ecuador.) In August 1994 the first known nest of this macaw in Ecuador was found in Cerro Blanco. The staff and volunteers from Pro-Bosque set up a program to protect this highly endangered bird with round-the-clock guards at the nest site.

This is also one of the easiest places to see the White-tailed Jay, a species restricted to the tropical dry forests of coastal southern Ecuador and extreme northern Perú. Two species of monkeys occur here, the Mantled Howler Monkey and the White-fronted Capuchin. Neither is easy to see, but the best chance is in the moist *quebrada* forests. Two species of deer (including the White-tailed Deer that also occurs in North America), two species of wild pigs, several species of cats (including recent evidence of Jaguars), as well as Coatamundi and the Crab-eating Raccoon are the larger mammals present, but they are nocturnal or very shy and thus can be extremely difficult to see.

An **interpretive center** and student guides are available upon entry. Lists of birds, mammals and dominant plants can be purchased at the interpretive center. Several trails lead up to the crests of the hills and are quite steep. A shorter and less steep trail follows one of the main *quebradas*. To experience the range of habitats and species here, both types of trails should be taken. Camping areas are available. Morning and afternoon are the best times to visit the reserve because most animal activity ceases during the hot midday hours. During the rainy season, January–May, mosquitoes are extremely common in the forest, but this is also the breeding season for most birds and mammals. The dry season has few to no mosquitoes, and animals tend to be concentrated more in the moist evergreen portions of the forest, so they are somewhat easier to see.

The gates are open from 7:30 a.m. to 3:30 p.m., but with advance notice, special arrangements can be made for groups wanting to enter earlier or stay later. The reserve entrance fee is $5 for day use and an extra $7 per night for camping. From Wednesday to Sunday, guides are available. For visits on other days, arrangement must be made in advance for a guide through the reserve's downtown office in Guayaquil (Edificio Multicomercio, Calles Cuenca and Eloy Alfaro, local 16; 4-416-975, 4-417-004) or directly at the reserve.

GETTING THERE: By Bus: Buses to Progreso or Salinas will let you off here, at Km. 15 (*Kilómetro quince Vía la Costa*), and the walk to the headquarters is only a little over a kilometer from the highway.

By Car: Drive west from Guayaquil on the main highway to Salinas. Soon you will see tall hills on the north side of the highway with open-pit limestone mines. At Km. 14 you will pass the private Rocafuerte Club and resort on the north side of the highway. At Km. 15 you will see the white walls and entrance sign to the reserve, also on the north side of the highway, with its characteristic symbol of the head of the Great Green Macaw.

Just below the entrance to Cerro Blanco is the community of **Puerto Hondo** (Km. 17) on the south side of the main highway to Salinas and the coast. This community is 25 minutes from downtown Guayaquil and lies next to one of the nicest examples of **mangrove forest** in the area.

With help from Cerro Blanco personnel and Peace Corps volunteers, an ecological club was formed to deal with problems of deforestation of the mangrove forest, as well as pollution problems that were affecting the mangroves. The club began to attract tourists visiting the Cerro Blanco reserve to take **canoe trips** among the mangroves. Local youths have been trained to guide these trips using boats belonging to local fishermen. The profits from this service are used to advertise the importance of pristine mangroves and purchase more materials and equipment for the community's environmental education program. For a two-hour boat tour of the mangroves, the cost is between $10 and $20 per boat (depending on the size of boat). The tours are presently only available on weekends, and reservations should be made in advance through Fundación Pro-Bosque (4-871-900, 4-417-004).

The 45-minute ride will give you a fine view of the plants, animals and ecology of this endangered habitat. Flocks of more than a hundred Red-lored Amazon Parrots fly overhead late in the afternoon to roost together in mangrove islands. Here both the isolation of the habitat and their large numbers protect them from predators during the night. At dawn, clouds of these large parrots rise up noisily and almost simultaneously from their mangrove roosts. They may travel more than a hundred kilometers during the day seeking fruiting trees along the coast. Without too much trouble, you should also be able to see sleek Bat Falcons feeding at dusk on bats and swallows. These sharp-winged falcons hunt from high up in the sky. When they spot their prey, the falcons fold their wings and swoosh (stoop) down in a dizzyingly acrobatic dive. They are only successful about 10 to 15 percent of the time, but then can you imagine trying to catch a bat or swallow in the air with your fingers while falling at 62 miles per hour.

GETTING THERE: By Bus: Buses to Progreso or Salinas will let you off here, at Km. 17 (*Kilómetro diecisiete Vía a la Costa*). Cross the busy divided highway and walk south about a kilometer to the small village of Puerto Hondo and the edge of the mangrove forest. Ask anyone for the canoe trip into the mangroves. If you have prearranged the canoe through Cerro Blanco, this search for the canoe will be easier, as you will be expected.

By Car: Drive west from Guayaquil on the main highway to Salinas. Soon you will see tall hills on the north side of the highway with open-pit limestone mines. At Km. 14 you will pass the private Rocafuerte Club and resort on the north side of the highway. At Km. 15 you will pass the Cerro Blanco reserve entrance. At Km. 18 there is a place to turn left and cross the median divide of the four-lane highway. Make a U-turn, and head back toward Guayaquil for a kilometer. Turn south (right) and drive down the gravel road a little more than a kilometer to the village of Puerto Hondo.

Ten kilometers west of the entrance to Cerro Blanco Forest Reserve on the main highway toward Salinas and Playas, **Chongon Dam** (a recently constructed dam) has begun to attract native birds and mammals. The city water company CEDEGE, has constructed paved roads, picnic areas and a small snack shop at the southeast end of the reservoir. **Parque El Lago** is open to the public only on weekends and holidays (8 a.m.–5 p.m.), and there is no entrance fee. The reservoir here has a surface area of several square kilometers, and as the water chemistry and biology stabilize, more and more water birds are being attracted. Kingfishers, grebes, herons, cormorants and ducks appear in good numbers already. With further checking, the list of water birds is bound to grow dramatically. Vegetation along the edge is also growing and attracting land birds. Patches of natural forest have White-tailed Jays, Collared peccaries and deer.

Parrotlet

GETTING THERE: By Bus: Buses to Progreso or Salinas will let you off here at the entrance to the park.

By Car: On the main highway to Salinas and the coast go 2 kilometers west of the toll booth (10 kilometers west of Cerro Blanco entrance) and turn right into the arched sign "Parque El Lago."

If you wish to visit the beach while you're in Guayaquil, but have only a day to spare, the town of **Playas** is the closest (two hours) and easiest ocean beach to try. Along the highway on the drive out, you'll see that the vegetation of tall, multi-armed cactus and acacia trees has become covered with an introduced Morning Glory vine. Just as the Kudzu vine became a scourge in the southeastern United States when it was introduced there, here in coastal Ecuador the Morning Glory kills native vegetation by overgrowing it during the rainy season and blocking out the sun. Only because it dies back during the dry season do the native plants have even half a chance. Nevertheless, these extensive and impenetrable stands of bushes, trees and cactus are full of bird, lizard and insect life. Yellow Grosbeaks, White-tailed Jays and Gray-capped Cuckoos are only some of the more obvious birds here.

On weekends and during holidays, Playas is a zoo with every *guayaquileño* and his sister here who couldn't get into Salinas. On weekdays and non-holidays, however, it reverts to a more or less quiet fishing village. The modern highrise condominiums are vacant, the restaurants actually have tables available, and the beach is empty except for fishermen and kids collecting young shrimp for sale to the shrimp farms. The beach directly in back of the city itself is not the most pristine as the rivers emptying into the ocean are quite polluted. Avoid the makeshift restaurants along the beach unless you like courting dangers like hepatitis. Southeast of town toward Villamil and Data de Posorja, there are a few relatively clean restaurants associated with hostales and hotels, but Playas is not set up to accommodate the tastes of most gringos. Bring a picnic lunch, buy your drinks here and find a bit of beach to enjoy away from the buildings and small rivers. Watch the Magnificent Frigatebirds soaring overhead, the large American Oystercatchers courting and flying noisily from one end of the beach to the other, and the fishermen coming onto the beach with their catch—all are delightful goals for a relaxing day on the beach.

The only hotel we can recommend in Playas is the **Hotel El "Tucano"** (General Villamil, Kilometer 1 on the Playas-Data highway; private bath, hot water, cable TV, air conditioning; $45; phone/fax: 4-760-866). It has 26 clean rooms around a pool and is less than 300 feet from the ocean beach. A restaurant on the premises serves international and Ecuadorian cuisine. The hotel also features a jacuzzi, sauna, billiards and a bar.

GETTING THERE: By Bus: Buses arrive here directly from Guayaquil, but there are only a few each day. More likely, people catch one of the many buses going to Salinas and transfer at Progreso to the local bus between Progreso and Playas. On weekends these buses are packed to the gills, so when you try to return to Guayaquil, the few direct buses from Playas to Guayaquil are already full, and your chances of transferring in Progreso to a Guayaquil bus coming from Salinas are minimal. Go on a weekday or rent a car.

By Car: Take the main highway to the coast toward Salinas, but 62 kilometers west of Guayaquil in the town of Progreso turn off the main highway and go south. The intersection is a "Y" in the middle of the town and not well marked, but take the left arm of the "Y." This highway on a weekday is not so busy as the Salinas Highway, but note that on holiday weekends both this highway and the Salinas Highway are closed to beach-bound traffic (the road is one-way toward Guayaquil) between 1 p.m. and 9 p.m. Twenty-seven kilometers south of the intersection in Progreso you arrive in the tourist and fishing village of Playas. Continue straight south through the town center to the beach. Left (east) toward Posorja, the highway goes along beaches that are even less crowded.

To experience the native moist coastal forest of Ecuador, you must visit one of a few patches preserved by a chance coincidence of economics and accessibility. The **Jauneche Forest Reserve** is three and a half hours north of relatively dry Guayaquil, but it is in an area of seasonal downpouring rain, almost 80 inches per year, and it can often be inaccessible. Unfortunately, the reserve has only 345 acres, and it is now an island completely surrounded by fields and plantations.

Established in 1963 by the University of Guayaquil, this reserve is dedicated to biological research, environmental education and forest conservation. A concrete laboratory, dormitory, lecture room and kitchen are available for students and scientists on short- or long-term studies. The facilities here are also available by prearrangement with the dean of the Faculty of Natural Sciences at the University of Guayaquil (contact: Decano, Facultad de Ciencias Naturales, Universidad de Guayaquil, Avenidas 25 de Julio and Pio Jaramillo, Guayaquil; 4-492-270, 4-435-666; fax: 4-324-239). There are over 5 kilometers of paths, and arriving early in the morning is best so there will be enough time for you to see all this small but packed reserve has to offer. Be sure to remember your rubber boots during the rainy season, as many of the trails are muddy and flooded.

Well-maintained paths lead from the station facilities into the forest. Within this small biological island are a great diversity of habitat types and vegetation zones. This variety of vegetation results in a great diversity of animal life that, except for the local extirpation of some of the large species like Jaguars, macaws and guans, is representative of what the extensive coastal moist forests were like in the years before 1950. Dense populations of two monkey species makes them easy to see here. The small area of the reserve, however, ensures that each species in the forest is represented by a relatively small population, and thus local extinction is always hanging over the collective heads of each species.

GETTING THERE: By Car: The one drawback to this site as a day trip out of Guayaquil is that you are going to have to really want to see this area to get here. A trip by bus is extremely difficult, and a rental car becomes the only viable alternative. The three-plus–hour drive can be grueling—especially the last hour. The highway north from Guayaquil to Daule (42 kilometers) is well maintained and fast. At the city of Daule, however, the road becomes narrower and the town looks for all the world like a town from the banks of the Ganges River in India. Watch out for the confusing one-way streets and make your way north through town on the highway to Balzar (61 kilometers). Thirty-four kilometers north of Balzar, just past Km. 136, turn off the pavement onto a gravel road running east. A small, split palm–sided house on stilts is on the southeast corner of this intersection, but otherwise there are no signs. Take this narrow gravel road east and south, avoiding any temptation to turn off onto any of the many lesser side roads. There is a labyrinth of roads that can confuse even experienced Ecuadorians. If you have any trouble, ask for the way to the town of Jauneche (note it is *not* spelled or pronounced as Juaneche but instead is pronounced "Howneechi"). Six kilometers down this road you will pass a schoolhouse named *Benito Jurrez*. In another 8 kilometers (14 kilometers from the pavement) you come to a *very* narrow wooden bridge over a small river. This river is the boundary between the provinces of Guayas and Los Ríos. The bridge must be maneuvered with caution because it is so narrow and a drop into the river will definitely put you out of the traveling mode for some time. Just beyond this bridge is a "T" in the road. Take the right turn here (southeast) and drive another 4 kilometers to Jauneche. Drive 660 feet (200 meters) through the village and turn left at the sign indicating the *Estación Biologica, Universidad de Guayaquil*. At the bottom of the hill, park and lock your vehicle. Walk up the next hill 1650 feet (500 meters) to the **field station** and wait for the resident manager who lives in a house within shouting distance west of the station. After checking your entrance permit from the Universidad de Guayaquil, the manager or your guide will show you the path entrances into the forest.

A biologist colleague and friend from Guayaquil decided one day to share a pleasant surprise with us. He said it was his secret cloud forest, and one of his favorite places to go when he wanted to get away from it all. He also told us that it would be a thrill to share this secret and see visitors from other countries appreciating the **Yanayacu Cloud Forest** as such a spectacular and relatively pristine habitat so close to Guayaquil. This forgotten cloud forest is only a little over an hour and a half from downtown Guayaquil on an abandoned stretch of the old Cuenca highway. It is well worth the trip for anyone who has no other chance to see this type of habitat or who wants to check out a great place for lots of new butterflies, plants and birds typical of the Andes.

Perhaps because of a combination of steep slopes and unreliable transportation, large patches of uncut cloud forest are located right along the road for almost 20 kilometers here. There are few paths into the forest, but walking along this road early in the morning is sure to give even the mildly interested a thrill. The view of the coastal plain is breathtaking as the inevitable clouds and fog clear away or as a small opening in the cloud cover drifts through. Bird flocks with 20 species in them are easily seen and followed as they move from tree to tree. Whether just for a brief morning visit or to pass the entire day, this secret cloud forest is guaranteed to amaze you and please you—especially if you are not enamored with Guayaquil and want to get as far away as you possibly can.

GETTING THERE: By Bus: Take a Cuenca-bound bus and ask the driver to let you off either in Cochancay or 2 kilometers east of the town. After you get off, walk along the gravel road, and you will enter cloud forest patches within about 5 kilometers.

By Car: Take the main highway east toward Cuenca via El Triunfo. At El Triunfo the highway goes southeast toward La Troncal and then turns east to begin climbing the Andes toward Cuenca. About 10 kilometers beyond La Troncal is the small town of Cochancay. Two kilometers beyond Cochancay on the same main highway to Cuenca, a gravel road runs off at an angle to the left (north). This is the remnant of the old Cuenca highway that was abandoned years ago when the new route was constructed. This gravel road eventually loops around to reconnect with the new highway, but only those visiting the hot springs of Yanayacu 5 kilometers up the old road (a roadhouse restaurant here is at the "Y" with Yanayacu Hot Springs to the left and the cloud forest on the right fork) or local residents use this route regularly. The annual rains often cause landslides (*derrumbes*) along the way, and because of the light traffic, the priorities for clearing these roadblocks are so low that months or even a year can go by when the road is completely blocked somewhere or other along its length.

TWELVE

Central and Southern Coast

Ecuador's central and southern coast includes sandy ocean beaches, mangrove estuaries, extensive floodplain rivers and marshes, and increasingly dry tropical forests as you go south. This is a region of fishermen and shrimp farmers and small seaside villages. The influence of the cold, drying Peruvian Current makes itself felt all along the southern coast. The rainy season (January to April) is two months shorter here than on the northern coast, and the dry season has many days that are cool and foggy. With only 10 inches of annual rainfall (compared to 120 inches at Esmeraldas in the north), much of this region is in many aspects a desert. Most of the native trees lose their leaves during the long dry season, and cactus and thorny bushes predominate. During the brief rainy season, the major rivers between the low coastal range of mountains and the Andes flood and create marshy grasslands and swamps that extend for hundreds of kilometers.

A considerable number of plants and animals, especially in the tropical dry forests, are endemic to the southern coast and into northern Perú. This biogeographical area is called Tumbesia, after the tiny Peruvian department of Tumbes, which is adjacent to the Ecuadorian border (and which used to be part of Ecuador before the 1941 war). Plant and animal species unique to this area are called Tumbesian. Higher on the western slope of the Andes, the last of the cloud forests begins to give out as you go south toward the Peruvian border. The drying tentacles of the Atacama Desert reach north from coastal Perú and Chile to make their effect felt in extreme southern Ecuador. As a result, the desert-adapted plants and animals are found at higher and higher elevations.

Archaeological evidence dating from before 10,000 B.P. (Years Before Present) shows that the southern and central coast of Ecuador was home to the earliest cultures living in Ecuador, with evidence of several locations continually inhabited for 8000 years. Evidently the favorable ocean currents and prevailing winds off the southern coast encouraged settlement of the area along with the development of sailing and trade skills. Based on the number of archaeological sites and the extent of ancient agricultural fields, it is likely that well over a million people lived along the Ecuadorian coast by the 1400s.

For tourists today, the attractions of this area range from the intriguing ruins of these past civilizations to beautiful and isolated sandy beaches. For others, it's the unusual animals and plants specialized for life either in the tropical dry forest or the patches of evergreen forest kept moist by fog. Many who visit this part of Ecuador will do so only as a side trip while they await a tour to the Galápagos to begin. For those with more than a single day, some spectacular scenery can be visited that will take little more than two or three additional days.

MACHALA

Two and a half hours south of Guayaquil by car, Machala, the capital of the province of El Oro, is the gateway to the borderlands area along the Peruvian frontier. Machala was founded in 1758. In addition to the small gold mines (*oro* is Spanish for gold) in the mountains above the town, Machala's earliest economic development was based on cacao exportation. Until 1930, cacao was king and the reason for most major construction in the area during the early part of the century. Machala's nearby port (Puerto Bolívar) and its railroads to the cacao plantations are two examples of this chocolate largesse. In the 1930s, bananas (locally called *el oro verde* or green gold) began to become more important economically than cacao and eventually took over completely. In the early 1980s, shrimp farming became popular in the area, and it, too, quickly became an economic powerhouse.

Today, Machala is a city of over 200,000 and, because of its agricultural bonanzas, is one of the richest cities on the coast and perhaps in all of Ecuador. With such wealth you might imagine the approach to Machala would include a skyline filled with highrise apartments and towering bank buildings. It is instead a modest-looking, clean and bustling city with a few green plazas interspersed among its many offices and stores. Tourism is a growing industry in the city and province, but it is relegated to a relatively low economic status by most local and regional officials. Business and industry are what makes politicians sit up and take notice here. Machala is only 50 kilometers from the Peruvian border, and over the years, major economic ties have been formed across the frontier. During the border dispute between Perú and Ecuador in 1995, businessmen on both sides of the border—from Machala in

Ecuador and Tumbes in Perú—actively worked to stop the insanity of fighting. The economic interdependence of these businessmen transcended foolish politics and 18th-century machismo. In the future, it may well be that modern international business practices will help make ritualized border skirmishes and pseudopatriotism obsolete.

Those interested in the local environment and conservation have tried to control the economic juggernauts of bananas and shrimp farming, but with limited success. Little tangible consideration is given to the long-term results of wholesale mangrove destruction, total clearing of the coastal forests, and unmeasured contamination of the land, rivers, estuaries and ocean by herbicides, pesticides and fertilizers. Only tourist areas like the Jambelí Peninsula support some small portion of the extensive mangroves common here only 20 years ago. Besides lovely swimming beaches, here you can also still see some of the animals that were present before development, like Rufous-necked Wood-rails and Roseate Spoonbills, but the Coastal Crocodile is gone. Some patches of dry savanna forest still exist with their numerous endemic bird, insect and plant species, most of them preserved on military reservations near Arenillas on the Peruvian border. Remnant montane and cloud forests still exist above Machala near the towns of Piñas and Buenaventura. Many bird species are still found there that cannot be easily seen anywhere else, such as the El Oro Parakeet, which was only described as a new species in 1985.

You can expect fog and cool temperatures around Machala. The average annual temperature is 77°F. The average daily amount of sunshine at the port of Bolívar from December to March is four and a half hours, but from June to November it is only two and a half hours. Rainfall and warm temperatures are most likely in January and February—otherwise bring your sweater. As you go inland, temperatures rise and the landscape becomes drier. As you climb the mountains, fog and rainfall support evergreen forests until you get too high, and then treeless paramo areas appear.

LODGING   Machala makes an ideal base for day trips to sights in the surrounding area. Thanks to all the businessmen visiting town, Machala has a large number of hotels in a wide variety of prices. The best in town, and the least pretentious of the entire chain, is the recently constructed **Oro Verde** (Circunvalación Norte and Calle Vehicular V7, Urbanización Unioro; private bath, hot water, air conditioning, phone, cable color TV, minibar; $70–$140; 7-933-140, fax: 7-933-150). The 70 rooms are large and have every convenience you would expect in a luxury hotel in North America or Europe. There are two restaurants, large pool, fitness center with jacuzzi and sauna, large conference room and a small shopping center. If you want to stay longer in Machala, the Oro Verde even has condominiums available. Only ten min-

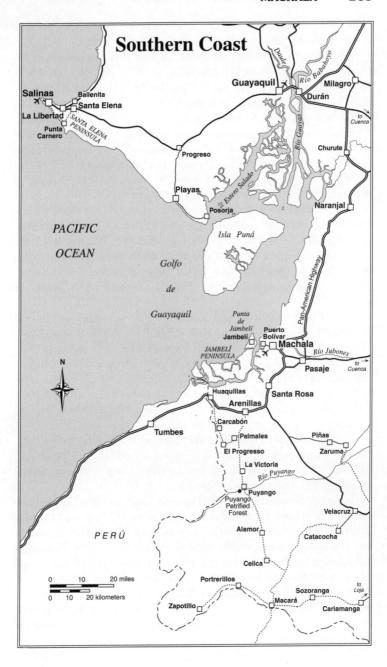

Southern Coast

Salinas
Ballenita
Santa Elena
La Libertad
Punta
Carnero
SANTA ELENA
PENINSULA

Daule
Río Babahoyo
Guayaquil
Milagro
Durán
to
Cuenca

Progreso

Churute

Playas

Posorja
Estero Salado
Río Guayas

Naranjal

PACIFIC

OCEAN

Golfo

de

Guayaquil

Isla Puná

Pan-American Highway

Punta
de
Jambelí
Jambelí
Puerto
Bolívar
Machala
Río Jubones
JAMBELÍ
PENINSULA
to
Cuenca

N

Huaquillas
Arenillas
Carcabón
Palmales
El Progresso
La Victoria
Río Puyango

Santa Rosa
Pasaje

Piñas
Zaruma

Tumbes

Puyango
Puyango
Petrified
Forest

Velacruz

PERÚ

Alamor
Catacocha

Celica

0   10   20 miles
0   10   20 kilometers

Portrerillos

Zapotillo

Macará

Sozoranga
Cariamanga
to
Loja

utes from the airport on the outskirts of Machala, it is a very handy place to drive in and out of town and avoid the traffic in the city center.

The **Rizzo Hotel** (Guayas and Bolívar; private bath, hot water, air conditioning, phone, cable color TV; $20–$25; 7-921-511, 7-921-906, fax: 7-923-651), built more than 20 years ago, is the oldest first-class hotel in Machala, and it has not aged well. The 38 rooms are dark, small and unexciting. The hotel is on a side street near, but not in, the city center, so it is relatively quiet. A restaurant and a coffee shop serve good food, and a large outdoor pool is available in the center of the complex. A sauna and a small casino are also on the premises. If you want a good place to sleep that is not in the city center but don't want to pay the prices of the Oro Verde, the Rizzo is probably your best bet. There is a parking garage for 30 cars.

Another first-class hotel is the **Oro Hotel** (Sucre and Juan Montalvo; private bath, hot water, air conditioning, phone, cable color TV, minibar; $30–$45; 7-930-783, 7-932-408, 7-937-569, fax: 7-933-751). However, it is in the city center and can be quite noisy with all the traffic. Although the 40 rooms on four floors are clean, they show the ten years that the hotel has been operating. A small restaurant, cafeteria and conference room for 300 people are also here.

Hotel Ejecutivo (Sucre and 9 de Mayo; private bath, hot water, air conditioning, phone, cable color TV; $15–$26; 7-923-162, 7-933-992, fax: 7-933-987) is also downtown, but it is a relatively quiet hotel. Its 16 rooms are clean but not sparkling; some of the rooms have a small refrigerator. The hallways, with impressive marble floors, are airy and light, but the dirt and smudges in the rooms have accumulated to give it a run-down appearance. For the price, however, we recommend it. There is also a very small restaurant for breakfast.

The **Marselle Hotel** (Avenida Las Palmas and 9 de Octubre; private bath, hot water, some with air conditioning, phone, TV; $13–$24; 7-935-577, 7-932-460) has 14 rooms on three floors, each with a large bathroom. Several small restaurants are on the same block.

In the middle price range, **Hotel Perla del Pacifico** (Sucre 722 and Paéz; private bath, hot water, air conditioning, phone, cable TV; $11–$14; 7-930-915, fax 7-937-350) has 60 rooms. The busy street below makes most of the rooms noisy all day long, and the view out most rooms is of telephone wires and adjacent buildings. However, the rooms themselves are clean and bright though somewhat run-down, with smudged handprints on the wall around the light switch. The perky restaurant and marble-topped counter remind us of a 1950s drugstore restaurant somewhere in Indianapolis, and is an inexpensive and excellent place to eat. They also have a casino and a small parking garage.

Another one of our favorites in the mid-price range is the **Hotel San Francisco Internacional** (Tarquí between Sucre and Olmedo; private bath, hot water, some with air conditioning, TV; $8–$15; 7-922-395, fax: 7-930-457). The 80 rooms are very simple but immaculately clean. Room prices vary depending on how many amenities you want. The hotel is in the city center and tends to have some rooms that are noisier than others, so ask to see the room first. There is a large restaurant and bar that serves simple Ecuadorian meals.

The **Araujo Hotel Internacional** (9 de Mayo and Boyaca; private bath, hot water, air conditioning, TV; $10–$23; 7-935-257, fax: 7-931-464) opened in 1993. Its 39 rooms on four floors are clean but small and spartan. To cram this many rooms into such a tiny space, not only was room size sacrificed, but the hallways and stairways are an obstacle course for anyone whose head is more than five feet above the floor. A tiny disco opens at 9 p.m. from Thursday to Saturday. The hotel is on a relatively quiet side street, but the disco music on the weekends may offset the tranquil locale. There is also a small garage for ten cars.

The newest hotel, and by our estimate the best of any in the central part of the city, is the **Hotel Montecarlo** (corner of Avenidas Guayas and Olmedo; private bath, hot water, some with air conditioning, cable TV, phone; $16–$30; 7-931-901, 933-642, fax: 7-933-104). Its 38 rooms on three floors (no elevator) are all sparkling with white tile floors. It has a small restaurant and bar on the ground floor. It has no garage.

Combined with a bus station, the **Hotel Ecuatoriana Pullman** (9 de Octubre and Colón; private bath, hot water, some with air conditioning; $5–$15; 7-930-197) is a budget hotel near the city center and is extremely noisy. It is set up to accommodate bus passengers making transfers or waiting overnight for the early morning bus. (The Pullman buses are express to Guayaquil every 30 minutes and take two and a half hours to make the journey; $4.50 one-way.) Its 60 rooms are simple and moderately clean and there are a telephone and TV in the lounge of each floor. A restaurant serves sandwiches, soups and quickly prepared dishes like rice and fried chicken.

For those on a very limited budget, the **Hotel Mosquera Internacional** (Olmedo between Guayas and Ayacucho; private bath, cold water, some with air conditioning, TV; $9–$23; 7-931-752, 7-931-140, fax: 7-930-390) is the best alternative. The hallways are dark and dingy, while the 44 rooms on four floors are tiny and stark but fairly clean.

There are many other hotels in Machala, but they go downhill drastically from those we have included here.

RESTAURANTS   Besides the excellent restaurants in the **Hotel Oro Verde**, **Hotel Ejecutivo** and the **Hotel Perla del Pacifico**, we found two other restaurants in town to have excellent food and service and one that could be good at times. They may not be as slick as the hotel restaurants, but we liked them.

Don Angelo Restaurant (9 de Mayo and Rocafuerte; 7 a.m.–4 a.m.; $2–$6, 7-923-577, 7-932-784) serves a luscious array of seafood and *criollo* (typical Ecuadorian food of the coast) food. The restaurant is somewhat of a hole-in-the-wall, but don't let that fool you into passing it up. The meals are inexpensive and you will likely meet Don Angelo himself if he's not out catering a dinner somewhere else.

Restaurant Chifa Central (Tarquí between 9 de Octubre and Sucre; 11 a.m.–11 p.m.; $2.50–$3; 7-932-761) is considered the best Chinese restaurant in town by many. It does not have a fancy ambiance, but the food is good and the portions generous.

The **Cafeteria Americana** (next to the Hotel Mosquera Internacional on Olmedo between Guayas and Ayacucho; 7:30 a.m.–midnight; $3.50) is somewhat inconsistent in its quality, but if you are there on a night when the cook is in a good mood, you can luck out. Ecuadorian national dishes like *corvina a la plancha* (fried fish), *pollo a la milanesa* (breaded chicken), *seco de gallina criollo* (fried chicken and rice), and *chulete a la criollo* (fried pork chops) are the mainstay of the menu.

GETTING THERE: By Air: TAME has two daily flights on weekdays between Machala and Guayaquil. Several air taxis also operate between Machala and Guayaquil, but their schedule is erratic. The airport is only ten minutes from the city center, and a taxi costs $2.

By Bus: Each of the many bus lines has its own office and miniterminal, and most of them are in the city center. There are several lines to Guayaquil (some express, some not), Loja, Cuenca and Quito. Locally, several buses daily go to Piñas, Arenillas and Santa Rosa. The bus lines, their routes, and schedules seem to change every month, so check with your hotel for the current best line going to your destination.

By Car: From Guayaquil (two and a half hours), take the main coastal highway south via Duran and Naranjal. A large traffic circle will indicate Machala off to the west. Drive the 12 kilometers into the city. Puerto Bolívar and boats to Jambelí and its beaches and mangroves are another 6 kilometers beyond the Machala city center. From Cuenca (three hours), take the highway south of Cuenca through Girón and Pasaje. Continue straight west to Machala. If you are passing through the town of Santa Rosa on the way to Loja or the Peruvian border, you will be stopped near here at a major military checkpoint. You will have to show your passport, visa or tourist card, and register. Loja is about three and a half hours away.

At Puerto Bolívar, 6 kilometers west of Machala city center, the road ends at a big estuarine bay protected from the Pacific Ocean by a series of large mangrove islands. Even though they have no dry-land connection to the mainland, the northernmost of these islands is called **Jambelí Peninsula**. There are many little seafood restaurants on the waterfront, and two blocks north is a small pier, from which ferries leave for the island of **Jambelí** every half-hour or until the boat fills with passengers ($1 per passenger, one-way).

The island of Jambelí is located 3 kilometers across the bay, and during the northern winter (November through February) the bay is filled with bird species like Osprey, Royal Tern, Sandwich Tern, Laughing Gull, a few Gray Gulls and hundreds of Magnificent Frigatebirds. Look for storm-petrels as you cross the water. Soon you enter the mangrove-lined canals of the island itself and pass for several kilometers through thick stands of this brackish-loving plant. Here you can see many species of herons, Roseate Spoonbills, and probably most exciting for birders, your easiest chance for Rufous-necked Wood-rail in all of Ecuador and probably in all of South America. This chicken-sized rail has a call that resembles a maniac laughing and can easily be heard over the roar of the boat's motor. The rail is most reliably found as it walks on the mudbanks in and out of the edge of the mangrove foliage at low tide. At high tide they tend to be back in the denser foliage. Until 20 years ago, the Coastal Crocodile could also be found here. Increased use and destruction of habitat for shrimp farming has wiped them out. Evidently, however, on the Peruvian end of this chain of mangrove islands, a population of crocodiles still persists, the only place in Perú where they can be found.

At the island pier, you can walk west through the village 550 yards (500 meters) to the beach. On weekends and holidays (January through March), this island is packed with vacationing Ecuadorians, and now you can understand why there are so many restaurants and food stands. If you avoid these crowded days, you will likely have the island largely to yourself. If you are not here on a holiday or weekend, be sure to check with your boatman as to the times for returning to the mainland. On these slow days, the last boat leaves in the early afternoon. There are a couple of small hotels on the island, but we do not recommend your staying there voluntarily.

GETTING THERE: Buses run between Puerto Bolívar and Machala every 15 minutes, or a taxi costs about $3. If you are driving your own car and will be leaving it here for a day trip to Jambelí, be sure to park to the south in front of the military police building or at the protected parking lot across from the municipal pier. Petty thievery is very common here. Boats leave Puerto Bolívar pier for Jambelí at 7:30 a.m., 10 a.m., 1 p.m. and 4 p.m.

SOUTH OF MACHALA

An interesting day trip from Machala takes you south to the Peruvian border and the heart of a special habitat full of endemic species of plants and animals. Only because much of this area is a military reservation (*Reserva Militar de Arenillas*) has the habitat been saved from degradation and development. Of the 140 species of birds found in this area, 32 are endemic to this dry forest and thornbush of southwest Ecuador and northwest Perú. Jaguarundi, Northern Tamandua Anteater and White-tailed Deer are among the common large mammals still found here.

Although the military does not permit tourists to wander into most parts of this reserve, we have found several areas legally accessible to tourists. At the checkpoint west of the city of **Arenillas**, ask if you can stop and look for birds, mammals and insects from the shoulder of the Pan-American Highway west toward the border town of Huaquillas. In the early morning, there is a lot of animal activity near the highway. Many large and fast trucks come by here, so be sure to park well off the pavement, and don't be tempted to wander off the highway shoulder into the reserve. There are mine fields here!

Just before entering Huaquillas, take the gravel road that goes south (left) along the border. This part of the reserve is much easier to take your time on as there is little traffic. The absolutely *best* place for observing animals and plants is right after the military control south of the town of **Carcabón** (the road leaves the town unobtrusively beyond the sandy plaza center). You quickly enter undisturbed forest along the Río Zarumilla. Stop and enjoy this area for as long as you want, but know that it can become very hot midday. Continue on the gravel road south and then east through the small towns of El Progreso and Palmales. Two kilometers east of Palmales, turn left (north) on the main highway back to Arenillas and Machala (60 kilometers or about an hour's drive), or turn right (south) to go to Puyango (36 kilometers or about an hour's drive).

GETTING THERE: *By Bus:* Buses leave Machala regularly for Arenillas. Between Arenillas and Huaquillas, immigration procedures make getting off and on the bus much more complicated.

By Car: From Machala take the main highway signed to Arenillas. A labyrinth of newly paved roads goes off left and right, and few of them have signs. Ask frequently for the highway to Arenillas. Then follow the signs of the Pan-American Highway toward the border and Huaquillas.

The tidy town of **Santa Rosa** is 25 kilometers south of Machala just off the Pan-American highway. It is a good alternative to Machala for those who want to visit the Puyango Petrified Forest on a day trip or need a stopover place on a trip from the coast to Loja.

LODGING   The best place in town to stay is the **Hotel América** (Avenida El Oro and Colón; 7-943-130, 943-339; private bath, hot water, some with air conditioning, TV; $10–$15). It has 30 rooms on two floors, and they are all clean and large. A restaurant on the ground flood serves sandwiches and a small fixed menu. Bakeries and grocery stores are nearby if you want to stock up on food and drinks for picnics and field trips.

Located 50 kilometers south of Arenillas in the opposite direction from Huaquillas but also near the Peruvian border, the 6645-acre **Puyango Petrified Forest Reserve** lies in an area of dry, second-growth vegetation. The trip there takes you through dry forest scrub with many species of plants and animals that occur no other place in Ecuador, and only extend a short way into northern Perú.

One hundred and twenty species of birds have been recorded from this reserve, including the Ecuadorian endemic Saffron Siskin. Some mammals like deer, Collared Peccary and armadillos are fairly common, but the real attraction here are the trunks of hundreds of large petrified trees lying on the ground. No other place in the hemisphere except the Petrified Forest National Park in northern Arizona in the U.S. comes close to the magnitude and diversity of this fossil forest. Some of these petrified trunks are more than 5 feet in diameter and 35 feet in length. The majority of these gigantic trees are primitive ancestors of pine trees and spruces. Today, living forms of this group are limited to the southern hemisphere, and in South America are found only in southern Chile and Argentina. Along with the fossil trunks, many smaller plant species such as tree ferns and primitive palms are perfectly preserved in rocks and provide an excellent record of the habitat in southern Ecuador many millions of years ago. Guides are available either in the town of Puyango or at the guard station. Camping is permitted.

LODGING   Simple but clean rooms for 14 people can be rented at the **reserve administration building**, some with private bath, cold water, no fans; $3 per person (Comisión Administradora de los Bosques Petrificados de Puyango: Ciudadela "Las Brisas" Manzana B-6, Villa 2, Apartado No. 5, Machala; 7-930-012, fax: 7-924-655). A small store across from the administration building serves meals, but you need to request this service at least several hours in advance.

GETTING THERE: To get to Puyango take the paved highway south and west from Machala 50 kilometers to Arenillas via Santa Rosa. In Arenillas take the gravel road south via the towns of Palmales and La Victoria 50 kilometers to the town of Puyango. This last 50 kilometers can be very slow during the rainy season (January to April) when giant potholes and mud are common. The reserve is located on both sides of the Río Puyango near the village of Puyango. However, the main part of the reserve, with its administrative offices, museum and interpretive center, is 5.5 kilometers west of the main road just before crossing the bridge over the Río Puyango. Turn right (west) at the large sign indicating the Puyango Reserve. The road is very narrow and rather rough in places. Just before arriving at the village of Puyango and the reserve's facilities, soldiers at a military checkpoint will register your passport. The camping area ($20 per night) and self-guiding trails are another 2 kilometers beyond the administrative offices. Pay your entrance fee ($10) here and buy trail guides and the bird list. If you would rather not drive your own vehicle, several hotels in Machala (100 kilometers one-way) and in Loja (225 kilometers one-way) have vans, drivers and guides that can be hired for a day trip.

MACARÁ

For the more adventurous, there are exciting opportunities to explore little-visited parts of Ecuador between Puyango and the border town of **Macará** (12,000 inhabitants). Although much of the area is agricultural land, there are patches of native tropical dry forest and montane cloud forest as well as spectacular vistas and landscapes. The town of Macará itself is unexciting, with deeply eroded streets and the atmosphere of a mean border town surrounded by fields of rice. The saving grace for ecotourists is a clean and comfortable hotel at the southern outskirts of town along with access to some of the most pristine and extensive tropical dry forest still found in Ecuador. The gravel road west to Potrerillos (30 kilometers) and on to Zapotillo (another 28 kilometers) has relatively little traffic but several military checkpoints. The forest in the early morning, especially after a March rain, resounds with bird and frog calls. The butterflies are thick and the verdant green plant life here will give you an idea of what the coastal forests from Guayaquil north used to look like. Do avoid walking in areas next to the border that have green and white signs indicating *CAMPO MINADO* (mine field). According to the local military, almost all of these mine fields are deactivated, and you can see cows and people wandering through them, but be cautious. The road east of Macará goes to the city of Cariamanga (81 kilometers). A paved road connects Cariamanga to Loja (103 kilometers or less than two hours) via Catamayo (see Chapter Ten).

Because of temporary civilian evacuations during the border wars, few tourists visit this area; those who do come between August and October. As the Pan-American Highway is improved and paving is finished in Ecuador and Perú, Macará is bound to become more frequently visited. Hopefully the wonderful habitat to the west and east of town will not suffer from this increased attention.

LODGING   The only place we can recommend to stay and eat in Macará is the **Parador Turistico Macará** (Panamericana Sur Vía Puente; private bath, cold water, table fans, color TV; $5–$10; 7-694-099). This hotel is run by the Ecuadorian government through CETUR, and it stands in marked contrast to the rest of the town. The multi-storied white hotel is on the south edge of town on the main highway to the border. Its 20 rooms are on the first and second floors and along with an immense lobby and lounge are very clean and relatively well-maintained. An efficient restaurant with good food

($2.50/meal) is located on the basement level. A large swimming pool is filled with water in the summer months (October–May). But the lack of air conditioning can make sleeping difficult during this part of the year.

GETTING THERE: By Bus: Served mainly by the bus company Loja International, Macará is connected by routes to Loja, Cariamanga and Catacocha, where transfers can be made to or from Guayaquil. Local bus companies also have frequent service between Macará and Zapotillo or Sozoronga.

By Car: From Loja take the paved highway 31 kilometers to Catamayo and another 72 kilometers south to Cariamanga. Follow the gravel road 81 kilometers west to Macará. From Guayaquil, take the Loja highway south from Machala. Then turn south on the Pan-Americana Sur Highway at Velacruz and Catacocha. From Puyango, take the gravel road through Alamor and Celica to the Pan-Americana Sur Highway. Turn south on this main highway and drive 44 kilometers to reach Macará.

SALINAS AND THE SANTA ELENA PENINSULA

In the 1930s, the first oil in Ecuador was found on the Santa Elena Peninsula, 140 kilometers due west of Guayaquil. Pumps still keep a small oil industry going, but tourism has by far taken over as the economic power. This area is the most popular vacation spot for Guayaquil's middle- and upper-class residents. On holidays and weekends from January to April, it is like Coney Island on the Fourth of July. Most people who come here have their own apartment or condominium in one of the numerous highrise buildings that fill the skyline. As you drive in from the east, the skyline of Salinas will be obvious long before you can smell the ocean. January through April is considered summer. Few visit even on weekends during the foggy and cool winter (June–August). Avoid visiting the peninsula on carnival week, the week of Easter (*semana santa*), Christmas and New Year, unless you like bumper-to-bumper traffic, the noise of three-wheeler cycles racing up and down the beach, and jet skis incessantly roaring along the surf's edge. In January and February, the mosquitoes can be especially vicious at night.

The towns of **La Libertad**, **Salinas** and **Punta Carnero** are separate municipalities on the Santa Elena Peninsula, but the boundaries between them are not obvious. For simplicity, we refer to these three locations primarily to indicate the eastern base of the peninsula (La Libertad), the western extreme point of the peninsula and the northern beach (Salinas), and the southern beach (Punta Carnero).

Besides the beaches, the main attractions here are the extensive salt lagoons on the south beach between Salinas and Punta Carnero. Saltwater is evaporated away and the salt mined into great white mountains for use throughout the country. Thousands of birds feed and rest in these humanmade lagoons. Brown Pelicans, North American migrating and wintering shore-birds, terns, gulls and occasionally Chilean Flamingoes that descend from the Peruvian Andes to winter here are all possible to view. The salt company offices of Equasal have been very generous about letting in birders if you stop and ask at the office next to the lagoons 5 kilometers southwest of Salinas. Otherwise, you can view most of the lagoons well with binoculars or a spotting scope from the road running along the coast toward Punta Carnero. From June to October, numerous species of whales move offshore. Two local tour companies in Salinas will arrange naturalist tours with guides: **Seretur** (Malecón 318 and Calle 36; 4-772-800, fax: 4-772-789) and **Ben and Brenda Haase** (at the Oystercatcher Bar, Avenida Malecón 888 and Calle 50; 4-778-329 or in Guayaquil, Whale tours, Casilla 0901-11905; 4-381-547). The Haases are English and are keen birdwatchers, naturalists and excellent guides. They know the area well and run an efficient operation.

If you want to stand on the westernmost point of land in mainland Ecuador, drive all the way west through Salinas (Chocolatera) and enter the army gate—not the navy (Marina) side to the right. A soldier will ask you to deposit your identification card (never give up your passport) or driver's license until you return. Follow the tiny signs with arrows first left then right to **Punta Santa Elena**. The scrub habitat is dry but as natural as you are going to see anywhere else on the peninsula. Seabirds fly by as you stand on the low cliffs overlooking the gigantic waves of the Pacific Ocean crashing onto both sides of the point. At sunset, the photographic opportunities are best. When you return to Salinas, don't forget to recover your identification card from the soldier at the gate. Occasionally, the point is closed because of national security, so check ahead in town.

For deep-sea fishermen, this is the best place in Ecuador for marlin and tuna. Contact Knud Holst at **Pesca Tours and Fishing Charters** in Salinas on the main street along the bay (in Guayaquil, 4-443-365, fax: 4-443-142; in Salinas, 4-772-391). There are six boats for charter. They can take one to six people per boat. Bait and equipment are included in the $350 rate for an entire day (7 a.m.–4:30 p.m.). There's food and drink on the boat at extra cost. October to December is the best season for marlin and tuna, and you must make reservations two to three months in advance. The rest of the year, usually one day in advance is all that is needed to charter a boat.

LODGING   At the east (La Libertad) end of the peninsula are four good hotels, none of which is on or near a sandy beach. The **Hotel Valdivia** (Urbanización Costa de Oro Fase III, Avenida Este; private bath, hot water, some with air conditioning, phone, TV; $35–$45; fax: 4-775-144) is the newest and most modern of them. It has 20 family-style apartments, each consisting of two floors with a master bedroom and two smaller bedrooms with bunk beds,

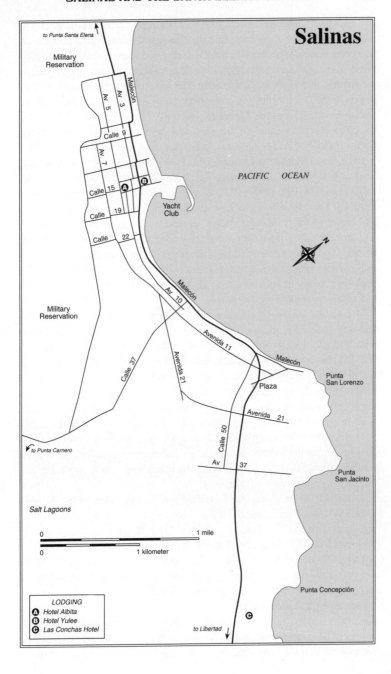

Salinas

to Punta Santa Elena

Military
Reservation

Malecón

Av 3

Av 5

Calle 9

Av 7

Calle 15

Calle 19

Calle 22

PACIFIC   OCEAN

Yacht
Club

Malecón

Av 10

Military
Reservation

Avenida 11

Malecón

Calle 37

Avenida 21

Plaza

Punta
San Lorenzo

Avenida 21

Calle 50

to Punta Carnero

Av 37

Punta
San Jacinto

Salt Lagoons

0   1 mile

0   1 kilometer

Punta Concepción

LODGING
Ⓐ Hotel Albita
Ⓑ Hotel Yulee
Ⓒ Las Conchas Hotel

to Libertad

two bathrooms, minibar and balcony overlooking the large central pool. The owner and his wife are French, and they manage the Valdivia as a combination private-members club and hotel. Members, however, always have preference over outsiders for reservations. The buildings, rooms and restaurant are spotless and of the highest quality. The service is excellent, and the food served in the hotel restaurant, a combination of French and Ecuadorian cuisine, is among the best on the entire peninsula. The wine list is also impressive. The hotel is located on the north side of the main Guayaquil–Salinas Highway right at the border between Salinas and La Libertad.

The **Hotel Samarina** (Avenida 9 de Octubre and Malecón; private bath, hot water, some with air conditioning, phone, TV, minibar; $30–$45; 4-735-167, fax: 4-784-100) is an excellent hotel at the west end of the town of La Libertad. The 43 rooms either have an ocean view or overlook the two pools and center of the compound. There are also ten cabañas (family-style with five beds) detached from the hotel at the west end of the property. The rooms are very light, enjoyable, well maintained and clean. The large restaurant is also pleasant and serves a menu of seafood and international cuisine. The ocean is directly in back of the hotel, but only during low tide is a narrow and relatively rocky beach exposed.

By far the largest hotel in the east part of the peninsula, **Las Conchas Hotel** (private bath, some with hot water, some with air conditioning, some with TV; $20–$36; 4-775-246, 4-775-937, fax: 4-775-830; in Guayaquil 4-405-702) has not aged well over its decade plus of operation. The 150 rooms are small and dark; the bathrooms are not always clean; the exteriors of the buildings are deteriorated; and the pool could use more than a good shocking of antifungal chemicals. The large restaurant serves seafood, but it is only open in the high season, so we have never been able to sample the menu. With the amount of advertisement and large signs on the highway just after passing across the Salinas boundary, we had high expectations for a place that has apparently quit trying harder. The beach here is also very rocky and largely nonexistent at high tide.

Also just at the municipal boundary into Salinas, **Hotel Don Mincho** (Vía a la Costa Highway; private bath, hot water, some with air conditioning, some with TV; $12–$28; 4-775-034, 4-775-655, fax: 4-285-452) is handily located on the south side of the main highway between Guayaquil and Salinas. Of course, if you want a beach, this hotel is a kilometer from the nearest beach and not very handy. Its 42 rooms are on two floors (no elevator) and are clean but a little run-down. A large restaurant (open 24 hours) attracts many Ecuadorians who are not even staying here, and we would add our recommendations if you like *criollo*-type seafood. A bar and two pools appear to be more for show than for use. If you want somewhere as a base for a few days while exploring the peninsula, this is a good place to sleep.

There are two very clean and nice hotels in downtown Salinas. The newest is the **Hotel Calypso** (Malecón de Salinas, next to the Capitan of the Port; private bath, hot water, air conditioning, TV, phone; $100–$200; 4-772-425; in Guayaquil: 4-281-056, fax: 4-285-452), which is part time-share condominiums and part hotel. All 48 rooms are suites with complete kitchens and balconies overlooking the harbor. There is a restaurant, pool, jacuzzi and private parking. The hotel is centrally located, within easy walking to restaurants and just across the highway from the beach. The other hotel we can highly recommend is the **Hotel El Carruaje** (Malecón 517; private bath, hot water, air conditioning, TV; $35–$45; 4-774-282, in Guayaquil 4-389-676). The only problem with it is that there are only eight rooms (on three floors with no elevator). All of them are sparkling clean, and most have individual balconies overlooking the main drag through town across to the main municipal beach. The Carruaje also has one of the best restaurants (8 a.m.–10 p.m.) in town, with delicious and very fresh seafood the specialty. It is on a terrace of the hotel with 15 umbrella-covered tables that spill out onto the sidewalk.

Farther west in town and away from the beach, the **Hotel Yulee** (private bath, hot water, ceiling fans; $23–$30; 4-772-028, in Quito 2-446-651) is an older and very family-oriented lodging. Its 25 rooms have a late 19th-century atmosphere to them without being run-down. Part of the hotel is like walking through an old mansion. The rooms themselves are simple but very clean. A few of the rooms are in the garden entrance on the first floor. The large restaurant and bar occupy the rest of the first floor together with reception. The restaurant (7:30 a.m.–8:30 p.m.) serves typical Ecuadorian food, but seafood is what most patrons eat here. The hours and menu are more extensive during the high season.

For budget travelers, the **Hotel Albita** (Barrio Bazán, Avenida 7 between Calle 22 and 23; some with private bath, cold water, desk fans; $5–$10; 4-773-211, 4-773-042) is the best bet. It has 13 rooms, all with low doors, so watch your head. The rooms are cool and clean, but very small. The beds are short, and don't expect any extras. Also, there is no garage or parking area. The people working here are helpful and friendly, and the two-block walk to the downtown area and the beach means less noise and less sand in your room. Driving there, you have to go all the way through town on the Malecón, which is one-way west, and then turn left. Go the two blocks to the main street going one-way east and turn left again to Calle 22.

For anyone more interested in nature and not so much in the party life of beach holidays, two hotels at Punta Carnero on the south shore are without question the best places to stay on the peninsula. The **Hotel Punta Carnero** (private bath, hot water, air conditioning, phone, TV, minibar; $50–$75; 4-775-450, 4-775-537, fax: 4-775-377) is built on a high cliff overlooking the Pacific Ocean. Except for the Hosteria del Mar next door, this point is relatively isolated and quiet. The hotel itself is luxurious, even if the prices are not. The 42 rooms are huge and elegant, with large picture windows and individual balconies looking out to sea or the large pool at the cliff's edge. A secluded beach can be reached by walking down steps along the cliff edge, and the tidal pools in the rocks on either side of the sandy beach are filled with sea stars, anemones and barnacles. The rocky promontory just before the cliff is a favorite roost of Blue-footed Boobies. The salt lagoons begin inland just below the entrance to the hotel, and several species of birds can be seen on the hotel grounds as you go up the hill.

If you choose to remain on the hotel grounds, it has an extensive entertainment and recreation area with large outdoor pool, volleyball court, children's recreation room, three bars, 120-person conference room, 24-hour cafeteria and superb restaurant (7 a.m.–11 p.m.) with a long menu of international cuisine emphasizing seafood. The restaurant, like virtually everywhere else in the hotel, has superb views of the ocean. This is the type of place that all the brochures like to picture as the ideal dream hotel on the ocean, but this one actually is.

Right next door to the Hotel Punta Carnero is the almost-as-attractive **Hosteria del Mar** (private bath, hot water, some with air conditioning, TV; $35–$60; 4-775-370, fax: 4-324-195). Its 38 rooms are on two floors but not all of them have a fabulous view of the ocean. All have balconies, but many of them look out onto the central pool area. Still, the rooms are large, airy and very clean. A tennis court, volleyball court and basketball court are available for those with restless energy to burn off. There is no convenient access to the beach, but the view from poolside is super. The restaurant (7:30 a.m.–9:30 p.m.) is partly inside and partly outside under a shaded porch and table umbrellas. The small menu emphasizes seafood.

RESTAURANTS   Besides the good hotel restaurants mentioned above, our favorite restaurant in Salinas is the **Restaurant Mar y Tierra** (left-hand side of the Malecón; 8:30 a.m.–12 midnight; $3–$8). The restaurant has a large porch section that looks out across the main street through Salinas to the municipal beach and the bay. You don't come here for anything else but seafood —conch, clam, shrimp, squid, octopus and fish. You can order your dish fried, baked, boiled or any other way you prefer, and it always seems to taste great. If you insist, beef and chicken are also served, but that's just to be able to keep the "Tierra" part of the restaurant's name.

The small **Oystercatcher Bar de Ostras** (Malecón 888; 10 a.m.–9 p.m.; $2–$9) serves delicious seafood. It is on the main street that is one-way west along the bay in downtown Salinas, on the right. The menu is short, but it makes up in quality what it lacks in quantity.

GETTING THERE: By Air: TAME has flights between Guayaquil and Salinas on Monday morning and Friday afternoon. These flights may be canceled during the low season, so check with a tour agent in Guayaquil.

By Bus: La Libertad is the main bus destination in the area, but it has no terrestrial terminal. If you are coming from Guayaquil, ask at the Guayaquil terrestrial terminal for the window that has buses going all the way to Salinas. There are far fewer of these than to La Libertad, especially in the low season. Even if it is going to Salinas, the bus will inevitably have a long stop in La Libertad before continuing on. From Machalilla National Park and the north coast, virtually all buses go only to La Libertad. You then have to transfer to a *ranchera* or other bus going to Salinas. Punta Carnero has little to no bus service, so you will probably have to hire a taxi ($4).

By Car: From Guayaquil, take the main highway west (Vía a la Costa) to Salinas. At the town of Progreso, take the right fork in the road (the left goes south to Playas). The entire drive is about 140 kilometers and takes three and a half hours with no traffic, but five hours on Friday afternoon or a holiday weekend. **NOTE:** From December to April, the main highway from Guayaquil to Salinas becomes a one-way road heading east toward Guayaquil on Sunday afternoons. This is also the case for the road to Playas. If you wish to drive from Guayaquil to Salinas or Playas on a Sunday afternoon, you will have to wait until after 6 p.m.

THE COASTAL ROAD NORTH

Until 1991, the potholes and dust in this highway were so bad that it took an entire day to wend your way north from La Libertad to Manglaralto. Now the road is entirely paved and very fast. This entire route along the coast has also received the overflow from Salinas as a vacation destination. Hotels, condominiums and apartments fill the skyline farther north every year. If you want to find some natural areas away from tourist development, there are extensive salt lagoons north of Ballenita (6 kilometers north of La Libertad), and they have many resident and migrant shorebirds, herons and gulls on them. Thirty minutes north of Salinas is the little fishing/tourist town of **Ayangue**. The town is actually 3 minutes off the road, but it is well signed and easy to find. Ayangue once was a sleepy fishing village tucked into a tight harbor surrounded by rocky bluffs. Now it is a popular weekend beach spot for *guayaquileños.* Just past Ayangue on the far southern point of the harbor is the secluded but sensational **Cumbres de Ayangue Hotel** (Manglaralto; private bath, hot water, phone, minibar; $35–$60; in Ayangue: 4-916-040, fax: 4-916-041, in Guayaquil: C. Ballén 1607 and G. Moreno, P.O. Box 48-52, 4-370-115, fax: 4-454-114). There are 25 very comfortable rooms in this new hotel, each with a terrace and an ocean view. Other amenities include an oceanside restaurant, two tennis courts, an exercise room, conference room and "private" beaches for guests to loll on. The most spectacular part of this hotel is the swimming pool. Built into the rocky point in front of the main buildings and surrounded by crashing waves, this pool is one of the most spectacular places in all of Ecuador to watch the sunset. There are horses for beach riding, a sailboat, and the hotel also will assist you in arranging diving and deep-sea fishing trips. If all of this were not enough, you can also watch passing whales right from the hotel. We recommend Cumbres de Ayange highly.

An hour or so north of Ayangue is the little beachside village of **Montañita**. Montañita has long been known as the surfing capital of Ecuador. While it remains so today, it has also become known as a perfect place for weekend getaways and sand-loving tourists. The best place to stay in Montañita, other than the numerous informal bungalows, is the **Hotel Baja Montañita** (Montañita: private bath, hot water, air conditioning, ceiling fan, phone, cable TV, minibar; $50–$90; 4-901-218, fax: 4-901-228). With its pool, jacuzzi, poolside bar, restaurant, beachside bar and ocean breezes in every room, the Hotel Baja Montañita is a little bit of Southern California nestled into the north bluffs of Montañita beach. The turn into the hotel is not well signed, but you can easily see the hotel from the main road.

Continuing north up the coast, the road veers away from the beach and heads over a low mountain ridge covered by a nice intact fog forest. Near the high point of the road is the most luxurious and elegant hotel on the road north of Salinas: the **Hosteria Atamari** (private bath, hot water, ceiling fans; $80–$150; in Quito: Barón Von Humbolt #279, P.O. Box 17-12-91, 2-226-071, fax: 2-508-369).

Look for Atamari's colorful concrete sign with the hummingbird logo on the west side of the highway. From here, the 2-kilometer private drive winds west through patches of fog forest and second-growth dry forest. Situated on a forested bluff (*Cinco Cerros*) overlooking the Ayampe Bay and the Pacific Ocean, the hotel's guest rooms are naturally air conditioned by sea breezes year-round. The ten rooms are spread out in bungalow-type cabins around the compound. Their exterior is white plaster with luxuriously rustic thatched roofs. The interior of the rooms is anything but rustic. Thick comforters cover each bed, the furniture is elegant, the bathroom immense, and an atmosphere of European luxury pervades. Owned by a German-Austrian couple and constructed in 1992, the reputation of this place has already made it hard to stay here most weekends without reservations made far ahead of time.

The restaurant and bar serve meals that are better than any other restaurant we have tried north of Guayaquil. Of course the prices also rival those of the luxury hotels and other exclusive restaurants in Quito and Guayaquil. The menu is gourmet, and the wine list goes on and on. A pool is centrally

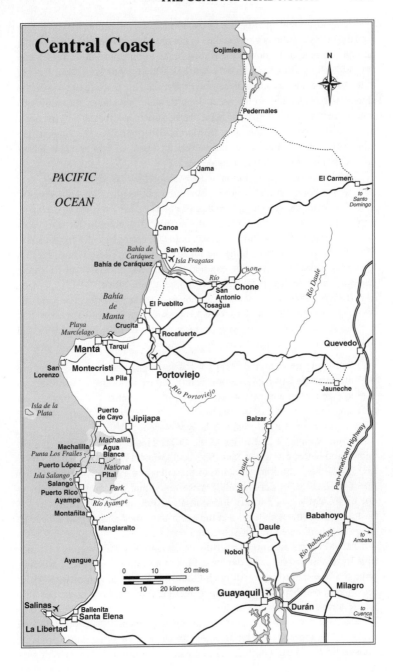

Central Coast

Cojimíes

N

PACIFIC

OCEAN

Pedernales

Jama

El Carmen

to
Santo
Domingo

Canoa

*Bahía de
Caráquez*
Bahía de Caráquez

San Vicente

Isla Fragatas

Río Chone

San
Antonio
Tosagua

Chone

El Pueblito

*Bahía
de
Manta*

Crucita

Rocafuerte

*Playa
Murciélago*

Manta

Tarquí

Quevedo

San
Lorenzo

Montecristi

La Pila

Portoviejo

Río Portoviejo

Jauneche

*Isla de la
Plata*

Puerto
de Cayo

Jipijapa

Balzar

Machalilla

Punta Los Frailes

*Agua
Blanca*

Puerto López

Isla Salango

Salango

*National
Pital*

Puerto Rico

Park

Ayampe

Río Ayampe

Montañita

Río Daule

Babahoyo

to
Ambato

Manglaralto

Daule

Nobol

Ayangue

0   10   20 miles

0   10   20 kilometers

Milagro

Salinas

Ballenita
Santa Elena

Guayaquil

Durán

to
Cuenca

La Libertad

located, and a small conference room is near the reception building. Obviously, access to the ocean beaches is not easy because of the steep bluffs, but a 15-minute drive down to Ayampe or 25 minutes to Puerto López can get you to long stretches of sandy beaches. There is one small trail leading down to a secluded beach with sea caves, but the best place to see wildlife is along the road leading to the hotel. June through November, the rainy season, is the best time to see birds here, and be sure to ask for the bird list compiled on the species in the area. In March, the grounds of the Atamari are aflutter with butterflies, in the summer months, pods of whales and dolphins can easily be seen from the poolside terrace.

Both because of its isolation and for economic reasons, the administrators of this hotel have a strong conservation philosophy. All gray water is used to irrigate the growing collection of plants on the property, and plastic, paper and aluminum are packed out to the recycling center in the nearby village of Puerto Rico. The hotel staff can help you arrange guides for trips into Machalilla National Park, along the forested Río Ayampe and other sites on the coast. Although there is no external telephone service at Atamari, direct two-way radio contact is maintained with the Quito office.

GETTING THERE: Most guests staying here arrive by personal or hired car. An eight-hour bus trip from La Libertad is possible, but it usually means at least two bus transfers and waiting time in between. Buses from Puerto López and Machalilla are only an hour's ride.

Continuing north up the coast a few kilometers, you come to the bridge over the **Ayampe River**, just before the little village of **Ayampe**. Birdwatchers should take the time to explore along the rough gravel road that travels east up along the river. It can be extremely "birdy," especially in the morning. Even if you are not into birds, it is a great place to hike.

From Ayampe, it is 3 miles to the ✪✪✪ **Hosteria Alandaluz** (private and shared baths, hot water, fans; $20–$30; 5-604-173, in Quito 2-543-042, fax: 2-525-671), 1 kilometer south of the village of Puerto Rico. Alandaluz refers to itself as an Ecological Tourist Center, and it is probably the most environmentally aware tourist lodge in all of Ecuador. Every aspect of the hosteria—from the architecture to the bathrooms, food and activist education program—is directed by environmental concerns.

The 40 rooms are spread over the compound in a wide variety of buildings from simple one-story duplex cabins to a multi-storied round building with an observation tower. All the buildings, however, are constructed from local palm, bamboo and tree products that grow quickly and make possible a long-term sustainable use of the local forest. The beds are simple but comfortable, and the rooms are rustic with rough floors and thatched walls and roofs. All bathrooms have biodigestion toilets, and the dried waste products are sterilized and used in their organic gardening program. The large, open-sided dining room serves no red meat, but a wide variety of vegetarian, fish and chicken dishes is available. The compound is right next to the beach, and you walk through sand to get anywhere on the compound. Camping areas are also available.

Playing volleyball, swimming in the ocean, hiking, reading in hammocks and relaxing on the beach seem to be the main diversions for guests staying here. The majority of visitors are under the age of 30, and most arrive with backpacks. The tour agency Pacarina has an office next to reception and can arrange tours of Machalilla National Park, find guides for hikes into the higher altitude fog forest, or rent boats for fishing or tours to Isla de la Plata (see Machalilla National Park section for more on this island).

An active environmental education program is not limited to guests at the hosteria. With the encouragement and help of staff from Alandaluz, a major recycling center has been operating in the village of Puerto Rico, just north of Alandaluz, for several years. To some extent, the lack of garbage on the beaches and along the highways that is so common in other parts of the coast can be attributed to the work of Alandaluz and local people living in Puerto Rico. To make this recycling center work, a continuing environmental education program has also been set up with the cooperation of Alandaluz and the residents of Puerto Rico.

Hosteria Alandaluz has teamed up with local farmers to develop a tourist package that combines wildlife viewing in tropical dry and river-edge (gallery) forest with the cultural experience of living with Ecuadorian families on small farms. Leaving from the village of Ayampe, participants hike along the gallery forest of the perennially flowing Río Ayampe for three hours, climbing and skirting the southern boundary of Machalilla National Park. All through this ascent, there are chances to see many of the bird and mammal species recorded from the nearby national park. At the end of the trail near the mountain ridge, Cerro Llovido, the forest becomes a transition zone between tropical dry and fog forest at an elevation of about 1000 feet (300 meters). Here the three cabins of **Cantalapiedra** have been built, and they can accommodate a maximum of 12 visitors at a time. All of the cabins are rustic with no electricity, and their construction reflects the local topography and availability of building materials. Some amenities, however, have been included, such as beds with orthopedic mattresses. If you prefer, hammocks can be a fun alternative. Mosquito netting is provided for everyone. Space for camping in tents brought by guests is also available. Shared latrines and showers are available, but when the river is flowing, most choose to bathe in it. Simple but wholesome meals are prepared by the staff.

The next day of the tour, you explore the area and visit nearby farms. You can see the techniques local farmers use to raise crops and visit the farmers and their families at home. Hopefully through this experience, visitors will gain a better appreciation for the great difficulties under which these hardy people till the land. Sometimes you are asked to help with planting, cultivating or harvesting. This excursion can be two or three days, costs $7 per day, and includes a bilingual guide and lodging. Meals are separate and cost $5 apiece, except for breakfast, which costs $2.50.

GETTING THERE: Tour companies can arrange vans or cars with drivers to get to Alandaluz with a minimum of problems. From the Manta airport, the drive is two hours. From Guayaquil, it is four hours via either Salinas to the south or Jipijapa to the north. Buses carry passengers north from La Libertad (usually involving several transfers) or from Manta via Puerto López (also involving at least one transfer).

MACHALILLA NATIONAL PARK

Declared a national park in 1979, the 137,500 acres of Machalilla National Park are the only national park lands on the entire coast of Ecuador. The goals of the park are to protect the unique coastal land and marine habitat (two nautical miles out into the ocean adjacent to all protected land are included in the park), as well as the abundant archaeological sites of the area. The park is divided into three physically separated units. A small mainland portion south of Puerto de Cayo has the driest portion of tropical dry forest and coastal scrub and is also the least visited area. Another, much larger mainland portion north of the towns of Salango and Puerto López includes a small offshore island, Isla Salango, considerable tropical dry forest on the mainland and patches of moister forest. A third portion is the entire island of Isla de la Plata, located 40 kilometers out into the ocean west of Puerto de Cayo.

The entrance fee for the park is $20 and can be paid at one of several guard stations or at the park headquarters in Puerto López. Bilingual guides, equipment, mules or boats for various trips can also be arranged through the park headquarters or through one of the several tour companies operating in Puerto López, Machalilla or Salango or out of Quito or Guayaquil. This park is not yet overridden with tourists, but the number of visitors has risen from 600 in 1989 to over 7000 in 1994.

Much of the vegetation in Machalilla National Park is tropical dry forest. Hugging tightly along the coast is another habitat, called coastal scrub, which is made up of thorny shrubs, low vegetation, and tall columnar cacti. This area of the park has had the longest interaction with human beings, and archaeological evidence indicates that a combination of human impact, extremely low rainfall, and stony soil have all contributed to the existence of this very poor habitat. Long-tailed Mockingbirds, several species of ground-doves and numerous lizards are the most common animals found here.

Another part of the park is made up of fog forest. When the fog, formed by cool ocean currents next to warm land, passes inland, the air currents carrying it are influenced by the shape of the coastline and the height of the hills and mountains over which the fog must pass. Much like the central coast of California between Monterey and San Francisco, some parts of the Ecuadorian coast have very high bluffs (like the area south of Ayamape), and the coastal range inland rises to almost 2640 feet (800 meters) elevation in places. These sites capture the moisture in the fog and form patches of humid fog forest. The plants found here are almost totally different from those of the dry forest, and the transition between the two zones is spectacularly abrupt. More moisture means more photosynthesis, more photosynthesis means more growth and vegetation, more vegetation means more herbivorous insects, frugivorous (fruit-eating) mammals and predacious birds. Of the 230 species of birds known from the park, for instance, over 140 of them occur in the fog forest patches, even though these patches make up less than 10 percent of the park's total area. The two species of monkey in the park, White-faced Capuchin and Mantled Howler, only occur in the fog forest.

Also part of the park, **Isla de la Plata** is physically and biologically very similar to the Galápagos. Low trees, shrubs and cactus dominate. It is *not*, however, just a "poor man's Galápagos" as several books have described it. It has many treasures of its own for ecotourists to enjoy. True, it is the only other place in the world besides the Galápagos where Waved Albatross nest (April to November), but it also has a suite of mainland species of plants and animals that have never made it to the Galápagos. It is a potential laboratory of species invasions and extinctions that could help clear up theories of species arrivals and occurrences on the more distant Galápagos. In addition, the waters around Isla de la Plata are a playground for more than 11 different species of cetaceans. From June to October, Humpback Whales concentrate here from the Antarctic to court and carry on with spectacular breaching, spy-hopping (rising in a vertical position to the ocean surface so that the eyes and head are out of the water) and competition for the females' attention. The rest of the year, Sperm Whales, Pilot Whales and False Killer Whales use the area together with several species of resident porpoise. The coral reefs around this island and on the adjacent coast are the only areas of coral off mainland Ecuador.

Isla de la Plata is two hours by boat from one of the several nearby towns on the coast. Besides the chance for seeing marine mammals, the surrounding coral reefs can be explored with scuba or snorkel gear (because

Red-Footed Booby

of the cool water temperature, wetsuits are needed for much of the year). On the island itself, two hiking trails wander its 6-kilometer length. Seabird colonies including three species of boobies and the Waved Albatross are exciting goals. Sir Francis Drake, among other notables, spent time on this island, and exploring an island with this kind of past is always intriguing.

Many other places in the park offer opportunities for nature viewing, vistas, archaeology and hiking. One of the most popular is Agua Blanca, with its museum, prehistoric ruins and trailhead to the fog forests of San Sebastian Mountain (a two-day hike). **Los Frailes**, near the village of Machalilla, is on the coast and includes a small island that is accessible at low tide. Here you will see nesting frigatebirds and Blue-footed Boobies and have beautiful photo opportunities of coastal scenery and harsh desert habitat meeting the crashing surf of the Pacific Ocean.

On the mainland, soon the village of Pital will be open to tourists, and this site just east of Puerto López will make more of the fog forest areas accessible via a three-hour hike. On the park's southern boundary, the perennially flowing Río Ayampe is a birder's paradise. Gallery forest is found along this stream all the way back up into the fog forest, and endemic bird species like Gray-backed Hawk along with most of the park's recorded species can be found along the road and hiking trail that follow the south side of the river. The river is easily accessible from the main coastal highway.

The lands that are now within Machalilla National Park have been under constant and unrelenting pressure from man for hundreds and likely thousands of years. Unlike national parks in the U.S., when national park boundaries are determined in Ecuador, private individuals already owning land within the park boundaries (inholdings) are often permitted to remain. Little of the park is pristine, and because 10 to 20 percent of the park's area is still privately owned, the pressure continues from tree cutting, burning, cattle and, most insidious of all, goats. Goats can survive where most other domestic animals cannot. They do so by eating plant parts like roots and bark that are indigestible for cows and horses. As a result, they can denude an area of vegetation so completely that the plants cannot recover.

The economic pressure from ecotourists and the increasing value of alternate noninvasive uses of these habitats, however, is having a positive impact. Initially, colonists and indigenous people from only one site within the park, **Agua Blanca**, were willing to take a chance and plan for tourism within their midst. They constructed a museum of anthropology and archaeology in their small village, elected a tourism committee to determine priorities, and trained guides to lead tourists through the museum and to archaeological digs, as well as to areas of natural history interest near their village. Working together with local NGOs and INEFAN, village residents began to see an economic profit from their efforts. Fewer goats are now grazed on their land and more residents are competing to become trained as guides. Most telling of all is the story of the residents of **Pital**, another village within the park, who initially resisted any attempt by NGOs and INEFAN to become involved in tourism. They reacted as if their land were about to be invaded, and they made it abundantly clear that any strangers approaching their village would not be treated well. That was their mindset for 15 years, just about the time it took for Agua Blanca's investment in tourism to show obvious economic profits. In 1995, the villagers from Pital did an about-face and asked INEFAN and Metropolitan Touring to help them do what Agua Blanca had done. Soon, a whole new set of trails and easier access to some parts of the park's higher ridges will be possible from Pital.

Archaeological ruins and evidence of thousands of years of human presence in this area are abundant. The most complete and modern museum in the area is at the town of Salango. The park headquarters in Puerto López also has a small museum, but the most intriguing and fun is at the village of Agua Blanca. To get there, go 5.5 kilometers north of Puerto López on the coastal paved road. Turn east at the national park kiosk and entrance gate ($20 entrance fee) and then drive 6 kilometers east on the gravel road to Agua Blanca. The museum is open all day long, and a $1 entrance fee includes a 20-minute guided tour of the museum and explanation of the history of the area. Guides can also be hired for a 20-minute hike to the remains of a large town, *Señorío de Salangone*, which is over 800 years old. Pottery, tools, graveyards and intriguing architecture all combine to give you a sense of the intellect and industry it took for these ancient people to survive and prosper in such a dry environment. That your guide is likely a descendent of these people adds a level of involvement and appreciation that no modern museum can ever offer.

Four-day package tours that include transportation from Puerto López, a guide, lodging and food cost $336 (Metropolitan Touring). The tours visit Los Frailes, Isla de la Plata, Agua Blanca and Salango. A six-day, five-night trek into the most extensive fog forest costs $440 and includes tents, guides, food, and transportation from Puerto López (everything except your own sleeping bag). Depending on your independence and ability to handle Spanish, many of these costs can be lowered by working directly with local guides. Camping is available at several sites outside and within the park.

GETTING THERE: By Bus: A bus from Guayaquil or Quito to Puerto López will involve a minimum of one to three transfers and will take 20 to 30 hours. Package tours will simplify this transportation problem by arranging pickup at Manta, Portoviejo or Guayaquil.

By Car: The alternatives for getting to Machalilla National Park include driving north from Guayaquil via Jipijapa to the coast at Puerto de Cayo and then south (three to four hours), or from Guayaquil east toward Salinas and then north at Santa Elena along the coast (five to six hours). Both of these routes are on good to excellent paved roads. Driving from Quito via Santa Domingo and then east to Chone and south through Portoviejo and Jipijapa is a long, 12-hour trip that has little scenic or natural history value. If you drive this route from Quito, take at least two days and enjoy a few stops along the way. The best route for the independent traveler from Quito is to fly to Manta (daily flights) and rent a car. The drive from Manta to Machalilla is only one and a half to two hours.

With its central location and the Machalilla National Park headquarters here, **Puerto López** (population 15,000) is probably the most convenient base for various trips in and around the park. Although it has been primarily a fishing village in the past, the increasing presence of tourists is quickly changing the economic emphasis of the village. The combination of high sea cliffs to the north and south, numerous fishing boats in the bay, and ocean sunsets makes the scenery outstanding and full of photographic opportunities. Many small restaurants have sprung up along the oceanfront, and the fresh seafood is exquisite. More restaurants and one of the most sophisticated archaeological museums on the southern coast are in the nearby town of **Salango** (4 kilometers south).

The small village of **Machalilla** is sandwiched in between the two mainland sections of the Machalilla National Park on the coast. It is a dusty town on a small bay that is primarily a fishing village. On the beach, frigatebirds swoop in, 10 or 20 at a time, to steal bits and pieces of fish and fish parts thrown from the small fishing boats returning in the morning from a night at sea. The bay itself is picturesque, and the beach is relatively clean. The tourist facilities are very limited here, but it is not a bad place to use as a base for day trips to other parts of the park and nearby coast.

Coming from Guayaquil via Jipijapa or from Quito via Portoviejo, **Puerto de Cayo** is the first place where you will see the Pacific Ocean. The garbage-strewn and often dry riverbed that runs along the road as you approach the village is not a good start, but after that initial bit of bad news, Puerto de Cayo gets better. The village is small and has few facilities, but it does have extensive beaches. The village's main economic base is fishing, and there is a colorful pageant of small fishing boats coming in to land on the beach after a day or two of fishing at sea. The scene at the beach is wild. The fish wholesalers and individuals trying to buy the fish compete with the frigatebirds zooming frighteningly close to the fish held in the hands of the fishermen.

LODGING   The only place we recommend staying in Puerto López is the **Hotel y Cabañas Pacífico** (private bath, hot water, some rooms with air conditioning, ceiling fans; $15–$30; in Manta 5-624-064, 5-621-516, in Puerto López 5-604-133, fax: 5-604-147). The three-story hotel was built in 1992 and is less than a block from the ocean bay in the village center. The 24 rooms are simple but spacious, airy and clean. Two cabins are available for larger groups and families and have rooms that sleep up to six. If you are allergic to insect fumigants, be sure to ask the administrator not to spray your room in the evening. Mosquitoes and biting gnats can be a problem some parts of the year (January–February). A tiny restaurant serves a limited menu and is best for breakfast. Try some of the small seafood places on the street running along the bay for other meals.

In Machalilla, one hotel, the **Hotel Internacional Machalilla** (private bath, hot water, table fans; $10–$40; in Guayaquil 4-331-343, 4-443-585) offers 25 adequate rooms that are somewhat run-down but are relatively clean (although dust and beach sand are an eternal problem). A broad, continuous balcony wraps around the building outside of each floor. From the balconies, hammocks hang strategically for a relaxing view of the beach and bay down across the Avenida Principal. Its small restaurant serves breakfast, lunch and dinner. The menu is international and, of course, emphasizes fresh seafood.

Puerto de Cayo is quite far from most of the destinations within Machalilla National Park, thus logistically more difficult than Puerto López or Machalilla to use as a base for day trips to the park and other points south along the coast. At some times of the year, however, there are no closer rooms available. The favorite of most tour companies, and an excellent choice, is the **Hosteria Luz de Luna** (private bath, cold water, table fans; $25–$60; in Quito: Avenida 10 de Agosto 7962; 2-400-562, 2-400-563). Follow the signs from Puerto de Cayo 6 kilometers north along the coast on a very rough dirt road to the hosteria with its brick-walled buildings surrounding the central pool area. Bright magenta bougainvillea flowers drape both sides of the walkways between the cabins. The hosteria is set in low coastal scrub vegetation right on the beach and has entertainment and recreation facilities to meet the demands of most families on a week's holiday.

Fourteen of the 18 cabins are set up for families, with six beds (including bunk beds for the kids); four of the cabins are doubles. A large restaurant serves popular Ecuadorian dishes like fried chicken and all kinds of seafood. A bar and recreation room are also available. The beach is clean, isolated and just a few steps from the buildings. The rooms are somewhat cramped (except for one large apartment on the second floor over the restaurant), but they are clean. All beds have mosquito netting, and the small bathrooms have doors that only very short people can enter upright. No telephone service is available here.

Hotel Torremolinos (private bath, hot water, table fans; $20–$60; in Quito: Calle Carlos Endara 160 and Avenida de La Prensa; 2-244-624, 2-243-990, fax: 2-444-594) is the tallest building in Puerto de Cayo and is down from the post office in the town center. The 11 rooms are very clean, but small; the bathrooms are tiny. A single color TV is available in the second-floor lounge, and it receives local stations via satellite. Fresh water can be a problem, as it must all be trucked in, and electricity can be intermittent.

The restaurant and bar on the first floor are done in a bullfighting motif, and the amazingly large menu of seafood, beef and chicken dishes is quite good. The beach is two blocks away, but it is not very crowded. There are no telephones in all of Puerto de Cayo except at the INETEL office, so to make reservations or communicate with the hotel, business must be conducted through the Quito office.

MANTA

After Guayaquil, Manta is the largest port on the coast of Ecuador. It is primarily a commercial center, but its beaches have long attracted tourists. The rapid growth of the city to over 250,000 people, however, has led to pollution and a tremendous increase in crime in the beach areas, especially the east end of town called Tarquí. The Murcielago Beach west of the city is the best and safest beach in the area. The old hotels around the Tarquí beach in the eastern part of the city are remnants of past glories, and much of this part of the city and its beaches have become run-down. Most foreign tourists will use Manta only as a one-night stopover to catch a flight back to Quito, meet their tour guides or rent a car.

If you do spend an evening in Manta, there are an amazing number of superb restaurants. If you are here in the early morning, go down to the Río Tarquí beach at the long jetty. Small bright-blue fishing boats return from

two to five days out at sea with their catch. Taxis, trucks and private individuals quickly gather around each boat as it arrives to barter for the fresh
catch. Hundreds of frigatebirds wheel overhead waiting for a chance to swoop
down and grab a meal left unguarded for even a few seconds. At sea, the two-
or three-man crew spends the whole time in an open boat with a single outboard motor using fishing nets to catch enough fish to sell for several hundred dollars. They sometimes have to go out as far as 300 kilometers to find
enough fish. These boats are little more than glorified rowboats, and the skill
and fortitude of the men who do this kind of work is mind-boggling. If you
want to do your own deep-sea fishing, boats can be chartered at the **Yacht
Club** (Malecón and Calle 14, 5-623-505).

LODGING   One of the best hotels in town is the **Hotel Manta Imperial**
(Malecón at Murcielago Beach; private bath, hot water, some with air conditioning, ceiling fans; $40–$55; 5-621-955, 5-622-016, 5-612-806, fax: 5-
623-016). It is a 50-room hotel built in 1972 right on the beach at the west
end of town. The Murcielago Beach is away from the less desirable east end
of town, and it is lighted and guarded all night long. The hotel itself has two
wings, each with two stories around the large central pool. The rooms with
balconies facing the ocean are the most delightful. The broad, sandy beach
extends for kilometers to the west, but on weekends and holidays it is packed
with people. The rooms are somewhat small and not very modern, but they
are generally clean. Besides sunbathing, guests can take advantage of surfing, tennis, soccer, an exercise room and a disco (Roberto's) that is open
weekends and holidays. An air-conditioned restaurant serves seafood and
other international cuisine.

   If a beachside place is not necessary for your stay in Manta, the cleanest
and most attractive hotel in town is the **Hotel Lun-fun** (Barrio Ensenadita;
private bath, hot water, air conditioning, TV, minibar; $25–$40; 5-622-966,
5-612-400), on the west side of the Río Tarquí. The Chinese motif is not just
a front, as the managers are Chinese–Ecuadorian. The entire building is spotless. The 26 rooms are elegant, spacious and comfortable. Artwork is tastefully hung throughout. The only problem is that the hotel is located in a
crowded part of town across the major highway through town and away from
the ocean beach. The restaurant (7 a.m.–9 p.m.), one of the town's best, serves
a mixture of tasty Chinese and Ecuadorian dishes.

   On the east (Tarquí) end of town, the overrated and overpriced **Hotel Las
Gaviotas** (Malecón 11090; private bath, hot water, air conditioning, phone,
TV; $40–$55; 5-620-140, 5-620-940, fax: 5-614-314) is the most popular. It
is very close to the airport, and the part of the beach and park across the main
street in front of the hotel is an interesting place to walk during the daytime.

The very broad beach has ponds and mudflats that attract birds and invertebrates despite the numerous trucks zooming by. The hotel itself appears older than its years. The service is poor, and the attitude of the employees borders on arrogance. Mainly businessmen stay here, so perhaps our problem was that we were among the few people not wearing a suit and tie. The 52 rooms are on four floors and are depressingly dingy. Some of the halls are so dark you can't see to put the key in the lock. But the view from the more expensive ocean (street) side rooms is impressive at night. The bay is always filled with large ships, their masts and decks lighted like Christmas trees. A coffee shop is open 24 hours for sandwiches and drinks, and a large restaurant (7:30 a.m.–10 p.m.) has a menu of seafood and national dishes. The food is okay but nothing to write home about. A small disco on the beach across the street is open on weekends.

Located in Tarquí two blocks from the beach, the **Hotel Las Rocas** (Calle 101 and Avenida 105; private bath, hot water, air conditioning, phone, TV; $25–$40; 5-612-856, 5-610-299, 5-620-607), offers 60 simple but clean rooms, and a friendly and helpful staff. This is a good hotel to stay in if you just need a place to sleep for one night. It has a large restaurant and bar, Los Caracoles, with a modest but good menu of regional and international food.

RESTAURANTS   Besides the hotel restaurants, there are six restaurants we recommend in Manta, all but one in the west end of town. The best Chinese restaurant (*chifa*) is the **Restaurant Chifa Popular** (Avenidas 109 and 4 de Noviembre; 9 a.m.–11 p.m.; $1.50–$2; 5-621-346) on the west end of Tarquí. There is no atmosphere here, but the menu is full of simple but delicious Chinese food. Most of the Chinese in town eat here. Look for the goldfish tank in the window.

For pizza, the **Topi** (Malecón and Avenida 15; 11:30 a.m.–1 a.m.; $2–$5; 5-621-180) is tops. Located on the west end of town across the road from the Murcielago Beach, it is an open-walled and airy structure with friendly and courteous staff. The menu includes 17 types of pizza, as well as other Italian dishes such as calzone, and some seafood.

La Parrillada del Che Marcelo (Avenida 24 and Calle 20; 5 p.m.–midnight; $3–$8; 5-620-664) is a typical Argentine-style restaurant. If you are vegetarian, stay away from here. Beef rules, and if the steak isn't bloody, it isn't worth eating. The large open grill sends off mouthwatering smells of cooking meat all evening. Chicken is also grilled for those who don't eat red meat. The brick-walled and open restaurant is in a quiet neighborhood in the west end of town.

One of the newest and trendiest restaurants in town is the **Jhonny Restaurant** (Avenida 24 and Calle 17; noon–3 p.m. and 6 p.m.–midnight; $3.50–$10; 5-610-670). It is a small restaurant in a residential neighborhood, but the elegant crystal and table settings quickly prepare you for the sumptuous menu. Seafood, chicken and beef are prepared in a unique French-*criollo* combination that will excite the palate of even those who generally eat only to live.

The **Charlat Restaurant** (noon–3 p.m. and 6:30 p.m.–midnight; $4–$8) is the oldest of the upscale restaurants in Manta. Its international cuisine, along with live entertainment (piano or organ) make it one of the most popular in Manta. Located in a quiet west-end neighborhood, every taxi driver knows immediately where it is.

Cheers Restaurant and Parrillada Peña (Malecón across from the Murcielago Beach; 4 p.m.–4 a.m.; $3–$3.50; 5-620-779) is a combination bar and barbecue steak house. An open-air restaurant with a small garden in the center courtyard, it looks out over the beach and specializes in seafood and beef steaks.

GETTING THERE: By Air: TAME has daily flights between Quito and Manta and on Monday and Friday between Guayaquil and Manta.

By Bus: The *terminal terrestre* is in the city center in back of the Banco Central. More than 20 different bus lines serve Manta. Most go to Quito (eight hours), Guayaquil (four hours) and Esmeraldas (eight hours), but many local destinations like Portoviejo, Jipijapa and Montecristi are also served.

By Car: From Guayaquil, take the highway 35 kilometers north toward Daule. Before entering Daule, turn northwest to Jipijapa at Nobol. After 120 kilometers, you will reach Jipijapa. Manta is another 56 kilometers north via Montecristi. From Quito, go through Santo Domingo (the bypass via Chone is the fastest way). At Chone, continue on to Portoviejo and Montecristi to Manta.

PORTOVIEJO

Although the capital of the province of Manabi, the city of Portoviejo is seldom visited by tourists except those passing through on the way to the coast. If you find yourself staying in this city, we can recommend only one hotel, **Hotel Ejecutivo** (18 de Octubre between 10 de Agosto and Pedro Gual; private bath, hot water, air conditioning, TV; $45–$75; 5-630-840, 5-630-872, fax: 5-630-876). This overpriced hotel caters to businessmen and has virtually no tourist trade. Its 30 rooms are small and somewhat run-down, especially relative to the prices they charge. The five floors are served by narrow stairs with head room that gives anyone problems who is more than average height. Avoid rooms that overlook the busy city street in front as they are very noisy. There is no protected parking, but if you can park your car directly in front of the hotel, the night guard will be able to watch it. The restaurant is expensive with mediocre service, but the food is fairly good. International cuisine, mainly seafood, is served. There are several small restaurants within six blocks of the hotel. Besides cheaper prices, they have better service and can introduce you to some local color.

The beaches of **Crucita** are only 20 minutes to the north of Portoviejo. The best and least disturbed beaches are north of Crucita near the mouth of the Río Portoviejo beyond El Pueblito. Small mangrove forests, tidal flats and salt works attract numerous shorebirds, herons and seabirds. Few visitors make it to these beaches, and their isolation makes them very relaxing. Restaurants in Crucita serve a delicious variety of seafood, but take a picnic lunch with you and avoid Crucita and its concentration of people if that suits you.

GETTING THERE: By Air: TAME has early evening flights between Portoviejo and Quito on Monday, Wednesday and Friday. The airport is 2 kilometers west of town, and a taxi ride to or from town costs about $2. A rental car agency office is next to reception in the Hotel Ejecutivo, and small cars cost $60 per day, with 100 kilometers free per day.

By Bus: The *terminal terrestre* is on the west end of Portoviejo. Bus routes include Manta, Bahía de Caráquez, Esmeraldas and Guayaquil on the coast and Santo Domingo, Quevedo and Quito inland.

By Car: From Guayaquil or Machalilla, take the Jipijapa Highway north. Thirty kilometers north of Jipijapa turn right (northeast) at La Pila to take the shortcut to Portoviejo. From Quito, take the Santo Domingo–Chone Highway.

BAHÍA DE CARÁQUEZ/SAN VICENTE/CANOA

Bahía de Caráquez is a white, shimmering seaside city of friendly people and quiet, safe streets. The city of Bahía de Caráquez (most people just say Bahía) lies at the mouth of the Río Chone. It is built on a sandy peninsula that separates the ocean from a large estuary that spreads inland for 30 kilometers. This estuary at one time had some of the most extensive mangroves north of Guayaquil, but in less than 20 years shrimp farming has eliminated all but a small remnant of this habitat. Tourism is the other major economic force in the area, but even tourism has changed the face of the area. What was once another sleepy coastal town is now a small city with highrise buildings and bigtime ambitions. The consequent construction of jetties and breakwaters has unfortunately changed the coastline. What was once a wide beach is now virtually gone except at low tide. Excellent beaches, however, are easily accessible on the north side of the bay near **Canoa** and **Pedernales**. For better or worse, Bahía is not what it once was, but it is still our favorite little city on the Ecuadorian coast.

Unfortunately the worst El Niño rains and floods of the century flooded much of coastal Ecuador between January and May of 1998. Bahía became entirely isolated as all roads to the city were wiped out by landslides and rising rivers. Then in August, just as hope for reconnecting Bahía to the rest of the country was rising, a devastating earthquake leveled many of the highrise apartments in town. Bahía's recovery, however, has been amazingly quick.

Much of the major damage may be under repair for years, but almost all the hotels escaped with little more than a few cracks here and there in the walls. The roads are also being quickly rebuilt, and they soon will be in good shape for vehicular traffic.

Numerous hotels in a wide price range are available in Bahía, but the prices are as much as 50 percent cheaper during the off-season (we've listed the low-season rates). During holidays and cool Highland weekends, the city fills with visitors from Quito and hotel prices go up dramatically. Many of the regular visitors from Quito have their own apartments in the tall highrises. On the other (north) side of the Río Chone is the much smaller town of **San Vicente**. The airport is located on the San Vicente–side of the river. Numerous family-style hotels and resorts are the economic center of San Vicente. North along the coast, there are more than 150 kilometers of almost continuous pristine beaches stretching past the Esmeraldas Province line. There are a few rustic hotels available along this route, and new ones are springing up every month. While the road is now very good, many people still drive on the beach at low tide instead of the road. From San Vicente, the beach at Canoa, 20 kilometers north, is the most accessible and convenient.

An alternative to crossing the Río Chone from San Vicente to Bahía by car ferry (every half-hour from 7 a.m. to 6 p.m.) or motor boat (every 15 minutes), is to drive east along the Río Chone and go around the estuary (55 kilometers). The north side of the estuary is best as the swamps, shallow pools and shrimp lagoons are close to the road. Herons, terns, gulls and shorebirds can be seen feeding here. At several places the road overlooks extensive swamps. Early in the morning or in the afternoon, these are good places to look for rails and the Pinnated Bittern. Boat rides can also be arranged to see the mangrove islands (Isla Fragatas) in the middle of the estuary that serve as nesting sites for thousands of Magnificent Frigatebirds. Bikes can also be hired, and several bike-tour routes have been mapped for day trips. Tours to visit and interact with the people of the region's small mountain villages are also available. Contact **Bahía Dolphin Tours** (Calle Salinas; P.O. Box 25; 5-692-097, fax: 5-692-088) or **Guacamayo–Marinatours** in Bahía (Avenida Bolívar and Arenas; 5-691-412, fax: 5-691-280) for information and details on these and other ecotourist destinations in the area.

Patricio Tamariz, operator of Bahía Dolphin Tours, offers an interesting alternative to the standard tourist fare. Just down the coast from Bahía, Patricio has developed a small nature/archaeology center with a lodge, museum and trails into the dry tropical forest. The location is known as **Chirije** and is the site of one of the most important archaeological excavations along the Ecuadorian coast. Chirije has been occupied for 25 centuries, and archaeology buffs can see many of the beautiful artifacts that have been recovered from the site and, with luck, perhaps even find some on their own. (Note: It is illegal to remove or export these relics without a permit.) The area is so rich in artifacts that centuries-old pots and chards drop out of the beach bluffs with every crashing wave. Chirije can be visited as a day trip or visitors can stay overnight in the comfortable cabins.

LODGING   The most luxurious hotel in Bahía de Caráquez, if not a little lacking in atmosphere, is the **Hotel La Piedra** (private bath, hot water, air conditioning, phone, cable color TV; $35–$75 low season; 5-690-780, 5-691-473, fax: 5-690-154). The hotel is at the northern end of the point that juts into the mouth of the Río Chone as it empties into the ocean. Its 41 rooms overlook the pool and ocean. They are large, clean and remind us of being in the United States at some good resort in California or North Carolina. There are three bars and a large restaurant that serve a wide menu of seafood and international cuisine. Steps lead down to the beach directly from the hotel, but except at low tide, there is no beach. Bicycles and kayaks can be rented at the hotel.

If you want a hotel loaded with atmosphere, stay at **La Herradura** (Avenidas Hidalgo and Bolívar, Bahía; private bath, hot water, air conditioning, phone, cable color TV; $30–$55 low season; 5-690-446, fax: 5-690-265). The owner and manager, Miguel Angel Viteri Molinari, took over the business from his father, who began the hotel in 1968. He takes great pride in his hotel and its guests, and you can count on being treated royally. Personally selected art objects decorate the rooms, hallways and restaurant, and each of the 31 rooms has its own personality. Rooms on the west side have balconies that look out at the ocean across the Avenida Circunvalación. Its Restaurant Isabela is one of the best in town and serves a wide variety of international cuisine and seafood.

Another very nice place to stay in Bahía is the new **Casa Grande** (on the Malecón; private bath, hot water, phone, TV; $50–$75; 5-692-097). The name means "big house," and that is exactly how you will feel, like a guest in a friend's big home. The guest house sits at the very tip of the peninsula, and the views are spectacular. The five rooms are upstairs, and they—as well as the living room and breakfast area downstairs—are all cozy. There is a pretty pool in back overhung by a beautiful fig tree for you to wash off the fatigue of the day. The Casa Grande is operated by Bahía Dolphin Tours, so contact them for reservations.

In Bahía's city center, the **Hotel Italia** (Avenida Bolívar and Calle Checa; private bath, hot water, some with air conditioning, ceiling fans, phone, cable color TV; $30–$50; 5-691-137, fax: 5-691-092) is the best choice. The building was originally built in 1953, but in 1992 it was completely remodeled and modernized. The 20 rooms are very clean and comfortable. A small res-

Right: A roadside orchid, one of many hundred Ecuadorian species, from the mountains above Baeza.

Below: Scarlet Macaws are loud and flashy residents of undisturbed rainforests.

Top left and right: Rainforest butterflies.

Middle left: A Marine Iguana, the only known saltwater lizard.

Middle right: A wild Galápagos Tortoise at Rancho Mairposa on Santa Cruz Island.

Below: A male Land Iguana from the Galápagos Islands.

taurant on the ground floor has an excellent menu of seafood and international cuisine. Although the hotel is on a busy city street, a park across the street helps keep the noise level down.

Also in the center of the city is the **Bahía Hotel** (Malecón and Vinueza Frente Muelle; private bath, hot water, ceiling fans, TV, no elevator; $8–$20; 5-690-509, fax: 5-693-833). There are 40 clean but simple rooms on five floors with a small restaurant downstairs. This is a good place to stay for the budget/student traveler.

Outside of Bahía, at the "Y" in the road 5 kilometers to the east, the family-oriented **Hosteria Quinta W** (private bath, hot water, air conditioning, TV; $18–$45, fax: 5-691-386) is an alternative to staying in the often noisy city. The 12 rooms, all on a single ground floor, are large, and each has three beds. A bar, restaurant, pool and tennis court are also on the grounds, but they are available only during holidays and high season.

For budget travelers, the **Hotel Palma** (Avenida Bolívar 910-914; private bath, cold water, ceiling fan, some with TV; $6–$12; 5-690-467) is a good choice. Located in the city center, it has 30 clean but starkly simple rooms on the second and third floors of its building. The floors are wooden, and the private bath is actually built into a corner of the room and separated with sliding-glass doors that do not reach the ceiling. A large restaurant on the ground floor is very popular and specializes in seafood.

The biggest surprise in Bahía is the **Bahía Bed and Breakfast Inn** (Ascazubi 322; private bath, hot water, table fan, cable color TV; $10 per person including American-style breakfast; 5-690-146). If it hadn't been for the small printed signs in English, we would never have noticed this recently opened establishment. If it hadn't been for the white-bearded owner working on fixing a door at the entrance, we would never have walked up the rickety stairs to the second floor. Here we talked to the two friendly Ecuadorian owners, both of whom had lived in Canada for years and between them speak three or four languages. They have purchased the entire building and their goal is to build an inn with a family atmosphere that is affordable. A family sitting room is available for the guests, and a dining room serves for the breakfast area. For budget travelers, this is without a doubt the best buy in Bahía.

Across the bay in San Vicente, all the hotels are along the main street. Most of the recommended hotels are at the north end of town, and except for one typical hotel, and a budget hostal, all the rest are family-type accommodations with cabins, multiple rooms and four or five beds. The most typical hotel is the **Hotel Vacaciones** (private bath, hot water, air conditioning, phone, TV; $15–$32; 5-674-116). From the street, you would never guess that such a nice large hotel is back there. The rooms are large and clean. A huge restaurant is open on weekends and holidays and specializes in *criollo* dishes and seafood. A beautiful flower garden and patch of natural vegetation can be reached by walking up a set of stairs behind the hotel. This is a delightful place to watch the sun set over the bay and ocean.

The **Hotel Cabañas Alcatraz** (private bath, hot water, air conditioning, TV; $60–$80; 5-690-842, fax: 5-674-179) has 14 family cabins with five beds per cabin. There are two swimming pools, a sauna, restaurant, bar and parking area on the compound.

Hostal El Montés (private bath, cold water, floor fans; $10 per person; 5-674-201) has ten family-style rooms with a double and bunk bed in each. The rooms are extremely clean. There is a bar but no restaurant.

Hotel Vel Velero (private bath, cold water, table fans; $25–$65; 5-674-122, 5-674-387, fax: 5-674-301) has eight family units on two floors. There is a pool, restaurant, bar and parking area on the compound.

Las Hamacas (private bath, cold water, floor fans, TV; $21–$60; 5-674-134, in Quito 2-542-700, fax: 2-568-664) has 16 family cabins, each with two floors and five to eight beds. There are also ten rooms for singles or doubles. There is a restaurant, bar, pool and air-conditioned disco (open in high season only).

For those with a yearning to get away from the tourists and enjoy a very secluded beach, the **Hotel Cocosol** (private bath, cold water, no electricity) will give you a sense of freedom to rest, recreate and enjoy. Situated on the beach between Cojimies and Pedernales 140 kilometers north of San Vicente, much of the route involves driving along the beach at low tide. Once there, the rustic hotel overlooks a 40-kilometer-long beach fringed with coconut palms, cliffs and sand dunes. The informal restaurant specializes, of course, in coconut dishes and foods typical of the region. Camping is available, and campers can use the showers and bathroom facilities. Trips to the Cojimies Estuary and mangroves will give you a chance to see some of the only untouched mangrove forest left on the coast. For prices, reservations and transportation, contact Guacamayo-Marinatours in Bahía (Avenida Bolívar and Arenas, 5-691-412, fax: 5-691-280).

RESTAURANTS   There are several good places to eat in Bahía, almost all of them specializing in seafood, especially shrimp. This is the place to try a seafood ceviche (with cooked seafood here) and in particular one with fresh conch or shrimp. Ecuador is the world's second-largest exporter of shrimp and Bahía is one of the primary producers.

The two most elegant restaurants in town (all restaurants in Bahía are informal) are the **Restaurant Isabela** in the Hotel La Herradura and **La Piedra** in the Hotel La Piedra. Both specialize in seafood, but nonseafood lovers will be happy too. Everything we tried was delicious.

There are several very casual places to eat in Bahía that also serve tasty meals. **La Chozita** (Calle Alberto Santos by the ferry dock; lunch and dinner, daily) is one of four open-air restaurants in a row serving essentially the same fresh seafood meals. From your table you can watch the fishing boats come and go and the chaos of birds trying to snatch a quick snack. Also near here is **Pablo's** (Calle Alberto Santos by the ferry dock; lunch and dinner, daily) located in a beautifully renovated old building and also specializing in seafood. If you don't want seafood (what are you doing here?), try **Pizzeria Donatello** (just south of the Municipal dock on Calle Alberto Santos; lunch and dinner, open daily). Donatello's not only serves pizza but also pasta and sandwiches and oddly enough has the best Chinese food in town!

On the outskirts of Bahía is **Saiananda** (all meals by reservation only; 5-398-399, 5-399-399, fax: 5-399-280). Saiananda is a strictly vegetarian restaurant, but the food is so good and the service so friendly you won't even notice. Besides the great food, the grounds have a virtual Noah's Ark full of animals. Unfortunately, some of these animals, such as the sloths, have been captured from the nearby forest.

GETTING THERE: By Air: TAME has flights between Guayaquil and Bahía on Friday and Monday. The regional airport is on the San Vicente side of the Río Chone and bay, so you can either hire one of the few taxis waiting at the airport and take the car ferry across to Bahía, or walk the kilometer from the airport past the car ferry landing down to the landing for launches and take one of them across the bay. Taxis will be waiting at the other side. Normally ferries do not run at night. The hotels in San Vicente are all on the main street, and unless you have mounds of baggage, they are walkable (all within 4 kilometers of the airport).

By Bus: In Bahía, bus lines serve Portoviejo (two hours), Manta (two hours), Quito (nine hours), Esmeraldas (eight hours) and Guayaquil (five hours). The offices are at the southern end of town on the main highway. In San Vicente, bus lines serve Pedernales (four hours), Cojimies (six to nine hours depending on the road and the tides) and Chone (one hour).

By Car: Driving from Quito, take the Chone road and bypass around Santo Domingo, and 6 kilometers west of Chone take either the right fork to San Vicente (30 kilometers) or the left fork to Bahía (33 kilometers). From Guayaquil, take the highway north through Jijipapa, Portoviejo, Rocafuerte and Tosagua. Here either turn west for Bahía or continue northeast to the village of San Antonio on the Chone–San Vicente Highway. Turn west and go to the Bahía–San Vicente "Y." Take the right branch 30 kilometers to San Vicente. Canoa is 19 kilometers beyond San Vicente on a good road. If you are driving north, the road gives out 48 kilometers farther north at Jama. The rest of the 46 kilometers north to Pedernales and then 41 kilometers to Cojimies is on the beach—watch out for high tide as the route can be completely cut off where the cliffs come down to the beach. Ask local drivers for the best time to drive. Usually the beach route is packed sand and as fast as a paved highway, but occasionally wet areas form, and a two-wheel-drive vehicle can get stuck easily. If you see pickups and *rancheras* waiting above the beach, don't pull around them and continue on your own, even if the route looks fine. They are probably waiting for the tide to go down at some impassable place up ahead.

THIRTEEN

Northern Coast

Isolated Pacific beaches, scenic jungle rivers and remote forest lodges await the adventurous ecotourist on a visit to Ecuador's northern coast. Out of the reach of the drying Peruvian Current most years, this northwestern corner of the country is both wetter and wilder than the central and southern coast. Indeed, some sites in the higher elevations of this region have the greatest rainfall in Ecuador. It's no surprise that the main town of the north coast is named Esmeraldas (emerald), although it is named for the gemstone, not the verdant scenery.

With relatively few roads and some places only accessible by boat, development of the north coast has been slow. As a result, many of the area's mangroves are relatively undisturbed compared to Ecuador's southern coast and the Colombian coast to the north. At present, the majority of tourists to this region are Ecuadorians and Colombians, and they come for one reason—fun in the sun and time on the beach. Many of the facilities and logistics for visiting natural areas other than the beaches tend to be relatively primitive and demand extra effort from anyone who wants to experience them. Besides the beaches, the diversity of cultures living here will intrigue you. One indication of the rewards of this cultural mixture is the unique food of the region. Typical foods here such as fish or seafood are soaked or cooked in coconut milk (*encocados*). The sweet result makes every dish seem like a dessert. Mixtures of honey and coconut are the actual desserts of the area and are called *cocados*. A common fruit is often served in a very sweet sauce called *bocaditos de guayaba*.

Esmeraldas and Santo Domingo are the principal cities of this region. Esmeraldas is right on the coast, and will serve as starting point for trips to nearby beaches or adventures to the forests of Río Cayapas. Santo Domingo is inland, and with its location about halfway between Quito and the coast, is both a convenient stopping place and a good starting point for excursions to destinations along the base of the Andes. The distances between cities in the northern coast region are relatively short, and many new sightseeing stops can be planned for a relatively short stay.

Although individual (artisanal) fishermen and local agriculture still predominate economically, in recent years, construction of new roads and uncontrolled economic development such as logging, are beginning to change the once-tranquil region. Industrial tuna fishing, corporate African oil palm and banana plantations and shrimp farming are all making inroads from the south. The oil pipeline from the Oriente terminates in the coastal city of Esmeraldas, and this economic juggernaut has had drastic environmental and cultural consequences.

Hopefully, the lessons learned from the impact of ecological, economic and cultural changes associated with large companies in other parts of Ecuador, especially on the southern coast, will be applied judiciously to the northern coast. Certainly, ecotourism dollars can have a positive influence on development decisions in the region.

ESMERALDAS

When Spanish explorers first arrived on the north coast of what is now Ecuador in the early 1500s, they found a native culture called the Atacames. These people and the earlier culture of the area (called La Tolita) had developed a sophisticated art of jewelry making. Gold and silver were used to make exquisite settings for clear green emeralds (*esmeraldas*). Although emerald mining is now an insignificant part of the economy in northwestern Ecuador, the Spaniards' name for the area (province and city) has stuck. Perhaps the emerald-green forests of the province of Esmeraldas, which still abound, are a more appropriate and hopefully longer-lasting legacy.

In 1533, the Spaniards began importing African slaves to supplement the small native Chachi (formerly called Cayapas) Indian workforce living in the area. The descendants of these slaves now make up more than 80 percent of the population of Esmeraldas Province. The influence of these Afro-Ecuadorians (locally called *morenos*) is obvious in the lifestyle of the people of Esmeraldas today. Typical of this influence and perhaps most obvious to the casual visitor are the marimbas, maracas and other musical instruments. The dance rhythms associated with these instruments evoke a peculiar mixture of African and Latin cultures unlike anything you will see or hear in the rest of Ecuador.

The remaining populations of the Indians are now found in the upper reaches of the Río Cayapas and its tributaries and a few isolated villages above

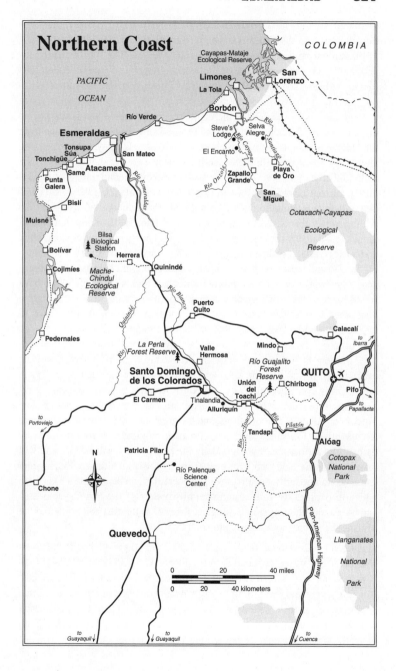

Northern Coast

COLOMBIA

PACIFIC

OCEAN

Cayapas-Mataje
Ecological Reserve

Limones

San
Lorenzo

La Tola

Borbón

Río Verde

Esmeraldas

Steve's
Lodge

Selva
Alegre

El Encanto

Playa
de Oro

Tonsupa
Súa

San Mateo

Zapallo
Grande

Tonchigüe

Atacames

Same

San
Miguel

Punta
Galera

Bislí

Cotacachi-Cayapas

Muisné

Ecological

Bilsa
Biological
Station

Reserve

Bolívar

Herrera

Cojimíes

Quinindé

Mache-
Chindul
Ecological
Reserve

Río Blanco

Puerto
Quito

Pedernales

Calacalí

to
Ibarra

La Perla
Forest Reserve

Valle
Hermosa

Mindo

Río Guajalito
Forest
Reserve

QUITO

**Santo Domingo
de los Colorados**

Unión
del
Toachi

Chiriboga

Pifo

El Carmen

Tinalandia

to
Portoviejo

Alluriquín

to
Papallacta

Tandapi

Pilatón

Alóag

Patricia Pilar

N

Cotopax
National
Park

Río Palenque
Science
Center

Chone

Llanganates

National

Quevedo

Park

| 0 | 20 | 40 miles |

| 0 | 20 | 40 kilometers |

Pan-American Highway

to
Guayaquil

to
Guayaquil

to
Cuenca

Río Verde
Río Esmeraldas
Río Cayapas
Río Onzole
Río Santiago
Quinindé
Río
Río Toachi

Quinindé. Living side by side in separate but interactive villages, the Afro-Ecuadorians and the Chachis have maintained distinctive cultures, but in a utilitarian harmony that could teach us all a lesson. The Afro-Ecuadorians and the Chachis recently have begun working together to attract ecotourists to their villages, and the result seems to be a positive economic impact without a serious negative cultural impact.

The city of Esmeraldas is the capital of the province and is the largest port in northern Ecuador. The terminal for the Trans-Andean oil pipeline from the Oriente is here, and it pumps about 450,000 barrels a day. Ever-expanding storage facilities and refining capabilities mean ever-expanding chances for leaks and contamination. The economic and environmental impact of this industry mirrors Ecuador's problem in general with balancing these two competing demands. Pollution is a constant price that Ecuador seems more than willing to pay for jobs. As a result, the city of Esmeraldas is not particularly attractive. Also, the presence of armed guards at every electronics store, bank and hotel is often less than reassuring to a first-time visitor. Everyone, including locals, will warn you not to walk the streets at night because of the muggers. However, if you are comfortable in New York City at night, we have found Esmeraldas is manageable at night, too. Except for passing through to visit other areas east or west, most tourists will probably find little reason to stay in Esmeraldas itself more than one or two nights.

Although the beaches of Esmeraldas have suffered from oil contamination, tourism is still a major industry. There are over 50 hotels, hosterias, cabañas and hostales in the area, and tourism is growing each year. This is an area, however, that relatively few North Americans and Europeans visit. Esmeraldas' population of 160,000 inhabitants grows by many thousands during school holidays and vacations, and the great majority of these visitors are from southern Colombia and the Quito area, only three or four hours away by car. The farther south you go along the beach, the fewer people you will have to share the sand with. However, there are fewer facilities for lodging and eating as you go farther south as well. Esmeraldas can be used as a base from which to explore the forests and natural wonders of the Río Cayapas area and the Cotacachi–Cayapas Ecological Reserve to the east and north and the Muisné–Bilsa area to the west and south.

LODGING   The **Costa Verde Suites** (Luís Tello 809 and Hilda Padilla; private bath, hot water, air conditioning, phone, TV; $35–$50; 6-728-717, 6-728-715, fax: 6-728-716) is by our estimation the best hotel in Esmeraldas. It is fairly new and everything seems to work. Located in the more upscale northern part of town called Las Palmas, it is only a block from the beach and in a much more secure area than hotels in the center of Esmeraldas. Each of its 12 suites is elegantly but simple furnished with efficiency kitchens,

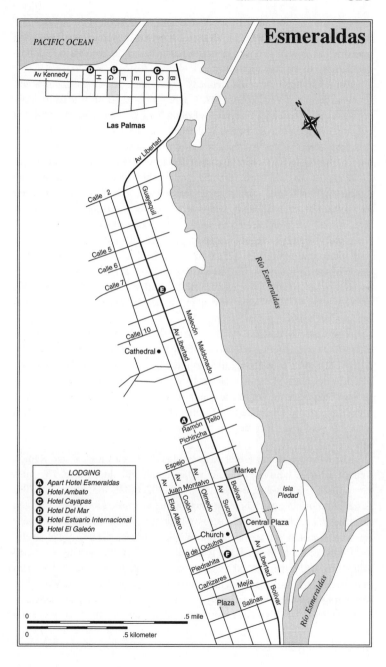

Esmeraldas

PACIFIC OCEAN

Av Kennedy

H G F E D C B

Las Palmas

Av Libertad

Calle 2

Guayaquil

Calle 5
Calle 6
Calle 7

Calle 10

Cathedral •

Malecón

Av Libertad

Maldonado

Río Esmeraldas

N

Ramón Tello

Pichincha

Espejo

Av Juan Montalvo

Av

Av

Eloy Alfaro

Colón

Olmedo

Av Sucre

Bolívar

Market

Isla
Piedad

Central Plaza

Av Libertad

Church •

9 de Octubre

Piedrahita

Cañizares

Mejía

Bolívar

Plaza

Salinas

Río Esmeraldas

LODGING
Ⓐ Apart Hotel Esmeraldas
Ⓑ Hotel Ambato
Ⓒ Hotel Cayapas
Ⓓ Hotel Del Mar
Ⓔ Hotel Estuario Internacional
Ⓕ Hotel El Galeón

0   .5 mile

0   .5 kilometer

separate sitting room and balcony. There are four floors and no elevator, but then no other hotel in town has an elevator either. It sports a small pool and poolside bar as well as a jacuzzi and separate sauna. Its restaurant, "La Fragata," is worth the stay on its own.

Hotel Cayapas (Avenida Kennedy and Valdez; private bath, hot water, air conditioning, TV; $22–$45; 6-721-318, fax: 6-721-320) is actually closer to the downtown area than most of the other Las Palmas hotels. Still it is only three blocks from the beach. With its tree-shaded location on a side street, it is very attractive and exudes a relaxing tropical setting. It also provides a good compromise for those who cannot decide to stay on the beach or in town. Its 16 rooms are rustic but clean and comfortable. Some have a balcony. Its restaurant, "La Tolito," specializes in seafood and colorful local dishes such as *sorpresa de coco Cayapas*, which would not be a surprise if we told you what it was. A bar and protected parking are also available.

Hotel Del Mar (Avenida Kennedy; private bath, cold water, some rooms with air conditioning; $15–$25; 6-723-707) is also located in Las Palmas. Some of the 27 rooms on the three floors look out across Avenida Kennedy to the ocean. A protected garage is available, and the bar has live organ music on the weekends. The "Fenix" restaurant on the ground floor serves good and inexpensive seafood.

A definite step down from all the previous hotels is **Hotel Ambato** (Avenida Kennedy and Antonio Guerra; private bath, cold water, ceiling fan; $9–$15; 6-721-144), even though it is in the city's trendy Las Palmas section. For the price, each of the 27 rooms is bare but clean. Although each room has its own bathroom, the commode, sink and shower are only a tiny partitioned area of the room. There are four floors but no elevator. Protected parking is available, and a small restaurant on the main floor serves very inexpensive meals.

The 44-room **Apart Hotel Esmeraldas** (Avenida Libertad and Ramón Tello, Casilla 292; private bath, hot water, air conditioning, phone, TV, minibar; $30–$55; 6-728-700, 6-728-701, 6-728-702, 6-728-703, fax: 6-728-704) is the best businessman's hotel in town but less focused on tourists. Located near the city center, it is easily accessible to most of the city's business centers and offices. If you are on the fourth floor, however, the absence of an elevator can get rather tiring. There is laundry service, room service associated with its bar and restaurant and a well-protected parking area in back. The main drawback to this hotel is its location near the city center where few feel like wandering after dark. You definitely have a feeling of being trapped here until morning. However, if you can wait until daylight, the central plaza, hustle and bustle of downtown, and sights and sounds of the open-air market are all within easy walking distance.

Hotel Estuario Internacional (Avenida Libertad and Gran Colombia; private bath, hot water, air conditioning, phone, TV; $25–$45; 6-721-300, fax: 6-721-348) has a location near the city center but not as close as the Apart Hotel. It is close to the city's piers and harbor facilities. Most of the 38 rooms are tiny, with doors and corridors adequate only for very short people. There is a bar and a new restaurant, and a protected parking area is available.

Hostal El Galeón (Piedrahita and Avenida Olmedo; private bath, cold water, some rooms with air conditioning, rest with ceiling fans; $7–$15; 6-723-918, fax: 6-723-821) is near the city center and is quite noisy. Rooms with air conditioning are quieter and cost more. The 21 rooms on three floors tend toward the seedy side of clean. A small restaurant and bar are attached, but they are dirty, smelly and right on a noisy street.

RESTAURANTS By far and away the best restaurant in town is **Restaurant Tiffany** (Avenida Kennedy 707; 10 a.m.–midnight; $3–$8; 6-710-263). Located at the north end of Las Palmas near the beach, Tiffany's serves an exciting array of European, Ecuadorian and North American cuisine. Not only is the service superb but the food is delicious, whether it is a steak cooked just like at home or seafood prepared in a local and exotic sauce. The wines and desserts reflect the international quality of this restaurant.

La Sultana del Valle (Avenida Libertad at Parada 10; noon–10 p.m., Tuesday–Sunday; $1.50–$3; 6-712-988) is probably the second-best restaurant in town, but it is at the other end of the spectrum from the Restaurant Tiffany. It is a long, narrow hole-in-the-wall with only 13 funky tables, and specializes in seafood, especially ceviche. The manager, Alvaro Fernando Diaz, has been running this restaurant for more than 16 years, and he claims whatever success he has had is due to his only serving fresh catch of the day. Indeed, the meals served from the simple menu are scrumptious.

With some Ecuadorian dishes that can challenge Restaurant Tiffany, **Apart Hotel Esmeraldas** (Avenida Libertad 407; 7 a.m.–10 p.m.; $3–$7; 6-728-700) is the best of the hotel restaurants. The service is only fair, but the menu is ample and the food consistently good. The small restaurant has tiny tables and can get very crowded when the hotel is full of salesmen and business clients. The food is quite pricey, but if you are staying in this hotel, this restaurant is handy and well worth a meal if you don't want to take the time and effort to seek out other restaurants in town.

La Fragata (Luís Tello 809 and Hilda Padilla; 7 a.m.–11 p.m.; $3–$10; 6-728-717) is associated with the Costa Verde Suites in Las Palmas. It is a small place, but the service is much better than at the Apart Hotel, and the fare, with an emphasis on seafood, is elegantly prepared. The cozy setting is light and informal without a feeling of being cornered. For an upscale but affordable evening meal, this restaurant would challenge Restaurant Tiffany as our favorite.

Fenix Restaurant (Avenida Kennedy; 7 a.m.–1 p.m. and 3 p.m.–10 p.m.; $1–$4; 6-713-910) is associated with the Hotel del Mar. For a sit-down meal that is inexpensive but still quite good, try this restaurant. Make sure you are interested in seafood, as chicken and beef are not emphasized on the menu. The ocean is a block away, but you wouldn't know it because of all the noisy traffic from the busy street below.

GETTING THERE: By Air: TAME has daily flights between Quito and Esmeraldas in the morning except on Sunday when it is in the afternoon. The Esmeraldas airport, General Rivadeneira de Tachina, is only 4 kilometers east across the Río Esmeraldas from town as the frigatebird flies, but the road to the city goes 10 kilometers south to cross the river at San Mateo and then 15 kilometers north to the city center. Count on 45 minutes and $5 per person to get to the city by taxi. If you have no need to go to Esmeraldas and are headed east for Borbón, La Tola or San Lorenzo, renting a taxi or catching a bus is much cheaper and closer from the airport.

By Bus: There is no terrestrial terminal Esmeraldas, but the individual bus offices tend to be clustered within a five-block stretch around the central plaza. Buses arrive and depart throughout the day and night between Esmeraldas and Quito (Trans-Esmeraldas, Occidentales and Aerotaxi), Guayaquil (Trans-Esmeraldas and Occidentales), Manta (Reina del Camino), Ambato (Cita Express) and many other locations (Empresa del Pacifico, La Costeñita).

By Car: The drive from Quito to Esmeraldas takes about four to five hours. If you take the paved highway south of Quito through Santo Domingo, at Santo Domingo take the Quinindé–Esmeraldas bypass road north. Some drivers prefer the new highway from the north part of Quito near the Mitad del Mundo that descends through Puerto Quito. This highway is not as broad as the Santo Domingo Highway, but it is paved most of the way and enables you to miss both downtown Quito and Santo Domingo. After Santo Domingo, the highway is broad, flat and fast. At San Mateo, 80 kilometers north of Quinindé, you will come to a major intersection and police check station. To the right is the bridge crossing the Río Esmeraldas and the road to the airport and Borbón. Straight ahead is the highway to Esmeraldas. The grassy hillsides are burned during the dry season, and this route can be obscured by smoke July to November. About 10 kilometers north of San Mateo you come to a major traffic circle. The route to Atacames and the western beaches is to the west (left), the route to the Esmeraldas city center is straight ahead another 5 kilometers.

TONSUPA–ATACAMES AREA

The better beaches begin just west of Esmeraldas on the Atacames Highway, which you can catch at the traffic circle just south of Esmeraldas. At last count, the Tonsupa–Atacames area sported more than 45 major hotels, hosterias and clubs. They all have a singularly unvarying architecture and atmosphere of stark white-plaster walls. Almost all of them are built to house families of four to five for the holiday vacations. Each resort is self-contained with swimming pool(s), access to the beach, a restaurant, volleyball court, playgrounds, bar(s) and rooms with four to six beds and private baths. The only differences are in the availability of hot water, air conditioning and color TV. This part of the coast is largely dependent on fresh water trucked in from inland; as a result, water shortages are always likely. In the off-season (weekdays and anytime other than a holiday like Holy Week, Carnival, Christmas and school vacation), many of these hotels go into hibernation, with few or no services available. If you can find one open in the off-season, you will probably be completely alone, and room prices will be almost half of those during the "high" season. During a holiday or high-season weekend, there is no room for anyone who didn't make a reservation months before. The roads are bumper to bumper with cars from Quito, and the beaches are cheek to jowl with sunbathers and screaming kids.

We found seven of these hotels to be open during low-season and appropriate for international tourists wanting to stay on the beach for a few days:

Hosteria Cabo Blanco (private bath, some with hot water, floor fans; $20–$35; phone/fax: 6-731-407) is at Km. 22 Vía a Atacames in Tonsupa.

Hotel Puerto Ballesta (private bath, hot water, fans; $15–$45; 6-731-538, in Quito 2-550-664, fax: 2-467-522) has 30 rooms (many with balconies) on two floors. It is next to the ocean and only 5 kilometers east of Atacames. A big disco is open during the high season and a large conference room is available for meetings.

Located right next to the beach but in the middle of town, **Le Castell Cabañas Turisticas** (private bath, cold water, some with air conditioning; $60–$80; 6-731-542, 6-731-408, in Quito 2-432-413, fax: 6-731-442) has 38 rooms and a pool for those who don't like saltwater.

Hotel and Club del Pacifico (private bath, hot water, ceiling fans, cable TV; $25–$65; 6-731-056, 6-731-053, fax: 6-731-368) provides an international atmosphere, which is especially reflected in the food served in the restaurant. It has a large pool and direct access to its own private ocean beach at Km. 20 Vía a Atacames in Tonsupa.

Resembling a stateside motel, **Hotel Castelnuovo** (at Km. 25 Vía a Atacames; private bath, hot water, fans; $30–$60; in Quito 2-223-608, 2-223-262, fax: 2-223-462) is not too far from the beach. It has three pools, including a gigantic pool for the adults. Palm trees shade the lounge area that has a restaurant and bar.

Hotel Casa Blanca (private bath, hot water, air conditioning, cable color TV; $30–$50; 6-731-031, 6-731-389, 6-731-390, fax: 6-731-096) is the grandmother of the beach hotels. With 18 cabins and 18 rooms, it is one of the largest of them all. Giant gates and walls isolate you from the rest of the world when you enter, and nature becomes a bit of sand and a couple of palm trees scattered here and there, but the beach is right next to the grounds of the hotel. An outdoor restaurant, coffee shop and bar are available on the compound. The hotel has a van to pick up guests at the Esmeraldas airport for $16 one-way.

Villas Arco Iris (private bath, hot water, air conditioning; $20–$30; 6-731-069, fax: 6-731-437) is in back of the main town of Atacames and harder than all get out to find, but is at last a place to stay with character, taste and relaxing surroundings. The ten thatched-roof cabins line the path through the sand and bushes to the beach. Hammocks on each porch encourage neighbors to talk to each other as they relax, and this place might even be fun. It has a small cafeteria and barbecue and sponsors a folkloric dance each Thursday evening.

GETTING THERE: By Bus: Numerous small buses leave Esmeraldas throughout the day and night for Atacames and points south and west. Few of them, however, drive right up to the hotel entrances. You will have to ask the driver to stop on the main highway as close to your destination as possible and then walk the kilometer or so down to the beach and your accommodations. Returning to Esmeraldas, you can flag down virtually any bus going east on the main highway.

By Car: Drive south out of Esmeraldas about 5 kilometers to the major traffic circle near the Petroecuador oil storage plant. If you are driving north from Santo Domingo, this traffic circle is about 10 kilometers north of the police check point at San Mateo. Go west here on the highway to Atacames (the Vía a Atacames). In about 7 kilometers you will come to the first hotels, but the hotels with beach access are 10 kilometers farther west. Look for large signs on the side of the highway and sandy roads leading down to the hotels 1 or 2 kilometers away. Atacames is 33 kilometers from the traffic circle, and on the north (right) side of the road. The hotels here are through the narrow and congested streets of the town next to the beach.

By Taxi: A taxi from the airport will cost between $20 and $30 one-way, and $15 from Esmeraldas. Several of the hotels provide shuttle service in their own vans to and from the airport at Esmeraldas, and they usually cost less than a taxi.

SÚA–SAME AREA

The **Súa–Same** area west and south of Esmeraldas and Atacames is much less developed, and both its beaches and forests give you an idea of what Esmeraldas looked like in the 1950s and 1960s. A small mountain range rises up to 990 feet (300 meters) and several small rivers enter the ocean along this stretch of coast. Recent highway construction makes the area easily accessible by car from Esmeraldas for a day trip. From Esmeraldas west to Atacames, Súa and Same, the habitat becomes somewhat less disturbed and tropical dry forest patches get bigger and bigger. **Club Casablanca** (private bath, hot water, ceiling fan; $50 per person including meals; 9-726-798, in Quito 2-467-848, fax: 2-467-580) is one of the area's most exclusive hotels. Located on the beach near the village of Same, it offers restaurants, pools, bars, disco, tennis courts and 42 villa-like rooms. Their bus meets every flight at the Esmeraldas airport (the one-hour bus trip is $15 one-way). At Tonchigüe, just west of Same, the road forks. To the right, a pleasant secondary road leads to the beaches and eventually, after 10 kilometers, to Punta Galera. The main paved road, however, takes the left fork to the south and climbs into the coastal range. This highway was constructed less than a dozen years ago, and there are still some large patches of moist forest along this route.

Even though the highway never gets above 990 feet (300 meters), the large Chocó Toucan and several species of tanagers and dacnis found here are typical of what you would see above 1980 feet (600 meters) almost 90 kilometers to the east in the Andes. This isolated, coastal-range forest even has bird species that otherwise are only known to occur in the Andes. We still regularly see King Vultures soaring over the highway here. These large, white-and-black vultures, locally known as *cóndor real*, generally are found in areas with extensive primary forest. They are a good indicator that the secondary growth and cutover forest immediately next to the road are not the only habitats around. Migrant warblers and flycatchers from North America are also common here in the winter and a reminder of how closely we in North America are connected to and dependent on the tropical rainforest.

Farther west toward Muisné, there are more isolated forests far away from the highway, especially in the vicinity of the town of Bislí. This extensive forest is classified as wet forest. Here, the valleys facing directly toward the ocean funnel rainfall relentlessly onto this habitat. This pristine forest still has many valuable lumber trees of types that have been completely cut down elsewhere in western Ecuador. Mantled Howler Monkeys are also common.

Although the vegetation is similar to species of the *Chocó* on the west slope of the Andes, a large number of the trees and plants here are endemic to this coastal range. Unfortunately, the very highway that gives you access to this area also now makes it easy for logging companies to enter. With no control or government management plan, these logging companies are having a heyday. Their unbridled profits are everyone else's loss, and this unique forest habitat with many undescribed species is likely to be gone within 20 years of being opened up. A report by the Coastal Resource Center (University of Rhode Island, Narragansett, RI 02882), *Atacames Special Area Management Plan*, was published in 1993, and if the Ecuadorian government chooses to heed any of its recommendations, some of these pristine coastal habitats will be saved. This same forest may be partially protected on its eastern side by the recently established Bilsa Biological Reserve, which is accessible via Quinindé on the Santo Domingo–Esmeraldas Highway.

GETTING THERE: By Bus: Numerous small buses leave Esmeraldas throughout the day and night for Súa, Same and Musiné. Unless your destination is one of these towns, you will have to ask the driver to stop on the main highway as close to your destination as possible and then walk the several kilometers to your accommodations. Returning to Esmeraldas, you can flag down virtually any bus going east on the main highway.

By Car: Drive south out of Emeraldas about 5 kilometers to the major traffic circle near the Petroecuador oil storage plant. If you are driving north from Santo Domingo, this traffic circle is about 10 kilometers north of the police check point at San Mateo. Go west here on the highway to Atacames called the Vía a Atacames. Súa is only 3 kilometers beyond (southwest of) Atacames. Few buses take the small road to Galera, so be prepared to wait or walk.

By Taxi: A taxi from the airport to Súa will cost about the same as to Atacames, between $20 and $30 one-way, and $15 from Esmeraldas.

After crossing the low coastal range, the highway from Esmeraldas eventually leads down to the coast again. Here the main part of the town of **Muisné** is located on an island ten minutes across the bay by motorized canoe. This town is in a beautiful and extensive estuary draining the coastal mountain range. Extensive tidal mud flats are surrounded by mangrove forests. Since 1969, when this estuary boasted almost 8750 acres of mangroves, only about a third have been cut down for charcoal and for constructing shrimp-rearing ponds. Compared to most other areas of the coast, this is minimal, and you can still get a feeling for relatively pristine mangrove forests and their wildlife here. Renting a canoe to view the mangroves and more remote parts of the estuary is easy. Ask one of the many motorized canoe operators waiting at the beach where the highway terminates. The price is completely dependent on your ability to bargain in Spanish. We have never stayed overnight at Muisné, but among the numerous pensiones and small hotels on the island, most who have stayed here recommend the **Hotel Galápagos**. Although Muisné is not on the main route for tourists to the beach, it receives just enough business to have a few beach cabañas and restaurants and even a disco place or two. Do not plan on staying or eating anywhere on the mainland side of the estuary. There are no adequate accommodations or restaurants on this side, and at night it can be somewhat reminiscent of Tombstone, Arizona, in the 1880s, but with no Wyatt Earp.

GETTING THERE: By Bus: A limited number of small buses leave Esmeraldas throughout the day and night for Muisné. They all stop at the mainland side of the estuary as there is no ferry here for buses to cross over to the island and main section of the town. Because there is no good place to stay on this side of the estuary, and there are few canoes crossing during the night, make sure you take an early morning bus from Esmeraldas to arrive in Muisné by late afternoon.

By Car: Drive south out of Esmeraldas about 5 kilometers to the major traffic circle near the Petroecuador oil storage plant. If you are driving north from Santo Domingo, this traffic circle is about 10 kilometers north of the police check point at San Mateo. Go west here on the highway to Atacames called Vía a Atacames. Muisné is 67 kilometers southwest of the traffic circle.

By Taxi: A taxi from the airport to Muisné will cost you about $50 to $75 one-way, and $35 from Esmeraldas. There will be great difficulty in getting a taxi for your return, so make arrangements for your taxi driver to return at a set time and day.

RÍO CAYAPAS REGION

Returning to Esmeraldas and points northeast, **Borbón** is a logging town on the banks of the Río Cayapas and a jumping-off place for anyone wanting to see the lower elevation portion of the Cotacachi–Cayapas Ecological Reserve. As a tourist site on its own merit, however, Borbón has little to offer. The commercial eating places are at best unappetizing, so choose the restaurant with the cleanest tables and fewest flies. Otherwise, bring your own lunch. Whatever Borbón lacks as a tourist mecca, however, is more than made up for when you get upriver from the town and are able to enjoy the splendors of the Cotacachi–Cayapas area. Four tourist lodges are now operating in the area. Steve's Lodge and El Encanto are 45 minutes to one hour by motorized canoe up the Río Cayapas from Borbón and are comfortable places to over-night or use as a base for two or three day trips into the Cotacachi–Cayapas Reserve. Newly built ecotourist lodges in the towns of San Miguel (three hours by motorized canoe south of Borbón on the Río Cayapas) and Playa de Oro (three hours east of Borbón by motorized canoe on the Río Santiago) are run by local people and provide direct access to the nearby reserve.

There is no good place in Borbón we can recommend for staying over-night. If you absolutely must stay the night, try **Pampa de Oro Hotel**. The owner is the local schoolteacher, and he is honestly interested in conservation.

GETTING THERE: By Bus or Taxi: The 102-kilometer highway from Esmer-aldas is now entirely paved. A taxi takes a little more than an hour and a half and costs between $35 and $50. Arrange a time and date for the taxi to pick you up for your return to the airport or Esmeraldas. There are no taxis in Borbón. One of the *rancheras,* converted trucks that pass for buses, will take about four hours and costs only $2.50. If you are arriving by air from Quito and have no need to go into Esmeraldas, hire a taxi at the airport or take one of the hourly buses passing directly in front of the airport. Make sure the bus you are getting on is going to Borbón and not La Tola. The airport is 25 kilometers closer to Borbón than Es-meraldas and you will save time and money. If you arrive in Esmeraldas by bus, the small buses going to Borbón leave from the same area as your Quito bus will drop you off. Esmeraldas does not yet have a central bus terminal, so you may have to ask which location the nearest Borbón bus leaves from.

By Car: If you are driving your own vehicle from Quito to Borbón, expect the trip to take about eight hours. If you do not need to first go to the city of Esmeraldas, turn right (northwest) at the police checkpoint in San Mateo (15 kilometers south of Esmeraldas), cross the suspension bridge over the Río Esmeraldas and continue past the airport on the coastal highway another 49 kilometers beyond the airport to a "Y" in the road. The left fork goes to La Tola at the mouth of the Río Cayapas (35 kilometers) and the right fork goes on to Borbón (38 kilometers). In Borbón, you can ask to leave your car in the enclosed American Missionary Church parking area. Whichever way you to choose to get to Borbón, arrange through your travel agent or local tour company to have your motorized canoe waiting for you. A fleeting glance at Borbón as you drive to the riverbank on the muddy or dusty paths that pass for streets will more than suffice for most tourists. Less than 15 minutes after getting into your motorized canoe and going up either the Río Cayapas or Río Santiago, the secondary forest and gardens (*chacras*) will look so good you will soon forget the town and its dreary images.

By Boat: If you have not prearranged with one of the four lodges or a tour agency for a canoe to meet you and take you to your destination on the river, you can take the daily water taxi that leaves Borbón for San Miguel each morning at about noon. This alternative means that you can only go up the Río Cayapas and cannot visit the Río Santiago, as there are no regular water taxis up this river. The advantages to the water taxi are its much cheaper price ($4 per person) and colorful memories of a 30-foot-long canoe packed with people and chickens stopping every 20 minutes at villages and individual homes. The local residents are very friendly, and if you understand Spanish, they will be explaining every turn and change in the river. If you do not speak Spanish, almost inevitably someone will take responsibility for you and become your godfather or godmother for the trip. Expect to arrive in San Miguel late in the afternoon. The water taxi leaves San Miguel early in the morning for Borbón, but because the hour varies from day to day and the taxi operator lives 15 minutes below San Miguel, prearrange the previous evening for him to pick you up.

One or two boats also leave Borbón daily for San Lorenzo, three hours to the northwest and usually via Limones. If the San Lorenzo–Ibarra train is running (a big *if*), you can return to the highlands on one of the most spectacular train rides anywhere. Completion of paved roads connecting the two towns will most likely hasten the train's demise. Buses now run regularly between San Lorenzo and Ibana.

Forty-five minutes north of Borbón up the Río Cayapas a major tributary, the Río Onzole, joins it. Here American-Hungarian expatriate Steve Tarjanyi and his wife, Laura, first opened a lodge for travelers some 25 years ago. As ecotourism became more common over the years, the Taranyis shifted more of their business to cater to the needs of foreigners looking for natural and cultural experiences in the Río Cayapas area. Because most of the habitat immediately surrounding ✪ **Steve's Lodge** (some private baths, cold water; $40 per person including meals) is now cattle pasture, the facilities are primarily used by ecotourists as a base for exploring up the river to more remote areas.

When you arrive at Steve's Lodge, you land at a large dock and walk up a gangplank and stairs to the main building. A reception area and dining room are on the first floor. On the second floor are six double rooms, each pair with a shared bathroom. Cold-water showers, flush toilets, comfortable beds and electricity make the lodgings quite satisfactory. The food here is good, with generous portions served family-style. The porch from the second floor is a good place to watch out across the river for Chestnut-fronted Macaws, Ringed Kingfishers and Pale-mandibled Araçaris flying by. If you listen carefully, you can hear Black Hawk-eagles soaring high up in the sky almost out of sight and unnoticed—except for their constant, high-pitched flight call.

Steve and his locally trained guides run three-day tours out of the lodge. The standard tour will begin at Steve's Lodge for the first night. Special arrangements can be made for someone to meet you in Borbón and take you to the lodge if you are uncomfortable making your own arrangements for transportation in Borbón and don't mind the extra cost. You then spend the next two days traveling by canoe up the Río Cayapas. You will visit Chachi Indian ceremonial centers, observe both Afro-Ecuadorians and Chachis making handicrafts, watch locals panning for gold, and visit a market at Zapallo Grande. At San Miguel, the last town on the river, you can visit local healers and see them using native plants as medicines. The day will end with an Afro-Ecuadorian musical presentation and dance with traditional instruments. Guests will stay either in the tourist lodge or in the homes of Chachi Indians. The final day is spent hiking through primary forest in the Cotacachi–Cayapas Ecological Reserve, with a late-afternoon return to Steve's Lodge. Optional tours include an overnight camping tour into the reserve or a day visit to La Tolita Island and the mangroves at the mouth of the Río Cayapas. Canoe lessons and water skiing are also available at the lodge.

Steve's Lodge can only be reached by canoe. The three-day tour package up the Río Cayapas starts at $250 per person and includes all food, lodging, transportation and guides after reaching the lodge. Optional trips can be arranged on an individual basis and the price determined when you make your reservations. To make reservations or request more details, write Steve and Laura Tarjanyi, Casilla 187, Esmeraldas, Ecuador. For faster service; e-mail: nagy@pi.pro.ec.

GETTING THERE: To get to the lodge if you made no previous arrangements with the Tarjanyis to pick you up in Borbón, take the passenger canoes that leave regularly from Borbón ($1.50 per person) or ask to rent an entire canoe to take you to Steve's Lodge ($15 to $20 depending on your bargaining skills in Spanish).

The **Cotacachi–Cayapas Ecological Reserve** was created in 1968, but it was not until 1987 that it was declared a National Protected Area. This immense reserve of 510,000 acres protects habitats in ten life zones—from the high-elevation paramo at 14,850 feet (4500 meters) to tropical lowland rainforest at less than 330 feet (100 meters) elevation. Even among Ecuador's many beautiful and biologically diverse natural areas, the Cotacachi–Cayapas Ecological Reserve stands out for its many unique and fragile ecosystems. The high-elevation parts of the reserve are only accessible from the Cotacachi area northwest of Otavalo along the Pan-American Highway (see Chapter Seven). The tropical lowland part of the reserve is accessible only from the small town of Borbón via canoe.

The local people who inhabit the area are native Chachi Indians and Afro-Ecuadorians, Both cultures have lived in this area for centuries and have developed a rich and colorful heritage. Although much of the history of their two cultures is intertwined, they also have culturally distinct beliefs. Each culture's oral tradition and knowledge of plant medicines, foods (ethnobotany) and general natural history is astounding, but often peculiar to each group. Faced with mounting pressures on their traditional ways of life, both groups have chosen to work to develop community-based ecotourism initiatives in their respective communities.

The communities of ⊙⊙ **San Miguel** and ⊙⊙⊙ **Playa de Oro** have taken the lead in establishing ecotourism-based projects (for more details and reservations contact ECOCIENCIA, P.O. Box 17-12-257, Quito, 2-451-338, fax: 2-451-339; e-mail: ecocia@hoy.net). Tours including food, lodging and guide cost $35 to $45 per day per person. These and other communities of the region are only accessible by river from the town of Borbón. Playa de Oro is three hours east of Borbón by motorized canoe on the Río Santiago, a main tributary of the Río Cayapas. This Afro-Ecuadorian community is located in the buffer zone of the Cotacachi–Cayapas Ecological Reserve. San Miguel, located three hours south of Borbón on the Río Cayapas, is a mixed Chachi–Afro-Ecuadorian community close to the reserve's northwestern boundary. While Spanish is the language spoken in Playa de Oro, both Spanish and Cha'palaachi are spoken in San Miguel. Playa de Oro is more isolated and removed from river traffic. The forest is less disturbed and from a wildlife-viewing perspective, perhaps more appealing. San Miguel, on the other hand, offers a richer mixture of cultural experiences and easier access to parts of the Cotacachi–Cayapas Ecological Reserve. A visit to either of these communities will provide an extraordinary insight into these peoples' cultures and daily lives, and how they coexist with the forest (upon which they still depend for so much of their survival).

Visitors to either community who plan to enter the Cotacachi–Cayapas Reserve should be in good physical condition and prepared for adverse weather conditions, including too much rain or too much sun. Insect repellent, long-sleeve shirts and anti-malaria pills are highly recommended, as this region has some of the highest incidences of malaria in Ecuador. However, we have been up these rivers for three weeks at a stretch, and with basic preventive tactics like these, we have never had a twinge of malaria. River blindness was introduced from Africa and has had its effects on people throughout the area, but this disease, spread by a small biting black fly, is generally contracted only after years of exposure. It is not considered a major health risk to tourists.

A trip to Playa de Oro or San Miguel usually includes a mix of cultural and natural attractions. Day trips into nearby primary forest are full of opportunities to see birds, flowers, insects and plants more closely related to what you might see in Central America than what is in the Amazon. On your walks through the forest, a strange contraption on the forest floor will soon become evident. Although hunting continues around all these villages, one peculiar source of meat is unique. Forest rats are considered a delicacy (they taste just like chicken), and you will see hundreds of traps on the ground anywhere in the forest within 5 kilometers of a village. Each trap is a heavy log held up at one end by a cord. The cord is attached to a stick in a narrow runway under the raised log. When the rat enters the runway for bait placed there, it trips the cord and the log falls on it. So as not to overhunt the rats, the traps are rotated from area to area every several weeks.

Overnight camping trips into the forest can be arranged. During day-long or overnight trips into the forest, one or more biologists will accompany you. Besides their duties as guides, these locals are currently carrying out biological monitoring of key indicator species of plants, birds, mammals and reptiles. Using techniques taught them by experts from EcoCiencia (Ecuadorian Foundation for Ecological Studies), these local biologist-guides have gone on to design their own projects in areas such as ethnobotany, captive breeding of forest rats, and land impact assessment of hunting in the area. Their dual role makes these guides exceptionally well trained and informative.

From either site, another very exciting adventure is to take a motorized canoe up the river into the reserve itself. From Playa de Oro, this trip up the Río Santiago quickly involves maneuvering whitewater rapids and white-knuckle turns in the river. From San Miguel, the Río San Miguel and Río Bravo are more placid as you enter beautiful canyons and forested cliffs.

Because these streams quickly become shallow and impassable by large canoes, you can generally only go upstream a few kilometers into the reserve from here. Even this taste of the sights and sounds of the reserve, however, are worth it. An obvious caveat is that the person in charge of the canoe must be *very* experienced and have reliable equipment. Don't forget your life jacket on this trip!

After being hunted for hundreds of years, few big mammals remain in even the more pristine-looking forest in the vicinities of these communities. However, birdwatchers will be particularly interested in the more than 270 species of birds known from the area. A published bird list is available.

Cultural events at both communities compliment these soirees into nature. Presentations of music and dancing have a distinctive marimba flavor. English-speaking guides present informal talks on the nature and culture of the area. Visits to the villages are conducted with great sensitivity. Always remember that putting a camera into someone's face can get old fast for the person being photographed. You are entering someone's town and in some cases someone's home. Consider how you would feel to have a constant stream of foreigners babbling and staring as they marched through your home. Try to be gracious and polite; otherwise stay back in the lodge or forest.

In both sites, you will find rustic but comfortable accommodations for up to eight tourists at a time. Amazingly modern kitchen facilities and adept kitchen staff offer a mix of local and international cuisine. All cooking and drinking water is purified. The guests' quarters have beds with orthopedic mattresses and mosquito netting. A bathroom with running water, cold showers and flush toilets is shared by every two rooms. There is a common meeting room and bar for talks, slide shows and relaxing after a day of activities. Solar panels supply electricity for several hours each evening, and the lodges in both communities are in direct contact with Quito via VHF radio.

GETTING THERE: To San Miguel, the directions are the same as for the Cotacachi–Cayapas Reserve through Borbón. For Playa de Oro, however, the new road from Ibarra to San Lorenzo provides an alternative route. Seven kilometers before San Lorenzo, turn left (southwest) onto the new coastal highway going to-

Poison arrow frog

ward Borbón. Go 23 kilometers (3 kilometers west of the town of Maldonado and the bridge over the Río Santiago) and turn left (south) onto a narrow road. Go 14 kilometers south to the village of Selva Alegre on the west bank of the Río Santiago. Here, by prior arrangement the canoe from Playa de Oro will meet you and transport you for the two hour ride upriver. *Rancheras* (small buses) also run several times a day between Borbón and Selva Alegre, if you want to come from that direction.

The road from Ibarra at 7290 feet (2210 meters) elevation ends at **San Lorenzo**, a bustling but often isolated town near the Colombian border. Although the road from Ibarra to San Lorenzo was pushed through in 1996, it has been paved only from Ibarra to Lita, and some of it can become impassable because of mud and landslides in the rainy season (January–April) (see Chapter Seven).

In San Lorenzo, there are three places we can cautiously recommend here —none of which is well set up for foreign tourists. The **Hostal Imperial** (Imbabura and 10 de Agosto; some rooms with private bath; $5–$10; 6-780-242), with 18 rooms, is the best in town. The **Hostal La Bahia** (José Garcas and Imbabura; some rooms with private bath; $6–$8; 6-780-267) has 45 rooms but is not very clean. The **Hostal Carondelet** (24 de Mayo and Isidro Ayora; some rooms with private bath; 6-780-202) has 24 rooms, and is definitely another step down in amenities.

From San Lorenzo, water taxis can take you to La Tola or Borbón, where you can catch a bus to Esmeraldas.

In 1995, Ecuador declared 126,711 acres of coastal mangroves and a small area of lowland humid forest as the **Manglares Cayapas-Mataje Ecological Reserve**. With the wanton destruction of most of Ecuador's coastal mangroves in the last decade, creation of this second reserve to protect Ecuadorian mangroves (see Manglares Churute Ecological Reserve in Chapter Eleven) is a welcome addition. Manglares is home to what are reported to be the tallest mangrove trees in the world. Some reach more than 100 feet (30 meters) in height! This area is also one of the last strongholds of the Coastal Crocodile.

Access to this reserve is not yet well organized, but motorized canoes can be rented by the hour or day in San Lorenzo or at Steve's Lodge to view the beaches, myriad islands and natural canals that make up most of this reserve.

SANTO DOMINGO DE LOS COLORADOS

Located on the main highway midway between Esmeraldas and Quito, the town of Santo Domingo de los Colorados makes a good base for day trips throughout the region. Its economy is now largely based on a wide range of business ventures from agriculture to electronics, and its location at the crossroads of north–south and east–west traffic is the key to its growth. Indeed, with 150,000 inhabitants and counting, Santo Domingo's growth rate is phenomenal even in comparison to the other fast-growing areas of the region. Businessmen and salespeople from Esmeraldas, Quito, Quevedo and Portoviejo fill the town all week long, and then Ecuadorians heading to the beaches from the mountains make themselves apparent on Friday and Sunday evenings. Santa Domingo has a more than reasonable number of restaurants, but most impressive is its incredible concentration of very good bakeries, ice cream parlors and sweet shops—especially in the city center and on the east side of town.

If you are passing through to or from Esmeraldas or Guayaquil, major bypass roads will conduct you around Santo Domingo, and you will see little of it. But if you want to take several days and explore the area around Santo Domingo, one of the hotels in this city can be a good alternative to the more expensive lodges outside the city. Exciting places like Palenque Science Center, La Perla Forest Reserve, the lower part of the Old Road to Santo Domingo, the road to Las Pampas de San Francisco and even day trips to Tinalandia itself are easy half- or whole-day trips from the city. In the evenings you can try one of several good restaurants, and then you will also have a chance to compare dessert shops. The outskirts of Santo Domingo are built up with wide streets, modern buildings, warehouses and residences. The older city center is hectic, crowded and confined. The Sunday market makes the city center feel even smaller and more crowded, but if you enjoy markets, this one is lively and colorful.

The people of Santo Domingo are as much a crossroads of cultures as is the physical setting of the city. Afro-Ecuadorians make up a large percent of the population, immigrants from the highlands and coast make up the majority of the population, and a very small population of Colorado Indians still live in the area. As recently as 20 years ago, it was not unusual to see Colorado men in their short skirts and red plastered hair strolling down the dusty streets of what was then a small town. Now this culture has been almost completely assimilated. Only a few still dress traditionally, and they are almost all weekend natives available for tourist pictures. Several package tours are advertised in the city to go see the native Colorado Indians, but this tour is completely staged and exploitative. We do not recommend that anyone visiting Santo Domingo make seeing a native village a priority.

LODGING   **Hotel Tropical Inn** (Avenida Quito; private bath, hot water, suites with air conditioning, table fans, phone, TV, minibar; $20–$50, 20 percent discount on weekends; 2-761-771, 2-761-772, 2-761-773, 2-761-774, fax: 2-761-775) is one of the newest and best places to stay in Santo Domingo. Located on the main highway from Quito on the eastern edge of town, it is right across the street from the Hotel Zaracay. Of the 45 units, 12 on the first floor are suites for three to four people. The rest of the ground-floor rooms and all of the second floor are doubles and singles. The rooms are a bit small but they are light and very clean, and are organized so that groups of three open out on the same landing. There is a lounge and meeting room on the second floor of the restaurant and a pool in back of the restaurant. The parking area is guarded 24 hours.

Well away from the busy downtown, **Hotel Zaracay** (Avenida Quito on the east of town on the main highway; private bath, hot water, some with air conditioning, phone, TV; $50–$70; fax: 2-754-535) sits directly across from the Hotel Tropical Inn. The hotel is designed after a Spanish hacienda with red-tile roofs and whitewashed walls built around a large interior garden with a central fountain. There are 72 spacious rooms facing the gardens and a beautiful open-air restaurant adorned with hanging ferns and hedges of impatients. Behind the restaurant is a lovely pool shaded by a large rubber tree and a tall stand of bamboo. Other amenities include a tennis court, casino and very comfortable bar. The hotel is built on 12.5 acres of garden and secondary forest that extend behind the hotel. There are several trails that crisscross this natural area making this a great hotel for birders or those folks who just want a bit of open space in which to wander.

Just a kilometer closer to the city center than the Hotel Zaracay and Hotel Tropical Inn, **Hotel Toachi** (Avenida Quito; private baths, hot water, table fans, phone, TV; $20–$30; 2-750-295) has 35 rooms, which are adequate and clean, but most are in need of renovation. There is a pool, as well as a restaurant that serves all meals, but there is little else to recommend.

Hotel La Siesta (Avenida Quito 606 and Yambo; private bath, hot water in some rooms, fans; $12–$35; 2-751-013, 2-751-860) is on the east end of town but closer to the city center than Hotel Tropical Inn or Hotel Zaracay on the main highway from Quito. It has 23 small rooms, none with a phone or TV. The hotel was built in 1974, and even though quite clean, its age is showing with peeling paint on the walls and some plumbing that doesn't work well. There is protected parking, and a small restaurant with a limited menu of national cuisine and sandwiches is open 7 a.m. to 9 p.m.

Offering 32 rooms and 2 cabins, **Rancho Hosteria Mi Cuchito** (Km. 2 Vía Chone; private bath, hot water, ceiling fans, except air conditioning in one cabin, TV; $25–$45; 2-750-636, 2-752-689, fax: 2-755-303) is the best hotel on the west end of town. Virtually all the hotel's clients are salesmen during the week, and, although open, the place is generally unused on the weekend. Apparently all the salesmen who stay in this hotel are very short, as the doorways and entrances to the rooms are well less than six feet high. The facilities are old and somewhat run-down, but for a single night they will serve more than satisfactorily. A relatively large restaurant is open 7 a.m. to 5 p.m. and offers big portions of Ecuadorian food. Because it is one of the few restaurants on the west end of town, you should plan on eating here if you stay overnight. We would not recommend it, however, for a longer stay.

Hotel Don Kleber (Km. 2 Vía Quinindé–Esmeraldas, private bath, hot water, fans, TV; $15–$35; 2-761-956, fax: 2-761-243) is the newest hotel in town, but it already has atmosphere and a good reputation. Besides the modern facilities, it has Don Kleber himself, who is the quintessential inn keeper

—portly, friendly and efficient—an ideal host. Each room is spacious and comfortably furnished. The 30 rooms are spread out over two floors and two wings of the hotel. The bar, lounge and restaurant are at the junction of the two wings and look out over the two pools (a large adult pool and shallow kiddie pool). The hotel is far enough out in the country that a noisy and persistent Pied Water Tyrant has taken up residence along the edge of the larger pool. On the other side of the pool is a building with a four-person jacuzzi and a separate sauna (*baño turco*). The restaurant serves delicious *criollo* food from the coast as well as from the sierra, and the chef is proud to show off his modern and very clean kitchen. Hotel Don Kleber is only 2 kilometers north of Santo Domingo on the Quinindé–Esmeraldas Highway (a large sign on the east side of the highway announces its location), and two hours from Esmeraldas. If you are taking the northern bypass around Santo Domingo, this hotel is the only one you will have available to you. It runs a close second to the Hotel Tropical Inn as our favorite in town.

Hosteria Valle Hermoso (Km. 24 Vía Quinindé–Esmeraldas; private bath, hot water, fans, TV; $13–$30; 2-773-208, fax: 2-759-095) is a nice surprise and a very pleasant place to stay a half-hour north of Santo Domingo on the Esmeraldas Highway. To reach the hotel you have to turn off the main highway at the town of Valle Hermosa. Large signs advertise the hosteria at Km. 24 where you turn east (right coming from Santo Domingo, left coming from Esmeraldas). Cross the large bridge over the Río Agua Blanca and continue straight ahead to the town center. Don't let the rather run-down appearance of the town discourage you. Signs somewhat ambiguously indicate which way to go, but turn right (south) when you come to a "T" in the town center and continue another 300 yards. A white arch and sign indicate a left turn into the hosteria. Be careful of the other signs advertising competing hosterias plastered right next to the arches into Hosteria Valle Hermoso. The reception building and parking lot are 100 yards farther in along the banks of the small Río Cristál.

Although much of the 200 acres of forest has been cleared, a line of trees and vegetation shade the small stream along which this hosteria is built. The reception building, restaurant, sauna and activities building are clustered around two swimming pools. Five small buildings with two to three bedrooms are across a small suspension bridge on the far side of the Río Cristál. The interior of the rooms (each have two to six beds) is stark white and scrupulously clean. The exteriors of the buildings are startling white plaster with red-tile roofs and shaded porches around the perimeter. Paths connect the buildings and plants have been placed generously throughout the grounds.

The very large restaurant has tables that overflow out onto the pool edge and onto an ample veranda. The cuisine is international, but specializes in seafood, chicken and beef dishes. Meals cost about $4–$9 apiece. Because of its isolation, there are no good alternatives to this restaurant for meals, but you will not be suffering if you eat here. The hosteria is primarily set up to accommodate vacationing families from Quito, so avoid Carnival, Easter, Christmas and other holidays. Weekdays are great as you can have virtually the whole place to yourself, and the nights will not be filled with loud dance music. Camping ($3) is permitted on the grounds.

RESTAURANTS   The best international and national cuisine is in restaurants associated with the better hotels. There are many restaurants in town that include everything from those specializing in chicken (Pollos Gus is a reliable chain of restaurants throughout Ecuador) to numerous *chifas* (Chinese restaurants), but most have varied quality even from night to night at the same restaurant. Many restaurants are closed Mondays, so you will have to eat at one of the hotel restaurants on Monday, whether you like it or not.

Hotel Tropical Inn (Avenida Quito on the east end of town; 7:30 a.m.–3 p.m. and 6 p.m.–11 p.m., $3–$8) is a restaurant that opened with the hotel complex in late 1994. The cuisine is international and emphasizes seafood, but chicken, pork and beef entrées are also offered. Of the several dishes we had, we were generally quite pleased. The restaurant itself is small but airy and clean. We rate this the best restaurant overall in the city.

Across the street is **Hotel Zaracay** (Avenida Quito on the east end of town on the main highway; 7:30 a.m.–3 p.m. and 6:30 p.m.–11:30 p.m.; $5–$9), the grand dame of hotel restaurants in Santo Domingo. It was evident to us, however, that this restaurant was operating on past glory. Besides having to maneuver around the numerous 18-wheeler trucks in the parking lot, the service was slow and verging on arrogant. The food was only moderately good and as expensive as the Hotel Tropical Inn. While the menu included national cuisine and seafood, choices were limited. The restaurant is very large, with walls that are open with a thatched-roof motif. Apparently it is outfitted with only a few lights to maintain some sense of romantic interlude. For us, it just made it almost impossible to read the menus.

Parrilladas Argentinas (Avenidas Quito and Tena; 7:30 p.m.–11 p.m.; $3–$6) is one of a couple of excellent steak houses in town. It is located on the traffic circle just as you enter the city center from the east. This relatively large restaurant offers a variety of beef steaks fried over immense beds of charcoal, but with its location right on a busy traffic circle, the noise and exhaust fumes of every truck traveling late through the city from or to Quito make enjoyment of the food quite difficult.

Restaurant "Elite" (Avenidas Quito and Sachíla; 10 a.m.–9:30 p.m.; $1.50–$3) is a small but clean and efficient restaurant on the southeast corner of the main city plaza. If you want a solid meal such as chicken and fries or beef stew and are pressed for time, eat here. The prices are very modest, but the service is good and the food amazingly tasty. In many ways this restaurant could be described as a mini-Denny's restaurant.

By Bus: Santo Domingo is serviced by so many bus lines from so many directions, it can be overwhelming. The city has grown so fast that a *terminal terrestre* terrestrial terminal has yet to be finished, and each bus company operates out of its own office. Most of these offices are within a few blocks of the central plaza, but some interprovincial bus lines use the bypasses around Santo Domingo and let you off or pick you up at these intersections far from the city center. All these peripheral bus stops, however, have lines of taxis waiting to pick up riders getting off these buses, so you are unlikely to be stranded.

By Car: The three-hour drive from Quito first goes south along the main highway to Latacunga–Cuenca and then turns west and down at a major intersection at the town of Alóag 36 kilometers south of Quito. The 108 kilometers of the rest of this highway to Santo Domingo are all paved, but it is curvy and adventuresome in the morning. In the afternoon and evening when the fog forms, the ride can be a series of heart attacks, even if you drive super cautiously. Buses and trucks careen down the mountainside and ignore little problems like pea-soup fog or keeping to the right on curves. The trip uphill to Quito in the afternoon can take five hours because of the weather.

Plan on five hours to drive between Santo Domingo and Guayaquil. The highway is all paved, flat and fast, but watch out for the bypass roads around the larger cities. They are often unmarked and very confusing. Take the route through Durán–Babahoyo as it is faster than the route through Balzar–Daule. During April and May, flooded streets and highways can make either route unpassable, so check with truckers and bus drivers to find out the road conditions and the better route.

LA PERLA FOREST RESERVE

La Perla Forest Reserve is a 625-acre patch of wet lowland forest that exists only because of the tenacity and feisty personality of Suzanne Sheppard. In 1949, this adventuresome spirit came from West Virginia with her husband to start a new life in the forests of western Ecuador where annual rainfall is between 78 and 120 inches. They started out with bananas and timber and then moved into cattle production. In those days, there was so much forest no one thought of the possibility that some day all of it would be cut down. Suzanne, however, already had a contrary streak in her. She did not like to see the big Ceiba trees cut down nor the colorful toucans and parrots hunted. Suzanne began to take action to preserve the forest habitat on her property. She first stopped removal of trees and vegetation along the streams running through her property. This helped prevent erosion during floods and also connected uncut forest patches to provide corridors that the animals and plant seeds could move through. Then she set aside 625 acres of primary forest in two blocks that would never be cleared for cattle, bananas or African palms. By the 1970s, most of the forest in the entire region was cut down, and Suzanne's protected patches of standing forest became more and more conspicuous. Neighbors and land-hungry colonists began to look enviously at all the uncut forest on her land. Ecuadorian law was unambiguous about this "undeveloped" land. Even if you wanted to preserve habitat, you could not, because uncut forest automatically became available to anyone who wanted to develop (cut down) the forest. The local government seized this forested part of her land and divided it among six colonists. Only through her energy, considerable time and personal finances was she able to fight this seizure in the courts and win. She worked with national parks (INEFAN) and Fundación Natura to have the forest declared an official protected forest (*bosque protectora*). Along with this fight to save the forest, she took on a long-term commitment to environmental education of the local youth. Much of her time now is spent leading tours of the forest for local school groups and presenting workshops on the biology of this last remnant of forest to local politicians and neighbors.

Although the Long-wattled Umbrellabirds, Jaguars, monkeys and macaws that were so common here when she arrived are now long gone, this forest is still home to many species of plants, insects and birds that are difficult or impossible to see anywhere else in the Santo Domingo area. The Rufous-headed Chachalaca and Purple-throated Fruit-crow are common, and a few Ocelots still roam the area. Immense Ceiba trees with buttress roots extending 50 feet (15 meters) from the trunk can be found in this forest. The beautiful and clear streams that flow through the forest give you an idea of what this area looked like when Suzanne first saw it some 50 years ago.

To plan a visit to La Perla Forest Reserve, first contact Suzanne Sheppard, Lucia Whitney or Inés de León by telephone (2-725-344 or 2-759-115) or write to Suzanne Sheppard, Bosque Protectora La Perla, Casilla 17-24-128, Santo Domingo de los Colorados, Ecuador, for a reservation. The entrance fee is $5 per person and includes the guide's services. Most of the guides only speak Spanish, but a few English-speaking guides are available, so make your needs known when you call or write for a reservation to visit La Perla. No groups larger than ten are allowed, and some very rustic cabins are available for those who want to camp out at the edge of the forest. All food, supplies and equipment must be supplied by the visitors.

GETTING THERE: Drive 41 kilometers north of Santo Domingo on the Quinindé–Esmeraldas Highway. At Km. 41 is a small driveway and entrance to Suzanne's home. Here she will meet you at a prearranged time, and a guide will accompany you to the forest entrance driveway another kilometer farther north (a large white sign indicates the entrance to the reserve at Km. 42). You can park your car in the grassy clearing at the thatched-roof assembly hall used for school classes, or you can drive on another 3 kilometers with your guide to a river cross-ing. Here you can follow various trails that can take one to three hours depending on your enthusiasm and interest.

BILSA BIOLOGICAL RESERVE AND MACHE–CHINDUL ECOLOGICAL RESERVE

The 8000-acre ✪✪✪ **Bilsa Biological Reserve and Station** is a center for field research, education, ecotourism and community service that was founded in 1994 by the Jatún Sacha Foundation. The reserve was created in memory of Al Gentry and Ted Parker who, along with Eduardo Aspiazu, the Ecuador-ian president of Fundacion Natura-Guayaquil, were killed in a 1993 airplane crash while surveying threatened forest areas of coastal Ecuador for Conser-vation International.

Located in the Mache Mountains, this area rises to 2640 feet (800 meters) and captures much of the moisture from the winds coming off the Pacific Ocean. Less than 1 percent of western Ecuador's tropical wet forest remains, and Bilsa's reserve is connected to much of what is left. This area is very remote, but this very isolation is the reason it still exists in pristine condition.

Large mammals such as Jaguar, Puma, Mantled Howler Monkey, White-throated Capuchin Monkey, Red-brocket Deer, Giant Anteater and Collared Peccary are still common. This forest harbors one of the last populations of the huge White-lipped Peccary on the entire coast of Ecuador. It is one of only three or four places in Ecuador where the grotesque Long-wattled Umbrella-bird be seen regularly, and Bilsa is the only place in Ecuador that the large turkey-like bird known as the Great Curassow apparently still exists. Until recently, only 12 individuals of the Río Palenque Mahogany Tree were thought to survive in the world. Now we know they are fairly common at Bilsa. Ex-citing studies of discovery are bound to reveal many more biological trea-sures unique to this last stand of virgin forest in coastal Ecuador.

This reserve and its future depend on many factors, not the least of which is purchasing additional land. If the plans for this reserve are fulfilled, it will be by far the largest stand of pristine wet forest protected in entire coastal Ecuador. If enough additional land can be purchased, it may be sufficiently large to be a self-sustaining ecosystem and not just another remnant forest island doomed to supporting small populations of plants and animals always verging on the brink of local extinction. The plans and future of this reserve are so exciting in the midst of so much pessimism, you might even consider supporting this effort financially, even if you will not have a chance to visit the reserve personally.

In 1997, in cooperation with scientists from Jatún Sacha and Bilsa, the government declared nearly 175,000 acres north and south of the Bilsa Reserve as the **Mache–Chindul Ecological Reserve**. This declaration will make it much more difficult for logging companies to operate unchecked in the region and will provide a legal basis for controlling colonization of this immense area that now buffers the private Bilsa Reserve. Be aware, however, that the logging companies have made serious threats against the Bilsa Reserve, and one serious assault by armed intruders was made on the researchers at the reserve complex in December of 1998. Although these intruders were never captured or identified, strong suspicions point to the logging companies as the instigators of this robbery and rape.

Before entering the reserve, you need to notify reserve personnel by radio through the Jatún Sacha Foundation office in Quito. Reservations to stay at Bilsa must also be made in advance through the Quito office (2-451-626). The cost for staying here is $20 per person, per day and includes all meals.

The cement-block building has ten private rooms on the second floor, with shared showers. A large kitchen and dining area occupy the ground floor. Toilets are outhouses. The station provides bunk beds, mattresses, sheets, pillows, blankets and mosquito netting. There is some solar-powered lighting, but candles and flashlights are needed at night. You will need to bring your own towels. Although ecotourists are welcome at all times, the staff and volunteers are so busy with reforestation projects and environmental education classes in local villages that unannounced visitors cannot be accommodated. You must arrange with the Quito office well in advance of your arrival. They will provide you with detailed directions (Jatún Sacha Foundation, 2-451-626, fax: 2-250-976; e-mail: jatunsacha@ecuadorexplorer.com). Visitors to Bilsa need to be not only independent but in relatively good physical condition. During the rainy season (January–May), much of the last part of the road is impassable except by foot. Mules can be arranged to carry baggage, but the paths through the forest are steep and muddy year-round.

GETTING THERE: By Bus: From Quinindé there is public transportation from the "cinqo esquinas" gasoline station to Herrera and during the dry season on to the cabins at Bilsa. During the wet season (January–May), the road from Herrera to Bilsa is a moderately difficult five-to-six hour hike.

By Car: Bilsa is accessible by car during the dry season from June to December. An ordinary car can make the trip at this time, but a four-wheel-drive vehicle is recommended. From Quinindé (on the main highway between Santo Domingo and Esmeraldas), drive 10 kilometers north and then turn left (west). Go 15 kilometers to Herrera and from there another 20 kilometers to the Bilsa station.

Leaf cutter ant

TINALANDIA

With very little exaggeration ✪✪ **Tinalandia** (Casilla 8, Santo Domingo de los Colorados, Ecuador in Quito, Urb. El Bosque, 2da Etapa, Avenida del Parque, Calle 3era, Lote 98; private bath, hot water; $35 per person; 2-449-028, fax: 2-442-638) can lay claim to being the oldest ecotourist facility in mainland Ecuador. In 1935, when it was a hacienda at the end of a long mule ride from the small pueblo of Santo Domingo, visitors were welcomed. Here they could relax, enjoy the cool breezes and escape the heat of the coastal plain. Tina Garzón, an emigree escaped from the Russian revolution, and her first husband began to change the emphasis of the hacienda from cattle to tourists. A nine-hole golf course carved out of the forest gave the hacienda a reputation unique for Ecuador and attracted even more tourists. Both because of Tina's interest in nature and an increasing number of naturalist-type tourists attracted to this area, Tinalandia evolved into a site emphasizing nature both physically and philosophically. Already by the late 1960s and early 1970s, access by highway from Quito made Tinalandia a must for birdwatchers, butterfly enthusiasts and nature lovers on tour in Ecuador.

In 1996, Tina died. Her son, Sergio Platonoff, no doubt influenced both by his mother and a lifetime spent breaking bread with nature-loving tourists and scientists every night, decided to resign his rank as captain in the Ecuadorian Army and take over the management of Tinalandia. Better facilities, more efficient services, improved collaboration with scientists, support for Ecuadorian biology students doing research and a more sophisticated environmental education program for all tourists visiting Tinalandia are now realized goals.

Tinalandia has 250 acres of forest at 1320–1980 feet (400–600 meters) elevation. A large part of this area is taken up by a nine-hole golf course, but the rest is preserved as native forest, which is only disturbed by 5 kilometers of paths. Adjacent to Tinalandia, a neighbor owns an additional 750 acres of relatively undisturbed forest called Tanti. Sergio and his neighbor are making plans to have their properties protected together as a unit. The burgeoning population of Santo Domingo, only 15 kilometers away, and the desire of many farmers to find new land for agriculture has turned virtually all of the surrounding mountainsides, as well as the flatter lowlands, into a treeless habitat. Tinalandia is another one of the proverbial islands of forest left in western Ecuador.

While it seems illogical, one of the best places to view wildlife, especially birds, is along the edge of the golf course. The isolated trees and shrubby borders are favorite spots for birds, and the openness of the habitat makes finding and seeing the birds quite easy.

The cabins and rooms reflect several decades of building styles and architecture, but all have 24-hour electricity supplied by a private hydroelectric generator. The restaurant serves plentiful, wholesome food family-style around large tables. Box lunches are available if requested the day before. Day use for those not wishing to stay overnight costs $10 per person.

There are 16 rooms in total, some in individual cabins, others in duplexes or in buildings with two floors. A maximum of 35 tourists can be accommodated at a time. The dining room is in the same building as reception near the entrance to Tinalandia. Some of the cabins are down at the base of the hill with the dining room and administration. The rest are up at the top of the hill. The road to the hilltop accommodations is almost a kilometer long and fairly steep. At one point on this road, you pass under the "automatic car wash." This is the sluice from the stream that passes over the road on its way to power the generator. Often extra water spills over onto the road, so make sure your windows are up when you pass under it. Plan your trips into the forest and its paths to take into account the extra time to walk down to the dining room for meals. Sergio is now planning a new dining room up above to avoid this inconvenience. Also, at the top of the hill is a large conference hall and bar near the first hole of the golf course. This hall is set up to accommodate classes or for large tour groups to assemble. On rainy days, it is often a place that many guests gravitate to just to read and look out the windows at the passing clouds.

Another plan that Sergio recently initiated was the conversion of several of the older cabins down at the bottom of the hill into dormitory-style accommodations for national and international students. Students wanting to do research at Tinalandia can stay here at very little cost ($25 per day). They have their own kitchen facilities and laboratory study area so they can be relatively independent of the tourist facilities. These students do, however, interact with the tourists and serve as guides from time to time. Guides who speak English, French or German are available at an extra cost and by prearrangement. They can show you around the grounds of Tinalandia as well as lead you on interesting day trips to other sites.

Tinalandia can also be used as a base for daily excursions to Palenque Research Center, La Perla Forest Reserve, Río Guajalito Forest Reserve and the lower part of the Old Road to Santo Domingo (see Chapter Six). If you only have a short time and can make one short trip away from Tinalandia, you should go up the road 15 kilometers to the junction with the Old Road to Santo Domingo (where the large metal sign indicates the Petroecuador oil duct passes). Turn north (left if you are headed toward Quito), and go about a hundred yards down this gravel road to a narrow concrete bridge. The bridge spans a rushing river squeezed at this point into a narrow channel between two cliffs. Look carefully on the rocks and in the vegetation on the canyon (west) side of the bridge for Cocks-of-the-Rock. The males are flame red with black and gray wings. The females and immatures are rusty colored. Early

morning and late afternoon are the best times to see these large and magnificent subtropical birds, as this is when the males assemble to attract the
notice of females. This bridge is also a good place to see sleek Torrent Ducks
swimming up impossible rapids and dumpy White-capped Dippers building
their nests under the bridge or along the moss-covered vertical cliff edges
next to the water. Be very careful standing on this bridge. There are no guard-
rails, and vehicles can come along to cross it with little warning. The long
fall into this rushing river would be an inadvisable way to get closer to the
Torrent Ducks and White-capped Dippers. For a better look at these white-
water birds or just for the thrill of descending a wild river, rafting can be
organized by prearrangement with Tinalandia.

GETTING THERE: By Bus: Buses between Santo Domingo and Quito run almost every half-hour day and night. Ask to be dropped off at Tinalandia. All the
drivers know where it is. Buses will also stop to pick you up at the side of the
highway in front of the driveway.

By Car: Tinalandia is on the main highway between Santo Domingo and
Quito. The trip takes about two and a half to three hours without stops. Arrangements can be made for the Tinalandia vehicle and a driver to meet you at the airport in Quito upon your arrival or pick you up at your Quito hotel. Coming from
Quito in your own car, 15 kilometers before Tinalandia a large metal sign on the
right indicates the oil duct from the Oriente, which along with the old road re-
joins this new road to Santo Domingo at this point. A few kilometers farther are
the towns of Tandapi and Alluriquín. This latter town will be obvious because of all
the people standing in doorways along the main highway pulling ten-pound strands
of taffy, locally called *melcocha*, attached to giant hooks on the door frame. The
pure sugar is brown when it is first prepared in sticky masses. The pulling action
turns it lighter in color. The whitish taffy is then broken off into thin sections,
rolled into colorful paper wrapping, and sold in bunches of ten to twenty.

Less than a kilometer before the Tinalandia driveway stands a large stone obe-
lisk and sign on the right with the name Tinalandia. The driveway goes off as the
left arm of a "Y" to the main highway. If you are coming from Santo Domingo 15
kilometers to the west, the acute angle of this driveway is very hard to take without turning wide into the left lane of the highway. Be very careful of oncoming
traffic. Trucks and buses barrel through here at 80 km per hour and are hard to see
coming over the hill at the entrance to the driveway. Head up the Tinalandia driveway to the first building and park. (This is the administration and dining area).

RÍO PALENQUE SCIENCE CENTER

Due to a long-term scientific presence, ✪✪ **The Río Palenque Science
Center** (Calaway Dodson, Centro Cientifico Río Palenque, Casilla 95, Santo
Domingo; both private and shared baths, cold water; in Quito: 2-561-646), a

remnant of 250 acres of primary lowland forest, is one of the best-known sites in western Ecuador. Located less than an hour south of Santo Domingo on the banks of the Río Palenque, the soils here have been deposited by the flooding rivers and are very rich. As a result, the pressure to cut the original wet forest for agricultural use was overwhelming, and the center and its forest reserve are now completely surrounded by palm, cacao, banana, soy and corn fields.

The **station house** and facilities are 1.5 kilometers in from the entrance. The station is a two-story concrete block building, and overnight visitors use the second floor. A caretaker and his family live on the ground floor. Six rooms with bunk beds are available for visitors, but scientists have first priority on this space. Private baths are attached to two of the rooms, while the rest share bathrooms. The showers are cold water, and electricity is usually available throughout the day. A large kitchen can be used to cook food. By prior arrangement, the caretaker's wife can do the cooking as well as purchase the food. A separate dining and lounge area is simple but adequate. Prices for staying here depend on the services required, but they range from $20 to $50 per person, per night.

The field station here was established in 1970 as a part of the University of Miami in Florida, and then eventually taken over under private deed by the well-known botanist and orchid specialist Calaway Dodson. In 1978, he and Al Gentry published a book called *Flora of the Río Palenque Science Center*, in which they detailed and illustrated 1112 species of plants from the site. Since that time, many additional plant species have been described from the forest, and an herbarium at the station has a collection with a representative specimen of each species.

Ornithologists, herpetologists, mammalogists and entomologists have also spent considerable time documenting the animal species found on the reserve. More than 360 species of birds and 350 species of butterflies have been recorded, many of which represent the only remaining small populations in Ecuador of species that formerly occurred throughout the coastal lowland forests. Published lists of these species are available at the center. The trail and road system make observations relatively easy within the forest, but do not expect to see large birds like macaws or mammals such as peccaries, as they were wiped out years ago.

GETTING THERE: By Bus: Buses between Santo Domingo and Quevedo or Guayaquil will drop you off or pick you up on the highway at the entrance to the center. Not all drivers know of this site, however, so check the kilometer signs to know where to tell the driver to stop.

By Car: To reach the Río Palenque Science Center from Santo Domingo, drive south on the road toward Quevedo 47 kilometers. The station entrance is on the left

(east) side of the road at Km. 48 and 2 kilometers south of the small town of Patricia Pilar. Look for a white sign with green lettering: *Centro Científico Río Palenque*. From Quevedo, the center is 56 kilometers north. Stop at the chain across the
entrance and pay the $5 fee to the person who will come out of the nearby house.
A map is available, and it indicates the roads, trails and station location within the
reserve.

QUEVEDO

Some 180 kilometers inland to the north of Guayaquil, Quevedo is a busy
commercial city of over 100,000 inhabitants. Few tourists are likely to visit
Quevedo except as a convenient stopover on a drive between Quito (two to
three hours) and Guayaquil (three hours) or Latacunga (three hours) and the
coast. Natural areas are few and far between, and densely farmed land extends
in all directions for many kilometers, a testimony to the rich floodplain soil
deposited by the many small rivers of the area. The Rio Palenque Science
Center is only 55 kilometers north, and several patches of wet montane forest still exist along the lower stretches of the highway east to Latacunga.

LODGING   The **Hotel Olimpico** (Ciudadela San José; private bath, hot
water, air conditioning, phone, TV, minibar; $35–$45; 5-750-539, 5-750-455,
fax: 5-751-314) is without a doubt the best place to stay in the city. Located
on the northeastern end of town, it was initially begun in 1975 as a sports
complex, and the hotel was then added on. The Olympic-size pool is gigantic, with waterslides, 3-meter diving platform and lanes for swimming laps.
The public is allowed in through another entrance, but guests of the hotel
have free access at all times. Basketball, volleyball, squash and handball
courts are also available.

From Tuesday to Friday, the 50 rooms are often filled with businessmen,
so reservations are a good idea. The rooms cover three floors and are large
and very clean. The wide hallways are open at the ends to the outside and are
at least 13 feet high, very welcome after so many close calls in other hotels
with low-clearance hallways and doorways. Six of the rooms have their own
saunas. The restaurant is the best in town, and also the most expensive ($3–
$7). The menu is varied but tends toward international cuisine. The food is
inconsistent in quality, with some dishes delicious and others marginal. The
service is good. A small casino is open Thursday to Sunday from 9 p.m., and
a disco that easily rivals the best in Quito and Guayaquil is also open Thursday to Saturday from 9 p.m. on. Bring your ear plugs if you go inside, but fortunately these vibrations do not reach the rooms.

As an alternative, the **Hotel Ejecutivo Internacional** (Cuarta 214 and 7
de Octubre; private bath, hot water, air conditioning, TV; $10–$15; 5-751-780,
5-751-781, fax: 5-750-596) is the next best hotel in town. Located in the city

center, it has its own bus line and terminal on the ground floor. Express buses go to Guayaquil hourly. The 32 rooms are smallish but clean. A small but efficient bus terminal–type restaurant is attached to the hotel. The food is simple but inexpensive with sandwiches and chicken with rice dishes emphasized. Many *chifas* (Chinese restaurants) are also in the city center close to the Hotel Ejecutivo Internacional.

GETTING THERE: Quevedo has no *terminal terrestre*, but it is served by bus lines to Guayaquil, Quito, Latacunga and Portoviejo out of individual offices throughout the city center. Quevedo has no scheduled airline service.

By Car: From Quito, Quevedo is best approached via Santo Domingo. Take the Quevedo bypass and continue south 106 kilometers on the major highway. From Latacunga (173 kilometers), much of the mountain highway is unpaved and fairly slow, but there is also less traffic. From Guayaquil (145 kilometers), the major highway is Vía Babahoyo and is well-maintained except during floods (March–May).

SECTION III

The Oriente (Amazon Lowlands)

Epithet after epithet was found too weak to convey to those who have not visited the intertropical regions, the sensation of delight which the mind experiences.

Charles Darwin

From exotic vegetation to rare and unusual birds and mammals—the Amazon region of eastern Ecuador (the "Oriente") is part of the most biologically rich area in the world. A great part of understanding Amazonia is recognizing its incredible biological diversity and how it came about. The best explanation comes from a combination of geological and biological studies. These studies showed that 10,000-year alternating cycles of drought and heavy rainfall changed large parts of this immense forest into savanna grassland and back to forest over and over again. This cycle of change and alternating upheaval in global climate helped fill this part of the world with more species than almost anywhere else on Earth.

Rainfall across the Amazon Basin is not, and probably never has been, uniform. Today, small pockets of forest with 120 to 160 inches of annual rainfall may be surrounded by forest receiving less than 60 inches of annual rainfall. During the most severe droughts, annual rainfall totals were probably cut by a third or more, and only the high-rainfall forest pockets were able to maintain themselves against the natural wildfires that changed the drier forest areas to grasslands and savanna. The patches of cool and moist forest in a great sea of open grasslands became islands of refuge for the plants and animals adapted to forests. Isolated for tens of thousands of years, many of these plants and animals changed (evolved) into different species and no longer were capable of breeding with members of their former species in other forest refuges. When the drought cycle shifted back to high rainfall, the plants in the forest islands began to expand out and reclaim the grassland habitat. Eventually the expansion of these forests brought them into contact with each other again. At the zones of contact where the forests met again, the vegetation once more formed a continuous forest habitat. The animal and plant species that formed during the period of isolation could now spread and mix into a newly connected forest, thus greatly enriching the diversity of species. As there were from 5 to 20 of these long-term cycles, we can begin to understand how so many species could come to live together here.

Scientists have been able to discern 15 to 20 Amazonian forest refuges that were formed at various times throughout the Pliocene and Pleistocene geological periods. The most persistent and largest forest island over and over was the area covering most of present-day eastern Ecuador—the Napo Refuge. As you walk along a forest path or canoe downriver toward your lodge in the Oriente, consider that the forest around you is unlike virtually any other part of Amazonia. It has been intact for hundreds of thousands of years and has served as a species factory to supply or resupply much of the rest of the present day forests of the Amazon Basin. If it has been a factory for species in the past, the likelihood is great that it also will be one in the future. Preserving national parks and reserves in the Oriente of Ecuador then takes on a much greater significance. These forests are likely the greatest center of evolution in all of South America, which makes them special indeed.

Cultural diversity, although it has a much shorter history, is another important part of understanding the Oriente. Less than 5000 years ago, human beings first made their way down from the Andes into the almost endless forests of the Amazon. In their exploration and settlement of these unfamiliar habitats, the earliest Amazonian people domesticated native forest plants such as manioc, sweet potatoes, peanuts and acari. All these food plants were easy to grow and simple to transport from place to place. (Strangely, no native animal species from the Amazon were domesticated.) Because of the poor soil, gardens had to be abandoned after only two or three years and new clearings made. This primitive agricultural system is called swidden or slash-and-burn. A swidden system of growing food led to a nomadic culture, and made difficult the establishment of large towns and cities except along major rivers.

Unfortunately, there is paltry evidence available to help archaeologists deduce the timing of colonization and the details of this early culture. The warm, humid conditions of the Amazon forests ensure that organic material will quickly rot and disintegrate. This natural destruction of skins, wooden tools and structures constructed with plant fibers, together with fast-growing foliage, quickly and permanently erased most traces of early settlers' villages and fields. Ceramic pottery has proven to be the most available evidence of these early cultures. Based primarily on pottery shards, at least 16 cultural phases have been described for the Ecuadorian Amazon. Later periods of development show influences from both the coast of Ecuador and areas of present-day Brazilian and Peruvian Amazonia. The most spectacular patterns on pottery, however, are from the Napo Period (around 1100 A.D.). Large burial urns, square bowls, jars and plates were covered with red, white and black paint, a design and technique common at that time throughout the Amazon. All of the evidence points to a well-established and sophisticated trading and transport system for the region.

The subsequent invasions of Ecuadorian Amazonia, first by the Incas and then the Spanish, drove many indigenous peoples deep into the forest far from the lands of their ancestors. These native cultures became fragmented as they sought more and more isolated areas, and this New World diaspora made the unwritten history of the Amazon peoples even more ambiguous. The Incas unsuccessfully tried several times to subjugate the people of the Amazon forests. The Spanish, however, in their almost maniacal quest for El Dorado and its legendary gold and treasure, were ruthlessly successful. In 1539, Francisco de Orellana and a small band of Spanish soldiers set out from Guayaquil to find gold in the Amazon. Hacking their way through vegetation and native people alike, they carved a bloody trail from Quito to the present-day city of Coca (otherwise known as Puerto Francisco de Orellana). Frustrated by their failure to find the fabled city of gold and too proud to return to Quito, Orellana and his men constructed rafts and drifted down the Río Napo and then through what are now Perú and Brazil down to the mouth of the Río Amazonas (Amazon River), which they reached in 1541—the first Europeans to travel from the Pacific to the Atlantic across Amazonian South America. Orellana did not keep an accurate written record of his trip. However, from the fragmentary reports published, he and his men encountered native people living by the thousands along the large rivers. By some estimates there may have been millions of inhabitants along these rivers. The next Europeans to travel down the Amazon, less than a decade later, found few people living there—likely because most had been wiped out by European diseases spread by Orellana and his men to the native people, who had absolutely no built-up resistance or natural immunity. The Spanish went on to establish a series of cities in the region, including Zamora in 1550, Baeza in 1559, Archidona in 1560 and Macas in 1600.

After thousands of years of cultural evolution, entire peoples and tribes were wiped out within a generation of the Spanish conquest—many leaving little or no record of their ever having existed. The Arda, Bolona, Bracamoro, Chirino, and Tetete are all cultures that once thrived in the Amazonian forest of what is now Ecuador. They no longer exist, and with them disappeared their myths, oral traditions and customs. The Zaparo at one time lived through-out the present-day province of Pastaza in southeastern Ecuador. They now number fewer than 20 individuals on a remote river near the Peruvian bor-der. In northeastern Ecuador, the Cofans can count fewer than 500 members, and the Siona/Secoya only 400 members. In central and eastern parts of Ecuador, the warrior-tribe of the Huaorani (the pejorative name Auca is no longer used) has about 1800 members. Only the politically savvy Amazonian Quichua (60,000 members) and the Shuar/Achuar (the pejorative name Jivaro is no longer used) Federation (45,000 members) have so far successfully sur-vived the dominant culture of Ecuador.

In a little less than 400 years, more than 80 percent of the Amazon tribes have been exterminated or reduced to such small numbers that their future remains doubtful. The discovery of oil in the Oriente in the 1960s, however, has had more impact on this region than all the previous effects of Europeans combined. The remaining indigenous peoples as well as the biological diver-sity of the region are under more severe pressure now than at any time in 5000 years, and the survival of neither is certain.

At the same time, the popularity and the mystique of the rainforest is growing rapidly throughout the world. Consequently, the business of show-ing people the "jungle" is expanding at a brisk pace. Realizing there is money to be made in ecotourism, countless companies have sprung up offering every-thing from day trips to week-long tours to the rainforest. Many companies have built lodges either in or near the forest to better serve visitors. But, buyer beware! There are many pitfalls into which naive tourists will fall on their way to a "jungle adventure."

The rainforest is not a uniform environment, and it is probably not what you imagine it to be. The Disneyesque version with exotic birds adorning every tree, bizarre insects under every leaf and Jaguars and panthers around every corner does not exist. This fact, however, has not stopped this imagi-nary portrayal of the rainforest from being advertised. When you do visit the rainforest, expect to experience a chaos of greenery, to hear exotic "jungle" sounds, to see beautiful butterflies and to catch glimpses of unusual animals. If you want to see more than just the surface, you will have to spend time in the rainforest looking. If a brochure promises everything in one trip, and it seems too good to be true—it is.

You should also know that the rainforest varies dramatically in quality. Most of the forest that is easily accessible has been more or less altered by humans. Even seemingly minor disturbances such as a new road or a cul-tivated field nearby leaves the once pristine forest less so. The big showy animals—howler monkeys, Jaguars, Harpy Eagles, macaws, curassows—are the first to leave when the forest is disturbed. If you want to see truly pristine primary rainforest, you have to travel well into the Oriente and find the most out-of-the-way places and lodges. Your effort and travel costs will increase but, hopefully, so will the quality of your experience.

Of course, every agency after the jungle dollar will say that they have the best trips to the most beautiful rainforest. Walk down the Avenida Amazonas in Quito, and you will be bombarded with fantastically appealing placards and banners advertising vividly the wonderful experiences awaiting you when you sign up inside. All the proper catch words will be included to describe the forest—primary, undisturbed, virgin—and many of the ads will have beautiful photos of the animals you will probably never see. If you want just a taste of the "jungle," most of these trips will be adequate. If you really want to experience the rainforest, take a longer trip to one of the more remote lodges, and select one with an attractive education program. La Selva, Yuturi and Sacha Lodge on the lower Río Napo, the Flotel and Iriparí sites on the Río Aguarico, and Kapawi on the lower Río Pastaza are probably the best places to be assured of wild experiences without too much suffering. Whatever your tastes, an entire range of opportunities await. You can stay in comfort and European elegance, or you can rough it with sleeping bags and cold showers. Whatever your needs, almost any trip to the world's richest environment will be worth it.

There are five primary jumping-off spots for almost all of the destinations in the Amazonian rainforest of Ecuador—Lago Agrio on the Río Aguarico and Coca on the lower Río Napo (see Chapter Fourteen), Misahuallí on the upper Río Napo and Shell-Mera or Macas for flights to extreme southeastern Ecuador (see Chapter Fifteen). Misahuallí is the closest to Quito and Cuenca and is easily accessible by bus through Tena (six–seven hours from Quito, seven–eight hours from Cuenca) or is an easy day's drive with stops for exploring. Lago Agrio, Coca and Shell-Mera are also served by bus from Quito and Cuenca (expect to take all day). Driving is also possible, but the time, discomfort and logistical difficulties make such a trip feasible only for the more adventuresome and durable. By far the easiest way to get to Macas, Lago Agrio and Coca is to fly. All three towns have regular commercial air connections to Quito. Typically, if you sign up with an agency in Quito or Cuenca they will make all the arrangements for you to get to the lodge.

FOURTEEN

Northern Oriente (Amazon)

Come to Ecuador's Oriente and you'll find one of the most vibrant and complex forests in the world. It is a region that fills you with the promise of adventure. Every river around you winds its way to the Amazon River in Brazil and eventually to the Atlantic Ocean, 3000 kilometers to the east. A path through the open undergrowth is shaded by a canopy that is only occasionally interrupted where a giant tree was blown over by a past storm. The canopy itself is so hard to study that most of its secrets have never been discovered by any human. For many visitors, this part of Ecuador cannot be matched for excitement and wonder. However, oil now dominates this region, and you will see its influence everywhere you turn. Paradoxically, mainly because of the oil, this is the most accessible part of the Amazonia forest in Ecuador. Airports, roads and towns have sprung up to support oil exploration and extraction, and even as you berate the destruction oil has brought to this area, you will fly in comfort from Quito to concrete landing fields convenient to the lodges you want to visit. These all-weather facilities are available to tourists largely because of the oil money that was used to chop the jungle down to build them. When you complain how hard it is to get to the forests near the Colombian and Peruvian borders that are still pristine, know that it is largely because oil companies have not yet built facilities there. As you explore this fantastic region, try to keep all these conflicting interests in mind. But most of all, be prepared for one of the most overwhelming sensory experiences of your lifetime.

CAYAMBE–COCA ECOLOGICAL RESERVE
This reserve was established in 1970 and its size (995,664 acres) is so immense it covers parts of four provinces and includes altitudes from 2640 feet

(800 meters) to almost 19,800 feet (6000 meters). The higher altitude parts of Cayambe–Coca Ecological Reserve range from paramo vegetation to alpine. Our two favorite mountains within the reserve for mountaineering and rock climbing are Puntas (14,850 feet/4500 meters) and Cayambe (18,810 feet/5700 meters). Over 80 alpine and paramo lakes lie throughout the northern part of the reserve, many of which are seldom visited and have huge Rainbow Trout. This area is perhaps the second-best place after Volcán Antisana to look for the dwindling population of Andean Condors. At last estimate, only about 100 individuals remain in all of Ecuador.

The lower altitudes of the reserve along the Baeza–Lago Agrio road are under considerable pressure by colonists, but even along this busy road there are large patches of montane and cloud forest. The reserve boundary is several kilometers from this road, and a guide is needed to find many of the trails.

No shelters or cabins are available, so backpacking and camping are your only option if you want to spend several days in the reserve. You are unlikely to see any other tourists here and even few Ecuadorians. It is a very wild and underutilized reserve.

GETTING THERE: The higher reaches of Cayambe–Coca Reserve are only accessible by vehicle north of Quito via the towns of Cayambe and Olmedo. The main road from Quito to Baeza parallels the southern boundary of the reserve, and hiking trails go into the reserve from Papallacata. On the eastern boundary, several trails enter the lower altitude forests of the reserve from the town of El Chaco and the San Rafael Falls area.

BAEZA

On the northern highway crossing the Andes to the Amazon, Baeza is the first major population center you come to after Papallacta (see Chapter Six for more details on Papallacta and the higher altitude sections of this highway). From Quito through the Pifo Valley and to Papallacta (61 kilometers) the highway is now paved and broad, but the last 38 kilometers from Papallacta to Baeza are gravel and winding. Many parts are so narrow that a car cannot pass a bus or truck unless a small pullout is found. In Ecuador there are only four major highways descending from the highlands to the Oriente. Because this one parallels the oil pipeline and is a direct connection between Quito and the oil fields around Lago Agrio and Coca, it is the busiest of all four highways. Any time of day or night you can expect to meet or be passed by semi-trailers and extra-long trucks. If you stop anywhere along this highway, be sure to pull way off the road.

This road was finished in 1972 as a way to access the pipeline, and much of the natural habitat along it is now cut down and colonized. Even in the remnant patches of forest, however, iridescent-green and bright-red quetzals call, and large tanager flocks move through trees in the middle of cow pastures. However, during the dry season (January–March), this road is very dusty, and wildlife viewing becomes more difficult. The billowing dust makes it harder to see and also keeps the flocks of birds away from the roadside. If you want to see birds and other wildlife at this time of year, you will have to find a track or trail that leads away from the dust into a forest patch.

Below Papallacta, locals still claim to see Mountain Tapirs occasionally crossing the highway at night. The southwestern boundary of the Cayambe–Coca Ecological Reserve runs parallel to the north side of the highway, but only after the Baeza–Lago Agrio intersection does the road run close to the boundary. On many parts of the road you can look across the raging mountain river to see uncut portions of the original forest that are too steep to farm or log. Check the large rocks in the river for Torrent Ducks sunning themselves. They are still fairly common away from farmhouses and villages. The whitish male and the rusty female are only found in fast-flowing mountain streams where they swim under water to find crustaceans, insects and fish.

At the "Y" in the road that either goes south to Baeza and Tena (see Chapter Fifteen) or north and east to Lago Agrio is the only gas station in the Baeza area. It also has a marginal hotel, **Oro Negro**, and a restaurant. If you are driving your own vehicle, it is a good idea to fill up here, especially if you are going south toward Tena. The Cosanga gas station has reopened. Otherwise, between Baeza and Archidona (65 kilometers), only emergency gas is available at a few houses along the highway. The price of this gasoline is very high and is unlikely to be filtered.

Baeza itself (2 kilometers south of the gas station at the "Y") was founded in the mid-1500s, and the older sections of town still have cobblestone streets. The main part of the town is now centered along the highway running south to Tena. Several grocery stores and bakeries here are handy for stocking up on supplies you might need for the rest of the day. A few moderately clean restaurants are also along this street. Only one hotel is available, the **Hotel Samay** (shared bath; $2–$4), and it is on the west side of this main street. The rooms are simple but clean.

SOUTH OF BAEZA

The road south goes along the west bank of the Río Cosanga, and orchids, birds, waterfalls and great scenery can be found around each bend. The traffic is not so bad here, but it is still a good idea to pull your vehicle completely off the road if you stop.

✪✪ **Cabañas San Isidro Labrador** (private bath, hot water; two days, one night, $60–$80 per person, all meals included; in Quito: Calle Carrión

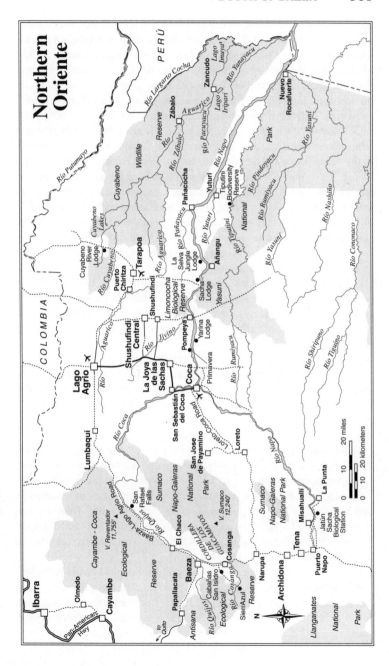

555-C and Juan León Mera, 2-465-578, 2-547-403, fax: 2-228-902) is located 17 kilometers south of Baeza (70 kilometers north of Tena and 120 kilometers southeast of Quito) and 1 kilometer north of the town of Cosanga.

San Isidro is a small but wonderful lodge on what was formerly a typical Ecuadorian dairy farm or "hacienda" situated in the center of the subtropical and cloud forest of the picturesque Quijos Valley. The hacienda's 1000 acres have been worked and maintained in an environmentally conscious way since the early 1970s, but today it is an oasis of ecotourism and reforestation within a setting of pristine forest. Besides the fabulous scenery of the valley below and the access to natural forest habitat, this lodge offers tourists the unique experience of living with an Ecuadorian family. From the moment you arrive, the manager, Carmen Bustamante, and her brothers make you feel like you are visiting their home. Carmen speaks fluent Spanish, English and French. Four separate cabins, each divided into two or four separate rooms as doubles or singles (20–26 beds), are clustered together overlooking the valley. A separate observation cabin serves as a conference center and has large windows to enjoy the view on rainy days. A separate dining area, living room and bar are in the main farmhouse. Each room has a private bath, 24-hour electricity and hot-water showers—a welcome luxury in this often cool and rainy climate. Because all food and supplies must be transported from Quito, advance reservations are mandatory. Prices include taxes, lodging and all meals ($78–$98 per person per night).

At an altitude of 6600 feet (2000 meters), daytime temperatures seldom rise above 68°F. At night the temperatures can fall to 41°F, but snuggled under alpaca blankets in your comfortable bed, sleep couldn't be better. The mean annual rainfall here is over 120 inches, so come prepared to walk in the rain and not see the sun every day. April to September are the rainiest months. The rest of the months are just rainy.

Several trails lead to various areas of interest. Although at first impression it appears that there is nothing but pasture around the cabins, primary forest, wooded streams and other native habitats are within short hiking distance.

In pre-Columbian times the Quijos region was home to a tribe known as the Curisetas. The name means "gold carver" or "goldsmith." This tribe was never conquered by the Incas, and ruins of their activities and habitations are within walking distance of the cabins. Of course, all archaeological artifacts are protected and cannot be removed.

The native plants of the area are typical of subtropical humid forest and well adapted to constant fog, gray skies and rain. The cedar, cinnamon tree and myrtle are common trees in the forest. Because of the constant high humidity, the trees are covered with mosses, orchids, and pineapple-type plants (bromeliads). On the ground between the trees is a thick mat of vegetation made up of ferns, ground bromeliads, orchids and climbing vines. Tall bamboo thickets are common in some of the more poorly drained parts of the forest.

A bird list is available, and its 270 species are likely only half of the actual number of species that will eventually be found in the area. All the animals here, including birds, butterflies and frogs, are adapted to cool rainy days, so just because it's raining doesn't mean there is no wildlife activity. If these animals were active only on sunny days, there would be little to see except for a few days each month. As a matter of fact, on warm, sunny days it can be difficult to see much wildlife. From October to April a small lek of male Cock-of-the-Rocks carry on noisily only a 20-minute walk from the cabins.

Because the hacienda permits no hunting on its land, mammals can sometimes be seen here more readily than in other areas. Large weasels called Tayra are regulars, even in the pastures running between forest patches. Several species of squirrels and a fox are also likely to be seen. The larger mammals like Puma, Mountain Tapir and Spectacled Bear are present, but because they are so shy and in such small numbers, the chances of seeing them are remote. Along the rushing mountain streams, otter occur together with Torrent Ducks, White-capped Dipper (a strange little bird that walks on the bottom of rushing mountain streams), and introduced Rainbow Trout. Fishing is permitted in many of these streams, so let the Bustamantes know if you are interested in trying your luck.

GETTING THERE: Just before you see the town of Cosanga (coming from Baeza) is a gravel road on the right (west) with signs indicating Cabañas San Isidro and SierrAzul. Three kilometers up this side road is a large cleared area of pastures on the left (south) side and a sign and gate leading to the lodge.

✪✪✪ **SierrAzul (Hacienda Aragon)** (both shared and private rooms, shared bath, warm or cold water; $35–$50 per day, per person; in Quito: SierrAzul, Paris 534 and Tomás de Berlanga, 2-254-484, fax: 2-449-464; e-mail: azul1@azul.com.ec) is an experience you will talk about the rest of your life. If you are ready for adventure and are willing to go rustic, you can find SierrAzul farther up the same road as Cabañas San Isidro. More than 20 years ago Bill Philips, a North American construction engineer, purchased 5000 acres of pristine cloud forest and trout streams. At that time Ecuadorian law dictated that any forest land purchased had to be "developed" or the owner lost title to the land. "Developed" meant cutting the forest down to put in some "useful" project. The engineer and his Ecuadorian wife are ardent conservationists, so they decided to cut only the minimum forest to start a small dairy farm. They called it Hacienda Aragon. More recently, Ecuadorian law has been changed so that "developed" can now include any use that brings economic return from the land, including ecotourism. Because the engineer's construction company is called Grupo Azul, he decided to rename the area SierrAzul and change its emphasis to ecotourism and scientific research. Already much of the forest originally cut for pastureland is being allowed to regrow into natural forest. Rustic cabins have been built, all-weather trails cleared, shelters in more remote areas constructed, scientists invited in to survey flora, fauna and soils, and plans laid to make SierrAzul an ecotourist mecca that will preserve one of the largest stands of pristine cloud forest left on the northern flanks of the Ecuadorian Andes.

Indeed, SierrAzul presents a unique combination of adventure, isolation and beauty untouched by human hands. Its land includes forest in elevations from 7260–8580 feet (2200–2600 meters). Annual rainfall is between 80 and 160 inches, and temperatures rarely rise above 75°F and often fall to 37°F. The coldest months are June to September and the wettest are April to August.

Ornithologists estimate that over 300 species of birds make their home in SierrAzul, including the quail-sized Giant Antpitta, which is common here. More than 15 species of mammals have already been found here. This is probably the easiest place in Ecuador to find Mountain Tapir (*Danta*). Tracks are on the forest trails almost every morning. The Puma and Spectacled Bear are also here in relatively good numbers, but because of their timidity, they are seldom seen. Frogs, many unique insects and Rainbow Trout are also present. One of the most eye-popping creatures you're likely to see is the local earthworm. In fact, often one and a half feet long and easily one inch in diameter, it's easy to mistake for a snake. During heavy rains they come out of the soil.

Upon your arrival at the reserve headquarters, Hacienda Aragon, you will be given a brief orientation emphasizing safety, conservation and the natural history of the area. The facilities at SierrAzul are comfortable but rustic. At Aragon, a building for guests has six rooms—some with twin beds and others with two bunk beds. For cold nights, each bed has three alpaca blankets. On the second floor of this building is an open-sided conference or class room. The quaint dining room and bar are on the ground floor. Small generators produce electricity for lights each evening until 9 p.m. The food is simple but good and provided in great quantities. The yogurt made from the hacienda's own cow's milk is so fresh, smooth and delicious, the stuff from the grocery store will never seem the same again. The bathrooms and hot-water showers are in a nearby building. Tents are available for those who prefer camping. Just bring your own sleeping bag, and the rest will be provided. Hacienda Aragon is also one of the few ecotourist sites in rural Ecuador with a small but well-stocked medical clinic. Normally, an Ecuadorian doctor is hired to accompany each tourist group into the hacienda and be available for any medical emergencies that may arise. A two-way radio is also in 24-hour contact with the Grupo Azul office in Quito.

Cabins and shelters have also been constructed at four more-remote sites on the property. Each one (Valle Hermoso, San Fernando, Estero Chico and Cedroyacu) has its own unique vistas, plants and animals to offer. The cabins on these sites are much more rustic, but are comfortable. Meals are also provided at these sites. On your own or with guides you can enjoy the cloud forest more individually. The trails (2–5 kilometers) to these sites have been corded with wood and gravel to make walking easier and to control erosion. If you come prepared with warm clothes and adequate rain gear, it is amazing how comfortable this weather and habitat can become. However, you may want to avoid coming from May to July. These are the rainiest months and when the rivers are most likely to be flooded.

Prices vary. They range from $35 per day, per person for the minimum basics (a mule ride in from the end of the road and back, Ecuadorian workers' food, bunk-bed lodging, central bathroom facilities with flush toilets, hot showers, and independent access to the trails and outlying cabins) up to $195 per day, per person for "luxury rustic" (transportation from and to Quito, special food, beds with orthopedic mattresses, private bilingual guides, etc.). You can design your own trip depending on your budget, the quality of the service desired and the number of people in your party. The money you pay all goes to underwrite operations, improve the reserve, and support Ecuadorian students and scientists who use the area for their studies.

GETTING THERE: If you are coming directly from Quito (three hours nonstop), a good idea is to stay at least the first night at Cabañas San Isidro. To begin the trip to SierrAzul, you must drive 13 kilometers beyond Cabañas San Isidro to the Río Aliso. Here, you cross the river by car and take a new, all-weather road for 5 kilometers. At the Río Cosanga you can choose to hike the final kilometer of corded path or ride in by mule.

Back out on the main highway south to Tena, you quickly come to the small town of **Cosanga**. The town itself has a gas station and a dirty restaurant but little else. A bridge at the south edge of town crosses the Río Cosanga and begins to climb the spectacular Cordillera de los Huacamayos ("Mountain Ridge of the Macaws"). The road south is mostly gravel, but some parts are paved with asphalt. Few people live here, and you pass through thrilling views of uncut forest. As you emerge from the cordillera going south, look off to the east (left). If the clouds clear, you will see a cone-shaped volcano rising out of the surrounding jungle. It is Volcán Sumaco and is 12,240 feet (3732 meters) high. Declared the **Sumaco Napo-Galeras National Park** in

1994, this 506,965-acre area protects lowland forest, cloud forest and paramo habitat. The cloud forest and paramo on its flanks and summit are completely disconnected from other cloud forest and paramo in the nearby Andes. There are few roads or trails into the park, so scientists have had little chance to study the area. As interest increases in exploring the park, both scientists and tourists who are willing to mount expeditions will undoubtedly encounter many new species and sights. The primary entrance into the park is via an often ill-defined trail from the Loreto-Coca Road (near the villages of Guamaní and Sumaco on the southern park boundary). A visit to the summit of Sumaco involves 30 kilometers of difficult and often steep hiking (one-way), and a round-trip excursion takes five to six days.

Twenty-three kilometers south of Cosanga is an intersection with a road going east. A few buildings and a small restaurant constitute the village of **Narupa**. Archidona is 24 kilometers farther south and has the next gas station after Baeza. Tena is another 7 kilometers south of Archidona. The road to the east from Narupa goes 78 kilometers to the small town of Loreto and then another 57 kilometers to Coca (Puerto Francisco de Orellana). This recently constructed **Loreto–Coca Road** is the shortest route to Coca from Quito or Tena. It is even asphalted some of the way and runs through many forest habitats with relatively few settlers. However, little traffic goes this way because there are no gas stations or services for the entire 135 kilometers if you break down. This is asking too much of many Ecuadorian vehicles, so they use the much longer but wider and more populated route from the northeast through Lago Agrio to get to Coca. Bus service is infrequent along this road, so if you are in your own vehicle, expect many people to ask for rides going either west or east.

BAEZA–LAGO AGRIO ROAD

Back at Baeza, if you continue on the north arm of the "Y" intersection near the Oro Negro gas station, you will follow the pipeline that carries the oil flowing from the oil fields of the Oriente all the way to Esmeraldas on the coast of Ecuador. This road follows the Quijos River Valley, and the western part is heavily settled and cut over. The Cayambe–Coca Ecological Reserve runs along the north side of the road, but with all the clearing and houses, it is hard to tell a difference from the other side of the road. Only after you go about 20 kilometers beyond the town of El Chaco does an eerie realization come over you. All of a sudden there are no houses, no cleared fields, no towns and no people. The highway takes strange turns and bridges stand where there is no road. This is because at 11 p.m. on the night of March 5, 1987, a tremendous earthquake hit this part of Ecuador. Great landslides of mud and rock buried countless hundreds of people living along this section of the road. It took over a year to reconstruct the road, and entire villages have yet to be unearthed. The plants have taken over many parts of the displaced mountainsides, but plenty of evidence of the force of this earthquake remains in bare hillsides and immense rocks still exposed.

San Rafael Falls (or **Coca Falls**) is a spectacular waterfall on the Río Quijos 48 kilometers northeast of the town of El Chaco. It is located in a protected forest reserve of 600 acres within the giant Cayambe–Coca Ecological Reserve. The entrance is on the south side of the road and is marked by a small concrete building. There are no signs, though, that mark the entrance road. The concrete block shelter at the entrance road is on a high bluff that rises above the Río Quijos. This bluff is the first uphill part of the road after you have traveled along the river bottom and is just after the road crosses a tributary marked Río Montana. The entrance road curves around and crosses a bridge over a pretty creek. Just after the bridge is a locked chain gate. If there is a group at the falls, the gate will be open. If not, there is a full-time caretaker here who you will have to find to unlock the chain. Fifty yards farther are the old electric company (INECEL) buildings, constructed here in the 1970s but now abandoned. The plan for this region was to build a dam on the Río Quijos for hydroelectric power, but the instability of the land prevented construction. In the late 1980s, the buildings were converted into sleeping and dining facilities for ecotourist groups wishing to visit the falls. Called ✪ **San Rafael Lodge** (shared bath, hot water; two days, three nights, $360 per person; in Quito: Hotel Quito, Avenida Gonzalez Suárez 2500, Casilla 17-01-2201, 2-544-600, 2-544-514, fax: 2-567-284), the cabins are maintained and administered by the Hotel Quito; and the rooms are simple but comfortable. The price for a stay at the San Rafael Lodge includes meals, guide and round-trip transportation from Quito.

These falls are the biggest in Ecuador. An immense volume of water goes over the 430-foot (130-meter) fall year-round. Several trails lead to overlooks or to the base of the falls. The main trail follows an old road that used to lead to the falls overlook before the 1987 earthquake made it impassable to vehicles. The road starts behind the buildings to the left of the parking area and is about a 30-minute walk to the lookouts. Most of the photos you see of the falls make them appear to be quite unimpressive, but don't let this fool you. The falls are breathtaking and well worth the easy walk to see them. The lookouts are at a flat spot along a ridge, which was once the turnaround for vehicles. The cross here is for the former caretaker, who was killed in his sleep by the earthquake when the ground beneath his home fell away. From the lookouts, the steep forests on either side are easily visible, a great spot to look for birds and monkeys. The other trails lead to the falls and the river below, but they are not well marked and are very difficult to follow. Ask for a guide if you want to explore more of the reserve.

The forest here in the morning is full of bird and monkey sounds. There are huge mixed flocks of tanagers, woodpeckers, flycatchers and humming-birds that traverse the treetops, and wrens and other skulkers that hide in the thickets. The star of the bird show is the spectacular Cock-of-the-Rock. Up to 80 brilliantly red and jet-black Cock-of-the-Rock males come together during the early morning and late afternoon to croon to females. The gathered males make quite a racket, so they are easy to find if you are in the vicinity. Look for the mating ground (lek) above the first stream crossing on the main trail to the lookouts over the falls. A male by himself apparently will not attract a female. Only if numerous males are calling together will a female come. It's like a beauty contest with reversed roles because it's the female that picks her mate. The male with the best call, brightest colors and other signals of his gene superiority can be quickly detected by the female when compared directly to the other males in the group. The hotel some-times puts out corn to attract Spectacled Bears, and several groups of tourists have been fortunate enough to see this usually shy creature at close range near the lodge.

The Hotel Quito runs the entire operation so you must plan ahead with them if you wish to stay at the site or use their guides. The Hotel Quito can also help make plans for explorations of nearby Volcán Reventador (11,755 feet/3562 meters elevation), which is still active. This trip involves consid-erable hiking and requires a high level of physical fitness. Rafting on the Río Quijos can also be arranged.

GETTING THERE: By Bus: From Quito, take the Baeza–Lago Agrio bus. Two hours east of Baeza or, if coming from Lago Agrio, half a kilometer west of the bridge crossing the Río Reventador, ask the driver to drop you off at the *Cas-cada San Rafael.*

By Car: It is a five-hour drive from Quito, two hours from Lago Agrio and an hour and a half from the little town of El Chaco.

LAGO AGRIO (NUEVA LOJA)

This oil boomtown of 30,000 people is probably the cleanest and least dis-agreeable of the oil towns in eastern Ecuador, but it is a place in which few tourists will linger. Although it is the capital of the new province of Sucumb-íos, most tourists will only see the airport on the way to one of the Cuya-beno or Aguarico river lodges. If you are driving or arriving by bus from Quito, you may decide to use this town as a place to stay overnight. The roads east and south of this town are confusingly unmarked, so be sure and ask directions for wherever you are headed.

LODGING   The only place we can recommend right in Lago Agrio is the **Hotel El Cofán** (in the town center at Avenida Quito and 12 de Febrero; private bath, ceiling fans, some rooms with air conditioning, TV; $20–$35; 6-830-009). It is located on a busy intersection and noise is unavoidable, especially on weekends. Although we have not visited it, friends have also recommended the **Gran Hostal del Lago**, which is 4 kilometers west of the city on the main highway to Quito.

RESTAURANTS   There are many restaurants in town, but the best one and one of the few we can recommend is in the **Hotel El Cofán** (7 a.m.–10 p.m.; $2–$3).

GETTING THERE: By Air: TAME has a daily flight except Sunday between Quito and Lago Agrio. The airport is located 5 kilometers east of the city, and taxis meet each flight.

By Bus: The ride from Quito takes about ten hours and can be very dusty and tiring. At least five different bus lines run between Quito and Lago Agrio and most go on to Coca and a few to Tena. There is no terrestrial terminal, but most of the bus offices are located in the southeast end of town on the road to the airport.

The **Amazon Jungle Resort Village** (Km. 33 Vía a Chiritza; private bath, hot water, ceiling fans; $75 per person, per day, including three meals; fax in Quito: 2-891-584) is 33 kilometers to the east of Lago Agrio on the road to Chiritza. Remodeled in 1996, this hotel is as elegant and luxurious as you will find anywhere in the northern Oriente. Located on the north bank of the Río Aguarico amid 200 acres of forest, the resort's grounds are immaculate and habitat for many species of birds and Titi Monkeys. An open-sided restaurant serves excellent food and a bar is available. Five oval-shaped cabins each have four double rooms with canopied beds and mosquito netting.

GETTING THERE: By Bus: Small *rancheras* pass often going from Lago Agrio to Chiritza. They will drop you off at the white entrance gates, and you can walk the 700-meter forested road to the reception building. The *ranchera* costs about $1.

By Taxi: A taxi from the Lago Agrio airport to the Amazon Jungle Resort Village costs about $15 one-way. The hotel manager can arrange for a taxi to pick you up to take you on to Chiritza and adventures on the Río Aguarico or back to Lago Agrio.

By Car: Take the main road east out of Lago Agrio toward Dureno. Continue through Dureno, avoiding any turnoffs, and follow the north side of the Río Aguarico. Stay on this road past the turn-off south to Shushufindi and Limoncocha. The white entrance gate will be on your right (south) 2 kilometers beyond the Shushufindi turn-off. Drive the 700 meters of gravel road to a large parking area just before you reach the river. Park here and walk the cobblestone path to the reception building.

CUYABENO WILDLIFE RESERVE

North of the Río Aguarico is a very large and very wild region, which makes up the Cuyabeno Wildlife Reserve. The reserve originally extended from just outside of the town of Lago Agrio southeast to the confluence of the Cuyabeno and Aguarico rivers and encompassed the entire drainage of the Río Cuyabeno. In the early 1980s, the oil exploration boom opened up the region between Lago Agrio and Tarapoa to development and spoiled the region's pristine wilderness. To compensate the indigenous people in the area for lost land, the government changed the borders of the reserve to include all the area around the Río Aguarico down to the Peruvian border and then removed the developed area from the reserve. The reserve went from 635,000 acres to 1,500,000 acres, and is now less accessible and far better protected.

The Cuyabeno Wildlife Reserve today is one of the most wild places in Amazonian Ecuador. About a third of all the birds found in the entire Amazon Basin can be found in the reserve, and botanists have counted over 240 species of trees per hectare. The reserve is comprised of a mixture of *tierra firme* (upland) and inundated (flooded) forests. *Tierra firme* forests are more common in the western part of the reserve and are what you typically think of when you think of rainforests—a dense understory of exotic plants crowned by a very tall canopy of trees with a few extraordinary trees topping the canopy and growing like a tall mushroom above the green forest roof. Inundated forests are typically flooded except during extreme dry periods. Both the understory and the canopy are less dense in an inundated forest, and in far eastern Ecuador the boundary between river-lake-marsh-forest is completely blurred. Here the landscape can best be compared to a flooded savanna with brushy thickets, pockets of forest, grassy rivers and giant, isolated waterbound trees.

The inaccessibility of the landscape, more than anything else, explains why the Cuyabeno Wildlife Reserve has remained wild and pristine. Travel is only practical by boat in most of the region, and even then only small, poled dugout canoes can navigate some areas. Oil exploration and colonization pressure, however, is always present. Development has been kept in check mainly by the very strong and politically active indigenous people and a strong ecotourist presence. The Cuyabeno Wildlife Reserve is a very good example of ecotourist dollars directly influencing government policy. The president of Ecuador visited the reserve in 1993 and vowed never to allow it to be developed.

GETTING THERE: The only practical way to see the reserve is through an organized tour group. There are three main operators that run tours in the area— Nuevo Mundo Expeditions, Paradise Huts and Ecuador Amazon Expeditions, a branch of Metropolitan Touring. Paradise Huts did not provide us with much detailed information. Both Nuevo Mundo and Ecuador Amazon Expeditions fly participants to either Lago Agrio or Tarapoa, bus them to the river and then transport them by comfortable motorized canoe to the lodges. It is about a 50-minute flight to either airport from Quito and then either a 45-minute bus ride from Tarapoa or a 90-minute bus ride to Puerto Chiritza from Lago Agrio. Puerto Chiritza is just a riverside gravel bar with a few rough buildings to provide shade and snacks for river travelers. There are bathrooms there and drinks are provided.

Passengers and guests are accompanied by several tour staff members to make sure the trip is both smooth and informative. This is an important advantage in using one of the large, well-established Ecuadorian tour operators. If something does not go smoothly or there is an emergency, only the large operators have the experience and the financial capability to make it better immediately. We have heard stories of stranded travelers and misplaced emergencies but only in reference to the small and/or haphazard operators. Using a first-rate tour operator means your trip will probably be a bit more expensive, but consider it insurance toward a successful and more enjoyable stay.

It would be possible to fly or take a bus to Lago Agrio on your own and catch a ride to the Río Aguarico. From there you could probably hire a canoe to take you into the reserve, but the only places to stay are the camps associated with the Flotel, the Cuyabeno River Lodge or at an indigenous village, and they do not favor strangers dropping in. You can camp but you will need stacks of permits. Sign up with Paradise Huts, the Cuyabeno River Lodge or the Flotel, so they can do all the work and you can enjoy yourself—it is a worthwhile experience.

✪ **Paradise Huts** (private bath, cold water; four days, three nights, $243 per person; in Quito: Orient Gal, Avenida Río Amazonas 816 and Veinti-

Spider Monkeys

milla, 2-561-104, 2-501-418, 2-501-420, fax: 2-501-419) is a small lodge located outside the reserve on the Río Aguarico about a hour downstream from Puerto Chiritza. The huts themselves are a group of round buildings connected by cobble walkways just back from the low river bluff. There are three rooms per building—each simple but clean, with two beds, screened windows and a private bath. Each building has a big porch with comfortable chairs and a pleasant view.

The grounds are small and parklike with many trees and flowering shrubs. The huts are surrounded by a wall of forest vegetation bringing the "jungle" practically into your room. To see wildlife, there are several trails that lead from the grounds into the forest, although there are many birds that are easily glimpsed from the grounds. Package tours to Paradise Huts are much less expensive than to the Flotel or Cuyabeno River Lodge, but the quality of the experience is not as high. If you want to see the Cuyabeno Reserve and price is very important and comfort is not, try the Paradise Huts. Four-day, five-day and seven-day excursions are available. The four-day, three-night excursion costs $243 per person, but does not include travel from Quito to Lago Agrio.

GETTING THERE: You will fly to Lago Agrio, bus to the river and then be picked up by Paradise Huts canoes.

✪✪✪ **Cuyabeno River Lodge (Cuyabeno Lakes)** (private bath, cold water; $500 per 4 days, per person; in Quito: Nuevo Mundo Travel and Tours, Casilla 1703-402-A, Avenida Corú 1349 and Orellana, 2-553-818, fax: 2-565-261; e-mail: nmundo@qui.telconet.net) can be found in the western part of the Cuyabeno Reserve at a series of large, shallow lakes that are only accessible via canoe from the Río Cuyabeno. Only in December and January, during exceptionally dry years when these lakes can dry up almost completely, is travel by canoe impossible. During these low-water months, however, special expeditions can be arranged to hike on foot into these lakes. The Cuyabeno Lakes and their surrounding forest provide access to an area rich in plant and animal life. More than 400 species of birds have been recorded, and it is one of the best places in Ecuador to see the gigantic Harpy Eagle. The plant species are more poorly known, but already well over 25,000 species of plants have been identified here.

After arriving in Lago Agrio on the daily flight from Quito, a private van will transport you 75 kilometers east to the Río Cuyabeno. Here you will walk or take a short canoe ride to the Cuyabeno River Lodge. After settling into your comfortable bungalow, constructed in native-style architecture and from native materials, you can cool off with a shower in your private bath. You will have the afternoon and evening to explore the flooded forest habitat with your guide, who will introduce you to the ecology and natural history of the area.

After a filling supper in the dining and lounge area overlooking the Río Cuyabeno, you will be ready for bed. A good night's rest with the Tropical Screech Owls whistling right outside your window will have you refreshed for the morning. An early departure in a motorized canoe will give you the best chance to see many animals on your exciting two-hour ride up the Río Cuyabeno to the Cuyabeno Lakes area. Mammals, birds, caiman, and all kinds of surprises are sure to be part of this adventure.

You can see the lakes as either a day trip from the Cuyabeno River Lodge or as an overnight on the shores of one of the larger lakes, Laguna Grande. Here, a permanent and comfortable tented camp makes more extensive exploring of the lakes area possible both by day and by night. Most of the exploring is by canoe, but several interesting trails lead to *tierra firme* forest on the other side of the lake where very different birds, mammals and plants can be found. On a full-moon night, the light can be so bright and the night noises from Boat-billed Herons, caimans, and five species of owls so distracting that sleep becomes an optional activity.

Four-day ($500 per person) or five-day ($597 per person) tours include round-trip air fare between Quito and Lago Agrio, private land and river transportation, lodging, meals, wildlife reserve entrance fee and multilingual naturalist-guide.

GETTING THERE: From Quito you either fly or take an overnight bus to Lago Agrio where you are met by a private van that takes you to Río Cuyabeno. From there you will take a canoe to the lodge.

If you prefer a cabin and more luxurious accommodations than tents, the **☻☻ Grand Cuyabeno Lake Lodge** (Neotropic Turis, Centro de Reservaciones Cultura, Robles 513 and Reina Victoria, Quito; $350-$400 plus $20 Reserve entrance fee; 2-564-956, fax: 2-554-902; e-mail: neotropi@uio.sat-net.net) is a good alternative for your stay on the Cuyabeno lakes. The lodge is built on the highest point overlooking the central lake area of the reserve. The seven cabins, built from native materials in the Secoya Indian style, each have two rooms and three of them have private baths. Mosquito netting protects you at night as the walls are largely open-sided. A central dining cabin, kitchen and bar has a large and open porch that overlooks the lake. Most of the exploring is by canoe, but several interesting trails lead to tierra firme forest on the other side of the lake where very different birds, mammals and plants can be found. On a full moon night, the light can be so bright and the night noises from Boat-billed Herons, caimans, and five species of owls so distracting that sleep becomes an optional activity. Tour price does not include transportation between Quito and Lago Agrio, but it does include a guide from Quito, private land and river transportation, lodging and meals from Lago Agrio on.

The ✪✪✪ **Flotel Francisco de Orellana** (private bath, hot water; three nights, $567 per person; in Quito: Transturi/Metropolitan Touring, Avenida República de El Salvador 970, 2-464-780, fax: 2-464-702; in the U.S.: Adventure Associates, 13150 Coit Road, Suite 110, Dallas, TX 75240, 800-527-2500), which most everyone just calls the Flotel, is a floating hotel designed to navigate the rivers of the Oriente while providing comfortable and clean hotel-like facilities and a base for environmental education and exploration. The Flotel was built in Coca in 1975 and operated on the Río Napo until 1991, when it was moved to the Río Aguarico, a major tributary of the Río Napo. It looks very much like a Mississippi river boat without the paddle wheels—three decks, blocky design, rooms inside facing out, upper sun deck, lower dining room and rails wrapping around each floor.

The Flotel is 140 feet long and 23 feet wide and is powered by three 100 horsepower diesel engines. It can hold 48 passengers in 22 cabins and, in addition to a spacious dining room where delicious meals and buffets are served, there is a large, upper-deck common room/bar that has reference books, interesting videos, maps and great chairs scattered about to plunk down in after a day's outing. The fully stocked bar extends outside to a broad sun deck, which is partially covered and is a magnificent place to watch the forest float by or capture the memories of the day in your journal.

All the cabins are basically the same except for two four-person cabins that would be suitable for a small family. Most of the cabins are located on the second deck away from the water-level engine room and a few are up on the third deck. Each room has a bunk bed with wide berths, a bureau, closet area, screened windows and a complete, if modest, private bathroom with constant hot and cold running water. While it is very much a ship's cabin, it is larger than any cabin you will find in the Galápagos, and it is refreshed daily with new towels and special treats.

Arriving visitors meet the Flotel at the confluence of the Río Cuyabeno, flowing from the northwest, and the Río Aguarico, here flowing from the west. During a three- or four-night stay (there are two schedules to choose from: Tuesday–Friday or Friday–Tuesday, both offering much the same daily programs), the Flotel travels downstream and then back up to the mouth of the Río Cuyabeno. Days are full of rainforest exploration at various sites (see below) and nights are spent tied up to a friendly riverbank tree for peaceful sleeping. A generator operates at night when the engines are turned off to provide 24-hour power.

While it is certainly remarkable to be staying at a floating Amazonian hotel, it is nothing compared to the spectacular rainforest you will be visiting. The Río Aguarico is like the Río Napo was 20 years ago, with uncut and undisturbed forests and few people. Consequently, the riverbank forests are alive with animal life. What you can see from the decks of the Flotel can make even hard-to-impress professional tour leaders drop their jaws in amazement.

There are several camps and day sites that are operated by the Ecuador Amazon Expeditions. Most of the day sites are visited on a typical Flotel tour depending, of course, on weather and river conditions. Passengers are transported to the sites in large, comfortable motor canoes with individual seats (not the typical wooden bench seats so common in most motor canoes) and a cloth canopy for sun and rain protection.

There are three camps run by Transturi. One, Río Pacuya Camp, is on the normal Flotel route and is usually visited during a day trip. The other two, Aguarico Camp and Iripari Camp, are farther downstream and are usually visited on a separate camp tour. There is also a program (Aguarico Trek) that offers participants the opportunity to travel and live with the native Cofans on a seven- to ten-day trek into the backcountry of the reserve. We heartily recommend all these programs.

The standard Flotel program typically includes daytime cruising on the Río Aguarico, morning and afternoon excursions, evening reviews of the day's activities and sightings and finally briefings for the next day. The briefings occur in the upper common room after dinner while the Flotel is tied to the riverbank. Afterward, most people wander out to the back deck with an after-dinner drink or hot tea or coffee to enjoy the spectacular star display and engage in quiet conversation. There are always several guides around to answer your questions or to help you find the proper reference book. The guides have interesting stories to tell and are very friendly, so try to get to know them. It will make your trip more fun.

There is a full-time medical doctor onboard the Flotel who provides medical care to both natives and tourists. Amazon Expeditions has negotiated solar collectors for the native villages from the oil companies. They directly support scientific research on river dolphins, endangered turtles and native agriculture. They employ 72 local people and work hard to provide them with education and opportunity. Every aspect of their operation is evaluated for environmental impact and lessened wherever possible. Ecuador Amazon Expeditions is one of the environmental leaders in ecotourism in Amazonian Ecuador.

PACUYA CAMP   The Río Pacuya forms a narrow peninsula where it enters the Río Aguarico. There is a day-long trip that starts with a slow catamaran (double canoes) paddle up this narrow tree-lined river to **Pacuya Camp**, where lunch is served and the afternoon can be spent relaxing, swimming or exploring a quiet backwater. The camp is a collection of connected thatched huts raised on stilts above water level. There are bathrooms, a small cooking area, lots of tables, benches and appealing hammocks. Visitors can decide to spend the night at this camp to experience the nocturnal rainforest, or they can head back to the Flotel. Nights here are spent on sleeping pads with linens provided and mosquito netting is available if needed. The other access to Pacuya Camp is along a 2-kilometer-long **boardwalk** that crosses the narrow river peninsula to the camp. This is a great way to see what an inundated forest looks like from the inside. Take your time on this boardwalk, and you are sure to see interesting things. Look in particular for tapir prints in the fresh mud and Squirrel Monkeys and Black-mantled Tamarins overhead. During high flood times parts of the boardwalk might be a bit wet, but it is still be a must-see experience.

The Cofans, one of three tribes of indigenous people in the Cuyabeno Wildlife Reserve (Secoya and Quichua are the other two), in partnership with Ecuador Amazon Expeditions, welcome Flotel visitors to an **interpretive center** across the river from their village of Zábalo. There is a 1-kilometer-long trail through the rainforest where a Cofan guide, with a Flotel naturalist as an interpreter, will show you the traditional uses of plants encountered along the trail. There is also a small cultural center where handicrafts made from sustainable rainforest material can be purchased.

Flotel guests will not be allowed to visit the village of Zábalo or to take photographs of the Cofan people. The Cofans are trying to keep both their traditions and integrity intact and choose to honor their privacy over our curiosity—a decision all visitors should respect. Unfortunately, too many native villages in Amazonia have opened up their lives to tourists and have been taken advantage of and abused. It is refreshing that the Cofans are working so hard to maintain their culture in the glare of tourism. However, if you want an authentic experience with Cofan guides and a camping adventure you will never forget, the Zábolo community has developed a tourist-guiding business. You can make arrangements with Metropolitan/Transturi Touring for an expedition into the forest ranging from several days to a week long.

AGUARICO CAMP   There are three camps that are not part of the regular Flotel program because they are too far downstream to be accessible to the Flotel. Guests signed up for the camp adventure arrive in Tarapoa with the Flotel guests and transfer to the river on the same bus, but do not go in the same canoes to the Flotel. They instead take faster, smaller motorboats for the four-hour, 200-kilometer trip past the Flotel to the ❀❀❀ **Aguarico Camp**. The camp is located on a wide bend in the river at what officially is known as Zancudo. There is a very small military outpost here as well, but the soldiers are friendly and usually outnumbered five to one by staff and guests of the camp.

The camp is located on top of a small bluff in a 12-acre grassy opening surrounded by a green wall of the rainforest. There are four main buildings connected by walkways: a dining/common room, two dormitories and a wash house. All are built in the typical native style. The dining/common room has a bar and lounge area as well as tables to seat 40. The food is quite good and nicely presented. Because a generator is provided, there is electricity at the camp. A TV in the bar is an unusual sight this far into the Oriente.

The sleeping quarters have 20 rooms with bunk beds and mosquito netting, large screened windows and private entrances. They are clean, well kept and perfectly suited for collapsing into after a long day. The bath house has private toilet and shower stalls and a long line of sinks for washing up. The accommodations at all the camps are not as nice as some Amazonian lodges and certainly not as nice as those on the Flotel, but if adventure and nature are higher on your list than ease, these camps are perfectly comfortable. If comfort and ease are more important to you, we recommend you stay on the Flotel.

IRIPARI CAMP   Iripari Lake is the largest lake in Ecuador. It is a relatively deep lake and therefore less prone to drastic changes in water level during the dry season. Consequently, it is home to a wide variety of freshwater rainforest animals such as piranhas, paiche (an important food fish that can be up to six feet long), manatees, giant otters and caiman. Visitors travel by paddled canoe across the lake to ✪✪✪ **Iripari Camp**, on the far shore directly opposite the trail head and shelter, about a 30-minute trip.

Iripari Camp was built in 1991 and extensively remodeled in 1994. It is a small camp made up of three palm-thatched, wooden buildings holding up to 20 guests in ten double rooms. It is a purposefully simple camp in order

Pink River Dolphin

to blend into its environment, yet it is comfortable. The rooms are of moderate size, plain but clean with two twin beds in each and large screened windows. There are shared bathroom facilities (biodigesters handle the human waste) and electricity is generated by solar collectors.

Because it is built on *tierra firme* (dry land), there is an extensive trail system that extends behind the camp. There are swampy areas, so rubber boots are recommended—available at the camp. This forest has never been disturbed and is wild for many kilometers in every direction. You have the chance to see Puma, Jaguar, tapir, large mixed flocks of birds and several different kinds of monkeys. Often the distant roar of howler monkeys can fool you into thinking a major wind storm is forming again. A very long list of animals could be accumulated at Iripari Camp if you were to stay several days and spend much time in quiet exploration. Not a bad idea come to think of it!

The entire trip from Iripari Camp to Aguarico Camp takes about three hours, but it would be criminal to do it in less than five. Half an hour away from the Río Aguarico just off the stream bank is a new canopy tower that is six stories high and big enough to sleep on.

GETTING THERE: Commercial flights on TAME fly daily to Lago Agrio except Sunday. Here a van will meet you and drive you 60 kilometers to the village of Chiritza on the Río Aguarico. Covered launches will then speed you down the river to your destination (two hours to the Flotel and four and a half hours to Aguarico Camp). Alternatively, charter flights will fly you to Tarapoa and vans then drive you the 40 minutes to Chiritza.

COCA (PUERTO FRANCISCO DE ORELLANA)

Driving the 93 kilometers from Lago Agrio to Coca takes about two to three hours because you have to wait to cross two rivers on ferries. Most of the road is paved and fairly fast, but for us it will always be depressing. When one of us (DLP) first worked in Ecuador in 1971, the oil pipeline road from Papallacta to the Oriente had just opened. The only way to get to Coca was by air or by canoe. All the area between Lago Agrio and Coca was pristine forest. Now it is a patchwork of towns, fields and overgrown gardens. Watch how many of the houses along the road have for "for sale" signs (*"Se vende este lote"*). The reason is simply a failure on the part of the Ecuadorian government and the oil companies to educate and logically control colonization of this type of habitat. There are so few nutrients in the soil of most tropical rainforests that after five or ten years of intensive agriculture, the soils become exhausted and are incapable of growing anything more. Expensive synthetic fertilizers can extend the agricultural viability of the area, but for only a few more years. For the sake of expediency, the Ecuadorian government did little to prepare these colonists for the special agricultural conditions they would face—especially if their experience had all been in the highlands. Unprepared colonists using the oil company roads for easy access to new areas is an equation for disaster. These are problems facing the rest of undeveloped Ecuador.

In the meantime, even though Coca has been around since the 1500s, it has the muddy, dusty, and transitory feeling of an oil boomtown. Since the road connections in the late 1970s, it has only gotten bigger and muddier and dustier. The bridge that now crosses the Río Napo at Coca has spread this unplanned development to the south side of the river as well. The streets are largely unpaved—dusty in the dry season and mud holes in the wet season. If you are flying into Coca to catch a canoe to one of the lodges on the lower Napo, you will get a fleeting view of a lively but disorganized city. From the airport on the north side of the city to the river takes only ten minutes, but for many tourists, even that is too long. Often tourists wait for their plane in one of the city hotels upon their return from the lodges and on the way to Quito. If it is the Hotel El Auca or Hotel La Mission, you will be able to experience a bit more of Coca without severe culture shock. The airport is tiny, hot and not a fun place to await your plane for an hour or more.

Note: Because Coca is an oil boomtown dominated by male oil workers, many consider it to be at least unfriendly and at worst dangerous to female travelers. For all visitors, but especially women, do not wander around the town at night and avoid the north end of town, which is the red-light district. There is nothing to see at night in Coca and plenty of trouble to find.

LODGING   For most foreign tourists forced for whatever reason to stay overnight in Coca, there is only one choice, **Hotel La Mission** (18 de Septiembre 413 and Avenida Amazonas, on the Río Napo riverfront; private bath, some with hot water, some with air conditioning; $35; 6-561-478, 6-553-960, 6-553-674, fax: 6-564-675). The 64 rooms are clean and have an honor bar/refrigerator. The reason for this hotel's presence and near-luxury is obvious from the breakfast menu—the continental breakfast costs $3, the American breakfast costs $4, but the oilman's breakfast costs $5.

For the more budget-minded, the **Hotel Oasis** (near the Hotel La Mission on the riverfront, Calle Malecón; private bath, cold water, fans, $5; 6-880-164, fax: 6-880-174) is the best alternative.

In the city center, the **Hotel El Auca** (some with private bath, cold water, unreliable fans; $6–$15; 6-880-127, in Quito phone/fax: 2-435-399) is another alternative but is in a very noisy location, and is a poor third choice.

There are at least 20 other hostales, hosterias and residenciales in the city. They cost $1–$2/night, and should be used only by those willing to endure noise, dirty linen (if any at all) and the possibility of new entomological discoveries emerging from your mattress at night.

RESTAURANTS   Only three places are worth taking a chance on if you must eat in Coca—the clean and restful **Hotel La Mission**, the new and clean **Hotel El Auca** and the **Ocaso Restaurant**, which caters to oilmen and is near the Auca. The Hotel El Auca has recently finished a two-story addition with a cement-block restaurant and disco on the second floor.

GETTING THERE: By Air: TAME flies a 40-passenger twin turbo-prop plane daily from and to Quito except on Sunday. Usually the flights are in the morning (9 a.m.) and at high season there are often two back-to-back flights (9 a.m. and 11:30 a.m.). Because it is impossible to make reservations on these domestic flights from the U.S. or Europe, work through an Ecuadorian travel agent. Be sure and give the return part of your ticket to the lodge's agent in Coca before getting on the canoe to go downriver to the lodge. They need to have your ticket to re-confirm the return flight to Quito, and you do not want to be stuck in Coca or have to take the 12-hour bus ride back to Quito.

By Bus: There are numerous buses going between Coca and Quito. Most go via Lago Agrio, and the entire trip will take 12 hours if you are lucky, 18 if you are not. A few buses go via the Loreto Road to Tena, but that often means a bus transfer in Tena. Water-taxis go up the Río Napo to Misahuallí, but that trip is not regularly scheduled and takes seven or eight hours when it does go. There you can get a tourist bus to Quito (if there is room) or a regular bus to Tena or Puyo–Baños. The reverse trip is also possible, but it takes an hour or so less because it is downstream.

By Car: Count on 10 to 12 dusty or muddy hours nonstop from Quito. The ferries that must be used to cross major rivers can slow you down even more. During the rainy season (July–November), landslides often close the highway for days at a time. If you are sightseeing along the way, we recommend that you make overnight stops at least once, preferably twice, in Baeza, San Rafael Falls and/or Lago Agrio. At an army and national police checkpoint just west of Lago Agrio, the wait can be interminable or so fast nobody will even look at your documents.

LOWER RÍO NAPO

For most tourists visiting this part of Ecuador, seeing the "jungle" is their top priority. Lodges on the lower Río Napo give you this opportunity. They provide some of the best wildlife viewing in pristine forest anywhere in the Amazon. In addition, several of them pamper you with luxury service in a rustic setting. Choosing among them is difficult—each has many positive points. Most have two-, three- and five-day packages that include canoe transport on the river, room and board, and guide. Airfare from Quito to Coca round-trip is $120 extra. Some have prices that are in the moderate to expensive range. Others are inexpensive but very primitive and for the independent, adventure traveler only. All but three are on the north side of the Río Napo. We include the current prices for a stay of four nights and three days only for a representative comparison of the costs at these lodges, but expect these prices to rise.

Upon landing at Coca from Quito, your guides will meet you at the airport and take you on a ten-minute bus ride through Coca to the Río Napo in a bus. Your 50-foot dugout canoes have a covered roof against the sun and rain, but the two powerful outboard motors mean you will be moving fast down the river to the lodge. The spray and wind make a light jacket comfortable. Be sure to tie your hat down, or it might blow off. You are advised to use the bathroom in the airport before getting on the canoe, as there are no facilities the rest of the way except bushes along the shore. On the trip you will see cleared fields (*chacras*) with pineapples, bananas and yuca growing. Some older areas have groves of orange trees. Cattle are also commonly raised in these clearings. Even though the Río Napo can be more than a kilometer wide in places, the water is often very shallow. Pushing a large canoe loaded with people off a sand bar is not something the crew wants to do, so the canoe will weave back and forth following the narrow deep-water channel of the river. Because of the high traffic on this part of the river, caiman (crocodile relatives) no longer haul out on the sand bars to rest. The large river turtles are also gone from here. However, you will see parrot flocks screaming overhead. Several trees along the way will have 10 to 20 long nests hanging from them. These are the nests of a colony of Russet-backed Oropendolas, related to the oriole. Look for a large paper wasp nest in the midst of the tree. The oropendolas often seek out trees with these wasp nests as the wasps are predatory on insects and protect the young oropendolas from parasitic flies as well as from marauding monkey troops after their eggs.

The newest, most affordable and closest lodge to Coca is ✪✪✪ **Yarina Lodge** (private bath, cold water; four days, three nights, $170 per person; Avenida Amazonas 1324 and Avenida Colón; 2-503-225, 2-544-166, fax: 2-504-037; e-mail: yuturi1@yuturi.com.ec). Finished in late 1998, this lodge is 30 kilometers or about an hour from Coca on the south side of the Río Napo. You enter a small side stream and go through a line of small hills (*colinas*) to this idyllic encampment of 21 cabins. Built and run by the same company as the Hosteria Yuturi, this new lodge is obviously constructed with care for the environment. So close to Coca, there are fewer large mammals and big birds than at the more remote lodges down the Río Napo. Nevertheless there are a surprising number of species of birds and even monkeys here. The tierra firme forest is largely uncut and covers the undulating hills of the area. Being on the south side of the Napo, many of the plant and animal species are different from those found on the north side. New trails are being built,

and because the company owns most of the land around the lodge and pro-
hibits hunting, it will likely become a refuge for more and more species as the
years go by. For this price and given the previous experience of this company in developing its other lodge, we can recommend it highly—both for its
comfort and for the wildlife. The lodge can be your primary destination, or
it can be combined with the more distant Yuturi Lodge for a longer adventure.

GETTING THERE: You will either be met at the airport or if arriving by bus
you make your way to the riverside Hotel Oasis. Here the Yuturi/Yarina canoes
will transport you directly to the lodge.

The **Limoncocha Biological Reserve** covers 11,500 acres and includes
one of the largest oxbow lakes in eastern Ecuador, as well as surrounding
flooded forest, Mauritius Palm forest, secondary forest and a 5-kilometer
section of the Río Napo and its islands. In its heyday from the 1970s to the
mid-1980s, Limoncocha Biological Reserve was *the* place to visit to see
breathtaking views of Amazonian forest and its flora and fauna. At that time,
there was no road into the area, and the only access was by missionary plane
from Quito or canoe from Coca via the Río Jivino. Jaguars roamed the
airstrip and Salvin's Curassows, Grey-winged Trumpeters and Harpy Eagles
were readily seen in the forest. In a giant Ceiba tree 130 feet high in the middle of the missionary compound, a pair of Orange-breasted Falcons nested
for at least ten years, and 20-foot-long Black Caiman were common in the
lake. With the construction of the road from Shushufindi to Pompeya in the
late 1980s and the resulting influx of colonists, all this pristine habitat and
its occupants were changed forever.

Even though Ecuador declared this site a biological reserve in 1985
when the missionaries left the area, dynamite in the lake destroyed the fish
and caiman populations, while poaching and tree cutting felled the last primary forest in the area. This site is now a sad memory of what it once was.
It is, however, still the only site known in Ecuador where the Pale-eyed
Blackbird can be found. This peculiar species only occupies the reedy-
shrubby edges of five large oxbow lakes in western Amazonia from Limoncocha to southeastern Perú.

This area is also well known for archaeological middens with ceramic
pot shards typical of the Napo Culture from the years 1150 to 1480. The pictures painted on these shards give us an idea of what the people of this culture looked like, how they dressed, and what activities they pursued. For
instance, they practiced double burials, in which an individual was first
buried in a regular grave, then after several years, the bones were exhumed,
placed in large ceramic pots decorated with snakes and other local fauna, and
then reburied in these containers. The density of these shards and graves has

led some archaeologists to estimate that the population of people along this stretch of the Napo was perhaps in the millions. After their first contact with white man in the late 1400s and early 1500s, however, these native populations crashed, presumably because of contact with the white man's diseases, against which they had no immunity.

INEFAN has a headquarters building here, and arrangements can be made for a boat to go out on the 3-kilometer-long lake. Check early in the morning, especially on the east side, for Hoatzins, Lesser Kiskadees, Pale-eyed Blackbirds, and other bird species still found here. The secondary forest along the airstrip can also be interesting.

Rustic accommodations are available at the **Cabañas Limoncocha** (some rooms with private bath, cold water; $2–$8; in Quito: Asociación Indígina de Limoncocha, CONFENIAE, Avenida 6 de Diciembre 159, 2-220-326, fax: 2-543-973). The local Quichua commune has taken over these facilities, built originally by the missionaries and Metropolitan Touring. Arrangements for meals can be made. The members of this commune can also provide guides for the trails and canoes on the lake. These guides cannot speak English, but their skill at locating wildlife and ability to communicate with hand signals and pointing with their chin is often adequate.

GETTING THERE: To visit Limoncocha, you can hire a canoe in Coca, go down the Napo two hours to the Río Jivino, and then go up this small tributary 30 minutes to the abandoned Limoncocha airstrip. Get out of the canoe and walk east along the old airstrip 2 kilometers to the village of Limoncocha.

Alternately, you can either take a canoe to Primavera on the Río Napo and walk the three hours north to Limoncocha, or hire a car in Coca and drive the gravel roads to Limoncocha via the Shushufindi–Pompeya route. This route south of Shushufindi is a labyrinth of gravel roads, so bring a guide along or ask the way to Limoncocha frequently. A few buses (*rancheras*) ply this route, too, but be sure you are on the right bus and expect an all-day trip from Coca.

✪✪✪ **Sacha Lodge** (private bath, hot water; four days, three nights, $525 per person; in Quito: Explorer Tours, Reina Victoria 1235 and Lizardo García, Casilla 17-211608; 2-522-220, 2-509-115, fax: 2-508-872) is the newest and closest lodge to Coca, 80 kilometers or two to three hours by motorized canoe. Sacha in Quichua means forest. Don't confuse this lodge with Jatún Sacha on the upper Napo. Construction began on this lodge in 1991, and the first guest visited in 1992. Explorer Tours, the owners of Sacha Lodge, also own Casa del Suizo on the upper Río Napo near Misahuallí, and they have used that experience to bring Sacha Lodge quickly into efficient and productive working order. The main building of the lodge is a two-story structure with dining room, bar and lounge. This main building also has a small observation tower above the bar that looks out over the adjacent lake. The rest of the lodge consists of seven duplex cabins, each with two separate twin-bed rooms and individual bath (maximum of 28 guests). The general construction is rustic wood except for the bathrooms, which are of modern tile and ceramic. The windows are all screened and no mosquito netting is needed over the bed. Gas water heaters for each duplex supply hot water for the shower. Electricity is available from dawn to 10 p.m. Meals are good and served individually or—when at capacity—by buffet. Covered and elevated walks connect most of the cabins with the main building.

Sacha Lodge owns 2000 acres of the surrounding forest on the north side of the Río Napo. With title to this land, the operators can be guaranteed long-term protection of the forest. The local people employed by Sacha Lodge all said they were treated well here and enjoyed the work. The lowland Quichua people have cooperatives and private land that abut the Sacha property, and receiving a fair profit through salaries and other services for tourists helps them in conserving the surrounding property.

When you are ready for a walk, your English-speaking guide will take you along some of the several kilometers of hiking trails through the forest. Some of the trips are half-day, some across the Río Napo are all-day. One of the highlights is climbing the canopy tower, about a 20-minute hike from the lodge. This solidly engineered structure is built around the trunk of a giant Ceiba tree 148 feet high. The steps lead to a comfortable platform near the top (130 feet). From this vantage point well above the forest canopy you can see to the horizon. Forest stretches in all directions. On a clear day you can see the peak of Volcán Sumaco 150 kilometers to the east. In the morning and afternoon, flocks of birds that you would normally break your neck to see from the forest floor flit around at eye level. The canopy is one of the last biological frontiers and harbors thousands of unknown animal and plant species. Here you have a rare opportunity to see what few others have been able to experience.

Each day's events are planned out the evening before with you and your guide. Bird lists, a small library and the experience of the guides will make this an educational as well as thrilling time. Calf-height boots can be borrowed free for the length of the stay. Limited laundry services are available.

The various habitats around the lodge include trails through primary *tierra firme* forest, flooded palm forest (with a fast ride on a cable seat crossing for those up to it), secondary forest, and canoe rides up quiet forest streams. On the south side of the Napo, longer trails are available directly across from the lodge or downriver 20 minutes into the northwest corner of the Yasuní National Park at the Añangu Ranger Station. Another memorable experience is to go early in the morning to the parrot salt lick cliffs near the military out-

Jaguar

post at Añangu. On a good morning, thousands of Blue-headed Parrots, Mealy Parrots, Yellow-headed Parrots, White-eyed Parakeets and Dusky-headed Parakeets congregate here to eat salts and other essential minerals from the near-vertical surface of this exposed cliff over the river. Several species of birds and monkeys live on the south side of the river that are not found on the north side and vice versa. The south side has rolling hills and steep climbs that are not present on the flat north side. The more different types of habitats you experience, the more chances you have for seeing different plants and animals.

GETTING THERE: Trips begin and end on Monday and Friday. When the covered canoe brings you to the Sacha Lodge dock on the Río Napo, your bags are loaded on carts, and you walk about 1.5 kilometers through secondary vegetation, gardens and on raised walkways through palm flood forest. Then you get into small dugout canoes that are paddled for about 15 minutes across the small lake, Pilchicocha. On the far side of the lake is the lodge.

✪✪✪ **La Selva Jungle Lodge** (private bath, cold water; four days, three nights, $547 per person; in Quito: La Selva Jungle Lodge, 6 de Diciembre 2816 and James Orton, 2-550-995, 2-554-686, fax: 2-567-297; e-mail: laselva @uio.satnet.net) was constructed in 1985 by Eric and Magdalena Schwartz; it received international recognition when it won the World Congress on Tourism and the Environment award in 1992. The lodge guides have been so well trained that they can "spoonfeed" you almost any of the 500 bird species here. The mammal list includes Giant Anteater, fourteen species of monkeys, Bicolored Porcupine, Bushdog, Puma, Ocelot, Jaguar, White-lipped Peccary, Collared Peccary, Three-toed Sloth, Coatimundi and many species of bats. The butterflies, plants and frogs are also well known in the area.

Part of the reason for such intimate knowledge of the local fauna is the amount of time this lodge has been here, but a big part of the natural history success here at La Selva is due to Eric Schwartz's far-sightedness. He developed a commercial butterfly house to sell 25 species of pupating butterflies to botanical gardens in Texas, Louisiana and Florida. To do this correctly, he needed help from butterfly scientists (Lepidopterists) who not only knew biology but were also sensitive to the environment. Scientists in his employ had to study butterfly behavior, understand plants that served as food for larval species, and how to get butterflies to breed in captivity. By law, adult butterflies reared from captivity must be released to make up for adults taken earlier from the forest. It turns out that breeding successive generations of butterflies in captivity results in poorly surviving individuals after a few generations. Their gene pool has to be revitalized regularly by wild caught individuals.

When you reach the dock of La Selva on the north bank of the Río Napo after three hours in the canoe, your baggage will be carried by employees, and you begin a 20-minute walk on a raised boardwalk through a Mauritius Palm swamp forest. The walk through the swamp forest is interesting. The low whistled song you hear in the distance that ascends in three long steps and then slurs up on the end of the third step is the Undulated Tinamou. It has got to be one of the most common birds around, but this ground-dwelling bird is so sneaky only rarely is anyone lucky to see one running on the forest floor or flying up noisily like a short-tailed pheasant. Soon you come to the end of the boardwalk and get into small dugout canoes paddled by the lodge personnel. Have your camera ready as the 25-minute ride across Garzacocha to the lodge is one of the most spectacular sights anywhere. Here you will begin to see lots of butterflies, birds, dragonflies, turtles and even a Black Caiman if you are lucky. Look up in the treetops along both sides of the lake for howler monkeys and Three-toed Sloths. The lake itself reflects the sky and the forest and is so beautiful, often all the tourists spontaneously stop their conversations and just take it in quietly.

At the other end of Garzacocha is the lodge itself. All the buildings are constructed from native materials and reflect the architecture of the lowland Quichua style. The main building is a combination reception lounge and bar. Next door is the dining room and kitchen. The individual cabins (15 doubles, one single and one family cabin for up to eight persons) are all connected by raised walkways but without cover. They are rustic but comfortable, and all have twin beds with mosquito netting except for cabin 9, which has a double bed (*matrimonio*). The private bathroom in each is also rustic, but with a flush toilet and cold-water shower. Only the kitchen, bar and administration building have electricity from a small generator if you need to recharge batteries. All the tourist facilities are lighted with kerosene lamps only, so don't forget your flashlight. The food here at La Selva is without a doubt some of the most delicious of any lodge we have visited anywhere in South America. From roasted turkey to beef and fish, the courses just keep on coming. And the desserts—Wow! You will find yourself eagerly waiting the sound of the bamboo whistle announcing meals.

The trail system is very well laid out. Your guide will take you on any number of alternatives. Because the lodge is basically surrounded by water, most hikes also include at least a short canoe ride. A visit to the canopy tower is a must. Climbing 130 feet up the stairs around this monstrous tree may seem daunting, but it is worth every effort to climb to the viewing platform at the top. The view is scenic, and the chances for seeing wildlife from an angle not normally possible from the forest floor makes every trip up there different and exciting. Visiting the butterfly house is another pleasure not to be missed.

The parrot salt licks near Añangu on the south side of the Río Napo should be made early in the morning. Thousands of parrots congregate here to eat essential chemicals from the riverbank. A trip to the river islands for Umbrellabirds and several other unique bird species can sometimes be pleasantly finished with Pink River Dolphins surfacing on the river as you return to the lodge in the late afternoon. A night trip out onto Garzacocha almost always results in sighting the bright red-orange glow of Black Caiman eyes reflected in the beam of a high-powered flashlight. During the day, you can swim in this lake or catch piranhas. If you do catch a piranha, make sure you have shoes on when it begins to flop around in the bottom of the canoe. Wherever you go on your stay at La Selva, there is the chance for an exciting observation or learning experience around every turn in the trail.

If you want a more rustic—although not less expensive—experience, La Selva Lodge offers a program called The Light Brigade. With guides, good food, and plenty of help with logistics, you can enjoy a seven-day camping experience based out of the nearby lake called **Challuacocha**. You visit four camp sites and have a lot more contact with the forest, day and night.

La Selva is interesting from another point of view in that it has passed through many of the initial problems and experiences that the newer lodges are just now facing. It is breaking ground in solving problems such as an aging sewage system and accumulated garbage buried in deep pits for ten years. Now little plastic is used in the kitchen, and garbage that is not biodegradable is packed out to Coca. The lodge itself only owns 250 acres, on which the buildings are concentrated. Two neighboring Quichua communes control the 125,000 acres that make up the forest around the lodge. In the early days, the local people believed that the tourists and the lodge were good for them because La Selva helped raise their living standards by purchasing and maintaining electric generators, constructing four schools and providing salaries. Now, however, rising expectations and greater desires for goods and services have put more and more strains on the relations between the lodge and the communes. Because the future of La Selva is so tightly dependent on the cooperation of the communes, it will be intriguing to see how the Schwartzs respond to the dynamics of this social dilemma. If their past innovations are any clue, the future resolutions of these problems could well serve as a model for ecotourist sites throughout Ecuador.

GETTING THERE: Trips begin and end on Wednesday and Saturday. From Coca you will take a 3-hour canoe trip on the Río Napo. After you reach the La Selva dock you will walk for 20 minutes and paddle in a canoe another 20 minutes to the lodge.

✪✪✪ **Hosteria Yuturi** (private bath, cold water; four days, three nights, $320 per person; in Quito: Amazonas 1324 and Colón, 2-503-225, fax: 2-504-037, in Coca: 6-880-164, 6-880-172; e-mail: yuturi1@yuturi.com.ec) is the least expensive of the "luxury" lodges here but also the farthest downriver from Coca (five hours). Built in 1990, this lodge is associated with the Oasis Hotel in Coca, and queries can also be made there. The lodge is not on the Río Napo itself, but rather 20 minutes up the Río Yuturi, a small tributary on the south side of the Napo. Because of its presence on the south side of the Napo, there are many opportunities to see flora and fauna not found on the north side of the Napo (where the other lodges are). The habitat is flat and includes blackwater lakes, swamps, inundated forest and some *tierra firme* forest, as well.

Anyone in relatively good physical shape will have a great time here. This area has been heavily hunted, so do not expect to see large birds such as curassows and trumpeters. We did, however, find tracks of a White-lipped Peccary and Jaguar on the trail one morning. This area is the most reliable site in Ecuador to see the Black-necked Red Cotinga. A lek of these large and brilliant red and black birds is active near the canopy tower. This 25 meter-high tower is also good for viewing birds, monkeys and plants that otherwise are rarely seen from the ground.

The compound is on high ground next to the river. Fifteen cabins are lined up on either side of a well-manicured lawn. The cabins are very rustic and mosquito netting is a necessity over the two single beds at night. Heavy rain leaks through, so make sure your clothes and equipment are always covered. The private bathroom attached to each cabin is concrete and clean. Electricity is available from a small generator for a few hours each evening, but don't plan on using your hair dryer as the power produced is basically for lights and little else. The combined dining room, bar and lounge is very comfortable and overlooks the river. The food is amazingly tasty and served with wine. All-day and half-day hikes, canoe trips and fishing for piranha are the alternative activities available. The turkey-sized Hoatzin is common here in the bushes along the edges of the lakes and rivers. This bird eats only leaves and has a digestive system that ferments the plant material to enable the fibers to be broken down and digested, very much like a cow except the Hoatzin doesn't chew its cud. Their stick nests are in bushes over the water, and young Hoatzins dive from them into the water at the approach of danger. They then pull themselves up out of the water on branches using an extra finger on the wing. They look for all the world like some prehistoric Archaeopteryx emerging from the primordial ooze.

The 550,000 acres used by the lodge are leased from the nearby Quichua cooperative (280 individuals live in the area), and the monthly rent of $125 helps them develop their community. Tourists are also taken to their village on the Río Napo to visit families and buy locally made *shigras* (net-like purses carried over the shoulder) and replica blowguns. Another side trip is to a large island in the Río Napo, Isla de los Chorongos. Here you can spend the day wandering on paths looking for monkeys and endemic island species of birds, insects and plants, or camp out for the night in a rustic Quichua-style cabin.

GETTING THERE: From Coca you will take a 4.5-hour canoe trip to the Hosteria Yuturi, which is on the Río Yuturi, a tributary of the Río Napo.

○ **Cabañas Jarrín** (communal bathrooms and showers, some private baths, cold water; $15 per person, per night; Ejarsytur Cía. Ltd., Calle La Mason, Coca; 6-880-251; in Tena: A. Pan, 6-880-251; in Quito: C. C. Espiral Local 154 Jorge Washington and A. Amazonas, 2-569-852, 2-569-853, fax: 2-223-245) is a lodge located just 4 kilometers upriver from the Cabañas Pañacocha. Recently refurbished and expanded, the lodge can accommodate up to 40 visitors. The lobby and kitchen-dining buildings are on stilts right over the river's edge. The simple cabins are built from local materials and situated on higher ground 50 meters from the river. The tourists who stay here are primarily young Europeans and budget travelers. When we asked them what they wanted to see, many of them said they wanted a good time in the jungle relaxing, swimming and dancing. There are hiking trails and canoe excursions on the Río Pañayacu. Unfortunately, the loud swimming parties that visit Pañacocha Lake from Cabañas Jarrín can be very disturbing for those who want to enjoy the tranquil beauty of natural surroundings.

GETTING THERE: Arrangements can be made in Coca (the office in Coca is opposite the Hotel La Mission south of the bridge across the Río Napo) or in

Tena to hire a canoe to take you down the Río Napo and up the Río Pañayacu to the Cabañas Jarrín. These canoes are small and lack a roof, so be prepared to fry in the sun or shiver in the rain. The canoe takes four to five hours from Coca and seven to nine hours from Tena, depending on the condition of the river and the motor.

YASUNÍ NATIONAL PARK

The largest national park in Ecuador, with a total area of 2,500,000 acres, Yasuní was established in 1979, but its borders have been changed several times. Fortunately, with each change, at least on paper, the total area protected has increased. Its present boundaries were last changed in 1992 to establish a large reserve for the Huaorani Indians. If this area is used reasonably, it will serve as a valuable buffer zone for the national park and extend considerably the effective area that protects its flora and fauna. There are only a few parts of this immense park that are accessible to tourists. From Sacha and La Selva lodges, entrance for day trips are possible via trails near the Añangu Ranger Station. Some of these trails are hunting trails that penetrate all the way to the Río Tiputini where a new lodge, Tiputini Biodiversity Station, has facilities for ecotourists. Obviously, an expedition would have to be mounted with guides and supplies for a week or more to see many parts of the park.

We have gone in two other ways. One is to enter by canoe from the eastern end of the park at Nuevo Rocafuerte (12 hours downriver from Coca by motorized canoe). Here the Río Yasuní empties into the Río Napo at the Peruvian border. Special permits are needed from INEFAN in Quito and at the ranger station in Nuevo Rocafuerte, and from the national police—probably the army, too, if they want to be stringent. Ecuador is very sensitive about its border with Perú and somewhat intimidated by its much more powerful and not always so friendly neighbor. This trip up the Río Yasuní, however, is worth all the red tape. The lower part of the river flows through large blackwater swamps surrounded by flood forest. Jatuncocha and Tambococha are the most attractive destinations on this part of the Río Yasuní. As you go farther upriver, the banks get higher and patches of white-sand forest appear. This habitat is from geologically ancient rock shields to the east and tends to be very nutrient poor. It probably occurs nowhere else in Ecuador and has many unique animal and plant species associated with it. The extremely high costs for renting a canoe, hiring guides and buying sufficient supplies have been a major barrier to tourists entering the park here. If you are planning on visiting the upper parts of the Río Yasuní, you will come into contact with Huaorani villages, and they will expect payment for visiting the area. One last caveat: The Río Yasuní is not fed by water from the mountains and depends primarily on local rains for its flow. The water level of the upper portions of the river can fall overnight and become unnavigable by even small canoes for weeks at a time. Being trapped upriver is always a possibility. Because virtually no one enters this part of the park, however, you are in a habitat that has changed little in ten thousand years. This unique aspect of the park more than offsets the hardships and danger of visiting the Río Yasuní.

The other entrance to Yasuní National Park is through virgin *tierra firme* forest on a beautiful gravel road built and maintained by YPF Oil Consortium. With some trepidation we were introduced to how YPF has chosen to deal with oil extraction and the environment. To their credit, and in spite of our many years of built-up prejudice against oil companies, we were duly impressed. Instead of building a bridge from the access road north of the Río Napo at Pompeya (35 kilometers southeast of Coca), they chose to use a barge system for transport of heavy trucks, supplies and personnel. An army of private security guards are everywhere. Nowhere else in Ecuador have we seen such strict and unrelenting enforcement of regulations. Entrance to the road on the south side of the Río Napo is by boat only. Because YPF chose not to build a bridge, colonist invasions along new roads can be controlled. YPF seems to be willing to invest in this extra effort to extract the oil and profits from the habitat. There is little doubt that the primary force behind this "green" effort is public relations pressure, but if it works, don't knock it. The only worry is that when YPF eventually finishes its work or its lease runs out, the Ecuadorian government will not have the means or desire to control colonists, or to properly maintain the oil line, and an ecological disaster similar to what happened on the north side of the Río Napo will be repeated.

The only facilities for staying in this area are at the fantastic ✪✪✪ **Tiputini Biodiversity Station** (private bathrooms and showers, cold water, floor fans; $155 per person, per night for *minimum group of six people*, which includes canoe and ground transportation from Coca; education groups can receive reduced rates; Universidad San Francisco de Quito, Campo Alegre, Casilla 17-12-841, Quito; 2-895-723, 2-895-724 or 2-895-725, ext. 243; fax: 2-890-070; e-mail: tbs@mail.usfq.edu.ec; in the U.S., TBS, P.O. Box 2006, Boerne, TX 78006, phone/fax: 830-336-2721; e-mail: tiputini@ aol.com). Two North American scientists, Carol Walton and Kelly Swing, combined more than 25 years of research and ecotourist experience in Amazonia to build their dream of a combined research-education and ecotourist facility in one of the most untouched areas of the Oriente. The Tiputini Biodiversity Station was finished in 1996.

You can now share their dream, and we unabashedly recommend it as the best place in all of Ecuador to see wildlife. Except for a few Huaroani who lived in this area 20 years ago, no one has lived here or even hunted here for decades. We have seen no other natural area in South America with so much wildlife that is so accessible and so well protected. This is the *best* place in Ecuador to see Jaguars! Nowhere else in Ecuador have we been able to stand under a large troop of Squirrel Monkeys and be ignored. The Spider Monkeys and Wooly Monkeys are so arrogant they will move right over you and challenge with much branch shaking and grimacing. Capybaras and tapirs are abundant; three species of caiman are common; and dolphins regularly swim along the river and its hidden cochas. On a two-hour canoe trip, we saw more of the huge and shy Salvin's Currasows than we had seen previously in our entire lives.

The 1500 acres owned by the Universidad San Francisco is immediately adjacent to and isolated by the Yasuni National Park boundary. More than a dozen trails cover at least 30 kilometers of forest and river edge, and more are planned. The compound itself has eight solidly built buildings spread out over five acres of small clearings within primary *tierra firme* forest or at the edge of the river. Nearby a 120 foot (36 meter) canopy tower sits on the top of a forested ridge in primary forest. In September 1998, Tiputini Biodiverity Station constructed the first canopy walk in Ecuador. It is a series of cable bridges suspended 120 to 130 feet (36 to 40 meters) above the ground. Six-hundred sixty feet (200 meters) long, it bridges primary forest canopy by connecting the tops of five giant trees. At each interconnected tree there is a platform for making observations, and at one end is a "crow's nest" in which you can sit even higher in the tree than you get during the rest of the walk. Although it is not for the faint of heart or those in mediocre physical condition, it is an adventure and exciting experience for those who want to try it. The initial climb of 120 feet straight up a tree trunk on a series of ladders permanently attached to the tree will immediately separate out the candidates for the high walk. Safety helmets, ropes, harnesses and instruction on how to use them are required before ascending.

A large generator makes electricity (110 v) available every evening from 6 p.m. to 9 p.m. The large open-air dining room building with views on all sides of the forest seats more than 40 persons. The modern kitchen is spotless and efficient, and the food is tasty and served in generous portions. A bar serves soft drinks and beer. The sprawling laboratory and air-conditioned library building houses research facilities and a large collection of books and research articles. The dormitory building is nearby, and it has eight rooms, each with two bunk beds and a large modern bathroom. Toward the back of the compound are two buildings with wide common porches for visitors.

Between them they have seven large rooms, each with two single beds and a bathroom. These rooms are so large that two extra beds can easily be put in temporarily. All sleeping and studying areas are screened, and no mosquito netting is needed. The water system collects rainwater for use in bathrooms and toilets. Water for drinking and cooking is additionally filtered. The buildings are all connected by a network of brick walkways.

The Tiputini Biodiversity Station is owned and operated by the Universidad de San Francisco in Quito with collaboration from Boston University in Massachusetts. Its top priority of education and research is a real plus for ecotourists, who are also welcome. International experts in several fields of Biology and Conservation are almost always in residence, and the guides available for ecotourists have all served as field assistants in scientific projects, from botany, frog taxonomy and primatology to tropical agriculture. This means you are being guided by local people who have had first-hand training and in many cases the equivalent of several university field courses.

GETTING THERE: You fly or take a bus from Quito to Coca. Here you get in a motorized canoe and go downriver one and a half hours to the "town" of Pompeya. On the south side of the river you get out at the YPF oil pier. Because entrance is through "Block 16" administered by the YPF Oil Consortium, company policy must be followed for everyone entering Tiputini Biodiversity Station. After checking in with the security guard and exchanging your passports and yellow inoculation cards (**NOTE:** you must have a current yellow fever inoculation registered and you *cannot be younger than 16 years old*—no exceptions!) for a YPF visitors badge, you board a comfortable bus and ride 50 kilometers (one and a half hours) south on the oil company road. Don't lose your plastic badge as it must be returned to get your passport back at the end of your stay. At the Río Tiputini bridge you transfer to another motorized canoe for an often exciting 50 kilometers (two-hour) trip down the Río Tiputini. Wildlife is abundant along the edge of this intermediate-sized river, so watch around every bend.

FIFTEEN

Central and Southern Oriente

Including some of the least known and least accessible parts of the country, southeastern Ecuador also has places that were colonized by the Spanish more than four hundred years ago. Agriculture is dominant in the area, but oil has had its influence in the past and is likely to be more important in the near future. Apart from the popular tourist areas around Tena and the upper Napo area of Misahuallí, few tourists visit this region. Incredible stretches of unexplored Amazon forest, beautiful cloud forests along the east slope of the Andes, and indigenous cultures are only some of the rewards awaiting those who are willing to try something different. Access to this area is most generally via the Quito–Baeza Road, but entrance from Cuenca via the Gualaceo–Macas Road or from Zamora in the extreme south are also possible for the more adventuresome.

The ever-present cloud of border disputes and war with Perú has probably had as much to do with the lack of tourist development in this area as anything. In the skirmish in February of 1995, the towns of Macas and Zamora were evacuated and Puyo was placed off-limits to foreigners because of national interest and the military posts here. In addition, much of this region is under the local control of the Shuar Nation, who have been among the most active tribes in gaining their autonomy and right to self-determination. Only recently have they begun to change their attitudes toward tourists.

ARCHIDONA/TENA

If you are driving from Quito and Baeza, continue south on the Baeza–Tena Highway to the pleasant little town of Archidona. If you take the truck bypass, you will miss the town center and its attractive town square. If you want to get to Tena quickly, take the bypass. If you are a spelunker or just like to look at caves, the **Jumandí Caves** are north of Archidona after the town of Cotundo. The caves themselves are well organized for visitors and local guides will take you into the caverns. Be prepared to wade if not swim a 200-foot (60-meter) stretch near the cave entrance to gain access to the interior of the cave. A tourist complex has been built outside the entrance to the cave, and it has 16 cabins (double beds in each), swimming pools, volleyball and a restaurant. Archidona is a chance to experience a quiet Ecuadorian town not frequently visited by foreign tourists.

Tena is a pleasant town that is obviously used to foreign tourists. There are many small and inexpensive hosterias and hostales. The town is divided in half by the Río Tena, with the older part on the west bank and the newer, more up and coming part on the east side of the river. A single-lane bridge (watch for the traffic signal to let you know if you can proceed or have to wait for cars coming from the other direction) and a foot bridge a block south are the only crossing points in town and are also the only way to go on south to Puyo. On both sides of the river, the town advertises cafés and restaurants in English. Many cater to backpackers and vegetarians as the town is a convenient stopover for younger or budget tourists who can't afford the more expensive places out of Misahuallí. However, changing money can be a problem here as in many parts of rural Ecuador. The local gas stations, even in the most remote areas, tend to be sophisticated about money exchange and are often willing to exchange U.S. dollars at a rate favorable to them. In Tena, the gas stations are all on the south end of town across the bridge over the Río Tena. In the city center on the north side of the bridge, the **Comercial Moscoso** advertises money exchange—and is also a good place to buy supplies, from food to rubber boots. They offer the best exchange rate in town. Be aware of smooth-talking salespeople selling jungle ecotourism packages to passersby. Our experience with tour companies in Tena is that if you have to rely on a hustler to approach you on the street to arrange a trip to the jungle, you are likely to be disappointed. Make arrangements out of Quito or at one of the reputable lodges on the upper Napo. **Jatún Sacha** and **Cabañas Aliñahui** (Butterfly Lodge) have an office in Tena two blocks north of the *terminal terrestre* on the east side of the river (on the road south to Puyo).

LODGING   The best hotels for budget travelers are the **Residencial Napoli**, **Residencial Aleman** and **Residencial Hilton** (all have shared bath, hot water and cost $2–$5). They are all clustered together on the east (Puyo) side of the river just after you cross the vehicle bridge. The **Hotel Mol** and **Hostal Sheraton Amazonico**, both on the west side of the river in the town center, are better, if a bit more expensive (private bath, cold water; $8–$15). If you have transportation, the best hotel is on the river at the north end of town—the **Hotel Auca** (private bath, hot water; $12–$20). This hotel has a restaurant and disco and overlooks the Río Tena. It is an interesting place to look for birds. The broad sand and gravel beaches also offer a fun place to enjoy the sun and have a cool swim. Avoid the weekends, however, when the beach becomes crowded with locals and very loud beach parties.

RESTAURANTS   The restaurants in Tena are numerous and varied, but be very cautious of sanitation. Many of them are not meticulous in keeping food and serving areas clean. According to Barbara Roth, the former manager of Cabañas Aliñahui, the following are the best and most reliable restaurants in Tena. They average in price from $4–$10.

Cositas Ricas (Avenida 15 de Noviembre 422, uphill from the foot bridge over the river; 2-886-372) offers a variety of national dishes as well as vegetarian meals. It has good-sized portions and most are very tasty. They cater to tourists and have gone out of their way to provide safe food preparation procedures for gringos. **Chuquitos** (Calles J. Montalvo and L. Mera) specializes in typical Ecuadorian meals of meat and potatoes and especially delicious soups. This is a favorite restaurant of the locals and is exceptionally clean. It is located at the upper end of the main plaza kittycorner from the bank and on the same side of the street as the Hotel Amazonas.

La Estancia (2-886-354) is a thatch-roofed restaurant on the main highway south of the river. It is a handy place to stop and eat for those driving on through to Misahuallí or Puyo. The food is excellent and quickly prepared.

El Tico Rico (Avenida Amazonas) also serves typical Ecuadorian food and is relatively clean. It is two blocks north of the city park and main plaza.

Hotel Auca at the north end of town serves a limited but very tasty menu. Soups, yuca and typical national dishes are available along with standard chicken and rice, as well as beef dishes. American breakfasts are served in the morning, and snacks are available all day long. The prices, although more expensive than restaurants in town, are not excessive.

GETTING THERE: By Bus: The *terminal terrestre* is across the bridge in the south part of town. Buses arrive and depart for Quito several times a day either via Puyo–Baños–Ambato (nine–ten hours) or via Baeza (seven hours). Buses also go to Lago Agrio and Coca.

By Car: Without stopping, the trip from Quito takes about five hours by car. Be wary of night driving, especially in the rain. The asphalt part of the road lacks white lines and sucks up the light. Staring into the headlights (often on bright) of oncoming traffic gets old fast.

MISAHUALLÍ AND THE UPPER RÍO NAPO

Starting high in the cloud forests and paramo of the east slope of the Andes, the Río Napo runs the entire length of Amazonian Ecuador to join the

Amazon River in Brazil. It drains the northern portion of the Oriente and therefore is a primary route of commerce in a land of few roads and far-flung villages. It is the riparian artery that pumps life into the region and along which human life travels, lives, acquires food, communicates and celebrates.

The upper Napo still retains the rollicking exuberance of the countless mountain streams that feed it. There are erratic turns and dramatic cutbanks, playful rapids, and sharp sweeps that contrast with the languorous Río Napo farther downstream. On the upper Napo, you will see people poling small

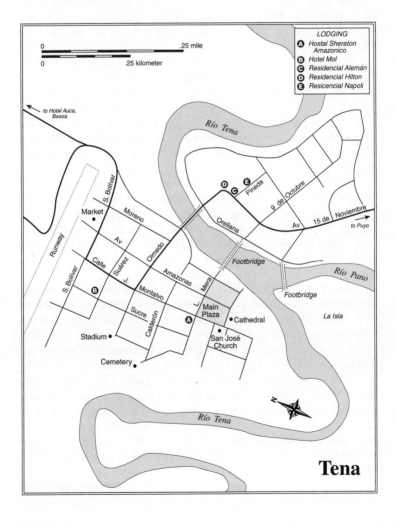

dugouts through the bankside eddies with a child or pile of crops up front, gold miners washing sand for the glint of dreams, thatch huts with backyard banana plantations and elegant hotels perched on high bluffs. There will be mothers washing babies and pounding laundry on boulders, missionary churches and small government schools, steps carved into the riverbank clay and clothes hung on volleyball nets, Yamaha outboard motors and Coca-Cola concessions, bewildered and bewondered pale-skinned gringos with stuff draped all over them, and amber-skinned natives—shirtless and at ease. You will see parrot flocks and granite rocks, long-winged hawks black as the night, great aerial kettles of vultures, splashes of red-flowering trees and dapper swallows dancing over the waves. And you may not even have gotten in the canoe yet!

Misahuallí (also called Puerto Misahuallí) is located at the end of the road on the northwest corner of the confluence of the Río Napo and the Río Misahuallí. It is a dusty cluster of boom-town outfitters, hostales and profiteers arranged around a central square, all of which would fit into a large city block. On the square there are numerous small cafés and general stores that cater to the waiting or under-provisioned tourist. They sell everything from sodas and candy bars to rubber boots, ponchos, blue plastic tarps and outboard motors.

There are only two places we can recommend to stay: the **Misahuallí Jungle Hotel** across the Río Misahuallí (see below) and the **Hotel Alberque Español** just off the southwest corner of the square. Both have clean, comfortable rooms and nice restaurants. The other places to stay and eat in town—**Dayuma Lodge**, **Residencial Sacha**, **Hotel Etsa**, **Hotel 55** and the **Hotel Jennifer** are very inexpensive ($1–$8), less predictable and are more for the adventuresome and broad-minded.

Although Misahuallí may look and feel like the frontier, it is not. Ninety-nine percent of the land around Misahuallí is disturbed or developed in some way—mostly by agriculture and cattle ranching. The last remaining and protected primary rainforest in the area can be found on the grounds of the Misahuallí Jungle Hotel and in a relatively large area protected by the Jatún Sacha Ecological Reserve just downstream and across the Río Napo.

Twenty years ago there was one building in Misahuallí—a military guard station. When oil extraction began, Misahuallí mushroomed with petroleum workers, bars and cheap pensiones. As eager colonists, hungry for cheap land, followed the new oil roads, the Huaoranis were pushed farther into the forest. Now, most Huaoranis have been absorbed into Ecuador's modern culture, although some try to retain their native lifestyle and live in small, isolated villages accessible only by foot or small dugout canoe.

GETTING THERE: Misahuallí is 17 kilometers east of Puerto Napo, which in turn is 7 kilometers south of Tena, the provincial capital. Buses leave the

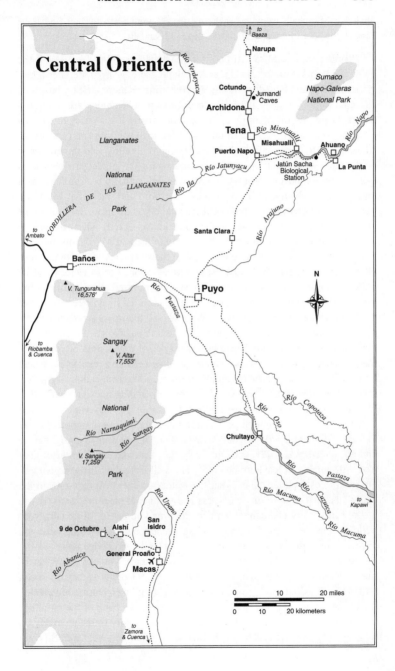

square in Misahuallí every half-hour for the 30-minute trip to Tena and leave Tena on the hour (more or less) for the trip to Misahuallí.

People pour into Misahuallí not for Misahuallí itself but because it is the point of embarkation for the Upper Río Napo. Here, gringos are after a jungle adventure, and Ecuadorians are after the gringo's money. Every business, it seems, offers some sort of jungle excursion, and guides are a sucre a dozen. There are few other places in Ecuador where it is so easy to spend a lot of money and get so little in return—other than wet, tired and frustrated. If you come to Misahuallí looking for an impromptu trip into the rainforest (something we do not recommend), make sure the guide you choose is licensed by the government, and make sure you actually see the license. If you do not speak enough Spanish to ask questions and state what you want, you may have a less than positive experience. If you do speak Spanish, make sure everything is spelled out and the guide knows exactly what you expect.

All **boat trips** leave from the beach where the Río Misahuallí joins the Río Napo (walk out the southeast corner of the square and down to the trees ahead, approximately 50 yards). At any time, a dozen or so canoes will be pulled up on the sand with boat drivers standing around chatting and telling stories. At this point, you will most likely be escorted by a representative of the lodge you are going to, so they will make all the travel arrangements.

If you are not part of a tour package, it is still easy to get a canoe to take you where you want to go. There are two styles of travel, both of which use the same boats. A water-bus is a canoe that operates like a regular bus where you share the ride with other people going to different locations. A water-taxi is a canoe you hire specifically for your trip and do not share with other people. The cheapest and most interesting way to go is by water-bus. You may have to wait for enough people wanting to go in your direction in order to leave, but the ride will cost only a few dollars. If you want to go right away and no water-bus is ready, you can easily hire a private canoe or water-taxi. You will be able to leave immediately and will have the canoe to yourself, but it will cost you ten times what the water-bus does. We recommend the water-bus, as it is more fun, costs less and you get to meet the locals. If you are still in a hurry and cannot wait by the time you get to Misahuallí, your building impatience and frustration will prevent you from enjoying what you have set out to do. Either relax or go back to Quito and dodge taxis.

As you relax on the beach waiting for your canoe, you can enjoy watching the local semi-domesticated Capuchin Monkey bandits as they try to con tourists for handouts and snatch goodies from their bags. During high water, the beach disappears, and the boats are tied up to the back of the buildings around the square. The water level can vary dramatically from day to day, so what appears as solid beach may in fact be very soft and wet sand. Be careful where you walk if you want dry feet, or buy a pair of high rubber boots and walk with impunity.

If you have hours to wait, there is a pleasant hike known as the **waterfall walk**. Take the bus toward Tena, and ask to be let off at *el camino a las cascadas*—the cascade trail—about a ten-minute ride. It takes about an hour to get to the waterfall as you walk along the stream through a small forest. To get back to Misahuallí, just wave down a bus going in the right direction.

A quiet, comfortable place to wait for your boat is at the ✪ **Misahuallí Jungle Hotel** (Ramírez Dávalos 251; private bath, hot water, ceiling fan; $20–$42; 2-520-043, fax: 2-454-146), across the Rió Misahuallí. They serve breakfast, lunch and dinner and have sodas available in their open-air dining room. Even better, stay a few days and enjoy the relaxed atmosphere. Although it is just across the river from the bustling town, the hotel's perch high on a bluff keeps it above the noise and commotion of Misahuallí.

The centerpiece of the Hotel Misahuallí is a large pyramid-shaped building that overlooks the Río Napo. A set of winding cement stairs leads up to the reception area from the sandy landing beach below. Most of the ground floor of the building is an open-sided space containing the dining room, bar, reception, meeting and lounging area. It is attractively designed, with exposed wooden posts and beams and large white tiles throughout. Only the kitchen is enclosed, so there is a sense of eating on an open-air terrace. Invariably, most guests end up in the comfortable padded wicker chairs and rockers to relax and recount the day. Upstairs are seven rooms and three shared baths designed for groups.

There are 15 cabañas on the grounds—ten of modern design with wooden construction and glass windows with screens, and five of more traditional style with split-bamboo siding and screened windows on three sides—all hold one to four guests. Each is very comfortable and well kept, with one to three beds, standing closet, bedside tables with reading lamps, electric ceiling fan, screened windows and small porch with comfortable wooden chairs. The private baths are spacious, completely tiled and have an enamel sink, large mirror and a large tiled shower with plenty of hot and cold water. We recommend the modern cabins for their comfort and views of the river.

There are some **trails** that can easily be explored from the hotel. Two short trails lead down to a small stream that wraps around the eastern side of the grounds. One crosses the stream to a small clearing and the other parallels it to where it empties into the Río Napo. For a longer excursion, there is a trail that roughly follows the Río Misahuallí. It begins at the back corner of the grounds where the cement walk ends along the Río Misahuallí. The trail has muddy spots so ask to borrow rubber boots from the hotel if you didn't pack your own.

Tapir

A *mirador* (lookout) is one popular destination that guides can take you to from the hotel. It sits on top of a small hill about an hour's walk and a gain in elevation of 578 feet (175 meters). You get great views of the Río Napo valley and the Andes to the west. There are no formal trails to the *mirador*, so a guide is necessary. This would make a great destination for a general rainforest discovery hike with the guides or a walk to look for birds or medicinal plants.

The hotel also offers a guided half-day trip to a neighboring Quichua village where there is a display of native hunting techniques and some artifacts. Another trip goes to an animal rehabilitation center where you can see native mammals waiting to be released back into the forest. You can also ask to be taken to the Jatún Sacha Reserve across the river if you are interested in exploring the largest parcel of rainforest in the area.

Across the Río Napo is a gravel road that parallels the southern banks of the river. The road is known locally as the Ahuano Road but it actually never gets to Ahuano, which is on the north side of the river. The landscape here is not much different than that found around Misahuallí except for one large patch of undisturbed forest at the Jatún Sacha Biological Station.

GETTING THERE: Puerto Napo used to be the point of embarkation for the upper Río Napo before the road to Misahuallí was established. Almost all boats leave from Misahuallí now and avoid the dangerous currents upstream.

Cabañas Cotacocha (Km. 10 Ahuano road, Misahuallí; private baths, hot water; several multiple day packages; four day, three night, $180 per person; in Quito: Lizardo Garcia 544 and Reina Victoria, phone/fax: 2-541-527) is a new ecotourist lodge that we have not yet had the chance to visit but of which we have had many good reports. Built on a bluff overlooking the Río Napo, Cabañas Cotacocha offers trips via canoes or trails for birdwatchers, jungle lovers, native culturists and those interested in medicinal plants. Bilingual guides are always available as are rubber boots and rain ponchos. Guests report a relaxed and comfortable atmosphere with a friendly and knowledgeable staff. There is a restaurant on the grounds serving all meals.

GETTING THERE: By Canoe: Cabañas Cotacocha is a two-hour motorized canoe ride downriver from Misahuallí. Most trips are arranged through their office in Quito, and a tour includes transportation by car to Misahuallí, escort by a guide, and the canoe trip to the cabañas. If you are planning to arrive in Misahuallí on your own, arrangements can be made for their canoe to be waiting for you.

❁❁❁ Jatún Sacha Biological Station (Isla Fernandina N43-98 and T. Berlangs; $25 for cabins, shared bath, cold water; in Quito: Box 17-12-867, phone/fax: 2-250-976) is a model ecotourist/research facility dedicated to conservation education and scientific investigation that directly benefits all the lives connected to the intact rainforest. Supporting this foundation either through contributions or by a visit enhances and supports this far-reaching mission.

Jatún Sacha was founded in 1989 by three landowners, who combined their adjacent property and created a 500-acre reserve. Since then, Jatún Sacha has become a nonprofit foundation that promotes conservation, research and education throughout Amazonia and through donations has grown to its present size. They provide in-class educational programs for area schools, college-level courses for Ecuadorian and international students and basic scientific investigations of rainforest ecology. In 1993, Jatún Sacha was named the second International Children's Rainforest (the first is Monteverde in Costa Rica).

Today, Jatún Sacha is a 4000-acre wet tropical rainforest island in an ocean of cut and disturbed agricultural land. It sits only 20 kilometers east of the crest of the Andes and is in a transitional zone between mountain and lowland forests. Because of the combined pressures of hunting and civilization, some of the large mammals are extremely rare, but monkeys, tapirs and Pumas are its least-shy residents. It is an extraordinarily rich environment: over 500 species of birds have been recorded, 200 species of trees per hectare (in comparison, there are only 600 species of trees in all of North America), more than 120 kinds of reptiles and amphibians, including 68 species of frogs in 50 hectares, the most from any site in the world, and the most diverse fauna of the colorful Dendrobates (poison arrow) frogs known—and more than 1500 species of plants including more than 120 kinds of orchids.

Jatún Sacha translates as "big forest" in the Quichua language. (Quichua are Ecuadorians—Quechua are Peruvians.) More than 70 percent of the preserved area is primary forest, the rest is made up of disturbed secondary forest and research plots. From the **administration building** at the road, there is an extensive network of trails that crisscross the reserve. Stop in at the office first to pay the entrance fee (10,000 sucres), pick up a trail map and ask for suggestions for trail walking. (They also have other information and great T-shirts.)

The trail system is a series of long parallel crisscrossing trails that go to the farthest corners of the forest. Tall rubber boots for the muddy parts of the trails are essential anytime of the year. November through March are generally the driest, sunniest months—April through June the wettest, but it can be sunny and dry or rainy and wet for a week anytime of the year. All trail junctions are marked with two-way arrows—the red arrow leads you away from the main entrance, the yellow arrows leads you back to the entrance.

Just to the west of the main building is a trail that quickly ascends a long series of steps to the lodging complex. The facilities are mostly for college student groups (up to 22 people) and are quite primitive, suitable only for the young and those tolerant of discomfort. There is electricity and a fully operational kitchen, but we strongly recommend staying just down the road at the Cabañas Aliñahui. The Jatún Sacha cabins sit in a small clearing on top of a little knoll and would be a good spot for lunch and one of the better spots for finding birds, assuming the cabins are not occupied.

GETTING THERE: By Bus: There are local buses that depart from below the Río Tena footbridge in Tena several times a day from the *terminal terrestre*. Make sure you are not taking the bus to Misahuallí (wrong side of the river).

By Car: Jatún Sacha is 30 kilometers from Tena and 200 kilometers from Quito. The trip from Quito takes six hours with inspired driving, more after heavy rains (there are often landslides) or if you are exploring along the way. It is best to leave Quito early and expect to take all day getting to Jatún Sacha. Twenty-three kilometers east of the turn at the Río Napo bridge along the Ahuano road is the administration building of Jatún Sacha and the place to begin your exploration of this beautiful forest.

By Boat: The Jatún Sacha forest is only 8 kilometers downstream from Misahuallí and can be easily reached by canoe as can the Cabañas Aliñahui.

☺☺☺ Cabañas Aliñahui (Butterfly Lodge) (shared bath, solar-heated water; $53 per adult, $32 per child, food included; in Quito: Isla Fernandina N43-78, Casilla 17-12-867, 2-253-267, fax: 2-253-266; e-mail: alinahui@jsacha.ecuanex.net.ec) pronounced (ah–lee–neYAH–wee) occupy about 3 acres of parklike grounds that have been extensively landscaped with splashes of red and lavender flowering plants and fruit trees. Cabañas Aliñahui are half-owned by Health and Habitat, a nonprofit California company (76 Lee Street, Mill Valley, CA 94941; 415-383-6130, fax: 415-381-9214). Arrangements and details can be made through them for two- to eight-day tours of the area.

The lodge sits at the edge of the river bluff where a short, staired trail leads down to canoes along the Río Napo and where on a clear day four snow-capped Andean volcanoes are visible. The area was initially a cattle ranch with pastures extending out to the main road and the family living in what is now the administration/office building. In 1988, tourist cabins were built to supplement the cattle income, and a rudimentary ecotourist program was begun. The Health and Habitat Foundation, a nonprofit organization, and the Fundación Jatún Sacha co-purchased the entire property in 1993, expelled the cattle, and began a more sophisticated and comfortable tourist operation. Caged animals were released, pastures were allowed to revert back to woodlands, the cabins were remodeled and an extensive trail system instituted. It is now, in conjunction with Jatún Sacha, one of the most eco-tourism-sensitive facilities in Amazonian Ecuador. To walk to Jatún Sacha takes about 45 minutes, if done quickly, or two to three hours if you are looking at things along the way. About a kilometer east of Jatún Sacha is a road-side beverage stand that is a great place to stop, have a drink and rest on a hot day.

Each of the ten cabins at Aliñahui is made of wood and raised on posts to a second-story level. There are two rooms per cabin, divided by a covered porch. Beneath each cabin is a shady concrete terrace with a table, comfortable chairs and two hammocks that are perfect for a midday siesta. The rooms are simple yet comfortable with two beds, a closet, reading lamps and large screened windows. There is one bathroom per cabin, located on the ground level and outfitted with a toilet, sink and solar-heated shower. While it is inconvenient to have to walk outside and downstairs to get to the bathroom, they are clean and well maintained and not enough of a problem to worry too much about. If there are any problems, the staff is exceptionally friendly and helpful. There is an on-site manager who speaks Spanish, German and English.

The cabins are spaced around the grounds and surrounded by tall trees so that each has a feeling of privacy. Cobblestone walks, lit by oil lamps at night, connect the cabins to the other buildings. There is a large open-air dining area, bar and library centrally located, and a thatched roofed barbecue hut for special meals. The meals are very good and served buffet style with hot soups and native fruits and vegetables featured. There is always safe drinking water available in a large cooler, and all the cooking and washing is done with boiled water.

On the edge of the river bluff are three thatched-roof, wooden-deck *miradores* that have a spectacular view east down the Río Napo and west to

the Andes (Aliñahui means "good view" in Quichua). We cannot recommend these *miradores* enough as a quiet spot for early-morning coffee or
late-afternoon tea and snacks. It would be a worthwhile day to just sit here
and watch the sun rise and fall, the play chase of cloud shadows across the
rolling green forest, the slow wind waltz of a circling vulture and listen to
the double-time tap of a foraging tanager while being rocked by the sounds
of the Río Napo below.

Several day trips are offered: a full-day canoe trip to the Guambuno, a
beautiful small river where Hoatzins and caimans can be seen; a half-day
canoe trip to the Río Arajuno for more sightseeing, gold panning (where
specks of gold are almost always found) and a visit to a local shaman who
explains the medicinal use of the plants in the area. They also offer a trip to
Amazoonico, a rainforest wildlife rehabilitation center, where up-close views
of the area's usually elusive wildlife are possible.

The Cabañas Aliñahui do not have the European elegance or the appearance of luxury that other Amazonian lodges have, but they provide a high-
quality experience while at the same time preserving the rainforest. For the
independent traveler, Cabañas Aliñahui and the Jatún Sacha Biological
Station are a very good and worthwhile destination.

GETTING THERE: By Car: Just a couple of kilometers east of Jatún Sacha
along the Ahuano road is the sign for Cabañas Aliñahui. Take a left turn toward the
river at this sign and then a 1.5-kilometer drive takes you to Cabañas Aliñahui.

❂ **Casa del Suizo** (private bath, hot water; $40–$60; in Quito: Explorer
Tours, Reina Victoria 1325 and Lizardo García, 2-522-220, 2-508-871, fax:
2-508-872) represents the edge. Physically, it is built on the edge of a Río
Napo riverbank and from this perch you can see the edge of the great sprawl
of the primeval rainforest. It is the edge of familiarity as well. You can travel this far into the Oriente along the upper reaches of the Amazonian basin
and still carry with you the full shadow of civilization. Located in the little
village of Ahuano and the most elegant and comfortable lodge in the
Oriente, Casa del Suizo is where to get your feet muddy and your spirits
buoyed on the trails of the forest but still have the safetyline of comfort to
bide you upon your return to your room—where European elegance and familiar comforts welcome you. Casa del Suizo is an experience too tame for
some folks, who want to hear the sunrise roar of a monkey troop, but perfect
for those who wish just to sample the jungle on their own familiar terms.

Ahuano is a very small village of several hundred people, mostly poor
farmers and small shopkeepers. On the west edge of the village, built on a shel-
tering riverbank bluff and rising above the tiled roofs and twisted antennae of
Ahuano sits Casa del Suizo. From the village it looks like a densely encrusted

growth of thatched-roof walkways and cabañas culminating at a large, blue-roofed main building. To step from the dirt streets of Ahuano to the beautifully landscaped gardens of Casa del Suizo is to cross from the hardscrabble life of jungle colonists to the ease and opulence of a tourist's vacation.

There are 30 individual cabañas and 20 motel-like rooms that can accommodate up to 130 guests altogether. The cabañas are very, very nice—far more comfortable than any other lodge we have visited in the Oriente. Dark, exotic tropical woods are used for the walls, floors and furniture. There are electric lights, and each room has a private bath and reliable hot water. We recommend the cabañas built over the river. They have a large veranda with comfortable chairs and a hammock to enjoy the river view. It is a delightful place to welcome the day or watch the day melt away as you are serenaded by the flow of the Río Napo. All the rooms and cabañas are connected by a maze of boardwalks that take you past pocket gardens and live animal displays that feature snakes, caiman, turtles and tortoises, guatusa (large forest rodents) and parrots.

Such displays of captive animals are common at lodges in the rainforest. Unfortunately, a number of animals die in order to get a few in captivity. This is particularly true and critically important with regards to parrots. Ten or more parrots will die and several nest trees will be destroyed for every one or two parrots you see at a jungle lodge.

There are a number of day trips that are offered by the hotel. One full-day trip goes up a small river to a wilder part of the forest. Guests have the option of riding a balsa raft back to the hotel. Another trip is a half-day walk through farming country with a visit to a shaman who will make a potion for you and demonstrate his herbal medicinal powers. You will probably be offered a local drink known as *chicha* made from fermented sweet potatoes. It tastes either like grapefruit juice with a tang or wine gone bad. Any interest you may still have in this drink will probably be diminished when you learn that the fermentation process is initiated by spitting into the mix. You might want to ask before trying *chicha* if any human byproducts were added to the beverage.

As we mentioned earlier, Casa del Suizo is for those travelers who want comfort and elegance first and are less interested in seeing the true rainforest. All the land surrounding the hotel is developed or disturbed and consequently there is little exotic flora or fauna to be seen. There are birds in the hedgerows and overgrown fields, but what primary forest is around is patchy and inaccessible. All the large, showy animals are long gone and even on the excursions you are very unlikely to see much more than a rudimentary version of the rainforest. Remember, as comfort and elegance increase, wildness often decreases.

Still, Casa del Suizo is a very popular jungle destination and justifiably so. The quality of service and accommodation is extraordinary. We recommend the Casa del Suizo as a place for those who are unsure and wary of a jungle adventure but who are willing to give it a chance. You will be well taken care of.

GETTING THERE: By Car: Just down the road (east) from the turnoff to the Cabañas Aliñahui is La Punta and the end of the road. La Punta is the typical place to cross the river to get to the Casa del Suizo. If you are going to the lodge they have a protected place to park your car at La Punta, although you should not leave valuables there. It costs 4000 sucres, about two dollars, for the five-minute ride over to Ahuano and Casa del Suizo. La Punta is just a wide river gravel bar where cars can be parked and canoes hired for your trip downstream. If you are not in a rush to jump in your canoe, there is usually a very informal market on the gravel bar that caters to both tourists and the local people.

Just downstream and across the river from Ahuano is Anaconda Island, a large island that marks the mouth of the small Río Arajuno. Five minutes from Ahuano on the downstream end of this island is ○○ **Cabañas Anaconda** (private bath, cold water; $25–$35; 2-545-426), another lodge, but one that offers a different rainforest experience.

The Cabañas Anaconda are situated in a small forest clearing on the east end of Anaconda Island in the Río Napo just on the opposite bank from the little village of Ahuaño and the Casa del Suizo. It feels, though, like it is miles and decades away, and that is the intent. The owners have made a conscious effort to keep the commotion and concerns of the outside world beyond the tall trees and dense vegetation that encircle the grounds. There are no saws, radios and loud trucks to be heard, and the current news of the day is whatever is picked up on the muddy flow of the Río Napo. You will not find all the European elegance and creature comforts of other lodges, but you will find a sanctuary where guests are invited to relax and encouraged to let their cares slip downstream. If you ever wanted to disappear someplace for a week to read books or just relax in comfort and friendship, this is it.

When you first walk into the grounds, the feeling is that of entering a friendly native village carved out of the surrounding forest. There are a dozen cabañas placed around a clearing, each built of local materials by a different native craftsman. The Hurtado family, who owns the Cabañas Anaconda, says that a native man puts part of himself into each cabaña and thus each is unique and special to that builder. The cabañas are widely spaced for privacy and connected by a web of wide, hard-dirt paths. Between the paths are well-kept grassy lawns and scattered large trees where a tame curassow and monkeys are often found.

Generally the cabañas are wooden-frame structures built on short stilts with bamboo siding and thatch or metal roofs. There are two to four rooms in each cabaña with private baths (cold water only), large screened windows with curtains, no electricity (there are candles for light) and no ceiling so noises are freely exchanged. The rooms, though rustic, are comfortable and clean and other than to sleep there is no reason to spend much time in them anyway.

Beside the sleeping cabañas, there is a gift hut, an office, a small museum displaying indigenous clothing, a meeting building, a thatched-roof dining room and the Hurtado family cabaña. The dining room is attractively decorated with tropical plants and heliconia blossoms and has electric lights from a gas generator, a full bar and a sitting area. The tables are attractively set and uniformed waiters serve a fixed meal that is ample and delicious.

The surrounding forest is an interesting mix of scattered emergent trees forming a thin canopy and a dense, impenetrable heliconia understory. There are more and less disturbed areas including a small pond that would be worth watching as animals come to drink and pocket plantations of cocoa, banana and papaya. While it is not a primary rainforest and evidence of disturbance is common, there are still many birds and butterflies present. Toucans, parrots and large cuckoos, among other birds, can be observed here. In fact, because the forest has been thinned, this is one of the easiest lodges in the Oriente to see interesting birds.

There are several excursions for an additional price that you can take into relatively undisturbed rainforest or to visit a native village. Ask the staff about the details of each trip. The entire staff of the Cabañas Anaconda is unusually friendly and helpful. They invite guests to become part of their large extended family and want you to feel both at ease and at home. This would be a great spot for a university group to come for an extended stay to catalog and explore the area or for someone who wants a friendly introduction to Amazonia.

Following the Río Napo downstream from Ahuano and the Cabañas Anaconda carries you farther into the wilder reaches of the upper Napo. There are still huts and crops carved out of the riverside forest but they are smaller and farther apart now than they were near Misahuallí. Consequently, parrot flocks are larger and more common, you are more likely to see herons prowling the backwaters and the intact forest will have its typical large emergent trees and gaudy splashes of flowers and fruit. If you continue too far downstream, the shadow of development from Coca again diminishes the forest and wildlife.

GETTING THERE: The Cabañas Anaconda is a 30-minute motorized canoe ride from Misahuallí. Most trips are arranged through their office in Quito and a tour includes a bus ride to Misahuallí, escorted by a guide, and the canoe trip to the Cabañas. If you are planning to arrive in Misahuallí on your own, arrangements can be made for their canoe to be waiting for you. If you are unsure when you are going to arrive, it is easy to hire a canoe at the Misahuallí beach that will take you to the Cabañas. Passengers disembark at a low undercut bank and follow a flat sandy trail to the compound. The trail is just long enough that you will have to switch hands if you are carrying a heavy duffel. It is best to leave your luggage at the canoe bank and let the staff of the Cabañas carry it to your room. There are no other buildings or people living on the island so your gear will be safe.

Just upstream from the Cabañas Anaconda the Río Arajuno flows into the Río Napo from the south. An hour or so down the Río Arajuno at the junction of the Río Puni is the **Dayuma Camp** (shared baths, cold water. Prices vary greatly depending on the type of program and number of people in your group, but $60 per person per night is average; in Quito: Avenida 10 de Agosto 3815 and Mariana de Jesús, Office 301, 2-506-204, fax: 2-564-924). Although we have not visited this new rainforest lodge yet, it is operated by the people who also run the Dayuma Lodge in Misahuallí, and hopefully their expertise and concern for the environment will be continued in this new venture. It is located in a section of mostly undisturbed rainforest. There are 16 two-room huts built in traditional style with native materials. A larger building with a restaurant and common area is centrally located on the grounds. Guides are available for birdwatching, nature and medicinal-plants walks, and arrangements can be made to visit the nearby native community of Sinchiruna. On the grounds of the Dayuma Camp is a very large zoo-like area where native animals are on display and are apparently waiting for release back into the forest. The camp has several package options, some with transportation from Quito included in the price.

GETTING THERE: By Canoe: Dayuma Camp is a two-hour motorized canoe ride from Misahuallí. Most trips are arranged through their office in Quito and a tour includes transportation by car to Misahuallí, escort by a guide and the canoe trip to the camp. If you are planning to arrive in Misahuallí on your own, arrangements can be made for their canoe to be waiting for you.

Forty-five minutes or so from Cabañas Anaconda is a wild, pristine section of the rainforest and the only building in sight—✪✪ **Hotel Jaguar** (private bath, hot water; $20–$50; in Quito: Luís Cordero 1313, 2-239-400, fax: 2-502-682). Upon arrival, guests disembark on a small cobble beach just below the hotel. On the walk up the concrete steps to the hotel, notice the three or four dark, bull-necked birds perched on top of the tree over the stairs. They are Swallow-wing Puffbirds and look like barn swallows on steroids. The steps curve up to a thatched-roof terrace, which also serves as the entry to the hotel. From the terrace there as a magnificent view of the river, especially as the sun rises, and you will now be looking down on the puffbirds. The flash of the puffbird's white rump patch will be easy to see whenever they sally out to catch a passing meal. You do not need to rush to see the puffbirds—they seem to always be there, at their post in the top of the tree. The name "puffbird" comes from an inconspicuous white fluff of feathers on each thigh. (For some reason, ornithologists prefer to name birds after their least-conspicuous field mark.)

The main building is modern, with a sweeping two-story glass front and a large covered terrace that overlooks the river. It is built right on the edge of the bluff so there are no trees to obscure the magnificent view. Inside, the large open floor plan holds a meeting area, bar and dining room. It is comfortable and attractively decorated with large floor tiles, cushioned chairs and benches and several sofas. The dining area has heavy wooden tables that are nicely set at all times with condiments and coffee, tea and sugar. Wooden beams traverse the ceiling from which hang lights in locally woven baskets; indigenous artifacts decorate the white plaster walls.

Behind the main building are 12 rooms enclosing a courtyard with a reflecting pool and the customary toucan in a cage. Each room is comfortably large, with white plaster walls, exposed wooded beams, attractive dark wooden furniture, and private bath. There is hot water and electric lights when the generator is on—which is most of the time—and when not, invigoration and candles. As with most of the lodges of the Oriente, the rooms are for sleeping—almost everyone relaxes, reads and converses on the terrace or around the bar inside.

What is special about the Hotel Jaguar is the uninterrupted primary rainforest that crowds the lodge in back. There are several ways to explore this forest. Walk down the cement walk behind the rooms as it descends through the nicely landscaped backyard to a beautiful little creek—the Huanbunolito. At the landing where the walk stops, the great green wall of the forest rises. Behind you, the cleared grounds around the hotel are the only pocket of disturbed forest within miles. Ahead are the delights and wonders of the forest.

*Yellow-headed
Parrot*

To those unfamiliar with the secrets of the forest the manager of the Hotel Jaguar, Edwardo Gomez, cannot be too highly recommended. Eduardo and his family (his wife is the cook and his little boy is the one causing mischief) have run the hotel for many years. He is a sturdy man with an expressive face and a smile that lingers. Edwardo has an encyclopedic knowledge of the plants and history of the region and will enthusiastically share it with those who ask. He genuinely wants you to see the forest through his eyes.

During the quiet times of the day and when the daylight has faded, Edwardo plays beautiful songs on a well-worn guitar. The true character of the Hotel Jaguar is revealed when you linger on the terrace before dinner watching the ever-present puffbirds hawk insects over the river below while you are serenaded by Edwardo's soft music. The Hotel Jaguar is farther away and therefore harder to get to, but if you want to explore a splendid piece of primary rainforest with comfort and a special guide, visit here.

GETTING THERE: The Hotel Jaguar sits on a low bluff above the Río Napo about half the distance between Misahuallí and Coca. Canoe arrangements can be made by the lodge. It takes about an hour and a half going downstream with high water, a bit longer during the dry months of December–February when the water is lower and navigation is a bit trickier. During extreme low water, your adventure may be enhanced by some necessary canoe pushing and river wading. The canoe drivers seem to delight in yelling *"¡Gringos al agua!"* when it is obvious the water is too low and the gringo passengers need to get out and push. When you walk in any river in Amazonia shuffle your feet along the bottom. Sting rays are often on the bottom, and if you step down on one, you are likely to be stung, putting you out of commission for a day.

On the south bank of the Río Napo near the Hotel Jaguar is the new lodge **Cabañas El Albergue Español** (private baths, cold water, solar energy lights; four day, three night, $145 per person; in Tena: P.O. Box 15-01-254). We have not had the opportunity to visit here yet, but we have had high recommendations from several people who have. The facilities are simple but clean. It is near undisturbed rainforest, so wildlife watching can be quite good. Native guides are available for excursions into the forest and a restaurant serves three meals a day for guests. The Cabañas El Albergue Español is for travelers who want the feel of the wild rainforest but don't want to travel two days to get there.

GETTING THERE: By Canoe: The cabañas are a two-hour motorized canoe ride from Misahuallí. Arrangements for canoe transportation from Misahuallí can be made at the office in Tena. Transportation from Quito or Tena to Misahuallí must be made on your own.

Two hours down the Río Napo by motorized canoe (almost halfway to Coca) is the new ✪✪✪ **Yachana Lodge** (in Quito Francisco Andrade Marín and Diego de Almagro; private or communal baths, solar electricity; four days and three nights $320, including ground transport from Quito and canoe from Misahuallí; 2-543-851, fax: 2-220-362; e-mail: info@yachana.com). The lodge is solidly built with native materials, and the buildings are connected by thatch-roofed walkways. There are ten comfortable double rooms with closets and sinks overlooking the Río Napo. These are connected to communal washroom facilities and showers. There are also three large family cabins, each with a sitting room, a balcony and a private bath. The dining room is centrally located and serves mainly vegetarian meals (the argument against beef being that cattle help destroy the forest). There is also a small bar and gift shop where local artisans sell their handicrafts.

Built by the NGO called FUNEDESIN, the goals of this lodge are specifically to support local conservation, health, agriculture and community development among the Quichua Indians living here. More than any other lodge on the upper or lower Napo, this one clearly uses ecotourism to better the lives of the local people. Although a little primary forest and lots of secondary forest are available for hikes and jungle viewing, tourists who come here are also exposed to local culture by visiting nearby villages, learning about logical agricultural practices and seeing firsthand ways in which this part of the Amazon can be used for long term and sustainable economic returns. The nearby clinic, built by FUNEDESIN and the villagers, has the best medical facilities for 100 miles, and it is largely supported from the profits of the ecotourism venture. We enthusiastically support and recommend this lodge for anyone who is interested in the human side of rational development of the Amazon.

GETTING THERE: The cost of staying at Yachana includes a van and driver to transport you from your hotel in Quito to Misahuallí and return. Normally you leave early in the morning from Quito for the six- to seven-hour drive. A lunch at a restaurant in Misahuallí is also included. The Yachana motorized canoe meets you at the port in Misahuallí and takes two hours downstream to the lodge. By prearrangement, you can make your own way to Misahuallí and meet the canoe directly. Also by prearrangement you can take a canoe down to Coca (two and a half hours) after your stay in Yachana and fly back to Quito. Departures from Quito are on Wednesday and Saturday with the return trip on Saturday or Wednesday, depending on the length of your stay.

PUYO

A small town of 35,000, Puyo has a major military base and air base, and is not a major center for tourism. It is on the crossroads of the north-south highway between Tena and Macas (six hours to the south), as well as at the lower end of the highway descending from Baños. Probably a majority of the tourists visiting Puyo come for a day of warm temperatures and a change from Baños.

LODGING   There are few good places to stay or eat in Puyo, but we highly recommend the **Hosteria Turingia** (Ceslao Marín 294; private bath, hot water, TV; $25–$35; 3-885-180, fax: 3-885-384). This pleasant compound in the middle of town is quiet, with bungalow-type rooms. Tropical plants and trees shade the buildings, and the restaurant in the main building next to reception is the best in town. Both national and international cuisine are served.

Five kilometers north of Puyo on the road to Tena is the **Hosteria Safari** (Km. 5 vía a Tena; private bath, hot water; $20–$40; 3-885-466, 3-851-424, fax: 3-828-574; in Ambato: American Park, Calle Luciano Guerrero, Casilla 18-01-1073, phone/fax: 3-850-593). The 33 rooms are in individual cabins spread out on the grounds of this extensive compound. There is a pool, sauna, convention hall, sports facilities and a restaurant (*El Jardín*) that serves national cuisine. Tours are also made to nearby "jungle"—mainly cutover areas with secondary forest.

GETTING THERE: By Bus and Bicycle: Buses leave hourly from Baños, and the ride to Puyo takes two hours. A challenging alternative is to rent a bicycle in Baños and make the descent at your leisure. The downhill coasting is not much work, but dodging trucks and buses on the very narrow upper section of the road as well as choking on clouds of dust over the gravel parts of the highway can be trying. In Puyo, the bicycle can be put on top of a bus and you return without facing a 3000-foot (1000-meter) climb of pedaling uphill. There are many pullouts, side trails and beautiful vistas of waterfalls and steep valleys, so bring your camera. Be sure to carefully inspect your bicycle before you start your trip. Some outfitters in Baños do maintain their bicycles very well, others don't. Also be sure to ask for a spare tire just in case you get a flat.

By Car: Puyo is 87 kilometers, about a two-hour drive south from Tena, and 68 kilometers, about an hour and a half's drive, from Baños. Expect to take all day to drive to Puyo from Quito.

MACAS

The gravel road from Puyo to Macas has been open for only a few years. The 200 kilometers can be done easily in a day if no landslides block your way or a bridge doesn't get washed away during the rainy season. The suspension bridge over the spectacular canyon of the Río Pastaza is so narrow that only regular cars and small trucks can cross it. Before the bridge was finished, you had to ferry across the river on rickety canoes that were lashed together. This area, around the village of **Chuitayo**, is without a doubt has the most interesting scenery and also has the most intact forest of the entire route between Puyo and Macas. Most of the rest of the road is cutover forest with considerable agriculture.

The road takes you through the edge of the Shuar Nation, so you are likely to see much of this intriguing culture. They are most renowned for their development of a process to shrink the heads of their enemies taken in battle. No longer do you see shrunken heads displayed in the villages, and the colorful feathered head crowns and long blowguns are reserved for special ceremonies, but the Shuars still retain much of their culture—not the least disarming of which is their propensity to converse among themselves nose to nose and screaming like they are about to kill each other. The Shuars are not interested in foreigners intruding upon their villages. They are independent enough and aggressive enough to take serious displeasure in your snooping, so don't even be tempted.

Macas itself is a contrast to Puyo in that it has had 400 years to grow and develop. It has only 15,000 inhabitants, and is built on cobblestone streets in a colonial style that's largely unmarred by modern buildings. Its cleanliness and friendliness make it easy to like this city, and we rate it as one of the better towns in all of Ecuador to visit. Unfortunately, the facilities for tourists are scarce, but those that are available are comfortable and inexpensive.

New lodges like Kapawi are opening up around Macas, and the city airport serves as a handy base for connections between commercial flights from Quito and small charter flights to jungle airstrips in the eastern parts of Morona Santiago Province or Pastaza Province—the wildest and most unexplored part of Ecuador. Sangay National Park has a headquarters building near the town of General Proaño north of Macas.

After five years of work, a huge suspension bridge was completed over the Río Upano in 1995, 2 kilometers east of Macas, which gave access for large buses and trucks to the southern portion of the Macas–Puyo road. Three months after its inauguration, an earthquake collapsed it flat, but the old narrow bridge next to it was not affected. The old bridge, however, is so narrow that only small trucks, cars and pedestrians can safely use it. As a result, passengers and cargo must be moved over the bridge in small pickups to transfer to awaiting buses or trucks on either side of the bridge.

LODGING   We recommend the **Hotel Peñon del Oriente** (Calle Domingo Comin 837 and Amazonas; private bath, some rooms with hot water; $20–$25; 7-700-132, fax: 7-700-450). Its 35 rooms are on four floors (no elevator), and many of them have great views of the city and the forested hills across the Upano River to the east. The hotel has seen better days, but perhaps with a resurgence of tourism after the 1995 war with Perú, its owners will be able to restore it to its former delightful ambience.

RESTAURANTS   The **Pagoda Restaurant** (Amazonas and Domingo Comin; 6:30 a.m. to 10:30 p.m. daily; $3–$5; 7-700-280) is around the corner and across the street from the Hotel Peñon. It is without a doubt the best place in town to eat, with a long list of Chinese dishes as well as national cuisine. The restaurant is large, immaculately clean and serves delicious food.

GETTING THERE: By Air: TAME has afternoon flights between Quito and Macas Monday, Wednesday and Friday.

By Bus: Buses are available at the terminal terrestre for trips north to Puyo, west to Cuenca and south to Zamora.

By Car: No rental cars are available in Macas, but a taxi and driver can be arranged for less than $60 per day depending on your bargaining skills and Spanish. From Cuenca via the marvelous and birdy route through Gualaceo, there are only a few places to stay between Macas and Gualaceo. Nonstop in a rental car, this 200-kilometer trip between Gualaceo and Macas takes about six hours. Numerous roads can be explored out of Macas to the east and south. The route south to Zamora and Loja via Gualaquiza should only be considered in a four-wheel-drive vehicle and with plenty of camping provisions along. There are few places for food and lodging, and what's available is fairly primitive.

The most isolated of all of Ecuador's national parks, the lower altitude portions of **Sangay National Park** on the eastern boundary are the most difficult of all to enter. The approach to the lower parts of this immense park (677,500 acres) are only by trails from the village of 9 de Octubre, west of Macas or San Isidro north of Macas. The park staffs an education center at the town of General Proaño just outside Macas. Here you can arrange for guides and pay the entrance fee of $20. Routes, camping sites and schedules can be worked out with the rangers. A minimum of three to four days is needed to reach the interior of the park and have time to enjoy the seclusion and unending views of scenery and wildlife. All camping equipment and supplies must be brought with you and then packed out.

GETTING THERE: Sangay National Park is not accessible by vehicle, and backpackers should plan on several days to reach this remote but lovely park via the village of 9 de Octubre above Alshí.

KAPAWI

After visiting ✪✪✪ **Kapawi** (private bath, hot water; three nights $750, plus $300 transportation, per person, double occupancy; in Guayaquil: Canodros, S. A., Luis Urdaneta 1418 y Avenida del Ejercito, Casilla 09-01-8442; 4-285-711, 2-222-203, fax: 4-287-651; e-mail: eco-tourism1@canodros.com.ec), we find ourselves struggling to find enough superlatives to do this ecotourist lodge justice. The lodge, in the middle of the most extensive virgin rainforest in Amazonian Ecuador, is not only far from any other ecotourist projects but there are also no cattle, no oil exploration, no colonists—nothing but forest extending to the horizon in all directions. If the natural beauty and isolation weren't enough, the company that built the lodge, Canodros, practices a level of cultural and environmental sensitivity that sets standards so high all other ecotourist lodges in Ecuador will have to reconsider their goals.

All the land in this area of Ecuador belongs to the Achuar Indian Federation. When we went to talk to the president of the Achuar Federation in his humble office in the town of Puyo, we were impressed by his wisdom and farsightedness. He told us the Achuar have learned from the mistakes made by indigenous groups north of the Río Napo. The Achuar want to conserve their culture and their environment by learning to use it in a long-term sustainable way. Ecotourism is a major part of this long-term plan, and the development of Kapawi is a high priority.

There are no roads into this entire area of Ecuador, so access is via an hour to an hour and a half ride in a small plane over uncut Amazonian forest. Once you leave the departure airport, you will soon be lost in the view of a canopy of leaves stretching as far as you can see and interrupted only by meandering rivers and an occasional small clearing of the Achuar Indians—almost exactly as it likely looked a thousand years ago. At the 800-meter-long dirt airstrip of Sharamentsa, you will step out of the plane into a time long-past. Achuar Indian men will help unload your baggage and supplies for the lodge and lead you down to the Río Pastaza and your awaiting canoe, but village life will go on around you. Men returning from a forest hunt with game over their backs and a blowgun or muzzle-loading *chiminea* gun will pass by. Women and children will be working in the nearby *jea* (house) whose elliptical shape, thatched roof and east-west orientation have gone virtually unchanged by the presence of tourists. Your English-speaking guides will caution you not to stare at the women (Achuar men are notoriously jealous) or take pictures here.

The canoe trip down the Río Pastaza takes about an hour and a half in a covered and motorized canoe. On the way you will see flocks of Green-winged and Blue and Yellow Macaws as they return to their roosts in the late afternoon. Flocks of Orinoco Geese sit on the beaches of sandy islands. Unlike travelers to the Río Napo lodges in northern Ecuador, you probably will see no other canoes on the river until you reach the military post across from the village of Kapawi. Here your canoe maneuvers the sandbars and proceeds north up the much smaller Río Capahuari another 15 minutes to the dock of the Kapawi Lodge. It is only a short five-minute walk on an elevated boardwalk to the lodge. If the river is high, the canoe will enter a small canal and go directly to the lodge situated along the edge of the Kapawi Cocha.

The lodge can accommodate 40 tourists in 14 single and duplex cabins. All the buildings were built following the Achuar architectural style. Not a single metal nail was used, and fast-growing forest products make up the roof, floors and walls. This is not to say they are shanties. The construction, although rustic, is elegant and luxurious. Each cabin has a view of the lake through screened windows and a covered porch. A combined sitting area and bedroom takes up most of the cabin's space, but an immense bathroom, whose floor and walls are covered with graceful terra-cotta tiles, reassures you that suffering is no part of this adventure. Each cabin has lights powered from photoelectric cells, and hot-water showers (each person, however, is rationed to a limited amount of hot water). The flush toilets drain into an elaborate digester septic system that is, as is everything else, state-of-the-art. You are not allowed to use your own soap and shampoo. Dispensers in each bathroom have liquid biodegradable soap that will not cause contamination.

Three large buildings are in the center of the complex—a separate hammock building; a ballroom-size building with a lecture hall, library, lounge and bar; and a building that houses the kitchen-dining room—all of which are connected to the cabins by raised boardwalks.

The food is prepared by European-trained chefs and is the best we have had in any lodge in the Oriente of Ecuador. Virtually no plastic is used anywhere. Even the "box" lunches sent out with you on day trips are elegant, with glassware, plates and silverware. All refuse is recycled, and separate garbage cans for aluminum, paper and batteries are strategically placed around the lodge. Organic refuse is mulched and eventually used to fertilize nearby *chacras* (gardens).

The number of options for field trips is so overwhelming you will quickly ask yourself why you chose to stay here only five days. Canoe trips to the blackwater river Río Ispingo may be an overnight trip. Day hiking trips down any number of trails can be for a morning or an entire day. Paddle canoe trips into isolated rivers and small cochas or a combination of hiking and canoeing can give you access to a profusion of habitat types, from marsh and flooded forest to *tierra firme* forest. Because of Kapawi's isolation, it has high populations of some species—such as Orinoco Goose, Giant River Otter and Pink River Dolphin—that are very difficult or impossible to see now in other parts of Ecuador. However, because active hunting continues by the Achuars, large mammals like monkeys and large birds like currasows are extremely shy and hard to see.

The Achuar culture is evident in every field trip. One of your guides will be a Spanish-speaking Achuar man. He will make sure you break no taboos and learn about his culture without interfering. If you come to a *jea* (house), it is considered insulting to pass by without stopping and talking. Inevitably, this stop involves a sip of *chicha* (fermented beer made from yuca). Even if you don't like the taste, good manners dictate you pretend to sip from the gourd bowl. Never set the unconsumed portion or even an empty bowl on the ground and leave. It must be handed to the woman directly with a polite *"Máketai"* (thank you). Men are not allowed in the female (*ekent*) portion of the house, usually on the east end of the house (look for the fireplace). The presence of foreign tourists will inevitably have an effect on these people, but with education of both the tourists and the Achuars the interference can be minimized and the changes thoughtfully planned. The worst alternative is to try to isolate the Achuars with some idealistic notion that they can keep their culture untainted by the dominant Ecuadorian culture. This isolation, no matter how well-intentioned, would never be perfect. Changes will come, and the best option is to prepare the Achuars for the changes without losing their dignity or pride in their own culture. Kapawi seems to be on target with this goal.

GETTING THERE: From Quito, you will either travel by comfortable chartered bus five hours to the Shell-Mera airstrip just west of Puyo, or you will take the daily TAME jet flight (40 minutes) to Macas. Single- or two-engine planes that seat up to 12 people will fly you the 140 kilometers from Macas or the 180 kilometers from Shell-Mera to the Sharamentsa airstrip about 25 kilometers from Kapawi. Because the TAME flight from Quito to Macas is so late in the afternoon, it is difficult to make the connections with the small plane to fly you to the airstrip at Sharamentsa before dark, and most trips into Kapawi are via Shell-Mera. At Sharamentsa you will be transferred to large, covered dugout canoes with powerful outboard motors. The canoe ride down the Río Pastaza and up the Río Capahuari will take about an hour to an hour and a half. Leaving Kapawi, you will most likely fly from Sharamentsa to Macas for the afternoon TAME flight and arrive in Quito about 5 p.m. A WORD OF CAUTION: Because rainfall and inclement weather can delay or postpone flights into and out of Sharamentsa, it is essential that you allow a "buffer" day when scheduling your itinerary. Following your stay at Kapawi, plan an extra day in Quito to visit Otavalo or Papallacta instead of flying to the Galápagos or back to the States the very next day. That way if there is a day's delay in leaving Kapawi, you will not miss your important flight to your next major destination.

MIAZAL

Although we have not yet had a chance to visit this ecotourist site, **Miazal** (semi-private bath; three nights $416 to $680, depending on size of group, plus $200 transportation per person; in Cuenca: Ecotrek Expeditions, Calle Larga 7-108 y Luis Cordero, Casilla 01-01-1858; 7-841-927, 7-834-677, fax: 7-835-387; e-mail: ecotrek@az.pro.ec) is already earning a reputation as an exciting place for more adventurous travelers. It is managed by some of the same personnel as Kapawi, and by all reports continues with the same consideration of local traditions carefully melded with travel to one of the wildest places in the Oriente.

The lodge is located at the base of the eastern slope of an isolated and virtually uninhabited range of low mountains called the Cutucú. This range lies only 75 kilometers southwest of Macas and the crowded Upano river valley, but because of the lack of roads and its isolation within Shuar territory, the mountains themselves are basically devoid of permanent human habitation. The lodge is located at the edge of this vast wilderness and local villages supply the guides and provide a respectful introduction to the Shuar culture. The lodge is constructed from native materials in the Shuar tradition. Each double room shares a bathroom and shower with the adjacent room. The rooms are comfortable but rustic. A common meeting area and dining room follow the Shuar custom of socializing.

The Río Tsuirim forms a natural pool in front of the lodge. Hikes to nearby areas include extensive forest on the slopes of the Cutucú, natural thermal baths, and visits to a Shuar center. Canoe rides in native dugout canoes take you deep into wild areas with rugged beauty and isolation. However, the rainy season from March to June can make logistics into the area difficult.

GETTING THERE: Depending on the weather conditions and the number of tourists, you will fly via a four-passenger plane from Shell-Mera to the small airstrip at Miazal. It is then a 30-minute hike or 20-minute canoe ride down the Río Mangosiza to the lodge.

ROAD SOUTH TO MÉNDEZ, LIMÓN & GUALACEO

The road south of Macas is narrow, bumpy and slow. If you have the patience, however, it offers access to parts of Ecuador that few tourist experience. Much of the habitat is cut over and agricultural, but large patches, especially along steep valleys and rivers, is verdant and full of native plants and animals. Gas stations, clean but simple hotels, and restaurants are conveniently available at Méndez and Limón. If you are traveling to Gualaceo, the trip is not rigorous. However, if you are traveling south to Zamora, the road south of Gualaquiza quickly deteriorates, and gas stations, hotels and restaurants become few and far between—to say nothing of marginal in cleanliness.

The 1995 border skirmish between Ecuador and Perú has opened up a new road 45 kilometers south of Sucúa or 3 kilometers north of the side road to Méndez. Turn south off the main Limón–Macas road and drive 3 kilometers to the town of Patuca. At Patuca, take the right fork in the road. This road is smooth gravel, wide and by far the best highway in this part of Ecuador.

It leads eventually 152 kilometers southeast to the town of **Morona**, an important garrison town for the Ecuadorian army. Many large expanses of forest are along this road, and the scenery is breathtaking as you drive through the foothills of the Andes toward the lowlands along the Río Pastaza. Don't plan on staying in Morona unless you have camping equipment. Otherwise you can return to the Macas–Limón road and continue 6 kilometers to the town of Méndez or another 43 kilometers south to the town of Limón, both of which have clean but simple hotels and restaurants.

Only 5 kilometers west of the main Limón–Macas road, **Méndez** is a delightful surprise. Tucked into a scenic valley of the Río Paute, its classic city square provides a comfortable and photogenic place to stay a night. A long-term highway construction project to connect Azogues in the Highlands to Méndez is underway. When this major highway is finished, Méndez will never again be the idyllic, sleepy town that it is now. Already the presence of construction company money apparently has driven up the cost of food and lodging here. Méndez is now about 30 percent more expensive than Limón.

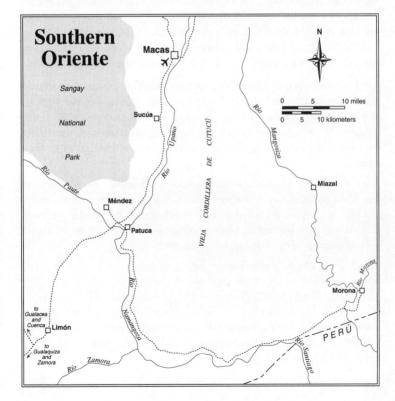

LODGING **Hostel Los Ceibos** (shared bathroom and shower, cold water; $5.50 per person) is the best place in Méndez to stay. It is located off the northwest corner of the main square in the town center and is clean and efficiently run. On weekends avoid the rooms that face the street. Between the singing party-goers and the 5 a.m. sermon blasted over loudspeakers by the priest at the local church, you will get little sleep unless your room is at the back of the hotel.

RESTAURANTS   At least five simple but clean restaurants are around the main plaza in Méndez. The **Restaurante de Turismo** is the biggest and most expensive ($3.50–$5), but it also has the best food.

GETTING THERE: By Bus: Unlike Limón, Méndez is not on the main highway between Macas and Gualaceo. Smaller buses and *colectivos*, however, regularly run the 5 kilometers between the main highway and the Méndez town plaza. There is also regular service between Méndez and Sucúa.

By Car: The turnoff for Méndez is 43 kilometers north of Limón (left just after the high bridge crossing the Río Paute) or 71 kilometers south of Macas (right just after the gasoline station on the left). The road is rough and slow, but there are many opportunities to stop and look at views of the magnificent Cordillera del Cóndor. Turn west at the sign to Méndez and drive 5 kilometers paralleling the north shore of the Río Paute. Cross a small bridge and drive into the main plaza.

The small town of **Limón** with its cobblestone main street is a pleasant relief from the dust and mud of the road. Don't expect any luxuries here, but if you are looking for a convenient place to stay over or experience a side of Ecuador few tourists see, Limón can supply an abundance of atmosphere. Because of frequent disruptions in electricity, carry a flashlight at all times at night.

LODGING   We recommend the **Residencial Limón** (shared bathroom and showers, cold water; $3 per person). The very clean rooms come in doubles and triples. Protected parking is provided in the interior courtyard. The owners have planted orchids on bushes and trees around the courtyard, and when they are blossoming, it is a delightful scene.

RESTAURANTS   Several simple but clean restaurants are on the main street north and south of the Residencial Limón. They all serve national dishes and cost $1.50–$2. If your group has more than four or five, it is a good idea to let the proprietor of the restaurant know that you will be coming to eat later on in the evening. Because the restaurants do not normally open until 8 a.m., ask to have them open earlier if you want to leave at the crack of dawn the next morning.

GETTING THERE: By Bus: Limón is on the main road between Macas and Cuenca, and buses stop here going both ways almost every hour day and night. There is no *terminal terrestre*, but the offices of the various *cooperativas* are obvious along the five-block-long main street.

By Car: The road to Gualaceo is winding and steep in places, so plan on three to four hours from Limón with no stops. From Macas to Limón the drive takes about an hour. Because the road is not well maintained, recent rains and mudslides can cause long delays. Going toward Gualaceo, take the right fork in the road 5 kilometers southwest of Limón (the left fork goes south to Indanza, Gualaquiza and eventually Zamora and Loja). There is an army traffic control post 2 kilometers after (west of) the right fork where you will have to get out and show your car registration and passport. The drive over the mountain pass to Gualaceo is one of the most scenic of all the east slope roads and certainly the least traveled (see Chapter Nine).

SECTION IV

The Galápagos Islands

The Galápagos Islands, 97 percent of which is national park land, have captured the imagination of the world ever since Charles Darwin popularized them over a century ago. The islands are synonymous with exotic adventure travel and are renowned for being a land of unique and tame animals and bizarre landscapes in a remote corner of the world. Indeed, all who visit the Galápagos return home with tales to tell about the otherworldliness of these "Enchanted Islands." If you like getting close to animals and intermingling with them, you will love the Galápagos Islands.

A BRIEF HISTORY

The Galápagos were officially discovered in 1535 by Fray Tomás de Berlanga, the Bishop of Panamá. Fray Tomás arrived in the Galápagos as many of the other plants and animals did—by accident. Becalmed in a sailing ship, he drifted west on the strong Humboldt Current from the Ecuadorian coast. He searched the islands in vain for fresh water but finally made his way back to the Peruvian mainland. As might be expected, his opinion of the "dry and inhospitable" Galápagos Islands was far from favorable. However, the bishop was impressed with the giant land tortoises he encountered and mentioned them in his report of his journey. His discovery first put the islands on the map, in a 1574 atlas of the world, and introduced them as "the Islands of the Tortoises"—or the Galápagos Islands.

From that time on, despite their isolation, the Galápagos Islands became a increasingly popular place to visit. Buccaneers and pirates (depends on which side you are on when captured) used the Galápagos as a base to raid Spanish galleons transporting Incan riches back to Spain. One of these buccaneers, William Ambrose Cowley, drew the first maps of the islands and named them after various British kings, dukes and admirals.

By the early 1800s, the ships of pirates and buccaneers seeking fortunes in gold were replaced by those of whalers and sealers seeking fortunes in oil from marine mammals. Sperm whales, fur seals and sea lions were numerous in the rich upwelling waters around the Galápagos and were heavily hunted. By the mid-1800s there were 2300 whaling ships in the region and hundreds more that would pass through on their way to Arctic hunting grounds. Fur seals were particularly hard hit and are to this day still recovering their numbers. Only with the discovery and increased reliance on cheaper, more reliable, underground petroleum in other parts of the word did this hunt slow and eventually stop in the late 1800s.

Also sought were the Giant Tortoises. Ship captains soon learned that tortoises could be carried down to the ship, stored upside down below deck and survive for many months to provide fresh meat for the crew. Each ship would take up to 500 tortoises per visit, with as many as 200,000 tortoises taken in total—15,000 off Floreana Island alone. This practice caused the extinction of the three unique subspecies of tortoise once found on Floreana, Santa Fe and Rábida islands, and decimated the population of tortoises on the other islands.

Ecuador gained its sovereignty in 1830 and annexed the Galápagos Islands in 1832. As the islands became better known, they received an increasing stream of visitors that has not stopped to this day. One of the first to write about the Galápagos was perhaps its most famous visitor, Charles Darwin, who visited the islands in 1835. Another author who helped popularize the Galápagos was the scientist William Beebe. He traveled to the Galápagos in 1924 and wrote a best-selling book of his experiences— *Galápagos: World's End*. During this period, the islands' main visitors were scientists on research vessels and wealthy lay people who could afford to visit the Galápagos on private vessels. By the early 1900s, there was a grow-

Frigatebird

ing population of full-time residents in the Galápagos. The first to arrive were convicts and other societal misfits, but soon entrepreneurs began to exploit the natural resources of the islands. The first protective laws were passed in 1935, and the entire archipelago was proclaimed a national park in 1959. At the same time, the world scientific and conservation community helped establish the Charles Darwin Research Station, which ever since has led the way in the protection and research of the Galápagos. Now over 60,000 tourists visit these magical islands every year. It is a journey not soon forgotten.

SIXTEEN

The Galápagos Islands

The Galápagos Islands lie 960 kilometers off the Ecuadorian coast. Costa Rica is more than 1000 kilometers to the north and Easter Island is 3200 kilometers to the south. There are 60 named islands, islets and rocks ranging from Isabela Island—128 kilometers long and boasting more than half of the land area of the archipelago—to tiny wave-washed rock ledges and pinnacles. The northern points of Isabela Island and Genovesa Island lie north of the equator—all the other islands you are likely to visit are south of the equator. The northernmost islands in the archipelago, Darwin and Wolf, require a very long boat trip and are seldom visited except for advanced diving trips. Volcán Wolf on Isabela Island is the tallest mountain in the Galápagos at 5975 feet (1707 meters) high. (Fernandina and Isabela are the most volcanically active islands.) From Darwin Island in the north to Española Island in the south, the Galápagos Islands extend for 430 kilometers.

Because the Galápagos lie on the equator, the temperature in the islands is pleasant throughout the year. Occasionally, extended periods of cloudy and rainy weather, especially from January to March, may occur. The weather in the islands is determined by the relative strength of two oceanic currents—the cold Humboldt from the south and the warm Equatorial from the north. The Humboldt Current starts in Antarctica and runs north in the deep Nazca Trench up the west coast of South America before deflecting off Ecuador and bumping into the Galápagos. This current dominates from June to December—the cool, *garúa* season. When the cool waters of the Humboldt come in contact with the warm air of the islands, condensation occurs, forming a thin layer of clouds over most of the islands. These clouds are densest over land where a mist—the *garúa*—falls in the highlands daily. During this season the lowlands, where most of the tourist sites are, are usually dry and the palo santo forests are leafless. The average water temperature during this cool season is 72°F and the sea can be a bit rough.

In January, the southeast trade winds and the strength of the Humboldt Current diminish, allowing the warm waters pooled in the Panamá Basin to flow south. This Equatorial Current brings warm waters to the islands and a more typical tropical weather pattern. The air temperatures are hot, the skies are clear and rainfall is restricted to occasional brief downpours in the afternoons. The average water temperature rises to 77°F. This hot season lasts from January to May and is when the Galápagos lowlands get most of their rain. This precipitation also causes the palo santo forests to become green and leafy and many of the flowers to bloom.

Every four or five years, the Equatorial Current is particularly strong and reaches all the way down to Perú. The resulting rise in water temperatures is called El Niño. The warm water kills the seaweed the Marine Iguanas feed on and displaces the fish the seabirds rely upon. The increased rainfall kills the cacti upon which the tortoises and Land Iguanas feed and increases erosion on the steep mountain slopes. Many plant and animal populations crash during this time. If it is just a brief event, the populations will quickly recover. If it is an unusually strong El Niño, it may take several generations for the plants and animals to return to their former levels of abundance.

GEOLOGY

Like many other oceanic island chains, the Galápagos are of volcanic origin. The islands are very young and still growing, much like the Hawaiian Islands. The geological structure of the earth is analogous to a peach—the solid core is surrounded by a cool, semi-solid interior and encased in a crust, like the skin of the peach. In fact, the relative thickness of a peach's skin is analogous to the relative thickness of the crust of the Earth. The Earth's crust is cracked into 12 major plates that move, dive, slide and collide while floating on the semi-solid interior. These movements of the plates periodically result in earthquakes and volcanic eruptions. In the crust of the earth under the Galápagos is what geologists call a "hot spot." A hot spot is a plume of rising magma that has pierced the earth's crust. This hot spot has formed an undersea platform from which individual volcanoes rise. Where these volcanoes break the surface of the ocean, an island is created. Isabela Island was once five separate islands, now melded together by continuing eruptions. The eruptions here are typically not violent as they can be on the mainland of Ecuador. The volcanic summits on the islands are not steep, conical, Mt. Fuji–type mountains, but instead are broad and gently sloping, the product of quiet eruptions.

The Galápagos Islands are on the Nazca Plate. This plate is creeping east toward South America at a rate of about 2.5 inches per year. South America is on the South American Plate, which is moving west toward the Nazca Plate at a rate of one inch per year. The two plates meet in a slow-motion collision zone off the western coast of South America. Along this zone, a deep trench is formed where the Nazca Plate dives under South America, remelts, rises and builds the Andes Mountains in a series of volcanic eruptions. Just to the north of the Galápagos is the Cocos Plate, which also dives under Central America. The Cocos Plate is responsible for Central America's volcanic activity.

Because the hot spot is stationary and the plate is moving toward South America, the Galápagos Islands are arranged by age on an east-west line. The oldest islands are the easternmost, including Española and Santa Fe, and are approximately 3.25 million years old. The youngest islands are the most volcanically active and include the westernmost islands of Fernandina and Isabela, approximately 700,000 years old. New geologic evidence suggests that earlier, proto-Galápagos Islands lie along an underwater ridge extending east from the present islands. These former islands are the victim of millions of years of erosion. The current islands come in basically two shapes: rounded mountains and tilted blocks. The mountains are volcanic cones, the tilted blocks are the result of faulting that has lifted the seafloor above water. Several of the islands are a combination of both forces.

The Galápagos are some of the most volcanically active islands in the world and recent lava flows and upheavals continue to add real estate to the islands. There is much evidence of the volcanic history on the islands—lava tubes, coarse *aa* lava and ropy *pahoehoe* lava, eroded cones, blocky cliffs, and so on. It was to this rocky landscape that plants and animals found their way, and upon which some of them became established. Española Island, the oldest, has the most diverse native plants and the most endemic species. Fernandina and Isabela islands are still volcanically active and have fewer plants and fewer unique animals. It is thought that a historically recent eruption on Fernandina wiped out its entire population of Giant Tortoises. In mid-September 1998, a large fissure opened up on the southeastern slope of Cerro Azul on the island of Isabela. Spectacular lava fountains flowed from this flank eruption and filled the night sky with red light and the day sky with billowing gas clouds. At one time, the lava was advancing at more than 12 miles per hour (20 kilometers per hour) toward the ocean. The Galápagos Tortoises inhabiting the slopes of this mountain (which have a noticeably flattened shell) are considered a distinct species by some scientists and number no more than 100 individuals. Because of the probable destruction of most of their remaining habitat, 20 adults of this rare form were removed by

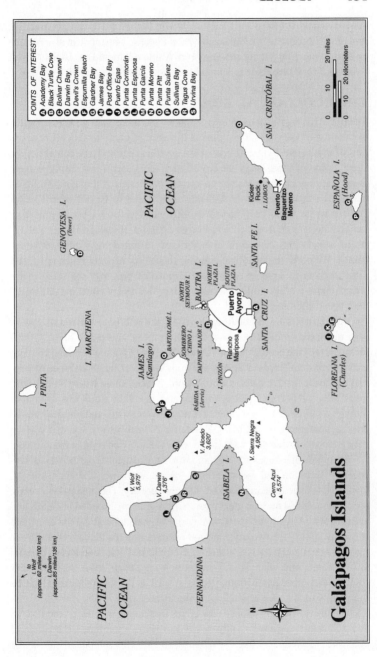

Galápagos Islands

POINTS OF INTEREST
- Ⓐ Academy Bay
- Ⓑ Black Turtle Cove
- Ⓒ Bolivar Channel
- Ⓓ Darwin Bay
- Ⓔ Devil's Crown
- Ⓕ Espumilla Beach
- Ⓖ Gardner Bay
- Ⓗ James Bay
- Ⓘ Post Office Bay
- Ⓙ Puerto Egas
- Ⓚ Punta Cormorán
- Ⓛ Punta Espinosa
- Ⓜ Punta Garcia
- Ⓝ Punta Moreno
- Ⓞ Punta Pitt
- Ⓟ Punta Suárez
- Ⓠ Sullivan Bay
- Ⓡ Tagus Cove
- Ⓢ Urvina Bay

helicopter and flown to the Charles Darwin Station for a captive breeding program. Evidence of the Galápagos' recent geologic history can also be seen on Bartolomé, Fernandina and Sombrero Chino (Chinese Hat) islands and at Sullivan Bay, where there is a broad lava flow about a hundred years old.

THE ECOLOGICAL ZONES

There are 13 large islands, 6 small islands and more than 40 islets that are named in the Galápagos. On a typical trip you are likely to visit six or seven of the large islands, three or four of the small islands and any number of the islets. Some of the islands are closed to visitors and a few are far enough away that they are only visited on special itineraries. Although they are all part of the archipelago, you will find each island to be different. Charles Darwin wrote when he returned to England that ". . . . by far the most remarkable feature in the natural history of this archipelago is, that the different islands to a considerable extent are inhabited by a different set of beings. We never dreamed that islands, about fifty or sixty miles apart, and most of them in sight of each other, formed of precisely the same rocks, placed under a quite similar climate, rising to a nearly equal height, would have been differently tenanted. . . ."

Before departing the boat, each visitor site will be described to you by your naturalist guide. The visitor sites have been selected to highlight different parts of the ecology of the islands. Some will feature breeding colonies of frigatebirds, Waved Albatross, sea lions or one of the three types of boobies of the Galápagos. Others will be along a rocky shore where Sally Lightfoot Crabs and Marine Iguanas are common, or follow a trail to a lookout or through a tall cactus forest. The sites are all wonderful, and you will not be missing something by not being able to land wherever you want. If you are patient, most of what you want to see will eventually be right in front of you.

There are five zones of vegetation in the Galápagos, defined by differences in elevation and moisture. The lowest two zones, the coast and the lowlands, receive little rainfall and thus are very dry. The highest two zones, the *Scalesia* forest and the grassy pampa, are often enshrouded in clouds and are very wet. Most tours spend a majority of their time along the coast and in the lowlands—the two dry zones—few tours visit the higher zones. To see the grassy pampa, a special effort must be made. Each zone has its characteristic plants and animals and unless you visit each zone, you will miss some of their specialties. Some animals, such as the Giant Tortoise, can be found in several zones depending on the time of year.

The lowest elevation zone is the coast. Depending on how protected it is, you will find mangroves, sandy beaches or rocky shorelines. The plants of this zone are evergreen, like the saltbush, and are very tolerant of salt. There are many animals that live along the coast including herons, crabs, sand-pipers, Marine Iguanas and fur seals. Almost every landing will be amongst or near a sea lion colony, and sooner or later you will find a sea lion nursery with a bunch of adorable pups frolicking in the surf. Directly behind the coastal strip is the arid zone, the largest zone in the archipelago. The plants in this zone are adapted to drought and are typically deciduous. Species of *Croton* and *Bursera* (palo santo) are very common and cactus, especially *Opuntia*, give this zone its characteristic look. Land Iguanas, Giant Tortoises and Darwin's finches are found in this zone. Interestingly, where Giant Tortoises are present or have been present historically, the Opuntia cactus grows in a tree-like fashion, and its pads are protected from the reach of the tortoise. Where there are no tortoises, the same *Opuntia* species will be short and bushy.

Where the *garúa* mist dampens the mountainsides, a thick cloud forest grows that is dominated by trees of the daisy family called *Scalesia*. Because the *Scalesia* zone is the most fertile and productive habitat in the islands, the forest has been extensively cut down for farming and cattle ranching. Giant Tortoises migrate up to this zone during the dry season, and it is rich in song-birds. Between the *Scalesia* and arid zones is a transitional zone made up of some unique trees and components from the neighboring zones. This zone is difficult for visitors to distinguish because of its intermediate nature. Unless you go to the highlands, you are unlikely to see either of these zones on a tour of the islands. The bus from the Baltra airport to Puerto Ayora passes through both of these zones on its way across Santa Cruz Island.

The *Scalesia* and transitional zones are generally found between 660 and 1980 feet (200 and 600 meters) in elevation. The zones are lower on the south sides of the islands because prevailing winds cause clouds to form and so there is more rainfall. The north sides of the islands are drier, being in a rain shadow, and the zones reach higher in elevation. Above the forest is the pampa zone characterized by low shrubby plants and a very moist climate. Two very rare and specialized birds are restricted to this zone—the Galápagos Rail and the Paint-billed Crake, but they are very hard to see in the dense vegetation. The pampa zone extends to the top of the highest mountains on Isabela Island.

DARWIN AND THE THEORY OF EVOLUTION

The Galápagos Islands are famous historically for their role in the develop-ment of the theory of evolution. Darwin spent five weeks exploring these isolated islands and their unique animals and plants in the fall of 1835 as a naturalist on board the *H.M.S. Beagle*, which was commissioned to map the coast of South America. Darwin was invited to go on the voyage not as a renowned scientist but as a companion to the captain (ship captains were of a different social class and did not mix with the crew) and only got the position because two others refused. His father, a prominent physician, forbade him to go—he thought nothing would come of such folly—but his uncle and future father-in-law, Josiah Wedgwood, of fine-china fame, interceded on his behalf. The official ship's naturalist jumped ship in Brazil and left the task of collecting and chronicling to Darwin. Although initially a very uninspired student, Darwin became an enthusiastic collector and blossomed with the new authority.

During the time he was in the Galápagos, Darwin collected many specimens of birds, reptiles and plants and spent much time wandering the bizarre landscape. Despite the prevalent myth of a great "Ah-ha" moment of insight, Darwin left the Galápagos impressed but not a changed man. At the time, religious edict explained the different plants and animals of each continent by different "centers of creation." To Darwin, who had studied to be a minister and who was a devoutly religious man, the Galápagos were simply another center of creation. Given this mindset, he initially overlooked and even mislabeled many of the key bits of evidence he later used in his famous treatise on evolution.

If the Galápagos were a center of creation, then there should be no variation of life on each island and every island should have the same plants and animals. Darwin noted but was not impressed when the governor of the islands told him that he could tell which island a tortoise came from by the characteristic shape of its shell. Darwin also failed to write the names of the islands on the tags he used when he collected birds—there was no need to. He figured they must be the same on all islands. Perhaps most ironically, he misidentified the soon-to-be-famous Galápagos finches (now known as Darwin's finches, and which became a cornerstone of his theory) as wrens, warblers and orioles.

Darwin thought that the animals he saw on the islands had an affinity to the animals on the mainland of South America. It was not until he showed his collections to scientists back in England and was told of the uniqueness of the species that he began to understand the significance of the animals he had seen on the Galápagos. When he was told that a group of birds he had collected were in fact all closely related finches, he began to formulate his famous theory of natural selection and the origin of species. Darwin realized that each island was inhabited by a unique set of plants and animals and yet all were very closely related. How could these closely related finches have become so unique and still show affinity to the birds of the mainland? In 1839, Darwin started the first of his Transmutation notebooks and began to gather evidence for the gradual transmutation or change of species when presented with a changing environment.

Volcán Antisana rising above the high elevation paramo vegetation.

BIRDS OF THE GALÁPAGOS

Top left: Swallow-tailed gull.

Top right: Blue-footed boobies.

Bottom right: A molting, juvenile Waved Albatross.

Middle left: Vermilion flycatcher.

Second middle left: A Magnificent Frigatebird.

Bottom left: Red-footed booby.

Darwin never used the word "evolution" in his writings. The word "evolution" in Victorian England meant progress. Darwin preferred the phrase "descent with modification." Darwin knew that life changed or adapted when presented with new environmental conditions, but that change was nondirectional. The word evolution implied change to a better, more advanced animal or plant. Darwin, however, lost this battle and the word "evolution" has become synonymous with Darwin.

Darwin filled several Transmutation notebooks with his thoughts and theories on descent with modification, but he did not initially publish or even tell anyone of his ideas. He did exhaustive studies of earthworms, barnacles—he was the first to describe male barnacles—and selective breeding of racing pigeons, but still he kept very much to himself. He did marry his cousin, Emma Wedgewood, and have a large family, but he was often sick and always tormented by his heretical ideas. Finally, in 1859 and only after another naturalist, Alfred Russel Wallace, wrote him detailing a very similar theory of evolution, did he write his now-famous book *The Origin of Species*.

Darwin's 20 years of hesitancy to make his ideas known seems ridiculous to us today, but his theory forever changed the way life and humanity are thought of. He directly challenged the great Church of England and many of the established scientists of his day and consequently he never received the praise or celebrity he deserved in his lifetime. It was not until the 1930s that the full significance and power of his theories were recognized. The theory of evolution by natural selection is the only unifying theory for all of biology and has guided studies from molecular biology and medicine to forestry management and conservation.

Evolution and natural selection, however, are not synonymous. Evolution is a change in the frequency of characters present in a population. Natural selection is one of several mechanisms by which this change is brought about. Natural selection is based on the variation all species show. Because no two individuals are identical, not all individuals in a species are equally well-adapted to new changes in the environment such as a cooler climate, less rain or smaller prey items. Some individuals are more likely to survive and pass on the genes for their characters than are other individuals. This survival of the fitter individuals brings about a change, or evolution, in the species or population.

THE NATURAL HISTORY OF THE ISLANDS

If populations are isolated from each other long enough, natural selection often leads to so many changes in the gene pools that if individuals from these isolated populations were to come back together again, they could no longer interbreed. They have formed new species. The Galápagos are the perfect laboratory of evolution because the islands are close enough to each other to be colonized, yet far enough apart to discourage constant immigration—the ideal isolating circumstances. Animals drifting on flotsam, birds blown off course by storms, plant seeds carried on the feathers of these birds or blown in by the same storms apparently arrived on the Galápagos from the South and Central American mainland to originally populate an island. As these populations of plants and animals grew, some individuals made it to other islands and were isolated long enough to become different from the population on the first island. Sometimes these individuals, now of a different species, made it back to the first island. Now there were two different species inhabiting that island, each species adapted to a special habitat or different resource on the island. Thus from a single invasion from the mainland, numerous species could evolve—often several occupying a single island. In this manner cacti, lizards, tortoises, mockingbirds and beetles radiated into new species or races on each island they colonized. That is why there are so many unique or endemic species of plants and animals in the Galápagos. Indeed, there are 13 species of finches in the Galápagos, each separable by the shape of its bill. They use these bills to catch insects, crack seeds or suck blood from the tails of resting boobies; one species has even learned to hold a cactus spine in its bill and use it to extract insect larvae from wood.

While there is only one species of tortoise, it has split into 14 unique races or subspecies (11 of which still survive), each isolated on its own island or volcanic peak. The finches of the Galápagos, Darwin's finches, played a central role in the development of his theory. Today, these finches continue to be studied and continue to help scientists better understand the process of change called evolution.

Twenty-two species of reptiles, of which 20 are endemic, are found in the Galápagos. They include the world's only marine reptile, the Marine Iguana, and the largest tortoise in the world, the giant Galápagos Tortoise, which can weigh up to 500 pounds and live to be over 200 years old. There are only six species of native mammals in the Galápagos—two rice rats, two bats and two members of the sea lion family. Land mammals are not as likely to survive the rigors of a two-week drift to the islands as are reptiles, so there are far fewer native mammals. There are, unfortunately, many introduced mammals that have generally had a negative effect on the islands. Black rats arrived with the whalers and prey on the eggs of iguanas and nesting birds. Early colonists brought dogs, goats, cattle and cats, all of which have become feral and have wreaked havoc upon the native plants and animals. There are over 100,000 goats on James Island alone.

There are 29 resident species of land birds, of which 22 are endemic. While many of these birds are interesting and easy to see, like the finches and flycatchers, by most visitors' standards the stars of the Galápagos avifauna are the seabirds. There are 19 species, of which five are endemic, and all can be expected to be seen with some effort on a typical Galápagos tour. Ornithologists estimate the total population of seabirds in the Galápagos at over 750,000 individuals. It is the sole nesting place for the Waved Albatross; it has the world's largest colony of both Masked and Red-footed Boobies and 30 percent of the world's Blue-footed Boobies. Each day when you visit the Galápagos, you will interact with several seabirds, either by stepping around a booby nest, marveling at the beauty of a Swallow-tailed Gull or photographing a funny-looking young albatross.

The Galápagos are also known for marine life. There are seven oceanic currents that intersect at the Galápagos, contributing marine life to the islands from as far away as the South Pacific and Antarctica. There are over 300 species of fish, of which 50 are endemic, and a seemingly countless variety of marine invertebrates. No trip to the Galápagos would be complete without some time spent either passively floating or actively diving to look at the magnificent fish and sea life. Doing so will also bring you into contact with the friendly sea lions in their natural environment and give you a chance to see swimming Marine Iguanas and Galápagos Penguins. It is an indescribable treat to swim with sea lions or to watch a penguin dart through a school of fish.

CONSERVATION

The Galápagos Islands have been recognized for years as a priceless and unique part of the world's natural heritage. Many people think that because it is now a national park of Ecuador, the conservation problems of the Galápagos have been addressed and solved. Unfortunately, that is not the case.

There are two persistent problems that still threaten the islands. The first is an ever-increasing human population. Eight hundred people lived in the Galápagos in 1949. The population increased to 3500 in 1971, the beginning of Galápagos ecotourism. The population is now over 15,000 people and rising some seven percent each year. Many of these newcomers arrive in the Galápagos expecting to get rich quick from the "easy" tourist dollar. Few of these people do, but they all require a place to live, food, fresh water and proper sanitation facilities. All of these requirements add stress to the islands' very limited resources.

Clear documentation of the direct effect of a growing human population on native species in the Galápagos is uncommon, but when records are available, they paint a clear picture. Although none of the Darwin's finches is known to have gone extinct since the arrival of man on the Galápagos, the entire population of one species, the Mangrove Finch, has been reduced to only 300 individuals. Historically, the Mangrove Finch was never abundant, and occurred only in six patches of mangrove forest on two islands, Isabela and Fernandina. Here it fed primarily on insect larvae found under the bark of the mangrove trees. This finch is now extinct on Fernandina and reduced to living in four small patches of mangroves on Isabela. The downfall of this highly specialized species can be traced to two causes: the illegal cutting of mangroves for firewood by colonists together with an introduced predatory wasp from the mainland that competes for insect larvae as food in this restricted habitat.

Increasing numbers of tourists are also part of human population problem in the Galápagos. Strict rules and enforcement by the national park service have controlled much of the negative effects of the additional ecotourists but the most-visited islands are still a shadow of their former richness. There is an annual quota for visitation to the Galápagos, but this number seems to be quite flexible. We do realize that we are promoting tourism to the Galápagos with this book, while at the same time lamenting the increased numbers of tourists. Our hope is that appropriate quotas are enforced and that tourists to the Galápagos respect the animals and land while contributing to the benefit of the park.

The other continuing conservation problem in the park has nothing directly to do with ecotourism. The diverse fauna of the offshore waters of the archipelago are well known to the international fishing industry. The same rich marine environment that underpins the entire Galápagos ecosystem is also an economic resource. Currently, there are three fishing practices that, if they continue, will threaten the health of the entire Galápagos ecosystem: inshore tuna fishing with huge, indiscriminate purse seine nets; shark trapping for the Asian shark fin market (the rest of the shark is tossed overboard); and the harvesting of sea cucumbers—another Asian delicacy.

There are laws that control or outlaw these practices, but they are sporadically enforced. If all the conservation laws concerning the Galápagos were actively enforced, the threats to the marine environment would dramatically lessen. Even easier than enforcing these laws is putting economic pressure on the Ecuadorian companies that support these outlawed activities. Incredibly, illegally harvested sea cucumbers are transported back to the mainland of Ecuador for processing by the same airlines that rely on a healthy marine environment to attract Galápagos ecotourists! Your voice and letters to the appropriate businesses and government agencies can exert significant pressure for the good.

WILDLIFE VIEWING IN THE GALÁPAGOS

There are few places on Earth where animals are easier to see and photograph than in the Galápagos. Not only are they unique and seldom found in such numbers elsewhere, but they are easy to locate and get close to. For centuries, despite decades of exploitation (read killing) by buccaneers, whalers, sailors, villagers and the U.S. Navy, to name just a few, the animals remain fearless of the thousands of humans that parade by them every year. At some visitor sites, not a day goes by in which humans are excluded from the animals' lives. Yet they still remain unafraid and allow you to approach very close.

The maintenance of this behavior is largely the result of the strict park rules and diligent enforcement by the naturalist guides. Much of the animal's fearlessness is passed from parent to offspring through the generations. Each individual animal accepts humans as just another inconsequential part of their environment—a nonevent. Humans, too, have to pass respect for the animals through the many generations that visit the Galápagos by not touching the animals, not altering behaviors and not pushing them to flight or apprehension. All it takes is a few insensitive acts for an animal to become wary and to pass that wariness on to its progeny. If this becomes the rule, the experience that we know as the Galápagos will be forever altered. Consider it a privilege to see these special animals, not a right.

One of the biggest problems visitors have in the park is trying not to step on the wildlife, whether it a basking iguana or a Blue-footed Booby egg. Always be careful where you place your feet, especially if you are backing up to take a picture. Despite their "tameness," the animals still need a zone of privacy. Do not get so close that they have to move. It is especially important to keep a respectful distance from babies and eggs, both of which can become overheated and quickly die without their parent's shade. If you do disturb a bird sitting on an egg, do not linger to take photos—back away immediately so the parent can return.

When you arrive on your first island, the temptation will be to walk off the paths to get closer to the subject. Do not do this. It is illegal as well as unethical! Besides, sooner or later, what you want to see or photograph will be standing, sunning, lying or sleeping in the trail or alongside it. The best time for animal watching is early morning or late afternoon. The reptiles, being cold-blooded, take a while to warm up, so in the morning they are sluggish and reluctant to move. By mid-day, most of the Marine Iguanas have headed for the sea and the birds that are sitting on nests are hot and bothered with droopy wings and fluttering throats.

On almost every island you will see sea lions, Marine Iguanas, Sally Lightfoot Crabs, Lava Lizards and Darwin's finches. On most islands you will see herons, Blue-footed Boobies, Swallow-tailed Gulls and mockingbirds. On some islands you will see Masked Boobies and penguins, and on just a few you will see tortoises, Red-footed Boobies, Land Iguanas, fur seals, Flightless Cormorants, frigatebird colonies and flamingos. After a few days you will not even notice the Marine Iguanas and Blue-footed Boobies, and only the most impressive or cutest sea lions will divert your attention.

PHOTOGRAPHY IN THE GALÁPAGOS

If you are an avid photographer, be sure to select a tour that emphasizes photography and, even better, has a professional photographer as your tour leader. The tour leader will give you tips to improve your photos and will be able to cater the trip to the interests of the group. Also, photography trips have fewer passengers, get on the islands at the best times for photography— early morning and late afternoon—and linger at the best photography situations. If you are an avid photographer and go on a general tour of the islands, you will probably go to the visitor sites at mid-day and be hurried along to keep up with your group—not conducive to good photography.

Wildlife photography doesn't get any easier than in the Galápagos. Subjects pose patiently while you fiddle with your gear and adjust your angles. Every new day reveals another amazing critter or landscape. Long telephoto lenses are not necessary in the Galápagos. The most handy lens is a 70–210 mm zoom for both portraits and shots of the landscape. A 300 mm lens will let you get close-up pictures of less cooperative animals. A short zoom, 35–70 mm is good for the big picture or in tight spots such as inside your boat.

Photography here is not foolproof, however. Despite the sophistication of modern cameras, only the photographer can think. If you take a little extra time and consider what would be the best picture, your pictures will greatly improve. When shooting very bright subjects such as a sunlit beach or a Masked Booby, overexpose a bit to bring out the whiteness. You have to do this no matter how sophisticated your camera might be. If you don't, the beach will be dull and the white Masked Booby will be grayish.

The most compelling angle to photograph animals is at their eye level. Kneel down to photograph boobies and tortoises and lie down for great shots of iguanas. When photographing from the *panga*, use autofocus and the fastest shutter speed you can for the most reliable results. A polarizing filter will eliminate a lot of the glare and is especially useful when shooting into the water. And be sure to bring lots of film—none of the boats sell film and even if you could find it in one of the two towns, you couldn't afford it. Even though some boat operators say tripods are inconvenient and unnecessary, if you prefer shooting with a tripod, take one.

Do not just take portraits—try some photos of the animals in their environment or interacting with other animals. For your slide show back home, be sure to take some photos of the landscapes and also some of the details like lava patterns and flowers. The best landscape photos have something of interest in the foreground—a rock, a flower, a nesting booby—to draw your viewer into the picture. There are new, inexpensive underwater cameras that do a pretty good job of taking pictures of fish. Try to get as close as you can when doing any underwater photography—the stronger the light from your camera flash, the better the photo. And always remember that no picture is more important than the welfare of the subject.

GETTING THERE

There are jet flights to and from the Galápagos on two airlines—TAME flies daily to Baltra Island and SAN, part of SAETA, flies to San Cristóbal Island every day except Sunday. Both airlines start in Quito, land in Guayaquil and then continue to the Galápagos. The return flights follow the same itinerary in reverse. The flight from Guayaquil to the islands takes about an hour and a half. The islands are on central standard time, so remember to set your watches back. There are advantages and disadvantages to each airline. Baltra is a little island that sits just off the north side of the much-larger Santa Cruz Island in the central part of the archipelago. It is a former U.S. Army base and not very pretty, but its central location makes it easier to get to the other islands. Unfortunately, only the cruise ship *Santa Cruz* and some of the ships operated by the company Quasar Nautica depart from Baltra—most visitors have to take a three-hour bus ride to the other side of Santa Cruz Island to the town of Puerto Ayora to board their boat.

San Cristóbal Island is on the eastern edge of the archipelago and thus a long boat ride to any other island, but the airport is just 5 minutes away from your boat, so you can be off and on your way very quickly. If you fly on SAN into San Cristóbal, you will be photographing sea lions and boobies that afternoon, but your boat ride to the next island will take longer. If you fly TAME to Baltra, your afternoon will probably be spent on the bus getting to your boat, but the trip to your next island will be shorter. Also, San Cristóbal is the closest island to Española Island, which has, perhaps, the most interesting visitor site. San Cristóbal is the island we prefer to start at.

Whichever airline you choose, there is an $80 entrance fee payable at the Quito or Guayaquil airport and a $30 tax, payable when you get off the plane in the islands. These fees are likely to increase, so inquire about the current rates before you go. Most tours do not include the fees in their price, so expect to pay out of your own pocket.

GETTING STARTED

There is really only one way to see the Galápagos—as part of a group. You will either arrive as part of a group or if you come as an individual, you will be put into a group on a boat. If money is no object, you can hire your own boat, but it would be hideously expensive. There are many companies offering tours to the Galápagos, and there are major differences among them. Some have no escort, some have a tour leader, some can have as many as 90 passengers, some as few as six. Some tours concentrate on photography, some on diving, some on birdwatching. It is best to choose your group beforehand based on your interests rather than roll the dice and see who you end up with once you are onboard. If you are an avid photographer, go with a group that emphasizes photography. If you are a scuba diver, go on a dive trip. If you want to see as many birds as possible, go on a birding trip. If you are interested in everything, go on a trip with 12 or fewer passengers. This will give you more time on each island and less time waiting for the logistics of a big group to be cleared up. If you are someone who thinks all trips to the Galápagos are the same and select a tour only because it has the lowest price, you are likely to get your money's worth. If you are unlucky, it could be even more dangerous. In early 1998, a newly constructed boat, the *Moby Dick*, turned belly up on its maiden voyage and killed several tourists. The crew evidently forgot to put sufficient ballast in the hold. Choose your tour company and boat on reputation and quality—not on cost alone.

All visitors to the Galápagos Islands must be accompanied by a licensed Galápagos guide in order to visit any of the islands. This is true whether you are part of a group with its own leader or arrive by yourself. Finding a guide is not a problem because, to really see any part of the islands, you must hire a boat and all boats will have a guide on board. The guide must be with you whenever you are on park land and groups cannot split or disperse unless there is a guide for each part. Some guides are very strict and keep groups tightly together—others are more relaxed and let the groups spread out a bit.

There are two types of guides in the Galápagos. Level 2 guides have a high-school degree and can more or less speak English. Level 3 guides have a college degree in biology or environmental science, speak English well and have graduated from the Galápagos naturalist guide course. In other words, Level 2 guides are basically escorts who probably will not enhance your trip. Level 3 guides are obviously what you want. The best guides are in great demand and are found on the best boats. These guides have years of experience and are capable of tailoring a trip to best suit your interests. You will not know it at the time, but if you try to economize with an inexpensive boat and a mediocre escort, your trip to the Galápagos will be a thin shadow of what it could have been for just a bit more money.

Ninety-seven percent of the archipelago is national park land. The other three percent is either towns or agricultural land. Visitors cannot just land anywhere and wander about. There are 50 or so official visitor sites where tourists are permitted to land. There are two kinds of visitor sites: open and restricted. At open sites, visitors can wander freely within the boundaries of the site. These beaches and sites usually always include sea lion colonies and small rocky headlands. You will be spending most of your time at restricted visitor sites. These are areas of significant natural history interest that are accessed by wide, clearly marked trails. Visitors must stay on the trail at all times to prevent disturbance to both the wildlife and vegetation.

To many, this system seems unnecessarily strict and inhibiting, but in fact it is essential and quite easy to live with. In 1994, over 60,000 people visited the Galápagos Islands. Everywhere the vegetation is fragile and the animals prone to disturbance. By staying on the trails, vegetation is preserved and the animals can adjust their territories to the human horde. At first you will be frustrated by not being able to walk over to look more closely at a particular bird or flower, but you will learn that sooner or later that bird or flower will appear again, either next to the trail or in the trail. A bit of patience is worth the continued trust of the animals and integrity of the environment.

There are currently more than 100 tourist boats operating in the Galápagos, with more likely in the future. They range from four-passenger converted old wooden trawlers built on a beach in the Galápagos to 90-passenger ships with all the comforts of home. By far the best are the 6- to 16-passenger boats specially built for ocean cruising. These include motor cruisers, sailboats and motorsailers. All the major tour operators have very nice boats. The best, we think, are operated by Quasar Nautica. For luxury-class boats you should expect a private room with private bath, comfortable lounging areas, good food, safe water and an experienced guide. For a complete review of the Galápagos operators and their boats, get a copy of *A Traveler's Guide to the Galápagos Islands* by Barry Boyce (available from Galápagos Travel, P.O. Box 1220, San Juan Bautista, CA 95045; 800-969-9014).

PRACTICAL INFORMATION

Life aboard your boat will quickly assume a regular daily pattern—a morning walk, mid-day swim and travel, an afternoon walk, dinner in a protected anchorage and evening travel to the next day's destination. You will always take a small boat to and from each visitor site—in the Galápagos, this boat is called a *panga*. The *panga* can be an old wooden rowboat, used by the economy boats, or a nice new zodiac, used by the better boats. Space in the *panga* can be tight, so bring just what you are going to need. Usually a daypack is sufficient to carry whatever you may want while on the island.

There are two types of landings—wet and dry. Wet landings are the easiest and get their name because they require you to step out of the *panga* into the shallow water and walk up the beach. Either wear sandals (Tevas are our favorites) or sling your shoes over your shoulder and put them on once you're on the beach. Avoid wearing socks because they stay wet all day and hold lots of sand. Dry landings do not require you to get wet but at times they can turn into a wet landing if you are not careful. For dry landings the *panga* lets you off at a convenient (or not) rock where you must adroitly scramble up and out of harm's way. The problem is that many of the rocks are slippery, and footfalls are not always where you would like them to be. Always ask for assistance when you are unsure or unsteady. Instead of grabbing someone's hand for help, however, grab each other's wrists. It's much more secure. Also remember to always wear your life vest, even onto the beach. You can take it off there, but not in the *panga*.

All the better boats make their own fresh water, so it is safe to drink. If you are concerned, ask just to be sure. Motion sickness medication is a must for all but the most hardened old salts. There are several very effective prescriptions available. Home and folk remedies are great until you actually get into some rough waters. Also, remember, you are on the equator so the sun is very strong. Use lots of sun protection, including a good hat, and do not forget sun lotion for your feet if you are wearing sandals. Binoculars will dramatically improve your view and appreciation of many sights. If you do not own a good pair it is well worth investing $100 for some new ones. Most boats have a collection of misfit snorkeling gear that is really only good to replace gear of your own that might have broken. If you are a serious snorkeler, be sure to bring at least your own mask and snorkel. For eyeglass wearers, you can order a dive mask with your prescription glass from any good dive store. No sense looking underwater if everything is out of focus. Your boat or guide will probably have a small library of books on the Galápagos on board. If you want to study up before your trip, see the list at the back of this book.

The islands of Española (Hood), Genovesa (Tower) and James (Santiago) are our favorites. They each have visitor sites that feature both interesting landscapes and many animals. Puerto Egas on James Island is a wonderful intertidal walk that ends at fur seal grottos. The trail at Punta Suárez on Española Island takes you through large Blue-footed Booby and Wandering Albatross colonies. Darwin Bay on Genovesa is special for its delightful Red-footed Boobies and the thrill of possibly seeing Hammerhead Sharks.

THE ISLANDS

The islands and visitor sites listed below are the ones you are most likely to visit. (For a complete description of every visitor site, refer to *A Traveler's Guide to the Galápagos Islands* by Barry Boyce.) Each Galápagos island often has several names—at least one Spanish and one English. Here we will refer to the most commonly used name, with the other in parentheses; when in doubt, favor the Spanish.

SAN CRISTÓBAL ISLAND

San Cristóbal Island is the fifth-largest and the easternmost island in the Galápagos archipelago. The town of Puerto Baquerizo Moreno, the capital of Galápagos Province, is located on the southwest corner of the island. The town is roughly rectangular in shape, stretched out along the small harbor—eight blocks by three blocks or so. One side of the harbor is a large military complex with low buildings with red-tile roofs. On the other side is the dock where you board your *panga* in a small inlet where boats are built and repaired. The streets are cobbled and a pleasant waterfront park with benches, nice plantings and the Banco de Pacifico building extends along the main street—Avenida Charles Darwin. Even though it is the administrative center of the Galápagos, it is sleepier and of less interest to most tourists than Puerto Ayora on Santa Cruz Island. There are fewer gift shops here, but more commercial stores to buy hardware and groceries.

The post office is on the main street on the airport side of town, and there is a small **natural history museum** two blocks off the main street next to the modest cathedral. It costs a dollar to enter the museum, but there is not much to see. They claim to have a live tortoise, but we have never seen it. The rest of the displays are artifacts and stuffed animals you have seen looking better alive. If you are arriving as part of a tour, you will be whisked from the plane to your boat and will not have time to explore. You may have a few hours to wander around town on the last morning of your trip before you catch your plane.

One of the more interesting things to do here is to watch the boat-building. On the beach past the post office and in the small inlet near the docks there is always a boat or two going up or going out to sea. Note how carefully the work is done—and without the help of many power tools. Launchings are always a big deal, with a big crowd and a bulldozer pushing the craft down the beach. It is always amazing to us that a design with so little hull and so many decks does not topple over as soon as it hits rough water. Then again, you don't see too many of these boats outside the harbor.

The tourist dock is marked by a large cement whale perched on top of the entrance. Opposite the whale is **Ed & Liz** souvenir shop for last-minute T-shirt buying and the **Casa Blanca Bar and Restaurant**, which is a good place to have a soda and relax as you wait for the plane. There are three places to stay in town that we can recommend. They have clean, private rooms, friendly service, a place to eat and very reasonable rates. They are not destination resorts, but they are fine for the time you will have to explore the islands if you are doing day trips from town. The **Gran Hotel San Cristobal** has a private beach out front. Near the Gran Hotel is the **Hotel Orca** and the **Hostal Galápagos**. All of these are located past the small inlet on the southeast side of town away from the airport and range in price from $6 to $15.

There are animals to see around town if you look closely. Small Marine Iguanas and Sally Lightfoot Crabs are on the black wave-washed rocks. Frigatebirds are always soaring over the harbor, and sea lions haul out on the old boats to sleep away the day. There is an endemic mockingbird on this island, the Chatham Mockingbird, that can be seen in the plantings around town or near the small beach in front of the Gran Hotel San Cristobal. **Frigatebird hill** is a visitor site that lies just outside of town. Both Greater and Magnificent Frigatebirds nest here, so it is a good spot to learn how to tell them apart. Greater Frigatebird males have greenish feathers on their nape—females have white chests and throats. Magnificent Frigatebird males have purplish feathers on their nape—females have all dark throats and chests. If you are planning on a visit, ask in town what the status of the colony is because they do not always nest at the same time every year.

Most tours that start from San Cristóbal make the short trip to **Isla Lobos** (the Spanish name for sea lions is *lobos* or "wolves of the sea") for your introduction to the wildlife of the Galápagos. Isla Lobos is named for the sea lions that bellow, cavort and loll around this small islet. It is a dry landing that can be slippery, so be especially careful here. There is always a colony of sea lions centered around the lone black mangrove tree—look underneath for moms with new pups. The afternoon light on the small beach on the far side is great for your first photos of sea lion pups and Blue-footed Boobies. Snorkeling is possible here as well, but be sure to stay away from the sea lion colony.

Off the western shore of San Cristóbal Island is a massive, angular rocky block called **Leon Dormido** or **Kicker Rock**. It is the Galápagos version of Gibraltar stuck out in the sea. Its size alone is impressive, but even more interesting is the cleft that splits the rock into a narrow passage—through which brave captains can navigate. Seabirds nest on the cliffs, and scuba diving is good all around the rock. Photographically, try to capture another boat as it passes through the cleft to give a sense of the size of the rock. It also makes a great subject for both sunset and sunrise photos, especially if you can get the sun setting through the cleft.

On the far northeastern point of San Cristóbal Island is **Punta Pitt**, a relatively new visitor site. It is an old volcanic cone that requires a bit of a hike to get into. This is the only site other than Genovesa Island, far to the north, where visitors can reliably see Red-footed Boobies. Even though this species of booby is by far the most common of the three species present in the Galá-pagos, it is the hardest to see. Blue-footed Boobies are the least numerous in the Galápagos, but are the easiest to see. This is because Red-footed Boobies fish far offshore and so nest on the outer edges of the archipelago where tourists seldom go. Blue-footed Boobies fish amongst the islands in the shallow nearshore waters where most of the visitor sites are located. Masked Boobies fish in deep nearshore water, so are somewhere in between the Blue-foots and Red-foots.

In addition to the Red-footed Boobies, there are Blue-footed and Masked Boobies, frigatebirds, Swallow-tailed Gulls, tropicbirds and storm petrels, so birdwatching and photography are excellent here. Take some time and notice the different technique each kind of seabird uses to catch food. Boobies dive from high over the ocean to catch fish and squid. Swallow-tailed Gulls are the only nocturnal gull in the world. They catch squid as they rise to the surface at night to feed. Tropicbirds and storm petrels snatch small fish from the surface of the ocean. Frigatebirds are avian pirates, what scientists term *klep-toparasites*. They pursue and outmaneuver smaller birds until they release their catch for the frigatebirds to grab in the air. Not many boats come to Punta Pitt, but it is a great site and also avoids the long, seasick ride out to Genovesa Island. There are also nice beaches nearby to wander and good snorkeling opportunities. If you want to see Red-footed Boobies, this is the easiest place to find them.

SANTA CRUZ ISLAND

Santa Cruz Island is the second-largest island in the Galápagos and is the hub for tourists. All tours of the islands will sooner or later anchor in Academy Bay at Puerto Ayora, the largest town in the Galápagos, to visit the **Charles Darwin Research Station** and to shop for T-shirts and trinkets. About half the people who live in the Galápagos live in or near Puerto Ayora. The National Park Service offices are also located in town.

The best strategy for visiting Puerto Ayora and the Darwin Station is to get to the station when they first open, and then go nuts buying T-shirts in town later. Of course, every boat has figured this out, so try to be first. *Pangas* dock at a long cement pier on the harbor's east side. The pier leads through a thick stand of Red and Black Mangroves (you can tell them apart by their leaves—the leaves of Red Mangroves are broad and bright green, those of Black Mangroves are narrow and gray-green) and usually there are some very large Marine Iguanas lying about. There are restrooms, an information kiosk and gift shop by the boat ramp. Continue straight ahead along the red, crushed-lava road following signs to the visitors center. It is about a five-minute walk through an interesting forest of manzanilla, *Parkinsonia*,

Scutia, *Jimnocerus* and *Opuntia* cactus trees. For birdwatchers, this is a great spot to look for several species of Darwin's finches, Galápagos Mocking-birds and flycatchers.

The **visitors center** is a large round building with interpretive displays on geology, climate, colonization by plants and animals, research and conservation. It is a good introduction to the park and an essential stop if you are not a member of a group. Continuing along the trail, a bit rougher now, is the **Tortoise Conservation Building**. There are displays inside on tortoise exploitation, conservation and ecology. Just behind this building are the tortoise rearing pens, arranged by age cohorts, and beyond them a boardwalk leading to the adult tortoises.

The efforts to rescue and restore the tortoise illustrate the heart of the struggle to conserve the Galápagos Islands. Three races of tortoises on three islands were wiped out by the early sailors and several other islands had populations that were devastated. In addition to collecting and killing the tortoises, the early settlers released domestic animals that either outcompeted the tortoises for food or directly preyed upon them. These feral animals—goats, pigs, donkeys, cats, rats and dogs—are the biggest threat to the ecological integrity of the Galápagos and much of the park service's efforts go to eliminating these animals. Islands that are most severely threatened are Santa Cruz, Santiago, San Cristóbal and Isabela. Santiago Island alone has over 100,000 feral goats.

On the islands where the park service has successfully eliminated the feral animals, the tortoises have been reintroduced. When park service scientists first arrived on Española Island in 1962 there were only 14 tortoises left. These were captured and brought to the captive breeding program at the Darwin Station. After three to four years and when they weigh at least three pounds, they are returned to their native island. Española Island now has a thriving population of several hundred tortoises roaming the landscape.

After the baby tortoise pens, the trail becomes a raised boardwalk that winds around large natural enclosures where adult tortoises live. The most famous of these tortoises is Solitario Jorge, or Lonesome George. George is the last member of his race from Pinta Island and a worldwide search of zoos has not uncovered another. For years, George was all by himself, hence the name, but now scientists have put two females of the most closely related race in with George and mating has occurred. Interestingly, it was not until George had daily human contact—petting—that he settled down enough to accept his female companions. Beyond Lonesome George, the boardwalk descends to a compound with six large tortoises that people are allowed to interact with. This may be your only chance to take head shots—E.T. was modeled after them—and to get really close to a tortoise. Please stay off their concrete feeding platform. Do not touch them, but linger if you have a chance to watch them move and listen to them creak about.

The walk ends just past the demo tortoises at two Darwin Station **kiosks**—one sells sodas and candy and the other T-shirts, postcards and books. If you are going to buy T-shirts, buy some here—the proceeds go directly to benefit the work of the station. Besides, the T-shirts are some of the nicest you will find and are not available anywhere else. There are more restrooms around the corner from the kiosks near the Tortoise Conservation building. After the kiosk, most people are allowed a couple of hours to explore Puerto Ayora. The town is about a 15-minute walk away—follow the exit signs to get back on the road you walked in on.

Puerto Ayora is a sleepy, slow-moving town wrapped around the rocky northern shore of Academy Bay. It is a pleasant place to wander, with clean public areas and nice plantings of trees and flowers. The west end of town is

a narrow harbor backwater where boats are maintained and supplies loaded. A post office, food store and hardware store are also near the loading pier. In addition to the numerous gift shops, there are many small stores that sell sodas and snacks and where you can get a streetside table to enjoy the view. Buses to the highlands or the other side of the island wait at the west-end park. Ask locally about their schedule, which changes often.

As you walk into town, the first sign of civilization is the stone arch of the **Hotel Galápagos** (private bath, cold water; 5-526-122). This is the nicest hotel in Puerto Ayora and a great place for a drink or to sit after walking around the station. There is usually a Great Blue Heron walking the grounds and Lava Gulls, the rarest gull in the world, are often seen hanging around the entrance. The hotel is built on a rocky point that commands the best harbor views, especially from the bar. The grounds are shaded by tall trees— under which separate buildings house the rooms. All guest rooms are comfortable, with electric lights and private baths. There is a separate shower building.

At the Hotel Galápagos the dirt road becomes a cobblestone street and the first wave of gift shops begins. There are dozens of stores in town. Most establishments sell T-shirts, but wooden carved figurines, books, jewelry and other knickknacks are also available. Please don't buy anything made from black coral, despite what the merchant may say. Black coral is a nonrenewable product whose collection causes great environmental damage—it simply isn't worth it. The best **gift shops** are: Galleria Johanna, Bambu Artesians, Galápagos Gallery, Art Mannys, Peer, Lorena's Boutique and the Travel Company.

There are several nice, inexpensive places to stay in Puerto Ayora, although none is exceptional. All the hotels range in price from $6 to $15. The two nicest are the above-mentioned **Hotel Galápagos** near the Darwin Station and the **Hotel Angermeyer** (Avenida Charles Darwin and Piqueros; private bath, hot water; 5-526-570, 5-526-186, fax: 5-526-571) on the main street in town. The Angermeyer is new and comes highly recommended. An interior courtyard with tall palms and hibiscus shrubs shades a small pool. The rooms are clean and very well maintained—each has a private bath with shower and hot water. The **Hotel Sol y Mar**, next to the Banco del Pacifico building, is smaller but has great views of Academy Bay. There is also the **Hotel Delfin** (5-526-297), with private beach and its own boat for day trips, and the **Hotel Lobo del Mar** (12 de Febrero and Avenida Charles Darwin; 5-526-569). The best food is in the best hotels, but you can also try **Cuatro Linternas** for international cuisine and either **Garrapata** or **Mas y Mas** for *comida típica*—typical food of Ecuador.

The **highlands** of Santa Cruz Island are well worth the extra time required to get there. In fact, we would not select a tour if it did not include some time in the highlands of this island. There are two important things to see in the highlands. One is the *Scalesia* forest that grows

Sea lion

in the zone of the *garúa*. Most tours go to **Los Gemelos**, or The Twins—two forest-draped craters easily accessible from the road. The *Scalesia* trees that you see are members of the sunflower or composite family. The forest has other interesting plants and is a haven for birds, especially Vermilion Flycatchers. There is also a lava tube nearby, with head lamps available so you can walk into the shadowy depths.

The other important part of the highlands experience is seeing the wild Giant Tortoises. A favorite way to do so is by visiting **Rancho Mariposa**, known locally as Steve Devine's farm. The farm is a series of rolling, dense green pastures that the tortoises migrate to, spending the months of October through June. There are seldom fewer than 40 tortoises here and sometimes as many as 90. At first, there doesn't seem to be any tortoises around, but when you begin to wander the meadows you start to see tortoises everywhere. A favorite spot for them to congregate is a small duckweed-covered pond where we have seen up to 17 of them mucking about. Try to get a photo of a head draped with the duckweed or one with its shell neatly embroidered in the green stuff.

There's a small restaurant on the hill overlooking the pond where light meals can be eaten if Steve is notified at least a day ahead. Even if you don't eat there, it's the perfect spot to meet and enjoy some hot lemongrass tea after your adventures with the tortoises. Some of the tortoises are not as friendly as others, so it is best to wander to find one that is comfortable with your being nearby. Also, remember to bring a raincoat and a plastic bag for your camera gear—the *garúa* mist can look and feel an awfully lot like rain at times. And please close each gate you come to—this is still a working ranch.

There are two other places to eat in the highlands that are available to groups by prior arrangement. One is **The Narwhal** located opposite the road into Rancho Mariposa and the other is the **Altair**, owned by Anita Salcedo. After a morning visiting the Darwin Station, shopping in town and having lunch in the moist highlands, followed by an afternoon with wild tortoises, you will feel that you have had a full and wonderful day. It is great to be able to enjoy the tortoises at the station, but seeing wild ones that you can sit near and spend time with is a special treat.

The other popular visitor site on Santa Cruz Island is **Black Turtle Cove**, sometimes called *Caleta Tortuga Negra*. The name is an unfortunate misnomer—they are actually green sea turtles that you will see (they looked black to the early sailors). Black Turtle Cove is a narrow inlet that winds through mangrove-lined shores to hidden backwaters. In these quiet lagoons sea turtles, White-tipped Reef Sharks and rays feed, congregate, rest and breed. Only small boats with 12 or fewer passengers are allowed to visit the cove and then only by paddled *panga*. The brown-stained water is surprisingly clear so that it is easy to see the sharks and turtles swimming around the *panga*. This is probably the best place to see the beautiful spotted eagle ray as it slowly wings through the water.

ESPAÑOLA ISLAND

Española (Hood) Island is the southernmost island and a favorite of ours. There are two visitor sites: Gardner Bay is a magnificent crescent beach and Punta Suárez is a walk across a rocky headland. **Gardner Bay** is one of the archipelago's nicest beaches, stretching in a lazy crescent for about one kilometer. The entire beach and tidal rocks are an open area. You are not allowed into the surrounding bushes. Several sea lion colonies are always present, with bulls roaring in the waves as they patrol their 70 feet of territory. While there are occasional skirmishes between neighboring bulls, most of the aggressive behavior is just territorial posturing. Dominance in sea lions is based on size, and size is in part determined by which animal can get its nose highest in the air. You will see even the newborns lifting their noses in the air when you approach. If you hover over them, they will be uncomfortable, but if you lie down at their level, the newborns will often come over to investigate you. If you walk, wade or swim along the water's edge, a bull may come over and challenge you (a battle you are unlikely to win), so walk up the beach or swim well offshore to avoid any confrontations.

As hard as it is to pull yourself away from the sea lions, be sure to explore the rest of the beach. There are Lava Lizards in the back beach rocks, Sally Lightfoot Crabs on the tidal rocks and the endemic Hood Mockingbirds fearlessly inspecting backpacks and big toes. The mockingbirds divide the beach by invisible lines in the sand into family territories. When a mockingbird interloper crosses the line, family skirmishes break out—with six or seven birds raising their tails, fluttering wings and much commotion facing off on either side. These small arguments mirror the similar territorial disputes going on at the water's edge among the sea lion bulls. If you happen to spill a bit of fresh water into your cupped hands a mockingbird or seven will surely come over for a drink—another fun opportunity for a photograph. Get to the beach early to enjoy these sights because it's a popular location and too many people and footprints will spoil your experience and your photos.

Gardner Bay is often visited on the first morning of the tour. It is a great place to get your feet wet with the Galápagos wildlife—it is a wet landing—and to try snorkeling. For beginners, start at the beach and swim out to the small rock 165 feet (50 meters) offshore. There are colorful fish in the crevices and maybe some rays on the sandy bottom. For the more experienced snorkelers, the panga will take you either to Gardner Rock where you can swim along the beachside cliff or to Tortuga Rock—the turtle-shaped rock past the beach—which has more open ocean species and higher numbers of fish and invertebrates.

Punta Suárez is around the west point of Española Island. Your *panga* will drop you at one of two pocket beaches that are a favorite spot for sea lions. Look for Galápagos Hawks in the trees or perched on the small rock monument. The trail crosses to the other side of the point passing the first of many Blue-footed Booby nests. The red form of the Marine Iguana, found only on this island, is best seen and photographed where the trail approaches the first rocky beach on the far side. In the early morning and late afternoon, the iguanas are massed on top of rocks for great group photos.

If you have a lens that allows you to focus closely but still keep some distance—in the 200–300 mm range—you will be able to get some great head shots of the Godzilla-like iguanas. If you watch the iguanas long enough, you will surely see them "spitting." What they are actually doing is spraying salt from their noses. Ingested salt is toxic to most animals. Those that live in a saltwater environment have ways, usually a gland, of concentrating the salt they swallow and then expelling it. Marine Iguanas blow salt out their noses, while many seabirds shake it out of their bills. Either way, do not take it personally, as the iguanas are not aiming for you. These are by far the most photogenic of the Marine Iguanas you will see, so try to get on shore early in the morning or late in the afternoon when the iguanas are sunning themselves and posing for you. If you get there during mid-day, the Marine Iguanas will have warmed up and headed off to feed in the waves.

From here, the trail hugs the high cliffs where Masked Boobies and Swallow-tailed Gulls nest. Masked Boobies are larger than their Blue-footed cousins and thus have a harder time getting airborne. This is why you will always see Masked Boobies with cliffside nests and perches and Blue-footed Boobies farther inland. It is not unusual for Masked Boobies to appropriate a Blue-footed Booby nest if they like its location. The trail then turns inland entering a very large Blue-footed Booby colony. If the wind is in your face you will know you are approaching the colony before you actually get there by the musty-chalky aroma in the air. You will have to step carefully over several nests and irate parents that are right in the middle of the trail. The nests are actually just shallow scrapings in the dirt where two to three eggs are laid. The eggs are laid a day or two apart so there is a difference in size between the first- and last-born chicks. During a year of plentiful fish, all the chicks are likely to survive. In years when fish are hard to find, the difference in chick hatching times gives the advantage to the older, bigger chick. Boobies are also unique in that they do not have any external holes on their bill to breathe through. They can only breath through their mouth. This adaptation, together with the sawtooth edge of their bills, enables them to dive after fish from 30 to 70 feet above the ocean surface. The rapid change in water pressure would otherwise force air up any openings in the bill. The toothlike edges of the bill make holding on to a slippery fish more effective. These same bills make very nasty weapons against bare human legs that get too close—so watch out.

Surrounding each nest is a wide band of guano forming a whitewashed ring around the eggs. The outer edge of this ring marks the nesting territory of the boobies. If a chick strays outside this boundary it is subject to attack by other adults. You will sometimes see a bigger chick pushing a smaller chick outside the guano ring. This is often how the older, bigger chick gets rid of its smaller siblings when food is scarce. This sibling food competition may seem cruel to us, but it ensures that when food is scarce, at least one chick will survive to leave the nest.

After the booby colony, the trail leads directly to the cliff ledge, where an impressive blowhole is visible below. If you have an adventurous guide, you can carefully negotiate your way down the cliff and stand next to the blowhole. As incoming waves release their concentrated energy out the small hole, water gushes up 50 feet into the air like a geyser. But do *not* stand too close to or over the hole as the power of the ejecting water is far beyond your imagination.

Past the blowhole, the trail follows the cliffs and enters an area of scrubby trees and a Waved Albatross colony. Española Island is the only place in the world where Waved Albatrosses nest. Between April and November, there are about 10,000 breeding pairs on the island in two sprawling colonies. The trail passes by the edge of one of these colonies, but there are almost always some albatrosses close by. Our favorite time to visit is mid-September to mid-November, when you can see both the young chicks that look like little poodles and the even funnier-looking older chicks as they begin to get their adult feathers. By December the adults are gone. The juveniles hang around until early January, waiting to get their full adult plumage.

Also in these months you will be likely to witness the courtship dance of the adults. Waved Albatrosses court after the breeding season is over. The courtship dance is so remarkable, it is worthwhile scheduling your trip to the Galápagos to be able to see it. The adults are large birds that stand three and a half feet tall and their bill is six to eight inches long. When they waddle about on land they look like a cross between a goose and a large penguin. Courtship begins with a lot of billing, sky pointing and synchronized movements, all accompanied by hoots, honks and rattles. After the courtship is over, the pair separates and spends a solitary four months cruising the South Pacific. It is an unusual system but these magnificent birds mate for life, produce many young and can live to be 50 years old.

The trail next turns inland to a large rocky area on the right. This is the albatross runway where perilous landings by the adults occur. Waved Albatross don't nest until they are five to seven years old. During this time, they spend their entire life out at sea skimming the waves and riding the tradewinds. Landings are perilous at the breeding colonies because the first-timers have not touched land since their first ever take-off years before, and even seasoned adults never get very good at it. The runway ends at a high coastal cliff where easy takeoffs are launched into the wind. The trail continues inland through the scrubby forest several hundred meters to a beach on the opposite side of the island. Then the trail skirts the rocky coastline, taking you back to the beach where you disembarked.

FLOREANA ISLAND

Floreana (Charles) Island is the sixth-largest and guards the south flank of the archipelago. This island has a long and fascinating human history that involves naked men on a beach, a countess, neighbor intrigue and even a mysterious disappearance/murder. For the complete tale, get the book Floreana by Margaret Wittmer. She has lived on the island for 60-plus years and played a part in the odd goings-on. Some tours still visit her house at Black Beach on the south side of the island. There are two land visitor sites—Punta Cormorán and Post Office Bay—and one water site—Devil's Crown.

The visitor site at **Post Office Bay** is a small beach on the north side of the island. Behind the beach is a tiny lagoon that may have herons and shorebirds hiding in the vegetation. A 70-foot (20-meter) trail leads into the scrubby forest to a clearing where what looks like a pile of junk and graffiti is located. This is the famous **post office barrel** (now a box with a door) that was started in the early 1800s as a mail exchange for passing whalers.

Sailors starting their voyage would leave mail in the barrel to be picked up by sailors returning home. It has been in use ever since as a mail drop and delivery system.

Open the door and pull out the mail. If any addresses are near your home, take and deliver—no stamps necessary. For fun, mail a card to yourself to see how long it will take or mail it with a note saying "please leave until _____ " and date it for your 50th anniversary or your daughter's 21st birthday.

Behind the barrel is the site of a former Norwegian fish processing plant that was started in 1926 and abandoned a few years later. Farther back into the forest is a lava tube that can also be explored. May tours do a *panga* ride from Post Office Beach through the offshore rocks looking for boobies, penguins and sea lions. Just down the coast is the other visitor site, **Punta Cormorán**. The landing is located on a light-green olivine beach—look for the mineral in the eroding beachside bank. A 330-foot (100-meter) walk to the right leads to a shallow lagoon that is a favorite spot for ducks and the Greater Flamingo. Look for the endemic Medium Tree Finch in the trailside vegetation.

The trail to the left leads along the lagoon, over a small hill (good for sunset photos) to a magnificent sand beach. The sand is incredibly fine and white—perfect for bare feet. During the winter months, December through March, look offshore for Green Sea Turtles. They come to this beach to lay their eggs, so walking is not allowed over the back beach area. In the waves and also just offshore, sting rays and White-tipped Reef Sharks are common. The rays are often in the shallow murky water where the waves break so be sure to shuffle your feet if you want to get a closer look at some. Swimming is not allowed here, but it is a beautiful beach to wander.

Just offshore from Punta Cormorán is the **Devil's Crown**—one of the best places in the Galápagos for snorkeling and diving. It is a broken crescent-shaped eroded volcanic cone that drops steeply on the outside, but is shallow and protected on the inside. Strong currents and high waves sometimes make swimming difficult, but the rewards are fantastic. Devil's Crown has huge schools of fish and turtles, and sleeping sharks are often seen. There are several underwater tunnels that strong swimmers can negotiate and a sandy, protected area inside that is better for less-confident swimmers. Some of the largest individuals of the garishly colored and festooned fish, the Moorish Idol, are found here. This is a must-see for all snorkelers and divers.

SANTA FE ISLAND

Santa Fe Island is a two-hour trip to the west from Puerto Ayora on Santa Cruz Island. Your boat will anchor in a cove protected by a small rockpile island studded with *Opuntia* cactus. A short loop trail heads inland through an interesting tall cactus forest. Some of the cacti are truly enormous on this island. *Opuntia* grow the tallest where there is dense vegetation and where Giant Tortoises occur. The tortoises eat the succulent pads of the cactus, so by growing tall the plant can both protect itself and rise into the full sunlight above the shading shrubs. An endemic race of the Land Iguana is also usually found on this trail. These iguanas are larger and have bigger spines than the ones you will see on the other islands. This is also a good area to look for the Galápagos Snake, mockingbirds and Galápagos Hawks. The cove has a sandy bottom where living sand dollars can be seen when snorkeling. There is a small coral head near the landing beach that is worth investigating. When swimming, stay away from the beach and the sea lion colony to avoid irate bulls.

SOUTH PLAZA ISLAND

South Plaza Island is one of two narrow islands (North Plaza is closed to visitors) just off the east coast of Santa Cruz Island. It is an uplifted, tilted block island with a loop trail that starts on the low protected side and traces the high windswept cliffs before returning to the natural rock dock. The island is very dry, with interesting vegetation. The most noticeable plants are the usually red ground cover—*Sesuvium* and the widely scattered *Opuntia* tree cacti. Around the cacti are a very yellow race of the Land Iguana. Look for them just as you get onshore, and also try to find one in the bright red *Sesuvium*—the yellow iguana and red plant combine for a great photo.

The trail climbs quickly to the rim of the cliff where seabirds are always very common. Red-tailed Tropicbirds, Swallow-tailed Gulls, frigatebirds, Audubon Shearwaters and Masked Boobies ride the updrafts created by the cliff. There is always much commotion and racket as the birds sail back and forth along the cliff trying to make the final approach calculations to their crevice nests. On the far side of the cliff is a bachelor sea lion colony that is home to bulls too young or too old or too lazy to fight for mating rights, but who lie around bellowing and posturing at each other. The amazing thing about this group of bulls is that they climb the cliff to get to their retreat. You can stand on the lip of the cliff and look down as the bulls flop out of the crashing waves and lumber up the cliff. This is a great spot for portraits of battle-scarred sea lion warriors. Snorkeling is sometimes offered between the two islands but be very careful. There are many bull sea lions around that do not want to be bothered or inadvertently challenged by swimming humans.

NORTH SEYMOUR ISLAND

North Seymour Island sits just north of Baltra Island (sometimes called South Seymour Island). It is another uplifted island like South Plaza and one that also features birds. There is a loop trail that takes between one to three hours to complete, depending on how far you go and how long you linger along the way. The major attraction here is the colony of frigatebirds—largest in the Galápagos. Most of them are Magnificent Frigatebirds, but there are some Great Frigatebirds here as well (Greats have greenish nape feathers while Magnificents have purplish). The trail passes very close to the colony, and it is usually possible to find males within camera range with their red pouches fully extended. The males extend their pouches to try to attract females. The females do most of the mate choosing and use the male's inflated gular pouch as a way to judge gene superiority among the many males, all more than ready to mate. Those males with the reddest and fullest pouch are evidently the ones most likely to pass on superior genes and thus the best prospect for a female looking for a breeding partner. To really turn the eye of a passing female, the males will often rattle their bills and shake their pouches in what is meant to be an irresistible display of male prowess. If you are susceptible to this kind of come-on, you might want to keep a safe distance!

Also along the path, before and after the frigatebirds, are breeding pairs of Blue-footed Boobies. You can tell the female and male apart quite easily. The female is a bit larger, has a bigger pupil and honks—the male is smaller with a smaller pupil and whistles. This becomes important (to us) only when you see a pair of boobies and decide to wait to see their remarkable courtship display. Make sure one is a female and the other is a male or else your wait will be longer than you would like. When a courtship does begin, it is at the same time comical and delightful. Done in what appears to be slow motion, first one and then the other booby lifts a startlingly blue foot in the air to show its mate and then points its bill, cocks its tail and flutters its wings in a synchronized dance of fidelity. The dance is often repeated, but it is always done the same way—a slow, mirrored booby pas de deux.

If the frigatebirds and boobies aren't enough, there are always clumps of Marine Iguanas on the shoreline rocks and the customary colony of sea lions at the landing to observe and photograph. This island is close to Baltra and the airport, so it is heavily visited. Try to get there early in the morning to avoid crowds.

DAPHNE MAJOR ISLAND

Daphne Major is a small cone that rises out of the ocean just west of Baltra Island. It is a seldom-visited island because it is sensitive to erosion and because the landing is tricky, especially when there are high waves. The park service limits visitation to Daphne Major to one visit per boat per month. If the sea conditions are favorable, the initial landing involves a bit of scrambling up a steep slope until the narrow trail is found. If the sea is rough, you should not attempt to land.

The trail spirals up to the lip of the cone and then traces the edge, giving walkers a view down into the flat interior of the cone and its colony of Blue-footed Boobies and frigatebirds. Along the way, there are numerous nests of Masked Boobies, typically right in the middle of the trail. Masked Boobies always lay two eggs, but only one chick ever survives. The other egg is insurance. In the clumps of cactus along the trail, Darwin's finches are very common. On this island, two scientists from Princeton University—after 20 years of research—were able to actually observe the finches adapting to their changing environment, by measuring every finch bill and the size of their food. As the rainfall patterns changed, different seeds became more or less available and finches with the best bill size survived better. This was the first time the process of evolution has actually been measured and documented—a very important accomplishment. For further information on these experiments, read *The Beak of the Finch* by Weiner.

JAMES ISLAND

James Island (also called San Salvador or Santiago) is the fourth-largest island in the archipelago and third-highest behind the youngsters Isabela and Fernandina. There are two popular visitor sites—James Bay and Sullivan Bay—and two satellite islands—Sombrero Chino (Chinese Hat) and Bartolomé.

James Bay is on the western coast of James Island, and is one visitor site that Charles Darwin stopped at. There are two walks possible at James Bay—one climbs the nearby cinder cone, Sugarloaf Mountain, and then leads to a salt lagoon Darwin visited. It takes about an hour to climb the mountain and another hour to visit the salt lagoon. If the other trail is crowded, this would be a good way to avoid the crowds, but otherwise the walk is dry and not very pretty. You will see far less here than on the other walk.

The most popular walk at James Bay is to explore **Puerto Egas**. The landing is on a black beach that at low tide has an interesting arch to photograph. Near the arch there is usually a sea lion nursery with playful pups. The trail, about 2 kilometers long, starts by crossing a dry interior past what was once a salt processing plant. The shack and foundation ruins are all that's left of the buildings now. Go right at the fork and head down to the rocky coast. The trail from here follows along the coast past several sea lion colonies and many photo opportunities of Sally Lightfoot Crabs, oyster-catchers, herons, Marine Iguanas, sandpipers and Galápagos Hawks. Scorpions are common under the rocks, so be careful where you sit. Take your time here and walk out on the rocks to see the most and get the best pictures.

The trail turns back to the landing beach at a series of very narrow channels, called the **Fur Seal Grottos**, that are now flooded and home to a small colony of fur seals. Fur seals are smaller and have blunter noses and longer whiskers and ears than sea lions. Actually, fur seals are not seals at all but members of the sea lion family (seals do not have external ears and cannot prop themselves up on their rotated forward flippers). Fur seals are very photogenic and friendly, and this is probably the only place you will be able to see them. Look for them sleeping on ledges and in narrow cracks. There is also often a Yellow-crowned Night-Heron that poses on the rocks at water's edge.

From the grottos the trail leads back through the dry scrub to the beach. The best time to visit Puerto Egas is in the morning. You will be walking with the sun at your back and will be at the grottos at just the right time for a swim.

On the far side of James Bay from Puerto Egas is **Espumilla Beach**. There is a wet landing on a black beach and interesting warped sedimentary formations in the surrounding cliffs. A short walk behind the beach leads to two small lagoons where Greater Flamingos are sometimes found. Greater Flamingos wander the islands from lagoon to lagoon searching for food—they eat mainly shrimp—so there is no guarantee that flamingos will be where you are. If you are a flamingo fan, ask your guide where they have been sighted most recently and keep your fingers crossed.

On the south end of James Island is **Sullivan Bay**. It is really more of a channel between James Island and Bartolomé. There are two very small beaches at Sullivan Bay that are used by sea turtles for nesting, but the main attraction is a very recent (around 1890) lava flow that added considerable real estate to the island. The typical walk is over the fresh lava to look at all the congealed swirls, loops and curlicues. Some very friendly sea lions are usually at Sullivan Bay to greet snorkelers off the beach.

SOMBRERO CHINO (CHINESE HAT) ISLAND

This is a very small island shaped, as you might expect, like an old Chinese hat. It forms the other side of a narrow channel that was almost closed by lava from the Sullivan Bay eruption. The walk follows the edge of the island around the tip to the open ocean side of the island. Along the way are several sea lion colonies and an interesting volcanic landscape. Try to get to the far end of the trail late in the afternoon when the light is best on the waves breaking against the rocky shore. Remember, wherever there are sea lion pups there are probably Galápagos Hawks around looking for the afterbirth or any sick pups. The hawks will usually sit and pose for you as you blow through rolls of film. The channel between the islands is a good spot for snorkeling, but there is a strong current so you will have to be picked up by your panga when you are tired. Where there is a strong current concentrating food, look for manta rays just under the surface of the water—a real treat.

BARTOLOMÉ ISLAND

Bartolomé Island is a recent volcanic island on the southeast side of James Island. There are two visitor sites on this popular island. Most boats anchor underneath the pointy spire of **Pinnacle Rock** and then take a *panga* ride along its rocky edge to look for resting Galápagos Penguins. Galápagos Penguins are very closely related to Humboldt Penguins found in the cold Humboldt Current off the coast of Perú and Chile. Galápagos Penguins are the only penguins found north of the equator—off the northern tip of Isabela Island. They are quite small, but are usually tolerant of humans, so you can often get very close to them.

To the left of Pinnacle Rock is a tight crescent beach. Around the beach and under the pinnacle is very good snorkeling, especially for beginners. Usually there are penguins swimming here just under Pinnacle Rock where large schools of small fish swarm around the sunken rocks. You will see a school suddenly part before you just as a penguin "flies" by underneath you. Don't bother to try to follow them; they are much too fast. It's better just to wait by the school and sooner or later the pudgy bullet will come by again.

There is an inconspicuous trail from the beach through the shrubs to another crescent beach just on the other side of the dunes. No swimming is allowed here, but during the months of December through March, it is a good spot to look for sea turtles resting in the waves before they come up on the beach at night to lay their eggs. Do not approach the turtles so closely that they have to retreat back into the water. These female turtles are exhausted and if forced to swim again they risk being mounted and even drowned by the amorous males patrolling just offshore.

The other visitor site is a moderately strenuous hike to the top of the **volcanic cone** that makes up most of the island. It takes about an hour at a leisurely pace to get to the top. There is interesting vegetation to see along the way and, where the trail steepens, wooden steps have been installed to save the easily erodible slope. There is much evidence visible of the volcanic history of this island, including lava flows and parasitic splatter cones (they are parasitic because they tap the main magma vein). The view from the top is perhaps the most famous in all the Galápagos. The twin beaches of Bartolomé and Pinnacle Rock are below you and the rugged outline of James Island stretches across the horizon beyond. Do this hike in the morning—in the afternoon you will be looking into the setting sun.

RÁBIDA ISLAND

Rábida (Jervis) Island, lying between James Island and Isabela Island, is considered the geographic center of the Galápagos. The visitor site is a red beach with a small lagoon behind that occasionally has flamingos in it. Brown Pelicans nest in the saltbushes between the beach and the lagoon, giving you an eye-level view of the nestlings. This is one of the best snorkeling spots in the Galápagos, with an incredible variety of fish present. The farther you swim out along the wall, the better the viewing.

GENOVESA ISLAND

Genovesa (Tower) Island is in the far northeastern corner of the archipelago. It is at least an eight-hour trip each way, usually done at night with rough seas. If you do not become seasick, you will at the least certainly lose several hours of sleep on the trip. So why does anyone want to visit Genovesa Island? Because of the wonderful animals and a wild, unspoiled feeling.

There are two visitor sites on Genovesa Island, each starting from **Darwin Bay**. Darwin Bay is circular and ringed by high cliffs, with a narrow, shallow entrance that's particularly thrilling when entering at night with only radar as your guide. Inside the bay, the water is pea-soup green because it is full of microscopic marine life. Because of the productivity of this bay, it supports a very rich animal community, evident by the numbers of birds perched on the cliffs and topside trees.

One visitor site is a small coarse shell and coral **beach** backed by tidal lagoons located where the cliffs recede to the interior. Behind the lagoons and along the cliffs is a large Red-footed Booby colony—the best place to photograph these birds in the Galápagos. Red-footed Boobies come in three color phases: white, brown and intermediate. In the Galápagos, the brown phase is common. In all phases they have pink bills and small red feet. The smallest boobies in the Galápagos, Red-foots are the only boobies to actually build a nest and they do so in trees to avoid predators.

Red-footed Boobies fish far out to sea to avoid competition with their Masked and Blue-footed cousins. Because so much time is spent finding and transporting the food, only one egg is laid, but the chicks have a high rate of survival. It does not seem likely, but the smallest booby with the longest flying time to food has by far the largest population in the Galápagos. There are also White-cheeked Pintail Ducks, frigatebirds, Blue-footed Boobies and both Lava and Swallow-tailed Gulls. You can spend hours just wandering around the beach and lagoons. There is a trail that leads back into the palo santo forest, but for many it will be more worthwhile to just stay around the beach. See if you can arrange to get on the beach at sunrise, stay a few hours, have a late breakfast, and then return to the beach. Because the lagoons are tidal, after a few hours they will change, with different viewing and photography opportunities.

Across the bay from the beach is the other visitor site, known as **Prince Phillip's steps** in honor of his visit in the early 1960s. The Steps are actually just steps with a handrail that follow a crack to the top of the cliffs (it is easier than it sounds). Once on top, the trail leads through a thin palo santo forest where Masked Boobies nest. At the deep fissure, look for a Short-eared Owl that roosts in the shadows. The trail eventually breaks into the open and overlooks a broad rocky plain where frigatebirds can be seen harassing boobies for food. At cliff's edge, swarms of storm petrels fly around before dashing into their nest holes. Unlike anywhere else in the world, storm petrels fly in the daytime here, returning to their island nests only at night to avoid predators.

Snorkeling is possible in Darwin Bay. The water is the least murky near the beach and just under the cliffs. As you get to deeper water the pea soupiness increases, which makes it difficult to see very far. Because the bay is so rich with food, it is a well-known spot for large schools of Hammerhead Sharks. It is a creepy feeling swimming around your boat and thinking there may be hammerheads under you. You can take some comfort in the knowledge that Hammerheads in the Galápagos have never attacked people.

It is a grueling trip to get to Darwin Bay, but definitely worth it. Don't kid yourself—take some serious seasickness medicine if you go. When you wake up in the morning, walk outside to your boat's railing. Not only will the fresh air feel good but there will be immature Red-footed Boobies perched all over your boat. If you approach them carefully, you can get close-up pictures! Is this not reason enough to make the effort to come to Genovesa Island?

ISABELA ISLAND

Isabela Island is by far the largest island in the Galápagos. It is made up of five volcanoes that over the years have coalesced into one island. When you are used to viewing the other, smaller islands, the immense size and height of Isabela is even more impressive as it sweeps along the horizon. Unfortunately, it is a logistically difficult island to visit and along with Fernandina is usually only included on two-week excursions.

Punta García is the only visitor site on the eastern side of the island and not much of one at that. If you are dying to see the Flightless Cormorant, this is the most convenient place to glimpse it. There are also penguins along the rocky coast, but the time it takes to get there, the typically rough water and the small numbers of animals, even though they are special, makes this a less favorable site.

Boats that do visit Isabela usually go up the west coast and pass through the **Bolívar Channel** between Isabela and Fernandina islands. This is a very rich marine environment and a great place to look for whales. Scan the horizon for spouts or look at the surface for circles of smooth water—whale "footprints." Along the way is Elizabeth Bay, where you take a *panga* ride past flightless cormorants and lots of penguins. There are two sites that require hard walking over rough volcanic terrain—**Punta Moreno** and **Tagus Cove**. These are both tough walks. If you are in shape, then you can expect to see interesting volcanic landscapes punctuated by freshwater pools that are a magnet to wildlife. Remember to bring some drinking water along.

Urvina Bay is on the southern edge of the Bolivar Channel. In 1954, in association with the eruption of Volcán Alcedo, 7 kilometers of coastline were suddenly raised up more than 13 feet (4 meters). At this visitor site you can now walk through what was once below water and see high and dry corals and other marine life. This is a good area for Flightless Cormorants and Marine Iguanas, which are particularly large here. It is also a good site to find the rare Mangrove Finch. There are three overnight hikes that are also possible on Isabela Island. The best goes up **Volcán Alcedo**, where you can camp on the caldera rim and visit with the largest population of Giant Tortoises in the islands. There are mud puddles and small pools chockablock with tortoises and Galápagos Hawks patrolling the area. All the wonderful and mysterious photos you have seen of the Giant Tortoises were probably taken here and probably by Tui de Roy, the photographer laureate of the Galápagos. The other two hikes ascend **Sierra Negra** (also called Santo Tomás) and **Cerro Azul,** volcanoes with similar sights and similar effort required. All the hikes require that you be physically fit and able to carry a heavy pack for six hours a day up rugged terrain. The hikes also must be arranged in advance to get the necessary permits.

FERNANDINA ISLAND

Fernandina Island is the youngest and farthest west of all the islands. It is also the most volcanically active, the latest eruption having occurred in 1991. In 1968, the floor of the caldera sank 990 feet (300 meters) in a geologic instant. You can never be too sure what to expect when you visit Fernandina. There is one visitor site on this island, **Punta Espinosa**, on the northeast corner of the island. The trail leads to the end of the point and back and then through another fresh lava landscape. The primary attractions are several sea lion colonies, the largest colony of Marine Iguanas in the Galápagos (often found in huge sunning masses) and, at the tip of the peninsula, a breeding colony of Flightless Cormorants. Try to get a photo of the cormorants with their wings extended to show that they are stumps and useless for flight. The trip to Punta Espinosa is typically combined with a visit to Tagus Cove just across the channel on Isabela.

GLOSSARY

adaptation—a characteristic of an animal or plant that increases its ability to survive

altiplano—the high-altitude valley running roughly north and south and between the eastern and western mountain ridges of the Andes

Amazon Basin—the area of northern South America drained by rivers that flow eventually into the Amazon River and then to the Atlantic Ocean

archipelago—a group of islands clustered together

biodiversity—all living forms of an area, their abundance and how they rely on each other

bromeliad—a common plant related to pineapple that grows perched on the branches or trunks of trees

canopy—the uppermost branches of trees that spread to connect and form a more or less continuous cover to the forest

cloud forest—moist forest found at mid-altitude on both slopes of the Andes characterized by abundant moss and plants growing on the branches of the trees, and which receives a large portion of its moisture in the form of clouds and fog (near coastal areas, low-altitude forests also receive most of their moisture from clouds, but they are called *fog forest*)

cocha—from the Quichua Indian language meaning lake

colonist—an individual or family who has recently moved into a pristine area to clear forest and start a farm

cordillera—Spanish for chain or ridge of mountains

criollo—local, typical food, language or custom

Darwin, Charles—an English naturalist of the 19th century who studied the plants and animals of the Galápagos Islands and co-authored the theory of natural selection and evolution

deforestation—the cutting down of native forest over extensive areas

diversity—the number of different species of plants and animals in an area

ecotourism—recreational and educational travel focused on enjoying and preserving nature and natural areas

El Niño—a movement of warm equatorial ocean currents south to displace the normal cold Humboldt Current off the western coast of South America

endemic—a species of plant or animal that is found only in a restricted region

equator—an imaginary line circling the earth that is halfway between the north and south poles at 0° latitude *evapotranspiration*—loss of water through evaporation from leaves of plants

evolution—in a species, the change over time of the percentage of individuals with a certain characteristic

extinction—disappearance of a species from a region

fauna—the animal species of a region

flora—the plant species of a region

frugivore—fruit-eating animal

habitat—the kind of place where an animal species or plant species normally lives

herbivore—a species that eats living plants

INEFAN—Ecuador's National Park Service

lek (sometimes spelled *lec*)—a gathering of dancing or singing male animals in a relatively small area to attract females for mating

monoculture—an agricultural field or area growing only one species of plant

montane—a habitat or region that is in the mountains

native—animal and plant species that occur in an area naturally and have not been brought in and released by humans

NGO—nongovernment organization

ocean currents—distinct rivers of water running through the ocean, often driven by prevailing winds

paramo—treeless area at high altitudes just below the snowline

Peruvian Upwelling (Humboldt Current)—a stream of cold Antarctic water moving north in the Pacific Ocean along the west coast of South America and causing cold water and nutrients from the ocean bottom to be pulled to the surface

photosynthesis—process by which green plants convert the energy in sunlight into plant matter

pollinator—an animal—like a hummingbird, bat or butterfly—that carries the pollen from the male part of one flower to the female ovary of another flower for fertilization

population—all the individuals of the same species found in an area

primary forest—an undisturbed forested area that has never been logged or cut down by humans and typically has a tall, dense canopy with many large and mature trees

quebrada—Spanish for ravine or gorge, usually with running water

rainforest—a forest habitat that receives more than 60 inches of rain each year *secondary forest*—a forest area that is generally made up of small trees with an open canopy and has recently regrown to replace a primary forest cut over or removed by humans

species—a group of individuals that breed exclusively among themselves (a group of closely related species is called a *genus* and a group of closely related genera is called a *family*)

sustainable use—an economic use of a habitat designed to be long-term and that does not destroy the habitat

swidden—temporary clearing of small forest plots for indigenous agriculture (slash and burn)

terrestrial—a plant or animal that lives primarily on land and not in the water

understory—the plants of the forest near the ground

xerophytic—plants adapted to very dry habitats (often used to describe animals as well)

RECOMMENDED READING

BOOKS

Balick, M.J., E. Elisabetsky, and S.A. Laird, *Medicinal Resources of the Tropical Forest*, Columbia University Press, 1996. *The* book for those interested in the latest on tropical plants and their uses as medicines. In addition to accounts of native medicines, the authors describe conservation efforts and ways in which pharmaceutical companies are working with the indigenous people to determine ethical rights to royalties, and to develop economic opportunity for these people through their knowledge of the forest. This book is fairly technical in places, but for a determined lay reader, it has more information on medicinal plants than any other source.

Bates, Henry Walter, *The Naturalist on the River Amazonas*, Penguin Books, 1988. A reprint of the original 1863 edition, this book is an astounding recount of the author's decade-long studies of the Amazon and its natural history.

Beebe, William, *Galapagos: World's End*, Dover Publications, 1988. An unabridged reprint of the first popular book on the Galápagos written by a renown scientist in 1924.

Best, Brinley and Michael Kessler, *Biodiversity and Conservation in Tumbesian Ecuador and Peru*, BirdLife International, Wellbrook Court, Girton Road, Cambridge CB3 ONA, UK, 1995. Although emphasizing birds, this is the best guide to natural history areas in southwest Ecuador. It documents endemic species of the area as well as past history and future needs for conservation.

Best, Brinley, Tom Heijnen and Rob Williams, *A Guide to Bird-watching in Ecuador and the Galápagos Islands*, Biosphere Publications, Buteo Books, Shipman, VA, 1996. With the most detailed information on how to get to birding sites in Ecuador and the Galápagos, this book is also ideal for independent travelers looking for natural sites even if birds are not your obsession.

Boyce, Barry, *A Traveler's Guide to the Galápagos Islands*, Second Edition, Galápagos Travel, San Juan Bautista, California, 1994. Arguably the best guide for travelers to the Galápagos.

Cameron, Ian, *Kingdom of the Sun God*, Facts on File, 1990. This book details the cultural history of the Andes and their indigenous peoples. It includes lots of photographs and maps.

Campbell, J. A., and W. W. Lamar, *The Venomous Reptiles of Latin America*, Cornell University Press/Comstock, 1989. For those with a fascination for poisonous reptiles, the color photos and informative text are a must, but be prepared to pay close to $100 for this book if you can't check it out of a local library.

Castro, Isabel and Antonio Phillips. *A Guide to the Birds of the Galápagos Islands*, Princeton University Press, 1997. The most complete book on the land and sea birds of the islands.

Collins, Mark (editor), *The Last Rain Forests*, Oxford University Press, 1990. An authoritative and comprehensive guide to people, plants, animals and conservation problems of the rainforests of the world. Stunning photos, maps, and colorful illustrations make this book easy to read and understand.

Constant, Pierre, *Marine Life of the Galapagos—A Guide to the Fishes, Whales, Dolphins and other Marine Animals*, Pierre Constant Books, 8 rue Erlanger, 75016 Paris, France, 1992. A nice field guide with extensive natural-history information.

Darwin, Charles, *The Voyage of the Beagle*, Penguin Books, Penguin Classic, 1989. A natural-history classic reprinted from the original 1880 edition.

Denslow, Julie and Christine Padoch (editors), *People of the Tropical Rain Forest*, University of California Press, 1988. One of the best books for understanding the life and history of people living in the rainforests of the world. It has beautiful photographs and illustrations throughout.

Emmons, Louise, *Neotropical Rainforest Mammals: A Field Guide* (2nd Edition), University of Chicago Press, 1997. This is the only field guide to the mammals of South America's rainforests.

Forsyth, Adrian and Ken Miyata, *Tropical Nature*, Charles Scribner's Sons, 1987. A delightful set of essays.

Gentry, Alwyn, *A Field Guide to the Families and Genera of Woody Plants of Northwest South America (Colombia, Ecuador, Peru)*, University of Chicago Press, 1996. The first and only guide to plants of this extremely species-rich region, it is user-friendly with lots of simple illustrations. Amateurs as well as professionals finally have a source that makes plant identifications relatively uncomplicated.

Hilty, Steven, *Birds of Tropical America*, Chapters Publishing, Ltd., Shelburne, Vermont, 1994. A book of ecology and natural history for those who want to look at birds for more than a checkmark on their lifelist.

Hilty, Steven and William Brown, *A Guide to the Birds of Colombia*, Princeton University Press, 1986. Until the long-awaited and eagerly anticipated *Birds of Ecuador* by Paul Greenfield and Robert Ridgely appears, the Colombia book is the only detailed field guide to the area's birds. It's useful for most of Ecuador, but it does not include many species from Ecuador's coastal and southern Andean regions.

Jackson, Michael, *Galápagos: A Natural History Guide*, University of Calgary Press, 1993. A detailed guide to the Galápagos, their history, ecology and descriptions of the islands' plants and animals.

Kricher, John, *A Neotropical Companion: An Introduction to the Animals, Plants, and Ecosystems of the New World Tropics* (2nd Edition), Princeton University Press, 1997. A primer on natural history and conservation in the New World tropics meant for the lay person.

Mabberley, D. J., *Tropical Rain Forest Ecology*, Chapman and Hall, 1992. A paperback book that takes the reader into sophisticated and detailed understanding of the complex interactions in the rainforest.

Merlen, Godfrey. *A Field Guide to the Fishes of Galapagos*. Ediciones Libri Mundi, Quito, 1988. This 60-page book highlights the common fish species of the islands with excellent color paintings, black-and-white illustrations and a succinct but readable text of species accounts.

Moore, Tui de Roy, *Galapagos—Islands Lost in Time*, Viking Press, 1980. A beautiful picture book by the photographer laureate of the Galápagos.

Parker, Ted and John Carr, *Status of Forest Remnants in the Cordillera de la Costa and Adjacent Areas of Southwestern Ecuador*, Rapid Assessment Program Working Papers 2, University of Chicago Press, 1992. This technical report describes the habitats and provides lists of plants and animals for sites throughout Coastal Ecuador. For many of the sites, these results of the RAP team are the only published natural-history data available anywhere.

Paymal, Noemi and Catalina Sosa, *Amazon Worlds: Peoples and Cultures of Ecuador's Amazon Region*, Sinch Sacha Foundation, Quito, 1993. The most detailed and informative publication on Ecuador's indigenous people of the Amazon, this coffee table book is illustrated throughout with beautiful color pictures and colored illustrations. The text (in English) is informative and accurate. It is available at better bookstores in Quito, Guayaquil and Cuenca but difficult to find in the U.S.

Pearson, David and Les Beletsky. *Ecuador and its Galápagos: The Eco-travellers' Wildlife Guide*. Academic Press, 1999. This book has more than 100 plates of color paintings and black and white illustrations of the common species of plants, insects, frogs, lizards, snakes, birds and mammals in Ecuador, the species an enthusiastic ecotourist is most likely to see in a two- or three-week trip to Ecuador. The illustrations are arranged in "field guide" format for easy comparison; the text provides details on the biology of these groups and places in the country you are most likely to find each species.

Rachowiecki, Rob, Mark Thurber and Betsy Wagenhauser, *Climbing and Hiking in Ecuador*, Fourth Edition, Bradt Publishing, 1997. The best guide for hikers, mountain climbers and serious backpackers.

Rodriguez, Lily and Bill Duellman, *Guide to the Frogs of the Iquitos Region, Amazonian Peru*, University of Kansas, 1994 (Publications Secretary, Natural History Museum, The University of Kansas, Lawrence, KS 66045). This is the only illustrated field guide to the frogs of the Amazon. Its coverage includes most of Amazonian Ecuador. The natural history section has many line drawings that introduce you to the world of frogs. The color photos are brilliant enough to capture the attention of every visitor with any interest in natural history.

Schofield, Eileen, *Plants of the Galapagos Islands*, Universe Books, 1984. A small but handy field guide to the common plants of the Galápagos.

Sienko, Walter, *Latin America by Bike: A Complete Touring Guide*, The Mountaineers, 1993. This specialized book gives information on biking throughout South America. A chapter dedicated to Ecuador includes detailed itineraries and maps as well as information on terrain, weather and scenery for coastal, highland and Amazonian areas.

Stephenson, Marylee, *The Galapagos Islands: The Essential Handbook for Exploring, Enjoying and Understanding Darwin's Enchanted Islands*, The Mountaineers, Seattle, 1989. Details of practical information for visitors to the Galápagos.

Terborgh, John, *Diversity and the Tropical Rain Forest*, Scientific American Library, 1992. A beautifully illustrated book, it is written for classroom use as well as for the sophisticated traveler who wants to understand the biology of rainforests in more detail.

Weiner, Jonathan, *The Beak of the Finch: A Story of Evolution in Our Time*, Knopf, 1994. A popularized account of current research on Darwin's Finches and the astonishing tests of evolution and natural selection that show Darwin's theory was very accurate. This book won a Pulitzer prize in 1995.

Wesche, Rolf, *The Ecotourist's Guide to the Ecuadorian Amazon*, Napo Province, CEPEIGE, 1995. An up-to-date inventory of ecotourism services for the entire Province of Napo, this book provides valuable details on out-of-the-way ecotourist locations in the Baeza–Coca–Nuevo Rocafuerte–Misahuallí area of Ecuador. Many of these areas are best visited by mounting expeditions, or by very independent and adventuresome individuals. It emphasizes indigenous-controlled ecotourism and has 25 detailed maps of the area that alone are worth the price of the book. Order from: World of Maps, 118 Holland Avenue, Ottawa, ONT, Canada K1Y 0X6.

Whitmore, T. C., *An Introduction to Tropical Rain Forests*, Oxford University Press, 1992. The standard book for college classes, this text is readable and interesting to professionals and laypersons alike.

CASSETTE AUDIO TAPES

Because so much of the way you will experience natural history in Ecuador is through your ears, it is a good idea to become familiar with the sounds of these settings. Both by listening to them before you leave for Ecuador, and using them while you are in each of the various habitats, your understanding and appreciation of Ecuador's natural settings will be dramatically enhanced. These cassettes and many others are available through specialized book stores such as the Los Angeles Audubon Society Bookstore (7377 Santa Monica Boulevard, West Hollywood, CA 90046-6694; 213-876-0202; fax: 213-876-7609).

English, Peter H. and Ted Parker, *Birds of Eastern Ecuador*, 1992.

Hardy, John W., *Voices of Galapagos Birds*, 1991.

Moore, John V., *Ecuador, More Bird Vocalizations from the Lowland Rain Forest, Vol. 1*, 1994.

Moore, John V., *Sounds of La Selva (Ecuador)*, 1993.

Index

Lodging Index

Dining Index

Notes

Notes

Notes from the Publisher

An alert, adventurous reader is as important as a travel writer in keeping a guidebook up-to-date and accurate. So if you happen upon a great restaurant, discover a hidden locale, or (heaven forbid) find an error in the text, we'd appreciate hearing from you. Just write to:

Ulysses Press
3286 Adeline Street, Suite 1
Berkeley, CA 94703
e-mail: readermail@ulyssespress.com

It is our desire as publishers to create guidebooks that are responsible as well as informative. We hope that our guidebooks treat the people, country, and land we visit with respect. We ask that our readers do the same. The hiker's motto, "Walk softly on the Earth," applies to travelers everywhere . . . in the desert, on the beach, and in town.

ECOCIENCIA
Fundación Ecuatoriana de Estudios Ecológicos

You're already helping!

Simply by purchasing the *The New Key to Ecuador and the Galápagos* you have helped preserve Ecuador's environment.

Would you like to do more?

At Ulysses Press, we believe that ecotourism can have a positive impact on a region's environment and can actually help preserve its natural state. In line with this philosophy, we donate a percentage of the sales from all New Key guides to conservation organizations working in the destination country—in Ecuador our environmental partner is *EcoCiencia*.

EcoCiencia (The Ecuadorian Foundation for Ecological Studies) is a private, nonprofit, scientific organization established in 1989 and committed to research, education and management for the conservation of wildlife species and their habitats.

EcoCiencia's projects promote the use and management of natural resources that may permit the fulfillment of human needs, and the conservation of biological diversity. As a nonprofit organization, it depends on contributions made by its members, proceeds derived from projects and donations received from national and international sources.

Ulysses Press encourages you to further support this organization. For more information or to make a donation contact:

EcoCiencia
Isla San Cristóbal 1523 e Isla Seymour
P.O. Box 17-12-257
Quito, Ecuador
Phone and fax: 593-2-451-338/593-2-451-339

HIDDEN GUIDES

Adventure travel or a relaxing vacation?—"Hidden" guidebooks are the only travel books in the business to provide detailed information on both. Aimed at environmentally aware travelers, our motto is "Adventure Travel Plus." These books combine details on unique hotels, restaurants and sightseeing with information on camping, sports and hiking for the outdoor enthusiast.

THE NEW KEY GUIDES

Based on the concept of ecotourism, The New Key Guides are dedicated to the preservation of Central America's rare and endangered species, architecture and archaeology. Filled with helpful tips, they give travelers everything they need to know about these exotic destinations.

Ulysses Press books are available at bookstores everywhere. If any of the following titles are unavailable at your local bookstore, ask the bookseller to order them.

You can also order books directly from Ulysses Press
P.O. Box 3440, Berkeley, CA 94703
800-377-2542 or 510-601-8301
fax: 510-601-8307
e-mail: ulysses@ulyssespress.com

Order Form

HIDDEN GUIDEBOOKS

____ Hidden Arizona, $14.95

____ Hidden Bahamas, $14.95

____ Hidden Baja, $14.95

____ Hidden Belize, $15.95

____ Hidden Boston and Cape Cod, $13.95

____ Hidden Cancún & the Yucatán, $16.95

____ Hidden Carolinas, $17.95

____ Hidden Coast of California, $17.95

____ Hidden Colorado, $14.95

____ Hidden Disney World, $13.95

____ Hidden Disneyland, $13.95

____ Hidden Florida, $17.95

____ Hidden Florida Keys & Everglades, $12.95

____ Hidden Georgia, $14.95

____ Hidden Guatemala, $16.95

____ Hidden Hawaii, $17.95

____ Hidden Idaho, $14.95

____ Hidden Maui, $13.95

____ Hidden Montana, $14.95

____ Hidden New England, $17.95

____ Hidden New Mexico, $14.95

____ Hidden Oahu, $13.95

____ Hidden Oregon, $14.95

____ Hidden Pacific Northwest, $17.95

____ Hidden Rockies, $16.95

____ Hidden San Francisco and Northern California, $17.95

____ Hidden Southern California, $17.95

____ Hidden Southwest, $17.95

____ Hidden Tahiti, $17.95

____ Hidden Tennessee, $15.95

____ Hidden Wyoming, $14.95

THE NEW KEY GUIDEBOOKS

____ The New Key to Costa Rica, $17.95

____ The New Key to Ecuador and the Galápagos, $17.95

Mark the book(s) you're ordering and enter total here ➩ [   ]

California residents add 8% sales tax here ➩ [   ]

Shipping: Check box for preferred method and enter cost here ➩ [   ]

☐ BOOK RATE   **FREE! FREE! FREE!**

☐ PRIORITY MAIL $3.20 first book, $1.00/each additional book

☐ UPS 2-DAY AIR $7.00 first book, $1.00/each additional book   [   ]

Billing: Enter total amount due here and check method of payment ➩ [   ]

☐ CHECK   ☐ MONEY ORDER

☐ VISA/MASTERCARD _____ EXP. DATE _____

Name_____ Phone _____

Address_____

_____

City _____ State _____ Zip_____

MONEY-BACK GUARANTEE ON DIRECT ORDERS PLACED THROUGH ULYSSES PRESS.

ABOUT THE AUTHORS

David L. Pearson is a Research Professor of Zoology at Arizona State University, where he teaches rainforest conservation and biology. His research on the ecology and conservation of tropical insects, birds and plants has taken him to rainforests around the world. Since 1968, much of his time has been spent working with Latin American colleagues and students throughout South America. Ecuador has been a focal point of his studies since 1971. He is co-author of *Ecuador and its Galápagos: The Ecotravellers' Wildlife Guide* (Academic Press, 1999). He is also a member of: the Board of Directors for the Organization for Tropical Studies and the Board of Editors for the Journal of the Society for Conservation Biology.

David W. Middleton is a professional photographer, writer and naturalist. He is the author and photographer of two other books: *Ancient Forests*, an artistic and conservationist overview of the old-growth forests of the Pacific Northwest, and *The Nature of America*, a joint project with other top nature photographers in America. He has led tours throughout the world for the last 20 years, but his love of Latin America began in 1984 when he first visited the Amazon. Since then, he has led numerous tours to Ecuador and the Galápagos. The color photographs in this book are by him.

ABOUT THE ILLUSTRATORS

Doug McCarthy has illustrated other Ulysses Press guidebooks including *Hidden British Columbia*, *Hidden Tennessee*, *Hidden Bahamas* and *Hidden Montana*. A native New Yorker, he lives in the San Francisco Bay area with his family.

Glenn Kim is a freelance illustrator residing in San Francisco. His work appears in numerous Ulysses Press titles, including *Hidden Tahiti*, *Hidden Southwest* and *Hidden Belize*. He has also done illustrations for the National Forest Service, several Bay Area magazines, book covers and greeting cards, as well as for advertising agencies.

The little highland town of San Bartolomé east of Cuenca.

Above: Independence Square in Quito with the Cathedral on the left and the edge of the Presidential Palace on the right.